A
GENEVA
SERIES
COMMENTARY

JEREMIAH

A COMMENTARY ON
JEREMIAH

John Calvin

Volume 2

THE BANNER OF TRUTH TRUST

THE BANNER OF TRUTH TRUST
3 *Murrayfield Road, Edinburgh* EH12 6EL
P.O. Box 621, *Carlisle, Pennsylvania* 17013, *U.S.A.*

*

First published in Latin 1559
This edition reprinted from the Calvin
Translation Society edition of 1851
First Banner of Truth Trust edition 1989

ISBN 0 85151 552 5 for the set

*

0 85151 548 7 Volume 2

*

Printed in Great Britain by offset lithography at
the University Printing House, Oxford

COMMENTARIES

ON

THE PROPHET JEREMIAH.

Lecture Thirty-Ninth.

CHAPTER X.

1. Hear ye the word which the Lord speaketh unto you, O house of Israel;

2. Thus saith the Lord, Learn not the way of the heathen, and be not dismayed at the signs of heaven; for the heathen are dismayed at them.

1. Audite verbum quod loquitur (sermonem quem profert) Jehova ad vos, domus Israel:

2. Sic dicit Jehova, Viam gentium ne didiceritis, et à signis cœlorum ne metuatis; quoniam metuunt ab illis gentes.

JEREMIAH enters here on a new subject. Though he had, no doubt, taught this truth often, yet I consider it as distinct from what has gone before; for he begins here a new attack on those superstitions to which the Jews were then extremely addicted. He exhorts them first to *hear the word of Jehovah;* for they had so hardened themselves in the errors which they had derived from the Gentiles, and the contagion had so prevailed, that they could not be easily drawn away from them. This, then, is the reason why he used a sort of preface, and said, *Hear ye the word of Jehovah, which he speaks to you, O house of Israel.*[1]

He then mentions the error in which the Chaldeans and the Egyptians were involved; for they were, we know, very attentive observers of the stars. And this is expressly stated,

[1] Here the preceding lecture ends in the original; but in order to keep the chapters distinct, this section has been transferred to the present lecture. A similar arrangement is adopted as to the last lecture in this volume.—*Ed.*

because the Jews despised God's judgments, and greatly feared what were foolishly divined. For when any one, by looking at the stars, threatened them with some calamity, they were immediately terrified; but when God denounced on them, as with the sound of a trumpet, a calamity by his Prophets, they were not at all moved. But it will be better to examine the very words of the Prophet, as then we shall more plainly see the drift of the whole.

Learn not, he says, *the way of the nations.* The Hebrew grammarians take אל, *al*, for את, *at.*[1] Way, we know, is everywhere taken for all those customs and habits by which human life is regulated. He then forbids them to pay attention to the rules of life observed by the Gentiles. And one thing he specifies, *Be not terrified by celestial signs.* He afterwards shews how vain were the practices of the Gentiles; being devoted to idols, they worshipped them in the place of God, though framed by the skill of man. But there are other words added, *For the heathens are terrified by them.* There is a threefold exposition of this clause. Some take כי, *ki*, properly a causative, in the sense of כ, *caph*, which denotes likeness, "as the Gentiles are terrified by them." Others regard it as an adversative, "though," and כי, *ki*, has often this meaning. There are also others who give this explanation, "For it is the case with the Gentiles, that they are terrified by them;" as though God had said, that it was extremely absurd in the Jews to be terrified by celestial signs, for they ought to have left this folly, or rather madness, to the Gentiles, as God regarded them as wholly blind. Let us now come to the subject.

Learn not, he says, *the way of the Gentiles.* This is a general precept. The law was to the Jews a rule which was sure, and prescribed to them the limits of duty; they ought, therefore, to have followed what God taught them in his law, and not to have turned aside either to the right hand or to

[1] The *Sept.* and *Vulg.* render it "according"—κατὰ—juxta. It is omitted in the *Syr.* *Blayney* renders the line thus:—

"Unto the way of the heathen conform ye not."

We may view it as a negative, thus:—

"No, the way of the heathen learn not."

But it is most probable a typographical error for את, as Jeremiah so writes at least in two other instances, ch. ii. 23, and ch. xii. 16.—*Ed.*

the left, according to what Moses also had said. But as human minds are always wanton, they were very desirous of knowing what the Gentiles observed ; but whenever this wantonness possesses men's minds, they necessarily blend darkness with light. It was then, for this reason, that Jeremiah reminded them, that nothing was to be learnt from the Gentiles ; as though he had said, "Ye ought to be satisfied with the simple doctrine of the law ; for unless ye are content with having God as your teacher, ye will necessarily go astray : unless, then, ye seek wilfully to err, keep the way which is pointed out to you in the law, and turn not aside to the rites and practices of the Gentiles."

After having given them a general command not to turn aside from the plain doctrine of the law, he specifies one thing in particular, *Be not terrified by celestial signs*, that is, "Do not suppose that prosperity or adversity depends on the position or aspect of the stars." There seems, however, to be here some inconsistency, for he mentions the stars as signs ; it hence follows that something is intimated by their position ; and Moses also says, that the sun and moon, and all the stars, (and especially the planets,) would be for signs. There are, at the same time, in the firmament, twelve signs by which astrologers especially make their calculations. Since then God has, from the beginning of the creation, appointed what they call the fixed stars in the firmament, as well as the planets, to be for signs, the Prophet seems not to have done right in forbidding the Jews to fear such signs ; for these signs in the heavens are not the vain fictions of men, but what God has created and appointed ; and we have already stated that the stars are not called signs through the foolish conceit of men, but this character was given them by God himself when they were first created ; and if the stars presage to us either prosperity or adversity, it follows that they ought to be dreaded by us.

But the Prophet here does not use the word signs in its proper meaning ; for he refers not to its true origin, but accommodates himself to the notions which then prevailed ;[1]

[1] *Blayney* gives a similar explanation—"The sun, moon, and stars are said indeed to have been created and set in the firmament for 'signs.' Gen.

and we must bear in mind what I have already said, that the Egyptians and Chaldeans were much given to that astrology, which is called at this day judiciary. The word itself may be allowed; but it has been long ago profaned by wicked and unprincipled men, whose object has been to make gain by mere falsehoods. There is no doubt but that the Egyptians and the Chaldeans were true astrologers, and understood the art, which in itself is praiseworthy; for to observe the stars, what else is it, but to contemplate that wonderful workmanship, in which the power, as well as the wisdom and goodness of God, shines forth? And, indeed, astrology may justly be called the alphabet of theology; for no one can with a right mind come to the contemplation of the celestial framework, without being enraptured with admiration at the display of God's wisdom, as well as of his power and goodness. I have no doubt, then, but that the Chaldeans and the Egyptians had learned that art, which in itself is not only to be approved, but is also most useful, and contains not only the most delightful speculations, but ought also to contribute much towards exciting in the hearts of men a high reverence for God. Hence Moses was instructed from his childhood in that art, and also Daniel among the Chaldeans. (Acts vii. 22; Dan. i. 17, 20.) Moses learned astrology as understood by the Egyptians, and Daniel as known by the Chaldeans; but the art among them was at that time much adulterated; for they had mingled, as I have already said, foolish divinations with the true and genuine science.

As then the Prophet's meaning seems evident, the truth remains fixed, that the sun, and moon, and other planets, and the fixed stars in the firmament, are for signs. But we must notice also here the purpose for which God intended the sun and moon to be signs. His purpose was, that the lunar course should complete one month, and that the solar course should complete one year. And then the twelve signs were designed to answer another purpose: for when

i. 14. But hereby is meant, that they should serve as natural marks, serving to distinguish, by their periodical revolutions and appearances, the various times and seasons; which, however, is a very different use from that of prognosticating future events, or causing any alteration in the fortunes of men."—*Ed.*

the sun is in Cancer it has not the same power and influence as when it is in Virgo; and it differs as to the other signs. In short, as to the order of nature, the stars, the planets, as well as the fixed stars, are to us for signs. We number the years by the solar course, and the months by the lunar; and then the sun, with respect to the twelve signs, introduces the spring, then the summer, then the autumn, and lastly the winter. There are other purposes; but we include in one sentence whatever can be said of the celestial signs, when we say, that they have a reference to the order of nature. Whosoever, then, seeks to make more of these signs, confounds the order established by God, as the Chaldeans formerly did, and also the Egyptians, when they sought to ascend higher than reason warranted: they tried to conjecture by the position of the stars what would be the fates of all nations; and then they dared to come down to the cases of individuals. Hence arose the casters of nativities. Then they first began more anxiously to philosophize, that the sun, when in a certain sign, portends the death of an only son, and happy events to another. But these are things, as we have said, which are beyond the usual order of nature. That there is to be, for instance, summer and winter, this is natural and common; but that there is to be war between one nation and another, this is not by the usual order of things, nor takes place according to what nature appoints, but through the ambition and avarice of men. The hidden providence of God, indeed, rules; but we speak of causes, which ought to be understood by us, and which can be comprehended by us, for they are within the reach of our understanding. It must at the same time be observed, that the course of the stars is in itself of no moment; for we see that God varies the seasons: there is not the same state of weather; we have no winters and no summers exactly alike; there is no year which is not dissimilar to the former; and the third which follows, differs from the second.

We hence, then, learn that God has so formed and ordered the sun, and the moon, and all the stars, that he himself still governs and changes the seasons as it pleases him. In this way we account for sterilities, and pestilences, and other things of this kind. When the air seems temperate, pestilence prevails, the year is less fruitful, and men are famished, and no cause appears. Then this diversity in nature itself shews that God has not resigned his power to the stars, but that he so works by them, that he still holds the reins of government, and that he, according to his own will, rules the world in a way different from what even the acutest can divine by the stars. Yet this is no reason why we should deny to them the office which I have mentioned. But they who exceed the limits fixed by God, and seek to form conjectures respecting war in this country and peace in that country—they who thus seek to learn from the stars what is beyond the order of nature, blend heaven and earth together. The Prophet, no doubt, intended to condemn this madness when he forbade the Jews to attend to the celestial signs so as to dread them.

But the reason also must be noticed, why the Prophet so severely condemned that fear which prevailed among the Gentiles: it was for this, because when the opinion prevailed that all events depended on the stars, the fear of God was removed, and nothing was ascribed to his judgments, faith was extinguished, and prayer to God, and all the ordinances of religion, were reduced to nothing. For all the astrologers, who falsely assume so honourable a name, yea those unprincipled men, who add to their impostures the name of judiciary astrology, hold and maintain, that a judgment respecting man's life ought to be formed by the horoscope, as though the fortune of every one depended on the stars. When, therefore, any one is born at a certain hour, this or that condition, according to them, awaits him. Thus they imagine that there is a fate, or some necessity, which holds a man bound to the influence of the sun, moon, and stars: for he was born when the sun was in the tail of that sign or in the head of another; his birth portends such and such fortune; he will live but a short time, or he will live long. Thus they judge. And they go still farther, and pronounce on every occurrence, "Such will be the issue of this expedition; this during the year will be unhappily undertaken, but that will succeed." Afterwards, when nativity is not taken into an account, they subject the whole human race to the uncontrollable influence of the stars: " See, if you undertake this business on such a day, you will succeed; but if you begin before mid-day, the issue will be unsuccessful." Thus they divine concerning the whole life of man with regard to each of his actions: but God never intended the stars to be signs for such purposes.

Now, as I have said, it hence follows that God does not rule, and that thus faith is extinguished, and all the exercises of religion are reduced to nothing. For whosoever is persuaded that he is bound by necessity, because the horoscope is of such a character, he must necessarily die at such an hour, and necessarily die of a certain kind of death,—will any one who has this conviction call on God? will he commend his life to his keeping? And then, when any adversity happens, who will bear it as a punishment for his sins? Will he acknowledge that he is called to judgment by God? And if he should prosper, will he be led to sing praises to God?

We hence see that this divination extinguishes all religion; for there will be no faith, there will be no recognition of punishment, no acknowledgment of God's blessings, and no concern for sin, whenever this diabolical error possesses our minds,—that we are subject to the stars, that such and such is our nativity, and that the stars portend some kind of death every day and every moment. This, then, is what is especially intended by the Prophet in forbidding the Jews to be *terrified by the celestial signs;* for the Chaldeans, no doubt, prophesied that they should have a new empire; and thus they frightened the miserable Jews: " It is all over with us, for the astrologers among the Chaldeans have so spoken; and on the other hand the Egyptians see also that this has been foreshewn by the position of the stars." Thus it happened that the Jews became, as it were, wholly lifeless. Nor did they remember what God had so often, and for so many years, threatened by his Prophets to do, in case they continued to provoke his wrath. Of God's judgment they made no account; and yet the persuasion, that the Chaldeans announced a judgment by the stars, and that there would be some convulsion, filled them with terror and amazement. Hence the Prophet, in order to lead them to repentance, as well as to faith, which are the two essentials of religion, and include in them the perfection of true wisdom, speaks thus to them in effect, " Fear not the stars, but fear God." For there is implied a contrast between God and the stars; as though he had said, " When any adversity happens to you, know that you are chastised by God's hand, who is a just avenger of sins." This was to teach them repentance; it was to shew them that they justly suffered, because they had been perverse in their wickedness. Then follows the other fact, that though the stars threatened calamity and destruction, they were to flee to God's mercy and never doubt of their safety, provided he was propitious to them. We now then understand the Prophet's object in telling them not to fear the stars.

More things might be said, but I study brevity as far as I can; and I trust that I have briefly included what is sufficient for the understanding of this passage. There are many, I know, at this day foolishly curious, and hence wish some account to be made of judiciary astrology; and this delirium has taken possession of some pious men and really learned: but we see what God here declares by his servant. And I wonder that some are thus credulous as to the stars, who yet speak with extreme subtlety on free-will. They would have the events of things fortuitous, they would have it that men act freely in both ways, and they hate and abhor fate; and yet they confine God as it were in a prison, and would have the stars to rule. This is to me a prodigy, not a sign. But all these things I leave. Let the plain doctrine of the Prophet be deemed sufficient by us, when he says, that we are not to be terrified by signs, for it belongs to the Gentiles to be thus terrified; for I am disposed to take this meaning,—that the Prophet says that this was a kind of blindness which belonged to them: " Leave," he says, " this folly to the Gentiles; it is no wonder that they labour under so many errors and delusions, for celestial truth has never shone upon them; but it becomes you to fear God and to rely on his mercy." It follows—

3. For the customs of the people *are* vain: for *one* cutteth a tree out of the forest (the work of the hands of the workman) with the axe.	3. Quoniam statuta populorum vanitas est: nam lignum à sylva scindit, opus manuum artificis dolabra (*vel,* in securi; *nam ponitur* ב, *quæ est nota instrumenti apud Hebræos.*)

The Prophet seems to break off his subject, and even to reason inconclusively; for he had said in the last verse, "Learn not the rites of the Gentiles, and fear not the celestial signs;" and he now adds, *Because the rites of the Gentiles are vanity; for wood they cut down from the forest.* He seems then, as though forgetting himself, to have passed off to idols. But we must observe, that the Jews were influenced by that ancient opinion, that the Chaldeans and the Egyptians were alone wise, and that they had acquired a fame of this kind among all nations. We find also that heathen writers, when speaking of the origin of the sciences, trace them up to the Chaldeans and the Egyptians; for with them, it is said, have originated astrology and all the liberal sciences. The Jews then, no doubt, allowed so much authority to the Chaldeans and the Egyptians, that their minds, being possessed by that prejudice, could discern nothing aright. The Prophet then shakes off from them this stupidity, and shews how foolish they were, who yet would have themselves to be alone deemed wise, and regarded others, compared with themselves, as barbarous and ignorant. We now then see why the Prophet connects idolatry with that false and spurious astrology which he had mentioned.

He says, *Laws:* the word, חקות, *chekut,* means strictly, statutes. The word, חק, *chek,* signifies to decree, or to write; and hence decrees are called חקות, *chekut.* The word Law is general; and one of those which are special and often occurs in Scripture, is the statute. Some render it "Edict;" and the verb means to publish by edict. But this word is often applied to ceremonies and rites. He then says, that *the rites of the nations* were *vanity.*

He then proves this, *Because they cut for themselves trees from the forest;* and after having polished them by art, they think them to be gods. How detestable was this madness, to think that a tree, cut from the forest, was a god, as soon as it assumed a certain form or shape! As then a madness, so great and so monstrous, prevailed among the Chaldeans and the Egyptians, what right knowledge or judgment could have been in them? The Jews then were very foolish in thinking that they were very clear-sighted. "They are," he says, "brute animals; for it is wholly contrary to reason to suppose that a god can be made from a dead piece of wood. When, therefore, the Chaldeans and the Egyptians amaze and astonish you through the influence of a false opinion, derived from nothing, that they are alone wise, do ye not see that ye are doubly and trebly mad? for where is their wisdom, when they thus make gods from trunks of trees?"

We now then perceive the design of the Prophet: but as these circumstances have not been considered by interpreters, they have only elicited a frigid doctrine and gathered some general thoughts. But when any one rightly and carefully examines the design of the Prophet, he will find how important is what he teaches; and no one can otherwise rightly understand what Jeremiah means.

A tree then *does* one *cut*, &c.: he uses the singular number.[1] He then adds, *the work of the hands of the artificer by the ax.* He shews that nature itself is changed through

[1] This is not correct, the verb is plural, and there is no different reading. The *Vulgate* has led *Calvin* and our translators astray here. The other versions never changed the form of the sentence. The verse may be thus rendered,—

3. Verily, the customs of the nations are very vanity;
For a tree from the forest they cut down,—
The work of the hands of the worker with the ax!

Then verbs in the plural number follow in the next verse,—

4. With silver and with gold they beautify,
With nails and with hammers they fasten them,
So that none may move *them.*

The verb for "move" is in Hiphil; it means in Kal to totter,—"that none may cause them to totter."

But the *Septuagint* have rendered the verb "cut down" as a passive participle, כרות, transposing the ו; and *Venema* takes this as the proper reading,—"For a tree from the forest is cut down." But this does not run well with the following verse. The nations or heathens, is the nominative to all the verbs.

Venema renders the last line of the fourth verse,—

That nothing may make *them* to reel.

He considers that לא means often "nothing;" but it means also sometimes "none," or no one.—*Ed.*

the false imagination of men; for as soon as it takes a new form, it seems to be no longer a tree. The tree, while it grows, when it produces fruit, is not worshipped as God; but when it is cut down, the dead and dry trunk is substituted in the place of God: for what reason? even because the ax has been applied. Some render it "hatchet," *hache, ou doloire,* which is the same; for there is no ambiguity in the meaning: they cut down trees from the forests; and then after the tree was formed by the ax and worked by the hands of the artificer, what follows was done to it—

4. They deck it with silver and with gold; they fasten it with nails and with hammers, that it move not.

5. They *are* upright as the palm-tree, but speak not: they must needs be borne, because they cannot go. Be not afraid of them; for they cannot do evil, neither also *is it* in them to do good.

4. Argento et auro pulchrificant (*hoc est,* exornant) illud; clavis et malleis fortificant (*hoc est,* bene defigunt;) et non movebitur (*hoc est,* ut non moveatur.)

5. Sicuti palma æqualis (*hoc est,* stat effigies illa æqualis tanquam palma, *id est,* assurgit in rectitudinem;) et non loquuntur; et tollendo tolluntur, quia non ambulabunt (*hoc est,* non possunt ambulare:) ne timeatis ab illis; quia non malè faciunt, atque etiam benè facere non penes ipsos.

He goes on with the same subject, and borrows his words from the forty-fourth chapter of Isaiah; for the passage is wholly similar. Jeremiah, being later, was induced to take the words from his predecessor, that his own nation might be more impressed, on finding that the same thing was said by two Prophets, and that thus they had two witnesses.

He then says that these wise men, who filled the Jews with wonder and astonishment, *adorned their images,* or statues, *with silver and gold,* and afterward *fixed them with nails and with hammers, that they might not move.* Some refer the last word to the metal, "that the pieces might not come off," as the verb sometimes means to depart. But the simpler meaning is, that the statues were fixed by nails and hammers, that they might not be moved. Then the Prophet adds by way of concession, *They are* indeed *erect as the palm-trees;* and thus there appears in them something remarkable: *but they speak not;* and then, *being raised they are raised,* that is, they cannot move themselves; *for they cannot walk.* Then he says, *Be not afraid of them; for they do no evil, nor is it in their power to do good.*

We now see what the Prophet meant to teach us,—that the wisdom of the Chaldeans, and also of the Egyptians, was celebrated throughout the world, and also so blinded the Jews, or so enraptured them, that they thought that nothing proceeded from them but what deserved to be known and esteemed. In order therefore to remove and demolish this false notion, he shews that they were beyond measure foolish; for what could have been more sottish than to think that the nature of a tree is changed as soon as it receives a new form? How? By the hand of the artificer. Can it be in the power of man to make a god at his will? This is a folly which heathen authors have derided. Horace has this sentence:—

"When the workman was uncertain whether to make a bench or Priapus,
He chose rather to make a god."[1]

That poet, as he dared not generally to condemn the madness which then prevailed, indirectly shewed how shameful it was to make a log of wood a god, because the workman had given it a form. The very richest worshipped a wooden god, while he despised the artificer! He who would not have condescended to give the workman a cup of water, yet prostrated himself before the god which the workman had made! This then is what our Prophet now says, "Behold, with silver and gold do they adorn trunks of trees; they indeed stood up, for they are erect statues;" and he compares them to palm-trees, because they stood high: and he says, "but they speak not; they are raised up, for they have no life; hence fear them not:" and then he adds, "*They cannot do evil, and it is not in their power to do good.*"

The Prophet seems to speak improperly when he says that they were not gods, because they could do no evil; for it is wholly contrary to the nature of the only true God to do evil: but the Prophet, according to what is common, uses the word for the infliction of punishment. God, then, is said to do evil, not because he does harm to any one—not because he does wrong to any mortals, but because he chastises them for their sins. And it is a way of speaking de-

[1] "Cum faber incertus scamnum faceretne Priapum,
Maluit esse Deum."—*Hor. Lib. i. Sat.* 8.

rived from the common judgment of man, for we call those things evils which are afflictions to us; for famine, diseases, poverty, cold, heat, disgrace, and things of this kind, are called afflictions or adversities. Now, the Prophet says, that the idols of the Gentiles, or their fictitious gods, do no evil, that is, they have no power to inflict punishment on men. And this is taken from Isaiah. God uses there a twofold argument, while claiming divinity to himself alone: he says, "I alone am he who foresees and predicts future things;" and hence I am God alone; and then he says, "I alone am he who do good and evil;" hence I alone am God. (Isaiah xlv. 22; xlviii. 3, 5.) He says, that he doeth evil, because he is the Judge of the world. We hence see that this expression is not to be taken in a bad sense, but, as I have said, it is to be taken in a sense used by men; for we consider and call those punishments, with which God visits us, evils. It follows—

6. Forasmuch as *there is* none like[1] unto thee, O Lord; thou *art* great, and thy name *is* great in might.	6. A non[1] (*vel,* ab eo quod non, *hoc est,* ab ultimis temporibus non) sicut tu Jehova reperietur; magnus tu, et magnum nomen tuum in fortitudine.

As the truth respecting the gods of the heathens, that they are mere figments, would be useless and of no moment, were not the knowledge of the true God added, the Prophet now introduces God himself. And there is another reason; for no one could know that these wooden and stony gods are of no account, were not the truth respecting the true God to shine forth. Whosoever does not understand that there is a God, and does not know who or what he is, can never be really influenced by this truth, that the gods of the heathens are demons, and that all their superstitions are sacrilegious.

We now then perceive why the Prophet turns to the true God: it was, that the brightness of God's glory might dissipate the darkness in which the Gentiles were involved,

[1] The word is, מאין: the מ here is not a preposition, but a formative, and the word means *none.* So all the versions and the *Targum* render it. The proper rendering of the verse is—

None *is* like thee, Jehovah;
Great *art* thou,
And great *is* thy name, in strength.—*Ed.*

and also, that true religion might really influence the hearts of men, so that by acknowledging the one true God, to whose power we ought to submit, they might not only despise and repudiate all idols, but also hate and abhor them. The rest to-morrow.

PRAYER.

Grant, Almighty God, that since thou hast made heaven and earth for our sake, and hast testified by thy servant Moses, that the sun, as well as the moon, to which foolish heathens ascribe divinity, are to be serviceable to us, and that we are to use them as though they were our servants,—O grant that we may, by thy so many blessings, have our minds raised upwards and contemplate thy true glory, so that we may faithfully worship thee only, and surrender ourselves so entirely to thee, that while we enjoy the benefits derived from all the stars, and also from the earth, we may know that we are bound to thee by so many favours, in order that we may be more and more roused to attend to what is just and right, and thus endeavour to glorify on earth thy name, that we may at length enjoy that blessed glory which has been provided for us by Christ our Lord.—Amen.

Lecture Fortieth.

We began yesterday to explain the sixth verse, in which Jeremiah says, *From no time has there been found any like the true God, for he is great, and great is his name in power.* This sentence appears, indeed, unmeaning or very common as to its idea, in negativing the notion that there has been any in all the ages like to God: but as the world by its figments has ever obscured the glory of the true God, there is in this sentence what is of great importance, for it says that God possesses his own peculiar dignity, and shines far above all fictitious deities. The same view is to be taken of the second clause, *Thou art great.* Who will not concede greatness to God? yet he is deprived of it by most; for when any one devises for himself a god, he robs the true God of his own greatness, and makes him as it were one like many other gods. If we bear in mind how men depreciate God's glory, it is easy for us to see, that he is not uselessly called here great, as he is in many other places. But I only touch here on these things briefly, as I have elsewhere discussed them more at large.

He says that *God's name is great in power;* for idols had a celebrated name among all nations, but had no power. Though many things have been related of their idols by the Grecians and Italians, as well as by the Orientals, yet it is certain that no proof has been given to shew that they worshipped true gods. Hence the Prophet declares here that greatness belongs to God alone, as his power has been made known, and has fully manifested his own peculiar glory. It now follows—

7. Who would not fear thee, O King of nations? for to thee doth it appertain: forasmuch as among all the wise *men* of the nations, and in all their kingdoms, *there is* none like unto thee.

7. Quis non timebit te rex gentium? quia tibi convenit; nam inter omnes sapientes gentium et in omnibus regnis eorum, à nullo tempore similis tibi, (*vel,* sicut tu, *ad verbum.*)

The Prophet exclaims, *Who will not fear thee?* This question is very emphatical, as though he indignantly rebuked the stupidity of all those who acknowledged not the only true God, as if he had said, "Whence is it that thou art not feared throughout the whole world? Surely were there a spark of right knowledge in men, they would acknowledge thee as the only true God, and having found this truth, would submit to thy power. When, therefore, men invent for themselves various gods, and when every one is led here and there without any judgment, it is a monstrous thing; for when the subject is pressed on the attention of the rudest, they confess that there is some supreme deity, and are at length constrained to allow that there is but one true God; whence then is it that there is such a multitude and variety of gods in the world? How is it that they who hold this principle—that God ought to be worshipped—fall away, and adopt many gods, and never can determine who the true God is, or how he is to be worshipped?" We now understand the object of the Prophet in exclaiming, as through astonishment, *Who will not fear thee, the King of nations?*

We know that the true God was then despised by the heathens; and we also know that his law was regarded with contempt, and even as an abomination: What then does this question mean? even what I have already stated: The Prophet indignantly says, that it was a monstrous thing, bordering on madness, that men paid no regard to the only true God, but went astray after their own foolish devices. And he calls him *the King of the nations*, not that the nations submitted to his authority, but because he manifested evidences of his power everywhere, which might have induced the rudest to shew him reverence, were they not extremely stupid. We then see that this is not said to the honour of the nations, but on the contrary, that their ingratitude might be exposed to shame in not honouring God, who manifested his power among them.

Then follows what confirms this: *For to thee it belongs; for among all the wise of the nations, and in all their kingdoms, from no time has there been one like to thee.* He says that it *belongs* to God, that is, that all the world should fear him. Some render יאתה, *iate*, as a noun, and take it as signifying "honour;" and others render it "government," or authority; but this cannot be received. He then says, it *belongs* to God. What? Some say, "glory or dominion belongs to thee." But it must be referred to the beginning of the verse: there is here a figure called Zeugma, and the meaning is, God deserves this, that is, to be feared by all. He then speaks of fear, and says that it belongs to God. What is meant is, that the glory of God shines so much as to be sufficient to arrest and engage all the thoughts of men, and that they are therefore extremely stupid when they pass by and forsake him, and turn to their own devices, and invent gods according to their own fancies.[1]

[1] This verse is omitted in the *Septuagint*. The sentence, "To thee it belongs," is in the *Vulgate* and *Syriac*, "Thine is the honour;" and in the *Targum* and *Arabic*, "Thine is the kingdom." *Blayney* gives this version,—

"When he shall approach unto thee."

But this has hardly a meaning here, and far less has the rendering of *Horsley*,—

"Surely unto thee shall be the coming;"

i.e., "The general coming, the universal resort." The bishop saw predictions everywhere. The explanation of *Calvin* is the most satisfactory. The act mentioned in the preceding clause, "fear," is to be understood as the nominative case.—*Ed.*

The Prophet then confirms what we have already said—that all men who worship not nor fear the only true God are detestable beings, because so much of his glory shines forth, that renders all bound to acknowledge him. It then follows, that those who are carried away into various superstitions are to the last degree stupid and brutish; for God renders his glory conspicuous everywhere, so that it ought to engage and occupy the thoughts of all men; and it would do so were they not led away by their own vanity.

We hence also learn that the pretext of ignorance made by unbelievers is wholly vain. There are those who on the first view seem to be excusable for their error, as they have not been taught, and never understood who the true God is; but yet there is in them the blame of neglect as well as of wickedness, for they wilfully neglect and despise the only true God. As then the unbelieving take delight in their errors, they are to be held guilty. And this is what the Prophet means by saying that God was worthy of glory—the glory of being feared by all: and this he more fully confirms when he says, "Among all the wise, and in all kingdoms," that is, among all the princes who seemed to excel in wisdom in governing the world, "no other God could be found throughout all the ages."

He repeats again the word מאין, *main*, of which we spoke yesterday.[1] It is the same as though the Prophet had said, "Let all the wise men and philosophers come forth, let all those counsellors who assume great wisdom appear, and let them adduce whatever they can allege; doubtless God will ever defend his own glory against all their frivolous arguments, so that they must depart confounded; nor shall they be able, however willing they may be, to bring any solid objection against him." By these words, then, the Prophet intimates that it is vain to boast of philosophic reasons, and that the counsels of princes, who esteem themselves very acute in civil affairs, will be adduced in vain; for all will be covered with shame, and be constrained to be silent, when God makes known his glory. Indeed the glory

[1] All the versions and the *Targum*, as in the former instance, do not regard the מ as a preposition, but render the word by "none," or no one.—*Ed.*

of God appears everywhere so conspicuously, that the rudest ought to perceive it, that the wise, who fly above the heavens as philosophers, who search all the secrets of nature, do not understand what is, as they say, abroad in the open air; for God manifests himself to the simple, and even to children. We now perceive the design of the Prophet, when he says, *From no times has been found any like to God,* not only among the vulgar or common men, but among the wise, and princes, and kings' counsellors. He afterwards adds—

8. But they are altogether brutish and foolish; the stock *is* a doctrine of vanities.	8. Et in uno stulti sunt et fatui sunt; eruditio vanitatum lignum est.

The Prophet shews here, in one sentence, that the wisest in the whole world could be proved guilty of the greatest madness, or of a twofold folly, because they willingly worshipped the trunks of trees, and they worshipped stones; for under one kind he includes the other. There is no one, he says, however intelligent, who does not approve of the superstitions of the people, who does not bend the knee before a wood or a stone. There have been, indeed, a few in the world who ridiculed such sottishness, but no one dared openly to condemn it, and no one introduced anything better. And even the Platonics hold that the Greeks had not without reason invented gods like men; and they say that there was not so much judgment among the barbarians as to form such ideas of the gods as were suitable to their nature. However this may have been, it is evident that the grossest superstitions of the nations were ever approved by all their wise men.

The Prophet then shews that there was no need of a long discussion to discover the vanity of the wise; *In one,* in one thing, he says; and there is emphasis in this word, when he says, *In one* thing *they are foolish and fatuitous;* for there is to be understood a contrast, as though he had said, "I will not here join together many heads of accusation against them to expose their folly, one thing is sufficient; this one sentence is enough to condemn them,—that *wood is the teaching of vanities.*"[1] We have stated what the Pro-

[1] The word באחת is rendered by the Versions and the *Targum, alike,*

phet means,—even that all the wise, who together with the vulgar worshipped gods made of wood and stone, were very foolish: but we must notice the import of the expression, *The teaching of vanities is the wood.* It is, as we have said, an instance of a part being put for the whole; for under "wood" Jeremiah includes statues of stone, and others made of different materials; as though he had said, "Every form or effigy, representing a god, is *the teaching of vanities.*" He takes this as granted; and yet there had been, as we have lately stated, a great and fierce contention among the wise men on this subject; but the Prophet deigned not to contend or seriously to dispute with them, for the thing itself was sufficiently evident, that is, that nothing can be more absurd than to worship the trunk of a tree or a stone.

Now we may from this passage draw a general truth,—that when men seek to represent God under any visible form, they give way to the delusions and impostures of Satan. Well known is that sentence of Gregory to Serenus, the Bishop of Marseilles, when that good man cast down the images which he saw led to ungodly worship, and purged the churches of Marseilles from such pollutions: Gregory, though a pious man, yet wrote very foolishly—that Serenus acted rightly and wisely in forbidding images to be worshipped, but that he yet acted inconsiderately by emptying the churches of them; for "they are," he said, "the books of the simple:" this is the conclusion of his epistle. And it is ever in the mouth of Papists—that images are the books of

equally or *together*. Literally, "in one," that is, altogether. *Calvin* rather refines here. The verse may be thus rendered,—

> But they are together brutish and stupid;
> The teaching of vanities, the wood is.

Literally, "the wood it," but as *Gataker* says, the pronoun is often used in Hebrew for the substantive verb. The phrase is elliptical, no unusual thing in Hebrew. It may be thus, rendering in full,—

> The teaching of vanities, is the teaching of the wood, or respecting the wood.

What they taught respecting the wooden idols was "vanities," that is, very or extremely vain; for so the plural often means. The version of *Blayney*, after *Castellio*, and approved by *Horsley*, is the following,—

> "The very wood itself being a rebuker of vanities."

But it is a sentiment not suitable to this place. The most strict meaning of מוסר is restraint, and not rebuke; it often means teaching or instruction.—*Ed.*

the simple. At the same time I would they retained this truth avowed by Gregory,—that they ought not to be worshipped. They worship and adore them, as it is well known, in the place of God. But as I have already said, that answer of Gregory was puerile and foolish: for we hear what the Prophet says,—that in wood and stone and in every outward representation there is vanity, as Habakkuk also in the second chapter, where he speaks of idols, calls an idol the teacher of vanity. Every statue, every image, by which foolish men seek to represent God, is a teacher of falsehood. So our Prophet says,—that the teaching of vanities is found in all statues, because God is thus misrepresented; for what can be in a wood or stone that is like the infinite power of God, or his incomprehensible essence and majesty? Men, therefore, offer a serious affront to God when they thus deform him, as Paul also in Rom. i. 25, says,—that the truth was thus changed into falsehood, that is, when he is supposed to have anything like to what external and dead figures have; as the same Paul further reasons in Acts xvii. 29, when he says, Do ye think that God is like to wood or stone, to silver or gold? And his argument was at that time suitable; for he had to do with heathens: he did not refer to the law, though he might have quoted a passage in Deuteronomy, where God reminded the people that he so appeared to them that they saw no similitude; and he might have referred to the testimonies of Isaiah, Jeremiah, and of the other Prophets; but as he addressed heathens, even the Athenians, he says, "One of your poets has said, that we are the offspring of God:" if we are then, he says, the offspring of God, do ye not draw God down from his celestial throne, when ye seek to delineate him according to your fancies, and suppose that he lies hid in wood or stone, in silver and gold? For some life appears at least in men, they are endued with mind and intelligence, and so far they bear some likeness to God: but a dead wood and stone, which are void of sense,—gold also and silver, which are metals without reason, which have no life,—what affinity, he says, can these have to God? This subject might be more copiously handled; but I merely explain what the Prophet means, and also shew the import of his doctrine, and how it may be applied for general instruction. It now follows—

9. Silver spread into plates is brought from Tarshish, and gold from Uphaz, the work of the workman, and of the hands of the founder: blue and purple *is* their clothing; they *are* all the work of cunning *men*.

9. Argentum percussum (*vel,* diductum, *hoc est, malleo sic contusum, ut redactum sit in laminas; hoc enim significat verbum* רקע *percutere, et ita contundere, ut res diducatur vel protrahatur:* argentum *ergo* laminatum, *ut ita loquar, vel,* malleo contusum) è Tharsis affertur, et aurum ex Ophas, opus artificis et manus conflatoris; hyacinthus et purpura, vestes eorum; opus sapientum omnes!

The Prophet, anticipating what might be said, refers to the splendour and pomp of idols, and declares that all was frivolous and extremely puerile. Whence was it that the world shewed so much honour to idols, except that their pomp dazzled the eyes of men? The devil has also by this artifice ever deluded the unbelieving; for he has exhibited in idols something that involved men's minds in darkness.

The Prophet then assails these foolish imaginations, and says, *Silver is brought from Tharsis,* that is, from Cilicia; for so the Scripture designates that transmarine country, which lies opposed to Judea; and we know that Cilicia was over against Judea; for the Mediterranean Sea intervenes between Syria and Cilicia; and the sea of Tharsis is what they call that part which extended towards Cilicia and Asia Minor. The Prophet then says that it was brought from a far country. Well, he says, the fact is so; and then it is added that *gold* was brought from *Uphaz.* Some have explained this last word wrongly, by saying that it means pure or fine gold; but it appears from this place and many others, that it is the name of a country, that is, Persia, or one not far from Persia: it was at least a country eastward of Judea. He then says, *gold* is brought *from Uphaz;* and he mentions the workmanship, *the work of the artificer;* that is, it is not silver and gold in its rude state; but they are so elegantly wrought, that they readily attract the eyes of men. Then he adds *the hands* (he speaks in the plural number) *of the melter;* that is, the silver and gold were melted and were made to assume a certain form; and then art was employed, which gave an increased polish to these forms which came out of the furnace. He afterwards says, *The hyacinth and purple are their vestments;* that is, it is not enough to have the precious metal, and that cast into an elegant and lovely form, but it must be clothed in purple and hyacinth. He says in the last place, that *the work* was that *of the wise;* that is, skilful men were chosen, who could in the most perfect manner give expression to every lineament; in short, nothing was left undone.[1]

But the Prophet, though he concedes generally to the unbelieving that they added whatever could add beauty to their idols, yet declares that they were mere trumperies: they are puppets, he says; for man, who is a mortal, cannot make a god: and then, what can art and the toil and labour of man do in this respect? can he change the nature of things? can he make a god from wood and stone? and when a vestment covers the idol of gold or of silver, can it raise it above the heavens, that it may attain a new divinity? We hence see that the Prophet mentions all that was done, that he might taunt the heathens and ridicule their fatuitous trifles; for in their idols there was nothing real, nothing that could be depended upon. He then subjoins—

10. But the Lord *is* the true God, he *is* the living God, and an everlasting King: at his wrath the earth shall tremble, and the nations shall not be able to abide his indignation.

10 Atqui Iehova Deus veritas (*qui vertunt,* Deus veritatis, *non observant syntax in Hebraicam; dixisset enim* יהוה אלהי אמת; Iehova *ergo* Deus veritas,) ipse Deus vita, et rex seculorum; à furore ejus contremiscet terra, et non sustinebunt gentes iram ejus.

The Prophet here exults and triumphs in the name of his God, as though he had overcome and put to flight the erroneous notions of the heathens: for he had spoken, as it ap-

[1] The verse is literally thus,—

9. Silver extended, from Tarsis it is brought,
And gold from Uphaz,—
The work of the artizan
And of the hands of the founder;
Blue and purple their garments,—
The work of the wise, all of them.

The *Septuagint* and *Arabic* have " Mophaz;" the *Vulgate,* " Ophaz;" the *Syriac* and the *Targum,* " Ophir." Probably the same country is meant, and that it had two names. " Blue" is rendered " hyacinth," violet-colour, by all the versions and the *Targum.*

" Uphaz," according to *Bochart,* was a country near the Ganges in India, and the same with Ophir.—*Ed.*

pears, contemptuously of their gross errors, and shewed that the wise men of the world were extremely sottish, who were so charmed with wood and stone. He now highly extols the glory of God, and says, *But Jehovah is God;* that is, let the nations worship their gods, let them recite fables as to their power, and falsely ascribe to them many miracles; but *Jehovah,* he says, *is God.* When all things are faithfully examined, it will appear evident that He is the only true God, and all the gods of the heathens will of themselves vanish into nothing. This then is the meaning of the Prophet, as though he had said, God himself is sufficient to put to flight all the errors of the heathens, when his majesty appears; for so great is its brightness that it will reduce to nothing whatever the world admires.

He then adds *truth.* He sets truth here in opposition to vanities. He had said that wood was the teaching of vanities; he now says, God is eternal truth; that is, he has no need of adventitious ornaments; they mask, he says, the idols of the heathens, they are clothed and adorned; but these things have nothing real in them: *Jehovah is God the truth;* that is, God borrows nothing from anything else, but is satisfied with himself, and his power possesses of itself sufficient authority. *God* then *is truth,* and *God,* he says, *is life.* After having said that God has real and solid glory in himself, he adds another proof, taken from what is known to men, even that God is *life;* for though God is in himself incomprehensible, yet he not only sets before our eyes evidences of his glory, but he also renders himself in a manner the object of feeling, as Paul says in Acts xiv. 17. What he means is, that though men were blind, they could yet by feeling find out God. Though the blind have no sight, yet they can find their way by feeling; they go round a hall or a room, and by feeling find the door; and when they wish to enter into a room, they find the door by the same means. But there is no need, says Paul, for us to depart from ourselves; for whosoever will examine himself will find God within; for in him we live and move and have our being. (Acts xvii. 28.) Were we then to object and say, that God is incomprehensible, and that we cannot ascend to the height of his glory, doubtless there is life in us, and as we have life, we have an evidence of his divinity; for who is so devoid of reason as to say that he lives through himself? Since then men live not of themselves, but obtain life as a favour from another, it follows that God dwells in them.[1]

Now, then, the Prophet, after having spoken of God's essence, descends to what is more evident. And doubtless it is a real knowledge of God, not when we speculate in the air as philosophers do, but when we know by experience that there is one true God—how ? because we exist. We exist not of ourselves, but in and through another, and that is, through the one true God. It hence follows that human life is a clear proof of one supreme God. *God* then *is life and the King of ages.* For as the world has also been made, as years succeed years, and as there is in this revolution variety and yet such perfect order, who does not see in all this the glory of God? Now, then, we also perceive why the Prophet calls God the *King of ages.*

He then adds, *Through his fury tremble will the earth, and the nations will not sustain his wrath.* As he could not succeed with the heathens, he warns here the Jews not to provoke the wrath of God, who will be the Judge of the whole world, and will destroy the unbelievers, however blind in darkness they may be. He then warns the Jews not to close their eyes to the glory, which had been more fully open to them. But the Gentiles might by the works of nature have known God, and were inexcusable; yet, the knowledge of him was made plain to the Jews by the law. For this rea-

[1] The verse, literally rendered, is as follows:—

> " But Jehovah, God the truth he,
> God the life and King eternal;
> At his wrath tremble will the earth,
> And not bear will the nations his indignation."

It is usual in Hebrew to put nouns for adjectives; divested of this peculiarity, and the future being taken for the present, the verse would run thus:

> " But Jehovah, the true God is he,
> The living God and King eternal;
> At his wrath tremble does the earth,
> And the nations cannot bear his indignation."

" The true God," and " the living God," is the version of the *Vulgate* and of the *Targum;* but that of the *Syr.* and *Arab.*, " the God of truth," and " the God of the living," but no doubt incorrect.—*Ed.*

son Jeremiah says, "Even though unbelievers now boldly despise God, yet when he shall appear as the Judge of the world, the whole earth must of necessity tremble, and will not be able to bear his presence, though they now proudly reproach true religion."

But it was not without reason that the Prophet took so much pains on this subject; for the ten tribes had been driven into exile, and the Assyrians and Chaldeans triumphed over God himself, as though he had been overcome, inasmuch as he did not defend the kingdom of Israel, which was under his care and protection; and the miserable Israelites could not but despond when they found themselves so distressed, and cruelly treated and oppressed by the most shameless tyranny; for what could they have thought, but that they had not been the objects of God's care, and that his promises were vain, or that he possessed no sufficient power to preserve them? It is, then, for this reason that the Prophet now so highly extols the power and glory of God, that is, that their calamities might not deject them and lay prostrate the faith of those who thought that they were forsaken.

And this will be more evident from the following verse, where the Prophet uses the Chaldee language; and this is the only verse in the whole book written in Chaldee; and the Chaldee differs much from the Hebrew. We have seen before that Daniel wrote in Chaldee, when he spoke of things pertaining to the Chaldeans; but when he addressed his own people and announced prophecies, belonging especially to the Church of God, he wrote in Hebrew. Hence the book of Daniel is written in Hebrew, except in those parts which he wished to be understood by the Chaldeans; and so does the Prophet in this place.

11. Thus shall ye say unto them, The gods that have not made the heavens and the earth, *even* they shall perish from the earth, and from under these heavens.

11. Sic (secundum hoc) dicetis illis (*inquit*) Dii (*prorsus diverso modo loquitur quam ante, et proximo etiam versu loquitur; dii ergo*) qui cœlum et terram non fecerunt, pereant è terra et de sub cœlis istis.

Now, the reason why he bids the Israelites to speak in the Chaldee language is, because they had been led into exile, and were mingled with the Assyrians and Chaldeans. He then required from those despised exiles an open and a bold confession, as though he had said, "Even though ye are now in the most miserable bondage, and though the Chaldeans disdainfully oppress you, as if ye were slaves, yet proclaim the glory of God and shrink not from an open confession of your religion, and say to them, in contempt of all their idols, *perish must your gods from the earth and from under heaven, for they have not made heaven nor the earth."* We now understand the meaning of the Prophet. But the rest I shall defer until to-morrow.

PRAYER.

Grant, Almighty God, that since thou hast exhibited thy glory to be seen by us, not only in the heavens and the earth, but also in the law, in the Prophets, and in the Gospel, and hast so plainly made thyself known to us in thine only-begotten Son, that ignorance can be no excuse,—O grant that we may make progress in this knowledge by which thou kindly invitest to thyself, and may so constantly cleave to thee, that none of the errors of the world may draw us aside; but may we stand firm in thy word, which cannot deceive us, until we shall at length come to that celestial blessedness, when we shall enjoy thee face to face in thy glory, having been made fully conformable to thine image in Christ Jesus our Lord.—Amen.

Lecture Forty-First.

We began yesterday to explain the declaration of the Prophet, in which he exhorted the Israelites to constancy, though scattered among the Chaldeans. Their condition was then miserable, because we know that it was that of bondage, and conquerors ruled in a very petulant manner, when a people were subdued by war; but they had been led into exile for the very purpose of degrading them. The Prophet therefore animates them here, that they might not be dejected, but continue in the pure worship of God, and faithfully profess his name.

What he said to them was, *May those gods, who created not the heaven and the earth, perish from the earth and from under heaven.* He assumed this principle—that no one ought to be counted God but he who is the creator and maker of heaven and earth ; and who could say that gods of wood and stone had created the world ? for wood, as well as stone, is a corruptible material. All the statues, which were created gods, had received their form and shape from mortal men. It is hence manifest, that to ascribe divinity to them was not only false, but foolish and monstrous. This, then, is the reason why he says, "May the gods who made not the heaven and earth perish." The verb is indeed in the future tense ; but we know that the future is often to be taken as an optative in Hebrew. If, however, any one prefers to retain this tense, "Perish shall the gods who made not the heaven and the earth," I shall not contend with him ; yet the other view is what I approve, that the Israelites were to imprecate destruction on all idols.[1]

[1] Critics have unnecessarily suggested a doubt as to the genuineness of this verse, written in Chaldee. They have nothing but conjecture, and even for that conjecture there is no solid reason. It is not omitted in any MS. but one, nor by any of the early versions, nor by the *Targum*, though paraphrased more than what is commonly done. As to the context, it seems to be wholly necessary ; for the meaning of the two following verses cannot be well understood without it, provided they are rendered correctly. I shall first give the three verses, and then point out the connection :—

11. Thus shall ye say to them,
"The gods, who have not made the heaven and the earth,
Perish from the earth, even from under heaven, shall they :
12. He who made the earth through his power,
Who has set in order the world by his wisdom,
And through his understanding expanded the heavens,—
13. At his voice when given,
Abundance of waters is in the heavens,
For he brings clouds from the extremity of the earth ;
Lightnings for rain he makes,
And sends forth the wind from his treasures."

The Prophet's object was to shew that the Creator of the world is its ruler. As false gods did not create the world, they do not rule it. The *name* of the true God is not given in these verses, nor are the gods of the Chaldeans specially named. The gods who were no creators are alone mentioned, and contrasted with them is he who made all things; and of him he says, that "at his voice when given," or literally, "at the voice of his giving," abundance of waters appear, which he brings from the extremity of the earth. He states things as they appear ; clouds arise from the horizon, said here to be the extremity of the earth. Then he mentions the most terrific things in nature, thunders, lightnings, and storms, (for that is what is meant here by wind,) as being under the entire control of him who made the heaven and the earth. Thus we see that when the passage is rightly understood, the eleventh verse is necessary as a portion of the context.

"He who made," &c. *He* is put as a sort of nominative absolute, as

Now that he uses the Chaldee language, is what deserves, as we said yesterday, to be observed; they had then to do with the Chaldeans, who insultingly triumphed over the true God, thinking that they were his conquerors; and they triumphed over him, as though he had been overcome by their swords. Then the Prophet bids the Israelites, boldly and courageously, to proclaim the name and the glory of the true God. Doubtless this could not have been done without immediate danger of death; but it was their duty, as God's true servants, to prefer his glory to their own lives, in opposing the fury of the enemies who then ruled over them, and who had led them to remote countries.

We see how much God makes of the confession of faith; and the whole Scripture shews that this sacrifice is especially approved by him. Hence also it appears how foolishly they talk who say that they cherish faith secretly in their hearts, though they may hide from the world their real sentiments. We see how frigid, nay, how foolish is this excuse, while they seek, by a perfidious silence, to save their own life and to remain in peace with the ungodly. They who at this day live under the Papacy, think that they justly exempt themselves by such an excuse as this—that they ought not rashly to endanger their lives, as facts prove that such is the rage of the enemies of the gospel, that were any to confess the truth, they would be immediately led to punishment. But we may compare the condition of the ancient people with our own; certainly ours is better than that of the ten tribes, who lived in a foreign land and were treated as slaves. As then the Chaldeans watched them, did they not find the sword daily and constantly ready to be used against them? And yet God bids them to close their eyes to their danger and faithfully to profess what they believed, yea, to detest the idols, which was still more displeasing to the Chaldeans; for he bids them to say, "The God whom we worship made himself known to Abraham our father, and we worship him, because we have found him to be a Redeemer and a constant preserver of our safety:" and this is not the only thing

"gods" is in the former verse. This kind of phraseology is often to be met with in Hebrew.—*Ed.*

that the Prophet bids them to say, but also, "May your gods perish." This was certainly enough to kindle rage in the Chaldeans, even if they had been men of temperate minds; but as they were elated with pride on account of their victory and hated the Jews, such a declaration must have been intolerable to them. What, then, can the Nicodemites of this day say, who indulge their own delusions? for they think it enough if they deny not God in their hearts; and yet being frightened with danger, they either pretend to deny him, or openly shew that they consent to errors.

In short, we see that there is no true religion in the hearts of men, except a confession is made, for there ought to be a consent between the heart and the tongue. But some one may object and say, Is it necessary for the faithful to cry through cross-ways and the streets of the city, "There is but one true God?" I answer, that all have not been chosen to the prophetic office, in order to preach everywhere; but it is commanded to all without exception, to detest idols, where they see the glory of God reproachfully traduced by enemies; for the Prophet meant, that they were to make this answer to the reproaches of those who then took the occasion insultingly to rise up against the true God. It now follows:—

12. He hath made the earth by his power, he hath established the world by his wisdom, and hath stretched out the heavens by his discretion.

13. When he uttereth his voice, *there is* a multitude of waters in the heavens, and he causeth the vapours to ascend from the ends of the earth; he maketh lightnings with rain, and bringeth forth the wind out of his treasures.

12. Faciens terram in virtute sua, disponens orbem in sapientia sua, et in sua intelligentia extendit cœlos.

13. Ad vocem dando sonitum aquarum (*vel potius* copiam aquarum) in cœlis; et ascendere faciens elevationes ab extremitate terræ, fulgura ad pluviam creans (faciens, *ut prius*,) et educens ventum è thesauris suis.

Jeremiah speaks now again in Hebrew, for he on purpose spoke in Chaldee, to shew that the ungodly were not to be given way to, if they blasphemed and wantonly derided the holy name of God. But as it is necessary that the confession of the mouth should proceed from faith, as fruit from the root, the Prophet here reminds the Israelites that there is but one true God; for, besides him who created the earth, set in order the world, and extended the heavens, there is no other to be found. Since, then, this cannot be said except of one, it follows that all the deities which the world devises for itself, are false and mere inventions of Satan, by which he deludes mankind. And doubtless no one can courageously oppose such errors, except he who believes in the one true God. We know that there were formerly some among the philosophers who jocularly and facetiously ridiculed the delirious notions of the vulgar; but no one in earnest undertook this cause, nor could they take upon themselves the defence of God's glory, for he was unknown to them. It is therefore necessary, as I have said, that we should be really and truly grounded in the faith before the building can be carried on; for the profession, by which we ascribe glory to God, is, as it were, the superstructure, but faith, concealed within the heart, is the foundation.

We now then understand the Prophet's design in saying, that there is but one, who made the earth. He speaks indeed concisely; but what he says has more force, when he does not mention God's name, but sets before us his power, as though he had said, "There is one, there is one, who has created the earth; there is one, who has set in order the world and extended the heavens; as these things cannot be ascribed to many, it follows that men are very absurd in imagining that there are various gods."

He says that God *created the earth by his power.* He alludes to the solid state of the earth. The philosophers indeed hold that the earth stands naturally in the middle of creation, as it is the heaviest element; and the reason they give that the earth is suspended in mid-air, is, because the centre of the world attracts what is most heavy; and these things indeed they wisely discuss. Yet we must go further: for the centre of the earth is not the main part of creation; it hence follows that the earth has been suspended in the air, because it has so pleased God. When, therefore, the Prophet commends God's power in fixing the earth, he refers to its firm state.

He then adds, There is one *who hath by his wisdom set the world in order.* He does not indeed say that he is one, but this is what is implied. Though the term תבל, *tabel*, is taken for the earth, it has yet a wider meaning. The Prophet, I have no doubt, includes in it at least the sea. And we know that the Spirit has not spoken in the Law and the Prophets with rigorous exactness, but in a style suited to the common capacities of men. He says then that the world was set in order by God's wisdom: for it is wonderful how the waters mingle with the earth, and yet retain their own habitation, and are restrained from covering the earth: in the earth also itself there is amazing variety; we see in one part mountains, in another small hills; there are meadows, forests, and fields for corn. Indeed, man's industry contributes to this variety; but we see how God hath fitted the earth for different purposes. Here then shines forth the wonderful wisdom of God. When again he speaks of the heavens, he says, that they have been *expanded* by God's *knowledge*. He indeed employs various expressions, but he means the same thing,—that God's singular wisdom may be seen in the earth and in the heavens.

Some connect the following verse and explain the verb נטה, *nuthe*, differently,—that God extends the heavens when he covers them with clouds; for the verb תתו, *tatu*, which means the same thing, follows: but the infinite mood is often to be taken for the preterite. As then this is a strained explanation, and too far-fetched, I reject it. The Prophet, no doubt, speaks of the original formation of the heavens: for when God covers the heavens with clouds, their true form does not appear; besides, the meaning of the verb is perverted, when taken to express the obscuring of the heavens by clouds. They who will impartially examine the passage, will be ready to admit, that the Prophet speaks of the expanding of the heavens. So the Scripture everywhere sets forth God's wisdom as displayed by this wonderful workmanship; and the heaven is said to have been expanded over the earth, so that it covers it around. (Psalm civ. 6.)

Now, though Jeremiah mentions only the word "heavens," yet he includes the wonders which appear in them, such as that the sun performs its daily course—that it changes its track daily—that the planets have two motions—that they appear in different parts—and that the sun seems now to ascend and then to descend. In short, Jeremiah here extols all the secrets of astrology, when he says, that the heavens have been expanded by God, and expanded with singular and incomparable wisdom. Though, then, he only briefly touches on this wonderful workmanship of God, yet he would have us carefully to dwell on it in our meditations; for all errors and all fancies will soon vanish, when we duly consider the power and wisdom of God, as manifested in the creation of the heavens and of the earth, and in the order observable in the world.

The Prophet then descends to the other works of God, to those which are changeable, for there is in nature a perpetual constancy as to the heavens and the earth; and there are many things subject to changes; as when God darkens the air, when he raises winds, when he pours down rain. These things happen not according to the settled order of the world of which he had spoken. We see then that the Prophet has hitherto referred to the fixed and regular government of the world, to what had been done at the creation. But now, as I have said, he sets before us things of another kind,—that God *gives* or sends forth, *by his voice, abundance of waters from the heavens.* Some render המון, *emun,* "sound;" but it is, on the contrary, to be taken for "multitude," or abundance. Moreover, he takes "voice" for thunder: for though it often rains without thunder, yet when God thunders from heaven, there is a sudden change, which not only disturbs the air, but also fills us with dread. As then in this sudden and unexpected change the power of God more strikingly appears, the Prophet says, *At his voice he gives abundance of waters.*

He then says, *he makes elevations to ascend;* for we see that vapours arise from the earth and ascend upwards. Philosophers shew how this happens: but yet the power of God cannot be excluded, when we say that anything is done according to nature. For we hence more clearly see what the Prophet means, that is, that God has so set in order the world, that when he causes vapours to ascend, he shews that he rules in the heavens and on the earth. And he adds, *from the extremity of the earth:* for we see that vapours rise at a distance and immediately spread over our heads. Is not this wonderful? And were we not accustomed to such a thing, it could not but fill us with admiration. The Prophet then rouses men here from their torpor, that they may learn to consider what is presented to their view. He goes on and says, *creating* or making *lightnings for the rain,* or with the rain: for ל, *lamed,* is taken by some, as though he had said, that lightnings are mingled with rain: and doubtless we see that these things, fire and rain, are contrary to one another; yet fire generates water, and it dwells also in the midst of a mass of waters: it rains, and yet the air is at the same time kindled with lightnings. Since then God thus mingles contrary things, and makes fire the origin and the cause of rain, is it not so wonderful that it is sufficient to move the very stones? How great then must be the stupidity of men, when they attend not to so conspicuous a work of God, in which they may see the glory of his wisdom as well as of his power!

He then says, that God *brings forth the wind from his treasures.* He calls hidden places the *treasures* of God; for whence the winds except from the caverns of the earth? Since, then, the earth, where it is hollow, generates winds, rightly does the Prophet say, that they were the hidden *treasures* of God. The philosophers also find out the cause why the winds arise from the earth; for the sun attracts vapours and exhalations; from vapours are formed clouds, snows, and rains, according to the fixed order of the middle region of the air. From the exhalations also are formed the thunders, lightnings, the comets also, and the winds; for the exhalations differ from the vapours only in their lightness and rarity, the vapours being thicker and heavier. Then from vapour arises rain; but the exhalation is lighter, and not so thick; hence the exhalations generate thunders as well as winds, according to the heat they contain. How, then, is it that the same exhalation now breaks forth into wind, then into lightnings? It is according to the measure of its heat; when it is dense it rises into the air; but the winds vanish and thus disturb the lower part of the world.

These are the things said by philosophers; but the chief thing in philosophy is to have regard to God, who brings the winds out of his treasures, for he keeps them hidden. We wonder that the wind rises suddenly when it is quite calm; who ought not to acknowledge that winds are formed, and are sent here and there at God's pleasure? And hence in Psalm civ. 4, they are called the swift messengers of God, "who makes spirits his messengers." It follows:—

14. Every man is brutish in *his* knowledge; every founder is confounded by the graven image: for his molten image *is* falsehood, and *there is* no breath in them.

14. Stultus est omnis homo à scientia (*vertunt alii*, præscientia; *sed perperam, meo judicio*,) pudefactus est omnis conflator à sculptili; quia mendacium conflatile, et non est spiritus in illis.

Some too refinedly explain the beginning of this verse—that their own subtlety or wisdom, which they arrogate, infatuates men, according to what Paul says, that men become vain in their minds, when they form an idea of God according to their own imagination. (Rom. i. 21.) But the Prophet speaks more plainly, for he says, that *all artificers were foolish*. The word knowledge is not to be taken here for knowledge of truth, but for the knowledge of artificers, whether carpenters or blacksmiths, or those who either melted or graved or formed gods of wood, stone, and silver, as we may learn from the second clause of the verse. There is no difficulty as to what is meant, if we duly consider the words of the Prophet; he expresses the same thing in two ways; *foolish*, he says, *are all our artificers;* then he specifies one sort, *every founder* or melter, &c. We hence see that the Prophet does not use the word knowledge according to its strict meaning, but extends it to skill in workmanship.[1]

[1] The first clause of this verse is rendered by the *Sept.* and *Vulg.*, "Foolish has become every man by knowledge;" by the *Syr.*, "Foolish have all men become without knowledge;" the *Arab.* and the *Targ.* convey the same idea with the last. *Gataker* takes this view and gives this version, "Every man is become brutish for want of knowledge." But as the framers of idols were called, in ver. 9, "wise" or cunning men, it is more probable that their boasted knowledge is what is meant here. The verse may be thus rendered—

14. Brutish has every man become by *his* knowledge;
Disgracefully has every founder done as to the graven image,
For deception *is* his cunning;
And no spirit is in them.

To render the different parts of this verse correspondent, it is necessary

But when he says that the *artizans were foolish*, he connects with them, no doubt, all the worshippers of false gods; but he reprobates their knowledge, who applied whatever skill and knowledge they had to so vain a purpose. Behold, he says, the worker in gold, and every other artificer, think that they are very ingenious when they elegantly form an idol; they spend all their wits on so vain a thing; what is this but folly? But they think that they make a god by their own hands; yet they cannot change the nature of gold and silver. It is the form only that they add; but this form contains no life. Hence he subjoins, *There is no spirit in them.* He had said before, that they who formed the graven image would be ashamed, or convicted of folly; for he had called them foolish and brutish. Now, בער, *bor*, in Hiphil, means to be foolish; but the noun means a brute animal. Hence he reproachfully compares these illustrious artizans, who gained repute by the elegant forms they gave to their gods, to asses, and oxen, and other brute animals. Some render נסך, *nusak*, "covering;" but it signifies, I doubt not, a molten image; for he repeats what he had said, that the founders would be *ashamed of the graven image.* In short, he says, that *the molten image was falsehood, for there was in them no spirit.* He changes the number, but the meaning is evident.

We have seen before that idols were said to be the *teaching of vanities;* for they were extremely deceived, and became wholly foolish, who ascribed the glory of God to wood and stone. The heathens might say, that they had never thought such a thing; but facts proved that they were liars and made only vain pretences; for why did they place confidence in their idols?—why did they bow down before them?

to take הוביש as a Hiphil. The connection is between the first and last line, and between the two middle lines. Every man, both the carver and the founder, or melter, were brutish, in employing their knowledge and skill in making idols or images, because there was, after all their toil, no spirit, no life in them. Then the founder acted shamefully in taking the carved thing or image, to cover it with gold or silver, because what he melted was a mere deception.

This verse is no prediction, but a representation of the extreme folly and stupidity of idol-makers. This is confirmed by the following verse.—*Ed.*

—why did they address to them prayers and supplications? They then believed that God was present in the visible form. Now the Prophet says, that this was the teaching of vanities; because they who made a figure or image of God thought that he was like to gold and silver, and that he had some affinity to dead elements, destitute of reason and understanding. For the same purpose he now adds, that the *molten image is falsehood;* why? because the truth of God is turned into falsehood, as Paul says, (Rom. i. 25.)

It is, therefore, a monstrous absurdity when men imagine that wood or stone is an image of God; for there is no similarity, nor can such a thing enter into man's mind without a grievous and an atrocious indignity being offered to God. The reason also is to be noticed, *For there is no spirit in them.* God, so to speak, is the life of all things living; now, to call a dead thing an image of God, a thing in which there is no mind nor life, is it not to turn light into darkness? This reason, then, ought to be remembered by us; and it is a sufficient refutation of all such errors, when the Prophet says, that there is no spirit in idols, that is, in wood, stone, gold, and silver, and that they are therefore a lie; for God will not have himself to be compared to dead things, without mind and life. He then adds—

15. They *are* vanity, *and* the work of errors: in the time of their visitation they shall perish.	15. Vanitas sunt, opus illusionum; in tempore visitationis ipsorum peribunt.

He confirms the same thing. What he called before falsehood, שקר, *shikor,* he calls now vanity, הבל, *ebel. They are vanity,* he says. He had said that they were falsehood, which means, that men were grossly deceived when they sought the presence of God in dead things. Now he says, that they were vanity, and also the *work of illusions;* but some render the last word "mockeries," taking it in a passive sense; and hence the Chaldee interpreter renders it, "a thing worthy of ridicule and laughter."[1] But I prefer to take it for imposture

[1] So, substantially, is the version of the *Sept.*, *Vulg.*, *Syr.*, and *Arab.*,—"ridiculous—worthy of laughter—foolish—ludicrous." But the word means no such thing. The verb תעה means to wander, to err, to go astray; in Niphal, to be led astray, to be deceived; and Hiphil, to lead astray, to seduce, to deceive; and it is a Hiphil participle in Gen. xxvii. 12. It is

or deception. Jacob said to his mother, "I shall be found in the eyes of my father a deceiver;" but some render the word there "a mocker." But Jacob, on the contrary, meant, that he should be found out as one of no credit, or acting in guile, as though he had said, "I shall be an impostor, and my father will find out the fraud." So also in this place, he calls idols the work of deceptions, by which men infatuated themselves. He does not then teach us here that idols deserved to be ridiculed, but he refers to the madness of those who imagined that they were gods, for he had before called them vanity and falsehood; and there is no doubt but that in these various ways he repeats and confirms the same thing.

He afterwards adds, *In the time of their visitation they shall perish.* The pronoun "their" may be applied to idols or to the Chaldeans: when the time of visitation shall come; that is, when God shall punish the enemies of his Church, then their idols shall perish: or, when the time shall come for God to visit the idols, they shall perish. Either sense may be admitted; and indeed as to the subject in hand, there is no difference.

The Israelites might have objected and said, "How is it then that false gods, whom men have devised for themselves, are worshipped, and are in great esteem and highly regarded? How does God suffer and overlook this?" The Israelites might have raised an objection of this kind. Therefore the Prophet answers them, *They shall perish;* but it shall be at the *time of visitation.*[1] It is an exhortation to

here a reduplicate noun; and *Blayney* takes it as referring to persons, and not as an abstract noun—those who greatly err; and this is the best view, as the Prophet has been throughout describing the idol-makers—

Vanity are they (*i.e.*, the idols,)
The work of the grossly deluded:
At the time of their visitation they shall perish;

that is, the grossly deluded.

He had before threatened ruin to idols; but he now threatens their makers.—*Ed.*

[1] *Scott* quotes a sermon of *Mede*, in which he says, "Ye have heard the state of the times, wherein this prophecy is commanded; now let us consider the event. We have heard of the admired oracles of the Gentiles, of Apollo at Delphos, of Jupiter Ammon in Egypt, &c.; but all of them are long since perished. Where is now Bel, the god of Babylon, Nisroch, the god of Assyria, Baal and Astaroth, the gods of Zidonians, Milcom of

patience, that the faithful might not despond or be weakened in their hopes, though they saw silver gods carried on men's shoulders, though they saw wood and stone set on elevated places, and incense burnt to them and sacrifices offered to them. Though then they saw idols in such esteem, they were not yet to despair or fall away from true religion, for the time of visitation was to be looked for, when God would execute his judgment on the false gods as well as on their worshippers. We now understand why he speaks of visitation. It follows—

16. The Portion of Jacob *is* not like them: for he *is* the former of all *things;* and Israel *is* the rod of his inheritance: The Lord of hosts *is* his name.

16. Non sicuti illi portio Iacob, quia creator omnium est; et Israel virga hæreditatis ejus, Iehova exercituum nomen ejus.

We have said before, that superstitions cannot be from the heart and boldly rejected, except the true God be known; for the heathens, even when they disapproved of the opinions of the vulgar, yet reasoned on both sides, and knew nothing certain, and had no sure faith. It is, therefore, necessary that we should have previously a knowledge of the true God. Hence the Prophets, whenever they spoke of idols, spoke also of the true God; for it would have been to little purpose to condemn these follies, except they represented God in his own real dignity. For this reason the Prophet says again, that God, who is the portion of Israel, is not like idols.

He calls God the portion of Israel, that he might preserve the people in the pure truth of the law which they had learnt, and with which they had been favoured; and thus he draws away the attention of the Israelites from all the inventions of men or of the heathens. *The portion* then *of Israel is not like idols*—how so? For *he is the former of all things,* that is, the creator of heaven and earth. Then he says, *Israel is the rod of his inheritance.*[1] Rod may be taken

the Ammonites, Chemosh of Moab, and Tammuz of the Egyptians? Even these also are perished with their names." The partial fulfilment of this prophecy is an evidence of its complete fulfilment, when "the spirit of evil," as *Scott* says, "whom all idolaters worship, shall be confined to the bottomless pit."—*Ed.*

[1] This clause is left out in the *Septuagint,* but retained by the *Vulgate,* the *Targum,* and the *Syriac,* though "rod" is rendered "tribe" in the

for a measuring rod; and I think it ought to be so taken, for he mentions inheritance: for he took the comparison from common practice; as men are wont to measure fields and possessions by a rod. He therefore says, *Israel is the rod,* that is, the measuring rod *of his inheritance.* He concludes by saying, *Jehovah of hosts is his name.*

PRAYER.

Grant, Almighty God, that as thou hast been pleased to shew thyself so plainly to us, and as thou art pleased to confirm us in thy truth,—O grant that we may not turn aside either to the right hand or to the left, but depend entirely on thy word, and so cleave to thee that no errors of the world may draw us aside: may we constantly persevere in that faith which we have learnt from thy Law and thy Prophets, and especially from thy gospel, where thou hast made thyself more clearly known to us, through Christ Jesus, until we shall at length enjoy thy full and perfect glory, when we shall be transformed into it in that inheritance, which has been purchased for us by the blood of thy only-begotten Son.—Amen.

Lecture Forty-Second.

17. Gather up thy wares out of the land, O inhabitant of the fortress:

18. For thus saith the Lord, Behold, I will sling out the inhabitants of the land at this once, and will distress them, that they may find *it so.*

17. Collige è terra merces tuas, quæ habitas in munitione:

18. Quia sic dicit Iehova, Ecce ego funda projiciens habitatores terræ vice hac, et coarctabo eos (*vel,* faciam ut obsideant eos) ut inveniant.

The first verse which we have recited, the Rabbins think, is addressed to the Chaldeans, but in my view very incorrectly. Jeremiah had indeed said that all the nations who devised gods of stone and of other corruptible materials, were very foolish; but we have seen for what purpose he said this, even to confirm the Israelites, who were captives, and in addition to the disgrace of exile were greatly hated by the Chaldeans and the Assyrians; it was, I say, to confirm them, lest they should depart from the true worship of God, but constantly defend the honour of their God, from

last; and so it may be rendered, for שבט means a tribe as well as a rod or sceptre: and this meaning is the most suitable. God was the portion of Israel, and Israel was the tribe or nation whom God inherited or possessed as his inheritance, there being no other nation so favoured.—*Ed.*

whom they expected restoration. It is, therefore, absurd for the Rabbins to explain this verse of the Chaldeans; for the two verses ought to be connected, *gather thy merchandise, because thus saith Jehovah.* It is then strange that these interpreters apply the second verse to the Israelites, while they read the first by itself, as though they were not connected: yet a reason is given why he bids all wages to be gathered.

But the meaning is simply this,—that the whole country would be exposed to the will of their enemies, that they might plunder it: as then devastation was nigh at hand, the Prophet bids those in fortified places to gather their wages, or to gather a gathering, (we shall hereafter speak of this expression.) Now, we have already stated in several places, that the Prophets ironically touched on the torpidity of the people; for plain truth would have had no effect, except it was urged on them as it were vehemently. The Prophet then undertakes the character of a man, who brings warlike tidings, as we shall more clearly see presently. But in this place, as in some other places, he declares that nowhere in Judea would there be safety, except in fortresses; which yet would not be able to resist the attacks of enemies, as we shall hereafter see.

As to the words, some give this rendering, "gather thy humiliation," as כנע, *cano,* means to be humble; but they apply the words to Babylon, as though the Prophet had said, "Now cease to subdue the remaining nations." Thus they take the verb אסף, *asaph,* in the sense of contraction, when some moderation is observed. But I have already said that this verse cannot refer to Babylon or to the Chaldeans. As then the Prophet addresses the Jews, and speaks of their effects, or of their merchandise, or precious things, which were wont to be gathered and laid up; as though he had said, "Gather thy gathering;" for the word כנע, *cano,* means also to collect or to gather: and this is a suitable meaning, it being taken afterwards for doing business. But as to the subject itself there is no obscurity; for the Prophet shews that in a short time the whole of Judea would be laid waste by enemies; and as it was to be exposed to plunder, what is usual was to be done, that is, to gather whatever was valuable into fortified cities. In short, the Prophet here declares that war and ruin would come on the Jews, which would extend through the whole land; for by land he means the country, as distinguished from fortified towns.

Then follows the reason, *For thus saith Jehovah, Behold, I will with a sling cast out the inhabitants of the land.* Land here is to be taken in another sense, even for the whole country. Wherever then the Jews dwelt, the Lord, says the Prophet, will draw them forth, yea, cast them out as with a sling. We now then see that the vengeance which the Jews despised is denounced on them, because they remained securely in their own delusions; and what still more provoked God's wrath, they regarded all that Jeremiah said of his judgment as a fable. But he compares their violent exile to slinging, and represents the Lord as the slinger. We know that when a sling is flung and a stone is cast, the motion is very violent. Such a casting away is then what God here threatens the people with,—that he would violently throw them here and there, like stones when cast by a sling.

And he says *at this term* or time, in order that the Jews might know that their calamity would be like a sudden storm. For they had often been subject to the assaults of enemies; but at one time they had delivered themselves, at another the Chaldeans and Assyrians had been constrained to turn aside to other quarters; or they had been miraculously delivered by God's aid. They hoped that it would be the same always; and they thought also that by protracting the war they could disappoint their enemies, as they had often done; and further still, they expected aid from various quarters. Hence the Prophet says, that they would be so taken away, that God would at once cast them all out of the land, and cast them out as it were in one day: *at this time then will I fling out the inhabitants of the land.*

Then he says, *And I will straiten them.* Some render the verb transitively, as it is in Hiphil, "I will cause them to be besieged by their enemies," and then, "that their enemies may find them." But this seems forced. Others more correctly give this explanation of the last clause, "that they may find," that is, as true, what had been so often foretold them. For, as we have said, the Prophets and their threatenings had been despised, as the Jews had hardened themselves in their impiety: therefore this interpretation may be allowed. But I prefer a more general meaning,—*that they may find*, even what they had sought; for they had in many and various ways provoked the wrath of God: it was therefore right that they should at last find that which they had by their perverse doings procured for themselves, according to what is said in Isaiah lvii. 10, "They shall find the fruit of their own ways." The Jews sought nothing less than the calamity which Jeremiah denounced on them: but they had really long sought it; for it was right that they should receive the wages due to their wickedness. Then it is, that they may find, that is, the reward of their own works.[1] It follows—

19. Woe is me for my hurt! my wound is grievous: but I said, Truly this *is* a grief, and I must bear it.	19. Hei mihi super contritione mea; dolore plena est percussio mea: et ego dixi, Certè (*vel*, utique) hæc plaga mea, et feram eam.

The Prophet here no doubt speaks in the name of the whole people; for he saw that no one was moved by threatenings, though very grievous and severe; and this mode of speaking must be sufficiently known to us, for it is commonly used by all the prophets. They first addressed the

[1] As to these two verses the early versions all differ from one another, as well as from our version and that of *Calvin*. The *Targum* comes the nighest to our version. I offer the following rendering,—

17. Gather from the land thy gains,
Thou who dwellest in a fortress!
18. For thus saith Jehovah,—
Behold I will sling out
The inhabitants of the land at this time,
And will fortress them, that they may be taken.

The first verse is spoken ironically, recommending what they were doing. Then the Lord says what he would do: They were gathering their goods into fortresses in order to secure them, and the Lord says that he would violently fortress (as the word means literally) or drive into fortresses all the inhabitants of the land, and would do so, that they might be found or taken, that is, captives; there would be no need of collecting the people, for they would be driven into fortified cities, where the enemies would find them. This seems to be the meaning of this verse, which *Horsley* deemed "very obscure," and elucidated "by no expositor."—*Ed.*

people; but when they saw that they produced no effect, in order to shew their indignation, they speak of themselves as in the presence of God: thus they rebuked the hardness and torpidity of men. So now does Jeremiah speak, *Woe to me for my bruising!* He did not grieve on his own account; but, as I have said, he represents the grief which the whole people ought to have felt, which yet they did not feel at all. As then they were so stupid, and proudly derided God and his threatenings, the Prophet shews to them, as it were in a mirror, what grievous and bitter lamentation awaited them.

We must then bear in mind that the Prophet speaks not here according to the feeling which the people had, for they were so stupified that they felt nothing; but that he speaks of what they ought to have felt, as though he had said,—"Were there in them a particle of wisdom, they would all most surely bewail their approaching calamity, before God begins to make his judgment to fall on their heads; but no one is moved: I shall therefore weep alone, but it is on your account." There is yet no doubt but he intended to try in every way whether God's threatenings would penetrate into their hearts.

He says that his *smiting was full of pain;* and then adds, *And I said, Surely it is my stroke, and I will bear it.* As I have already said, he does not relate what the Jews said or thought, but what would have been the case with them had they the smallest portion of wisdom. Some connect this with the following verse, as though the Prophet had said that he thought himself able to bear his grief, but was deceived, as he was at length constrained to succumb. But this is an incorrect view, and the passage runs better otherwise. The Prophet here reminds his own people with what feeling they ought to have regarded the fact, that God was angry with them; for he no doubt indirectly condemns their sottishness, because God's hand was put forth to chastise them, and yet they disregarded the hand of him who smote them. He then relates what they ought to have thought and felt, when God shewed tokens of his wrath,—that they ought to have acknowledged that it was their own stroke, and that it was therefore to be borne: for it is the best preparation for repentance when the sinner acknowledges that he is justly smitten, and when he willingly receives the yoke. When, therefore, any one proceeds thus far, his conversion is half effected.

The Prophet then teaches us here that the only remedy which remained for the Jews was to be fully convinced that they deserved the punishment which they endured, and then patiently to submit to God's judgment, according to what a dutiful son does who suffers himself to be chastised when he offends. The word is used in another sense in Psalm lxxvii. 10, "To die is my lot." The Prophet has חלי, *cheli*, here; but there it is חלותי, *cheluti*. That passage is indeed variously explained; but it seems to be an expression of despair, when it is said, "To die is my lot;" that is, it is all over with me. But the Prophet here shews that it was the beginning of repentance, when the Jews confessed that they deserved their stroke; for no doubt there is here a comparison made between sin and its punishment, as though the Prophet had said, "We have thus deserved, and God allots to us the reward due to our sins." It is one thing,—to give glory to God, by confessing that he inflicts due punishment; but it is not sufficient unless patience be added,—*I will bear it;* that is, I will submit to God. For there are many who, when convinced of their sins, do yet complain against their judge, and also raise a clamour. Hence the Prophet joins together these two things,—the confession of sin and patience; so that they who experience the severity of God quietly submit to him as long as he exercises towards them the office of a judge.[1] He afterwards adds—

[1] Our translation, as to this verse, is nearly the *Syriac*. The *Septuagint* and *Arabic* have wandered much from the original; and so have the *Vulgate* and the *Targum* in some degree. The most literal is the version of *Calvin*. The terms here used, *bruising, smiting*, are commonly employed to designate great trouble and affliction, or distress; and this distress he describes in the verse that follows; and in the twenty-first verse the cause of it is set forth. And the distress corresponds with what he says in the eighteenth verse, where he says that the inhabitants would be driven from the land into fortresses, so that he would have none to set up his tent. All these verses seem connected. The literal rendering of this verse is as follows,—

20. My tabernacle is spoiled, and all my cords are broken: my children are gone forth of me, and they *are* not: *there is* none to stretch forth my tent any more, and to set up my curtains.

20. Tabernaculum meum vastatum est (*vel,* dirutum) et omnes funes mei rupti sunt; filii mei egressi sunt à me (*particula* ני *tantundem valet ac* ממני,) et nulli sunt (*hoc est,* nulli restant amplius:) nemo qui extendat amplius tabernaculum meum, et erigat (*vel,* disponat) cortinas meas.

This metaphor may have been taken from shepherds, and it seems suitable here; yet the prophets often compare the Church to a tent. Though indeed it is said elsewhere that the Church is built on the holy mountains, (Psalm lxxxvii. 1,) and great firmness is ascribed to it, yet, as to its external condition, it may justly be said to be like a tent, for there is no fixed residence for God's children on earth, for they are often constrained to change their place; and hence Paul speaks of the faithful as unsettled. (1 Cor. iv. 11.) But as, in the next verse, mention is made of shepherds, the Prophet seems here to refer to the tents of shepherds. Though indeed he takes hereafter the similitude more generally, or in a wider sense, yet there is no reason why he should not allude to the shepherds of whom he afterwards speaks, and yet retain the metaphor which so often occurs in all the prophets.

He then says that his *tent was pulled down,* and that *all his cords were broken.* Some take the tent for the city of Jerusalem, but this is a strained view, and unsuitable. We have already said that the Prophet speaks here in the name of the whole people; and it is the same as though he compared the people to a man dwelling with his family in a tent. He adds, *My children are gone forth from me.* The people then complain that they were deprived of all their children; nor was this all, but they were scattered here and there, which was worse than if they had been taken away by death. He afterwards says, *And there is no one to extend my tent, and to set up my curtains.* Jeremiah shews that the people would be so bereaved as to have none to bring them any assistance, though in much want of it.

19. Woe is to me, because of my bruising, (distress;)
Grievous is my stroke; I have said,—
Surely, this *is* grief! but I must bear it.

Then he proceeds to state his distress: he had none even to assist him to pitch his tent, the people having all been driven to fortified cities.—*Ed.*

No one then thought that such a thing would take place, and Jeremiah was held in contempt, and some raged against him, and yet he shewed what would be. And that what he said might be more forcible, and produce a stronger effect, he speaks in their name, like a poet in a play, who describes a miser, and mentions things suitable to his character, making use of such words and actions, so that he cannot but see, as it were in a mirror, his own disposition and conduct. So also the Prophet does here; for when he saw that the stupid people could not be moved by the simple truth, he told them what they all ought to have felt in their hearts, and to have testified by their mouths,—that they were solitary, deserted by all who belonged to them, and that there was no one to bring them any help.[1] But he pursues, as we have said, the same metaphor. It follows—

21. For the pastors are become brutish, and have not sought the Lord: therefore they shall not prosper, and all their flocks shall be scattered.

21. Quia infatuati sunt pastores, et Jehovam non inquisierunt; propterea non egerunt prosperè (*alii, non intellexerunt,*) et omnis pascua eorum (*hoc est,* quicquid in pascuis eorum erat) fuit destructum.

In the first place, he assigns a cause for the dreadful devastation of which he had spoken, and that was, because the shepherds were without thought and understanding. He still, as we see, goes on with his metaphor. Some confine this to the kings of Israel; but I do not agree with them: for I include under the name shepherds, the priests and the prophets as well as the king and his counsellors. But Jeremiah did not mean to exempt the people from fault, when he, in an especial manner, accused the shepherds; but he only mentioned the origin and the primary cause of evils,—that the kings, the prophets, and the priests were blind, and thus destroyed the flock of God. We have observed elsewhere the same mode of speaking; and yet the prophets

[1] I should render the verse as follows—

My tent, it is laid waste,
And all my curtains, they are broken;
My sons, they have left me, and there are none of them;
No one extends any more my tent, and sets up my curtains.

When the noun precedes its verb in Hebrew, I consider that it ought commonly to be rendered as above. "There are none of them," that is, with me; not that they "were not," that is, that they were dead.—*Ed.*

did not intend to extenuate the vices of the people, nor to absolve the lower orders. But as it mostly happens that the lower ranks, and those in humble stations, rely much on the chief men who occupy places of authority, it was necessary that the prophets should notice this evil: and we also know how much pride and arrogance there is in kings and priests, and in all those who enjoy any honour or dignity; for they think themselves exempt from the restraint of laws, and will not be reproved, as though they were sacred persons. It was, therefore, for this reason, that the Prophet reproved such with so much vehemence and severity. Hence, he says, *The shepherds are infatuated.*

The people, indeed, at that time repudiated the prophets, as the case is now under the Papacy. For even when the truth of God is clearly and perspicuously set forth, there are many who set up this shield,—that they believe their bishops, prelates, and kings, and others of a similar kind. When, therefore, Jeremiah saw that the pure truth of God was subverted by vain splendour, he found it necessary to expose the disguise, and, so to speak, to pull off the mask. It was, then, for this reason, that he said that the shepherds were infatuated. If the prophets were under this necessity, what ought to be done by us at this day, when we see that all those who unblushingly boast that they are the representatives of the Church are sheer impostors, and draw miserable souls into destruction? What else, I pray, ought to be done by us, but what we learn was done by the prophets? And how foolishly and childishly do the Papal bishops prattle, when they would have themselves exempted from all reproofs, because power and government is in their own hands! For they cannot surely assume to themselves more than what belonged formerly to the Levitical priests; for God had chosen them, and all the priests under the law might have justly boasted that they were appointed by divine authority: yet we see that they were reproved, and were said to be infatuated. The Pope and his bishops have not been appointed by God, nor have they any evidence of their calling. Though, then, they arrogate all things to themselves, and seem to do so by divine right, yet they cannot be deemed superior to the ancient priests: they must, therefore, become subject to the judgment which God denounces here by the mouth of his Prophet.

He gives a reason why they were infatuated, because *they sought not Jehovah.* We hence see, on the other hand, that true wisdom is to seek God. When, therefore, there is no care taken to seek God, however acute men may be, they must necessarily be altogether infatuated: and it was for this reason that Jeremiah called them who had not sought God foolish or fatuitous. This passage teaches us, that the only way of governing rightly is, when they who rule strive to give glory to God, and regard him in all their thoughts and actions: but when they act otherwise, they must necessarily play the fool and become infatuated, however wise they may appear to be.

Hence he says, *they have not prospered.* The verb שכל, *shical,* means to understand, and also to prosper. I see no reason for rendering it here, "they have not understood" or acted wisely; for it seems frigid, nor do I see what sense can be elicited. But the Prophet may be considered to have justly said, that neither the kings and their counsellors, nor the priests and the prophets ruled with any success, *because they sought not God;* and that as they had no care for true religion, they were become infatuated.[1] And what follows confirms this view, *And all that was in their pastures,* &c.;

[1] The meaning of the verb שכל here is determined by the verb בער at the beginning of the verse: it is what is the reverse of that. Now בער is a verb derived from the name, which means a beast. To be like the beast is to be ignorant, stupid, void of reason and understanding: then שכל means here to act with knowledge, like one who possesses mind and reason. But then the shepherds did not act but like beasts who have no understanding. Then the verse may be thus rendered,—

20. For stupidly-ignorant have become the shepherds,
And Jehovah they have not sought;
Therefore wisely have they not acted,
And every one from their pastures is scattered.

The "scattering" was from the land or country to the fortified towns, referred to in verse 18. They left the country, like sheep quiting their shepherds' pastures, and visited towns. Then, in the next verse, the Prophet says, that even the towns also would be destroyed. In the first instance God would terrify them, and fling them, as it were, from the land, so that they would take shelter in fortresses: this would be owing to the foolish conduct of their shepherds. They would be driven, then, that their enemies might more easily find or take them: and in the following verse for the Prophet seems here to add to his general statement a particular thing, and thus to prove that the government was unhappily conducted, being under the curse of God, because true religion had been neglected. He then adds this special thing,—that the *pastures had been deserted,* that is, that the flock in the pastures had been wholly scattered. It follows—

22. Behold, the noise of the bruit is come, and a great commotion out of the north country, to make the cities of Judah desolate, *and* a den of dragons.	22. Vox rumoris, ecce venit, et strepitus (*vel,* tumultus) magnus (commotio, *alii vertunt*) è terra Aquilonis, ad ponendas urbes Jehudah in vastationem, domicilium draconum.

Jeremiah shews in this verse that prophetic doctrine was useless to an obstinate people; for there is a contrast, no doubt, to be understood between the voice of God, which had constantly resounded in Judea, and the tumultuous clamours of enemies; for the prophets, one after another, had reproved the people, but without effect. Now, then, as they were deaf to God's voice, the Prophet declares that new teachers were now come who would address them in another way, and in an unusual manner. *The voice* then *of rumour is heard;* "ye would not hear me and other servants of God; but a *voice of rumour comes from the north:* the Chaldeans shall be your teachers; I send you to their school, since I have spent my labour for many years in vain, as all those have done who before me diligently sought to lead you to the right way, whom God employed, and who faithfully endeavoured to secure your safety; but they were no more attended to than I am, and therefore they ceased to teach you. I now turn you over to the Chaldeans; they shall teach you." This is the simple meaning.

The voice of rumour, he says, or literally, of hearing, שמועה, *shimuoe,* comes; that is, the voice which shall be heard, for they had closed their ears to the prophetic warnings; *and a great tumult* or commotion *from the land of the north.* We now then see that the Chaldeans are set in opposition to the prophets, who had laboured in vain among

he announces the approach of their enemies who were coming to lay waste their towns.

All the versions give the idea of knowledge or wisdom to שכל here; but the *Targum,* that of prosperity. To act foolishly is what they all render the verb בער.—*Ed.*

the Jews; as though Jeremiah had said that the Jews would, willing or unwilling, be made to attend to this tumultuous noise; and he says that it would be for the purpose of *turning the cities of Judah to desolation and an habitation of dragons.*[1] It follows—

23. O Lord, I know that the way of man *is* not in himself: *it is* not in man that walketh to direct his steps.	23. Novi, Jehova, quod non sit penes hominem via ejus, non sit penes virum ambulantem, ut dirigat grassum suum.

The Jews confine this to Sennacherib, who had, according to his own will, at one time resolved to attack the Ammonites, at another the Moabites, and to reduce them under his own power; but had been induced by a sudden impulse to go to Judea. But this is frivolous. The Prophet, I doubt not, referred to the Jews, who had for a long time been accustomed to dismiss every fear, as though they were able by their own counsels to consult in the best way for the public good: for we know, that whenever any danger was apprehended from the Assyrians, they usually fled for aid to Egypt or to Chaldea. Thus, then, they provided for themselves, so that they thought that they took good care of their affairs, while they had recourse to this or that expedient; and then, when the prophets denounced on them the vengeance of God, they usually regarded only their then present state, as though God could not in one instant vibrate his lightnings from the rising to the setting sun.

Since then this security produced torpor and obstinacy, the Prophet in this passage justly exclaims, *I know, Jehovah, that his way is not in man's power;* nor is it in the *power of a person walking to direct his steps.*[2]

[1] The verse may be thus rendered,—

A sound is heard!—behold it comes,
Even a great commotion, from the land of the North,
To make the cities of Judah a desolation,
The habitation of dragons.

Blayney is right in taking the first words by themselves, but, " Hark, a voice!" is not a true version. שמועה is here a passive participle.—*Ed.*

[2] Literally rendered the verse is as follows:—

I know, Jehovah,
That not to a mortal *is* his way;
Nor *is it* for man to walk
And to stablish his steps.

Such substantially is the meaning of the *Targum*, and of all the versions, except the *Syriac*, which *Blayney* has followed thus:

We now perceive what the Prophet had in view; and this is ever to be remembered—that if we desire to read what has been written with profit, we must consider the meaning intended by the Holy Spirit, and then the purpose for which he has spoken. When we understand these things, then it is easy to make the application to other things: but he who does not weigh the end in view, ever wanders here and there, and though he may say many things, he yet does not reach the chief point.[1] But we must observe that the Prophet, as he had done before, spoke as though he had God alone as his witness, for he saw that his own people were so hardened, that he addressed his words to them in vain: he therefore turned to God, which was a proof that he despaired as to the disposition of the people, as though he had said, "I shall have nothing to do with this perverse people any more; for I have already found out by my experience that their perverseness is untameable. I am now therefore constrained, O Lord, to address thee as though I were alone in the world." This is the reason why he spoke to God himself. We shall defer the rest till to-morrow.

PRAYER.

Grant, Almighty God, that as we are in like manner at this day so torpid, that we are not moved by thy threatenings, nor do the kind and friendly warnings, by which thou invitest us to thyself, prevail with us,—O grant that we may at length learn to attend to the truth, in whatever form thou settest it before us, and

I know Jehovah, that his way is not like that of men,
Nor like a human being doth he proceed and order his going.

This construction is wholly inadmissible. Had Jehovah been in the objective case, it would have את before it. See 1 Sam. iii. 7. Then the rest of the verse is a paraphrase and not a version; and such a paraphrase as the original will not bear. To "walk" and to "stablish" are in the same predicament, both infinitives; and so they are rendered in all the versions and the *Targum*.

The design of the passage seems to be more correctly intimated by *Gataker* than by *Calvin*:—"Lord, we know well, that this army cannot come in but by thy permission; but since thou art resolved to chastise us, we beseech thee, in wrath remember mercy." So in the next verse the Prophet says, "O Lord, correct me, but with judgment."—*Ed.*

[1] Or, as the French version has it, "does not reach the burden and knot of the subject."

that we may be teachable and obedient, when thou only invitest us, and that if we become hardened, we may be also touched by thy threatenings, and not tempt thy patience, but suffer ourselves to be brought under thy yoke, and so submit to thee, that thou mayest through our whole life rule over us, and shew to us thy paternal love, so that, after having faithfully served thee in this world, we may come at length into that blessed rest which is prepared for us in heaven by Christ our Lord.—Amen.

Lecture Forty-Third.

We stated yesterday why the Prophet exclaimed, that man's way is not in his own power: for as the sentence is brought in abruptly, it is made to signify different things. But I have briefly shewed that the Prophet condemns the security of his own people, because they thought that they were beyond the reach of danger, as they hoped for aid from neighbouring nations in league with them, or because they supposed that they had sufficient help and protection in their own resources. Hence the Prophet derides this foolish confidence, and says, that *his way is not in the power of man,* and that *it is not in the power of man while walking to direct his steps.*

It must be farther noticed, that he treats not here of counsels, but that though men wisely guided their affairs, the Prophet denies that the issue is in their own hands or at their own will: and hence he expressly speaks of a *man walking.* He concedes that men walk, but yet he intimates that they cannot move a foot, except they receive strength from God. We now then perceive what the Prophet had in view.

We may hence gather a general truth—that men greatly deceive themselves, when they think that fortune or the issue of events is in their own hands: for though they may consult most wisely, yet things will turn out unsuccessfully, unless God blesses their counsels. And this is what we ought carefully to notice, because we see how presumptuously men promise themselves this and that; and this presumption can hardly be arrested while men arrogate to themselves what belongs peculiarly to God alone. There are many warnings given in Scripture in order to check this rashness; but almost all proceed in their own course, and cannot be induced to allow themselves to be ruled by God. James condemns this madness[1] when he says, that men resolve what they would for a long time do: the merchant determines on a long voyage, not only for three or four months, but for many years; another undertakes war; another ventures to take this or that business in hand; in short, there is no end to such instances. The Holy Spirit has by this one passage checked the boldness of those who claim for themselves more than they ought: but the greater part, as I have already said, think that the event is in their own power. On this account Solomon says,[2] that man deliberates, but that it is God who governs the tongue. He had said in the former clause, that it is man who sets in order his ways; but he said this ironically, as it is what most believe; for when they undertake anything, they are not so solicitous about the event, but they always promise to themselves more than what they have a right to do. Men, he says, set in order or arrange their ways, but God governs the tongue; that is, they cannot speak a word unless the Lord lets loose the bridle of their tongues; and yet we know that many things are vainly said by men, for they are never accomplished. Since then the voice itself is not in the power of man, but depends on the will of God, what ought we to think of the issue?

We now then see the truth which may be learnt from this passage,—that men deceive themselves when they dare to undertake this or that business, and promise themselves a happy issue. But we must farther observe, that not only events are at the disposal of God, but counsels also; for God directs the hearts and minds of men as it seemeth him good. But all things are not said in every passage. The Prophet does not here avowedly speak of what men can do, but grants this to them—that they consult, that they decide; yet he teaches us that the execution is not in their own power.

Some foolishly elicit from this passage, that something

[1] James iv. 13. [2] Proverbs xvi. 1.

belongs to man, that he possesses some power of free-will. There seems indeed to be here something plausible at the first view. Jeremiah says, that his way is not in man's power, and that it is not in the power of him who walks to direct his steps; he then, it is said, has left something to man—he walks; it hence follows that free-will is not reduced to nothing, but that a defect is proved, for man of himself has no sufficient power unless he is helped from above. These are only puerile trifles; for, as we have said, the Prophet does not shew here what are the powers of free-will, and what power man has to deliberate, but he takes this as granted; yet the children of this world, though they seem to themselves to be very acute in all things, and take their own counsels, and rely on their own resources, are yet deceived, because God can in one moment dissipate all their hopes, as the events of things are wholly in his power. It is therefore by way of concession that he says that *man walks*, according to what Paul says in Rom. ix. 16, though in that passage he ascends higher; yet in saying, that it is not of him who wills nor of him who runs, he seems to concede to men the power of willing and running. But there is to be understood here a species of irony; for we know that men can never be stripped of that vain and deceptive conceit which fills them, while they think that they can obtain righteousness by their own strength. They dare not, indeed, actually to boast that they are the authors of their own salvation, and that righteousness is within their own power, but they wish to be associates with God. Though they admit him as a partner, they yet wish to divide with him. This is the folly which Paul ridicules; and he says, that it is not of him who wills, or of him who runs, but of God only who shews mercy; that is, that man's salvation is alone from the mercy of God, and that it is not from the toil and running of man.

When the Pelagians sought by this cavil to evade the sentence of Paul, " It is not of him who wills and runs," deducing hence, that man has some liberty to will and to run, Augustine said wisely, " If it be so, then, on the other hand, we may infer, that it is not of God who shews mercy, but of him who wills and runs."[1] How so? If men co-operate in half with God, and if there is a concurrence of human power with the grace and aid of the Holy Spirit, and if this sentence, "It is not of him who wills, or of him who runs," is true according to the sense given to it, so we may also say, that it is not only of God who shews mercy, but also of him who wills and runs. Why? Because the mercy of God is not sufficient if it is to be aided by man's power. But this is extremely absurd, and there is no one who does not abhor the thought, that man's salvation is not from God's mercy, but from their willing and running. It then follows, that all human power, and all labours, are wholly excluded by these words of Paul.

Now, the Prophet does not speak of eternal salvation, but only of the actions of the present life. As then the Israelites thought that they had sufficient protection in their own wisdom, in their own power, in their own numbers, and also in their confederacies with other nations, the Prophet says, that they were deceived, for they arrogated to themselves the ruling power, which belongs to God alone; for what men commonly call fortune is nothing else but God's providence. Since then God by his hidden counsel governs the affairs of men, it follows that all events, prosperous or adverse, are at his will. Whatever, then, men may consult, determine, and attempt, they yet can execute nothing, for God gives such an issue as he pleases.

We now see what the Prophet speaks of, and also see that he touches not on the powers of free-will; for he does not refer here to man's will, but only shews that after men have arranged their affairs in the best manner, all their counsels, strivings, and toils come to nothing, and that God disappoints their confidence, because they dare rashly to promise to themselves more than what is right. It now follows—

24. O Lord, correct me, but with judgment; not in thine anger, lest thou bring me to nothing.	**24. Castiga me, Jehova, tantummodo in judicio, non in ira tua, ne imminuas me.**

The Prophet again indirectly reproves and condemns the stupor of the people, because he saw that all his threatenings

[1] Epist. 107, ad Vitalem.

were despised. They had indeed been often punished, and they thought that they had escaped ; and though an extreme calamity was approaching, they yet supposed that God was far from them ; and thus they cherished their own delusions. Hence the Prophet alone personates the whole people, and undertakes a common and public lamentation. *Chastise me, Jehovah,* he says, but *in judgment.* The Prophet doubtless is not here solicitous about his own safety only, nor does he plead his own private cause, but he supplicates for the whole people.

But why does he speak of himself alone ? Because he personated, as I have already said, the whole community, and thus reproved them for their insensibility, because they were not more attentive to the approaching judgment of God. In short, the Prophet here teaches them how they must all have felt, were they not wholly blinded and, as it were, given up to a reprobate mind ; and thus he shews, that the only thing that remained for them was suppliantly to ask pardon from God, and that they were not wholly to refuse all chastisement, but to supplicate forgiveness only in part, even that God would not exercise such severity as altogether to consume them. In this way he shews how atrocious were the sins of the people ; for they were not simply and unreservedly to ask God to pardon them, but only to moderate his vengeance. When any one sins lightly, he may flee to God's mercy, and say, " Lord, forgive me !" but they who have accumulated evils on evils, and after having been often warned have not repented, as though they purposely sought to arm God against themselves and to their own ruin,—can such seek entire exemption from all punishment ? This would not be meet nor reasonable.

The Prophet then shews here briefly, that the Jews had so far advanced in wickedness that God would not wholly forgive them, and that they were not to seek pardon without any chastisement, but only to ask of God, as I have said, to moderate his severity. David did the same thing, though he pleaded his own cause only, and not that of the people. He deprecated God's wrath and indignation ; he sought not to be so forgiven as to feel no chastisement ; but as he dreaded God's wrath he wished it to be in a measure averted. And hence, in another place, he thanks God that he had been lightly smitten by his hand, "Chastising, the Lord has chastised me, but doomed me not to death." (Ps. cxviii. 18.) But this ought to be especially observed as to the words of Jeremiah,—that the people ought not to have asked pardon unless they submitted to God's chastisement, for they had most grievously and perversely sinned.

We may hence also gather a general truth: the real character and nature of repentance is, to submit to God's judgment and to suffer with a resigned mind his chastisement, provided it be paternal. For when God deals with us according to strict justice, all hope of salvation is extinguished, so that it cannot be that we shall from the heart repent. Let us then know that this is necessary in repentance—that he who has offended God should present himself willingly, and of his own accord, before his tribunal and bear his chastisement. For they who are so delicate and tender, that they cannot endure any of his scourges, seem to be still refractory and rebellious. Wherever, then, there is the true feeling of penitence, there is this submission connected with it,—that God should chastise him who has offended. But a moderation is needed, according to the promise, "I will chastise them, but with the hand of man; for my mercy will I not take away from them." (2 Sam. vii. 14; Ps. lxxxix. 33, 34.) This was God's promise to Solomon; but we know that it belongs to all the members of Christ. Though then God indiscriminately punishes the sins of the whole world, there is yet a great difference between the elect and the reprobate, for God grants this privilege to his elect,—that he chastises them paternally as his children, while he deals with the reprobate as a severe judge, so that all the punishments which they endure are fatal, as they cannot see anything but God's wrath in their judgments. The elect also have ever a reason for consolation, for they know God to be their Father; and though they may at first shun his wrath, and being smitten with terror, seek some hiding places, yet having afterwards a taste of his kindness and mercy they take courage; and thus their punishments, though much more grievous than those endured by the reprobate, are yet not fatal to them, for God turns them to remedies. We now then see what is the use and benefit of what the Prophet teaches, when he says, *Chastise me, Jehovah, but only in judgment.*

Judgment is to be taken here for moderation. The word משפט, *meshephcth*, has indeed various meanings: but it is to be regarded here as signifying a measured portion; not that God ever exceeds due limits in inflicting punishment, but because men faint when he exercises rigour, as then there appears to them no hope of pardon. When God therefore executes only the office of a Judge, men must necessarily faint altogether: so Jeremiah means, that there would be no measured dealing, that is, that God's judgment would not be endurable, except he dealt mercifully with him.[1] There is also set in opposition to this another clause, *not in fury*, or, not in wrath. Here then the want of moderation or excess is not opposed to a measured proportion, but the wrath of God. We also know that no passions belong to God; but when God's wrath or rigour appears, men must necessarily not only be terrified, but be also reduced to nothing: and yet in many places we read that God is angry with his elect and the whole Church: but this is to be referred to the outward appearance; for it is certain that the punishments with which God visits his own children are evidences of his paternal love, as in this way he promotes their salvation. Hence the Apostle says, that they are bastards whom God does not favour with any correction. (Heb. xii. 8.) But yet as to the outward ap-

[1] The word judgment, though usually given as the version of the original word, does not convey its meaning here. Of the twelve senses mentioned by *Johnson* as belonging to the word judgment, not one of them is applicable to this place. There is perhaps not a word in any language which includes all the ideas conveyed by a word of a similar general import in another. The word משפט is rendered in our version. "judgment," Ex. xxiii. 6,—"manner," 1 Sam. xxvii. 11,—"custom," 1 Sam. ii. 13,—"ordinance," Isaiah lviii. 2,—"due," Deut. xviii. 3,—"right," Deut. xxi. 17,—"measure," Jer. xxx. 11; the last is in the sense of moderation; and this is its meaning here; or, it may be rendered, "due measure."

Chastise me, Jehovah, but yet in moderation;
Not in thy wrath, lest thou diminish me,
or,
render me small.—*Ed.*

pearance, the punishments which God inflicts on his elect differ nothing from those by which he manifests his wrath, and which he executes on the reprobate. Therefore it is by a sort of impropriety in language that punishments are always said to be evidences and signs of God's wrath, and that God is said to be angry with his Church. But the Prophet speaks here strictly correct when he sets God's wrath in opposition to his judgment, that is, to that moderation which he exercises towards his elect, when he withholds his hand, which would otherwise overwhelm them in an instant.

Hence he subjoins, *Lest thou shouldest diminish them.* By diminishing he means destruction: as in many other places. It could not be otherwise but that God should diminish us, were he only to touch us with the end of his finger, as we know how dreadful is his power: nor is there any need for him to thunder from heaven, but were he only to shew an angry countenance, it would be all over with us. But the Prophet takes diminution here for demolition. We hence see that he so subjects himself and the whole people to God's chastisement as yet to seek some moderation; for otherwise God's rigour would have consumed them all, from the least to the greatest, according to what is also said by Isaiah, "I have tried thee, but not as gold and silver, for thou wouldest have been consumed." (Isaiah xlviii. 10.) God then so deals with miserable sinners, that he regards what they can bear, and not what they deserve. This is simply what the Prophet means.[1]

[1] The *Septuagint* and *Arabic* render this verse as though spoken by the people, "chastise us," &c., and the last clause, "lest thou make us few." The *Targum* has, "chastise them," and, "lest they be diminished." These are interpretations and not versions. The *Vulgate* and the *Syriac* render the Hebrew literally, "chastise me," and the last clause, "lest thou reduce me to nothing," or, according to the *Syriac*, "to a small number," which is literally the original; and this verb clearly shews that this verse was spoken, as *Calvin* observes, in the name of the people: but diminution, and not destruction, is meant, as the verb has never the latter meaning. Hence our version is wrong, and also *Blayney's*, "lest thou crush me to atoms." Diminution, and not annihilation, is what the word means; and this diminution was one of the judgments that would come upon them in case of disobedience, as mentioned by Moses, Lev. xxvi. 22. —*Ed.*

But we may hence learn, that there is no one who can bear the strict rigour of God; and that therefore our only asylum is his mercy; not that he may pardon us altogether: for it is good for us to be chastised by his hand; but that he may chastise us only according to his paternal kindness. It follows—

25. Pour out thy fury upon the heathen that know thee not, and upon the families that call not on thy name: for they have eaten up Jacob, and devoured him, and consumed him, and have made his habitation desolate.

25. Effunde iram tuam super gentes, quae te non noverunt, et super cognationes (*vel*, familias) quae nomen tuum non invocaverunt; quia comederunt Jacob, comederunt inquam ipsum, et consumpserunt eum, et tabernacula ejus vastarunt.

The Prophet confirms his prayer by this reason—that God had sufficient ground for executing his vengeance on the wicked and ungodly heathens who were alienated from him; and there is no doubt but that he had respect to the promise to which we have referred; for the Prophet knew that what had been said once to David was promised to the whole Church throughout all ages. Hence he reminds God, as it were, of the difference which he had made between domestics and foreigners; as though he had said, "O Lord, though it is right and also useful for our salvation to be chastised by thy hand, yet thou dost not indiscriminately visit with vengeance the sins of men; for thou hast promised paternally to chastise thy children: but as to aliens, thou art their judge, so that they may be wholly destroyed. Now then, O Lord, shew that this has not been said in vain; and as thou hast been pleased to adopt us as thy peculiar people, forgive us according to thy paternal kindness." Hence we see that the Prophet did not inconsiderately pour forth his prayer into the air, but had a regard to God's promise, and referred to that difference which God himself was pleased to make between his Church and unbelievers.

He then says, *Pour forth thy wrath on the nations who know not thee:* and he exaggerates what he says by adding, that *Jacob* had been *devoured* by these heathen nations as by wild beasts; as though he had said, "We have indeed sinned, O Lord; but dost thou shew thyself to be the Judge of the world for our destruction, and yet sparest the Egyptians, the Assyrians, and the Chaldeans, who have so cruelly distressed us, yea, who have not only torn us, but have also wholly devoured us? (For he uses the word devour twice; and then he adds, *they have consumed him;* and lastly, *His tents have they laid waste.*) Since then they have so atrociously raged against thy people, are they to go unpunished, when thou castest us down, who are thine? Even had we given thee ever so great a cause for punishing us, still thine adoption should avail us; and thou mightest in the meantime execute thy judgment on the heathen nations."

There is no doubt but that the Prophet, or whoever he was who composed the seventy-ninth Psalm, borrowed the words used here, for it is there said, "Pour forth thy wrath on the nations who know not thee, and on the kingdoms which have not called on thy name; for they have consumed Jacob and his inheritance." (Psalm lxxix. 6, 7.) It may be that Jeremiah himself wrote that Psalm, after having been driven into Egypt, when that city had been destroyed. It was, however, suitable to the time when dreadful scattering had happened; for the Psalm seems to have been composed for the benefit of the miserable, and as it were of the lost Church. It is yet more probable that it was written under the tyranny of Antiochus, or at the time when the cruelty of God's enemies raged against his people. However this may be, the author of that Psalm wished to repeat what is contained here.

It may now be asked, Whether it is right to pray for evils on the ungodly and wicked, while we are doubtful and uncertain as to their final doom. For as God has not made it known how he purposes to deal at last with them, the rule of charity ought on the contrary to turn us another way,—that we are to hope for their salvation and to pray God to forgive them: but the Prophet consigns them only to destruction; and he speaks not according to his own private feeling, but dictates a prayer which all the faithful were to use. To this I answer,—that we are not to denounce a sentence on this or that man individually, and that our prejudging would be presumptuous, were we to consign individuals to eternal death and to pray for evil on them: but we may use this form of prayer generally with regard to the obstinate enemies of God, so as still to refer to him the certainty of the issue; and yet we are not to mix in one mass all those whom we know to be now ungodly, for this, as I have said, would be presumptuous It would then be more becoming in us to pray for the good of all and to wish their salvation, and, as far as we can, to promote it. Yet when we thus entertain love towards every individual, we may still so pray in general, that God would lay prostrate, consume, scatter, and reduce to nothing his enemies. There is then no doubt but that the Prophet here turns his own thoughts to God's judgment, as though he had said, "Lord, it was thy work to make a distinction between domestics and aliens; it has pleased thee to adopt this people; what now remains, but that thou shouldest deal mercifully with them, inasmuch as thou sustainest towards them the character of a Father? As to the heathen nations, as they are aliens to thee and belong not to thy flock, destruction awaits them; let them therefore perish."

Now the Prophet in thus speaking of heathen nations, does not anticipate God's judgment so as to restrain him from doing what he pleased: but he only mentions, as I have already said, what he derived from God's word,—that some are elected, and that others are reprobates. He infers God's election from his vocation or his covenant; and, on the other hand, he regards all those reprobate on whom God has not been pleased to bestow the privilege of his paternal favour.

The question then is now solved: and hence it appears how it is lawful for us to pray for the destruction of the reprobate, and of those who despise God,—that our prayers ought not to anticipate God's judgment,—and that we are not to determine as to individuals, but only remember this distinction—that God acts as a Father towards his elect, and as a judge towards the reprobate.

Pour forth then *thy wrath:* as he had subjected himself and the whole people to God's chastisements, so he says, *Pour forth thy wrath;* that is, deal with them with strict justice; but yet moderate thy wrath towards us, lest like the deluge it should swallow us up; for the word "pour forth" conveys this meaning. By saying, *on the nations which know not thee, which have not called on thy name,* he uses words which ought to be carefully noticed; for we are by them taught that the beginning of religion is the knowledge of God. He then mentions the fruit or the effect, which is invocation or prayer. These two things are connected together: but we must bear in mind the order also; for God cannot be invoked, except the knowledge of him previously shines on us. Indeed all everywhere call on God; even the unbelieving commonly cry on him when urged by danger; but they do not rightly address their prayers to him, nor offer them as legitimate sacrifices. How so? "How can they call on him," says Paul, "in whom they have not believed?" Hence it is necessary, as I have said, that God himself should shew us the way before we can rightly pray: and therefore where there is no knowledge of God, there can be no way of praying to him. But when God has once given us light, then there is a way of access open to us. Invocation then is ever the fruit of faith, as it is an evidence of religion; for all who call not on God, and that seriously, prove that they have never known anything of religion. If then we desire to pray aright, we must first learn what is God's will towards us: we must also know that we then only advance as we ought in the attainment of salvation, when we flee to God and exercise ourselves in prayer.

He lastly adds, *For they have consumed Jacob, they have consumed him, they have consumed him,*[1] *and his tents have they laid waste.* Two things are to be observed here: we see how sad and miserable was the state of the Church; for he says not that the Israelites had suffered many wrongs, or had

[1] *Blayney* for no good reason has omitted the verb "consumed," following the *Septuagint* and one MS. The *Vulgate*, the *Syriac*, and the *Targum*, retain the two verbs. So far is the last verb from being without meaning, as this author says, that it has an especial emphasis, it being stronger than the preceding verb,—

24. Pour forth thine indignation on the nations,
Who know not thee, and on the families,
Who on thy name have not called;
For they have devoured Jacob,
Yea, they have devoured him and consumed him,
And his habitation have they made desolate.—*Ed.*

been treated violently and reproachfully, but that they had been *devoured* by the nations, and he repeats this twice; and then he adds, that they had been consumed, and that their *tents had been laid waste.* Since then we see how cruelly afflicted were God's children formerly, let us not wonder if the Church at this day be exposed to the most grievous calamities, and let us not be frightened as though it was something new and unusual; but as the same thing happened formerly to our fathers, let us bear such trials with a submissive mind. The other thing to be observed is,—that as the Prophet was not here led to pray by the impulse of his flesh, but by the guidance of the Spirit, we may hence with certainty conclude, that though the enemies of the Church triumph at this day, and think that they have everything in their own power, while they cruelly treat the innocent, they shall at length be punished; for the Spirit who guided the tongue of the Prophet intended this form of prayer to be unto us like a promise, so that we may feel assured that the more atrociously the ungodly rage against God's children, the heavier punishment is nigh them as the wages of their cruelty. They indeed devour, at this day, like wild beasts; but God will sooner or later put forth his hand, and shew how precious to him is the blood of his people.

PRAYER.

Grant, Almighty God, that since we are so torpid in our sins, except thou rousest us, that we profit not by the severe warnings by which thou didst formerly stimulate thine ancient people, and since we have also been already warned by many signs of thy wrath to seek repentance with increasing assiduity,—O grant that we may earnestly persevere in this course, and so submit to thee, that with patient and calm minds we may bear thy corrections: and may we in the meantime be fully assured that thou wilt ever be our Father, and never hesitate, even in death itself, to flee to thy mercy, until thou pourest forth thy wrath on the ungodly and the profane despisers of thy name, and shewest such compassion towards us, that we may know that thou hast not in vain promised that thy chastisements would ever be kind and paternal, in visiting the sins of those who hope in thee, through Christ our Lord.—Amen.

Lecture Forty-Fourth.

CHAPTER XI.

1. The word that came to Jeremiah from the Lord, saying,

2. Hear ye the words of this covenant, and speak unto the men of Judah, and to the inhabitants of Jerusalem;

3. And say thou unto them, Thus saith the Lord God of Israel, Cursed *be* the man that obeyeth not the words of this covenant,

4. Which I commanded your fathers in the day *that* I brought them forth out of the land of Egypt, from the iron furnace, saying, Obey my voice, and do them, according to all which I command you: so shall ye be my people, and I will be your God;

5. That I may perform the oath which I have sworn unto your fathers, to give them a land flowing with milk and honey, as *it is* this day. Then answered I, and said, So be it, O Lord.

1. Sermo qui directus fuit ad Jeremiah à Jehova, dicendo,

2. Audite verba (sermones) fœderis hujus, et dicite viro Jehudah (viris Jehudah, *enallage est numeri,*) et habitatoribus Jerusalem;

3. Et dices ad eos, Sic dicit Jehova, Deus Israel, Maledictus vir qui non audierit verba fœderis hujus;

4. Quæ (*vel,* quod fœdus) mandavi patribus vestris die quo eduxi eos è terra Egypti, è fornace ferrea, dicendo, Audite vocem meam, et facite ea quæ (*hoc est,* quæcunque) præcipio (*relativum sine antecedente;* secundum omnia quæ præcepi vobis) et eritis mihi in populum, et ego ero vobis in Deum; (*cohærent hæc omnia inter se, ideo non disjungo;*)

5. Ut statuam (*vel,* stabiliam; *alii vertunt,* suscitem, *sed improprie*) jusjurandum quod juravi patribus vestris ad dandum illis terram affluentem lacte et melle, secundum diem hanc: et respondi et dixi, Amen, Jehova.

HERE the Prophet teaches us, that the Jews, though they continued to profess God's holy name, were yet wholly perfidious, and had departed altogether from the law. The import of this discourse is, that the Jews gloried in the name of God, and yet were violaters of his covenant, for they had broken their faith pledged to God, and wholly cast aside the doctrine of the law. The Jews, no doubt, were often greatly exasperated against Jeremiah, as though he was pleading his own cause: it was therefore necessary to set before them their departure from the law, so that they might feel assured that their contention was not with Jeremiah but with Moses, and with God himself, the author of the law. They were doubtless exasperated with his doctrine; but Jeremiah could not spare them when he saw that they were so perverse.

We may understand this better by an example: Though

the Papists at this day openly repudiate everything adduced from the law, and the prophets, and the gospel, yet they dissemble on this point, and even affirm that they receive whatever proceeds from God. As they then shuffle and do so shamelessly, he who seeks to restore the pure worship of God and true religion, may deal with them in the same manner. As for instance, when any one of God's servants meets the Papists, he may thus address them:—"Let not the dispute be now between us individually, but hear what God commanded formerly by Moses, and what he has more fully confirmed by his prophets, and at last by his only-begotten Son and his apostles; so that it is not right to do anything any longer against his word: now then attend to the law and the prophets."

We now understand what was God's design in bidding his servant Jeremiah to speak these words. For, except we duly consider the unfaithfulness of that people, we shall feel surprised that the word covenant is so often mentioned, and it will appear unmeaning to us. But the Prophet, as I have said, when he saw that the Jews by their cavils made evasions, could not deal with them in any other way than by shewing that they had violated God's covenant and had thus become apostates, having wholly departed from the law. And he says that this was commanded them by God: nor is there doubt but that God not only suggested this to his servant, but dictated also to him the way and manner of speaking.

Rightly then does Jeremiah begin by saying, that this *word was given* to him. By using the plural number in the second verse, he no doubt shews that he had a few assistants remaining, whom God addressed in connexion with him, that they might unite together in delivering his message. For though there were very few good men, yet Jeremiah was not wholly deprived of colleagues, who assented to and confirmed his doctrine. Baruch was one of them, and there were a few like him. These, then, God addresses in the second verse, when he says, *Hear ye the words of this covenant, and say ye*[1] *to the men of Judah and to the citizens of*

[1] So the *Vulgate* and the *Targum*, but the *Septuagint*, the *Syriac*, and *Arabic*, have the verb in the singular number, "and thou shalt say."

Jerusalem. Jeremiah indeed knew, and also those who were with him, that they brought forward nothing but what was in the law: but however conscious they were of their own sincerity, and could testify before God and his angels that they drew nothing from puddles but from a pure fountain, yet God intended to strengthen them against the contumacy of the people; for they had this objection ready at hand, "Ye indeed boast that whatever it pleases you to bring forward, is the word of God; but this we deny." Since then the prophets had to undergo such a contest, it seemed good to God to strengthen their hands, that they might first be themselves assured, and then become fit and bold witnesses of his truth to others, having good authority, as it was derived from the law itself, and not from the devices of men.

And we see to whom God intended this to be proclaimed, even *to the men of Judah and to the citizens of Jerusalem.* The ten tribes, as it has elsewhere appeared, were now driven into exile; and here was the flower, as it were, of the chosen people; and having survived so many calamities, they thought that they had been preserved by Divine power, because religion and God's worship prevailed among them. Thus they were inebriated with false notions and self-flatteries. Hence the Prophet, and those who were with him, are expressly bidden to declare, what we shall hereafter notice, to the citizens of Jerusalem and to the inhabitants of the land

The ם at the end of the verb may be rendered "them;" so *Blayney* regards it. We may consider the end of this verse and the following as parenthetic; otherwise the particle "this" seems singular. It will thus appear to be "this covenant which I commanded your fathers." Still the whole passage seems not to run well. I am disposed to render הזאת, "even these," and to put a part in a parenthesis, thus,—

2. Hear ye the words of the covenant, even these, (and thou shalt speak
them to every man of Judah and to the inhabitants of Jerusalem,
3. and thou shalt say to them, Thus saith Jehovah, the God of Israel,)
4. "Cursed is the man who hearkens not to the words of the covenant,
even these, which I commanded your fathers in the day I brought
them up from the land of Egypt, from the iron furnace," saying,
"Hearken to my voice, and do ye according to all that I shall com-
5. mand thee; and ye shall be to me a people, and I shall be to you a
God; that I may confirm the oath which I have sworn to your
fathers, to give them a land flowing with milk and honey, as it is
this day."—And I answered and said, Amen, O Jehovah.—*Ed.*

who remained, and thought that they were the chosen of God and would continue safe, even if all others were to perish.

The Prophet afterwards shews more clearly that the command was especially given to him, for he uses the singular number, *Thou shalt say to them.* Nor is it inconsistent that at first he joined others with himself; for God might have united the suffrages of the few who wished the restoration of pure religion among the people, while yet Jeremiah, who was superior to the rest, sustained the chief part. There is no doubt but that others were anxious by their consent to confirm his doctrine: but there was no emulation among them; and though he excelled them, he yet willingly admitted into a connection with himself all those whom he found to be united with him in so good and holy a cause. God then, in the last verse, spoke of them in common, for he wished all his servants to add their testimony to that of his Prophet; but now he addresses the Prophet alone, for his authority was greater.

It follows, *Thus saith Jehovah, the God of Israel, cursed the man who does not hearken to the words of this covenant.* As often as the word covenant is mentioned, Jeremiah no doubt cuts off every pretext for all those evasions to which the Jews, according to what we have said, had recourse: for they never willingly allowed that they took away anything from the law, though they yet despised Jeremiah, who was its true and faithful interpreter, who had blended with it nothing of his own, but only applied what had been taught by Moses to the condition of the people at that time. There is then to be understood an implied contrast between the word covenant and the doctrine of Jeremiah; not that there was any difference or contrariety, or that Jeremiah had anything apart from the law, but that he formed his discourse so as to suit the condition of the people. And there is a kind of concession, as though he had said, " I do not now demand to be heard by you, but hear only the law itself: I have hitherto brought forward nothing but what God has commanded; and I have taught nothing at variance with Moses; there has been nothing additional in my doctrine:

but as I cannot convince you of this, I now give over speaking to you; Moses himself speaks, hear him."

By adding the pronoun demonstrative, "Hear ye the words of *this* covenant," it is the same as though he had openly shewed them as by his finger, so that there was no room for any doubt.[1] He then upbraided them by pointing out the covenant, as though he had said, "What avails you to feign and to pretend that what we say is ambiguous, and to hold it as uncertain whether we are or not the servants of God? whether we speak by his Spirit? whether he himself has sent us? The thing is clear; *this* is the *covenant.*" We now perceive the force of this pronoun.

But in referring to the *curse*, his purpose, no doubt, was to bend the stubbornness of the people. Had the Jews been teachable and submissive, God would have used a milder strain, and allured them by words of kindness and love: but as he had to do with perverse minds, he was under the necessity of addressing them in this manner, in order to strike them with terror, and to render them more attentive, and also to make them to hear with more reverence, as they usually treated with contempt what he had spoken before. We hence see why he began with mentioning a curse. God followed in the law another order; for he first introduced the rule of life, and added also promises to render the people willing to obey; and then he subjoined the curses. But Jeremiah here begins by saying, *Cursed* are all those who *hear not the words of this covenant.* Why was this done? Even because he had already found out the hardness and the obstinate wickedness of the people. He then does not propound a simple doctrine, but before all things he sets before them the curse of God; as though he had said, "It is very strange that you have not hitherto been moved, since God's curse has been so often denounced on you: as then ye are so stupid, before I begin to speak of God's commands, his curse shall be mentioned to awaken your torpidity."

But we learn from the Prophet's words that he alluded to

[1] *Gataker* says, "It is not unlikely that the Prophet held out the book or volume of the law, wherein the covenant was engrossed and recorded, then in his hand."—*Ed.*

the form prescribed in the law: for after Moses rehearsed all the precepts, he added, "Cursed is every one who turns aside to foreign gods;" and he commanded the people to respond, Amen; and, "Cursed is every one who curses father and mother," and he bade them to respond, Amen; and after having narrated all the precepts, he added, "Cursed is every one who fulfils not all the words of this law," and the people responded, Amen. (Deut. xxvii. 15, 16, 26.) The same form does Jeremiah now adopt when he says, "Declare then to the people, that they are all accursed who obey not my precepts;" and then the Prophet adds, *I answered and said, Amen, O Jehovah.* But it must be observed, that the Prophet here personates as before the whole people; as though he had said, "I subscribe to God's judgment, even though ye should be all gainsayers, as ye really are. Though then ye think that ye can escape from God's hand, as though it were easy to elude the curse which is pronounced in his law, yet I subscribe with my own name, and answer before God, *Amen, O Jehovah.*

But we must notice also the other words, *Cursed,* he says, *is every one who hears not the words of this covenant.* To hear, in this place, and in many other places, is to be taken for obeying. He then speaks of the words or of the covenant itself; for the expression may be taken in either sense, as God had made a covenant with the Jews and at the same time expressed words. I am inclined to consider the covenant itself as intended. God then says that he *had made a covenant* with them. There is yet a fuller explanation, *The words which I commanded your fathers,* he says, *in the day when I brought them up from the land of Egypt.* God shews here by a circumstance as to the time how inexcusable the Jews were; for he says that he gave the law to their fathers at the very time when they were extricated from death; as they were drawn out of the grave, as it were, when God made them a passage through the Red Sea. That redemption ought to have made such a deep impression as to constrain them wholly to devote themselves to God; yea, the memory of such a benefit ought to have been deeply fixed in their hearts.

We hence see how aggravated here is the sin of ingratitude; for the law was given to the Israelites when they had before their eyes the many deaths to which they had been exposed, and from which the Lord had miraculously delivered them. For the same reason also he mentions their miserable state as an *iron furnace,* according to what we find in the third chapter of Exodus and in many other places. He then compares their Egyptian bondage to a furnace; for the Jews were then like wood and straw in a burning furnace; and he calls the furnace *iron,* as it could melt and reduce to nothing things harder than wood, even gold or silver or any other metal. In short, the deplorable state of the people is here set forth; and the Prophet, by the comparison, magnifies the favour shewn to them—that God, beyond all hope, had delivered them from death. Since then the authority of the law was sanctioned by so great a benefit, it became evident how much was the impiety of the people, and how unbecoming and wicked their ingratitude; for they did not willingly suffer God's yoke to be laid on them.

He says that God *commanded these things.* This expression, as I have said, is to be applied to the words of the law, and not to the covenant. But the Prophet speaks indiscriminately, now of the covenant, then of the things it embraces, that is, of all the precepts it includes. In other words, he expresses how inexcusable was the sin of the people; for God, in substance, required of them no other thing but to hear his voice: and what can be more just than that they who have been redeemed should obey the voice of their deliverer? and what could have been more detestable and monstrous than for the Israelites to refuse what God had a right to demand? We now then perceive the design of the Prophet in saying, that God *commanded* this only to his redeemed people, even *to hear his voice,* and to do what he commanded.[1]

[1] There is no need of any alteration in the text, as proposed by some: the literal rendering is, "Hearken to my voice, and do ye according to all that I shall command you." The אתם, "ye," after "do," seems to be placed there instead of with "hearken." Some MSS. have אותם, which is evidently wrong. It is only the *Targum* that countenances this reading: all the versions read according to the meaning given above.—*Ed.*

He further adds a promise, which ought to have softened their stony hearts, *Ye shall be,* he says, *to me a people, and I will be to you a God.* God might have positively required of the Jews what is implanted in all by nature; for they who have never been taught acknowledge that God ought to be worshipped; and the right way of worshipping him is when we obey his precepts. God then might have thus commanded them according to his supreme authority. The commands of kings, as it is said, are brief, for they are no soothing expressions, nor do they reason, nor employ any persuasive language. How much greater is the authority of God, who can intimate by a nod what he pleases and what he demands? But as though he descended from his high station, he seeks by promises to attach people to himself, so that they may willingly obey him. Thus God recommends his law by manifesting his favour, and does not merely assert his own authority. Since then God thus kindly addresses his people, and promises so great a reward to obedience, how base and abominable is the contumacy of men when they repudiate his law? Hence the Prophet shews here more clearly why he began by saying, *Cursed is every one who obeys not,* &c.: for kindness had profited nothing; friendly and tender words, the paternal invitation of God, produced no effect; as though he had said, "God could not, doubtless, have treated you more gently and kindly than by reminding you in a paternal manner of your duty, and by adding promises sufficient to soften even the hardest hearts; but as this has been done without effect, what now remains for God to do but to thunder and announce only his curses?"

We now understand what the Prophet had in view. But it may be here objected,—that all this was useless and without any benefit, for the Jews could not have undertaken the yoke of the law, until it was inscribed on their hearts. To this I answer, that of this very thing they were here at the same time reminded: for though the teaching of the letter could do nothing but condemn the people, and hence it is said by Paul to be what brings death, (2 Cor. iii. 6,) yet the faithful knew that the Spirit of regeneration would not be denied them, if they sought it of God. Then, in the first place, it was their fault that the law was not inscribed on their hearts ; and, in the second place, a free promise of forgiveness was added ; for why were those sacrifices and expiations under the law, and so many ceremonies, which had respect to their reconciliation to God, but in order that the people might feel assured that God would be propitious and appeasable to them, though they could not satisfy the law? This teaching then was not useless as to the faithful; for God, when he required from the Israelites what they ought to have done, was at the time ready to inscribe the law on their hearts, and also to forgive their sins. But when through obstinate wickedness they rejected the whole law, the Prophet justly declares here that the curse of God was on them ; because they basely rejected God's promises, by which he testified his paternal kindness towards them.

He adds, *That I may establish the oath which I have sworn to your fathers, to give them a land abounding in milk and honey, according to* what it is at *this day.* Here he does not refer to the chief part of their happiness ; but only the land of Canaan is mentioned as the pledge or the earnest of God's favour ; for his promise had regard to something much higher than to the land of Canaan. God had indeed promised this as an inheritance to the Israelites : but when he says, that he would be their God and they his people, the promise of eternal life and of celestial glory is included, according to what is said elsewhere, that he is not the God of the dead but of the living. (Matt. xxii. 31.) And we must ever bear in mind what is said by the Prophet Habakkuk, "Thou art our God, we shall not die." (Hab. i. 12.) God then promised to the Israelites something far greater than the possession of the land, when he said, that *he would be their God.* But that land was a symbol, an earnest and a pledge of his paternal favour. All these things well agree together.

And to the same purpose is what the Prophet adds, that God had formerly *sworn* to their *fathers,* that he would give them that land by an hereditary right: and this promise had been fulfilled to their posterity. Were any to lay hold on this only,—that God's favour was seen in the land of Canaan, because they had obtained it through the expulsion of the heathens by God's kindness, the view would be frigid, and the Prophet would diminish much from that promise which far exceeds all that man can conceive. Hence, as I have said, in speaking of the land of Canaan, he accommodates himself no doubt to the comprehension of a rude and ignorant people, and mentions the earnest and the pledge, that they might see by their eyes, exhibited to them even in this world and in this frail life some evidence of that favour, which far surpasses all that can be desired in the world.

Now, when he says, *That I may establish*[1] *the oath which I have sworn to your fathers,* God doubtless shews that though the Jews should obey him, they had not yet deserved by their obedience the inheritance promised before they were born. God then here proves that it was through his gratuitous kindness that they became heirs of the land. How so? because they were not created when God sware to Abraham that he would give that land to him and to his posterity. As then the promise had been given long before, it follows that it could not be ascribed to the merits of the people, that they had at length in due time obtained the land. As to the oath, God by referring to it extols his favour; for he not only promised the land for an heritage to the children of Abraham, but he also added an oath, that the covenant might appear more sure. But the Prophet at the same time intimates, that they, if ungrateful to God, might justly be deprived of the promised inheritance; as though he had said, "There is no ground for you to expostulate with God, as though he defrauded you, were he to cast you out of the land; for God himself does not disinherit you, but your own wickedness; and ye are now unworthy, for God regards you not as his children." While then the Prophet takes away every ground for boasting, that the Jews might not think that they possessed the land as a

[1] "Establish—στήσω," is the *Septuagint;* "awaken—suscitem," is the *Vulgate;* "perform," is the *Syriac;* "confirm," is the *Targum.* "To make to stand" is the literal meaning of the verb. Hence the most correct word is "confirm." The connection of this verse is not with the immediately preceding words, but with "Hearken" and "do," &c., at the middle of the former verse. Hearken and do, that I may confirm the oath, &c.—*Ed.*

reward for their merits, he also reminds them that they might be justly deprived of their land, and that on account of their own fault, as they rendered not to God the service they owed to him. Hence he says, *that I might establish the oath which I have sworn to your fathers.*

A land, he says, *flowing with milk and honey:* this mode of speaking was often adopted by Moses, (Ex. iii. 8, 17; xiii. 5; xxxiii. 3; Lev. xx. 24.) The land was no doubt from the beginning very fertile; but it is probable that it became more fruitful after the people entered into it, for it was in a manner renewed; and it was God's design to shew in a visible manner how great was the efficacy of his covenant. It was not then to no purpose that Moses said so often that it was a land flowing with milk and honey.

He afterwards adds, *According as* it is *at this day.* He produces witnesses; as though he had said, "God has dealt faithfully with you, for he has performed the faith pledged to your fathers, and has fulfilled his oath: but now since ye have polluted this land, and the memory of God's favour is as it were buried among you, and ye even tread under your feet his law—since then such great impiety averts his blessing from you, what remains for him to do, but to drive you away into exile?" We hence see that there is here to be understood an implied threatening, when he says that God had performed what he had promised to the fathers, and promised with this condition—that they were to obey his commands.

We have already spoken of the Prophet's answer. When he answered, Amen, he did not wait for what the people would say; for the greater part no doubt made a clamour and sought to make shifts with God. So great was their effrontery, that they often rose up insolently against the Prophets. Then as he knew that they were so refractory, he subscribed to the curse in his own name. It follows—

6. Then the Lord said unto me, Proclaim all these words in the cities of Judah, and in the streets of Jerusalem, saying, Hear ye the words of this covenant, and do them.

7. For I earnestly protested unto your fathers, in the day *that* I brought

6. Ex dixit Jehova ad me, clama (*hoc est,* clamosa voce promulga) verba hæc in urbibus Jehudah et in compitis Jerusalem dicendo, Audite verba fœderis hujus et facite ea.

7. Quia contestando contestatus sum patribus vestris die qua feci as-

them up out of the land of Egypt, *even* unto this day, rising early and protesting, saying, Obey my voice.

cendere eos è terra Egypti usque ad diem hanc, mane surgendo et contestando et dicendo, Audite vocem meam:

8. Yet they obeyed not, nor inclined their ear, but walked every one in the imagination of their evil heart: therefore I will bring upon them all the words of this covenant, which I commanded *them* to do; but they did *them* not.

8. Et non audierunt et non inclinarunt aurem suam; et ambularunt quisque post pravitatem cordis sui mali: et (ideo, *copula hic illativè accipitur*) venire feci (*hoc est*, immisi) super eos omnia verba fœderis hujus, quod mandavi ut facerent; et non fecerunt.

Here the Prophet explains more clearly why he had been commanded to promulgate the words of the covenant: for the greater part of the people were no doubt ready boldly to object and say, "What dost thou mean? Are not we the disciples of Moses? Thou, forsooth! thinkest that thou hast to do with a barbarous people. Have we not been from our childhood taught the law of God? Is it not daily enjoined on us? We are sufficiently instructed in this doctrine of which thou pretendest that we are ignorant. Be gone hence; and go either to the Chaldeans or to the Assyrians or to the Egyptians; for we understand what the law teaches."

There is then no doubt but that Jeremiah had been repulsed by this kind of insolence: he therefore shews that he had a just cause to set before them the law of God; for so great an oblivion had prevailed, that they did not know what God had formerly taught in his law: and besides, they and their fathers had been always rebellious, so that they had ever need of being taught, according to what is said by Isaiah, that the people were to be treated like children and taught, A, A; B, B, and that though the same things were repeated, they yet stopped at the rudiments and never made any progress. (Isaiah xxviii. 10, 13.) As then Isaiah reproached the people with tardiness in learning the law, so Jeremiah shews now that they were not to think it strange that God commanded his law to be proclaimed to them, because it had been hitherto despised by them. The rest we shall defer.

PRAYER.

Grant, Almighty God, that since thou hast been pleased daily to invite us to thyself with so much benignity and kindness, we may not with deaf ears turn aside from the doctrine which is set forth for our salvation, but that we may attend to it and persevere also in that obedience which thou justly requirest from us, so that we may make increasing progress in true religion, and so form the whole course of our life according to thy righteous law, that we may fight as good soldiers to thee in this world, until we shall at length come to that blessed rest, which is prepared for us in heaven, through Christ our Lord.—Amen.

Lecture Forty-Fifth.

We observed in the last Lecture the complaint which God made against his people,—that he had tried every means to reconcile them to himself, but all in vain. But there is great weight and emphasis in these words,—that by *protesting he protested*, &c.; as though he subjected himself to the judgment of a third party; for we are wont to protest against those who do not willingly come before the tribunal of a judge. God then takes this figure from the common practice of men, and says that he *protested*, and that not only once, but repeatedly. He afterwards adds that he had done this not only in one age, but from the time their fathers came forth from bondage to that day. It was then extreme perverseness, when God ceased not to call them to himself, and yet spoke to the deaf. But what follows is still more emphatical,—that he *rose early:* for to take this transitively as some do, is what I do not approve. God then says, that he was so solicitous about their welfare, that he rose early to call them. There is no doubt but that God applies here to himself what properly belonged to his Prophets, as he also concedes to his servants what rightly belongs to him, and what cannot be applied to men, except by way of concession.

But God does here extol the authority of his word, when he says that he rose early; and at the same time he amplifies their ingratitude, inasmuch as they had despised him, when they saw that he, like the head of a family, provided for their welfare. We hence then learn how much God values his word; for he testifies that there is no difference between him and his servants, whose labours he employs in teaching his Church. We also hence learn how inexcusable is our wickedness when we reject God speaking thus familiarly to us. We now then perceive the import of this passage. But it may, in the third place, be observed, that God's name is in vain pretended, except when he himself speaks. The Papists of this day would have whatever they say, according to their own fancies, to be received without any dispute; but God shews in this place that he is not offended except when he is himself despised; and he at the same time declares that he is so connected with his prophets, that they bring nothing of their own, nor anything else except what proceeds from him.

He now adds, that this only he required from his chosen people, *to obey his voice.* The justness of this precept shews how base and wicked was the impiety of the people; and God also shews that they had not the pretext of error or of ignorance; for the only way of evading was to pretend that they wished no other thing than to render to God the worship due to him; but the rule he had prescribed in his law was such as could not be mistaken. It hence follows that they wilfully went astray after superstitions, for they were sufficiently taught in the law what God approved. This then is the reason why he so often repeats that he required nothing from the children of Abraham except to *hear* his *voice.*

It afterwards follows, *Yet they heard not, and bent not,* or inclined not *their ear.* Here the Prophet does not accuse a few men of perverseness, but says that, from the time they had been redeemed, they had been rebellious against God: and he exaggerates their sin by saying that they *inclined not their ear;* for this was no doubt added for the sake of emphasis, as though the Prophet had said,—that it was only their own fault that the right way was not quite evident to them, for they deigned not to give ear to God. Now, it is a proof of extreme contempt, when we not only repudiate what God says to us, and refuse to obey his authority and advice, but when we close up every avenue, and, as far as we can, forbid him to speak to us; this is surely an extremity of insolence. It may indeed be, that one will hear another speaking, and yet will not do what he says; he still will shew some courtesy, lest a complaint of inattention be made; but it is an intolerable barbarity when we do not listen to the words of another. God here complains that the Israelites had not only been disobedient to him, after having been instructed, but that they had been so refractory, that they insolently rejected all the words of the prophets; which was not only a proof of base impiety, but also of barbarous perverseness. We now then understand what the Prophet means.

He says, that *they walked every one in the wickedness of his own evil heart.*[1] As he had before shewn that they had been in due time warned, it is clear that they followed not through mistake their impious superstitions, but because they rejected the true worship of God, and hearkened not to the teaching of the prophets. By saying that they *walked every one,* &c., the Prophet doubtless intended to include them all as it were in one bundle; as though he had said, that they had not been drawn away by a sudden impulse, as it is often the case when an agitation is made by a few, and when the most follow, being driven as it were by a storm, and think not what they do; for thus some terror often seizes on the minds of the many, so that they go here and there without knowing where they are going. But the Prophet here teaches us that every one followed his own counsel; as though he had said that the worship of God had not been thus rejected by the influence of the multitude, but that each one had his own object, and had concocted the wickedness and the great sin of rejecting God. There is then more meaning and force in this way of speaking, than if he had said that they all walked in the wickedness of their own hearts. He further shews that they were all, from the least to the greatest, implicated, as they say, in the same impiety.

He afterwards adds, that God had *brought upon them the words,* that is, the threatenings *of the covenant.* By the words of the covenant he means not here the doctrine or

[1] On the meaning of these words, see a note in vol. i. p. 187.

precepts of the law. He indeed mentioned before the words of the covenant for the commands of God; but now, on finding that he had to do with refractory men, who were not capable of receiving any doctrine, he comes to threatenings. But God prescribes first in his law what he wills to be done, and then adds not only kind invitations, but also what is alluring, in order to conciliate the minds of men: but when there is no attention to obedience, and no care for it, he then comes to threatenings. Though the Prophet had omitted the promises, he had yet spoken previously of the law itself; but he says now that God had executed what he had denounced on them.

He further says, *Which I have commanded to be done; and they did them not.* There seems indeed to be a confusion here; for by *the words of this covenant,* he no doubt means threatenings, as I have stated: then he immediately adds, *which I have commanded to be done, and they did them not.* But, as I have already reminded you, the Prophet had previously, with sufficient clearness, taught them that the rule of a godly and holy life was set forth in the law; but he now refers especially to threatenings. It is then not strange that he speaks thus indistinctly, for the people had in a manner perverted the law. There were indeed in the law these two distinct things—doctrine, or a rule of life; and threatenings, which were added as stimulants to rouse the sloth of men, or rather to subdue their perverseness. But as the Israelites and the Jews had not attended to the voice of God, the Prophet here blends threatenings with precepts.[1]

[1] There is certainly an incongruity in taking the expression, "the words of the covenant," in two different senses. The verse is omitted in the *Septuagint,* but retained in the other versions and the *Targum.* This clause, in the *Vulgate* and *Syriac,* is thus given: "I have brought on them the words of this covenant." The *Targum* is, "I have brought vengeance on them, because they undertook not the words of this covenant." To bring words on one, seems to mean to enforce, to enjoin them. I cannot find the phrase anywhere else. Taken in this sense, the expressions will be wholly suitable to the rest of the passage, which I render thus:—

6. Then said Jehovah to me, Proclain these words in the cities of Judah, and in the streets of Jerusalem, saying,—

Hear the words of the covenant,

We now understand what the Prophet means in this passage, when he says that he was sent by God to cry, *Hear ye the words of this covenant;* for they were forgetful of true religion; and such was their oblivion and impious contempt of the whole law, that they had need of being taught its first rudiments. This is one thing. He then shews how solicitous God had been about their welfare, so that he had not neglected any of the duties of the best of fathers, and that yet his labour had been all in vain; for they had not only been led away by their own lusts, but their inward wickedness had closed their ears, so that they deigned not to listen to God's voice; and this had not been in one age only, but from the time they came out of Egypt to that day. It hence follows that they were justly punished, for God had tried all means before he had recourse to severity; but since he had adopted all kinds of ways to reform them, and all in vain, the only thing that remained was to punish them as men past all remedy. This is the import of the whole. He now adds—

9. And the Lord said unto me, A conspiracy is found among the men of Judah, and among the inhabitants of Jerusalem.

9. Et dixit Jehova ad me, inventa est conspiratio (*ad verbum,* colligatio; *nam* קשר *significat proprie ligare vel connectere, sed metaphorica est significatio cum transfertur ad conspirationem*) in viro (*hoc est,* in viris) Jehudah et in civibus Jerusalem.

10. They are turned back to the iniquities of their forefathers, which refused to hear my words; and

10. Reversi sunt ad iniquitates patrum suorum superiorum (*qui ante fuerunt,*) qui noluerunt audire

Even these, and do them:
7. Verily, testifying I testified to your fathers
In the day I brought them from the land of Egypt;
And to this day, early-rising and testifying,
Saying, "Hearken to my voice:"
8. Yet they hearkened not, nor bent their ear,
But walked, every one, according to the resolutions
Of their own wicked heart;
Yea, I urged on them all the words of the covenant,
Even these, which I commanded them to do;
But they did *them* not.

To "testify," rather than to "protest," is the meaning of the verb, when followed by ב, as here. To this testifying was added that of urging or pressing on them the duty of attending to all the words of the covenant; but all was to no purpose. To introduce punishment here comports not with the passage.—*Ed.*

they went after other gods to serve them: the house of Israel and the house of Judah have broken my covenant, which I made with their fathers.

verba mea; et ipsi ambularunt post deos alienos, ut servirent ipsis; dissoluerunt domus Israel et domus Jehudah fœdus meum, quod pepigeram cum patribus ipsorum.

Here the Prophet joins closer battle with the men of his age, and says, that they were worse than their fathers; for this is the meaning of the word, banding or joining together. For when the Israelites concurred in a body in ungodly superstitions, it was more excusable at the beginning, for they had not yet struck deep roots in true religion; but when God by his prophets had endeavoured many times, and in various ways, to restore them to the right way, and when his diligence and assiduous efforts had proved fruitless, it was an evidence of confirmed and hopeless obstinacy. He then says, that this had been discovered; for this is what he means by saying, that it *had been found out.* This verb is often used in Scripture in another sense, but it means here the same, as though he had said, that the conspiracy of the people had been discovered or proved, as it is said of thieves when found out, that they are caught in the very act. So God says here, that it was no matter of dispute whether the people had designedly and from sheer wickedness perverted his true and lawful worship; *the conspiracy,*[1] he says, *is sufficiently notorious.*

We then understand the meaning of the Prophet to be,—that not a part of the people was implicated in impiety, but that all, from the least to the greatest, were together defiled, and that this was done, not by some foolish impulse of the moment, but designedly, for they *banded together;* and further, that this was *sufficiently evident,* so that they could no longer contend as to the fact, for their wickedness was sufficiently manifest.

And he says *between Judah and Israel.*[2] There is here

[1] Rendered "σύνδεσμος, binding together," by the *Sept.*,—"conjuratio, confederacy, *or* conspiracy," by the *Vulg.* and *Arab.*,—"rebellion," by the *Syr.* and *Targ.*,—"combination," as given by *Gataker* and *Blayney*, would express better the meaning of the original word.—*Ed.*

[2] There is here an oversight. "Israel" is not mentioned here, but the men of Judah and the inhabitants of Jerusalem. "Israel" is mentioned at the end of the next verse, as having with "Judah" annulled the covenant.—*Ed.*

implied a sharp reproof; for we know that these two kingdoms had not only entertained a hidden grudge, but fiercely contended with one another. Since then the discord had been such between the ten tribes and the tribe of Judah, that it was as it were an insane hatred, so that they wished wholly to destroy one another, for the Jews sent for the Egyptians when the Israelites had called to arms the Syrians and the Assyrians for the destruction of Judah. Since then they so inimically treated one another for so many ages, what did this now mean? What a monstrous thing it was, that they conspired together to subvert the worship of God, to overturn everything true in religion, and to set up their own idols! We now then perceive the meaning of the Prophet; he intimates, that they had in all other things been enemies, and that they only united in this one thing, that is, in carrying on war against God, in subverting his worship, and rendering void his law. We hence see what the Spirit of God had in view in saying, that a *conspiracy was found out;* which was, that the Prophet might not use many words, as though the matter was doubtful. God then bids him positively to declare this fact, like a scribe who records the sentence of a judge; and thus God shews that he dealt with the Jews, as men deal with those who are condemned.

He also adds, that they *had returned,* &c. He shews for what purpose they had conspired, even to *return to the vices of their fathers, who had been before them.* Some render the word "ancestors;" but the meaning of the Prophet is not thus sufficiently expressed, for what he means is, that the Israelites had been refractory from the very beginning, so that God could never subdue their wayward dispositions. It must however be observed, that he speaks not of the most ancient, as הראשנים, *erashnim,* are the ancient who were before them;[1] but as there had been a continued succession

[1] The *Sept.* have "τῶν πρότερον—who were before;" the *Vulg.* improperly joins it with "iniquities,"—"the former iniquities of the fathers;" the *Syriac* renders it "ancient," and the *Targum,* "former," both connecting it with "fathers." The word means the "first," rather than the "former." If we take it as connected with "fathers," then the first fathers with whom the covenant, after they came out of Egypt, was made, are meant; but it may be taken as in apposition with "fathers;" then the first who refused

or series of impiety, the Prophet calls them here, the former fathers, who had first begun to shake off the yoke of God even to that day. And he again mentions what we have before noticed, that *they were unwilling to hear.* Though ignorance does not wholly clear or absolve us, it yet extenuates a crime ; but God shews that the Israelites had been disobedient from the beginning. Though he had by Moses sufficiently taught them, we yet find that they often rose up against Moses. If we inquire of their origin, it appears to have been marked with resolute impiety ; they were unwilling to obey God.

He then adds, that *they walked after alien gods that they might serve them.* There is ever an implied contrast between God and idols. God had given them evidences enough of his power and glory, and we may justly say, that he had sufficiently proved himself to be the only true God. How then was it that the Israelites had given the preference to fictitious gods ? Doubtless no unwilling error could have been pretended. We hence see that they had rejected the true God and wilfully followed their own devices. He then says, that they *might serve them.* But God had already bound them to himself, as he had redeemed them ; when, therefore, they devoted themselves to alien gods, was not their ingratitude thus most fully proved ?

He at length subjoins, by way of explanation, *Therefore the house of Israel and the house of Judah have dissolved my covenant.* He confirms what I have just said,—that they had not erred because the way was unknown, but because they

to hear God, are referred to. Taking this view, we may render the verse thus—

10. They have turned to the iniquities of their fathers—
The first who refused to hearken to my words;
And they have walked after alien gods to serve them :
Annulled have the house of Israel and the house of Judah
My covenant, which I made with their fathers.

The word for "iniquities" means perversions, distortions, the turning of things to purposes not intended. These are the kinds of iniquities which are meant. Perverting the truth rather than denying or renouncing it, had ever been the sin of the Jews. Instead of worshipping God himself, they worshipped him by means of idols, and through the mediation of inferior gods. This was the perversion. Alien gods were mediators ; hence they never renounced God's worship. But God deemed this as an annulment of his covenant, by which they were required to worship him alone.—*Ed.*

were refractory and untameable in their disposition, and would not bear to hear God, though he kindly shewed to them what they were to do. But the word covenant expresses more than this,—that God had not only delivered them his precepts by Moses, but had also adopted them as his own people, and at the same time pledged his faith to them, "I shall be your God, be ye my people," (ver. 4, above.) Since then God had so kindly allured them to himself, how monstrous was their rebellion, when they refused to hear his voice! With reference to this the word ברית, *berit*, is used; for God had not only delivered to them a rule of life, but also adopted them as his people, that they might be obedient to him.

By saying that he made a covenant *with their fathers*, he refers to that time when he brought the people out of Egypt, for then was the race of Abraham united. They were indeed twelve distinct tribes; but there was one head over the people, there was one priesthood, and they formed afterwards one kingdom. God then shews, that though the ten tribes made for themselves in after time another king, and the tribe of Judah was then divided, and there were in this separation some special causes of enmity, they yet had always been of the same disposition, and proved how like their fathers they were, as though he had said, "They were formerly one people, they are now two, yet they have *conspired together;* their iniquity is the same, in this they are united; and there is among them a binding together." It follows—

11. Therefore thus saith the Lord, Behold, I will bring evil upon them, which they shall not be able to escape; and though they shall cry unto me, I will not hearken unto them.

11. Propterea sic dicit Jehova, Ecce ego inducam (inducens, *vel*, induco) super eos malum, à quo non poterunt exire (*hoc est*, se explicare; *ad verbum*, quod non poterunt exire ab ipso;) et clamabunt ad me et non audiam eos.

The Prophet now denounces on them a calamity; for it is probable that for many years he had been as their teacher threatening them, but all in vain. Hence he now confirms what we have before observed,—that their impious conspiracy was fully known and proved, so that they were not now to be called or drawn before the judge's tribunal, as they had so openly procured for themselves their own ruin.

He then says, that God was, as it were, armed to take vengeance; *I will bring,* he says, *upon them an evil from which they shall not be able to go away.*[1] Then he adds, *and they shall cry to me, but I will not hear them.* By this latter clause he shews that no hope remained, as they could get no pardon from God, for he would no longer be entreated by them. The import of the whole is,—that they were so given up to destruction, that it was in vain for them to expect God's mercy. God had indeed often promised in his law that he would be reconciled to them; but the Prophet says now that every hope was cut off, because they had rejected God's covenant. Hence, whatever God had promised respecting his kindness and mercy, belonged to them no longer.

Let us now learn also how to accommodate this doctrine to ourselves. And, first, we may remark, that there is a great difference between us, who have been plainly, and for a long time, taught what is the true and lawful worship of God, and those miserable people who were blind in darkness; hence much more atrocious is our sin and worthy of much heavier punishment. Then we may also add this,—that though God may for a time bear with us, the whole time of his forbearance will have to be accounted for. There is no day in which God does not accuse us; and thus he rises early, and thus he shews us what concern he has for our salvation; but if we remain asleep in our sloth, a threatening this day is suspended over our heads, and especially when we consider that God comes nearer, as it were, to us than to his ancient

[1] The literal rendering is as follows:—

11. Therefore thus saith Jehovah,—
Behold, I will cause to come on them an evil,
From which they shall not be able to go forth:
And they shall loudly cry to me,
But I will not hearken to them.

The third line in Welsh is literally the Hebrew,—

Yr hwn nis gallant vyned allan ohono.
Which they will not be able to go forth from it.

The verb זעק is not merely to cry, but to cry loudly, or vehemently, or clamorously; the effect of great distress impatiently endured. Our version and *Blayney* are wrong in rendering ו "And though." It is not what *may* have been, is meant, but what *would* be. It is expressly foretold what they would do; and corresponding with this are all the versions and the *Targum.*—*Ed.*

people. And hence we may also learn how much less tolerable is our ingratitude. It ought, therefore, to be carefully noticed, that God is armed against those before whom he has set his word, not only for one day but for many years, when he has found that he has laboured in vain; and that when he is offended with their obstinate wickedness, there is no more any remedy.

But it may be asked here, How is it that God declares here that he would not be propitious to the Israelites, though they even cried to him, when yet this promise so often occurs, "Call on me, and I will hear thee?" (Psalm l. 15.) Though God does not everywhere use such words, yet in many places he makes this promise. But still it may appear inconsistent that he closes up the door of mercy against those who flee to his mercy. But in the next verse he shews what this cry would be; for had they from the heart repented, doubtless his pardon would never have been denied: but we shall presently see that these cries would be rambling, vagrant, and confused; so that they would not direct their prayers to God, nor observe the way which is made known to us all; for they would cry without repentance and faith, according to what follows; for the Prophet says—

12. Then shall the cities of Judah, and inhabitants of Jerusalem, go and cry unto the gods unto whom they offer incense; but they shall not save them at all in the time of their trouble.

12. Et ibunt urbes Jehudah et cives Jerusalem et clamabunt ad deos quibus ipsi fecerunt suffitum; et servando non servabunt eos in tempore afflictionis.

The Prophet then shews in these words that they were not touched by a true and sincere feeling of repentance who cried thus indiscriminately to God and to idols.[1]

But another question may be here raised, How could they flee to God and to foreign gods too? The ready an-

[1] But the most obvious meaning of the passage is, that the Jews would first cry to God, and that being not heard, they would then cry to alien gods. Hence our version renders the ו at the beginning of this verse, "Then," and rightly too: so does the *Syriac*, though the other versions render it "And," as *Blayney* does: and if so rendered, the connection would appear the same,—

And go shall the cities of Judah and the inhabitants of Jerusalem,
And they shall loudly cry to the gods,
To whom they burn incense;
But saving they will not save them
At the time of their calamity.—*Ed.*

swer is this, that the unbelieving, in a turbulent state of mind, turn here and there, so that they lay hold of nothing certain, or sure and fixed. This we see in the Papists—they cry to God and at the same time to a great number of gods. Let us therefore know, that there is in all the unbelieving a spirit, as it were, of giddiness, which turns them into different expedients, so that now they call on God, then they flee to their idols. Men naturally are led to God when any distress holds them bound; hence they call on God: but afterwards, being not satisfied with him alone, they betake themselves to their own devices, and heap together, as I have said, a vast multitude of gods. Since then we see this to be done under the Papacy in our day, we need not wonder that it was done formerly, and that the Jews were on this account condemned.

The Prophet now addresses the Jews only; he had before spoken of the Israelites, but he now speaks especially to his own people, *Go shall the cities of Judah and the citizens of Jerusalem*, &c. What shall they do? *They shall cry to their gods.* We hence see that their prayers were rambling, as though they poured them unto the air: therefore God could not have heard them. For whenever God promises to be propitious and appeasable he requires faith and repentance: but there was in this people an impious wantonness, and no faith, for they were entangled in their own superstitions.

The meaning is, that the Jews, when oppressed by calamities, would make their prayers to the true God, but without understanding, without any discrimination, but on the contrary, in a confused state of mind: and that this would be sufficiently evident, for they would at the same time seek the aid of various idols, but that they would gain no help, either from God or from their idols; and why? because they would be unworthy to be heard by God, as they would not call on him in a right spirit, not with faith and repentance; and their idols would not be able to bring them any help. It hence follows that they would be altogether in a hopeless state.

PRAYER.

Grant, Almighty God, that since thou hast been pleased, in so kind a manner, according to thy paternal kindness, to invite us to thyself, we may not be refractory, but willingly and quietly submit ourselves to thee, and not wait until thou shakest us with terror, and shewest us signs of thy wrath; but may we anticipate thy dreadful judgment, and thus always go on, so as to have no other object in view but to glorify thy name through the whole course of our life, until we shall at length be made partakers of that glory which thine only-begotten Son has obtained for us.—Amen.

Lecture Forty-Sixth.

13. For *according to* the number of thy cities were thy gods, O Judah; and *according to* the number of the streets of Jerusalem have ye set up altars to *that* shameful thing, *even* altars to burn incense unto Baal.

13. Quia pro numero urbium tuarum fuerunt dii tui, Jehudah; et pro numero platearum, Jerusalem, posuistis altaria in opprobrium, altaria ad offerendum suffitum Baal.

THE Prophet shews here that the Jews were not only polluted with one kind of superstition, but that they sought for themselves fictitious gods from all quarters, so that the land was filled and, as it were, deluged with innumerable superstitions. He says, that in proportion to the *number of cities were the gods* in the kingdom of Judah, and that in every city, in proportion to the number of *streets, altars* were built, that they might *burn incense to Baal.*

There seems, however, to be some inconsistency in the words; for if they all worshipped Baal, where could be found the multitude of gods which the Prophet condemns? It then follows, that there was everywhere the same form of superstition, or that they did not in every place burn incense to Baal. But from this place and from others we may gather that this is a common name; for though all idols had their distinctive names, yet this name was applied indiscriminately, and all idols had it in common. For what does Baal mean but a patron, or an inferior god, who procured the favour of the supreme God? The prophets often use the word in the plural number, and call the lesser or inferior gods Baalim, who were regarded as mediators or angels; and farther, they often mean all kinds of idols by Baal. There is to be understood here a figure, by which a part is taken for the whole; for the Prophet intended by the word to include all those gods which the Jews had devised for themselves, though their names were different.

But what the Prophet condemned in the people was, as we see, daily practised. For there is no end, when men once depart ever so little from the pure worship of the only true God: for when anything is blended with it, one error immediately produces another; so various errors will cumulate, till men fall into a labyrinth from which there is no exit. This is clearly seen under the Papacy. At first Satan, by spurious pretences, led men away from the simple worship of God and his pure doctrine; and as there is in all an inbred curiosity, every one had a desire to add something of his own. Hence then it happened that so great a mass of errors and superstitions has prevailed. It is nothing strange, then, that the Prophet condemned the Jews, not only for having departed from the true and lawful worship of God, but also for having as many idols as cities, and for having so many forms of worship as there were streets in their cities. And we hence also learn that all the superstitions among the whole people had the same root; for though they differed in particulars, they all yet proceeded from the same principle; for every one wished to have his own God. It hence happened, that every city had its patron, and every family also devised a god for itself; for no one was satisfied with the common worship. It is then wholly necessary that we should faithfully worship the one true God; otherwise the Devil will immediately bring in strange gods and a mixed multitude of gods: so that it hence evidently appears, that we thus justly suffer for our impious levity in forsaking the fountain of living waters.

He says that *altars were built for reproach.*[1] This may

[1] The word is בשת. "*Bosheth,* shame," says *Lowth,* "was a nickname for Baal. (See Hos. ix. 10.) So Jerubbaal is called Jerubbosheth in 2 Sam. xi. 21." The word is left out in the *Septuagint;* the other versions and the *Targum* render it differently; its meaning was evidently not understood. It may be rendered here "baseness," or a base thing; the last clause is explanatory of this,—

be referred to God, because they offered to God a heinous effrontery in setting up their profane altars in opposition to that one true altar which God had commanded to be built for him in the temple. But this is a strained interpretation. It is more suitable to refer this to the people, because they erected altars for themselves to their own shame, as though he had said that the Jews were themselves the authors of all their evils, so that they ought to consider them as due to their impiety, being the punishments inflicted by the Lord. It is the same as though he had said, "God will indeed chastise you, as ye are worthy of being so treated, but ascribe the whole fault to yourselves; for the altars, raised by your own hands, will be to you for reproach and shame."

He at length adds, *To offer incense to Baal.* They sought doubtless the favour of the supreme God; but as they devised for themselves patrons, as mediators between them and God, according to the Platonic figment, which has prevailed in all ages, the Prophet here declares that their gods were as many as their cities, and even as many as their streets; for God does not admit those sophistical subtleties by which hypocrites seek to escape; for whenever his glory is transferred to others, he complains that new gods are introduced.[1] It follows—

14. Therefore pray not thou for this people, neither lift up a cry or prayer for them: for I will not hear *them* in the time that they cry unto me for their trouble.	14. Et tu ne ores pro populo hoc, et ne tollas pro ipsis clamorem et precationem; quia ego non audiens (non audiam) in tempore quo clamabunt ad me pro (*vel*, super) malo suo (super afflictione sua.)

That the Jews might understand that a sore calamity was nigh, and that God would not be appeasable, the Prophet

Ye have set up altars for a base thing—
Altars to burn incense to a Baal.

By putting the indefinite article we avoid the contrariety which *Calvin* refers to. It is given in the singular number in all the versions except the *Vulgate*, which has Baalim.—*Ed.*

[1] The connection of this verse has not been pointed out by *Calvin.* It begins with "For," or because; so that a reason is given for what has been said previously, and that is not found in the immediately preceding verse, but at the end of the 11th, "I will not hearken unto them;" then what is said here is given as a reason. But if we render כי "though," as it is often done, and not "For," the connection is with the next preceding verse; their gods would not save them, "though" they were as many as their cities, &c. This seems to be the most natural connection.—*Ed.*

himself is forbidden to intercede for them. There is no doubt but that even when he reproved the people in the severest strain, he made supplications to God for them; for he sustained a twofold character: when he went forth as the herald of celestial vengeance, he thundered against the ungodly and the despisers of God; but at the same time he humbly supplicated pardon in behalf of lost and miserable men; for had he not been solicitous for the salvation of the people, had he not diligently prayed, it would not have been necessary to prohibit him to pray. It hence appears that the Prophet was diligent in these two things, that he severely reproved the people according to God's command, and that he also was a suppliant in seeking God's favour to the unworthy. This is one thing.

Now then that God prohibits Jeremiah to pray, this was not done for his sake only, but he had a regard also to the whole people, that they might know that a sentence was pronounced on them, and that there was no hope left. We hence see that God positively declares that it was his purpose to destroy the people, and that therefore there was no room for prayer.

But it may be asked, Whether the Prophet, by going on in praying, offended God? for we shall see that he was still so anxious for the welfare of the people that he ceased not to pray: and what is said of Jeremiah is true also of all the other prophets; and the faithful have ever prayed for pardon, though the state of things had been brought to an extremity. But we must observe, that God, when he thus issues a simple prohibition, often stimulates the prayers of his people, according to what we read of Samuel; for though he knew from God's own mouth that Saul was rejected, he yet from love ceased not to seek his good and to intercede God for him. (1 Sam. xv. 35; xvi. 1.) But the prophets doubtless paid regard to God's counsel in this case: yet as God did not speak for the sake of Jeremiah, but of the people, the Prophet is not to be charged with rashness or presumption, or foolish obstinacy or inconsiderate zeal, for having afterwards prayed; for he knew that this was not so much for his sake as on account of the people.

But there is another thing to be observed,—that Jeremiah was not forbidden to pray for the remnant, that is, for the elect, and for the seed from which the Church was afterwards to arise; but he was forbidden to pray for the whole body of the people: and no doubt he felt assured from that time that no remedy could be applied, and that the people would be driven into exile. This then is to be understood of the whole mass of the people; Jeremiah might still pray for the elect, and also for the new Church, that is, for the renewal of the Church: he was not indeed to pray that the Lord would not execute the vengeance which had been already decreed, for that could not be turned aside by any prayers.

We now then understand the meaning of this passage,—that Jeremiah prayed daily for all men, and also for the renewal of the Church; but that he was to look for the calamity of exile as a certain thing, for this had been fixed by God.

As to the words, *Raise not for them a cry or a prayer*, we have said elsewhere that there are two ways of speaking, which though different in some respects, are yet the same in meaning—to raise up and to cast a prayer. Hence the saints are said sometimes to cast their prayers: "Let my prayer be cast in thy presence." For no one is rightly prepared to call on God, except he is cast down in himself and laid prostrate. Hence the prayers of the saints are said to be cast on account of their humility; they are also said to be raised up on account of the fervour of their zeal, and also on account of their confidence. And that he repeats the same thing in different words is not without a meaning; for it is the same as though he had said, "Thou wilt do nothing by beseeching, praying, interceding and supplicating." God then confirms by these several words that he would not hereafter be reconciled to the people.

It follows, *For I will not hear them at the time when they shall cry to me.* There seems not to be a suitable reason given here, for God might have conceded to the Prophet what had not been denied to the ungodly and the rebellious: but he simply means that he would be a severe Judge in executing punishment, so that there would be no room for mercy: *I will not* then *hear them;* that is, "If even they cry, I will not hear them, (it is an argument from the greater to the less,) much less then will I hear thee for them." But why was not God propitious to his servant? To this I answer, that God is more ready to shew mercy when any one himself calls on him, than when he is supplicated by others. The meaning is, that whether they themselves prayed or employed others to pray for them, God would not be reconciled to them.

What might be objected here has been elsewhere answered; for if they had from the heart and sincerely prayed, God would have no doubt heard them; for that promise never disappoints any, "Nigh is God to all who call upon him;" (Psalm cxlv. 18;) but it is added, "in truth." As then hypocrites are here spoken of who poured forth rambling and false prayers, and blended the worship of the true God with that of their own idols, it is no wonder that God rejected their prayers, for our prayers are sanctified by faith and repentance. When, therefore, unbelief prevails, and when the heart cleaves perversely to wickedness, our prayers are polluted and presumptuous; for then the name of God is profaned. It is therefore not strange that God rejects those who call on him hypocritically.[1] It follows—

15. What hath my beloved to do in mine house, *seeing* she hath wrought lewdness with many, and the holy flesh is passed from thee? when thou doest evil, then thou rejoicest.

15. Quid dilecto meo in domo mea? dum facit ipsa abominationem cum multis; et caro sanctuarii transierunt abs te; quia dum malè fecisti, tunc gloriaris.

As the words are concise, this passage is in various ways perverted by interpreters: brevity is commonly obscure. But the explanation almost universally received is this,—that the Prophet addresses God as his beloved. They who take the words of the Prophet in this sense, think also that the Temple is called his house, on account of his concern for religion, for which he was very zealous. As then he had preferred God's Temple to all earthly things, they think that he thus spoke, *What has my beloved to do in mine house?* But Jonathan much more correctly applies the words to God; and doubtless, whoever wisely considers the Prophet's words,

[1] See a note in vol. i. p. 384.—*Ed.*

will wonder that so many learned men have been mistaken on a point by no means doubtful. God then, no doubt, speaks here; and he calls his people *beloved* on account of their adoption.

But the expression is ironical: we cannot think otherwise when we consider how great was the impiety of the people, and how unworthy they were of such an honour on account of their ingratitude. It is yet not strange that they were called beloved, as in other places, for they had been chosen by God. They were in a similar way called "upright" in the song of Moses; and yet Moses, in that very song, declared how wickedly they had departed from their God. (Deut. xxxii. 15.) But he called them "upright" in reference to God; for though men do not answer to their vocation, yet the counsel of God remains firm, and can never be changed by the wickedness of men. Though then all had then become apostates, yet God did not suffer his covenant to be abolished. Hence Paul, in speaking of the Jews, in Romans xi. 28, when almost all had become the bitterest enemies to the gospel, and had, through their unfaithfulness, wholly forfeited their privileges, so as to become aliens, yet says that they were beloved on account of their fathers: "For you," he says, "they are indeed for a time enemies;" which means, that God designed to give their place to the Gentiles, and to adopt them; and yet that, on account of his covenant, they remain, and will remain beloved, that is, with regard to the first adoption.

I shall quote no other similar passages, for it is enough to understand the real meaning of the term: *What then has my beloved to do in my house?* which means, "Why do the Jews now pretend to come to the Temple to sacrifice to me? Why do they profess themselves to be my people? What have they to do with my house?" that is, "What have they to do with anything like holiness?" Hence he indirectly touches the Jews in two ways,—that they had precluded themselves from the advantage of offering sacrifices in the temple,—and that it was an increase of their crime, that while they were God's friends, that is, when he bestowed on them his favour, and embraced them as a father his own children, they yet carried on war with him as his avowed enemies, according to what is elsewhere said, "Ah! I will take vengeance on mine enemies." (Isaiah i. 24.)

We now see that this meaning is the most suitable. God shews that his temple was polluted by the Jews, when they thoughtlessly rushed there to offer their sacrifices; *What have you,* he says, *to do with my house?* Nearly the same thing is said in the first chapter of Isaiah; for God there contemptuously reproves the Jews because they trod the pavement of his temple: "I truly do not owe you anything; ye indeed come to my courts, but for what purpose? Ye only wear out the pavement of my temple: Stay then at home, and think not that I am bound to you because ye come to the temple." So also in this place, *What has my beloved to do with my house?* He concedes to them the title Beloved, as though he had said, "Ye are, it is true, beloved, and ye think that God is bound to you; for, relying on the covenant which I made with your father Abraham, ye always continue to make this boasting—'We are the people of God and his heritage; we are a holy nation and a royal priesthood'—Beloved ye are," he says, "but what have you to do with my Temple?"

Then he adds, *For she has done abomination with many.* The gender is here changed, for the relative is feminine: but this mode of speaking is everywhere common, as the people are represented to us under the character of a woman. Then he in effect says, "Behold the daughter of my people hath done abomination with many." The Jews were not to enter the Temple except they remained as it were fixed in its pure worship; for as it was the only true Temple, and had in it the only true altar, so they ought to have worshipped none but the only true God, and also to have observed one rule only in worshipping him. But he says here that they had done abomination; and thus he charged them with those impious devices, those spurious forms of worship which they had adopted, and thus departed from what had been prescribed to them; for abomination is set here in opposition to the law. He says further, that they did this *with many.* We hence see that the gate of the Temple was closed against them, for the Temple could not be separated from the law, nor yet from God, to whom it was dedicated. The Jews, having forsaken the law, and adopted innumerable idols, thrust themselves into the Temple; and hence we see the reason why God complains that they still came to the Temple: "As then they have done *abomination*, and done it with *many*, they have no more anything to do with my law." The Temple was a visible image of the one true God, and also the holy receptacle of his law. They despised the law, and gloried in innumerable gods: they sought thus to blend the sanctity of the Temple with a multitude of gods, and with their own depravations and devices.

He says afterwards, that the *flesh of the sanctuary* had *passed away* from them: *The flesh of the sanctuary have passed away.* Some apply this to all the faithful, according to that saying, "Silent before God let all flesh be," (Hab. ii. 20;) but this is forced, and without meaning. He speaks no doubt of sacrifices, and says, that the flesh of the sanctuary, that is, sacrifices, had departed from the people. They no doubt still offered sacrifices very regularly; but God did not accept their sacrifices, because they had corrupted his true worship. This then is the reason why he says that the *flesh of the sanctuary* had departed from the people, as in other places he denies that it was offered to him. At the same time the Jews wished sacrifices to be regarded as offered to him, and doubtless they boldly referred to them in opposition to the prophets. But God did not accept them, though they sought thus to render him as it were a debtor. "It is not to me," he says, "that ye offer your sacrifices, but to idols." So also in this place he says, *The flesh of the sanctuary is taken away from them;* for their sacrifices had become polluted. They were then nothing but putrid carcases; for victims ought to have been offered in the Temple; but they had polluted the Temple, so that it had become a den of robbers, and like a dunghill, in short, a brothel, as Scripture speaks elsewhere. There was then now, doubtless, no *flesh of the sanctuary*;[1] that is, no lawful sacrifice, such as God approved.

[1] "Holy fleshes," κρέα ἅγια, carnes sanctæ, is the version of the *Septua-*

Let us then know that hypocrites, as soon as they depart from the true worship of God, do nothing that can avail them, though they may busy themselves much, and even weary themselves in worshipping God, for all that they offer is abominable. If then we desire to render to God such services as he will accept and approve, let us regard this truth—that obedience is more valued by him than all sacrifices. (1 Samuel xv. 22.)

He adds another complaint,—that when *they did evil, they gloried* in it. And there is a causal particle introduced, *Because,* he says, *thou gloriest when thou hast done evil.* The Prophet no doubt means, that they had by no means a right to contend, because they had not only corrupted true religion, but were also proud of their superstitions, and despised God, and set up their own devices against his law. But it was an intolerable thing for men to attempt to subject God to their own will, or rather to their own fancies. Indeed, the faithful do not so purely and so perfectly sacrifice to God, but that some vices are mixed with their offerings; but God nevertheless receives what they offer, though there be some mixture of defilement. How so? Because they acquiesce not in their own performances, but, on the contrary, aspire after purity, though they do not attain it; but when hypocrites exalt themselves against God, and proudly despise his teaching, and prefer their own inventions, and dare even to set up these against his authority, it is doubtless a diabolical presumption, such as contaminates what would otherwise be most holy.[1] It follows—

gint and *Vulgate,* and "holy flesh" is the *Syriac;* but the *Targum* has "the worship of my sanctuary." *Blayney* renders it "holy flesh." The word קדש means holy, or holiness, and מקדש is the sanctuary.—*Ed.*

[1] This verse has been variously rendered and explained. The versions all differ, and the *Targum* too; and none of them seem to render the original correctly. *Blayney,* following the *Septuagint,* has introduced corrections, but not authorized by any MSS. There is no different reading of any consequence. The literal rendering I consider to be as follows:—

15. What, as to my beloved, *is* in my house her doing?
Is not her plotting with many?—
Yea, the holy flesh do they take away from thee;
When thou doest evil against me, then thou exultest.

The word for "plotting" does not mean "lewdness," or "abomination," as rendered by all the versions, but devising, contriving, scheming, machinating; the reference is to the scheme of uniting the worship of God with the

16. The Lord called thy name, A green olive-tree, fair, *and* of goodly fruit: with the noise of a great tumult he hath kindled fire upon it, and the branches of it are broken.

17. For the Lord of hosts, that planted thee, hath pronounced evil against thee, for the evil of the house of Israel, and of the house of Judah, which they have done against themselves, to provoke me to anger, in offering incense unto Baal.

16. Olivam viridem, pulchram fructu, forma, vocavit Jehova nomen tuum; ad vocem sermonis (*alii vertunt,* tumultus) magni accendit (accendere fecit) super eam, et fracti sunt rami ejus (*alii vertunt transitivè,* et fregerunt ramos ejus.)

17. Nam Jehovah (*copula enim hîc accipitur vice causalis;* quia Jehova) exercituum, qui te plantavit, loquutus est (*vel,* pronunciavit) super te malum propter malitiam domus Israel et domus Jehudah, quam fecerunt sibi ad provocandum me, ad faciendum suffitum Baal.

The Prophet says first that the Jews had indeed been for a time like a fruitful and a fair olive; then he adds, that this beauty would not prevent God from breaking its branches and entirely eradicating it. He afterwards confirms this declaration, and says, *For God who had planted it, can also root it up* whenever it pleases him.' This is the import of the two verses.

The Prophet no doubt derides here the vain confidence by which he knew the Jews were deceived: for they were so inebriated with their privileges that they dared to despise the very giver of them. Hence the Prophet thus addressed them, "Do ye think that so many vices will be unpunished? Ye omit nothing to kindle God's wrath against you,—ye have polluted his Temple, ye have corrupted the whole of Divine worship, ye have despised the law; and can you think that the Lord will perpetually spare you?" But when the prophets thus assailed them, they had this answer, "What! will God leave his own Temple, concerning which he has sworn, This is my rest for ever? Is not this the Holy Land? And is not this also his heritage and his rest? And further, are we not his flock? Are we not his children? Are we not a holy people?" What then the Jews were wont ar-

worship of idols. The *Targum* gives the idea, "they have taken counsel to sin greatly." All the versions agree in giving a Hiphil meaning to יעברו, cause to pass from—to remove or take away. The "many" who advocated the worship of idols took away the holy flesh—the sacrifices, and took them away from her, "the beloved," as, when given to idols, they would be of no benefit. The words, כי רעתכי, are literally, "when thy evil *is* against me." It is a similar mode of expression with קמי, "those who rise up against me," (2 Samuel xxii. 40.) Though it was an evil against God, yet they exulted in what they did.—*Ed.*

rogantly to claim, the Prophet concedes to them. "So," he says, "ye are a green olive, a fair and tall olive, a fruitful olive; all this I grant; but cannot God kindle a fire to burn the branches and to reduce to nothing the whole tree?" We now then understand the design of the Prophet.

But the next verse must be joined, *For Jehovah of hosts, who hath planted thee,* &c.; as though he had said, "Your beauty and whatever that is valuable in you, is it from you? Surely, all your dignity and excellency have proceeded from the gratuitous kindness of God: know ye then that nothing comes from you, but from God and from his good pleasure. Then Jehovah, who has planted you, can, when he pleases, pull up by the roots a tree which he has himself planted."

He says that it was a *green olive, fair in fruit and form.* How so? Because God had favoured them with much honour. This similitude is found in many other places, but yet it is various as to its meaning. It might indeed with regard to God's dealings be applied to the whole people; but as hypocrites deserved to be spoiled and stripped of their privileges, so that which was offered to all in common, could only be really applied to the faithful, according to what David says, "I am a fruitful olive in the house of God." (Psalm lii. 8.) He then no doubt separated himself from hypocrites, as though he had said, "Even hypocrites seek to have a place in God's Temple, and are as it were tall trees, but they are unfruitful: I shall then be a green olive in the house of God; but they will wither." But the Prophet, as I have said, compares the Jews to a green olive on account of their adoption and the free favour shewn to them; for God had raised them unto a high state of excellency and honour.

But after having thus spoken by way of concession, he then adds, *At the sound of a great tumult,* or of a great word, *he will kindle his fire upon it, and broken shall be its branches.* Some, as I have said, render the last clause, "and they have broken its branches." As to what is intended, there is nothing dubious; but if we take the verb in an active sense, something must be understood, that is, that enemies, who will be like fire, shall break its branches.[1] Then follows

[1] This clause is difficult. The versions give no assistance. The word

what I have said to be a confirmation,—that *Jehovah, who had planted it, had spoken of* or pronounced *an evil,* or a calamity *against it.* He thus shews that there was no reason for them to trust in their present beauty; for they had it not from themselves, but possessed it only at the will of another; for God who had planted them, could also destroy them. But on this subject more shall be said.

PRAYER.

Grant, Almighty God, that as thou hast deigned to gather us into thy Church, we may never turn aside in the least from the purity of thy worship, but always regard what pleases thee, and learn to direct our doings and our thoughts in obedience to thy truth, and worship thee so purely both in spirit and in external forms, that thy name may be glorified by us, and that we may especially retain that purity which thou everywhere commendest to us, so that we may be indeed the members of thy only-begotten Son; and that as he has sanctified himself on our account, we may also through his Spirit be made partakers of the same sanctification, until he at length will gather us into his celestial kingdom, which he has obtained for us by his own blood.—Amen.

המולה, or rather המלה, is rendered "circumcision" by the *Septuagint,* "speech" by the *Vulgate,* "decree" by the *Syriac,* "tumult" by our version, and "clamour" by *Blayney.* It occurs only in one other place, Ezek. i. 24; where it stands in apposition with the "voice of the Almighty," which means there, and often elsewhere, "thunder:" and its meaning there is evidently the breaking of thunder or the thunderclap. It comes from מל, to cut, to break, to shiver. Then the noun is literally breaking, or crashing; it is the bursting noise of thunder. The other difficulty is עליה, rendered "upon it" in our version as well as in the early versions: but "it" is feminine in Hebrew, and "of it" after branches is masculine, the same gender with "olive." None have accounted for this anomaly. *Blayney* has indeed made the word a participle to agree with fire,—"a fire mounting upwards;" but this can hardly be admitted. I would render the verse thus,—

An olive, flourishing, beautiful in fruit, in form,
Hath Jehovah called thy name:
At the sound of a great thunderclap,—
Kindled hath he a fire by it,
And shivered have been its branches.

The verb for "kindled" is in Hiphil, and "by it" is the "thunderclap," which is feminine, and "its" is the "olive," which is masculine. *Houbigant* refers this passage to thunder.

The past tense is used for the future. He compares the nation to a flourishing tree, and then he speaks of its destruction by a fire kindled by the breaking of a thunder: the fire is the lightning.—*Ed.*

Lecture Forty-Seventh.

We mentioned yesterday why the Prophet reminded the Jews, that they had been *planted* by God; it was, that they might know that they did not stand through their own power, and that they had their roots elsewhere, even in the good pleasure of God. The import of the whole is, that whenever God pleased they would instantly perish; for they stood not through their own power, but only through his favour: and this is what he confirms elsewhere, by comparing God to a potter and the people to vessels of clay. Similar is the argument which Quintilian quotes from the Medea of Ovid, "I was able to save thee, and dost thou ask whether I can destroy thee?" As then the Jews, relying on their long tranquillity and on their forces, thought themselves beyond the reach of danger, the Prophet ridicules this confidence; he shews how vain it was, for God had planted them, and so he could easily root them up again.

But this metaphor is very common in Scripture: yet the comparison is the more suitable when the Church is said to have been planted by God; for as a tree draws juice and strength from a hidden root, so the faithful draw their life from the hidden election of God: but this refers to the hope of eternal life. The same is meant by Christ in Matthew xv. 13, when he says, "Every planting," that is, every tree, "which my Father hath not planted shall be rooted up." He then says, that the elect alone are planted by God, for they have their roots in the hidden life of God. But this is also extended much farther, even to the external state of the Church, according to what is said in Psalm xliv. 2, "Thou hast rooted out the nations, and planted our fathers;" as we find also in the eightieth Psalm and in other places. As God then plants his own elect, so also in gathering an external Church to himself, he is said to plant it: but they who are thus planted may be again rooted up, as the Prophet here testifies; while secret election cannot be changed.

We must then observe this difference,—that God's children have their roots in his eternal election, respecting which there can be no repentance and no change. But the external state of the Church is also compared to a planting: yet they who flourish for a time and are full of leaves and seem also to produce some fruit, are rooted up by God's hand, when they become degenerate. And this mode of speaking is to be taken sometimes still more generally, according to what we shall see in the next chapter, and also in other parts of Scripture.

The Prophet says that God had *spoken* concerning *the wickedness of Israel.* This refers to what had been taught: for though the Jews had already in part felt the just judgment of God, yet they still continued in safety. He then says that ruin was nigh them, for God had announced it by his servants. And he adds, that it was on account of the *wickedness*[1] of both kingdoms; and this was said in order to dissipate all their complaints; for we know that men are ever ready to clamour whenever God chastises them, as though they wished to contend with him. But the Prophet shews here, that God would deal thus severely with the Jews, because they had never ceased to provoke his wrath by their evil deeds. Hence he says, that they had *done it for themselves.* Some render the words, "And it shall therefore happen to them." But there seems to be much more force in the Prophet's words, when we say, that they had done evil for themselves, that is, to their own ruin. He adds, *To provoke me,* that is, their object is to provoke me. In short, God intimates, that he would justly punish the Jews, because they had procured evil for themselves; and at the

[1] It is literally "evil." There is here a striking instance of the same word used in two different senses—the *evil* of punishment and the *evil* of sin. The verse is thus,—

And Jehovah of hosts, who hath planted thee,
Hath spoken against thee an evil,
For the evil of the house of Israel and of the house of Judah:
Which they have done for themselves,
By provoking me in burning incense to Baal.

"For the evil," &c., is unintelligibly rendered by *Blayney,* "In prosecution of the evil," &c.; בגלל is a preposition, and is so rendered in all the early versions and the *Targum:* it is also so found in many other parts of Scripture. "Which they have done," &c., may be rendered, Which they have procured for themselves; for the verb עשה may sometimes be thus rendered. See Gen. xii. 5; xxxi. 1. But "which" refers to the first "evil," of which God had spoken, the evil of punishment.—*Ed.*

same time he points out the fountain of evil, for they had designedly provoked God by offering *incense to Baal.* It follows—

18. And the Lord hath given me knowledge *of it,* and I know *it:* then thou shewedst me their doings.	18. Et Jehova ostendit mihi (cognoscere me fecit) et cognovi; tunc patefecisti mihi opera (*vel,* instituta) ipsorum.

We know that they were all very wicked; and though they were proved guilty, yet they were not willing to yield, to acknowledge and confess their fault; but they raged against God and rose up against the prophets. And as they dared not to vomit forth their blasphemies against God, they assailed his servants and wished to appear as though their contest was with them. And this is not the vice only of one age, but we find that it prevails at this day; for when we boldly reprove hidden vices, immediately the profane make a clamour and say, "What! these divine; but who has made these things known to them? Have they this oracle from heaven?" As though, indeed, neither the word of God nor his Spirit can shew their power, except when children become judges! But the ungodly rise up against God's servants for this end, that they may with impunity do this and that, and everything, except what may draw them before an earthly tribunal, and be proved by clear and many evidences.

For this reason the Prophet says, that *made known* to him had been the vices of his own nation; as though he had said, "I see that you will be ready to raise an objection, as ye are wont proudly to resist all reproofs and threatenings, as though you contended only with men; but I testify to you now beforehand, that I bring nothing of my own, nor divine of myself what any one of you thinks within: but know ye that God, who knoweth the heart, has committed to me my office. He has then appointed me to be the herald of his vengeance, he has appointed me as a herald to denounce war on you. So I do not come nor act in my own name: there is, then, no reason for you to deceive yourselves, according to your usual manner, as though I presumptuously reproved you, when yet your vices are concealed, it being peculiar to God to know what is hid in the hearts of men. The recesses of the heart are indeed intricate, and great darkness is within; but God sees more clearly than men. Cease then to make this objection which ye are wont to raise against me, that I am presumptuous in bringing forth to light what lies hid in darkness, for God has appointed me to bring these commands to you: as he knows the heart, and as nothing escapes him, and as he penetrates into our thoughts and feelings, so he has also designed by his word which he has put in my mouth to render public what ye think is concealed."

We now see the design of the Prophet: but some take a different view, that God had made known to his servant Jeremiah the impious conspiracy of which he afterwards speaks, and thus connect the two verses. But I doubt not that the Prophet intended here to shew what and how much weight belonged to his doctrine, the credit and authority of which the Jews thought of detracting by boastfully alleging that he, a mortal man, assumed too much, and announced uncertain divinations. Hence, to repel such calumnies, he wished to testify that he threatened them not inconsiderately, nor spoke what he supposed or conjectured, when he exposed their sins, but that he only declared faithfully what had been enjoined by God and revealed also by the Holy Spirit. This is what is meant.[1] It afterwards follows—

19. But I *was* like a lamb *or* an ox *that* is brought to the slaughter; and I knew not that they had devised devices against me, *saying*, Let us destroy the tree with the fruit thereof, and let us cut him off from the land of the living, that his name may be no more remembered.

19. Ego autem quasi agnus, bos ductus ad immolandum (ad mactandum,) et non cognovi quod contra me cogitarent cogitationes (*hoc est,* inirent consilia, *nempe*) corrumpamus ligno panem ejus (*ad verbum est,* corrumpamus lignum in pane; *sed dicemus post de sensu verborum,*) et excidamus eum è terra vivorum, et nomen ejus non memoretur amplius.

[1] *Calvin* connects this verse with the foregoing, but most with what follows. The first verb in the *Septuagint* is a prayer, "Lord, make known to me, and I shall know." The *Syriac* and *Arabic* are the same. The *Vulgate* takes the verb in the second person, "O Lord, thou hast made known," &c. *Venema* seems to agree in part with *Calvin;* he connects the first clause with the foregoing, and the second with the following verse; and this appears to be the best construction. Then the ו is "when," as it may be rendered when followed as here by אז, "then,"—

The Prophet adds here, as I think, that he did not retaliate private wrongs: for the Jews might, under this pretext, have rejected his doctrine, and have said, that he was moved by anger to treat them sharply and severely. And doubtless, whosoever allows his own feelings to prevail in the least degree, cannot teach in sincerity; for he who prepares himself for the prophetic office, ought to put off all the affections of the flesh, and to manifest a pure, and, so to speak, a limpid zeal, and also a calm mind, so that he may seek nothing, and have no object but the glory of God and the salvation of those to whom he is sent a teacher. Whosoever then is under the influence of private feelings cannot act otherwise than violently, so that he cannot either faithfully or profitably discharge the office of a prophet or a teacher.

Hence the Prophet now adds, in the second place, that he did not plead his own cause, nor had respect, as they say, to his own person; for he *knew not* what the Jews had *devised* against him. They who join the two verses think that they have some reason for doing so, as they suppose that the Prophet now expresses more fully what he had before briefly touched upon: but if any maturely considers the whole passage, he will easily see that Jeremiah had another object in view, and that was, to secure authority to his doctrine. The Jews probably employed two ways to discredit the holy Prophet: "O, thou divinest!—the same thing, as we have said, is done now by many." He therefore summons the Jews here before God's tribunal, and shews that it was nothing strange, that he brought to light what they thought to be hidden, because it had been revealed to him by the Spirit of God. Even Christ said the same, "The Spirit, when he comes, shall judge the world." (John xvi. 8.) The Spirit did not appear except in the doctrine of the Apostles; but he exercised by the Apostles his own functions. The Apostle also seems to have this in view in Heb. iv. 12, when he says, that the word of God is like a two-edged sword,

When Jehovah made me to know, so that I knew *these things;*
Then thou didst shew me their doings.

That is, when Jehovah made known to him what he had previously related, he then shewed to him also the doings, or the purposes, of the men of Anathoth, which he afterwards more particularly mentions.—*Ed.*

which penetrates into the inmost thoughts and hidden feelings, even to the marrow and bones, so as to distinguish between thoughts and feelings.

Then the Prophet, in the first place, shews that it was nothing strange that he ascended above all human judgments, for he was endued with the authority of the Holy Spirit. And he adds, in the second place, that he was not influenced by carnal feelings, but by a pure zeal for God, for he *knew not* their wicked designs; and he says that he was *like a lamb and an ox*, or a calf. There is here no conjunction, and hence some join the two words, "And I am like a lamb a year old:" for the Hebrews, they say, call a lamb a year old כבש, *cabesh*, and then a ram; but this is, in my view, a forced meaning, and a copulative or a disjunctive may be supposed to be understood. *I am* then *as a lamb or as a calf, which is led to the slaughter* (to be sacrificed or killed.) Here the Prophet intimates that he was not violent, as angry men are wont to be, who are excited either by indignation or great grief. He then testifies that he was moved by no such feeling, for he differed nothing from a lamb or a calf that is led to the slaughter.[1]

For the sake of amplifying, he adds, *I knew not that they devised devices against me*, that is, this did not come to my mind. The Prophet, indeed, might have suspected or even have known this; but as he disregarded himself, and even his own life, he testifies here that he had acted with so much simplicity as not to regard what they planned and contrived.

[1] All the early versions, and the *Targum* render אלוף as a participle or an adjective,—"ἄκακον, innocent," by the *Septuagint;* "mansuetus, meek," by the *Vulgate;* "simple," by the *Syriac;* and "choice" or chosen by the *Targum.* The word used as a verb means to teach, to train, to guide; and it seems here to be a passive participle, taught, trained, and may be rendered here docile, meek or innocent,—

> But I,—as a meek lamb led to be killed *was I;*
> And I knew not, that against me they had devised devices.

The *Septuagint* render the last words, "they have thought an evil thought;" and, "I knew not," is connected with the former line thus,—

> But I, as an innocent lamb led to be slain, I knew not:
> Against me have they thought an evil thought.

But the construction in the other versions, and in the *Targum*, is according to the former rendering.—*Ed.*

He then adds, *Let us spoil wood in his bread.* They think rightly, according to my judgment, who consider that there is here a change of case; for it ought rather to be, "Let us spoil with wood his bread:" for that exposition is too unmeaning, "Let us spoil or destroy wood," as though they spoke of a thing of no value: for what has this to do with the subject? On the contrary, if we retain, as they say, the letter, the Prophet might think that wood would be spoiled in bread, as it would become rotten: but wood in bread, except by becoming rotten, would do no harm. But doubtless the Prophet speaks here metaphorically, as David does in Psalm lxix. 22, when he says, "They have put gall in my bread, and vinegar in my drink." Jeremiah also, in Lament. iii. 15, complains that his food was mingled with poison. Similitudes of this kind often occur; for when the very food of man is corrupted, there is no more any support for life. The meaning then is, that his enemies had acted cruelly towards the Prophet, as they sought in every way to destroy him, even by poison.

Some take wood for poison, but I know not whether that can be done. They indeed imagine that a poisonous wood is what is here meant; but this is too refined. I take the meaning to be simply this, as though they had said, "Let us spoil with wood his food," that is, "Let us give him wood instead of bread; and this, by its hardness, will hurt his teeth, ulcerate his throat, and cannot be digested so as to become nourishment." To spoil this bread with wood is to cause the wood to spoil the food either by its hardness or by its putridity. In this sense there is nothing ambiguous.

The ancients perverted this passage in the most childish manner when they applied it to the body of Christ. The Papists too, at this day, boast wonderfully of this allegory, though they make the most absurd use of it; for they seek to prove by it that bread is converted, or, as they say, transubstantiated into the body of Christ; and they quote Origen and Irenæus, and others like them: "Behold, explained is that passage of Jeremiah, let us send wood for his bread, (such is the meaning of the Vulgate,) for the body of Christ has been crucified;" and then they add,

"For he said, 'Take and eat, this is my body.'" We see how extremely absurd this is; and it must appear ridiculous even to children. But so great is the dishonesty and wantonness of the Papists, that they cast off all shame, and only boastfully pretend the authority of the ancients; and whatever Origen may have foolishly and falsely said, they will have it to be regarded as something oracular, provided their errors are thereby confirmed. But if we grant that the Prophet was a type of Christ, what has this to do with the similitude of his body, since he speaks here only of food? It is as though he had said, that his aliment was corrupted, as it were, with poison, and that he was so cruelly treated by his enemies, that they sought to destroy him by the means of his food.[1]

It then follows, *Let us cut him off from the land of the living.* This kind of speaking often occurs: the land or region of the living means the state of the present life. He at last adds, *That his name may not be in remembrance any more.* In short, the Prophet meant in these words to set forth the extreme savageness with which his enemies were inflamed; for they were not content with intrigues or with open violence, but wished to destroy him by poison, and wholly to obliterate his name. It follows—

20. But, O Lord of hosts, that judgest righteously, that triest the reins and the heart, let me see thy vengeance on them; for unto thee have I revealed my cause.

20. Et, Jehova exercituum, judicans justitiam, (*aut*, judex justitiæ,) scrutans (*vel*, inquirens) renes et cor, videam ultionem tuam de ipsis; quia tibi revelavi causam meam, (litem meam, *ad verbum.*)

[1] But the best meaning is that given by the *Syriac*, and has been adopted in our version, and by *Gataker*, *Venema*, *Henry*, *Horsley*, *Scott*, and *Adam Clarke*,—"Let us destroy the tree with its fruit;" that is, the Prophet and his prophecy. "In this case," says *Horsley*, "the man is the tree; his doctrine the fruit." But there seems to be an allusion in the words to "the olive" mentioned in verse 16, which was threatened with destruction: and Jeremiah's enemies, adopting his simile, by way of irony apply it to himself: "Well, thou comparest us to an olive devoted to ruin; we shall now deal with thee accordingly: thou art a tree, and we shall cut thee down and destroy thee and all the fruit thou bearest."

The whole verse I would render as follows,—

19. And I—as a meek lamb led to be killed *was I;*
And I knew not that against me they had devised *these* devices:—
"Let us destroy the tree with its fruit,
Yea, let us cut him down from the land of the living;
And his name, let it be remembered no more."—*Ed.*

Here the Prophet, after having found that the impiety of the people was so great that he was speaking to the deaf, turns his address to God: *O Jehovah of hosts*, he says, *who art a great Judge, who searchest the reins and the heart, may I see thy vengeance on them.* The Prophet seems here inconsistent with himself; for he had before declared that he was like a lamb or a calf, as though he had offered, as they say, his life a willing sacrifice; but here he seems like one made suddenly angry, and he prays for God's vengeance. These things appear indeed to be very different; for if he had offered himself a victim, why did he not wait calmly for the event; why is he inflamed with so much displeasure? why does he thus imprecate on them the vengeance of God? But these things will well agree together, if we distinguish between private feeling and that pure and discreet zeal by which the meekness of truth can never be disturbed. For though the Prophet disregarded his own life, and was not moved by private wrongs, he was nevertheless not a log of wood; but zeal for God did eat up his heart, according to what is said in common of all the members of Christ, " Zeal for thine house hath eaten me, and the reproaches of those who upbraided thee have fallen on me." (Psalm lxix. 9; John ii. 17; Rom. xv. 3.) The Prophet then had previously freed himself from all suspicion by saying that he was prepared for the slaughter, as though he were a lamb or a calf; but he now shews that he was, notwithstanding, not destitute of zeal for God. Here then he gives vent to this new fervour when he says, " O Jehovah, who searchest the reins and the heart, may I see thy vengeance on them."

The Prophet, no doubt, was free from every carnal feeling, and pronounced what we read through the influence of the Spirit. Since then the Holy Spirit dictated this prayer to the holy man, he might still have offered himself a voluntary sacrifice, while yet he justly appealed to God's tribunal to take vengeance on the impiety of a reprobate people; for he did not indiscriminately include them all, but imprecated God's judgment on the abandoned and irreclaimable.

It is indeed true, that we may regard the Prophet as predicting what he knew would happen to his people: and some give this explanation; they consider it as a prediction only and no prayer. But they are terrified without reason at the appearance of inconsistency, as they think it inconsistent in the Prophet to desire the perdition of his own people: for he might have wished it through the influence of that zeal, as I have said, which the Holy Spirit had kindled in his heart, and according to the words which the same Spirit had dictated.

He calls God the *Judge of righteousness;* and he so called him, that he might wipe away and dissipate the disguises in which the Jews exulted when they sought to prove their own cause. By this then he intimates that they gained nothing by their evasions, for these would vanish like smoke when they came before God's tribunal. He, in short, means that they could not stand before the judgment of God. He then adds, that God *searches the reins and the heart.* He says this, not only that he might testify his own integrity, as some suppose, but that he might rouse hypocrites. For he intimates that they stood safe before men, as they concealed their wickedness, but that when they came before God's tribunal another kind of account must then be given; for God would prove and *try* them, as the word בחן, *bechen,* signifies: he would search *the reins and the heart,* that is, their most inward feelings; for the Scripture means by reins all the hidden feelings or affections.

He says, *For to thee have I made known my judgment.* The Prophet, no doubt, appeals here to God's tribunal, because he saw that he was destitute of every patronage—he saw that all were against him. Few pious men indeed were left, as we have elsewhere seen; but the Prophet speaks here of the mass of the people. As then there was no one among the people who did not then openly oppose God, so that there was no defender of equity and justice, he turns to God and says, "I have made known my cause to thee;" as though he had said, "O Lord, thou knowest what my cause is, and I do not act dissemblingly; for I serve thee faithfully and sincerely, as thou knowest. Since it is so, may I see thy vengeance on them."[1]

[1] The beginning of the verse is differently rendered: "O Lord," in the

Now, we are taught in this passage, that even were the whole world united to suppress the light of truth, Prophets and teachers ought not to despond, nor to rely on the judgment of men, for that is a false and deceptive balance; but that they ought to persevere in the discharge of their office, and to be satisfied with this alone—that they render their office approved of God, and exercise it as in his presence. We may also learn, that the ungodly and hypocrites in vain make shifts and evasions, while they try to elude the authority of the Prophets; for they will at length be led before God's tribunal. When therefore we find teachers rightly and sincerely discharging their office, let us know that we cannot possibly escape the judgment of God except we submit to their teaching. And Prophets and pastors themselves ought to learn from this passage, that though the whole world, as I have already said, were opposed to them, they ought not yet to cease from their perseverance, nor be changeable, but to consider it enough that God approves of their cause. It afterwards follows—

21. Therefore thus saith the Lord of the men of Anathoth, that seek thy life, saying, Prophesy not in the name of the Lord, that thou die not by our hand:

22. Therefore thus saith the Lord of hosts, Behold, I will punish them: the young men shall die by the sword; their sons and their daughters shall die by famine:

23. And there shall be no remnant of them: for I will bring

21. Propterea sic dicit Jehova ad viros Anathoth, qui quærunt animam tuam, dicendo, Ne prophetes in nomine Jehovæ, et non morieris in manu nostra, (*hoc est,* ne moriaris manu nostra.)

22. Propterea sic dicit Jehova exercituum, Ecce ego visitans (visitabo) super eos; adolescentes eorum morientur gladio, filii eorum et filiæ eorum morientur fame:

23. Et residuum non erit ipsis, (*hoc est,* nihil erit ipsis residuum;) quia ve-

vocative case, by the *Septuagint,* the *Vulgate,* and the *Syriac;* "The Lord," by the *Arabic* and *Targum.* All the versions agree as to the imprecation, "May I see—ἴδοιμι—videam:" but the *Targum* has, "I shall see;" and so it is rendered by *Gataker, Venema, Scott,* and *Adam Clarke.* The verb is future, but the future in Hebrew has sometimes the meaning of the optative or the subjunctive, as well as of the imperative. But the future is the most suitable here; for the ו before "Jehovah" will not allow it to be in the vocative case. The verse then would be as follows,—

20. But Jehovah of hosts, *who art* a righteous judge,
The trier of the reins and of the heart,
I shall see thy vengeance on them;
For on thee have I devolved my cause.

"Jehovah of hosts" is a nominative absolute—a form of expression very common in the Prophets.—*Ed.*

evil upon the men of Anathoth, *even* the year of their visitation.

nire faciam malum super homines Anathoth anno visitationis ipsorum (*alii vertunt*, annum, *sed malè, meo judicio.*)

The Prophet here expressly denounces vengeance on his own people: for we have seen at the beginning of this book that he belonged to the town of Anathoth. Now it appears from this passage, that the holy man had not only to contend with the king and his courtiers, and the priests, who were at Jerusalem; but that when he betook himself to a corner to live quietly with his own people, he had even there no friend, but that all persecuted him as an enemy. We hence see how miserable was the condition of the Prophet; for he had no rest, even when he sought retirement and fled to his own country. That he was not safe even there, is a proof to us how hardly God exercised and tried him for the many years in which he performed his prophetic office.

As the citizens of Anathoth had grievously sinned, so he denounces on them an especial calamity. It is indeed certain that the Prophet was not kindly received at Jerusalem; nay, he met there, as we shall hereafter see, with enemies the most cruel: but when he hoped for some rest and relaxation in his own country, he was even there received as we find here. This is the reason why God commanded him to threaten the citizens of Anathoth with destruction. I cannot finish the whole to-day.

PRAYER.

Grant, Almighty God, that as thou remindest us in thy word of our many vices and sins, we may learn to direct our eyes and thoughts to thee, and never think that we have to do with a mortal being, but that we may anticipate thy judgment: and may we learn so to examine all our thoughts and try our feelings, that no hypocrisy may deceive us, and that we may not sleep in our sins; but that being really and truly awakened, we may humble ourselves before thee, and so seek thy pardon, that when we lie down in true repentance, thou mayest absolve us in thy mercy, through the virtue of that sacrifice by which thine only-begotten Son has once for all reconciled us to thee.—Amen.

Lecture Forty-Eighth.

CHAPTER XII.

1. Righteous *art* thou, O Lord, when I plead with thee; *yet* let me talk with thee of *thy* judgments: Wherefore doth the way of the wicked prosper? *wherefore* are all they happy that deal very treacherously?

1. Justus es, Jehova, si contendam tecum (si litigem, *vel*, quando litigabo;) tamen judicia loquar tecum (*hoc est*, disceptabo jure tecum:) Quousque via impiorum prosperabitur (*vel*, feliciter habebit;) quieti sunt omnes transgredientes transgressione?

The minds of the faithful, we know, have often been greatly tried and even shaken, on seeing all things happening successfully and prosperously to the despisers of God. We find this complaint expressed at large in Psalm lxxiii. The Prophet there confesses that he had well-nigh fallen, as he had been treading in a slippery place; he saw that God favoured the wicked; at least, from the appearance of things, he could form no other judgment, but that they were loved and cherished by God. We know also that the ungodly become thus hardened, according to what is related of Dionysius, who said that God favoured the sacrilegious; for he had sailed in safety after having plundered temples, and committed robberies in many places; thus he laughed to scorn the forbearance of God. And hence Solomon says, That when all things are in a state of confusion in the world, men's minds are led to despise God, as they think that all things happen on the earth by chance, and that God has no care for mankind. (Eccl. ix.) But with regard to the faithful, as I have already said, when they see the ungodly proceeding in all wickedness and evil deeds with impunity, and claiming the world to themselves, while God is, as it were, conniving at them, their minds cannot be otherwise than grievously distressed. And this is the view which interpreters take of this passage; that is, that he was disturbed with the prosperous condition of the wicked, and expostulated with God, as Habakkuk seems to have done at the beginning of the first chapter; but he appears to me to have something higher in view.

We have said elsewhere, that when the Prophets saw that they spent their labour in vain on the deaf and the intractable, they turned their addresses to God as in despair. I hence doubt not but that it was a sign of indignation when the Prophet addressed God, having as it were given up men, inasmuch as he saw that he spoke to the deaf without any benefit. Here then he rouses the minds of the people, that they might know at length that he could not convince them that they were doomed to ruin by God. For when Jeremiah spoke to them, all his threatenings were scorned and laughed at; hence he now addresses God himself, as though he had said, that he would have nothing more to do with them, as he had laboured wholly in vain. This then seems to have been the object of the Prophet.

But lest the ungodly should have an occasion for calumniating, he intended so to regulate his discourse as to give them no ground for cavilling. Hence he makes this preface,—that *God is*, or would be *just, though he contended with him.* This order ought to be carefully observed; for when we give way in the least to our passions, we are immediately carried away, and we cannot restrain ourselves within proper limits and continue in a right course. As soon then as those thoughts, which may draw us away from the fear of God, and lessen the reverence due to him, creep in, we ought to fortify our minds and to set up mounds, lest the devil should draw us on farther than we wish to go. For instance, when any one in the present day sees things in disorder in the world, he begins to reason thus freely with himself, "What does this mean? How is it that God suffers licentiousness to prevail so long? Why is it that he thus conceals himself?" As soon then as these thoughts creep in, if we possess the true principle of religion, we shall try to restrain these wanderings, and to bring ourselves to the right way; but this will be no easy matter; for as soon as we pass over the boundaries, there is no restraint, no limitation. Hence the Prophet wisely begins by saying, *Thou art just, though I contend with thee.* It is not only for the sake of others he speaks thus, but also to restrain in time his own feelings and not to allow himself more than what is right. We must still remember what I have said,—that the Prophet here directs his words to God, in order that the Jews might know that they were left as it were without hope, and were unworthy that he should spend any more labour on them.

He says, *And yet I will speak judgments with thee;* that is, I will dispute according to the limits of what is right and just. Some indeed take judgments for punishments, as though the Prophet wished the people to be punished; but of this I do not approve, for it is a strained view. To speak judgments, means nothing else than to discuss a point in law, to plead according to law, as it is commonly said. By saying, "I will legally contend," he does not throw off the restraint which he has before put on himself, but asks it as a matter of indulgence to set before God what might seem just and right to all. David, or the Prophet who was the author of that psalm which we have already quoted, (Psalm lxxiii.,) even when he expressed his own feelings and ingenuously confessed his own infirmity, yet made a preface similar to what is found here. But he there speaks as it were abruptly, "Yet thou art just;" he uses the same word אך, *ak,* as Jeremiah does; but here it is put in the last clause, and there at the beginning of the sentence, "Yet good is God to Israel, even to those who are upright in heart." The Prophet no doubt was agitated and distracted in various ways, but he afterwards restrained himself. But it was otherwise with Jeremiah; for he does not confess here that he was tried, as almost all the faithful are wont to be; but as I have already said, he advisedly, and by the guidance of the Holy Spirit, addressed his words to God; for he intended to rouse the Jews, that they might understand that they were rejected, and rejected as unworthy of having their salvation cared for any longer.

By saying then, *Yet will I plead with thee,* he doubtless intended to touch the Jews to the quick, as they were so extremely stupid. "Behold," he says, "I will yet contend with God, whether he will forgive you?" We now see the real meaning of the Prophet; for the Jews in vain brought forward their own prosperity as a proof that God was propitious to them; for this was nothing else than to abuse his forbearance. Jeremiah intended in short to shew, that though God might pass by them for a time, yet the wicked ought not on this account to flatter themselves, for his indulgence is no proof of his love; but, on the contrary, as we shall see, a heavier vengeance is accumulated, when the ungodly increasingly harden themselves while God is treating them with indulgence. This then is the reason why the Prophet says, that he would *plead* with God; he had regard more to men than to God. He yet does not set up the judgments of men against the absolute power of God, as the sophists under the Papacy do, who ascribe such absolute power to God as perverts all judgment and all order; this is nothing less than sacrilege.

Now the Prophet does not call God to an account, as though there was no rule by which he regulated his works and governed the world. But by judgments he means, as I have said, what God had declared in his law; for it is written, "Cursed is every one who continueth not," &c., (Deut. xxvii. 26; Gal. iii. 10.) Now then as the Jews were transgressors of the law, nay, as they ceased not to provoke God to wrath by their vices, they ought surely, according to the ordinary course of justice, to have been immediately destroyed. Hence the Prophet says here, *I will plead with thee;* that is, "Hadst thou dealt with this people as they deserved, they must have been often reduced to nothing." At the same time he had no doubt, as we have said, respecting the rectitude of the divine judgment; only he had regard to those men who flattered themselves, and securely indulged themselves in their vices, because God did not immediately execute those punishments with which he threatens the transgressors of his law.[1]

[1] "Emboldened," says *Blayney*, "as it should seem, by the success of his prayers against the men of Anathoth, the Prophet ventures freely, though with professions of confidence in the divine justice, to expostulate with God concerning the prosperity of wicked men in general, whose punishment he solicits, attesting the mischiefs that were continually brought on the land by their unrestrained wickedness."

I would render the verse thus,—

Righteous art thou, Jehovah;
Though I should dispute with thee;
Yet of judgments will I speak to thee,—

Hence he says, *How long shall the way of the wicked prosper? for secure are all they who by transgression transgress;* that is, who are not only tainted with small vices, but who are extremely wicked. They then who openly rejected all religion and all care for righteousness, how was it that they were secure and that their way prospered? We now then more clearly understand what I have stated,—that the Prophet turned his words to God, that he might more effectually rouse the stupid, so that they might know that they were in a manner summoned by this expostulation before the celestial tribunal. It now follows,—

2. Thou hast planted them; yea, they have taken root: they grow; yea, they bring forth fruit: thou *art* near in their mouth, and far from their reins.

2. Plantasti eos, etiam radicem egerunt; prodierunt, etiam fecerunt fructum (produxerunt fructum:) propè es in ore ipsorum, et procul es á renibus ipsorum (*hoc est,* ab intimo affectu, *renes enim alibi diximus accipi pro affectibus arcanis.*)

When the happiness of the wicked disturbs our minds, two false thoughts occur to us,—either that this world is ruled by chance and not governed by God's providence, or that God does not perform the office of a good and righteous judge when he suffers light to be so blended with darkness. But the Prophet here takes it as granted, that the world is governed by God's providence; he therefore does not touch the false notion, which yet harasses pious minds, that fortune governs the world. Well known are these words, "I am disposed to think that there are no gods."[1] It was thought there were no gods who ruled the world, because he died who deserved a longer life. And the wisest heathens have thus

How *is it?* the way of the wicked, it prospers;
Secure are all the dissemblers of dissimulation.

Perhaps the fourth line might be rendered thus,—

Why; the way of the wicked, it prospers.

The order of the words will not admit it to be rendered otherwise. *Blayney* renders the last line as follows:—

At ease are all they who deal very perfidiously.

The last words literally are, "all the cloakers of cloaking," or, "all the coverers of covering." But according to the secondary meaning of the word בגד, the phrase would be, "all the dissemblers of dissimulation." The version of the *Septuagint* is, "all who prevaricate prevarications." What is meant evidently is, that they were hypocrites, and that by hypocrisy they covered their hypocrisy,—a true and a striking representation.—*Ed.*

[1] Ovid, Eleg. 8.

spoken, "I see fortune, which yet no reason governs; I see fortune, which prevails more than reason in these matters."[1] But the Prophet, who was far removed from these profane notions, held this truth,—that the world is governed by God; and he now asks, How it was that God exercised so long a forbearance? The ungodly, the thoughtless, and inconsiderate might have said that this forbearance was far too scanty. But the Prophet, as I have said, clearly describes what the Jews deserved.

Then he says, that they had been *planted* by God; for they could not have prospered had not God blessed them. The metaphor of planting, as we have before seen, often occurs, but in a different sense. When the celestial life is the subject, God is said to have planted his own elect, because their salvation is sure. He is said also to have planted his people in the land which he had given to them as an heritage. Now, when he speaks of the reprobate, the Prophet says that they had been planted by God, and for these reasons, because they flourished, because they produced leaves, and because they brought forth some fruit. In short, as Scripture, for various reasons, compares men to trees, so it employs the word planting in a corresponding sense. The Prophet indeed says that the ungodly are supported by God, and this is certain; for were not God to deal kindly with them for a time, they could not but instantly perish. Hence their prosperity is a proof of God's indulgence. But the Prophet expresses his wonder at this, not so much through his own private feeling, as for the purpose of shewing to the Jews that it was a strange thing that they were tolerated so long by God, as they had a hundred times deserved to be wholly destroyed.

Yea, he says, *they have taken root.* By this metaphor he means their continued happiness. He says also, that they had *advanced aloft;* that is, were raised high and increased.[2] He then adds, that they had *brought forth fruit.*

[1] Ovid, Eleg. 8.

[2] The verb is ילכו, rendered "proficiunt—proceed or advance," by the *Vulgate* and *Syriac*. The *Septuagint* must have read ילדו, as the version is, "they have brought forth children," which is wholly inconsistent with te simile of a tree. To "advance in growth," as *Blayney* renders it, is

The fruit of which he speaks was nothing else than their offspring; as though he had said, that the ungodly were not only prosperous to the end of life, but that they also propagated their kind, so that they had children surviving them, so that their families became celebrated. But the import of the whole is this,—that God not only endured the ungodly for a time, but extended his indulgence to many ages, so that their descendants continued in the same wealth, dignity, and power, with their dead fathers.

He afterwards adds, *Thou indeed art nigh in their mouth, but thou art far from their reins.* Jeremiah no doubt intended to anticipate them; for he knew that the Jews would have objections in readiness,—"What art thou, who summonest us here before God's tribunal, and who pleadest with God that he may not too patiently bear with us? Are not we his servants? Do we not daily offer sacrifices in the Temple? Are we not circumcised? Do we not bear in our bodies the sign of our adoption? Do we not possess a kingdom and a priesthood? Now, these are pledges of God's paternal love towards us. But thou wouldest have thyself to be more just than God himself. Can God deny himself? He has bound his faithfulness to us by the sign of circumcision, by the Temple, by the kingdom, by the priesthood, and by the sacrifices; and when we do anything amiss, then our sins are expiated by sacrifices and washings, and other rites."

As then the Prophet knew that the Jews were wont thus loquaciously and perversely to defend their own cause, he says, "O, I see what they will say to me, even that which they are wont to say; for the common burden of their song

what is clearly meant. The *Targum* is a paraphrase, and the simile is wholly left out. To "become rich" is the corresponding expression, which gives the meaning. The גם, which occurs twice, would be better rendered "yea," as in our version, than "also," as by *Blayney*,—

Thou hast planted them, yea, they have taken root;
They thrive, yea, they have produced fruit:
Nigh art thou to their mouth,
But far from their reins.

"They thrive," is literally "they go on," that is, after having rooted, or taken root. The "reins" stand for the affections—fear, reverence, love, &c.—*Ed.*

is, that they are the children of Abraham, that they sacrifice, and have other ways of pacifying God, and then that they possess a priesthood and a kingdom. These things," he says, "are well known to me: but, O Lord, thou knowest that they are mere words; thou knowest that they act fallaciously, and that they do nothing but declare what is false when they pretend these vain shifts and evasions; for thou knowest the heart, (καρδιογνώστης;) thou therefore understandest that there is nothing right or sincere in their mouth; for their *reins* are far from thee, and thou also art far from their reins." We hence also perceive with more certainty the truth of what I have stated,—that the Prophet here pleads with God, in order that the Jews might know that they could in no way be absolved when they came before God's tribunal. It follows—

3. But thou, O Lord, knowest me: thou hast seen me, and tried mine heart toward thee: pull them out like sheep for the slaughter, and prepare them for the day of slaughter.	3. Et tu, Jehova, cognoscis me (cognovisti me), videbis me (vides me), et probasti cor meum tecum (*hoc est,* probasti quale sit cor meum apud te, *vel,* coram te:) extrahe eos tanquam oves ad mactationem, et præpara eos ad diem occisionis.

The Prophet is not here solicitous about himself, but, on the contrary, undertakes the defence of his own office, as though he had said that he faithfully discharged the office committed to him by God. Though then the Jews, and even the citizens of Anathoth, his own people, unjustly persecuted him, yet he was not excited by private wrongs; and though he disregarded these entirely, he yet could not give up the defence of his office. He then does not speak here of his own private feelings, but only claims for himself faithfulness and sincerity before God in performing his office as a teacher; as though he had said that he executed what God had commanded him to do, and that therefore the Jews contended not with a mortal being, but with God himself.

Hence he says, *But thou, Jehovah, knowest me and seest me, and triest my heart towards thee;* that is, thou knowest how sincerely I serve thee, and endeavour to fulfil my vocation, and thus to obey thy command. He afterwards glories over them as a conqueror, and says, *Draw them forth as sheep for the day of sacrificing, prepare them for slaughter.* Here no doubt the Prophet intended not only to touch, but sharply to wound the Jews, in order that they might know that they had been hitherto secure to no purpose, and to their own ruin, because God had spared them. They who consider that the Prophet was himself troubled, because he saw that God was propitious and kind to the ungodly, think that, with reference to himself, he took comfort from this,—that the judgment of God was nigh at hand; but I doubt not but that the Prophet had regard to the Jews, as I have already reminded you. When, therefore, he saw that they were torpid in their delusions, he intended to rouse their sensibilities by saying, "I see how it is, O Lord; thou dost indeed conceal thyself; but what else is thy purpose but that they should be fattened for the day of slaughter?"

He says, first, *Thou wilt draw them out:* others read, "Thou wilt lead them forth," and quote a passage in Judges xx. 32, where נתק, *nutak,* is taken in this sense. The word properly means to draw out with force, as when a tree is pulled up, or when any one is drawn out against his will; and this is the sense most suitable to the present passage. *Thou wilt* then *draw them out;* that is, thou wilt suddenly draw them out to slaughter. He then intimates that there was no reason for the Jews to be dormant in their prosperity, for God could in a moment act against them; and as the pain of one in labour is sudden, so also, when the wicked say, Peace and security, their ruin will come suddenly upon them. (1 Thess. v. 3.) This then is what the Prophet now means: but he goes on in his way of teaching; for he does not address men as they were all deaf, but speaks to God himself, that his doctrine might be more effectual: *Thou* then *wilt draw them out,* and *do thou prepare* them; for it is a prayer: do thou then prepare them *for the day of slaughter.*[1]

[1] This verse, according to the tenses of the verbs, is as follows:—

But thou, Jehovah, thou hast known me;
Thou seest me, and triest my heart towards thee:
Pull them out as sheep for the sacrifice,
And set them apart for the day of slaughter.

It is evident that "seest," which is here in the future tense, is to be taken as expressing a present act. It would be so rendered in Welsh,—

The last expression ought especially to be noticed. The Prophet indeed seems here in an excited feeling to imprecate ruin on the people; but there is no doubt but that he was here discharging the duty of his office, for he was the herald of God's vengeance. He therefore asks God to execute what he had commanded him to denounce on the people. He had often promulgated what God had resolved to do to them, but he had moved no one: he now then asks God to fulfil what he had foretold the Jews—that they should shortly perish, because they refused to repent.

We may also learn from this passage,—that when the ungodly accumulate wealth, they are in a manner fattened. When oxen plough, and sheep are fed that they may bear wool and bring forth young, they are not fed that they may grow fat, and a moderate quantity of food will suffice them; but when any one intends to prepare sheep or oxen for the slaughter, he fattens them. So then the feeding of them is nothing else than the fattening of them; and the fattening of them is a preparation for their slaughter. I have therefore said that a very useful doctrine is included in this form of speaking; for when we see that plenty of wealth and power abound with the ungodly and the despisers of God, we see that they are in a manner thus filled with good things, that they may grow fat:—it is fattening or cramming. Let us then not bear it ill that they are thus covered with their own fatness, for they are prepared for the day of slaughter. It follows—

4. How long shall the land mourn, and the herbs of every field wither, for the wickedness of them that dwell therein? the beasts are consumed, and the birds; because they said, He shall not see our last end.

4. Quousque lugebit terra, et herba omnis agri arescet præ malitia habitantium in ea? defecit bestiæ (*hoc est,* consumptæ sunt bestiæ,) et avis (*hoc est,* aves, *est enallage numeri tam in verbo quàm in nomine;*) quia dixerunt, Non videbit novissimum nostrum (*vel,* finem nostrum.)

Jeremiah confirms the former sentence and more strongly

Ond ti Jehova, adwaenaist vi;
Gweli vi, a phrovi vy nghalon tuag atat.

God had known him, he was still seeing him, and approved of his heart before him, as the *Septuagint* express the words. To prove here, or to "try," means a trial by which a thing is found to be genuine. *Blayney* gives the meaning by a paraphrase,—

Thou canst discern by trial my heart to be with thee.—*Ed.*

reproves the Jews, who still continued obstinately to despise what he had said: "What do you mean, he says? for God's judgment appears as to brute beasts and birds; and what have birds and sheep and oxen deserved? Ye know that there is no fault in miserable animals, and yet the curse of God is through them set before you; ye see that God is offended with brute animals, but the fault is doubtless in you. And will God spare you, when he has already begun, and long ago begun to inflict punishment on innocent animals? how can he bear with you to the end, who are full of so many and the most atrocious sins?" This then is a confirmation of his former doctrine.

And hence we also learn that he did not speak for his own sake, nor express his own private feelings, but that he defended the doctrine which he had announced, that the Jews might know that God was angry with them, and that they were not to expect that he would always conceal himself, though he for a time connived at them.

How long, he says, *shall the land mourn?* or, How long should the land mourn? for thus it ought to be rendered; *and should every herb become dry?* "What!" he says, "is not God's judgment visible in herbs and flocks and beasts and birds? Since it is so, and the whole fault is in you, shall ye be spared? Will God pour forth his whole wrath on herbs, on sheep, and on cattle? and shall you be at the same time exempted from his judgment?"

And more clearly still does he express his meaning, when he says, *Because they have said, He shall not see our end.* Here the Prophet briefly shews that the wrath of God was seen in herbs as well as in brute animals, because he was despised by the people. Since then evil proceeded from them, should it not return on their own heads? It could not surely be otherwise. But he speaks expressly of the end; for the Jews were so stupified by their prosperity, that they thought that God was no longer adverse to them: "Ha! what have we to do with God? we are already beyond the reach of danger." As then they thus perversely rejected God, he upbraids them with the thought, that they were to give no account to God. It is not indeed probable that they openly, or with a full mouth, as they say, vomited forth such a blasphemy; but we know that Scripture often speaks in this manner, "God shall not see;" "God will not look on Jacob." Though the ungodly did not speak so insolently, yet they no doubt thought that they could set up many hinderances to prevent God's hand from reaching them. Hence Jeremiah, according to the usual manner of Scripture, justly lays this to their charge,—that they thought that they were now as it were unknown to God and beyond the reach of his care, so that he would not see their end; in other words, that they had no concern with God, because they were on all sides so well fortified, that the hand of God could not reach them.[1]

PRAYER.

Grant, Almighty God, that though the same hardness is inbred in us as in thine ancient people, we may not become rooted in it; but do thou rouse us by thy Spirit, that we may suffer ourselves to be gently governed by thy word, and be so touched by thy threatenings, that we may not defer the time whenever thou announcest to us thy judgment, but strive to be immediately reconciled to thee: and as there is no other way of being reconciled except through thine only-begotten Son, may we in true faith embrace the favour which thou offerest to us in thy gospel, and also devote ourselves wholly to thee, being truly penitent of our sins; and as we ought to make progress to the end of life, may we strive more and more to put off all the lusts of our flesh, until we shall at length be made partakers of that glory which thine only-begotten Son has prepared for us.—Amen.

[1] Both *Gataker* and *Venema* regard the meaning of the last clause differently. Here ends the expostulation of Jeremiah; and they consider that he mentions here what his persecutors said of him, that he would not see their end, or their ruin, which he had foretold. Were כִּי, as in the first verse, rendered "though," the connection would be more natural,—

How long shall mourn the land
And the grass of every field wither?
For the evil of those who dwell in it,
Swept away has been the beast and the bird,
Though they have said, "He will not see our end."

The third line connects better with what follows than with what precedes it; and it is so rendered in the *Syriac*. The word for "beast," though in a plural form, is used elsewhere as a singular, Psalm lxxiii. 22; and so it is here, and so rendered by the *Vulgate* and the *Targum*.—*Ed.*

Lecture Forty-Ninth.

5. If thou hast run with the footmen, and they have wearied thee, then how canst thou contend with horses? and *if* in the land of peace, *wherein* thou trustedst, *they wearied thee,* then how wilt thou do in the swelling of Jordan?

5. Quia (*vel,* si) cum peditibus (*significat propriè pedes,* sed translativè significat etiam pedites; si *ergo* cum peditibus) cucurristi et fatigarunt te, quomodo miscebis te equitibus? et in terra pacis tu confisus es, quid facies (*vel,* quomodo facies, *vel* faceres) in altitudine Jordanis?

Many think that God here checks the boldness of Jeremiah, as though he had exceeded the limits of moderation when he contended with God, as we have seen, because he patiently endured the reprobate and did not immediately punish them. Hence they elicit this meaning from the words, "Thou hast hitherto been contending with mortals, and hast confessed that thou didst maintain an unequal contest; dost thou dare now to assail me, who am far greater than the whole world? Footmen have wearied thee, who walk on earth; but thou engagest now with horsemen, that is, with me."

But I have already shewn that the Prophet did not undertake this cause presumptuously, nor was he carried away by blind zeal when he disputed with God, but that he thus spoke through a divine fervour: he was indeed influenced by God, in order that he might by this mode of speaking more fully rouse an obstinate people. There was therefore no need to check him; for his object was no other than to shew by a lively representation, that God would be the Judge of the Jews, who had despised his teaching and esteemed it as nothing.

Some think that a comparison is made between the citizens of Anathoth and the citizens of Jerusalem: they hence suppose that Jeremiah is encouraged, lest he should succumb under the temptations which awaited him; as though it was said, "Thy citizens or thy people are like footmen; thou seest now how much they have wearied thee, for thou canst not bear their insolence: what then will become of thee, when thou comest to Jerusalem? for as there is more power there, so there is more arrogance; thou wilt have to contend with the king and his court, with the priests and with the people, who are blinded by their own splendour: horsemen will be there, and thou wilt have an equestrian contest. Thou mayest hence see how thou art to prepare thyself; for these things are only the beginnings, and yet thou complainest of them."

But when I maturely weigh all things, I come to another opinion, which both Jerome and Jonathan[1] have suggested, and yet obscurely, and so confusedly that the meaning cannot be correctly understood, and especially for this reason, because they did not state the exposition which we have hitherto given; hence the meaning of what they have said does not seem suitable. But the Prophet, I doubt not, here reproves the people and condemns their presumption, because they thought themselves furnished with so many defences that they despised the judgment of God. I regard then this verse as spoken in the person of God, for hitherto Jeremiah has been the accuser, and arraigned the whole people as guilty before God, and was also the herald of his judgment. Now that what he says might have more weight, God himself comes forth and says, *Thou hast hitherto run with footmen, and thou hast been wearied,* how will it be when thou comest to an equestrian contest? He intimates by these words that a much greater outrage was at hand than what the Jews had already experienced. Their country had been oppressed, their city had been exposed to extreme peril, there had been as it were a pedestrian conflict; but God now intimates that a heavier storm was nigh at hand, for horsemen would assail them, because the Chaldeans and the Assyrians were to come with much greater violence to lay waste the whole country and to destroy the city itself.

This then is not addressed to the Prophet, but to the people; as though it was said, that the Jews had but a slight contest with the Assyrians, and yet were conquered and oppressed by many calamities; but that they would have now to fight more seriously, as a greater violence was im-

[1] The author of the Targum—the Chaldee Paraphrase.—*Ed.*

pending over them: *how* then, he says, *canst thou contend with horsemen?*[1]

He then adds, *In the land of peace thou trustest, and how wilt thou do in the rising of Jordan?* The land of peace is commonly taken for the town of Anathoth, where the Prophet ought to have enjoyed a quiet life, as he lived there among his relations and friends. The rising of Jordan is also taken as signifying violent waves; but this has nothing to do with the subject. Were I to approve of this view, I would rather take the rising of Jordan as meaning its fountain, for we know that Jordan rose from Mount Lebanon, north of Jerusalem: so then would I interpret the words, and the explanation would be plausible. But as I feel assured that the words are not addressed to the Prophet, but to the people, I doubt not but that the *land of peace* is the land open to plunder, that is, not protected. As that is called the land of war, which is surrounded by defences, and fortified by towers, moats, and ramparts; so that is called the land of peace, which is not capable of repelling enemies. The Prophet derided the Jews, because they swelled with so much arrogance, though they possessed no fortresses: "Ye are," he says, "in the land of peace, having no means to carry on war, and possessing no forces to resist your enemies: as then ye swell with so much pride in your penury and want, what would become of you, were you in the rising

[1] Most commentators agree in the previous exposition,—that a comparison is made between the persecution which Jeremiah experienced from his countrymen at Anathoth, and the persecution he was to expect at Jerusalem. So thought the Jewish commentators, *Grotius*, *Venema*, *Gataker*, *Henry*, *Scott*, *Adam Clarke*, and *Blayney*. It must, however, be added, that *Jerome* and *Horsley* were of the same opinion with *Calvin*: but the most obvious and natural meaning seems to be the former.

The rendering of *Blayney* is as follows,—

If thou hast run with footmen, and they have wearied thee,
Then how wilt thou chafe thyself with horses?

More literally,—

If with footmen thou hast run, and they have tired thee,
Then how wilt thou heat thyself with horses?

"Horses" may indeed be rendered horsemen, as "feet" in the previous line is rendered footmen. As to the verb "heat thyself," the versions and the *Targum* differ, but the word in Hebrew is plain enough; it is חרה, to heat, to burn, or to be warm or hot, in Hithpael. To "contend" has been taken from the *Vulgate*.—*Ed.*

of Jordan? that is, were your cities on the banks of Jordan, where it widely spreads, so as to prevent any access?" Rising here means height or largeness: for גאון, *gaun*, signifies pride, and metaphorically it means the highest or chief glory. "What wouldest thou do," he says, "in the largeness of Jordan? that is, were that river a defence to you against enemies? for there is nothing that can hinder your enemies from coming to your gates, from breaking down your walls by warlike instruments; and ye glory: how great is your madness, for ye do not consider how weak you are?" We hence see that in the whole of this verse the foolish boastings of the people are beaten down; for they were proud without a cause, as they were destitute of all defences and auxiliaries. This then is what I consider to be the real meaning.[1] It afterwards follows—

6. For even thy brethren, and the house of thy father, even they have dealt treacherously with thee; yea, they have called a multitude after thee: believe them not, though they speak fair words unto thee.	6. Certè etiam fratres tui et domus patris tui, etiam ipsi perfidè agunt in te, etiam ipsi clamant post te plena voce (*vel*, turmatim, מלא *enim variè exponitur;*) ne confides ipsis, etiam si loquantur ad te (*hoc est*, tecum) bona (*id est*, amicè tecum loquantur.)

Here God addresses his Prophet, in order to confirm the whole of what we have observed. Jeremiah's object was, as we have said, to set forth the judgment of God: he therefore undertook the part of an accuser, and shewed how in-

[1] As in the previous clause, so in this, most interpreters are opposed to *Calvin*. The contrast here is between a quiet state and great troubles. If Jeremiah complained, when among his connections at Anathoth, what could he do when troubles, like the swelling of Jordan, overflowed the land? And this view is confirmed by the verse which follows,—

Blayney, following the *Vulgate*, renders the passage thus,—

And though in the land of peace thou mayest have confidence,
Yet how wilt thou do in the swelling of Jordan?

But rather as follows,—

And in the land of peace thou art secure;
But how wilt thou do in the swelling of Jordan?

That is, "Thou complainest though living secure in a land which enjoys peace and is not harassed with war: what then wilt thou do when the troubles of war shall come over the land like the overflowings of Jordan?" or, according to some, "Thou complainest though living in retirement among thine own people, where thou didst expect rest and peace, what wilt thou do when exposed to the violent persecutions of the great and powerful?" the swelling of Jordan being considered a proverbial expression, designating great and overwhelming troubles.—*Ed.*

tolerable was the impiety of the whole people. He afterwards shewed that he was a conqueror in the cause. And now God himself speaks: he first indeed reproves the people and condemns their insane presumption; and then he addresses the Prophet himself, as though he had said, "Thou hast faithfully pleaded my cause, and as thine own people are all perfidious, there is no reason for thee to doubt but that I will be thy defender."

The Prophet no doubt was commanded to preach and to write in God's name; and yet he had regard to the people, who would have hardened themselves against his preaching, had he not more fully set forth the dreadful judgment of God. Hence he says, *Surely even thy brethren and the house of thy father*, &c.: it is an amplification, when he says, that not only the citizens of Jerusalem and the whole people had conspired against the Prophet, but also his own relations and friends; *Even thy brethren*, he says, *and the house of thy father, even these*, &c. We see how emphatically God speaks; and there is an implied comparison between the citizens of Anathoth and the rest of the Jews, for they dealt not with a brother and one of themselves with any more courtesy than those not related to him. He repeats for the third time, *Even these have cried after thee;* that is, "They have so inimically persecuted thee, that even when thou hast yielded to their fury they were not pacified." For to cry after one is an evidence of settled hatred; for when an enemy stands his ground and offers resistance, it is no wonder that we assail him; but when he turns his back and allows that he is conquered, and declines fighting, it seems that we are burning with a furious hatred, when we follow him and draw him to fight against his will, even when he of his own accord avoids a contest. It was to set forth this blind fury that God said that they *cried after* Jeremiah.[1]

[1] It is necessary to understand אחרי here as meaning "behind," that is, "behind his back," as we commonly say; for his friends and relations acted perfidiously, they cried against him in his absence, while they spoke friendly to himself. The verse is as follows,—

For even thy brethren and thy father's house,
Even they have dissembled with thee;
Yea, they have cried behind thee vehemently

He adds the word מלא, *mela*, which some render "with a full voice;" others, "in a troop," or, "in a mass." Either sense may be admitted; I will not therefore dwell on the point; for it makes but little difference whether we say that they followed the Prophet with loud clamour, or that they in a troop conspired against him.

He afterwards subjoins, *Even though they speak to thee good things,* that is, though they pretend to be friends and profess peace, *yet trust them not.* God intimates by these words, that though the citizens of Anathoth did not openly rage against Jeremiah, they were yet full of perfidy: in short, he means that they were either wolves or foxes, for they fought against the Prophet, now by fraud, then openly. We hence see that God here condemns the people, and shews his approbation of what had been previously said by Jeremiah. He afterwards subjoins—

7. I have forsaken mine house, I have left mine heritage; I have given the dearly beloved of my soul into the hand of her enemies.

7. Reliqui domum meam, deserui hæreditatem meam, posui dilectionem (*aut,* desiderium) animæ meæ in manum inimicorum ejus.

He confirms what I have already stated; he testifies that the people were either openly furious or acting perfidiously and deceitfully; nor has it been the object hitherto merely to say that wrong had been done to the Prophet, but regard has been had to what he taught.

He now adds, *Forsaken have I my house and left my heritage.* God here declares that it was all over with the people. They were inebriated with vain confidence, relying on the covenant which God had made with their fathers, and thought that God was bound to them. Thus they wished to treat God with contempt according to their own humour, and at the same time to allow themselves every kind of licentiousness. The Prophet makes here many concessions, as though he had said, "Ye are the house of God, ye are his heritage, ye are his beloved, ye are his portion and his richest portion;

Believe them not when they speak to thee kind things.

"Vehemently," or more literally, "fully;" מלא is used here adverbially. The versions, except the *Vulgate,* which renders it, "with a full voice," have not given its meaning, nor the *Targum.* The "multitude" of our version is evidently wrong, distantly derived from the *Septuagint.*—*Ed.*

but all this will not prevent him to become your Judge, and at length to treat you with rigorous justice, and to vindicate himself." We now perceive the meaning of the Prophet. But as I have before said, the words have more weight having been spoken by God, than if Jeremiah himself had said them. God then, as though sitting for judgment, declares thus to the Jews, *Forsaken have I my house.* The Temple was indeed commended in high terms; but the whole country also was on account of the Temple regarded as the habitation of God; for Judah was overshadowed by the Temple, and was secure and safe under its shadow. This word then is to be extended to the whole land and people, when God says, "Forsaken have I my house;" that is, "Though I have hitherto chosen for myself an habitation among the Jews, yet I now leave them." He then adds, *Left have I my heritage.* (The verbs עזב, *oseb*, and נטש, *nuthesh*, have nearly the same meaning; the one is to forsake, and the other is to leave.) This distinction was a great honour to the Jews; and hence, how much soever they kindled God's wrath against themselves, they yet thought that they were safe as it were by privilege, inasmuch as they were the heritage of God. The Prophet concedes to them this distinction, but shews how vain it was, for God had departed from them.

He then says, *Given have I the desire* or the love *of my soul,*[1] &c. The word ידידות, *ididut*, may be rendered love; but in Latin we may render it darling, (*delitias:*) *the darling* then *of my soul have I put in the hand of her enemies;* for the pronoun is in the feminine gender. We hence see what is the subject here; for God intended to deprive the Jews of their vain confidence, and thus to humble and subdue them, so that they might know that no empty and vain titles would be of any help to them. These titles or distinctions he indeed concedes to them, but not without some

[1] "My beloved soul" is the version of the *Septuagint*, *Vulgate*, and *Arabic*, but very improperly; the *Syriac* is "the beloved of my soul." The three first versions betoken an ignorance of the construction of the Hebrew language. To express their idea, "beloved" must have followed "soul," and not preceded it. Besides, the word for "beloved" is in the plural number, but used as *delitiæ* in Latin, to express great affection; and it ought to be rendered, the very dear, or the very beloved, of my soul. —*Ed.*

degree of irony; for he at the same time shews that all this in which they gloried would avail them nothing when God executed on them his vengeance. But further, this passage contains an implied reproof to the Jews for their ingratitude, inasmuch as they were not retained in their obedience to God by benefits so remarkable; for how great was the honour of being called the heritage and the house of God, and even the beloved of his soul? They had deserved no such honour. As then God had manifested towards them such incomparable love, as he had rendered himself more than a father to them, was it not a wickedness in every way inexcusable, not to respond to so great a love, and that gratuitous, and also to so great a liberality? for what more could God have done than to call them the darling of his soul?

We hence see that the sin of the people is greatly amplified by these distinctions, on account of which they yet fostered their pride; as though he had said, "These words indeed are ready on your tongues,—that ye are God's heritage, and sanctuary, and his love; but ye are for this very reason the more abominable, because ye respond not to God's love and bountiful dealings: he has favoured you with incredible love, he has raised you to very great honour, and yet ye despise him and perversely resist his teaching, nor can ye bear him to govern you." We now then see what instruction may be gathered from these words. It follows—

8. Mine heritage is unto me as a lion in the forest; it crieth out against me: therefore have I hated it.	8. Fuit mihi hæreditas mea quasi leo in sylva; edidit contra me vocem suam; propterea odio ipsam habui.

God now shews the reason why he resolved to cast away the people; for it might appear at the first view very inconsistent, that God's covenant, which he had made with Abraham and his seed, should become void. Hence he shews here that he was not too rigid in heavily punishing the Jews, and that he could not be accused of levity or inconstancy in rejecting or repudiating them.

Mine heritage, he says, *has become like a lion in the forest;* that is, they have not only acted insolently towards me, but they have even dared furiously to attack me, like a lion who roars against men in the forest. God then here complains of their contempt, and then he declares how furious was their impiety: for the Jews, as though seized by the rage of a wild beast, dared to make a violent attack on him. And the words, as they are connected, render the sin the more atrocious, *My heritage,* he says, *has become to me as a lion in the forest:* one's heritage and patrimony, we know, is his delight; and then, they who possess small tenements live much more quietly than those who occupy large ones. God now shews that he was in his own heritage as though he was in a vast and wild forest, and also, that the fields which ought to have been his delight, and also his vineyards and meadows, were become places of the greatest horror, as though a lion were roaring and raging against unhappy men.

He says further, that it had *sent forth its voice.* By these words he accuses the people of extreme wantonness; and such is to be found in the world at this day; for how audaciously do the Papists vomit forth their blasphemies against God? The unprincipled and the dregs of society hesitate not with a full mouth to be insolent towards God; and courtiers also and epicures, and those who admire themselves for their splendour and wealth, with what haughtiness do they rise up against him; and how disdainfully do they reject every truth that is set before them! We therefore in this miserable age experience the very same thing which the Prophet deplores in the men of his own time,—that they raised their voices against God himself.

He therefore comes to this conclusion,—that he *hated* his own heritage. "Since then," he says, "the Jews are become to me as lions in a forest, since they have rendered themselves a horror instead of a delight to me, what am I to do with them? Can I treat them as my patrimony and heritage? But they have put me to flight by their treachery, yea, by their diabolical fury. It is therefore nothing strange that I hate them, though they have been my heritage." Thus the Prophet shews, that it availed the Jews nothing that they had been of old adopted, since they had repudiated themselves and had become alienated from God their Father.

Let us also hence learn, that whatever honour hypocrites at this day possess in the Church, they yet boast in vain; for though they may for a time be counted as the heritage of God, they are at the same time hated by God, inasmuch as they are within full of wickedness and of perverseness towards him; and then, when urged and pressed, they hesitate not to vomit forth their insolence. It follows:—

9. Mine heritage *is* unto me *as* a speckled bird; the birds round about *are* against her: come ye, assemble all the beasts of the field, come to devour.

9. An avis picta (*vel*, tincta, *aut*, colorata) hæreditas mea mihi? an avis in circuitu super eam? Venite, colligite vos (*alii transitivè accipiunt*, congregate omnes bestias, *sed subaudiendum est*, congregate vos) omnes bestiæ agri (*hoc est*, omnes bestiæ agrestes,) venite ad devorandum ipsam.

The beginning of this verse is variously explained, Some think that a kind of bird is here meant, which has various colours, one variegated, which excites all other birds against itself; but this is without meaning. Others are of the opinion, and the greater part too, that birds tinged with blood were against his heritage. They hence thus explain tho words, "Is a bird, tinged," that is, with blood, "my heritage," that is, about my heritage; "is there a bird around it?" They consider both clauses to be of the same meaning; and hence they think that the same thing is repeated in different words, that birds were flying against the Jews, like those which are drawn by the smell of carcases, and which come in great numbers, that each may have a part; and then, wild beasts follow them. But I approve of neither of these explanations; nor indeed have they even the appearance of being correct.

I therefore think that the people are now compared to foreign birds, as they were before to lions; as though he had said,—"I had chosen this people for myself, that they might be my friends, as birds which are wont to be gathered into their own cages, as sheep into their own folds, and as oxen, and other animals which are tamed, keep within their own enclosures. So when I gathered this people, I thought that they would be to me like domesticated sheep; but now they are like speckled birds; that is, like wild birds, or birds of the wood." For I have no doubt but that by a speckled or coloured bird is to be understood a strange bird, which by its novel appearance excites the attention of men. *Is* then *a variegated bird,* or a bird of the wood, *become mine heritage?* Questions, we know, were often used by the Hebrews; and the Prophet here simply affirms the fact; and as God had said before, that his heritage was become like a lion in the forest, so he adds now, that his heritage was like a speckled bird. A question has much more power and force than a simple declaration; for God assumes here the character of one in astonishment,—"What does this mean, that my heritage should become to me like some bird from the wood, or a foreign bird?" He then adds, *All birds* then *shall be around and all beasts of the field.*[1]

We now see how fitly the words of the Prophet run; God had complained that his heritage was like a lion in the forest, and also like a wild and foreign bird; and now he says, *Then all birds* will fly to the prey and *all the beasts of the field;* as though he had said,—"Since they have dared to act thus wantonly, and have dared to assail my servants like wild beasts, and have also become wild birds which cannot be tamed, I will shew what they will gain by their ferocity; for I will now send for all the birds of the air, and the wild beasts of the wood, that they may fly together quickly, and that they may come together to the prey." That we must thus understand the Prophet's meaning, we learn from the very words; for God not only says, "A speckled bird has mine heritage become," but he adds, *to me,* as he had before

[1] The most literal rendering of the verse is as follows,—

9. Is not my heritage to me a stripped bird of prey?
Is there not a bird of prey around against it?
Come, assemble, every beast of the field;
Hasten ye to devour.

The versions and the *Targum* all differ, and are wholly unsatisfactory. Some, as *Venema,* agreeably with our version, retain not the questionary form in the two first lines, and render them thus,—

A stripped bird of prey *is* my heritage to me;
A bird of prey *is* around against it.

The meaning is the same; but the ה before "bird of prey," or rapacious bird, seems to favour the interrogation. The צבוע, stripped or speckled, is a participle, and not the name of "a ravenous bird," as *Blayney* thinks, is evident from its location, for it follows the word עיט, a rapacious bird: it would have otherwise preceded it. The *Vulgate* renders it, "discolor—diversely coloured," and the *Syriac* is the same.—*Ed.*

said, that his heritage had become to him as a lion, so he says now, *Is not mine heritage become to me?* &c. This pronoun then ought to be carefully noticed; for we hence learn, as I have said already, that the intractable disposition of the people is here condemned, for they could by no means be tamed.

But the latter clause ought also to be especially observed; for it imports as much as though God had said, "As then your wickedness is such that ye are to me lions and wild birds, take your course; but I will yet check this your barbarous and untameable ferocity; for I have under my command all the birds of the air and all the wild beasts of the field; let them then come together to this one bird, and to this one beast. Ye are but one bird; ye are indeed terrible at the first view, for ye are worse than all the hawks; but ye are only one bird, and around you shall come all birds, which shall make war on you. Ye are as one lion in a forest, or one boar, or one wolf; but all the savage beasts of the wood shall come together against you, and shall come together to devour you."

This place deserves special notice; for we hence learn how foolishly men deceive themselves when they oppose God and perversely shake off his yoke, and suffer not themselves to be corrected by his word; they are lions, they are savage birds; but the Lord can easily destroy them, for all birds and all wild beasts are ready to obey him; and hence it follows:—

10. Many pastors have destroyed my vineyard, they have trodden my portion under foot, they have made my pleasant portion a desolate wilderness.	10. Pastores multi perdiderunt vitem meam, calcarunt (*aut*, vastarunt, *utrunque enim significat* בססו, *sed hic verbum quadratum*, perdiderunt *ergo*) portionem meam, dederunt portionem desiderii mei in desertum vastitatis.

He explains by another comparison what we have just observed; he calls those pastors or shepherds whom he had before compared to wild beasts; for by saying, "Come ye, all the wild beasts of the wood," he doubtless meant the same as those of whom he now speaks; and yet he calls them pastors. But he touched the Jews to the quick, for they could not bear him to discharge the office of a pastor towards them. God ought to have been the pastor of his chosen people; but they were wild beasts. "Forsaken them have I," he says, "for they were wholly unworthy. What now then? Other pastors shall come, but those of a very different character, being fiercer and more cruel than wolves or any savage wild beasts." Though then the Prophet blends various comparisons, we yet see that he handles the same subject; we also see why he thus changes his expressions, for there is a meaning in every word he uses. It is indeed certain that those also are called pastors who would come as leaders or chiefs from Assyria and Chaldea; but there is no doubt here an implied antithesis, such as I have referred to, as though he had said, "I have hitherto been a shepherd to you, and was willing to continue to be so perpetually; but as ye can no longer bear me, other shepherds shall come, who will treat you according to their own will and disposition."

PRAYER.

Grant, Almighty God, that as thou hast not only been pleased to offer thyself to be our Shepherd, but hast also set over us thine only-begotten Son, that he might gather us into his own fold, and as he sweetly invites us daily by his voice to continue collected under his power and government,—O grant that we may suffer ourselves to be governed by him, and never be like wild and untameable beasts, but so obey his voice, that wherever he may call us we may be ready to follow, and thus proceed through the whole course of our life, until we shall at length reach the goal which is set before us, and be thence led to the fruition of that eternal inheritance and glory which thine only-begotten Son has obtained for us by his own blood.—Amen.

Lecture Fiftieth.

We began yesterday to explain what the Prophet declared—that the Jews would be laid waste by shepherds; and we said, that there is implied in this expression what is ironical; for they ought to have allowed themselves to be governed by God, who was willing to discharge towards them the office of a shepherd; but as they had refused to receive such a favour, they had deserved to be given over by God to the Assyrians and Chaldeans, who are also called shepherds. As, however, there is mention made of vineyard, the Prophet alludes to the shepherds of sheep or cattle: for when any one brings his herd or his flock to a vineyard it is no small evil. Hence also this allusion is not unsuitable. However this may be, the Prophet intimates, that as they would not bear the yoke of God, such shepherds would come as they deserved.

He again repeats what we have before observed, that this people had not only been God's vineyard, כרם, *carem*, but also his portion or his heritage, and even a portion of desire: for God designed that it should be often testified, that no bounty towards the Jews had been omitted by him, in order that their ingratitude might appear less excusable. As then God had manifested so much love towards them as to call them the desire of his soul and a desirable heritage, what wickedness it was not to acknowledge such an incomparable kindness? It now follows—

11. They have made it desolate, *and being* desolate it mourneth unto me; the whole land is made desolate, because no man layeth *it* to heart.	11. Posuit vastitatem, luxit super me (*vel*, ad me) vastata (*vel*, vastatio, *quidam adjectivè accipiunt, quidam volunt esse nomen substantivum, sed propriè* שממה *secundum grammaticam est vastatio, sed appositivè loco participii capitur, quemadmodum continuò pòst subjicit,*) vastata est omnis terra; quia (*vel*, tametsi) nemo posuit super cor (*hoc est*, nemo animum adjecit, *quemadmodum alibi vidimus.*)

There is a change of number in the verb שם, *shem;* but there is no obscurity: for the Prophet means, that the Jews would be exposed to the outrage of all, so that every one would plunder and lay waste the land. He does not then speak only of all their enemies or of the whole army; but he also declares that every one would be their master, so as to vex, scatter, devour, and wholly to destroy them at his pleasure: in short, he sets forth the atrocity of their punishment,—that the whole land would not only be spoiled by the united army, but also by every individual in it.[1]

[1] The *Septuagint* and *Arabic* render the verb as passive in the singular number, "It has been set a desolation." We may take שמה as a passive participle, the ו being omitted, with ה, *it*, affixed. Then the verse would run thus,—

He then adds that the *land was in mourning* before him. The Prophet seems to me to touch here the torpor of his own nation, because there was no one who had any regard for God; nay, they laughed at the judgments which were nigh at hand, and of which he had often spoken. Hence God says, that they would at length come to him when calamities oppressed them and caused them to mourn. "As then in peaceable times," he says, "they are unwilling to come to me, but are so refractory and untameable, that I can effect nothing by so many warnings, they shall come," he says, "but in another state of mind, even in extreme mourning."

He afterwards adds, *No one lays on the heart.* What this means we have elsewhere explained. But the particle כי, *ki*, which is properly a causative, may be here rendered as an adversative. If we take it in its first and most proper sense, then a reason is here given why the Jews would be brought to a most grievous mourning, even because they had despised all the prophets, and wholly disregarded as a fable what they had so often heard from God's mouth: and this is the view taken by most interpreters. But it may be also taken as an adversative, as in many other places,—"Though no one lays on the heart;" and thus it will be a complaint as to their perverse stupor, inasmuch as, when smitten by God's hand, they did not perceive that they were punished for their sins, not that they were wholly insensible as to their evils. But what avails it to cry and to howl, as God's Spirit speaks elsewhere, except the hand of the smiter be perceived? The Jews then ought, had a spark of wisdom been in them, to have considered their sins, to have prayed for forgiveness, and to have repented, and also to have em-

11. Set it *is* an utter desolation;
It has mourned before me (or, to me) being utterly desolate:
Desolate has been the whole land,
Though no man lays *it* to heart.

"Utter desolation" is the meaning, for it is a reduplicate noun. Both the *Vulgate* and the *Targum* connect "being utterly desolate" with the next line, though not rightly: but both, as well as the *Syriac*, render the first verb, as though it were שמוה, "They have set it." *Venema* and *Houbigant* render עלי, in the second line, a preposition, and render the line thus,—

It has mourned on account of desolation.—*Ed.*

braced the favour promised to them. But when they perversely added sins to sins, God justly expostulated with them, because they did not attend to the signs of his wrath, by which they ought not only to have been taught, but also subdued. It follows—

12. The spoilers are come upon all high places through the wilderness: for the sword of the Lord shall devour from the *one* end of the land even to the *other* end of the land: no flesh shall have peace.

12. Super omnes oras (*vel, quomodo alii vertunt*, super omnia loca excelsa, שׁפים, *uno verbo dicere licebit*, prominentias; *accipitur etiam pro rupibus; sed loquitur de finibus extremis; ergo* super fines extremos) in desertum venerunt perditores; quia gladius Jehovæ voravit à fine terræ usque ad finem terræ; non est pax universæ carni.

Jeremiah here proceeds farther—that no corner of the land would be exempt from the attacks of enemies. Desert is not put here for solitude not inhabited, but for high places; and as such places for the most part are fit for pastures, there is no doubt but that he means here secluded places. It is, however, sufficient for our present purpose to consider, that the desert here is put in opposition to the level parts of the country. When, therefore, the enemies had rambled through the plains, the Prophet says, that no recesses, however hidden, would be safe; for there also the violence of the enemies would penetrate. And this is what he states more clearly at the end of the verse when he says that there would be no peace to any flesh: for he intimates, no doubt, that all, from the least to the greatest, would be rendered miserable, as God's vengeance would reach every one without exception; and he says this, because those who sought hiding-places might have hoped to escape, thinking that the enemy would be satisfied with a limited victory; but the Prophet declares, that God's wrath would so burn as to consume all, and to leave no part of the land without involving in ruin the rich and the poor, the country people and the citizens.

After having then threatened the plains, which were more open and accessible, he now adds, that neither the mountains nor the hills would escape the outrage of their enemies; and at the same time he reminds them that God would be the author of all their calamities; for had he only spoken of the Chaldeans, the Jews would not have thought that they were given up to punishment by God on account of their sins: it would have therefore been without any good effect had they thought that they had a contest only with the Chaldeans. Hence he calls their attention to God's judgment, and shews, that though ambition, avarice, and cruelty instigated and influenced their enemies, they were yet conducted by a divine power, because the Jews had for a long time provoked against themselves the vengeance of God. He, in short, intimates that the Chaldeans would fight for God and do his work, as he would be the chief commander in the war; and this he intimates lest the Jews should think that such great calamities happened to them by chance: hence he says, *The sword of Jehovah hath devoured*, &c. He indeed speaks of future things; but he uses the past tense, which is commonly done by the prophets.[1] It now follows—

13. They have sown wheat, but shall reap thorns: they have put themselves to pain, *but* shall not profit; and they shall be ashamed of your revenues, because of the fierce anger of the Lord.

13. Seminarunt triticum et spinas messuerunt; hæreditatem adepti sunt (*vel*, fatigati sunt) nec profecerunt; et confusi sunt à proventibus vestris, a furore (*vel*, excandescentia, *potius*) iræ Jehovæ.

Most interpreters understand this of the prophets, that they had been disappointed, after having faithfully cultivated the field of God and sown good seed, that thorns only had sprung up, and briars only had grown: but this is a strained exposition. The Prophet, I doubt not, sets forth the curse of God, which the people were soon to experience. I indeed readily admit, that when he speaks of sowing and reaping, the expression is metaphorical; but I have no doubt but that the Jews are said to sow in seeking aids here and there, in strengthening themselves by confederacies, and in devising means to repel dangers.

Hence he says, by way of concession, that they had *sown*

[1] The versions and the *Targum* render the first verb in the past tense, but the second, incorrectly, in the future. The verse is as follows,—

12. On all heights in the wilderness have wasters come,
For the sword has for Jehovah devoured;
From one end of the land to the other end of the land
No peace *has been* to any flesh.

The third line reads better with the last. No doubt, the past, as *Calvin* says, is used for the future. The same is the case in the next verse.—*Ed.*

wheat; for they had recourse to false counsels: but he speaks according to what they themselves thought; for they imagined that they were safe when they found that the Egyptians were ready to help them; and when they procured assistance from various quarters, they considered that they were acting wisely, and thus they flattered themselves with a prosperous issue. The Prophet now laughs to scorn this vain confidence: but yet in words he allows that they were going on successfully: as a husbandman, while sowing, expects that he will have a good harvest, so also the Jews thought that they would have good fruit after having thus sown. But the Prophet says that they would be disappointed; for instead of wheat briars and thorns would grow, so that the issue would not answer their expectations. Thus the words of the Prophet would well harmonize: but to explain the passage of the prophets would by no means be suitable, as it will hereafter appear more clearly.

He then says that they had *sown wheat* (he uses the plural number) *and reaped thorns.* He intimates that they hoped for a good harvest, for they sowed wheat, as they thought; that is, they wisely, or rather astutely, provided for themselves, as they left undone nothing that was necessary for their safety; but they *reaped,* or shall reap *thorns;* for he speaks of what was future. He means that God would frustrate their expectation; for their sowing, from which they promised themselves so much, would prove fruitless.

He then adds, that they had *obtained an inheritance,* or had endured grief, *but were not enriched.* Some render the first clause a little more harshly, that "they were rich." But I readily excuse its harshness, if it suits the place: then the meaning would be,—that they tormented themselves with continual labours, and thus became rich; for we know that they who are extremely anxious about anything wear out themselves, and become in a manner their own executioners; and this would not be unsuitable to this place. However, a different view may be taken,—that the Prophet uses the expression, that they had obtained an heritage, not in its ordinary sense, as signifying, not that God gave them the land of Canaan as their hereditary possession, or that they had accumulated wealth, but that they had thus increased in their own esteem, because they had the Egyptians as their friends, and looked for help to the neighbouring nations, and because they thought that they could by various stratagems prevent the Chaldeans from coming nigh them. Their heritage then was, that they were able to collect from various quarters such assistance as would render them safe, and repel all dangers. God then allows that they had obtained an heritage; but what then, he says? All this will not avail them, nor shall they be thereby enriched. He, in short, intimates that they would be thus deceived by trusting in helps so laboriously and sedulously acquired; for the aids in which they proudly trusted would vanish away, as well as all their counsels and designs; in a word, the vain attempts by which they thought to secure everything for themselves are laughed to scorn.

He adds, for the same purpose, that they were *confounded on account of their produce.* They who understand this of the prophets read thus, "they were ashamed," that is, "of their own labours;" but this is wholly foreign to the subject. He then continues in the same strain,—that the Jews were ashamed when they found the issue contrary to what they expected. He mentions "produce:" the noun comes from בא, *ba,* which means to come or to enter; it has also other meanings. But the Hebrews call it produce, because it comes every year. He says then, that they were *ashamed of their produce,* because they received no fruit such as they expected. Thus Jeremiah carries on the same metaphor: they had sown, but thorns were found instead of wheat; they also obtained for themselves an heritage, or they wearied themselves with labour, but it was useless: they further promised to themselves a great and rich produce, but it came to nothing. We now then understand the meaning of the words.

But we must at the same time consider what the Prophet had in view. Doubtless he intended to shake off from the Jews that arrogance by which they blinded themselves, as though he had said,—"I see that I effect but little; for the

Egyptians, who are to come to your aid, are as yet strong; ye think that they are prepared to oppose the Assyrians and Chaldeans, and ye have also other confederacies. As then ye are thus well fortified, ye consider yourselves to be out of the reach of danger; but the Lord will make you ashamed of this your presumption, for all your produce or provision will come to nothing." The produce, we know, was the successful issue with which they flattered themselves, so that they thought that nothing would do them harm. This then is the meaning of the Prophet.[1]

He adds, *Through the burning of the wrath of Jehovah.* They could not have been otherwise awakened, except they were made to think that God was angry with them. The Prophet then says, though the whole world might laugh him to scorn, that nothing would avail them, inasmuch as God fought against them. We must at the same time notice the change of person, *They have been ashamed of your produce.* Some have on this account applied the verb, בשו, *beshu*, "they have been ashamed," to the prophets; but it is an anomaly often found, and it is in this place very em-

[1] The *Septuagint*, the *Syriac*, and the *Arabic*, render all the verbs in the second person plural, and in the present tense, "Ye sow," &c.; but the *Vulgate* and *Targum* retain the Hebrew third person and the past tense, except in the third line, "Ye (not they) are ashamed," &c., which seems to be the correct reading, though not found in any MS., for it is what "your fruits," or produce, require.

The meaning of being "wearied," or sick with labour, is given only by the *Syriac* to the verb נחלו; all the other versions, as well as the *Targum*, give it the idea of "inheriting," or possessing as an heritage. So *Blayney* renders it, "They have possessed," &c. The verse then is as follows,—

13. They have sown wheats, but thorns have they reaped;
They have got an heritage, but have not succeeded:
Yea, ashamed have you been of your produce,
Through the burning of the wrath of Jehovah.

A conversive *vau* before "succeeded" is supplied by many MSS., and by the *Vulgate* and *Syriac*. The way in which *Calvin* accounts for the change of person in the third line is ingenious; but an instance of what he says can hardly be found in one and the same clause. All the versions and the *Targum* regard the verb as ותבשו, the *tau* only being supplied.

Venema takes the verb to be an imperative in the second person plural, and gives this version,—

Therefore be ye ashamed of your fruits,
By reason of the heat of the wrath of Jehovah.

But what the early versions warrant is more consistent with the context, and gives a better meaning.—*Ed.*

phatical. Had he said, in the third person, "They were ashamed of their fruits," it would have been less calculated to rouse their minds; but having previously spoken in disdain of the Jews, as he knew them to be deaf, he now, as he proceeds, turns his discourse to them, and says that they were ashamed; yes, he says, "Ye were ashamed of your fruits." It is therefore a kind of modification; but it is only used that the Prophet might more sharply touch their feelings; for they had need of this kind of speaking, as a plain discourse would have produced no effect. It follows—

14. Thus saith the Lord against all mine evil neighbours, that touch the inheritance which I have caused my people Israel to inherit; Behold, I will pluck them out of their land, and pluck out the house of Judah from among them.

14. Sic dicit Jehova, Super omnes vicinos meos malos qui tangunt hæreditatem meam, quam hæreditare obtinui, populum meum Israel; ecce ego evellam ipsos è terra ipsorum, et domum Jehudah evellam è medio ipsorum.

The Prophet now begins to mitigate what might have beyond measure exasperated the minds of the people; and this he did, not so much for the sake of the people in general, as for the sake of the elect, a few of whom still remained. We have indeed seen that it was all over with the body of the people; for it had been said to Jeremiah, "Pray not for them, for I will not hear them," (chap. xi. 14.) The Prophet then knew the immutable purpose of God as to the mass of the people. Nor did he intend here to soften what might have appeared grievous in what he had taught. But as we have said elsewhere, and indeed often repeated, the prophets used reproofs only as to the whole community, and then spoke as it were apart to the elect; for there ever was a remnant among that people, inasmuch as God never suffered his covenant to be made void. As then the Church was still existing, the Prophet had regard to the hidden seed, and therefore blended consolation with those grievous and dreadful predictions which we have noticed.

This is the reason why he now says that God would be the avenger of that cruelty which their neighbours had exercised towards the Jews. For this temptation might have greatly disturbed the minds of the godly,—"What means this, that God rages so violently against us, while he spares the heathens? Have the Moabites, or the Ammonites, or the Idumeans, deserved nothing? Why then does God bear with them, while he deals so severely with us?" The Prophet then meets this objection, and says, that punishment was nigh those nations, and such as they deserved, and that for the sake of the chosen people. If indeed he had only said that the Moabites and the Idumeans, and the rest, would be summoned before God's tribunal, that they in their turn might be punished, it would have given no relief to the miserable Jews; for it would have been a very empty consolation to have only so many associates in their misery: but the Prophet also adds, that God would be thus propitious to his elect; for it was a sign of his paternal favour, when he inflicted punishment on all those neighbours by whom they had been so cruelly treated.

He begins by saying, *Thus saith Jehovah;* and he says, *against all my evil neighbours*, &c. He speaks here in the person of God, who calls the Moabites and the Idumeans, as well as others, his neighbours, because he had chosen the land of Canaan as an habitation for himself; for it was, as it appears often from the prophets, an evidence above all other things of God's favour, that he dwelt among that people. He was not indeed confined either to the Temple or to the land of Canaan; but he had taken the people under his safeguard and protection, as though he had his hands extended for the purpose of defending them all. We now see why he calls the nations near to the Jews *his evil neighbours:* for though the Jews deserved extreme evils, yet that promise remained valid, "He who touches you, touches the apple of my eye." (Zech. ii. 8.)

Then he adds, *who touch my heritage.* Here he speaks not ironically as before, but regards simply his own election, as though he had said,—"Whatever the Jews may be, I will yet be consistent with myself, and my covenant shall not fall to the ground; for my faithfulness shall surpass their perfidy." We must yet bear in mind what I have already stated,—that the whole of this is to be confined to the elect, who were few in number and were hid like twenty or a hundred grains in a large heap of chaff. As then the Prophet addresses here especially the elect of God, it is no wonder that he calls them God's heritage, not for the sake of upbraiding them, as he had done before, but because God really loved them and would have them to be saved. There is another thing to be noticed,—that God had in view the Idumeans as well as the Ammonites, Sidonians, and Tyrians, who had unjustly oppressed his people. The Ammonites and the Moabites were by kindred connected, for they both derived their origin from Lot, the nephew of Abraham. As to the Idumeans, they were the descendants of Esau, all of the same family; and they knew that the Jews had been chosen by God. Hence God here shews that he himself was injured, when such wrongs were done to his people.

We hence see why God calls here Israel his *heritage; which*, he says, *by heritage I have possessed.* Here he takes away from the neighbouring nations every handle for evasion; as though he had said,—"Though the Jews have sinned, yet these are not their judges; nor have they any right to punish them for their unfaithfulness: it has been my will to choose them for mine heritage." We thus see that these words are emphatical, their import being, that God would punish the wrongs done to his people, because his own majesty was insulted, inasmuch as no regard was shewn to his adoption: nor had the heathens any right to inquire whether the Jews were worthy or not; for it had pleased God to take them under his protection.[1]

He then adds, *Behold, I will pluck them up from their land, and the house of Judah will I pluck up from the midst of them.* He mentions here two kinds of plucking up. He says first, that he would by force expel the Idumeans and

[1] No doubt the people of Israel were often called the heritage of God; but the word heritage means here evidently the land. The version of *Calvin* cannot be admitted; the verb is in Hiphil and must be rendered, "I have caused to inherit;" and so it is rendered in all the versions and *Targum*. The verse runs thus,—

14. Thus saith Jehovah,—As to all my neighbours,
Who have done evil, who have touched the heritage,
Which I have caused my people Israel to inherit,—
Behold, I will root them up from their land,
And the house of Judah will I root up from the midst of them.

There is here a promise of two removals,—that of heathens from the land of Canaan,—and that of the Jews from the land of heathens.—*Ed.*

drive them far into exile; for this is the meaning, when he says, *I will pluck them up*, as נתש, *nutash*, is to draw out by force. The word is often found in the prophets, especially in reference to the Church, " I have planted and will pluck up," (chap. xlv. 4:) We have also seen the following, "I have set thee to plant and to pluck up," (chap. i. 10;) this was to shew the power of prophetic truth. And he says here, " I will pluck up," or eradicate them, as some render it; but as this word (*eradicabo*) is not Latin, let us retain *evellam*—I will pluck up; only you must understand that what it properly means is, to draw up by the roots, and that by force: *I will pluck up*, he says, the Idumeans, the Ammonites, the Moabites, and all other neighbouring nations, from their land, because they have violated *mine heritage*, even the people chosen by me: therefore they themselves shall be driven into remote exile and into captivity, according to what is said elsewhere, " Remember the children of Edom, who said in the day of Jerusalem," &c., (Psalm cxxxvii. 7;) and we shall hereafter see that this was fulfilled; for the Prophet will presently speak of all these nations, in order that the Jews might perceive that God's judgment would extend to all parts of the earth. But here the Prophet briefly threatens these nations with vengeance, that he might alleviate the sorrow of the small portion which remained. For as we have said, the body of the people was without hope, as God had given them up, according to what they deserved, to final destruction.

But as God ever reserved a remnant, the Prophet says in this place, *The house of Judah will I pluck up from the midst of them:* for some had fled to the Moabites and to others, and some had indeed been taken captives and were held in bondage. The Jews, as we know, had been miserably plundered, and some of them had been exposed to sale by these nations. Hence God here promises that he would be at length entreated by his people, so as to gather the remnant from the Moabites as well as from the Idumeans and other heathen nations. This second plucking up is therefore to be taken in a good sense; for the Prophet promises deliverance here to God's elect: and yet he suitably employs the same word, in order to set forth the cruelty of these nations, who would have never willingly given them up, had not God by force rescued from their tyranny the innocent Israelites—that is, innocent with regard to them. "I will," he says, "draw them out by force;" as though he had said,—"However obstinate may be the cruelty of all these nations, by whom my people shall be taken captive, I will yet be stronger than they, so that I shall bring forth the captives, though they who consider them as perpetual slaves may resist with all their power."

And this also have we found in our time; for how hard was our bondage under the Papacy? and was not also its tyranny almost unconquerable? But God put forth his power and drew forth a few from under its cruel domination. In the same manner he promised formerly to the remnant of his people, that he would be so merciful to them as to rescue them from the yoke of tyranny. It follows—

15. And it shall come to pass, after that I have plucked them out, I will return, and have compassion on them, and will bring them again, every man to his heritage, and every man to his land.

15. Et erit postquam extraxero illos, revertar et miserebor ipsorum, et redire ipsos faciam (*vel*, reducam) unumquenque ad hæreditatem suam, et unumquenque ad terram suam.

God does not only promise mercy here to the Jews, but also to heathen nations, of whom he would be the Judge, to punish them for the sake of his people. And that this passage is to be extended to aliens is evident from the context; for the Prophet immediately adds, "And it shall be, that when they shall learn the ways of my people, to swear in my name, Live does Jehovah, as they have taught my people to swear by Baal, then shall they be built in the midst of my people." We hence see that God would not only shew mercy to the remnant of his elect people, but also to their enemies.

If it be objected,—that thus God's favour, manifested towards the children of Abraham, was obscured, the answer is,—that this availed much to confirm the hope of the faithful; for they had not only to look for their own salvation, but also for that of their enemies, whom God would gather together with them. Thus God rendered double his favour to the Israelites. The Prophet also in this place confirms in a striking manner the confidence of the faithful; for he says that God would be merciful even to their enemies for their sake, as they would be saved in common with themselves. We now then understand the object of the Prophet, when he declares, that God, after having drawn out the Gentiles from their own countries, would again be merciful to them, so as to restore every one of them to their own inheritance and to their own place.

PRAYER.

Grant, Almighty God, that as at this day such a dreadful scattering terrifies us on every side, we may learn to raise up our eyes above the world and to hope for that which is now hidden from us, even that in executing thy judgments on the Church as well as on aliens, thou wilt be so merciful to the whole world, as that we may be gathered into the unity of faith: and may we labour to devote ourselves wholly to thy service and cultivate brotherly concord among ourselves, until we shall at length enjoy that eternal inheritance, which has been obtained for us by the blood of thine only-begotten Son.—Amen.

Lecture Fifty-First.

We said in our last Lecture that God here promises pardon and salvation to alien nations, provided they repented, and that he did this, that he might more fully confirm his promises to his elect people. We indeed know that all nations were then excluded from the covenant of God: as, then, he would extend his mercy even to them, the Jews might with some confidence entertain hope, since they were already as it were near to God, he having adopted them as his peculiar people and heritage.

And this is what may be easily gathered from the context; for God declares that he would draw forth his own elect from these nations; and then he adds, that he would proceed still further, that he would even receive into favour those who had been previously his enemies. Hence he says,

After I shall draw them out, I will return,[1] *and shew mercy to them.* He speaks this of aliens: *And I will restore them,* he says, *every one to his heritage and to his own land.* It now follows—

16. And it shall come to pass, if they will diligently learn the ways of my people, to swear by my name, The Lord liveth; (as they taught my people to swear by Baal;) then shall they be built in the midst of my people.

16. Et accidet, Si discendo didicerint vias populi mei ad jurandum per nomen meum, vivit Jehova, sicuti docuerunt populum meum jurare (*ad verbum,* ad jurandum) per Baal, tunc ædificabuntur in medio populi mei.

We see that this refers to the Gentiles, who were previously aliens to the grace of God; nay, they entertained the most dire hatred towards his chosen people. In short, God declares that he would be merciful and propitious to these miserable nations, of whose salvation no hope was entertained, for they had been rejected by him, and they had often and long, and in various ways, provoked his vengeance; and though he speaks of neighbours, as we have seen, yet this prediction belongs generally to the whole world, and was at length fulfilled in the call of the Gentiles; for God then gathered a Church indiscriminately both from the Jews and the Gentiles.

But a condition is here laid down—If the Gentiles, who had hitherto opposed the true worship of God, received his law. We indeed know how much hated was true religion, especially by the neighbouring nations; for their hatred was increased, because they saw that their superstitions were condemned by this one people. As then they had been greatly incensed against God and the pure doctrine of his law, he now requires a change in them; *If they will learn,* he says, *the ways of my people.* By the *ways* of his people he understands what he had commanded. The people of Israel had indeed often departed from true religion; but God here refers to himself rather than to their perverse conduct, for the law had not been abolished by the wickedness

[1] Rather, "I will turn," *i.e.,* from the course he had pursued. This is often the meaning of שוב. It is rendered here adverbially by *Blayney* and others; though it may at times be so rendered, yet not suitably in this place. It means here a change in God's proceedings: he had plucked them up; but now he will deal differently with them.—*Ed.*

and ingratitude of his people. We hence see that, by the *ways* of his people, we are not to understand those glosses which the Jews had devised, but the law itself, which God had delivered to them. The authority of men, therefore, cannot be hence established, as though they had power to frame a religion for themselves; but God means only that by his good pleasure alone the Jews had been taught what was right. In short, Jeremiah understands the *ways* of the people passively, not those which the people had contrived for themselves, but such as they had received from above.

It is then added, *That they may swear in my name.* The expression is a part for the whole, for in it is included the whole worship and service of God. Swearing, as we have said elsewhere, is a part of God's worship and of true religion, for we profess that we ourselves and our life are in God's hand when we swear by his name; and we also refer judgment to him, and own that he is really God, inasmuch as he knows our hearts and judges of hidden things. All these things are included in swearing. It is therefore no wonder that, in this place and in many other places, the whole of religion is designated by this expression, according to what is said elsewhere, "Swear shall they all in my name, Live do I, saith Jehovah; to me shall bend every knee, and by me shall every tongue swear." (Isaiah xlv. 23.) And as by the altar, in another place, is meant the worship of God, so here by swearing. The meaning is,—that if the Gentiles became so changed as to submit their neck to the yoke of the law, and allow themselves to be ruled by God, they would be made partakers of the mercy which the Jews had before enjoyed.

Then follows the common form of swearing, *Live does Jehovah.* So the Scripture speaks everywhere; and by these words men do not merely testify that they swear by the life of God, but they also ascribe eternity to him, as though it was said, "God alone exists:" for no life is anywhere to be found but in God. Men, indeed, and brute animals, and even trees, are said to live; but in trees there is only vigour without the senses, in brutes the senses without reason and understanding; but in men the life is light; yet they live not by or of themselves, but they derive life from God, according to what we see on the earth, on which light shines; but we know that there is really no light where we dwell but what descends and is conveyed to us by the rays of the sun. In the same manner it may be said that life dwells in men, being conveyed to them by the hidden power of God. Nor do angels, properly speaking, live of themselves. We hence see the meaning of the words, *Live does Jehovah.* The eternity of God is hereby set forth; he is also owned as the Judge of the world; and further, whatever he claims for himself, men thus testify that it is justly and by right his due.

It afterwards follows, *As they taught my people to swear by Baal.* The corruptions of heathens had greatly prevailed among the chosen people; and the greater part, when they saw that the nations prospered, had cast aside every care for true worship and sincere religion. As then the Jews had been so much given to the superstitions of the heathens, the Prophet says, speaking in God's name,—"If the Gentiles, who have hitherto taught my people to swear by Baal, who have drawn them away to their own idolatries and fictitious and false forms of worship, begin now to swear by my name, faithfully to worship me alone, they shall be built in the midst of my people." The metaphor of building is very common; but in this place God intimates no more than that the Gentiles would become a part of his flock, when they cast away their superstitions, and embraced the pure worship prescribed in the law. Nor is this to be applied to any particular place, as some have frigidly explained it, but "in the midst of the people," is the same as though he had said,—"I will count those nations my people, as a part of my Church," according to what is said in the Psalms,—that though the Tyrians and Sidonians, and Egyptians, and others who had been hostile nations, were born here and there, yet they would boast that they were all born at Jerusalem when God owned them as members of his own people. (Psalm lxxxvii. 3, 4.)[1] It follows—

[1] The verb למד, to learn, in this verse, has evidently two meanings, as "learn" has in old English. In the first instance,—"If they will learn the ways of my people," it means what is commonly understood by the

17. But if they will not obey, I will utterly pluck up and destroy that nation, saith the Lord.	17. Quòd si non audierint, tunc evellam (*copula* etiam *hic accipitur pro adverbio temporis*) gentem illam, evellendo et perdendo, dicit Jehova.

As he had shewn that there was a sure hope of salvation to his own people, when the Gentiles would embrace his mercy, so he now threatens the Gentiles with destruction in case they repented not; for he had promised to be merciful to the Gentiles conditionally, and said,—" If they *learn the ways of my people*, if they submit to my authority:" but now he says, *If they will not hear*, &c. We hence see that God here threatens extreme vengeance to the Gentiles if they subjected not themselves to his yoke, so as to render obedience to him. His object, no doubt, was to terrify the Jews as well as the nations; for as the Gentiles could not with impunity despise God, though unknown to them, how inexcusable would the Jews be, who had from their infancy imbibed the true knowledge of the law, if, after the manner of the Gentiles, they were perverse and intractable?

We in short see that God, on one side, sweetly allured the Jews to render a willing obedience to his law, and, on the other, he threatened them; for as he could by no means bear with the perverseness of the Gentiles, much less could the Jews hope to escape punishment. This is the import of the passage. Now follows another prophecy—

CHAPTER XIII.

1. Thus saith the Lord unto me, Go and get thee a linen girdle, and put it upon thy loins, and put it not in water.	1. Sic dicit Jehova mihi, Vade et compara tibi cingulum lineum, et pone illud super renes tuos, et in aquas ne inferas illud.

term; but, in the second instance,—" As they have learned my people," it signifies to teach. Though in English the word is not now used in this sense, yet in Welsh the word still continues to have this double meaning; and the same word, " dysgu," is used in these two clauses, according to what is done in Hebrew.

There is here a clear instance of ו, following אם, being rendered " then," and it cannot be rendered otherwise,—" If learning they will learn, &c., then shall they be built up," &c. In the first clause there is also a striking correspondence between the Welsh and the Hebrew,—" Os gan ddysgu y dysgant."—*Ed.*

2. So I got a girdle, according to the word of the Lord, and put *it* on my loins.	2. Et comparavi mihi cingulum (paravi, *ad verbum*) sicuti mandaverat Jehova, et posui (*vel*, applicavi) illud ad renes meos.
3. And the word of the Lord came unto me the second time, saying,	3. Et factus est sermo Jehovæ ad me secundò, dicendo,
4. Take the girdle that thou hast got, which *is* upon thy loins, and arise, go to Euphrates, and hide it there in a hole of the rock.	4. Tolle cingulum quod comparasti, quod est super renes tuos, et surge, proficiscere (*vel*, surgens proficiscere) ad Euphratem, et absconde illic in foramine petræ.
5. So I went, and hid it by Euphrates, as the Lord commanded me.	5. Et profectus sum et abscondi in Euphrate, quemadmodum præceperat Jehova mihi.
6. And it came to pass after many days, that the Lord said unto me, Arise, go to Euphrates, and take the girdle from thence, which I commanded thee to hide there.	6. Et accidit post finem (à fine *ad verbum*) dierum multorum, et dixit (*hoc est*, ut diceret) Jehova mihi, Surge et proficiscere ad Euphratem, et tolle illinc cingulum, de quo præcepi tibi ut absconderes illic.
7. Then I went to Euphrates, and digged, and took the girdle from the place where I had hid it; and, behold, the girdle was marred, it was profitable for nothing.	7. Et profectus sum ad Euphratem, et fodi et sustuli cingulum è loco ubi illic absconderam; et ecce corruptum erat cingulum, non proderat ad omne (*hoc est*, ad quicquam.)
8. Then the word of the Lord came unto me, saying,	8. Et factus est sermo Jehovæ ad me, dicendo,
9. Thus saith the Lord, After this manner will I mar the pride of Judah, and the great pride of Jerusalem.	9. Sic dicit Jehova, In hunc modum corrumpam excellentiam Jehudah et excellentiam Jerusalem magnam (*vel*, altitudinem.)

I have said that there is here a new prophecy; for the Prophet is said to buy for himself a girdle or a belt, or, according to some, a truss or breeches; and as mention is made of linen, this opinion may be probable; but אזור, *asur*, means not only the breeches which they then wore, but also a girdle or belt, according to what Isaiah says, when, speaking figuratively of Christ's kingdom, that faithfulness would be the girdle of his loins. (Isaiah xi. 5.) It may here, however, be taken for breeches as well as for a girdle.[1] As to

[1] It is rendered "περίζωμα—a girdle," by the *Septuagint*;—"lumbare—a garment for the loins," by the *Vulgate*;—"sudarium—a napkin," by the *Syriac*;—"cingulum—a girdle," by the *Targum* and *Arabic*. The Hebrew word never means anything but a girdle or belt, as the verb signifies to surround, to bind.

Calvin makes no remark on the command, not to put it in water before he wore it. Various has been the explanation. The view the Rabbins give is inconsistent with the passage,—that it was to be left dirty after wearing, that it might rot the sooner; for the Prophet is bidden, when

the matter in hand, it makes no great difference. The Prophet then is bidden to buy for himself a linen girdle or a linen breeches, and he is also bidden to *go to Euphrates, and to hide the girdle in a hole.* He is again bidden to go the second time to Euphrates, and to draw the girdle from the hole, and he found it *marred.* The application follows; for God declares that he would thus deal with the Jews; though he had had them as a belt, he would yet cast them away. As he had adorned them, so he designed them to be an ornament to him; for the glory of God shines forth in his Church. The Jews then, as Isaiah says, were a crown of glory and a royal diadem in God's hand. (Isaiah lxii. 3.) Hence he compares them here most fitly to a belt or a girdle. Though then their condition was honourable, yet God threatens that he would cast them away; so that, being hidden, they might contract rottenness in a cavern of the Euphrates, that is, in Assyria and Chaldea. This is the meaning of the prophecy.

But no doubt a vision is here narrated, and not a real transaction, as some think, who regard Jeremiah as having gone there; but what can be imagined more absurd? He was, we know, continually engaged in his office of a teacher among his own people. Had he undertaken so long a journey, and that twice, it would have taken him some months. Hence contentious must he be, who urges the words of the Prophet, and holds that he must have gone to the Euphrates and hidden there his girdle. We know that this form of speaking is common and often used by the prophets: they narrate visions as facts.

We must also observe, that God might have spoken plainly and without any similitude; but as they were not only ignor-

commanded to wear it, not to wash it. *Grotius* and others think that he was to wear it as made, in its rough state, in order to shew the rude condition of the Jews when God adopted them. *Venema* is of the opinion that it was to shew that it was newly made, and had not been worn by another, nor polluted. *Gataker* says that the purpose was to shew that nothing was to be done by the Prophet to cause the girdle to rot, as wet might have done so, in order to prove that the rottenness proceeded only from the Jews themselves. *Lowth* regards it as intended to teach the Jews their corrupt state by nature, so that it was through favour or grace only that God adopted them; and he refers to Ezekiel xvi. 4. The last, which is nearly the same with the view of *Grotius*, seems the most suitable.—*Ed.*

ant, but also stupid, it was found necessary to reprove their torpidity by an external symbol. This was the reason why God confirmed the doctrine of his Prophet by an external representation. Had God said, "Ye have been to me hitherto as a belt, ye were my ornament and my glory, not indeed through your merit or worthiness, but because I have united you to myself, that ye might be a holy people and a priestly kingdom; but now I am constrained to cast you away: and as a person throws from him and casts a girdle into some hole, so that after a long time he finds it rotten, so it will be with you, after having been hidden a long time beyond Euphrates; ye shall there contract rottenness, which will mar you altogether, so that your appearance will be very different, when a remnant of you shall come from thence:" This indeed might have been sufficient; but in that state of security and dulness in which we know the Jews were, such a simple statement would not have so effectually penetrated into their hearts, as when this symbol was presented to them. The Prophet, therefore, says, that he was girded with a belt, that the belt was hid in a hole near Euphrates, and that there it became marred; and then he adds, so shall it be done to you. This statement, as I have said, more sharply touched the Jews, so that they saw that the judgment of God was at hand.

With regard to the similitude of girdle or breeches, we know how proudly the Jews gloried in the thought that God was bound to them; and he would have really been so, had they been in return faithful to him: but as they had become so disobedient and ungrateful, how could God be bound to them? He had indeed chosen them to be a people to himself, but this condition was added, that they were to be as a chaste wife, as he had become, according to what we have seen, a husband to them. But they had prostituted themselves and had become shamefully polluted with idols. As then they had perfidiously departed from their marriage engagement, was not God freed from his obligations? according to what is said by Isaiah, "There is no need to give you a bill of divorcement, for your mother is an adulteress." (Isaiah l. 1.) The Prophet then, in this place, meant in a few words to shake off from the Jews those vain boastings in which they indulged, when they said that they were God's people and the holy seed of Abraham. " True," he says, " and I will concede more to you, that you were to God even as a belt, by which men usually adorn themselves; but God adopted you, that you might serve him chastely and faithfully; but now, as ye have made void his covenant, he will cast away this belt, which is a disgrace to him and not an ornament, and will throw it into a cavern where it will rot." Such is the view we are to take of this belt, as we shall hereafter see more clearly.

The Prophet, by saying that he went to the Euphrates, confirms what he had narrated: he did not indeed mean that he actually went there, but his object was to give the Jews a vivid representation. It is then what Rhetorians call a scene presented to the view; though the place is not changed, yet the thing is set before the eyes by a lively description.[1] Thus the Prophet, as the Jews were deaf, exhibited to their view what they would not hear. This is the reason why he says that he *went.* For the same purpose is what follows, that at *the end of many days* God had bidden him to take out the *girdle.* Here also is signified the length of the exile. As to the *hole in a rock,* what is meant is disgrace; for without honour and esteem the Jews lived in banishment, in the same manner as though they were cast into a cavern. Hence by the hole is signified their ignoble and base condition, that they were like persons removed from the sight of all men and from the common light of

[1] Many agree with *Calvin* that this was a vision and not an actual transaction, such as *Gataker, Lowth, Blayney, Adam Clarke,* &c. *Henry* hesitates, but *Scott* seems to be strongly in favour of a real transaction. *Bochart* and *Venema* hold also the latter opinion, only they think that פרת here does not mean " Euphrates," but Ephrata, that is, Bethlehem, in Judea; but this cannot be maintained. *Lowth* refers to an instance where a vision is related as a fact, without any mention being made that it was a vision, that is, Gen. xv. 5: God brought Abraham forth and shewed to him the stars; and yet it appears from verse 12 that the sun was not set. *Blayney* remarks, that " the same supposition of a vision must be admitted in other cases, particularly chap. xxv. 15-29." *Gataker* refers to similar instances in Ezekiel viii. 3; xi. 24. It was most probably a vision; and the Prophet related to the people what God had in a supernatural way exhibited to him.—*Ed.*

day. By the *end of many days,* is meant, as I have said, the length of their exile, for in a short time they would not have become putrified, and except indeed this had been distinctly expressed, they would have never been convinced of the grievousness of the calamity which was nigh them. Hence he says that the days would be many, so that they might contract putridity while hidden in the hole.

As to the application of the Prophecy, the Prophet then distinctly describes it; but he sets forth with sufficient clearness the main point, when he says, *Thus will I mar the stateliness* (*altitudinem,* the altitude or height) *of Judah and the great stateliness of Jerusalem.* Other interpreters unanimously render the word, pride; but as גאון, *gaun,* may be taken in two senses, it means here, I have no doubt, excellency, and this will appear more fully from what follows.[1] The word then signifies here that dignity with which God had favoured the seed of Abraham, when he intended them to be an ornament to himself. So it is said in Exod. xv. 7, "In thy greatness thou wilt destroy the nations." And in Isaiah he says, "I will make thee the excellency of ages." (Isaiah lx. 15.) There no doubt it is to be taken in a good sense. And these things harmonize together,—that God had prepared the Jews for himself as a belt, and then that he cast them from him into a cavern, where they would be for a time without any light and without any glory.

The import of this clause then is, "Though the dignity of Judah and Jerusalem has been great, (for the people whom God had adopted were renowned according to what is said in Deut. iv.,) though then the stateliness of Judah and Jerusalem has been great, yet I *will mar* it." We see how the Prophet takes from the Jews that false confidence by which they deceived themselves. They might indeed have gloried in God, had they acted truly and from the heart: but when they arrogated all things to themselves, and deprived God of his authority, whose subjects they were, how great was their vanity and folly, and how ridiculous always to profess

[1] It is strangely rendered "reproach—ὕβριν," by the *Septuagint,* but "pride" by the *Vulgate,*—"the haughty ones," by the *Syriac,*—"insolence" by the *Arabic,* and "strength" by the *Targum. Blayney* agrees with *Calvin* and renders it "excellency," and *Horsley,* "glory."—*Ed.*

his sacred name, and to say, We are God's people? for he was no God to them, as they esteemed him as nothing; nay, they disdainfully and reproachfully rejected his yoke. We hence see that the word גאון, *gaun,* is to be taken here in a good sense. The Prophet at the same time reproachfully taunts them, that they abused the name of God and falsely pretended to be his people and heritage. The rest we cannot finish; we shall go on with the subject to-morrow.

PRAYER.

Grant, Almighty God, that as so many of the people who have been gathered by thee, that they might be the body of thine only-begotten Son, have fallen away, and have by their ingratitude alienated themselves from the hope of eternal salvation,—O grant, that they may again at this day be united together, and hold with us the true unity of faith, so that with one heart and one mouth we may profess thee as our God and Father, and so learn to swear by thy name, that we may acknowledge thee as our Judge, and ascribe to thee all power over us, until we shall at length enjoy that eternal inheritance, into the hope of which thou hast called us and daily invitest us, through Christ Jesus our Lord.—Amen.

Lecture Fifty-Second.

10. This evil people, which refuse to hear my words, which walk in the imagination of their heart, and walk after other gods, to serve them, and to worship them, shall even be as this girdle, which is good for nothing.

10. Populus hic malus[1] renuentes audire verba mea, ambulantes in pravitate cordis sui; et ambulant post deos alienos ut serviant ipsis et adorent ipsos; et erunt (*collectivum nomen populi est singulare*) tanquam baltheus hic, qui ad nihilum prodest (*qui ad quicquam non est utilis.*)

The Prophet said, according to what we observed yesterday, that the people would be like the belt which he had

[1] These words are in the *Septuagint* and the *Vulgate* put in apposition with the last words of the preceding verse; but in the *Syriac* and *Targum* they form the nominative case to the verb "shall be," as in our version, near the end of the verse, the ו before it being omitted; but the simpler mode of construction is to consider the substantive verb, is, to be understood in the first clause; then the whole verse would run thus,—

This *is* a wicked people,
Who refuse to hear my words,
Who walk in the resolutions of their own heart,
And walk after foreign gods,

hidden in a hole and found putrified: but now the cause is expressed why God had resolved to treat them with so much severity. He then says that he would be an avenger, because the Jews had refused to obey his voice, and preferred their own inventions in *walking after the hardness*, or the wickedness *of their own heart.* We hence see that the cause of this calamity was, that the people had rejected the teaching of the prophets. This indeed was far more grievous than if they had fallen away through mistake or ignorance, as we often see that men go miserably astray when the teaching of the truth is taken away. But when God shews the way, and prescribes what is right, when by his servants he exhorts his people, it is an inexcusable hardness if men repudiate such a kindness. But as this subject has been elsewhere largely treated, I shall only touch on it now briefly.

We see then that God threatens his people with extreme calamity, because they would not bear to be taught by his prophets. Then he adds, that they had *walked after the wickedness of their own heart*, and had *walked after foreign gods.* He in the first place complains that they had been so refractory as to prefer to obey their own impious inclinations than to be ruled by good and salutary counsels. But it was necessary to specify their crime; for had the Prophet only spoken of their hardness, they might have had their objections ready at hand; but when he said that they had walked after foreign gods, there was no longer any room for evasion. The word to walk has a reference to a way. This metaphor has indeed a relation to something else; for men are not wont to take a course without going somewhere: we must therefore have some end in view when we walk along any way. Now, there is to be understood here a contrast, that the people despised the way pointed out to them by God, and that they had preferred to follow their own errors. God was ready to guide the Jews by his own law; but they

To serve them and to bow down to them;
And they shall be as this girdle,
Which will not be good for anything.

On "the resolutions," see vol. i. p. 187. "For anything," the כל here evidently means "anything," as it means in some other places "any," or any one.—*Ed.*

chose rather, as I have said, to abandon themselves to their own errors, as it were designedly.

He says, that they had walked after alien gods, *that they might serve them and prostrate themselves before them;* for such is the meaning of the last verb. The Prophet no doubt repeats the same thing, for to serve is not only to obey, but also to worship. And hence is refuted that folly of the Papists, who imagine that worship (*duliam*) is not inconsistent with true religion; for they say that service (*latriam*) is due only to God, but that worship may be given to angels, to statues, or to dead men, as though God, forsooth! in condemning superstitions, did not use the word עבד, *obed*, to serve. It hence follows that it is extremely ridiculous to devise two sorts of worship, one peculiar to God, and another common to angels as well as to men and dead idols. We now understand the import of this verse: the Prophet draws this conclusion, that the Jews would become like a useless or a putrified belt. It afterwards follows—

11. For as the girdle cleaveth to the loins of a man, so have I caused to cleave unto me the whole house of Israel, and the whole house of Judah, saith the Lord; that they might be unto me for a people, and for a name, and for a praise, and for a glory: but they would not hear.

11. Quia sicut adhæret (*vel*, conjunctus est) baltheus renibus viri, sic conjunxeram (*vel*, conjunxi) mihi totam domum Israel, et totam domum Jehudah, dicit Jehova, ut esset mihi in populum et in nomen et in laudem et in decus; et non audierunt.

He confirms what we noticed yesterday,—that the Jews entertained a foolish confidence, and promised themselves perpetual happiness, because God had chosen them as his people. This indeed would have been a perpetual glory to them, had they not violated their pledged faith; but their defection rendered void God's covenant as far as they were concerned: for though God never suffered his faithfulness to fail, however false and perfidious they were, yet the adoption from which they had departed availed them nothing. But as they thought it an unalienable defence, the Prophet again repeats that they had been indeed adorned with singular gifts, but that, as they had not remained faithful, they would be deprived of them.

He indeed says, by way of concession, *As a belt cleaves to the loins of man, so also have I joined to myself the house of*

Israel; for given to them is what they claimed. But at the same time, he reminds them that they only swelled with wind; for the less tolerable was their impiety, because they were so ungrateful to God. What, indeed, could have been more base or less excusable, than when those whom God had favoured with so much honour rejected his bounty? Jeremiah then concedes to them what they proudly boasted of; but he retorts it on their own heads, and shews how they deserved a heavier judgment, as they had despised so many of God's blessings.

We said yesterday that the people is elsewhere compared to a crown and a diadem, as though God had declared that nothing was more precious to him than the children of Abraham. But the same thing is now expressed in other words,—that he had prepared them for himself as a girdle, that they *might be his people.* This was indeed a great dignity; but what follows exceeds it,—that they might be to me a name, that is, that I might be celebrated by them; for it was his will to be called the God of Israel. What likeness there is between God and men! And yet, as though descending from his celestial glory, he united to himself the seed of Abraham, that he might also bind them to himself. The election of God was therefore like a bond of mutual union, so that he might not be separated from his people. Hence he says that they had been thus joined to him, that they might be for a *name,* and also *for a praise and glory.*[1] Though these words are nearly of the same meaning, yet no doubt they are put together for the sake of amplification. God, therefore, intended to exaggerate more fully the sin of the people, by saying that he had done so much for them, in order that he might be celebrated by them, and that his praise and his glory might dwell among them.

He at last adds, *They have not heard.* Had God only commanded what he might have justly required, not to obey his authority would have been an inexcusable wickedness in

[1] "Name" means here renown; "praise," celebrity or commendation; and "glory," ornament, decoration, or beauty. The three words are found together, though not in exactly the same order, in Deut. xxvi. 19. There the order is, praise, name, and honour, which is rendered here "glory." See Isaiah xliii. 21; lxi. 11; lxiii. 12.—*Ed.*

the people; but as he had so freely offered himself and all other things to them, what a base and detestable ingratitude it was in them to reject blessings so many and so valuable? We hence see that the mouths of the Jews are here completely closed, so that they could not expostulate with God, and complain that he was too rigid, for they had in an extreme degree provoked his wrath, having not only rejected his yoke, but also refused his offered favours. It follows—

12. Therefore thou shalt speak unto them this word, Thus saith the Lord God of Israel, Every bottle shall be filled with wine; and they shall say unto thee, Do we not certainly know that every bottle shall be filled with wine?

13. Then shalt thou say unto them, Thus saith the Lord, Behold, I will fill all the inhabitants of this land, even the kings that sit upon David's throne, and the priests, and the prophets, and all the inhabitants of Jerusalem, with drunkenness.

14. And I will dash them one against another, even the fathers and the sons together, saith the Lord: I will not pity, nor spare, nor have mercy, but destroy them.

12. Dices etiam illis (*hoc est*, annuntiabis) hunc sermonem, Sic dicit Jehova, Deus Israel, Omnis lagena (*alii vertunt*, utrem, *sed hoc loco parum interest*, omnis *ergo* lagena) implebitur vino: et dicent tibi, An non sciendo scimus (*hoc est*, An nesciendo non scimus) quòd omnis lagena implebitur vino?

13. Tunc dices illis, Sic dicit Jehova, Ecce ego implens (*vel*, impleo) omnes habitatores terræ hujus, et omnes reges qui sedent pro Davide super solium ejus, et sacerdotes et prophetas, et omnes incolas Jerosolymæ ebrietate.

14. Et collidam eos (*alii vertunt*, dispergam; *propriè significat violenter disjicere; hic* aptè reddetur collidere; collidam *ergo*) quenque ad fratrem suum et patres et filios simul, dicit Jehova; non parcam et non ero propitius, (*idem significant*, sunt synonyma,) et non miserabor à perdendo (*hoc est*, quin perdam) ipsos.

The Prophet denounces here by another similitude the vengeance of God, for he says that all would be *filled with drunkenness:* but he is bidden at first simply to set before them the metaphor, *Every bottle*, or flagon, he says, *shall be filled with wine.* The word נבל, *nubel*, means a bladder; but the word bottle is more suitable here.[1] Bladders were wont in those countries to be filled with water and with wine, as the custom is still in the east; as we see at this day that oil is put in bladders and thus carried, so

[1] It is not true that the word ever means a bladder, though so rendered by the *Septuagint* and the *Targum.* The *Vulgate* has "laguncula—a little flagon," and *Syriac* "dolium,—a tub." It means a jug or jar. *Blayney* has "vessel."—*Ed.*

bladders are commonly used there to carry water and wine; but as it is added, *I will dash them against one another*, it is better to use the word bottles, or flagons.

This general statement might have appeared to be of no weight; for what instruction does this contain, "Every bottle shall be filled with wine?" It is like what one might say,—that a tankard is made to carry wine, and that bowls are made for drinking: this is well known, even to children. And then it might have been said that this was unworthy of a prophet. "Eh! what dost thou say? Thou sayest that bottles are the receptacles of wine, even as a hat is made to cover the head, or clothes to keep off the cold; but thou seemest to mock us with childish trifles." We also find that the Prophet's address was thus objected to, for they contemptuously and proudly answered, "What! do we not know that bottles are prepared for the purpose of preserving wine? But what dost thou mean? Thou boastest of the inspiration of the Holy Spirit: how strange is this? Thou art like an angel come down from heaven; thou pretendest the name of God, and professest to have the authority of a prophet; now, what does this mean, that bottles are filled with wine?" But it was God's particular object thus to rouse the people, who were asleep in their delusions, and who were also by no means attentive to spiritual instruction. It was then his purpose to shew, by the most trifling, and as it were by frivolous things, that they were not possessed of so much clear-sightedness as to perceive even that which was most evident. They indeed all knew that bottles were made for wine; but they did not understand that they were the bottles, or were like bottles. We have indeed said that they were inflated with so much arrogance that they seemed like hard rocks; and hence was their contempt of all threatenings, because they did not consider what they were. The Prophet then says that they were like bottles; though God had indeed chosen them for an excellent use, yet, forgetful of their frailty, they had marred their own excellency, so that they were no longer of any use, except that God would inebriate them with giddiness and also with calamities.

We hence see why God had commanded a general truth

to be here announced which was received with indifference and contempt; it was, that an opportunity might be given to the Prophet to touch to the quick those stupid men to whom their own state was wholly unknown. It had been said that they were like mountains, because they had as their foundation the free election of God; but as they had in them no firmness and no constancy of faith, but had decayed, their glory had as it were melted away; and though they still retained an outward appearance, yet they were like brittle vessels; and so their fragility is here better expressed by the Prophet than if, in a plain sentence, he had said, "As a bottle is filled with wine, so will the Lord fill you with drunkenness." Had he thus spoken, there would not have been so much force in the prediction; but when they answered with disdain, "This is known even to children," they were then told what more sensibly touched them,—that they were like bottles.[1]

It may now be asked, What was this drunkenness which the Prophet announces? It may be understood in two ways,—either that God would give them up to a reprobate mind,—or that he would make them drunk with evils and calamities; for when God deprives men of a right mind, it is to prepare them for extreme vengeance. But the Prophet seems to have something further in view,—that this people would be given up to the most grievous evils, which would wholly fill them with amazement. Yet it appears from the context that the former evil is intended here; for he says, *I will dash them one against another, every one against his brother, even the fathers and sons together;* and thus they were all to be broken as it were in pieces. God then not only points out the calamity which was nigh the Jews, but also the manner of it; that is, that every one would draw his own brethren to ruin, as though they inflicted wounds on one another. But God says first generally, *I will fill all*

[1] With regard to this comparison, *Gataker* says, "A type taken from what they much loved, liked, and looked after; for they loved and looked after the *flagons of wine,* Hosea iii. 1; and those prophets best pleased them who prophesied of *wine and strong drink,* Micah ii. 11. God therefore sendeth his prophet to them with a prophecy of *wine,* but of other wine than they expected."

the inhabitants of the land with drunkenness, and then he explains the effect such as I have stated.

But he afterwards speaks of the whole people, including the *kings, priests,* and *prophets,* so that he excepts no order of men, however honourable; and this express mention of different orders was altogether necessary, for kings thought that they ought not to have been blended with the common people. The priests also regarded themselves as sacred, and a similar pride possessed the false prophets. But Jeremiah includes them all, without exception, in the same bundle, as though he had said,—"The majesty of kings shall not deliver them from God's judgment, nor shall the priests be safe on account of their dignity, nor shall it avail the false prophets to boast of that noble and illustrious office which they discharge." This prediction was no doubt regarded as very unjust; for we know with what high commendations God had spoken of the kingdom of David. As to the priesthood, we also know that it was a type of the priesthood of Christ, and also that the whole tribe of Levi was counted sacred to God. It could not therefore be but that Jeremiah must have greatly exasperated the minds of all by thus threatening kings as well as priests.

But we hence gather,—that there is nothing so high and so illustrious on earth, which ought not to be made to submit, when the power and glory of God, and the authority of celestial truth, are to be vindicated. Whatever then is precious and excellent in the world must come to nothing, if it derogates even in the least degree from the glory of God or from the authority of his truth: and yet kings and priests dared to oppose the word of God. No wonder then, that the Prophet should thrust them down from their elevations and compare them to bottles: he thus treads under foot that frail glory by which they sought to obscure God himself. And as the name of David was, as it were, sacred among that people, in order to shake off this vain confidence, the Prophet says,—"Though kings sit on the throne of David and be his successors and posterity, yet God will not spare them."[1]

[1] The clause, literally rendered, would convey this meaning,—
And the kings who sit for David on his throne.

And hence also it appears how foolishly the Papal clergy at this day bring forward against us their privileges and their dignity. Doubtless, whatever these unprincipled men may claim for themselves, they cannot yet make themselves equal to the Levitical priests: and yet we see that it availed them nothing, that God had set them apart for himself, because they had abused their power. There is, therefore, no reason for the Pope and his clergy, the very filth of the world, to be at this day so proud. We now perceive the design of the words, when mention is made of kings, priests, and prophets.

It must, however, be observed, that he does not speak here of faithful prophets, but of those who wore the mask, while yet they brought nothing but chaff instead of wheat, as we shall hereafter see. He then uses the word prophets in an improper sense, for he applies it to false teachers: as we do at this day, when we speak of those savages who boast that they are bishops and prelates and governors: we indeed concede to them these titles, but it does not follow that they justly deserve to be counted bishops, though they are so called. In the same way then does Jeremiah speak here of those who were called prophets, who yet were wholly unworthy of the office.

He then speaks of the collision to which we have referred, —I will cause them to *tear* or break *one another* in pieces. Some render the word "scatter;" but scattering does by no means comport with the words, *every one against his brother*, &c.[1] We hence see that the meaning is much more suitable

"For David," that is, as his representatives. "In David's stead," is the rendering of *Gataker* and *Blayney*. The word "even" before "the kings" in our version, is improper; for what follows is not a specification of what is gone before, as "the inhabitants of Jerusalem," at the end of the verse, is in contrast with "all the inhabitants of this land," that is, the people of the country.—*Ed.*

[1] The word seems to mean shattering or breaking in pieces, and in a secondary sense, scattering, as the effect. The early versions give the latter meaning, scattering, but, as *Calvin* says, inconsistently with the rest of the clause. The *Targum* gives in effect the first sense, "I will cause them to rush, each on his brother." The word "dash" is the most suitable, or dash to pieces,—

> And I will dash them to pieces, each against his brother,
> Both the fathers and the sons together, saith Jehovah.

The allusion is to the bottles: they would be broken like brittle vessels, when thrown one against another.—*Ed.*

when we render the words, *I will dash them, every one against his brother*, and then, *even the fathers and the sons together;* so that they might tear one another by a mutual conflict. And hence, as I have said, Jeremiah not only foretells the destruction of the people, but also points out the manner of it; for they would become so void of common prudence, that they would wilfully destroy one another, as though they were given up to mutual slaughter. They gloried, we know, in their number, but the Prophet shews that this would be no protection to them, but, on the contrary, the cause of their ruin; for the Lord would so blind them, that they would fight with one another, and thus perish without any foreign enemy.

He then adds, *I will not spare, I will not spare,*[1] *I will not have mercy.* He repeats three times that he would not be propitious to them. It would have been sufficient to declare this once, were they so teachable and attentive as really to consider the threatenings announced to them; but being so torpid as they were, it was necessary to repeat the same thing often; not as though there was anything ambiguous or obscure in the message itself, but because hardly any vehemence was sufficient to rouse hearts so obstinate. We hence see why the Prophet repeated the same thing so often. He, however, does not employ words uselessly: whenever God repeats the promises of his favour, he does not utter words heedlessly and without reason; but since he sees that there is in us so much dulness, that one promise is not sufficient, he confirms it by repetitions; so also when he sees that men, owing to their stupidity, cannot be moved nor terrified by his threatenings, he repeats them, that they may have more weight. He in short declares, that it was all

[1] The verbs are different, and so *Calvin* renders them in the text; but not here. There is no unanimity in the versions as to these verbs and the one which follows. The first means to be tender so as to relent; the second, to spare so as not to inflict punishment, to connive; and the third, to feel pity or compassion. They may be rendered thus,—

I will not relent, nor will I spare;
Nor will I pity, so as not to destroy them.

The two lines announce the same thing, only the last is stronger and more specific. Pitying or commiserating is stronger than relenting, and not destroying describes the act, while sparing is a general term.—*Ed.*

over with that people, so that he does not now call the wicked and the rebellious to repentance, but speaks to them as to men past remedy. This is the meaning.

And he adds, *Until I shall consume them.*[1] This refers to the whole body of the people. God, in the meantime, still preserved, in a wonderful manner and by hidden means, a remnant, as it has appeared elsewhere: but yet God took that vengeance, which is here denounced on the people as a body; for it was as it were a general death, when they were all driven into exile and everywhere scattered. Now as the Lord in so great a ruin never forgot his covenant, but some seed still remained safe and secure; so what is said here, *I will not have mercy until I shall consume them,* is not inconsistent with the promise of mercy elsewhere given, when he declares that he is long-suffering and plenteous in mercy. (Num. xiv. 18; Psalm ciii. 8.) Though God then destroyed his people in so dreadful a manner, yet he did not divest himself of his own nature, nor cast away his mercy; but he executed his judgments on the reprobate in a way so wonderful, that he yet lost nothing of his eternal mercy and remained still faithful as to his election. It follows—

15. Hear ye, and give ear; be not proud: for the Lord hath spoken.

16. Give glory to the Lord your God, before he cause darkness, and before your feet stumble upon the dark mountains, and, while ye look for light, he turn it into the shadow of death, *and* make *it* gross darkness.

15. Audite et auscultate; ne elevemini, quia Jehova loquutus est.

16. Date Jehovæ Deo vestro gloriam priusquam obtenebrescere faciat, et priusquam offendant pedes vestri ad montes tenebrarum, speretisque lucem, et ponat in umbram mortis et in caliginem.

The Prophet shews here more fully what we have stated, —that so refractory was the temper of those with whom he had to do, that it was necessary to use various means to subdue them. And it was not in vain that he added this

[1] The sentence literally is, "From consuming," or destroying, "them." The preposition מ, *mem,* here has the force of a negative. It is a sort of an elliptic phrase, which, though understood in the original, yet requires a supplement in a translation,—"I will not pity, *so as to abstain* from consuming them." But a literal rendering in Welsh would be understood,—

Ac ni resynav rhag eu difetha.

The preposition "rhag," which ordinarily means *from,* signifies here *from not,* which is exactly the Hebrew.—*Ed.*

exhortation, which manifests indignation; nor was it without displeasure that he required a hearing, *Hear ye, and give ear; be not lifted up, for the Lord is he who speaks.* Then we may hence gather, either that Jeremiah was derided, or that his words were disregarded by the Jews; for this is intimated by the words, *For Jehovah has spoken;*[1] for were they of themselves persuaded, that he announced what God had commanded him, these words would have been used to no purpose. But we shall elsewhere see, that he was deemed an impostor, and that he was assailed by many reproofs and curses.

He therefore defends here his calling from their calumnies and reproaches, when he says, that God had spoken; for by these words he affirms that he brought nothing of his own, but spoke as it were from the mouth of God, or, which is the same thing, that he was the instrument of the Holy Spirit; and he said this, in order that they might know that they in vain contended with him, as the contest was between them and God. And on this account he says, *Hear ye, and give ear;* for he saw that they were deaf and torpid, and had need of many stimulants. He at the same time points out the cause and the source of evil by saying, *Be ye not lifted up.*[2] The cause then of their contumacy was pride, for they dared to quarrel with God. So also the main principle of obedience is humility, that is, when men acknowledge that they are nothing and ascribe to God what is due to him.

PRAYER.

Grant, Almighty God, that as we are by nature frail vessels, and our frailty is such that we of ourselves melt away, and when we become stronger we cannot stand by our own power,—O grant, that being supported by thy power, we may indeed rejoice in the perpetuity of our salvation, not indeed relying on any earthly

[1] This may be rendered more consistently with the context, "For Jehovah speaks," or *is* speaking: for the reference evidently is to what was now addressed to them.—*Ed.*

[2] So all the versions and the *Targum*. *Gataker* renders it, "Be ye not haughty," which is no doubt the meaning. The verb means to be high, lofty, or elevated, and so to be elevated as to be haughty, proud. See Isaiah iii. 16. Men, creatures of the dust, too high and elevated to hear what God said to them! This is the case still. What a monstrous thing!—*Ed.*

protection, but because thou hast been pleased to choose us as thy people: and may we at the same time so pursue the course of our life, that we may not by our perfidy exclude thy grace from us, but give place to thee, that we may be more and more enriched by those gifts which pertain to the hope of a future life, until we shall at length come to that full and perfect happiness, in thy celestial kingdom, which is laid up for us by Christ our Lord.—Amen.

Lecture Fifty-Third.

16. Give glory to the Lord your God, before he cause darkness, and before your feet stumble upon the dark mountains, and, while ye look for light, he turn it into the shadow of death, *and* make *it* gross darkness.

16. Date Jehovæ Deo vestro gloriam priusquam obtenebrescere faciat (*tenebras immittat,*) et priusquam offendant pedes vestri ad montes tenebrarum, et speretis lucem, et ponat in umbram mortis, ponat in caliginem.

JEREMIAH pursues the subject, which we began to explain yesterday, for he saw that the Jews were but little moved by what he taught them. He bid them to regard what he said as coming from God, and told them that they could by no means succeed by their pride. For the same purpose he now adds, *Give glory to Jehovah your God.* To give glory to God is elsewhere taken for confessing the truth in his name; for when Joshua abjured Achan, he used these words, "Give glory to God, my son;" that is, As I have set God before you as a judge, beware lest you should think that if you lie you can escape his judgment. (Josh. vii. 19.) But here, to give glory to God, is the same as to ascribe to him what properly belongs to him, or to acknowledge his power so as to be submissive to his word: for if we deny faith to the prophets, we rob God of his glory, as we thus disown his power, and, as far as we can, diminish his glory. How indeed can we ascribe glory to God except by acknowledging him to be the fountain of all wisdom, justice, and power, and especially by trembling at his sacred word? Whosoever then does not fear and reverence God, whosoever does not believe his word, he robs him of his glory. We hence see that all the unbelieving, though they may testify the contrary by their mouths, are yet in reality enemies to God's glory and deprive him of it.

This subject ought to be carefully noticed; for all ought to dread such a sacrilege as this, and yet there is no one who takes sufficient heed in this respect. We then see what instruction this expression conveys; it is as though he had said, that the Jews had hitherto acted contemptuously towards God, for they trembled not before him, as they had no faith in his word: and that it was now time for him to set God before them as their Judge, and also for them to know that they ought to have believed whatever God declared to them by his servants.

He says, *Before he introduces darkness.* Others render it by a single word, " Before it grows dark," but as the verb is in Hiphil, it ought to be taken in a causative sense. Some consider the word sun to be understood, but without reason; for the sun is not said to send darkness by its setting. But the Prophet removes all ambiguity by the words which immediately follow in the second clause, *And turn light to the shadow of death,* and *turn* it *to thick darkness.* In these words the Prophet no doubt refers to God, so that the word God, used at the beginning of the verse, is to be understood here.[1]

Before God, he then says, *sends darkness, and before your feet stumble on the mountains of obscurity.* The word נשף, *neshiph,* means the evening and the twilight; it means also the obscure light before the rising of the sun; but it is often taken for the whole night. We can render the words, " the mountains of density." But the word, no doubt, means here obscurity. Some think that mountains are to be here taken metaphorically for Egypt; for the Jews were wont to flee there in their troubles. But there are safer recesses on mountains than on the plains; yet I know not whether this sense will be very suitable here. On the contrary, I prefer to regard the words as preceded by כ, *caph,* a particle of likeness, which is often understood, and the meaning would be thus suitable, " Before your feet stumble as on obscure

[1] All the versions and the *Targum* render the first verb intransitively, " Before it grows dark:" but *Montanus, Pagninus, Piscator* and *Junius and Tremellius,* give it a transitive meaning, as *Calvin* does, and no doubt correctly, for it is in Hiphil, " Before he causes *or* brings darkness;" or it may be rendered, " Before he makes it dark." *Blayney* follows the early versions, but *Gataker, Lowth,* and *Venema,* the latter versions; and the conclusion of the verse confirms, as *Calvin* says, this meaning.—*Ed.*

mountains:" for there is more light on level grounds than on mountains, for darkness often fills narrow passes: the sun cannot penetrate there; and also the evening does not come on so soon on plains as in the recesses of mountains; for the Prophet refers not to the summits but to the narrow valleys, which receive not the oblique rays of the sun but for a few hours. But what if we give this rendering? "Before your feet stumble at the mountains of darkness;" for אל, *al*, has the meaning of *at*,[1] as though the Prophet had said, that the darkness would be so thick that they could not discern mountains opposite them. As in the twilight or in darkness a traveller stumbles at the smallest stones, so also, when the darkness is very thick, even mountains are not perceived. It thus often happens that a person stumbles at mountains, and finds by his feet and his hands a stumblingblock before he perceives it by his eyes. As to myself, I wholly think that this is the right explanation, *Before* then *your feet stumble at the dark mountains.*

He afterwards adds, *When ye hope for light, he turns it to the shadow of death.* The word צלמות, *tsalmut*, as I have said elsewhere, is thought by grammarians to be composed of צל, *tsal*, "shadow," and of מות, *mut*, which means "death;" and they render it "fatal darkness." Then what he says is, "Before God turns light to darkness, turns it to thick darkness, give to him his glory." And hence we perceive

[1] This is a mistake, the preposition is על, which means *on*, *upon*, &c. Our version of this sentence is in accordance with the early versions: it is indeed literally the *Septuagint* and the *Vulgate*. Yet it is not the original. The verb is in Hithpael, and means to strike or smite together, or against one another. The literal rendering is the following,—

Before your feet smite one against the other,
On the mountains of gloominess (*i.e.* gloomy mountains.)

It is true the word for "gloominess" means sometimes the twilight; but here it seems to signify a state somewhat dark or obscure. To wander and to stumble on gloomy mountains betokens the miserable condition of fugitives: and this is what is meant here. See chap. xvi. 16; Ezekiel vii. 16. Then what follows might be thus rendered,—

When ye shall look anxiously for light,
Then will he make it the shadow of death,
He will turn it to thick darkness.

When two *vaus* occur in a sentence, they may often be rendered *when* and *then.* The change proposed as to the last verb is not at all necessary. Literally it is, "He will set it (to be) for thick darkness."—*Ed.*

more clearly what I have already referred to, that the verb יחשיך, *icheshik,* " will cause darkness," ought to be applied to God.

But the sum of the whole is this, that they could anticipate God's judgment by admitting him in time as their Judge, and also by receiving his word with more reverence than they had previously done. At the same time he declares that their hope was vain if they promised themselves light. But we must know that light is here to be taken metaphorically, as in many other places, and darkness also, its opposite, is to be so taken. Darkness means adversities, and light, peace and prosperity. The Prophet then says that the Jews deceived themselves, if they thought that their happiness would be perpetual, if they despised God and his prophets; and why? because it would have been the same as to disarm or to deprive him of his power, as though he was not the Judge of the world. He in short shews, that there was nigh at hand a most dreadful vengeance, except the Jews in time anticipated it and submitted themselves to God. It now follows—

17. But if ye will not hear it, my soul shall weep in secret places for *your* pride; and mine eye shall weep sore, and run down with tears, because the Lord's flock is carried away captive.

17. Quod si non audieritis hoc, in arcanis (*hoc est,* in secreto) lugebit anima mea à facie superbia (*hoc est,* propter superbiam,) et lachrymando lachrymabitur, et descendet oculus meus in lachrymas (*de hac locutione vidimus cap.* 9; diffluet *ergo* oculus meus in lachrymas; *ad verbum,* et descendet oculus meus lachryma;) quoniam abductus est (captus est) grex Jehovæ.

The Prophet had indirectly threatened them; but yet there was some hope of pardon, provided the Jews anticipated God's judgment in time and humbled themselves before him. He now declares more clearly that a most certain destruction was nigh at hand, *If ye will not hear,* he says, *weep will my soul in secret.* But much weight is in what the Prophet intimates, that he would cease to address them, as though he had said, " I have not hitherto left off to exhort you, for God has so commanded me; but there will be no remedy, if ye as usual harden yourselves against what I teach you. There remains then nothing now for me, except to hide myself in some secret place and there to mourn; for my prophetic office among you is at an end, as ye are unworthy of such a favour from God."

He does not state simply, *If ye will not hear*, but he adds a pronoun, this, *If ye will not hear this*, or it: for the Jews might have raised an objection and said, that they were not disobedient to God, and had prophets among them, as it appeared yesterday; for there were those who deceived them by their flatteries. The Prophet then does not speak indistinctly, for that would have had no effect; but he expressly declares that they were to hear what he had said in the last verse: "Except then," he says, "ye give glory to God, I will leave you or bid you farewell, and will hide myself in some corner, and there bewail your miseries." When the Prophet said that nothing remained for him but weeping, he intimated that it was all over with them, and that their salvation was hopeless. The sum of the whole is, that they were not to be always favoured with that which they were now despising, that is, to be warned by God's servants; for if they continued to despise all the prophets, God would withdraw such a favour from them.

The Prophet at the same time shews with what feelings he exercised his prophetic office; for though he knew that he was to perform the part of an herald, and boldly to denounce on the Jews the calamity which we have observed; he yet ever felt so much pity in his soul, that he bewailed that perverseness which would prove their ruin. The Prophet then connected the two feelings together, so that with a bold and intrepid spirit he denounced vengeance on the Jews, and at the same time he felt commiseration and sympathy.

He then mentions the cause, *For taken captive is the flock of Jehovah.* Jeremiah might have had indeed a regard also for his own blood. When, therefore, he saw the nation from which he himself sprung miserably perishing, he could not but mourn for their ruin: but he had an especial regard to the favour of God, as was the case also with Paul, (Rom. ix. 2, 4, 5,) for though he refers to his descent from the Israelites, and assigns this as a reason why he wished to be an anathema from Christ on their account, there were yet other reasons why he spoke highly of them; for he afterwards adds, that the covenant was theirs, that they derived their origin from the fathers, that from them Christ came according to the flesh, who is God, blessed for ever. Paul then so honoured and valued the benefits with which the Jews were adorned, that he wished as it were to die for their salvation, and even wished to be an anathema from Christ. There is not the least doubt but Jeremiah for a similar reason adds now, that he would seek retirement or some hidden place where he might bewail the destruction of his people, for it was the *flock of Jehovah.*[1] We hence see that it was God's covenant that made him to shed tears, for he saw that in a manner it failed through the fault of the people. It follows—

18. Say unto the king, and to the queen, Humble yourselves, sit down: for your principalities shall come down, *even* the crown of your glory.	18. Dic regi et dominæ, Humiliamini (descendite) sedete (*hoc est,* jacete;) quia descendet à capitibus vestris corona decoris vestri (*alii vertunt,* descendet altitudines vestræ, *pro* altitudo vestra; *et appositivè legunt quod sequitur,* corona decoris vestri.)

The Prophet is here bidden to address his discourse directly to King Jehoiakim and his mother; for the term lady is not to be taken for the queen, the wife of Jehoiakim, but for his mother, who was then his associate in the kingdom, and possessed great authority.[2] And there is no doubt

[1] The whole verse may be thus rendered,—

But if ye will not hear, weep in secret places
Will my soul, on account of your haughtiness;
Yea, bewailing it will bewail,
And pour down will mine eye the tear,
When taken captive is the flock of Jehovah.

The word for "haughtiness," גוה, is rendered "insolence" by the *Septuagint* and *Arabic;* "pride" by the *Vulgate,* and "affliction" by the *Syriac.* The word is commonly derived from גאה, to swell, to be high, to be elated. It is found in this sense in two other places, Job xxxiii. 17, and Daniel iv. 37; and in a good sense, elevation, in Job xxii. 29. It seems to be a contraction, in full גאוה. See Psalm xxxvi. 12; Prov. xxix. 23. This being the meaning of the word, the view of *Calvin* cannot be admitted. There is an evident reference to what is said in verse 15, "Be ye not lifted up," or, "be ye not haughty." The cause of his weeping was their haughtiness in not hearing God speaking to them.—*Ed.*

[2] So *Gataker* and *Lowth;* and they refer to 2 Kings xxiv. 12, and to ch. xxii. 26. From this circumstance it is gathered that this prophecy was delivered in the short reign of that king, which lasted only three months.

The word "queen," in our version, is rendered "mistress *or* lady—do-but that God thus intended to rouse more fully the community in general; that is, by shewing that he would not spare, no, not the king nor the queen. But we may hence also learn what has already been observed, that the truth announced by the prophets is superior to all the greatness of the world. For it was said before to Jeremiah, "Reprove mountains and rebuke hills;"[1] and still farther, "Behold, I have set thee over kingdoms and nations, to pull down and to pluck up," &c., (ch. i. 10.) This ought to be carefully noticed; for kings and those who are eminent in the world, think that they are not only, by a singular privilege, exempt from all laws, but also free from every obligation to observe modesty and to avoid shame. Hence it is, that they from their elevation despise God and his prophets. Here God shews, that he supplied the prophets with his word for this end,—that they might close their eyes to all the splendour of the world, and shew no respect of persons, but pull down every height, and bring to order everything that is elevated in this world. Paul also teaches us, that ministers of the gospel are endued with this power; "Given to us," he says, "is power against every height that exalteth itself against Christ." (2 Cor. x. 5.)

And hence we must observe, that all who are chosen to the office of teaching, cannot faithfully discharge their duty except they boldly, and with intrepid spirit, dare to reprove both kings and queens; for the word of God is not to be restricted to the common people or men in humble life, but it subjects to itself all, from the least to the greatest. This prophecy was no doubt very bitter to the king as well as to the common people; but it behoved Jeremiah to discharge faithfully his office; and this was also necessary, for the king Jehoiakim and his mother thought that they could not possibly be dethroned.

He therefore bids them to *descend* and *to lie down*; that

mina," by *Calvin*, but "potentates" by the *Septuagint*, *Syriac*, and *Arabic*; "governess—dominatrix," by the *Vulgate*; and "queen" by the *Targum*. The word means governess; it is rendered "mistress" in Gen. xvi. 4, 8; "lady" in Is. xlvii. 5, 7; and "queen" in 2 Kings x. 13.—*Ed.*

[1] There is an oversight here; the passage referred to is in Mic. vi. 1; nor is it a right view of it. See vol. iii. on the Minor Prophets, p. 328.—*Ed.*

is, he bids them to forget their ancient greatness. He does not simply exhort them to repent, but shews, that as they had been so refractory in their pride, the punishment of disgrace was nigh at hand, for the Lord would with a strong hand lay them prostrate. It is not then an exhortation that the Prophet gives; but he only foretells what they little thought of,—that they in vain flattered themselves, for the Lord would in a short time expose them to reproach by casting them down.

And this is evident from what is added, *For descend shall the crown of your honour;* that is, it shall be taken away from your highnesses, or from your eminencies, or from your heads; for the word ראשה, *rashe,* means sometimes the head.[1] But some think that it means here eminencies, and that "the magnificent crown" is put here in apposition.

I have omitted, if I mistake not, to notice one thing; that is, the pride mentioned by the Prophet; *except ye hear, weep will my soul in secret on account of pride.* Interpreters render it "your pride;" that is, the pride with which the Jews were filled; but I am inclined to take a different view, that the Prophet speaks here of the pride or the great power of those enemies whom the Jews then did not in any degree fear. "Since then," says the Prophet, "ye are so secure, I will retire and weep by myself, and my soul by mourning shall mourn, yea, my eye shall flow down with tears, on account of the pride of the enemies, who are now so much despised by you." Let us now proceed—

19. The cities of the south shall be shut up, and none shall open *them:* Judah shall be carried away	19. Urbes Austri clausæ sunt, et nemo qui aperiat; traductus est (*vel,* transmigravit) Jehudah totus, trans-

[1] All the early versions render the words, "Fallen from your head has the crown of your glory." Our version is that of *Montanus.* If מ be a formative, then the word, in every instance in which it occurs, means bolsters or pillows, things for the head to rest on. The word for head has commonly a masculine termination in the plural number; but here it is feminine. The most literal rendering is the following:—

For bring down from your heads will he the crown of your glory.

The latter words mean "your glorious crown," the expression being an Hebraism.

Our common version, as *Blayney* observes, violates grammar; for the gender of the verb ירד (which, the same author thinks, ought to be יורד, future in Hiphil) is masculine, while the noun made its nominative is feminine.—*Ed.*

captive all of it, it shall be wholly carried away captive.

latus est perfectè (perfectione, *hoc est*, in totum abductus est in captivitatem.)

By the *cities of the south*, almost all understand the cities of the tribe of Judah, whose portion was towards the south; and by the cities being shut up, they consider that what is meant is, that they would be forsaken; for they say, that cities are open when they are frequented. But I am constrained here also to take another view. I take the cities of the south to have been those of Egypt; for we know that the Jews looked there for a refuge, whenever they were attacked by the Assyrians or the Chaldeans. Since then they thought that Egypt would be to them a sort of an asylum, the Prophet declares that all these cities would be closed against them, and that there would be no one to open them; as though he had said, "The Lord will drive you out, and will prevent you to take refuge there."

He would doubtless have spoken more clearly had he meant the cities of Judah; and besides, as he was at Jerusalem, this way of speaking must have been ambiguous, and even improper; and we shall find him presently speaking of the Assyrians as being in the north. He now then warns them, that Egypt would be closed against them, though they at the same time expected that they would be safe there, and that an easily-borne exile was in their power. As then they foolishly trusted that they would be received by the Egyptians, the Prophet says, that the gates would be closed, and that there would be no one to open them. It then follows, *carried away wholly has been Judah, carried away completely;*[1] that is, "Ye shall all be led away into Assyria and

[1] The ancient versions render these last words of the verse in the same way with our version and that of *Calvin;* but the Hebrew, as *Blayney* remarks, is not rightly rendered, though he unnecessarily makes כלה a verb, and according to his construction it ought to be כלתה; and he does not satisfactorily account for the last word, שלומים. The literal version I regard to be the following:—

> The transmigration of Judah *has been* entire,—
> The transmigration of retributions.

The past time, as in the beginning of the verse, is to be used, though it is used for the future. The word שלומים, is never found in an adverbial sense; and indeed it is found only once elsewhere as here, in the plural number, Is. xxxiv. 8; but thrice in this sense in the singular number, Deut. xxxii. 35; Hos. ix. 7; Mic. vii. 3. The *Targum* favours this rendering, as it retains the idea of retribution.—*Ed.*

Babylon ;" which is the north country, according to what afterwards follows,—

20. Lift up your eyes, and behold them that come from the north: where *is* the flock *that* was given thee, thy beautiful flock ?

20. Levate oculos vestros, et aspicite venientes ab aquilone: ubi grex qui datus fuerat tibi ? oves decoris tui ?

We here see that Egypt and Chaldea are set in opposition, the one to the other; as though the Prophet had said, " Whenever anything is said to you about the Chaldeans, ye turn your eyes to Egypt, as though that would be a quiet residence for you ; but God will prevent you from having any escape there. Now *see,* see your enemies who are coming from another quarter, even from Chaldea. *Lift up* then your eyes." As they were so very intent on their present ease, he bids them to lift up their eyes, that they might see farther than they were wont to do.

He then says, *Where is the flock which had been given to thee ? and the sheep of thy glory ?* It is through pity that the Prophet thus speaks ; for he saw by the Spirit the whole land deserted, and in wonder he asks, " What does this mean, that the flock is scattered which had been given to thee ?" He addresses the people under the character of a woman, as he does often in other places.[1] In short, he confirms what he had said before,—that he would go to some secret place, if the people were not influenced by his doctrine, and that he would there by himself deplore their calamity ; but he employs other words, and at the same time intimates, that he alone had eyes to see, as others were blind, for God had even taken from them understanding and discernment. The Prophet then shews here that he saw the dreadful desolation that was soon to come ; and therefore as one astonished he asks, Where is the flock with which God had enriched the land ? and further he asks, Where are the sheep which possessed a magnificent honour or beauty ? It follows—

21. What wilt thou say when he shall punish thee ? (for thou hast taught them *to be* captains, *and*

21. Quid dices, cum visitaverit super te ? Et tu (*hoc est,* atqui tu) docuisti (*hoc est,* assuefecisti) illos super

[1] May not the queen regent, or governess, mentioned with the king in verse 18, be here meant ? Sovereigns are called shepherds, and hence "flock" and "sheep" are here mentioned.—*Ed.*

as chief over thee;) shall not sorrows take thee, as a woman in travail?

te duces in caput: annon dolores apprehendent te tanquam mulierem parturientem?

As the Prophet observed that the Jews were in no way moved, he addressed them still further, and set before them what seemed then incredible, even the calamity, from which they thought they were able easily to defend themselves by means of their auxiliaries.

He then adds, *What wilt thou then say?* For the false teachers made a clamour, and whenever Jeremiah began to speak, they violently assailed him, and the common people also wantonly barked at him. As then they thus petulantly resisted God and his truths, the Prophet intimates that the time would come when they should become mute through shame: *What wilt thou say then?* he says, "Ye are now very talkative, and God cannot obtain a hearing from you; but he will check your wantonness, when the enemy shall distress you." It is the same as though he had said, "It will not be the time then for your loquacity, for the Lord will constrain you to be silent."

Some refer to God what follows, *When he shall visit you;* but it ought on the contrary to be applied to the Chaldeans; for he immediately adds, *But thou hast accustomed them*, &c. There is indeed a change or an anomaly of number, but this is common in the prophets. When he uses the singular, the head of the army is referred to, but afterwards the whole forces are included. *What* then *wilt thou say*, when the enemy *shall visit thee?* He then adds, *But then*, &c.; that is, "If thou seekest to cast blame on others, when the Assyrians and the Chaldeans shall overwhelm thee, thou wilt attempt it in vain? for thou hast opened a passage for them, and *hast accustomed them to be thy leaders over thy head.*" For the Assyrians had a long time before been sent for by the Israelites; and the Jews also had formed confederacies with the Chaldeans against the Assyrians, before these monarchies were united. As then they had called them in as auxiliaries, they had accustomed them to rule, and, as it were, had set them over themselves. The case was similar to that of the Turks at this day, were they to pass over to these parts and exercise their authority; for it might be asked the French kings and their counsellors, "Whose fault it is that the Turks come to us so easily? It is because ye have prepared for them the way by sea, because ye have bribed them, and your ports have been opened to them; and yet they have wilfully exercised the greatest cruelty towards your subjects. All these things have proceeded from yourselves; ye are therefore the authors of all these evils." So also now the Prophet upbraids the Jews, because they had accustomed the Chaldeans to be their leaders; and as they had set them over their own heads, he says to them, that it was no wonder that they were now so troublesome and grievous to them.[1]

He afterwards says, *Shall not sorrows lay hold on thee as on a woman in travail?* By this comparison he intimates, that the Jews gained nothing by their vain hopes; for when they should say, peace and security, destruction, such as they by no means expected, would suddenly come upon them. This similitude we know often occurs, and it is a very apt one; for a woman with child may be very cheerful and quietly enjoying herself, and yet a sudden pain may seize her. So also it will be with the wicked; they cannot now bear to hear anything sad or alarming, and they drive from them every fear as far as possible; but the more they harden themselves, the heavier is God's vengence which follows them, and which will overtake them suddenly and unexpectedly. As then it was incredible to the Jews, that the Chaldeans would soon come to lay waste their land, he says to them, "Surely sorrows will take hold on you, though you look not for them. Though a woman with child thinks not of her coming pain, yet it comes suddenly and cannot be driven away; so you will gain nothing by heedlessly promising to yourselves continual peace and quietness." I cannot finish what follows to-day if I go on farther; I shall therefore put it off to the next Lecture.

[1] The best rendering of this clause is as follows:—

For thou hast taught them *to be* over the leaders in chief.

It is the feminine gender that is still used; and the queen or governess may be addressed as the representative of the ruling power in the land.—*Ed.*

PRAYER.

Grant, Almighty God, that as we are so slothful to hear thee, yea, inasmuch as our minds are taken up with so many vanities so that we deceive ourselves,—O grant, that thy Holy Spirit may so illuminate us, that we may not despise thy threatenings, but may learn to anticipate in time thy judgment, and thus obtain pardon; that being mindful of thy mercy, we may pursue the course of our calling, until we shall at length be received into that blessed rest, which has been obtained for us by thy only-begotten Son.—Amen.

Lecture Fifty-Fourth.

22. And if thou say in thine heart, Wherefore come these things upon me? For the greatness of thine iniquity are thy skirts discovered, *and* thy heels made bare.

22. Quod si dixeris in corde suo, cur (*vel,* ut quid) hæc mala acciderunt mihi (*occurrerunt mihi?*) in multitudine (*hoc est,* propter multitudinem) iniquitatis tuæ discoopertæ sunt fimbriæ tuæ, et nudati calces tui (*vel,* plantæ tuæ nudatæ sunt.)

The Prophet again declares that God's judgment would be just, which he had previously foretold; for hypocrites, we know, do not cease to quarrel with God, except they are often proved guilty; and it is always their object, where they cannot wholly excuse themselves, to extenuate in some measure their fault. The Prophet therefore here removes every pretence for evasion, and declares that they were wholly worthy of such a reward.

But his manner of speaking ought to be noticed, *If thou wilt say in thine heart,* &c. Hypocrites do not only claim for themselves righteousness before the world, but they also deceive themselves, and the devil so dementates them with a false persuasion, that they seek to be counted just before God. This then is what the Prophet sets forth when he says, *If thou wilt say in thine heart, Why have these evils happened to me?*[1] that is, if thou seekest by secret murmuring to contend with God, the answer is ready,—*Because of the multitude of thine iniquity, discovered are thy skirts, and thy*

[1] The verb is here in the singular, and is followed by a nominative in the plural; the very same anomaly exists in *Welsh.* The line would be literally the same in that language,—

Pam y digwyddodd i mi y pethau hyn?

But if "these things" preceded the verb, it would be in the plural.—*Ed.*

heels are denuded." The multitude of iniquity he calls that perverse wickedness which prevailed among the Jews; for they had not ceased for a long time to provoke the wrath of God. Had they only once sinned, or had been guilty of one kind of sin, there would have been some hope of pardon, at least God would not have executed a punishment so severe; but as there had been an uninterrupted course of sinning, the Prophet shews that it would not be right to spare them any longer.

As to the simile, it is a form of speaking often used by the prophets, that is, to denude the soles of the feet, and to discover the skirts. We know that men clothe themselves, not only to preserve them from cold, but that they also cover the body for the sake of modesty: there is therefore a twofold use of garments, the one occasioned by necessity, and the other by decency. As then clothes are partly made for this end—to cover what could not be decently shewn or left bare without shame, the prophets use this mode of speaking when they have in view to shew that one is exposed to public reproach.[1] It afterwards follows—

23. Can the Ethiopian change his skin, or the leopard his spots? *then* may ye also do good, that are accustomed to do evil.

23. An mutabit (*sic propriè vertitur*) Æthiops pellem suam, et pardus maculas suas (*aut*, varietates, *nam nomen hoc duplicatum deducitur à* חבר, *quod significat congregare, significat etiam livorem, accipitur vero hic pro maculis;*) etiam tu poteris ad benefaciendum, doctus ad malum?

God declares in this verse, that the people were so hardened in their wickedness, that there was no hope of their repentance. This is the sum of what is said. But it was a very bitter reproof for the Prophet to say that his own nation were past hope—that they had so entirely given themselves up to their vices that they were no longer healable.

[1] The three last lines are as follows:—

For the number of thine iniquity
Discovered have been thy skirts,
Violently stripped off have been thy heels.

"Skirts" here stand for the parts covered by them, and "heels" for the sandals which were worn. Both the *Septuagint* and the *Vulgate* mention the parts, and not skirts—"the hinder parts," "the uncomely parts," but they retain the word "heels." The metonomy exists, no doubt, as to both. The *Syriac* has "skirts" and "ankles." The *Targum* gives the meaning, "confusion" and "ignominy." The past time is used for the future. —*Ed.*

But he uses a comparison,—*Can the Ethiopian,*[1] he says, *change his skin?* Blackness is inherent in the skin of the Ethiopians, as it is well known. Were they then to wash themselves a hundred times daily, they could not put off their blackness. The same also must be said of leopards or panthers, and we know that these animals are besprinkled with spots. Such then is the spotted character of the leopard or panther,[2] that whatever might be done to him he would still retain his colour. We now then see what the Prophet means—that the Jews were so corrupted by long habit that they could not repent, for the devil had so enslaved them that they were not in their right mind; they no longer had any discernment, and could not discriminate between good and evil.

Learned men in our age do not wisely refer to this passage, when they seek to prove that there is no free-will in man; for it is not simply the nature of man that is spoken of here, but the habit that is contracted by long practice. Aristotle, a strong advocate of free will, confesses that it is not in man's power to do right, when he is so immersed in his own vices as to have lost a free choice, (7. *Lib. Ethicōn,*) and this also is what experience proves. We hence see that this passage is improperly adduced to prove a sentiment which is yet true, and fully confirmed by many passages of Scripture.

Jeremiah, then, does not here refer to man's nature as he is when he comes from the womb; but he condemns the Jews for contracting such a habit by long practice. As, then, they had hardened themselves in doing evil, he says that they could not repent, that wickedness had become inherent, or firmly fixed in their hearts, like the blackness

[1] The word in Hebrew is "Cushite;" and many learned men contend that the "Ethiopian" is not meant, though all the early versions so render it except the *Syriac,* which has "Indian." *Blayney* agrees with *Bochart* and others in thinking that the Cushites were the inhabitants of Arabia, on the borders of the Red Sea, and he refers in proof of this to 2 Chron. xxi. 16. The skin is not said here to be black, but it was no doubt of a particular colour, different from that of the Jews.—*Ed.*

[2] "Panther," πάρδαλις—pardus, is the rendering of the *Septuagint* and the other versions. The word rendered "spots," found only here, is translated "varieties" by the *Septuagint* and *Vulgate,* but "spots" by the *Syriac* and *Targum.*—*Ed.*

which is inherent in the skin of the Ethiopians, or the spots which belong to the leopards or panthers.

We may at the same time gather from this passage a useful doctrine—that men become so corrupt, by sinful habits and sinful indulgence, that the devil takes away from them every desire and care for acting rightly, so that, in a word, they become wholly irreclaimable, as we see to be the case with regard to bodily diseases; for a chronic disease, in most instances, so corrupts what is sound and healthy in the body, that it becomes by degrees incurable. When, therefore, the body is thus infected for a long time, there is no hope of a cure. Life may indeed be prolonged, but not without continual languor. Now, as to spiritual diseases it is also true, that when putridity has pervaded the inward parts, it is impossible for any one to repent. And yet it must be observed, that we do not speak here of the power of God, but only shew, that all those who harden themselves in their vices, as far as their power is concerned, are incurable, and past all remedy. Yet God can deliver, even from the lowest depths, such as have a hundred times past all recovery. But here, as I have already said, the Prophet does not refer to God's power, but only condemns his own nation, that they might not complain that God treated them with too much severity.

The meaning then is, that they ought not to have thought it strange that God left them no hope; for they became past recovery, through their own perverseness, as they could not adopt another course of life after having so long accustomed themselves to everything that was evil: *Wilt thou also,* he says, *be able to do good?* that is, wilt thou apply thy mind to what is just, *who hast been accustomed to evil,* or who hast hitherto learnt nothing but to do evil?[1] We now perceive

[1] Neither this sentence nor the preceding is put interrogatively in the *Septuagint*, the *Syriac*, and the *Vulgate*, but in this way,—"If the Ethiopian," &c.; "Even so can ye," &c. The *Arabic* and the *Targum* have both sentences in an interrogative form, and more consistently with the Hebrew. *Blayney* renders the first part interrogatively, as in our version, but not the second, and he gives a meaning to the second part which the original will not bear, and which is not countenanced by any of the versions. The most literal version is as follows,—

Can the Cushite change his skin,
Or the panther his spots?—

the design of the Prophet—that they unreasonably sought pardon of God, who had contracted such hardness by a long course of sinning that they were become incurable. It afterwards follows—

24. Therefore I will scatter them as the stubble that passeth away by the wind of the wilderness.	24. Et dispergam (*vel,* dissipabo) eos quasi stipulam transeuntem ad ventum deserti.

This is an inference which Jeremiah draws from the last verse. As long as there is any hope of repentance, there is also room for mercy; God often declares that he is long-suffering. Then the most wicked might object and say, that God is too rigid, because he waits not until they return to a sound mind. Now the Prophet had said that it was all over with the people: here therefore he meets the objection, and shews that extreme calamity was justly brought on them by God, because the Jews had obstinately hardened themselves in their vices and wickedness.

After having shewn, therefore, that corruption was inherent in them, as blackness in the skin of an Ethiopian, and as spots in panthers, he now comes to this conclusion—*I will scatter them as stubble which passes away by the wind of the desert.* This scattering denotes their exile; as though he had said, "I will banish them, that they may know that they are deprived of the inheritance in which they place their safety and their happiness." For the Jews gloried in this only—that they were God's people, because the Temple was built among them, and because they dwelt in the land promised to them. They then thought that God was in a manner tied to them, while they possessed that inheritance. Hence Jeremiah declares, that they would become like stubble carried away by the wind.

He mentions *the wind of the desert,* that is, the wind of the south, which was the most violent in that country. The south wind, as we know, was also pestilential; the air also was more disturbed by the south wind than by any other, for it raised storms and tempests. Therefore the Scripture,

Also ye, can ye do good,
Who have learned evil?

The future tense in Hebrew ought often to be rendered potentially, and sometimes subjunctively.—*Ed.*

in setting forth any turbulent movement, often adopts this similitude. Some think that Jeremiah alludes to the Egyptians; but I see no reason to seek out any refined explanation, when this mode of speaking is commonly adopted. Then by this similitude of south wind God intimates the great power of his vengeance; as though he had said, "Even if the Jews think that they have a firm standing in the promised land, they are wholly deceived, for God will with irresistible force expel them." And he compares them to *stubble*, while yet they boasted that they were like trees planted in that land; and we have before seen that they had been planted as it were by the hand of God; but they wanted the living root of piety, they were therefore to be driven far away like stubble.[1]

Let us then learn from this passage not to abuse the patience of God: for though he may suspend for a time the punishment we deserve, yet when he sees that we go on in our wickedness, he will come to extreme measures, and will deal with us without mercy as those who are past remedy. It follows—

25. This *is* thy lot, the portion of thy measures from me, saith the Lord; because thou hast forgotten me, and trusted in falsehood.	25. Hæc sors tua, portio mensurarum tuarum à me, dicit Jehova; quia oblita es mei, et confisa in mendacio.

The Prophet no doubt wished to strip the Jews of their vain confidence, through which they acted arrogantly and presumptuously towards God, while yet they professed his

[1] Our version begins with "therefore," giving this meaning to ו, *vau*, but *Gataker* considers this verse as connected with the 22d, and regards the 23d as parenthetic; and then he renders the *vau* "and." The literal rendering of the latter part is, "Passing to the wind of the desert," that is, the stubble which is exposed to that violent wind. The meaning may be thus given,—

And I will scatter them like the stubble
That is subject to the wind of the desert.

To pass over to a thing is to become within its range, or to its possession. The sense would be given by the following version,—

That is carried away by the wind of the desert.

The meaning is not what the *Septuagint* give, "carried by the wind to the desert;" nor what the *Vulgate* presents, "carried by the wind in the desert;" but what is meant is, "the wind of the desert," or, as *Calvin* says, the south wind. When the stubble was exposed to that, it is carried away with the greatest violence: such would be the scattering of the Jews. —*Ed.*

name and claimed his favour. They said that they had obtained that land by an hereditary right, because it had been promised to their father Abraham. This indeed was true. They also said, that the land was God's rest; and they derived this from the prophets. They said farther that God was their heritage; and this also was true. But since they had wickedly profaned God's name, he takes from them these false boastings, and says, *This is thy lot.* But still they said, When God divided the nations, his lot fell on Israel, for so says Moses. (Deut. xxxii. 8.) As then they were wont to say, that God afterwards deceived them, the Prophet here on the other hand reminds them, that they foolishly confided in that lot, because God had rejected them, and did not acknowledge them now as his children, as they were become degenerate and perfidious. *This,* he says, *is thy lot.*[1]

We see that there is to be understood here a contrast: God was the lot of the people, and they were also the lot of God, according to the passages to which we have referred. They were the heritage of God, and they boasted that God was their heritage; the land was a symbol and a pledge of this heritage. The Prophet now says, "This lot shall be to thee *the portion of thy measures from me.*" He alludes to an ancient custom; for they were wont to divide fields and meadows by lines, as they afterwards used poles; and we call such measures in the present day perches (*perticas.*)

We now then understand what the Prophet means; for he intimates that the Jews vainly and presumptuously and foolishly boasted, that God was their heritage; for he owned them not now as his children: and he also declares that another lot was prepared for them, far different from that of heritage,—that God would banish them from the promised land, which they had polluted by their vices. Thus we see

[1] It may be thus rendered,—

This thy lot *is* the share of thy measures
From me, saith Jehovah.

The "lot" was the scattering threatened in the previous verse. "The share of thy measures," is a Hebrew idiom for "a measured share," or "a measured portion," as rendered by *Blayney*. Some say that "measures" are mentioned, because the length and breadth were included.—*Ed.*

that we ought not presumptuously and falsely to pretend or profess the name of God; for though he has been pleased to choose us as his people, it is yet required of us to be faithful to him; and if we forsake him, the same reward for our impiety will no doubt await us as Jeremiah threatens here to his own nation. Let us then so use the favour of God and of Christ, and all the blessings which are offered to us by the gospel, that we may not have to fear that vengeance which happened to the Jews.

He adds the reason, *Because thou hast forgotten me and trusted in falsehood.*[1] By falsehood the Prophet means not only the superstitions in which the Jews involved themselves, but also the false counsels which they adopted, when at one time they had recourse to the Egyptians, at another to some other ungodly nations, in order to get aids in opposition to the will of God. For wherever there was any danger, they thought they had a remedy at hand by having the favour and help of the Egyptians, or of the Assyrians, or of the Chaldeans. In the word falsehood, then, the Prophet includes those perverse designs which they formed, when they sought to defend themselves against God, who would have protected them by his power, had it not been necessary to punish them for their sins. What Jeremiah then condemned in the people was, that they placed their *trust in falsehood,* that is, that they sought here and there vain helps, and at the same time disregarded God; nay, they thought themselves safer when God was displeased with them: and hence he says, *Thou hast forgotten me.* For the Jews could not have sought deliverance from the Egyptians or from other heathen nations, or from their idols, without having first rejected God; for if this truth had been really fixed in their minds,—that God cared for their safety, they would no doubt have been satisfied with his protection. Their ingratitude was therefore very manifest in thus adopting vain and impious hopes; for they thus dishonoured God, and distrusted his power, as though he was not sufficient to preserve them. It now follows—

[1] It is better to render אשר here "because" or for, according to all the versions and the *Targum,* than "who," as by *Blayney.*—*Ed.*

26. Therefore will I discover thy skirts upon thy face, that thy shame may appear.

26. Et etiam ego nudabo, (*vel*, discooperiam) fimbrias tuas in faciem tuam (super faciem tuam,) et aspicietur ignominia tua (*potest etiam in præterito tempore exponi hic versus; sed quoniam vaticinium est, ideo non insisto curiosè in verbis aut in syllabis, sed sensum duntaxat respicio; quamquam non malè etiam conveniet, si vertamus in tempore præterito, quasi propheta de re jam facta disserat.*)

He continues the same subject,—that God did not deal with his people with so much severity without the most just cause; for it could not be expected that he should treat them with more gentleness, since they rejected him and had recourse to vain confidences. *I also*, he says; for the particle גם, *gam*, denotes something mutual, as though he had said, "I also will have my turn; for I have it in my power to avenge myself: I will retaliate," he seems to say, "this thine ingratitude; for as thou hast despised me, so will I expose thee to reproach and shame." For God was shamefully despised by the Jews, when they substituted the Egyptians and their idols in his place: they could not have done him more dishonour than by transferring his glory to the ungodly and to their own figments. We hence see that there is an emphasis in the particle *also*, *I will also make bare*, or discover, *thy skirts on thy face;* that is, I will cast thy skirts on thy face.[1]

This mode of speaking often occurs in the Prophets; and as I have elsewhere explained, it means the uncovering of the uncomely parts: it is as though a vile woman was condemned to bear the disgrace of being stripped of her garments and exposed to the public, that all might abhor a spectacle so base and disgraceful. God, as we have before seen, assumed the character of a husband to his people: as then he had been so shamefully despised, he now says, that he had in readiness the punishment of casting the skirts of his people over their faces, that their reproach or baseness

[1] This is no doubt the meaning. See Nah. iii. 5. The verb means to strip off, so as to make bare. The threatening is, to strip off the skirts and throw them over the face; and this is the rendering of the *Syriac*. Probably the most literal rendering would be the following,—

And I also will strip (or roll) up thy skirts over thy face.

The versions all differ, but the *Septuagint* convey this idea. *Blayney's* uncovering "thy skirts before thee," imparts no meaning.—*Ed.*

might appear by exposing their uncomely parts. It then follows—

27. I have seen thy adulteries, and thy neighings, the lewdness of thy whoredom, *and* thine abominations on the hills in the fields. Woe unto thee, O Jerusalem! wilt thou not be made clean? when *shall it* once *be?*

27. Adulteria tua et hinnitus tuos, cogitationem scortationis tuæ super montes in agro vidi, abominationes tuas: væ tibi Jerusalem; non mundaberis posthac? quousque adhuc?

Here the Prophet explains at large what I have before stated,—that the people were justly punished by God, though very grievously, because they had provoked God, not at one time only, but for a long time, and had obstinately persisted in their evil courses. Moreover, as their sins were various, the Prophet does not mention them all here; for we have seen elsewhere, that they were not only given to superstitions, but also to whoredoms, drunkenness, plunders, and outrages; but here he only speaks of their superstitions,—that having rejected God, they followed their own idols. For by *adulteries* he no doubt means idolatries; and he does not speak here of whoredom, which yet prevailed greatly among the people; but he only condemns them for having fallen away into ungodly and false forms of worship. To the same thing must be referred what follows, *thy neighings;* for by this comparison, we know, is set forth elsewhere, by way of reproach, that furious ardour with which the Jews followed their own inventions. The word indeed sometimes means exultation; for the verb צהל, *tsel,* is to exult; but here, as in chap. v. it signifies neighing.

He then says, *Thy adulteries and thy neighings,* &c. Now this is far more shameful than if he had said thy lusts, for by this comparison we know their crime was enhanced, because they were not merely inflamed by a violent natural lust, such as adulterers feel towards strumpets, but they were like horses or bulls: *Thy adulteries* then *and thy neighings;* and he adds, the *thought of thy whoredom,* &c. The word זמת, *zamet,* is to be taken here for thought, and this is its proper meaning. It is indeed taken sometimes in a bad sense; but the Prophet, I have no doubt, meant here to wipe off a colour with which the Jews painted themselves; for they said that they intended to worship God, while they accumulated rites which were not prescribed in the law. The Prophet therefore condemns them here as being within full of unchastity, as though he had said, "I do not only accuse you of open acts of wickedness, but ye burn also within with lust, for impiety has taken such hold on all your thoughts, that God has no place at all in you; ye are like an unchaste woman, who thinks of nothing but of her filthy lovers, and goes after her adulterers: ye are thus wholly given up to your whoredoms.

Some read the words by themselves and put them in the nominative case, "Thy adulteries and thy neighings, and the thought of thy whoredom on the mountains;" and then they add, "In the field have I seen thine abominations." But I prefer to take the whole together, and thus to include all as being governed by the verb ראיתי, *raiti,* I have seen; "Thy adulteries and thy neighings, the thought of thy whoredom on the mountains in the field have I seen, *even* thy abominations." The last word is to be taken in apposition with the former words. But the Prophet introduces God here as the speaker, that the Jews might not seek evasions and excuse themselves. He therefore shews that God, whose proper office it is to examine and search the hearts of men, is the fit Judge.[1]

[1] In all the versions, as well as in the *Targum,* the words in the beginning of this verse, as far as "whoredom," are read in apposition with "shame" in the preceding verse, and what follows as connected with the verb "I have seen," in this manner,—

On hills in the field have I seen thy abominations.

Another arrangement, suggested by *Gataker,* is more consonant with the Hebrew style, by considering the substantive verb to be understood in the first clause, as follows,—

27. Thy adulteries and thy neighings,
The scheming of thy fornication,
Have been on hills in the field;
I have seen thine abominations.

The word זמת, which I render "scheming," is from a verb which means to devise, to contrive, to scheme, to plot. It is rendered "wickedness" by the *Vulgate,* "alienation" by the *Septuagint,* "fornication" by the *Syriac,* and "design" or counsel by the *Targum.* It never means "lewdness." It seems to mean here the contrivances and devices formed by those given to fornication. *Blayney* considers it a verb in the second person: he connects the first line with the preceding verse, and renders thus what follows,—

Thou hast devised thy whoredom upon the hills,

He mentions *hills* and *field.* Altars, we know, were then built on hills, for they thought that God would be better worshipped in groves; and hence there was no place, no wood, and even no tree, but that they imagined there was something divine in it. This is the reason why the Prophet says, that their abominations were seen by God on the hills as well as on the plains. And he adds *fields,* as though he had said, that the hills did not suffice them for their false worship, by which they profaned the true worship of God, but that the level fields were filled with their abominations.

We now then perceive the meaning of what is here said, that the Jews in vain tried to escape by evasions, since God declares that he had *seen* them; as though he had said, "Cease to produce your excuses, for I will allow nothing of what ye may bring forward, as the whole is already well known by me." And he declares their doings to be abominations, and also adulteries and neighings.

At length he adds, *Woe to thee, Jerusalem!* The Prophet here confirms what we have before observed, that the Jews had no just ground of complaint, for they had provoked God extremely. Hence the particle *woe* intimates that they were now justly given up to destruction. And then he says, *Will they never repent?* But this last part is variously explained; and I know not whether it can to-day be fully expounded. I will however briefly glance at the meaning.

Jerome seems to have read אחרי, *achri,* "after me," "Wilt thou not then return after me?" as though God here intended to exhort the Jews to return at length to him, as he was ready to be reconciled to them. But as it is simply אחרי, *achri,* and he may have read without the points, I do not wish to depart from what is commonly received. There is further a difficulty in the words which follow, for interpreters vary as to the import of the words מתי עד, *mati od,* "how long yet?" In whatever sense we may take the words, they are sufficient to confute the opinion of *Jerome,* which I had forgotten to mention, because the malediction in that case

In the fields I have seen thine abominations.

The simplicity of this order recommends it, but the former seems preferable.—*Ed.*

would be improper and without meaning, "Woe to thee, Jerusalem, wilt thou not be made clean after me?" for what can this mean? It is therefore necessary so to read as to include all the words in the sentence, "Wilt thou not hereafter *or* at length be made clean?" Some, however, read the words affirmatively, "Thou shalt not be cleansed hereafter," as though it was said, "Thou shalt not be cleansed until I first drive thee into exile." But this meaning is too refined, as I think. I therefore take the words in their simple form, *Wilt thou not at length be made clean? how long yet?* as though God again reproved the hardness of the people, as indeed he did reprove it. Hence he says, "Wilt thou not at length be made clean?" for I take אחרי, *achri,* as meaning "at length." Then follows an amplification, מתי עד, *mati od,* "how long yet?"[1] that is, "Wilt thou never make an end? and can I not at length obtain this from thee, since I have so often exhorted thee, and since thou seest that I make no end of exhorting thee? how long yet shall thy obstinacy continue, so that I cannot subdue thee by my salutary admonitions?" This is the meaning.

PRAYER.

Grant, Almighty God, that as thou hast once cleansed us by the blood of thine only-begotten Son, to the end that we might worship thee in true sincerity of heart, and that we might also strive to regulate our whole life according to the rule of righteousness,—O grant that we, being mindful of our vocation, may labour to render ourselves approved by thee, so that thy name may through us be glorified, and that casting far away from us all pollutions, we may retain the simple worship of thee, and preserve ourselves within the limits of thy word, so that we may not be led astray after vanities and the sinful superstitions of this world, but advance towards the mark which thou hast been pleased to set before us, until we shall be at length gathered into that celestial kingdom in which we shall enjoy that inheritance which thine only-begotten Son has provided for us.—Amen.

[1] The meaning seems to be right, but it is better to construe אחרי, "after," with these words,—

Woe to thee, Jerusalem! thou wilt not be cleansed
After what time *wilt it* yet *be?*

Literally it may be rendered, "After when yet?"—*Ed.*

Lecture Fifty-Fifth.

CHAPTER XIV.

1. The word of the Lord that came to Jeremiah concerning the dearth.	1. Quod fuit verbum Jehovæ ad Jeremiam super verbis prohibitionum.

THOUGH the Prophet does not distinctly express that what had not yet happened was divinely revealed to him, yet it may be easily gathered that it was a prophecy with reference to what was future. Of this sterility nothing is recorded in sacred history: there is, however, no doubt but God had in an unusual manner afflicted the Jews, as previously in the days of Ahab. As then a drought was near at hand which would cause great scarcity, his purpose was to forewarn the Jews of it before the time, that they might know that the dryness did not happen by chance, but was an evidence of God's vengeance. And we know that whenever any adversity happens, the causes of it are sought in the world, so that hardly any one regards the hand of him who smites. But when there is a year of sterility, we consult astrology, and think that it is owing to the influence of the stars: thus God's judgment is overlooked. As then men contrive so many expedients by which they throw aside the consideration of Divine judgment, it was necessary that the Prophet should speak of the sterility mentioned here before it happened, and point it out as it were by the finger, though it was yet not made manifest.

He therefore says that the word of God came to him respecting the *words of restraints.*[1] Though דבר, *deber*, signifies a thing or a business or concern, yet, what seems here to be intended is the contrast between דבר, *deber*,

[1] The *Septuagint* express it in one word, "ἀβροχία—the want of rain;" the *Vulgate*, by "words of dryness," or drought; and the *Syriac*, by "defect of rain." We may take "words" here in the sense of effects; so we may render the Hebrew, "concerning the effects of restraints;" and the last word is put in the plural number because there was a twofold restraint,—that of the heavens from rain, and that of the earth from producing fruit. The "effects" of these restraints are described in the following verses.—*Ed.*

the word of God, and דְּבָרִים, *deberim,* the words of men; for he says, עַל דִּבְרֵי הַבַּצָּרוֹת, *ol deberi ebetserut,* because the Jews, as it is usual, would have many words of different kinds among themselves respecting the sterility: when anything uncommon or unexpected happens, every one has his own opinion. But the Prophet sets up the word of Jehovah in opposition to the words of men; as though he had said, "They will inquire here and there as to the causes of the scarcity; there will yet be but one cause, and that is, God is punishing them for their wickedness."

He calls sterility *prohibitions* or restraints: for though God could in an instant destroy and mar whatever has come to maturity, yet, in order to shew that all the elements are ready to obey him, he restrains the heavens whenever he pleases; and hence he says, "In that day the heavens will hear the earth, and the earth will hear the corn, and the corn will hear men." (Hosea ii. 21, 22.) For as this order of things is set before us, it cannot be otherwise but that, whenever we are hungry, our eyes turn to the corn and bread; but corn does not come except the earth be fruitful; and the earth cannot of itself bring forth anything, and except it derives moisture and strength from the heavens. So also, on the other hand, he says, "I will make for you the heaven brass and the earth iron."[1] (Lev. xxvi. 19.) We hence see the reason for this word, *prohibitions,* by which the Prophet designates the dryness of the heavens and the sterility of the earth; for the earth in a manner opens to us its bowels when it brings forth food for our nourishment; and the heavens also pour forth rain, by which the earth is irrigated. So also God prohibits or restrains the heavens and the earth, and closes up his bounty, so as to prevent it to come to us. It now follows—

2. Judah mourneth, and the gates thereof languish; they are black unto the ground; and the cry of Jerusalem is gone up.	2. Luxit Jehudah et portæ ejus debilitatæ sunt, (*vel,* dissipatæ sunt;) obtenebrati sunt in terra (*referunt quidam ad portas, sed malo ad homines referre;*) et clamor Jerusalem ascendit.
3. And their nobles have	3. Et proceres eorum (*hoc est,* qui

[1] There is a little inadvertence here: "iron," in this text, is applied to heaven, and "brass" to the earth.—*Ed.*

sent their little ones to the waters: they came to the pits, *and* found no water; they returned with their vessels empty; they were ashamed and confounded, and covered their heads.

pollent dignitate) miserunt minores (*hoc est,* homines plebeios et mercenarios) ad aquas; venerunt ad cisternas, non invenerunt aquas; reversi sunt cum vasis inanibus (*vel,* reversa sunt vasa eorum vacua;) confusi sunt, et erubuerunt, et operuerunt caput suum.

The Prophet intimates in these words, that so great would be the scarcity as to appear to be a manifest and remarkable evidence of God's vengeance; for when God punishes us in a common way, we for the most part refer the event to some fortuitous circumstances, and the devil also ever retains our minds in the consideration of secondary causes. Hence the Prophet declares here that an event so unusual could not be ascribed to natural causes, as that the earth should become so sterile, but that it was the extraordinary judgment of God. This is the reason why he employs so many figurative expressions. He might indeed have said, in one sentence, that there would be in the land a most grievous famine; but hardly one in a hundred would have been moved by words so simply expressed. Therefore the Prophet, in order to arouse their stupor, uses terms the most forcible.

Hence he says, *Mourned has Judah.* Though he speaks of what was future, yet, according to his own usual manner and that of others, he uses the past time in order to shew the certainty of what he said. He then declares that there would be mourning in Judah. He afterwards says, *His gates have been weakened,* or scattered. In mentioning gates, he takes a part for the whole, for he means the cities: but as judgments were wont to be administered at the gates, and as men often assembled there, he says that the gates would be reduced to solitude, so that hardly any one would appear there. He in the third place adds, *They have become darkened to the ground,* or, in plainer words, they became overwhelmed with grief; but the proper meaning of the word is to become darkened: and he says, *to the ground,* as though he said that they would be so cast down as to lie in the dust, and would not dare to raise up their heads, nor would be able to do so, being worn down by want and famine. We hence see what he means, even this,—that the scarcity would be so great that men would lie down on the ground, and in a manner seek darkness for themselves, as it is the case with us when we flee as it were from the light and lie on the ground; for we then shew that we cannot enjoy the light, it being disagreeable to us: and hence we see more clearly what I have stated,—that the Prophet uses very strong terms to produce an impression on the Jews, that they might know that the earth was so sterile, not through any natural or common cause, but through the judgment of God.[1]

He afterwards adds, *The cry of Jerusalem has ascended.* Here he sets forth their despair: for in doubtful matters we are wont to deliberate and to devise remedies; but when we are destitute of any counsel or advice, and when no hope appears, we then break out into crying. We hence see that it was an evidence of despair when the *cry of Jerusalem* ascended; for they would not be able to complain and to disburden their cares and griefs by pouring them into the bosoms of one another, but all of them would cry and howl.

It is then added, *Their chiefs will send the common people to the waters.* The Prophet's object was again to point out something extraordinary,—that the great, possessing authority, would constrain and compel the common sort to draw

[1] The versions connect the two verbs with gates: and if we take "gates" metonymically for those who attended them, the meaning will be evident. We may then render the verse thus,—

> Mourned hath Judah,
> And her gates, they have languished;
> Grieved have they for the land;
> And the cry of Jerusalem hath ascended.

In the gates was the court of justice; there the chief men or governors assembled. The languishing belonged, not to the gates, but to those who attended them, and so the grief or lamentation. The first meaning of the verb is to be dark, to be black, but it is used to signify extreme grief or lamentation. See Psalms xxxv. 14; xxxviii. 6; Jer. viii. 21. As light denotes joy, so darkness is a symbol of grief or mourning. We use a similar kind of metonymy, when we say, "The court is in mourning." The *Septuagint* render the verse thus,—

> Mourned hath Judah,
> And her gates have been emptied,
> And have become dark for the land;
> And the shout of Jerusalem hath ascended.

Blayney's version of the third line is as follows,—

> They are in deep mourning for the land.

The *Targum* paraphrases the verb thus,—"Their faces are covered with blackness."—*Ed.*

water. They have *sent* them, he says, that is, by authority; they who could command others sent them to the waters.[1] *They came,* he says, *to the cisterns.* By the word גבים, *gabim,* he means deep ditches, or pits; but some render them cisterns. With regard to the subject in hand, it signifies not; for the Prophet no doubt meant that they would come to the deepest wells or pits, as it is usually done in a great drought; for many springs become often dry, and pits also, situated in high places; but in valleys some water remains, and there it may be had: there are also some wells ever full of water, where its abundance never fails. It was therefore the Prophet's design to refer to such wells. *They came,* he says, *to the wells,* where they thought they could find a sufficient supply; but he adds, *They found no waters; they returned with their empty vessels.*[2]

We now perceive what I have said,—that the Prophet here reproves the Jews for their stupidity in not understanding that God was angry with them when the order of nature, which ought ever to continue the same, thus failed. Droughts indeed often happen when there are no waters in most places; but when no well supplies any water, when there is not a drop of water to be found in the most favourable places, then indeed it ought to be concluded that God's

[1] The persons here mentioned are called by the *Septuagint* "chieftains—μεγιστᾶνες," and "young men—τους νεωτέρους;" by the *Vulgate,* "the elder ones—majores," and "the younger ones—minores;" by the *Syriac,* "the chiefs," and "the common sort;" and by the *Targum,* "chief men," and "subjects." The first word is well expressed in our version, "nobles,"—the illustrious; and the most suitable word for the others is "menials;" they were the servants.—*Ed.*

[2] I would render the verse thus,—

3. When their nobles sent their menials for water,
They came to the reservoirs, they found no water;
They brought back their vessels empty:
They were ashamed and confounded,
And they covered their heads.

The word I render "reservoirs" means literally arches or vaults. They were places arched over to preserve water. *Parkhurst* thinks that the reservoirs made by King Hezekiah are intended, 2 Chron. xxxii. 30. That the verb שב has the meaning of bringing back is evident from Isaiah lii.8; and this is according to the *Vulgate* and the *Septuagint* in this place. *Gataker* and *Venema* think that the shame and confusion refer to the nobles, and not to the servants. This verse speaks of Jerusalem, the last mentioned in the former verse; and what follows refers to Judea, spoken of in the former part according to the usual manner of the prophets.—*Ed.*

curse is on the people, who find nothing to drink; for in nothing does God deal more bountifully with the world than in the supply of water. We do not speak now of wine; but we see fountains everywhere pouring forth waters, and rivers also flow through countries: moreover, pits are dug through the labours of men; there are also cisterns in which the rain is preserved in places that are commonly dry: but when in cisterns no water remains, and when the fountains themselves refuse any supply, we may hence surely know that it is the special judgment of God; and this is what Jeremiah intended here to shew; and therefore he says that they were *confounded* and *ashamed*, and that they *covered their head.* It now follows—

4. Because the ground is chapt, for there was no rain in the earth, the plowmen were ashamed, they covered their heads.

4. Propter terram afflictam (contritam, *vel,* scissam; *cum enim verbum hoc proprie significat* conterere, *non dubito, quin Propheta hic terram vel pulverulentam vel concisam significat,*) quia non fuit pluvia in terra, confusi sunt agricolæ (*vel,* pudefacti sunt, *repetit illud verbum* בשו) et cooperuerunt caput suum (*etiam eandem dictionem repetit.*)

The Prophet had said, that though the whole common people were sent to the waters, yet none would be found. He now adds the same thing respecting the husbandmen. *Ashamed,* he says, *shall be the husbandmen, for the ground shall be turned into dust,* and God will pound it small. When the heavens supply moisture, the earth retains thus its solid character; but in a great heat we see the earth dissolving into dust, as though it was pounded in a mortar.

So he says, *On account of the chapt ground, because there is no rain, ashamed shall be the husbandmen, and they shall cover their heads;* for sorrow shall not only seize on them, but also fill them with such shame as to make them to shun the light and the sight of men. These things were intended for the same purpose, even to make the Jews to know that they were not by chance deprived of water, but because God had cursed their land, so that it yielded them no water even for the common wants of nature. It follows—

5. Yea, the hind also calved in the field, and forsook *it,* because there was no grass.

5. Quin etiam cerva in agro peperit et deseruit (*nempe,* fœtum suum,) quia non fuit herba.

6. And the wild asses did stand in the high places, they snuffed up the wind like dragons; their eyes did fail, because *there was* no grass.

6. Et onagri steterunt super excelsa (*diximus de hoc nomine*, super labia, *vel*, eminentias, *vel*, rupes,) traxerunt (*vel*, hauserunt) ventum sicut serpentes; defecerunt oculi eorum, quia non fuit herba (*utitur alio nomine, posuerat* דשא *prius, nunc ponit* עשב, *sed eodem sensu.*)

Jeremiah now comes to animals: he said before, that men would be visited with thirst, and then that the ground would become dry, so that husbandmen would be ashamed; he now says that the wild asses and the hinds would become partakers of this scarcity. *The hind*, he says, *has brought forth in the field*, which was not usual; but he says that such would be the drought, that the hinds would come forth to the plains. The hinds, we know, wander in solitary places and there seek their food, and do not thus expose themselves; for they have a natural timidity, which keeps them from encountering danger. But he says that hinds, big with young, shall be constrained by famine to come to the fields and bring forth there, and then flee away: and yet they prefer their young to their own life. But the Prophet here shews that there would be something extraordinary in that vengeance of God, which was nigh the Jews, in order that they might know that the heavens and the earth and all the elements were armed against them by God, for they had so deserved. But he says, *Bring forth shall the hind*, and then he adds, *and will forsake* its young: but why will it bring forth in the field? even because it will not find grass in the mountains, and in the woods, and in the usual places.

The same thing is said of the wild asses, *And the wild asses*, he says, *stood on the rocks:* and yet this animal, we know, can endure want for a long time. But the Prophet, as I have said, intended to shew that there would be in this scarcity some remarkable evidences of God's vengeance. *Stood* then *did the wild asses on the rocks*, and *thence drew in wind like serpents:* for great is the heat of serpents; on account of inward burning they are constrained to draw in wind to allay the heat within. The Prophet says, that wild asses were like serpents, for they were burning with long famine, so that they were seeking food in the wind itself, or by respiration. He then adds, *Failed have their eyes, for there was no grass.*[1]

We now understand the object of this prediction: It was God's purpose not only to foretell the Jews what was soon to be, but also to point out, as it were, by the finger, his vengeance, that they might not have recourse, as usual, to secondary causes, but that they might know that they suffered punishment for their sins; for the scarcity would be so extraordinary as far to exceed what was usual. It now follows—

7. O Lord, though our iniquities testify against us, do thou *it* for thy name's sake: for our backslidings are many; we have sinned against thee.	7. Si iniquitates nostræ testificantur contra nos, Jehova, fac propter nomen tuum; quia multiplicatæ sunt aversiones nostræ, in te sceleratè egimus.

The Prophet, no doubt, intended here to exhort the Jews by his own example to seek pardon; nor does he so assume the character of others, as though he was free himself from guilt; for he was not more righteous than Daniel, who, as we find, testified that he confessed before God, not only the sins of the people, but also his own sins. (Dan. ix. 4, 5.) And Jeremiah, though not one of God's despisers, nor of the profane, who had provoked God's wrath, was yet one of the people; and here he connects himself with them; and he did this in sincerity and not in dissimulation. But he might have prayed silently at home; why then did he make public his prayer? What was his purpose in consigning it to writing? It was that he might rouse the people, as I have already said, by his example, so that they might flee as suppliants to God's mercy, and seek forgiveness for their sins. This then was the Prophet's object. Thus we see

[1] The three foregoing verses I render as follows,—

4. On account of the ground being cracked,
As there has been no rain in the land,
Ashamed were the husbandmen,
They covered their heads:
5. When also the hind *was* in the field,
It brought forth young, and it was forsaken,
Because there was no grass:
6. And the wild asses, they stood on the cliffs;
They drew in the wind like serpents;
Fail did their eyes,
Because there was no herbage.—*Ed.*

that the prophecy concerning the scarcity and the famine was announced, that the people might through repentance escape the wrath of God; for we know that when God has even taken his sword he may possibly be pacified, as he is in his nature merciful: and besides, the design of all such predictions is, that men, conscious of their sins, may by faith and repentance escape the destruction that awaits them. We now then understand the design of the Prophet in this passage.

He says first, *Even though our iniquities testify*, &c. The verb ענה, *one*, properly means to answer; but it means also to testify, as in this place. *O Jehovah,*[1] he says, there is no reason now to contend with thee, or to expostulate, or to ask why thou dealest so severely with us; let all such excuses be dismissed, *for our sins testify against us;* that is, "Were there no angels nor men to accuse us, our own conscience is sufficient to condemn us." But when do our iniquities testify against us? Even when we know that we are exposed to God's judgment and are held guilty by him. As to the reprobate, their iniquities cry to heaven, as it is said of Sodom. (Gen. xviii. 20, 21.) But the Prophet seems here to express something more,—that the Jews could not make evasions, but must confess that they were worthy of death.

For he says, *For thy name's sake deal* with us. We see that the Prophet first condemns himself and the whole people; as though he had said, "If thou, Lord, summonest us to plead our own cause, we can expect nothing better than to be condemned by our own mouths, for our iniquities are sufficient to condemn us. What then remains for us?" The Prophet takes it as granted that there was but one remedy, —that God would save his people for his own name's sake; as though he had said, "In ourselves we find nothing but reasons for condemnation; seek then in thyself a reason for forgiving us: for as long as thou regardest us, thou must

[1] All the versions connect "Jehovah" with the next words; and so do *Venema*, *Gataker*, and *Blayney*. The particle אם, if, or though, is omitted by the *Septuagint* and the *Arabic;* but is retained by the *Vulgate*, *Syriac*, and the *Targum*. It may be rendered verily, or truly,—

Verily, our perversities, they have responded against us.

The word עון means perverse or headstrong wickedness. There is an allusion in responding to a trial. "They have stood against us," is the *Septuagint*. See Job xv. 6.—*Ed.*

necessarily hate us and be thus a rigid Judge; cease then to seek anything in us or to call us to an account, but seek from thyself a reason for sparing us." He then adds, *For multiplied have our defections, and against thee have we done wickedly.*[1] By these words the Prophet shews that he did not formally, like hypocrites, confess sins, but really acknowledged that the Jews would have been found in various ways guilty had God dealt with them according to justice.

As we now perceive the import of the words, let us learn from this passage, that there is no other way of being reconciled to God than by having him to be propitious to us for his name's sake. And by this truth is refuted everything that has been invented by the Papists, not less foolishly than rashly, respecting their own satisfactions. They indeed know that they stand in need of God's mercy; for no one is so blinded under the Papacy, who does not feel the secret misgivings of his own conscience: so the saintlings, who lay claim to angelic perfection, are yet self-convicted, and are by necessity urged to seek pardon; but in the mean time they obtrude on God their satisfactions and works of supererogation, by which they compensate for their sins, and thus deliver themselves from the hand of God. Now this is a remarkable passage to confute such a diabolical delirium, for the Prophet brings forward the name of God; as though he had said, "This is the only way by which we can return to God's favour and obtain reconciliation with him, even by having him to *deal with us for his name's sake,* so that he may seek the cause of his mercy in himself, for in us he can find none." If Jeremiah said this of himself, and not feignedly, what madness is it for us to arrogate so much to ourselves, as to bring anything before God by which he may be induced to shew mercy? Let us then know that God forgives our sins, not from a regard to any compensation, but only on account of a sufficient reason

[1] The latter part may be thus rendered,—

Jehovah! deal *with us* for thy name's sake:
For many have been our defections,
Against thee have we sinned.

The *Syriac* renders fitly the first line,—

O Lord, spare us on account of thy name.—*Ed.*

within himself, that he may glorify his own name. Now follows a clearer explanation and a confirmation of this verse.

8. O the Hope of Israel, the Saviour thereof in time of trouble, why shouldest thou be as a stranger in the land, and as a wayfaring man *that* turneth aside to tarry for a night?

9. Why shouldest thou be as a man astonied, as a mighty man *that* cannot save? yet thou, O Lord, *art* in the midst of us, and we are called by thy name; leave us not.

8. Spes Israel (*vel*, expectatio; קוה *est expectare*,) servator ejus in tempore angustiæ (*vel*, tribulationis,) cur eris quasi peregrinus in terra? quasi viator divertens ad pernoctandum?

9. Quare eris vir territus? quasi gigas qui non potest servare? atqui (*copula enim valet hic adversativum*) tu in medio nostri Jehova, et nomen tuum super nos invocatum est, ne deseras nos.

I have said that the former verse is confirmed by these words; for since the Prophet mentions to God his own name, we must consider the cause of the confidence with which he was supported, which was even this,—because God had chosen that people, and promised that they should be to him a peculiar people. It is then on the ground of that covenant that the Prophet now prays God to glorify his name; such a prayer could not have been made for heathen nations. We hence perceive how the Prophet dared so to introduce God's name, as to say, *Deal* with us *for thy name's sake.*

He calls God, in the next place, *the hope of Israel;* not that the Israelites relied on him as they ought to have done, for the ten tribes had long before revolted from him, and so great a corruption had also prevailed in Judah, that hardly one in a thousand could be deemed faithful. Hope then among the people had become extinct; but the Prophet here regards the perpetuity of the covenant, as though he had said, "Even though we are unworthy to be protected by thee, yet as thou hast promised to be always ready to bring us help, thou art our hope. In short, the word *hope* or expectation, is to be referred to God's promise, and to the constancy of his faithfulness, and not to the faithfulness of men, which did not exist, at least it was very small and in very few.

To the same purpose he adds, *His Saviour in time of trouble.* He had in view the many proofs by which God had manifested his power in the preservation of the faithful.

And he expressly mentions *trouble* or distress, as though he had said, that the aid of God had been known by evidences sufficiently clear; for had the people never wanted his help, his favour would have been less evident; but as they had been often reduced to great straits, the bounty and the power of God had become more manifest by delivering them from extreme dangers.

It is then added, *Why shouldest thou be as a stranger in the land? as a traveller, who turns aside for a short time in his journey to pass the night?* Here must be noticed a contrast between a stranger and one that is stationary, spoken of afterwards. God would have his name to be invoked in Judea; it was therefore necessary that his favour should continue there; and hence he called the land his rest, and he had also promised by Moses that he would ever be in the midst of his people. The Prophet no doubt had taken from the law what he relates here, *Thou art in the midst of us, Jehovah, thy name is called on us.* He therefore reasons from what seemed inconsistent, that he might obtain pardon from God; for if he was inexorable, his covenant would have failed and perished, which would have been unreasonable, and could not indeed have been possible. Hence he says, "Lord, why shouldest thou be as a stranger and as a traveller, who seeks only a lodging for one night, and then goes forward?" God had promised, as I have already said, that he would rest perpetually in the land, that he would be a God to the people; it was not then consistent with the covenant that God should pass as a stranger through the land. As he had then formerly defended the Jews, and made them safe and secure even in the greatest dangers, so the Prophet now says, that it was right that he should be consistent with himself and continue ever the same.

As to the words which follow, *Why shouldest thou be as a man astonished* or terrified? I take "terrified" for an uncultivated person, as we say in our language, *homme savage.*[1]

[1] The word נדהם, rendered "astonished," is only found here; it is evidently a Niphal participle, and rendered by the *Septuagint* "sleeping—ὑπνῶ,"—by the *Vulgate*, "wandering—vagus,"—by the *Syriac*, "weak—imbecillis,"—by *Montanus* and *Pagninus*, "astonished." *Parkhurst*, after

It is then added, *As a giant who cannot save;* that is, a strong helper, but of no skill, who possesses great strength, but fails, because he is rendered useless by his own bulk. And so the Prophet says, that it would be a strange thing, that God should be as a strong man, anxious to bring help and yet should do nothing.

After having said these things, he subjoins the contrast to which I have referred, *But thou art in the midst of us, Jehovah, thy name is called on us, forsake us not.* We now see that the Prophet dismisses all other reasons and betakes himself to God's gratuitous covenant only, and recumbs on his mercy. *Thou art,* he says, *in the midst of us.* God had bound himself by his own compact, for no one else could have bound him. Then he says, *Thy name is called on us.* Could the people boast of anything of their own in being thus called? By no means; but that they were so called depended on a gratuitous covenant. As then the Prophet did cast away every merit in works, and every trust in satisfactions, there remained nothing for him but the promise of God, which was itself founded on the free good pleasure of God. Let us hence learn, whenever we pray to God, not to bring forward our own satisfactions, which are nothing but filthy things, abominable to God, but to allege only his own name and promise, even the covenant, which he has made with us in his only-begotten Son, and confirmed by his blood.

Grotius, derives it from an Arabic verb, which means to "come upon one unexpectedly," or to overwhelm, and renders it overwhelmed, astonied. It may then be rendered, surprised. *Grotius* says, that it means a precipitant person, coming to the aid of one in danger, and not capable of delivering him.

As in the former instance, "the sojourner" and "the traveller" are the same, only what is said of the latter is more specific; so it seems to be here: the man, taken by surprise, is only farther described as one who is not able on that account to save. The two verses may be thus rendered—

8. The hope of Israel! his Saviour in time of distress!
Why art thou like a sojourner in the land?
Or like a traveller turning aside to pass the night?
9. Why art thou like one taken by surprise—
Like a man who is not able to save?
Yet thou *art* in the midst of us, Jehovah;
And thy name, on us is it called:
Do not forsake us.—*Ed.*

PRAYER.

Grant, Almighty God, that since we are taught by the Teacher whom thou hast set over us, to seek our daily bread from thee, we may know that whenever thou chastisest us with scarcity, we are justly visited by thy hand; and shouldest thou at any time deal severely with us, may we never cease to implore thy mercy, and feel assured that thou wilt ever be merciful and propitious to us, provided we decline not from the way which thou hast pointed out to us, even that thy Son will reconcile us to thee, and that his blood is our only satisfaction; and may we not look to anything else, even in seeking our salvation, but that thy name may be more and more glorified through Jesus Christ our Lord.—Amen.

Lecture Fifty-Sixth.

10. Thus saith the Lord unto this people, Thus have they loved to wander, they have not refrained their feet; therefore the Lord doth not accept them: he will now remember their iniquity, and visit their sins.

10. Sic dicit Jehovah ad populum hunc (*vel*, de populo hoc; ל *utrunque significat*,) Sicut dilexerunt ad vagandum (*hoc est*, sicut amarunt vagari,) pedes suos non cohibuerunt, ideo Jehova non placuit sibi in illis; nunc recordabitur iniquitatum eorum, et visitabit peccata ipsorum.

The Prophet goes on with the same subject; but he reproves the Jews more severely and shews what their sins were. He says then that they were given to inconstancy; but by saying, "to wander," לנוע, *lenuo*, which means to move here and there, he no doubt mentions this inconstancy as a contrast to that quietness and rest, of which Isaiah speaks, when he says, "Behold the Lord hath commanded, In returning and in confidence shall be your strength, in quietness and tranquillity. (Isaiah xxx. 15.) He then wished the Jews to adopt different counsels, and not to run here and there when any danger was at hand, but to wait until he, according to his promise, came to their aid. Hence Jeremiah now accuses them of inconstancy, because they would not rely on God's help and remain firm in their purpose, but run here and there for vain helps; besides a diabolical frenzy led them after idols, as Isaiah says in another place, "Thou hast wearied thyself in thy ways and without profit," (Isaiah xlvii. 13.)

This fact is often mentioned by the prophets,—that they were like roving strumpets who seek paramours everywhere; for their confederacies with the Egyptians and the Chaldeans cost them much, and yet they spared no expenses. They might have waited quietly for the aid of God, which had been promised; but they did not.

We now then perceive the meaning of the Prophet when he says, that they *loved to wander*,[1] or to move here and there, and that they *restrained not their feet.* At the first view, indeed, this seems to have been but a small offence; but if we consider its source, that they distrusted God and his power, and placed their safety in the Egyptians, or the Chaldeans, it will appear to have been a shameful and an intolerable sacrilege. Unbelief, then, is here condemned; for the Jews looked around for foreign aids, and made no account of God.

Now this passage is worthy of being especially noticed, for unbelief is here painted to the life. It is indeed true that even the children of God are not so tranquil in their minds that they never fear, that they are never solicitous or anxious, that they dread no danger; but yet, though the faithful are disturbed by many inquietudes, cares, anxieties, and fears, still God ever preserves them; and the firmness of their faith within continues, though it may happen that they are apparently not only shaken, but even stagger and fall. But God gives to the unbelieving their just reward, who derogate from his power, while they place their safety on men or on idols, for they never find where they may safely stand. They therefore weary themselves without any advantage. On this account he says, *Therefore Jehovah will not be pleased with them*, that is, God will not give them

[1] The כן, *so*, before "loved," is not well accounted for, nor is it given in any of the versions. The previous complaint was that God was like a "traveller" in the land, who made no stay: the answer given is, "so have ye been; ye have loved to wander here and there." It is an ironical retort. The verse may be thus rendered,—

> Thus saith Jehovah of this people,—
> "So have they loved to wander,
> Their feet have they not restrained."
> And Jehovah has not been pleased with them;
> He will now remember their iniquity,
> And he will visit their sin.—*Ed.*

courage: nay, he says, *he will now remember their iniquities and visit their sins.* In short, he teaches us, that so grievous was the wickedness of that people, that there was no place for the mercy of God. He afterwards adds—

11. Then said the Lord unto me, Pray not for this people for *their* good.

12. When they fast, I will not hear their cry; and when they offer burnt-offering and an oblation, I will not accept them: but I will consume them by the sword, and by the famine, and by the pestilence.

11. Et dixit mihi Jehovah, Ne ores in gratiam populi hujus in bonum, (*hoc est*, ut benefaciam.)

12. Quum jejunaverint, ego non exaudiam ad clamorem eorum, et quum obtulerint sacrificium et oblationem, ego non habebo gratum (*idem est verbum*, in illis non placebit mihi, non placabor, non ero propitius;) quoniam in gladio, in fame, et peste ego consumam eos.

God first forbids the Prophet to pray for the people, as we have before seen, (ch. vii. 16; xi. 14.) But we must remember what I have said before, that this prohibition is to be understood as to their exile; for as God had already decreed that the people should be banished from the promised land, the Prophet was forbidden to pray, inasmuch as that decree was immutable. It is not, therefore, a general prohibition, as though the Prophet was not allowed to ask God's forgiveness in behalf of the whole people, or at least in behalf of the godly who still remained. The Prophet might indeed pray in a certain way for the whole people, that is, that God, being satisfied with their temporal punishment, would at length spare the miserable with regard to eternal life: he might have also prayed for the remnant; for he knew that there was some seed remaining, though hidden; nay, he was himself one of the people, and he not only knew that some true servants of God were still remaining, but he had also some friends of his own, whose piety was sufficiently known to him. God, therefore, did not strictly exclude all his prayers, but every prayer with regard to the exile which was soon to be undergone by the people.

Except we bear in mind this circumstance, the prohibition might seem strange; for we know that it is one of the first duties of love to be solicitous for one another before God, and thus to pray for the wellbeing of our brethren. (James v. 16.) It is not then the purpose of God to deprive the Prophet of this holy and praiseworthy feeling, which is necessarily connected with true religion; but his design was to shew, that it was now in vain to implore him for the remission of that punishment which had been determined.

We hence see first, that under the name of people every individual was not included, for some seed remained; and we farther see that this prohibition extended not to eternal life, but on the contrary to temporal punishment. And the demonstrative pronoun *this* indicates contempt or disdain, as though he had said, "What! why shouldest thou pray for a people wholly unworthy of mercy; let them perish as they deserve." So when he says, *for good*—לטובה, *lethube*, it ought also to be referred to their exile, by which he intimates, "Hope not that what has been once fixed by me respecting this people can be changed by any prayers; they must therefore suffer the punishment which they have deserved, for I will banish them from the land."

He afterwards adds, *Even when they fast, I will not hear their cry,* and when they present a sacrifice and an oblation, *I will not be pleased with them.* He doubtless touches the hypocrites, who, though void of all sincerity, yet professed to be the true worshippers of God, and by sacrifices and fastings and other external rites wished to prove themselves to be so. He therefore says that he would not be propitious or appeasable, though they fasted, and prayed, and offered all kinds of sacrifices. The words, as I have said, were especially addressed to hypocrites; for we know that that declaration remains unchangeable—that God is nigh to all those who call on him in sincerity. (Psalm cxlv. 18.) Whosoever, then, calls on God with a true heart, infallibly obtains his favour; for in another place it is ascribed to God as a thing necessarily belonging to him, that he hears prayers. Whenever then God is invoked, he cannot divest himself of what essentially appertains to him—his readiness to hear prayer. But here he intimates that there was no sincerity in the people; for even when they fasted and prayed, and offered sacrifices, they did not truly worship him; for, as it was said before, they could no more put off the wickedness which adhered to their marrow than the Ethiopian could change his skin or the panther his spots, (ch. xiii. 23.) He then shews, in this place, that though they wearied themselves in pacifying God by an external profession, they did nothing but act falsely, and that therefore their efforts would be all in vain; for they profaned the name of God when they thus grossly dissembled with him. This is the meaning.

Fasting is expressly mentioned, and it hence appears, that when there is nothing wanting as to outward appearance, God still ever regards faith, as we have seen in the fifth chapter. Hence God values not what is highly esteemed by men, and excites their feelings: why? because he regards the faith of the heart, and faith is taken for integrity. So then God abominates a double and a false heart; and the greater the fervour hypocrites display in external rites, the more they provoke him.

We pray to God daily, it may be said, and yet we do not fast daily. It is indeed true that prayer is more intent when we fast; but yet God requires not daily fastings, while he enjoins prayer both in the morning and in the evening, yea, he would have us to implore his grace continually. (1 Thes. v. 17.) But when fasting is joined to prayer, then prayer becomes more earnest; as it is usually the case when there is any danger, or when there appears any evidence of God's wrath, or when we labour under any heavy affliction; for we then not only pray but we also fast that we may be more free and more at liberty to pray. Besides, fasting is also an evidence that we are deprecating the wrath of God, while we confess that we are guilty before him; and thus also they who pray stimulate themselves the more to sorrow and to other penitential feelings. It is therefore the same as though he had said, "Even if they pray in no common manner and every day, and add fasting, so that greater fervour may appear in their prayers and extraordinary attention, yet I will not hear their cries, even because their heart is false."

We further gather from this passage that fasting is not in itself a religious duty or exercise, but that it refers to another end. Except then they who fast have a regard to what is thereby intended—that there may be a greater alacrity in prayer—that it may be an evidence of humility in confessing their sins—and that they may also strive to subdue all their lusts—except these things be regarded, fasting becomes a frivolous exercise, nay, a profanation of God's worship, it being only superstitious. We hence see that fastings are not only without benefit except when prayers are added, and those objects which I have stated are regarded, but that they provoke the wrath of God as all superstitions do, for his worship is polluted.

But under the Papacy the reason given for fastings is, that they merit the favour of God. The Papists seek to pacify him by fasting as by a sort of satisfaction ; they will have fasting to be a work of merit. I will not now speak of the numberless trifles which also pollute their fasting ; but let us suppose that they are not superstitious in their choice of meats, in their hours, and in other childish follies, which are mere trumperies, nay, mockeries also to God—let us suppose them to be free from all these vices, yet the intention, as they call it, is nothing else but a diabolical error, for they determine that fasting is a work of merit and of satisfaction, and a kind of expiation. Let us then know, that though Jeremiah speaks of hypocrites, yet he briefly points out the design of fasting by mentioning prayer. So also Christ, when recommending fasting, makes mention of prayer. (Matt. xvii. 21 ; Mark ix. 29.) The same is done by Paul. (1 Cor. vii. 5.) But it ought to be noticed here, that though hypocrites joined before men prayer with fasting, they were yet rejected, for there was no sincerity in their hearts, but only an outward profession, a mere disguise. But God, as we have seen, regards the heart, and sincerity alone pleases him.

The same thing is said of sacrificing, *When they present sacrifices*, or burnt-offerings, *and an oblation*, מנחה, *meneche*, that is, the daily offerings, *I will not hear them*, or, as he says in the second clause, *I will not be pleased with them.* Sacrifices without prayers were no doubt vain and worthless, for as prayers were not acceptable to God without a sacrifice, so when sacrifice was without prayers it was only a vain shew. These two things are then united as by an indissoluble knot, to offer sacrifices and to pray. Prayers, as I have said, cannot be acceptable to God without a sacrifice ;

for what can proceed from mortal man but what is abominable before God? Our prayers must therefore be sanctified in order that they please God; and the only way of sanctification is through the sacrifice of Christ. When they offered sacrifices under the law they also joined prayers; and by this ceremony they who made any request professed themselves unworthy except a sacrifice was offered. The Prophet then mentions here what God had commanded under the law, but he shews that hypocrites separated the principal thing from the external signs. God indeed neither disregards nor rejects signs, but when what they signify is separated from them, there is then an intolerable profanation. Let us then know, that though nothing may be wanting in the external worship, yet whatever we seek to do is abominable to God except it be accompanied with sincerity of heart.

But I will consume them,[1] he says, *with the sword, and with famine, and with pestilence.* I render the particle כי, *ki,* "but." He refers here to three modes of destruction, that the Jews might surely know that they were to perish, according to what is said elsewhere, "He who escapes from the sword shall perish by the famine, and he who survives the famine shall perish by the pestilence." God shews, in short, that he was armed with various kinds of punishment, so that they who had so provoked him as wholly to lose the hope of pardon, could by no escapes deliver themselves from destruction. God might indeed have consumed the Jews by one punishment, he might have also threatened them in general terms without specifying anything, but as the unbelieving ever promise themselves some way of escape, so his purpose was to hold them bound in every way, that they might know that they were shut up on every side, and that no way of escape could be found. This is the meaning. It follows—

13. Then said I, Ah, Lord God! behold, the prophets say unto them, Ye shall not see the sword, neither	**13. Et dixi, O, ho, Domine Jehovah; ecce prophetæ dicunt illis, Non videbitis gladium, et fames**

[1] As it is a participle in Hiphil, preceded by a pronoun, it ought to be rendered causatively,—

But with the sword, and with famine, and with pestilence,
Will I cause them to be consumed.—*Ed.*

shall ye have famine; but I will give you assured peace in this place.

non erit vobis; quoniam pacem veritatis (*id est*, stabilem) dabo vobis in hoc loco.

The Prophet no doubt relates what he had expressed in prayer to God; but yet he has a reference to the people. He then prayed in the manner he now relates; but he renders public the prayers he offered by himself and without a witness, in order that he might restore the Jews from their impiety. Now Jeremiah's colloquy with God availed not a little to touch the Jews; for as though they themselves had been present, he set before them what he had heard from God's mouth. We now then understand why he made known his secret prayers; it was not for the sake of boasting, but for the sake of doing good to the Jews. It was then his object to consult their benefit, when he declared to them what he had previously poured forth without any witness into the bosom of his God.

And I said, Ah, Lord Jehovah! He uses an expression of grief, *Ah!* and thus he shews what concern he felt for his people, being not less anxious on account of their ruin than on account of his own. It may yet be an expression of astonishment, as though the Prophet was filled with surprise, "What can this be, O Lord?" And doubtless an expression of astonishment is not unsuitable, so that the Jews might feel horrified together with him, when they saw that they had been led astray by the false prophecies, by which they had been deceived. He then says, "How is this, O Lord? *for the prophets say to them*, &c.[1]

Here the word, prophets, is emphatic, as though he had said, They are not thus mad wilfully in promising to themselves peace, contrary to thy will, but these prophets who profess and boast of thy name, these are the authors of this so gross a security; for they say, *Ye shall not see the sword, famine shall not happen to you; nay, I will give you*, &c. Here they assume the person of God; for it is not said, "God shall give you sure peace," but "I will give you," &c. We hence see that the Prophet here expresses his horror, while

[1] "Alas!" is commonly the meaning of this exclamation, being an expression of grief rather than of astonishment. "Ah!" is the *Vulgate*,—"Oh!" the *Septuagint*. It is rendered "Alas!" by *Blayney*.—*Ed.*

he compares false prophecies with the oracle which he had received from the mouth of God. *The prophets,* he declares, *say,* &c. They assumed an honourable title, and one connected with the power and authority of God himself. "Even the prophets then, who seem endued with the authority of heaven, and seem to have been sent by thee, as though they were angels,—even these *promise men peace,* not in a common manner, but in a way the most imposing, as though they had thine authority, and brought from thy mouth their fallacies, *I will give you.*"

We now then understand the design of the Prophet; for it was necessary to shake off from the Jews that false confidence, by which the false prophets, who pretended to have been sent from above, and boasted that they were God's servants, the agents of the Holy Spirit, had inebriated them. As then it was necessary to take away from the Jews this confidence, the cause of their ruin, because they hardened themselves in contempt of God, and despised all his threatenings; he therefore says, "What! the false prophets speak thus, *I will give you sure peace*[1] *in this place.*"

We hence learn that Jeremiah had almost a continual contest; for the fiercest antagonists immediately presented themselves, whenever he threatened the people either with exile or with famine, or with any other judgment of God. "What! be secure, for God has chosen this place where he is worshipped. It cannot be that he will banish his Church from its quiet rest. There is no reason then to fear that he will ever suffer this kingdom to perish or his Temple to be destroyed." Hence the complaint of the Prophet, not that he himself was affected by such falsehoods, but he regarded the good of the people, and sought to recover those who were as yet healable from these deceptions. Hence it follows—

14. Then the Lord said unto me, The prophets prophesy lies in my name: I sent them not, neither have	14. Et dixit Jehova mihi, Mendacium prophetæ prophetant in nomine meo; non misi eos, et non

[1] Or, "constant peace—pacem firmam." It rather means "true or real peace," literally, "the peace of truth." The version of the *Septuagint* is "truth and peace,"—of the *Vulgate* and *Targum,* "true peace," and of the *Syriac,* "peace and security."—*Ed.*

I commanded them, neither spake unto them: they prophesy unto you a false vision and divination, and a thing of nought, and the deceit of their heart.

præcepi illis, et non loquutus sum cum illis: visionem mendacii (*hoc est*, mendacem) et divinationem et vanitatem (*vel*, rem nihili) et fraudem cordis sui ipsi prophetant vobis.

We now see more clearly why the Prophet related his own complaint, and also his astonishment, of which God alone had been the witness, and that was, that the people might be more attentive to his warning. For had he only said, "The prophets deceive you, and God would have this to be made known to you," his address would not have been so powerful, as when this question precedes, "Lord God, what is this? the prophets promise peace to this people, and forbid them to fear pestilence and war." As then the Prophet had set forth this according to his own view and the common view of the whole people, the answer, as I have said, becomes more forcible, and more easily penetrates into the mind. God then gives this answer, *Falsehood do the prophets prophesy in my name.*

In my name, is emphatical; for God reminds us, that we ought to beware of every appearance of falsehood, that we ought not easily and rashly, and without discrimination, to believe all prophecies; for not everything boasted of as being divine is really so. We then see that this is a remarkable passage; for God reminds us, that we ought to exercise judgment as to prophecies, so that we may not be inconsiderately led away by anything brought forward under the pretext of his name. He would have us therefore wisely to distinguish between things; and hence I have said that this passage deserves to be specially noticed. The Papists at this day vainly boast of their titles, and say that they are the real Church, that they are the pastors, and that the Church of God is the pillar of the truth; and thus they astonish and confound the simple, so that every discrimination is taken away, and whatever it pleases them to determine is to be received as an oracle. But God shews here, by the mouth of Jeremiah, that we are not rashly to believe every kind of prophecy. *In my name,* he says, the prophets prophesy, as though he had said, "My name is often impiously profaned by men. As then there are many who pass themselves as my servants and prophets, and who also occupy a place of dignity and exercise the ordinary office, yea, as there is such depravity in men, that they are not ashamed to abuse my name, wisdom and discretion ought to be exercised." This is the first thing; for God intimates, that it is not enough for men to claim the prophetic office, except they also prove that they are true and faithful prophets.

He afterwards adds, *I have not sent them, nor have I commanded them, neither have I spoken to them; a vision of falsehood*, &c. He here takes away authority from the false prophets; for he had not sent them, nor commanded them to speak, nor spoken to them. The latter clause is more general than the rest: but these three things ought to be carefully noticed, for they serve to distinguish true from false prophets. It was then God's purpose to mention here certain marks by which the difference between true and false prophets may be known.

He says first, that they were not *sent*, for they obtruded themselves. Hence a call is necessary, for God would not have disorder and confusion in his Church. It is indeed true that the call of Jeremiah was extraordinary; for when the state of the Church was rightly formed, the chief priest was the teacher of religion and true doctrine, who was now the adversary of God's faithful servant. There were indeed some, like Amos, who were taken from the common people; yet there were none more fit for the prophetic office than the priests, for they were, as Malachi says, the messengers of the God of hosts. (Mal. ii. 4, 7.) But when they became degenerate, God, in order to reproach them, raised up other prophets from obscure villages and from the common people. It was then sometimes an interior call only; but when the Church was duly formed, a regular outward call was also necessary. However this may have been, it is certain that such as were not called by God, falsely and wickedly pretended to have his authority, being both without the outward call and without the guidance of the Holy Spirit. This is the first thing.

It then follows, *I have not commanded them.* Here is the second mark of distinction; for God testifies that no credit is due to the prophets, except as far as they faithfully deliver, as it were from hand to hand, what has been committed to them. If then a prophet mingles anything of his own, he is proved to be false and is not worthy of any credit. Let us hence know, that prophets are not endued with any other power, but to deliver faithfully what has been committed to them from above.

But the third mark, which is added, is still more clear: God says, that he had *not spoken* to them; for he thus intimates that no voice but his ought to be heard in the Church. Why then does he bid honour and reverence to be payed to his prophets? Even because they bring nothing but what he has delivered. We hence see how God allows men no power of their own to rule in his Church; but he will have obedience to be rendered to himself, so that their duty is faithfully to declare what he has committed to them. Therefore as to the command, it refers to what was particular; but when he says, I have not spoken to them, what was general is intended; it is the same as though he had said, that it was not lawful nor right for prophets and teachers to bring forward anything but what they had received from heaven.

Hence he concludes, that they spoke *falsehood and impostures, and divination and vanity, and the deceit of their own heart.*[1] We hence see that as soon as men depart even

[1] I render the verse as follows,—

14. And Jehovah said to me,—
Falsehood do the prophets prophesy in my name;
I have not sent them, nor given them a command,
Nor have I spoken to them:
A vision of the falsehood and divination,
And vanity and delusion of their own heart,
Do these of themselves prophesy to you.

God had not *sent* them, the final act; he had given them *no command* or commission, the preceding act; he had not *spoken* to them, the first act. God first speaks, then gives a commission, and afterwards sends forth his servants. The vision the false prophets had was that of the falsehood of their own heart, of the divination, of the vanity, and of the delusion of their own heart. Such seems to be the meaning given by the *Septuagint* and the *Vulgate.* It was the lying vision of their own heart, it was the divination or the presage, the vanity, and the delusion of their own heart. The word for "prophesy" in the last line is in *Hithpael;* and hence "of themselves" is added.

Blayney gives a different view; his version is,—

in the smallest degree from God's word, they cannot preach anything but falsehoods, vanities, impostures, errors, and deceits: and all who thoughtlessly give credit to men, without considering whether they have been sent by God, and faithfully deliver what he has committed to them, wilfully perish. But on this subject more shall be said.

PRAYER.

Grant, Almighty God, that as thou dealest so kindly with us as daily to shew to us our sins and to exhort us to repent, and teachest us that thou art ready to give us forgiveness,—O grant, that we may not be of a refractory mind, nor flee away from thee, while thou so kindly invitest us to thyself, but learn seasonably to repent, and be touched with the fear of thy judgment, so that we may truly and from the heart seek that reconciliation, which has been procured for us by the blood of thine only-begotten Son; and as we can bring nothing of our own, may we submissively humble ourselves before thee, and also by faith embrace the gift of thine only-begotten Son.—Amen.

Lecture Fifty-Seventh.

15. Therefore thus saith the Lord concerning the prophets that prophesy in my name, and I sent them not, yet they say, Sword and famine shall not be in this land; By sword and famine shall those prophets be consumed.

16. And the people to whom they prophesy shall be cast out in the

15. Propterea sic dicit Jehova super prophetas, qui prophetant in nomine meo, et ego non misi eos, et dicunt, Gladius et fames non erit in terra hac; in gladio et fame consumentur prophetæ illi:

16. Et populo cui ipsi prophetarunt (*illis, est supervacuum*) erunt

A false vision, and divination, and vanity,
And the guile of their own heart, do these prophesy unto you.

He considers "a false vision" to be an imaginary revelation; "divination," to be something discovered by that art; "vanity," to be the oracular response of an idol; and "guile," to be the fraudulent suggestion of their own heart.

But the simplest exposition is what I have stated: The vision, being that of their own heart, was false; it was their own divination or prognostication; it was worthless, vain, and empty; it was the effect of their own delusion. This was the character of what they prophesied. We may render the words thus,—

The false vision and the divination
And the vanity and the delusion of their own heart,
Do these of themselves prophesy to you.—*Ed.*

streets of Jerusalem, because of the famine and the sword; and they shall have none to bury them; them, their wives, nor their sons, nor their daughters: for I will pour their wickedness upon them.

projecti in compitis Jerusalem à facie famis et gladii (*hoc est*, coram fame et gladio *vel* prælio,) et non erit qui sepeliat eos, ipsi, uxores eorum, et filii eorum, et filiæ eorum, et effundam super eos malum ipsorum.

Jeremiah, after having declared to the false prophets, that as they had by their flatteries deceived the people, they would have to suffer the punishment they had deserved, turns now his address to the people themselves. God might, however, have seemed to deal with them rather hardly, that he inflicted so severe a punishment on men who had been deceived; but the answer to this is evident; for it is certain that except the world willingly sought falsehoods, the power of the devil to deceive would not be so great. When men therefore are led astray by impostures, it happens through their own fault, inasmuch as they are more ready to embrace vanity than to submit to God and his word. And we must remember that saying of Paul, that all the reprobate are blinded and given up to a reprobate mind, because they wilfully seek falsehood, and will not obey the truth. (Rom. i. 28.) And on this account God declares that he tries the hearts of men, whenever false prophets come abroad; for every one who really fears God shall by no means be led away by the deceits of Satan and of impostors. Hence, whenever men are too credulous and readily embrace deceptions, it is certain that their hypocrisy is thus justly punished by God. And it was well known to the Prophet, that the Jews ever wished for such prophets as soothed their ears and promised them an abundant harvest and a fruitful vintage. (Micah ii. 11.) As then they had itching ears, a liberty was justly given to Satan to deluge the whole land with falsehood; and so indeed it happened. There is then no wonder that the Lord was so severe in chastising the people; for they had not been deceived except through their own fault. The same thing happens at this day. Though we are touched with pity when we see the ministers of Satan prevail in deceiving the common people: yet we must remember that a reward is rendered by heaven for the impiety of men, who either extinguish or smother the light of God as much as they can, and seek to plunge into darkness.

This then was the reason why God so severely visited the Jews, who had been deceived by false teachers: it was owing to their previous impiety and ingratitude. And on this account also he adds at the end of the verse, *I will pour forth upon them their wickedness.* Some think that the word רעה, *roe,* may denote punishment as well as wickedness, as עון, *oun,* also is taken for both. But the Prophet seems to give a reason why God had resolved to execute so dreadful a judgment on the Jews; and the reason was, because they were worthy of such a reward. I am therefore inclined to render the word wickedness, as though he had said, "A dreadful calamity indeed awaits this people; but that they may not complain of my severity, they shall receive the reward of their own wickedness." However this may be, the Prophet no doubt wished here to close the mouths of the Jews, that they might not proceed in their evasions, as though God treated them with too little kindness. Hence then it appears, that God does not heedlessly execute his vengeance on the innocent; but that the teachers and the whole people, who approved of them, were involved in the same punishment.[1]

[1] These two verses are differently connected by some: the words, "these prophets," at the end of the fifteenth verse, are joined with the "the people" in the next verse; and this construction is evidently the best,—

15. Therefore, thus saith Jehovah,—
As to the prophets who prophesy in my name,
(Though I have not sent them, yet they say,—
The sword and the famine shall not be in this land)
By the sword and by the famine shall they perish:
16. These prophets, and the people, to whom they prophesy,
Shall be cast out into the streets of Jerusalem,
On account of the famine and the sword;
And there *will be* none to bury them—
Neither them, *nor* their wives, nor their sons, nor their daughters;
Thus will I pour upon them their own wickedness.

The preceding connection is favoured by the *Septuagint* and the *Arabic,* but the other versions do not join the "prophets" and the "people" together. "Their own wickedness" is "their own evils" in the *Septuagint,*—"their own evil" in the *Vulgate,*—and "their own wickedness" in the *Syriac.* If rendered "wickedness," then it is a metonymy for the fruit or effect of wickedness; if "evil," then the meaning is, the evil due to them.—*Ed.*

And he says, *They shall be cast out in the streets of Jerusalem by the famine and the sword,* or on account of the famine and the sword. They shall then all of them, that is, their carcases, be cast out; for their carcases are evidently meant, as he immediately adds, *and no one shall bury them;* and he mentions their wives and children. And these had no excuse for themselves, for we have seen in the seventh chapter that this charge was brought against them, —that the children gathered wood, that the parents kindled the fire, and that the women kneaded the dough to make cakes for their idols. The Prophet then intimates, that no one would escape, because they were all implicated in the same wickedness, some more and some less, but so far, however, that the children were not to go unpunished, because they followed their fathers, nor the wives, because they followed the example of their husbands. It follows—

17. Therefore thou shalt say this word unto them, Let mine eyes run down with tears night and day, and let them not cease: for the virgin daughter of my people is broken with a great breach, with a very grievous blow.

17. Dices igitur (*copula enim loco illativæ particulæ sumitur*) ad eos verbum hoc, (*hoc est,* annunciabis illis hoc verbum) Deducent oculi mei lachrymam (*vertunt alii,* descendent oculi mei in lachrymam; *Hebraicum nomen est singulare*) nocte et die, et non quiescent; quoniam contritione magna contrita est virgo, filia populi mei, plaga ægra (*vel,* acerba) valde.

God shews here again how tardy, yea, how stupid the people were, whom no threatenings could induce to return to a right mind. When, therefore, they daringly neglected all threatenings, God bids a sad spectacle to be presented to them, justly calculated to fill them with fear and shame; he bids his Prophet to speak thus to them, "Behold, I shall be wholly dissolved into tears, and that on your account." The Prophet, no doubt, wept sincerely when he saw his own people wilfully drawing upon themselves the wrath of God and their final destruction; nor could he divest himself of his humane feelings: but he speaks not here only of his own solicitude, but God himself bids him thus to speak, in order that the Jews might be ashamed of their carelessness, as they ridiculed or despised, with dry eyes, the calamity which was nigh them, and the Prophet alone wept for them. We have spoken of this in the ninth chapter and in other places. There indeed the Prophet wished that his eyes were fountains of tears; but his object was, no doubt, not only to shew his concern for his own nation, but also thus to try whether they could be turned to repentance, their hardness being so great: and in this place the same thing is shewn still more clearly; for God bids the Prophet to weep, not in secret, but to declare this to the whole people, *Behold, my eyes come down into tears, and there shall be no rest,* no cessation.

We now perceive the design of the Holy Spirit; for as the obstinacy of the people was so great that they shed no tears, though God often terrified them with the most dreadful threatenings, it was necessary that this coming calamity should be set before their eyes, in the person of Jeremiah, as in a mirror, in order that they might at length learn to fear. Whenever such passages occur, let us remember that at this day also men are equally stupid, so that they ought not to be less sharply urged, and that God in the gospel adds vehemence and sharp goads to the truth; for such is not only the sloth of our hearts, but also their hardness, that it is necessary to constrain those who will not suffer themselves to be drawn and led.

Some render the words, "Descend shall tears from mine eyes;" but more correct is the other version, "Mine eyes shall descend into tears," as ב, *beth,* is to be prefixed to דמעה, *damoe,* or ל, *lamed;* and it is added, *night and day, because the daughter of my people is broken with a great breach.* As yet the Jews were indeed existing as a nation; but the Prophet gives here a striking representation, as though the scene was present, that they might know that a sudden destruction was at hand, though they as yet trusted in their own auxiliaries; nor indeed could they have been led to fear God in any degree until their quietness was disturbed.[1]

[1] More consistent with the character of the Hebrew is to render the verse thus,—

17. And thou shalt say to them this word,—
Pour down shall my eyes the tear
Night and day, and shall not cease;
For great *has been* the breach,

He calls them *the virgin daughter* of his *people,* not for honour's sake, but because God had hitherto spared the Jews. Virgin is sometimes taken in a good sense; for God, when speaking of the holy marriage, by which he had bound the Jews to himself, compares his people to a virgin. But the daughter of Babylon is also often called a virgin, because the Chaldeans, through long peace, had accustomed themselves to delicacies. So also in this place the Prophet, by way of concession, says that his own nation were soft and tender, because they had been borne with through the indulgence of God. But as in war virgins are exposed to violations, and the lust of men rages without shame and beyond all limits, so God intended here to set forth the fierceness of his vengeance; as though he had said, "Now indeed ye are tender and delicate young women, but in a short time your condition will be changed; nor is there any reason why the constant happiness which ye have hitherto enjoyed should deceive you."

And for the same purpose he adds, that *the smiting* would be *very bitter.* It was indeed necessary by many words to exaggerate that vengeance, of which the people made no account. It now follows—

18. If I go forth into the field, then behold the slain with the sword! and if I enter into the city, then behold them that are sick with famine! yea, both the prophet and the priest go about into a land that they know not.

18. Si exiero in agrum, ecce (*copula enim redundat*) occisi gladio; et si ingressus fuero in urbem, ecce dolentes fame (*alii volunt esse nomen substantivum,* dolores famis, *vel,* ægritudines;) quia tàm propheta quàm sacerdos circumeunt ad terram, et nesciunt (*alii vertunt,* quam nesciunt.)

He confirms the same thing in other words, not on ac-

> Broken has been the virgin of the daughter of my people;
> The smiting has been very grievous.

The event, though future, is represented as having past; for he relates a vision. The "daughter" is not in apposition but in construction with "virgin." *Vitringa* says, that a state, or a kingdom, is often called a virgin in the prophets. It is rendered here "kingdom" by the *Targum.* See Is. xxxvii. 22; xlvii. 1; Jer. xxxi. 21; xlvi. 11.

"Those cities," says *Lowth,* "are called virgins, which never came into a conqueror's hands." Jerusalem was in this sense a virgin. He says further, "The dissolution of the body politic is called a *breach,* in allusion to the breaking of the limbs of the human body." The "smiting," or the stroke, was "very grievous," because the body politic, or the state, was shattered into pieces."—*Ed.*

count of the obscurity of what he had said, but because he knew that he was speaking to the deaf, or that such was their sloth, that they needed many goads. He says, in short, that there would be in the city no defence for the people to shield them from the punishment that was at hand, and that if they went into the fields the whole land would be covered with enemies, who would destroy them. This is the sum of the whole.

But he speaks as though he saw the event with his eyes, *If I go out into the field*, he says, their carcases meet me; for the enemy destroys with his drawn sword all who venture to go forth. Then he says, *If I go into the city*, there famine kills those whom the enemy has not reached.[1] As he had said before, "Behold, all were cast forth in the streets of Jerusalem because of the famine and the sword." But what he had said of the streets of Jerusalem he extends now to the fields; as though he had said, that there would be no place of rest to the Jews; for if they attempted to flee away, they met with the swords of enemies, and if they sought hiding-places, the famine would meet them, so that they would perish without being destroyed by any enemy.

The prophet, he says, *as well as the priest shall wander*, shall go round *to the land and know not.* Some explain the last part of the verse as though the Prophet had said, When both the prophets and the priests shall be driven into exile, after many wanderings, they shall not understand that exile is a punishment due to their sins. They therefore take the words, ולא ידעו, *vela idou, and they shall not know*, in a general sense, as though the Prophet here condemned that brutal blindness which possessed the minds of the people, nay, even of the priests, who did not consider that God punished them for their sins. Others explain the words more simply,—that they would go round to the land, that is, that they would come to Chaldea by various windings and by

[1] I take the words before "sword" and "famine" to be nouns substantive,—"the piercings of the sword," and "the wastings of the famine,"—

If I go out to the field,
Then behold the piercings of the sword;
And if I enter the city,
Then behold the wastings of the famine.—*Ed.*

long circuits, and would come to a land they knew not, that is, which was before unknown to them. But I know not whether this was the meaning of the Prophet. Certainly a third view seems more suitable to me, though it has none in its favour, that is, that the priests and prophets would go round to seek subterfuges, as they would be destitute of all means of escape, not knowing what to do; and *they shall not know,* that is, they shall find that a sound mind is by God taken from them, because they had demented others. Hence I doubt not but that the Prophet had especially denounced this punishment on the wicked priests and the false prophets, because they thought that they would have some way of escape; but they would be mistaken; for their own conceit would at length disappoint them; and when they thought of this and of that, God would bring to nothing their crafty ways. And they were worthy of such a punishment, because they had fascinated the wretched people with their lies; and we also know that they were proud of their own crafts and wiles. The Prophet therefore derides this false confidence and says, *They shall go round through the land and shall not understand,* that is, all their counsels and plans shall be without any fruit or benefit, though they may be long in forming them.[1] It follows—

19. Hast thou utterly rejected Judah? hath thy soul loathed Zion? why hast thou smitten us, and *there is* no healing for us? we looked for peace, and *there is* no good; and for the time of healing, and behold trouble!

19. An abjiciendo abjecisti Jehudah? an in Sion (an Sion, ב *redundat*) abominata est anima tua? quare percussisti nos, et nulla nobis medela? expectando pacem (*id est,* expectavimus pacem) et nihil boni (*vel,* non bonum,) et tempus medelæ (*idem est verbum,*) et ecce terror.

The Prophet now turns to prayer and to complaints, that by his example he might at length rouse the people to lamentation, in order that they might humbly implore God's

[1] *Venema* agrees with *Calvin* as to the meaning of the latter part of the verse: it is indeed the only one that comports with the context; the other explanations are quite foreign to it. Our version is according to the *Septuagint* and *Vulgate;* but it is no doubt wrong. *Blayney,* in some measure, following the *Targum,* gives the following version,—

Yet both the prophet and also the priest
Go trafficking about the city and take no knowledge.

Meaning, that they went about with their false predictions, like pedlars, for gain, and paid no regard to the miseries of the country. This sense suits the passage, but the other is the most obvious and natural.—*Ed.*

forgiveness, and sincerely confess their sins and be displeased with themselves. At the same time he indirectly reproves that hardness of which we have before spoken. As then he effected nothing by teaching, he changed his manner of speaking, and leaving the people he addressed God, according to what we have before noticed.

He then asks, *Repudiating hast thou repudiated Judah? Has thy soul abominated Sion?*[1] Jeremiah seems to reason here from what is inconsistent, as though he had said, "Is it possible that thou hast rejected the tribe of Judah and Mount Sion?" For God had promised that he should ever have a lamp at Jerusalem. The ten tribes had already been overthrown, and their kingdom had not only been distressed, but wholly demolished: still there remained a seed, because the tribe of Judah continued, which was as it were the flower of the whole people; and from him the salvation of the world was to proceed. Hence the Prophet does here, as it were, expostulate with God, as though he had said, "Thou hast chosen the tribe of Judah for this end, that it might be safe perpetually; thou hast also commanded the Temple to be built on Mount Sion for thy name; thou hast said that it would be thy rest for ever: hadst thou then by rejecting rejected the tribe of Judah? does thy soul abominate Mount Sion?

There seems, however, to be a kind of irony implied: for though Jeremiah prayed sincerely, he yet intended to remind the people how foolishly they promised themselves impunity as to their sins, because God had his habitation in the Temple, and because Jerusalem was as it were his royal palace. It is indeed evident that the Prophet recalled to mind the promises of God; but yet he wished briefly to shew, that though God should apparently destroy the remnant, and suffer the Temple to be demolished, he would be still faithful to his promises. In asking therefore these

[1] The first verb means to reject with contempt, and the second, to reject with abhorrence,—

Despising, hast thou despised Judah?
Has thy soul abhorred Sion?

Had he despised Judah as a worthless thing, and had he abhorred Sion as a filthy thing?—*Ed.*

questions, as in astonishment, he had partly a regard to God, and partly also he reminded the people, that though God delivered the body of the people to destruction, he would yet be faithful and constant in what he had promised.

He then says, *Why hast thou smitten us, and there is no healing?* There is no doubt but that the Prophet in this place also wished to turn God to mercy for this reason, because he had promised to be merciful to the posterity of David, though sometimes he punished them for their sins; for there was this remarkable promise, "If his children shall offend and violate my covenant, I will smite them with a rod and chastise their iniquities; yet my mercy will I not take from them." (2 Sam. vii. 14; Psalm lxxxix. 31-33.) And to the same purpose is what he said in chap. x. 24, "Chastise me, O Lord, but in judgment," that is, moderately, "lest thou bring me to nothing." There the Prophet, as we have said, reminded God of his covenant; and he does the same here, *Why hast thou smitten, so that there is no healing?* For the punishment which God inflicts on his Church would be, as he declares, a kind of medicine; but when there is no hope of healing, God seems to render void what he had promised. Hence Jeremiah goes on in drawing his argument from what is inconsistent, as though he had said, that it was not possible that God should so severely smite his people as not to allow a place for forgiveness, but that he would at length be intreated and heal the wound inflicted.

We have expected peace, and there is no good; and the time of healing, and behold trouble, or terror.[1] This latter part of the verse confirms what I just stated, that the Prophet had partly a reference to God in this mode of prayer,

[1] The proper construction of these lines, and of the preceding, is not commonly given. The "why" before "smitten" is to be understood here,—

> Why hast thou smitten us, and *there is* for us no healing?
> *Why has there been* hope for peace, and *there is* no good?
> And for the time of healing, and behold terror?

The word for "hope," or longing, or looking for, is a participial noun, but rendered by the versions as though it were a verb in the first person plural. As "smitten" is in the past tense, so *has been* is to be understood before "hope."—*Ed.*

and that he partly reproved the Jews, because they thought, being deceived by false confidence, that they were beyond the reach of danger, inasmuch as God had consecrated Jerusalem, that his name might be there called upon, and that the Temple might be his perpetual habitation. As then he saw that his nation were inebriated, as it were, with this foolish notion, he intended briefly to shew to them that God would have an unknown way by which he would retain his faithfulness, and yet punish the ungodly and the transgressors; for by saying, "We expected peace, and there is no good," he certainly does not commend the fidelity of the people; for relying on God's promises, they sought comfort in evils, and hoped that God would at length be exorable and propitious. The word expecting is not to be taken in a good sense; but he on the contrary reproves the Jews, because they put too much faith in false prophets. We hence see that he condemns that false expectation by which they had been deceived. Hence also we learn what has been before stated, that the Jews foolishly promised to themselves impunity, because God had chosen his habitation among them; for he shews that God had not in vain threatened their ruin by his servants. This then is also the meaning when he says, We expected *the time of healing, and behold terror*. It now follows—

20. We acknowledge, O Lord, our wickedness, *and* the iniquity of our fathers; for we have sinned against thee.

20. Cognoscimus, Jehova, scelus nostrum, et iniquitatem patrum nostrorum; quoniam scelerate egimus in te (חטאנו, *quanquam* רשע *et* חטא *idem ferè sunt, tamen simpliciter concludit, quòd sceleratè egerint adversus Deum.)*

The Prophet here prescribes no doubt to the Jews the way of appeasing God. He before uttered a prayer, partly in order to reprove the people for their wicked obstinacy, and partly to shew to the godly and the elect that there remained some hope. But now he uses a simple form of prayer, when he says, *O Lord, we know*, &c. Hardly one in a thousand then did know; but the Prophet does not assume the character of the whole people; and why not? He doubtless knew that the faithful among the people were very few; but he dictates for posterity a right form of prayer, so that they might in exile know that this one thing only remained for them—to confess their sins, as otherwise they could not obtain pardon.

He therefore says, *We know our wickedness and the iniquity of our fathers; for we have done wickedly against thee.* We have already explained the Prophet's meaning in these few words,—that when God puts forth his hand against us, there is no hope of salvation, except we repent. But confession is here put for repentance. Hypocrites are indeed very free in confessing their sins; but the Prophet speaks here of real confession; and by stating a part for the whole, everything included in repentance, as I have said, is intended. But the object here is to shew, that they were humbly to seek forgiveness, which could not be done, except they condemned themselves before God, and thus anticipated his judgment.

He speaks of *the iniquity* of the fathers, not that the faithful seek associates, here and there, for the sake of extenuating their guilt; but it was an aggravation of their sins, when they confessed that they were not only guilty themselves before God, but that they had brought from the womb what was, as it were, hereditary, so that they deserved death because they were the descendants of ungodly parents. Whilst hypocrites allege the examples of fathers, they think themselves thus absolved, or at least not so culpable, because they had learnt what they practise from their childhood, because a bad education had led them astray. But the faithful are of a far different mind; for they confess themselves worthy of God's vengeance, though he inquired not into the wickedness of their fathers; and they think also that God acts justly, when he executes vengeance on account of their fathers' sins, being thus worthy of a twofold vengeance.

We now then understand what the Prophet means; and hence we learn how foolishly the Papists set up this shield against God; that is, by having the word fathers often on their lips; for they ought on the contrary to confess the wickedness and iniquities of their fathers, according to what is more fully enlarged upon in the ninth chapter of Daniel, where he confesses that he himself and the fathers and kings had done wickedly. And in these words we may also notice, that it was not some slight fault that Jeremiah refers to when he said, "We acknowledge our iniquity and the iniquity of our fathers;" he mentions first the iniquity of the living; then the iniquity of their fathers, and adds, in the third place, "We have acted wickedly against thee." We hence see that he did not formally acknowledge some slight faults, but he confesses most plainly, that they were all ungodly and transgressors of God's law, and were worthy, not merely of a moderate chastisement, but of dreadful perdition, as they had thus provoked the wrath of God.[1]

PRAYER.

Grant, Almighty God, that though we have been once reconciled to thee, and reconciliation has been testified to us in thy gospel, we yet cease not daily to provoke thy wrath,—O grant, that we may at least groan, and undissemblingly so condemn our vices, that we may be touched with real and deep sorrow, and thus learn to flee, not only once in our life, but every moment, to thy mercy, that thou mayest be reconciled to us, and not deal with us according to our merits; but since thou hast been once pleased to embrace us with paternal love, for the sake of thy only-begotten Son, continue this favour to us, until having at length been cleansed from all filth and pollution, we shall become partakers of thy celestial glory, through Christ our Lord.—Amen.

[1] There is no *and* in Hebrew, nor in the *Septuagint,* nor in the *Vulgate,* between "wickedness" and "iniquity;" it is found in the *Syriac* and the *Targum.* In case it be excluded, *Blayney* proposes to render the passage thus, "We acknowledge, O Jehovah, that we have wrought wickedly the iniquity of our fathers;" that is, as he adds, "We have practised over again the same wickedness, of which our fathers set the example." But a meaning is given to רשע, which it never has; nor is this rendering necessary in order to convey this idea, which is probably what is intended. They confessed their wickedness, which was the iniquity of their fathers; it was the same: the latter is in apposition with the former,—

We acknowledge, Jehovah, our wickedness,—
The iniquity of our fathers;
For we have sinned against thee.

Their wickedness, the same with the wickedness or iniquity of the fathers, was, that they sinned against God.—*Ed.*

Lecture Fifty-Eighth.

21. Do not abhor *us*, for thy name's sake; do not disgrace the throne of thy glory: remember, break not thy covenant with us.

21. Ne rejicias propter nomen tuum, ne rejicias (נבל *significat interdum respuere, floccipendere, significat etiam projicere, et eadem est ferè significatio alterius verbi* נאץ, *significat enim projicere, et pro nihilo ducere et vilipendere;* ne *ergo* projicias *vel* vilipendas) solium gloriæ tuæ; recordare, ne irritum facias (*alii vertunt,* dissolvas) fœdus tuum nobiscum.

JEREMIAH goes on with the same prayer; and he made it from love, and also for the purpose of encouraging the faithful, who remained among the people, to seek forgiveness; for he undertakes here to represent the true Church, which was then very small. All indeed boasted that they were the children of God, and gloried in the covenant made with Abraham; but hardly one in a thousand called on God in truth and from the heart. The Prophet then represented the common feeling of a very small number; and yet he proceeded, as I have said, with his prayer.

Hence he says, *Reject not, overthrow not, the throne of thy glory;* or the meaning of the two verbs may be the same, which seems to me more probable.[1] But the Prophet joined together two verbs, not so much for the sake of ornament as

[1] The versions differ as to the two verbs: "Cease for thy name's sake, and destroy not," &c., is the *Septuagint* and the *Arabic;* "Reproach us not, &c., nor dishonour," &c., is the *Vulgate;* "Be not angry, &c., nor dishonour," &c. is the *Syriac;* "Cast us not away, &c., nor make vile," &c., is the *Targum*. Neither of these renderings is correct. The two verbs here used have a similar meaning, though they are different, with those in the 19th verse; the first signifies the rejection of a thing as worthless, and the second as vile, or filthy. They may be thus rendered,—

Scorn not, for thy name's sake,
Abominate not, the throne of thy glory.

The same form is adopted in what follows; two verbs are used, which have the same objective case,—

Remember, break not, thy covenant with us.

Which means, Remember thy covenant, and break it not, or annul it not.

Blayney renders the first two lines thus,—

Spurn us not for thy name's sake.
Dishonour not the throne of thy glory.

But "us" is not in the original, nor do the versions give it, except the *Vulgate;* and dishonour has also been borrowed from that version, and is not the meaning of the verb. No doubt the two verbs refer to the throne. —*Ed.*

rhetoricians do, as for the purpose of expressing the intenseness of his concern and anxiety; for he saw that the kingdom of Judah was in extreme danger. He then did not in an ordinary way try to turn aside God's vengeance, but he hastened as one to extinguish a fire; for the obtaining of pardon was difficult.

He calls Jerusalem the *throne* of God's *glory*, because God had chosen that city where he was to be worshipped, not that he was confined to the Temple, but because the memorial of his name was there, according to what had been usually said, especially by Moses. (Ex. xx. 24.) Nor was the ark a vain symbol of his covenant, for God really dwelt there; for the presence of his power and grace was evidenced by the clearest proofs. But as this mode of speaking is often found in the Prophets, it was sufficient for Jeremiah briefly to notice the subject. God indeed, as it is well known, fills heaven and earth, but he gives symbols of his presence wherever he pleases; and as it was his will to be worshipped in the Temple, it is called his throne, and it is elsewhere called his footstool; for the Scripture describes the same thing in various ways. The Temple is often called the rest of God, his dwelling, his sanctuary, the place of his habitation; it is also called his footstool, "We will worship at his footstool." (Psalm cxxxii. 7.) But these various forms are used for the same purpose, though they are apparently different; for where the Temple is called the habitation of God, his palace or his throne, the presence of his power is set forth, as though God dwelt as a friend among his worshippers; but when it is called his footstool, it is for the purpose of checking a superstition which might have crept in; for God raises the minds of the godly higher, lest they should think that his presence is confined to any place.

We then perceive what the Scripture intends and what it means, whenever it calls Jerusalem or the Temple the throne or the house of God.

But we must carefully notice what is here mentioned by the Prophet, *For thy name's sake.* We know that whenever the saints pray to be heard for the sake of God's name, they cast aside every confidence in their own worthiness and righteousness. Whosoever then pleads God's name, in order to obtain what he asks, renounces all other things, and fully confesses that he is unworthy to find God propitious to him ; for this form of speaking necessarily implies a contrast. As then the Prophet flees to God's name as his only refuge, there is included in the words a confession, such as we have before noticed,—that the Jews, inasmuch as they had acted wickedly towards God, were unworthy of any mercy ; nor could they pacify him by any of their own satisfactions, nor have anything by which they could obtain his favour. This then is the meaning ; and as this doctrine has been elsewhere more fully handled, it seems to me sufficient briefly to shew the design of the Prophet.

He calls it the *throne of glory,* to intimate that God's name would be unknown and unnoticed, or even despised and exposed to reproaches, if he did not spare the people whom he had chosen. The genitive case is used in Hebrew, we know, instead of an adjective ; and to enlarge on the subject is useless, as this is one of its primary elements. The Prophet then in calling the Temple the glorious throne of God, in which his majesty shone forth, in a manner reminds God himself not to expose his name to reproaches ; for instantly the ungoldly, according to their evil dispositions, would vomit forth their blasphemies ; and thus God's name would be reproached.

He afterwards adds, *Remember, make not void, thy covenant with us.* Here also the Prophet strengthens his prayer by calling to mind the covenant : for it might have been said, that the Jews had nothing to do with the holy name of God, with his glory, or with his throne ; and doubtless they were worthy of being wholly forsaken by God. As then they had divorced themselves from God, and were wholly destitute of all holiness, the Prophet here brings before God his covenant, as though he had said, " I have already prayed thee to regard thine own glory and to spare thine own throne, as thou hast favoured the place with so much honour as to reign among us : now, though our impiety is so great that thou mayest justly cast us away yet thou didst not make a covenant with Mount Sion, or with the stones of the Temple, or with material things, but with us; render not void then this thy covenant."

We hence see that there is great emphasis in the words of the Prophet, when he implores God not to *make void*, or not to undo, *the covenant*, which he had made with the people. For though God would have continued true and faithful, had he obliterated the name of the whole people, yet it was necessary that his goodness should contend with their wickedness, his fidelity with their perfidiousness, inasmuch as the covenant of God did not depend on the people's faithfulness or integrity. It was, as it may be said, a mutual stipulation; for God made a covenant with Abraham on this condition—that he should walk perfectly with him: this is indeed true; and the same stipulation was in force in the time of the Prophets. Yet at the same time Jeremiah assumed this principle—that the grace of God cannot be wholly obliterated; for he had chosen the race of Abraham, from whom the Redeemer was at length to be born. But Jeremiah intended to extend God's grace still farther, according to what has been already said, and we shall again presently see the same thing. However this may be, he had a just reason for praying, "Undo not thy covenant with us." But God had hidden means of accomplishing his purpose; for he did, according to the common apprehension of men, abolish the covenant by which the Jews thought him to be bound to them; and yet he remained true; for his truth shone forth at length from darkness, after the time of exile was completed. It now follows—

22. Are there *any* among the vanities of the Gentiles that can cause rain? or can the heavens give showers? *Art* thou not he, O Lord our God? therefore we will wait upon thee; for thou hast made all these *things*.

22. An in idolis (*vel*, vanitatibus) gentium, qui pluere faciat? et an cœli dabunt pluviam (*vel*, et an ex cœlis dabunt pluviam) an non tu ipse Jehova Deus noster? et speravimus in te (expectavimus ad te:) quoniam tu fecisti omnia hæc.

In order to conciliate the favour of God, Jeremiah says here, that with him is the only remedy in extremities; and it is the same as though by avowing despair he wished to turn God to mercy; as if he had said, "What will become of us, except thou shewest thyself propitious? for if thou remainest implacable, the Gentiles have their gods from whom they seek safety; but with us it is a fixed principle to hope for and to seek salvation from thee alone." Now this argument must have been of great weight; not that God had need of being reminded, but he allows a familiar dealing with himself. For if we wish stoically to dispute, even our prayers are superfluous; for why do we pray God to help us? Does he not himself see what we want? Is he not ready enough to bring us help? But these are delirious things, wholly contrary to the true and genuine feeling of piety. As then we flee to God, whenever necessity urges us, so also we remind him, like a son who unburdens all his feelings in the bosom of his father. Thus in prayer the faithful reason and expostulate with God, and bring forward all those things by which he may be pacified towards them; in short, they deal with him after the manner of men, as though they would persuade him concerning that which yet has been decreed before the creation of the world: but as the eternal counsel of God is hid from us, we ought in this respect to act wisely and according to the measure of our faith.

However this may be, the Prophet, according to the common practice of the godly, seeks to conciliate the favour of God by this argument,—that unless God dealt mercifully with his people and in his paternal kindness forgave them, it was all over with them, as though he had said, "O Lord, thou alone art he, from whom we can hope for salvation; if now we are repudiated by thee, there remains for us no refuge: wilt thou send thy people to the idols and the inventions of the heathens? but *we have looked for thee alone;* thou then seest that there remains for us no hope of salvation but from thy mercy."

But the Prophet here testifies in the name of the faithful, that when extremities oppress the miserable, they cannot obtain any help from the idols of the heathens. *Can they give rain,* he says? He states here a part for the whole; for he means that the idols of the heathens have no power whatever. Hence to give rain is to be taken for everything necessary to sustain mankind, either to bring help, or to supply the necessaries of life, or to bestow abundance of blessings. Paul also, in speaking of God's power, refers to rain, (Acts xiv. 17 ;) and Isaiah often uses this kind of speaking, (Isaiah v. 6.)

He then says, *Are there any among the vanities of the heathens?* &c. He here condemns and reproaches all superstitions; for he does not call them the gods of the heathens, though this word is often used by the prophets, but the *vanities* of the heathens. Are there any, he says, *who can cause it to rain? and can the heavens give rain?* I may give a more free rendering, "Can they from heaven give rain?" for it seems not to me so suitable to apply this to the heavens. If, however, the common rendering is more approved, let every one have his own judgment; but if the heavens are spoken of, the argument is from the less to the greater; "Not even the heavens give rain; how then can vanities? how can the devices of men do this, which only proceed from their foolish brains? Can they give rain? For doubtless there is some implanted power in the heavens? but man, were he to devise for himself a thousand gods, cannot yet form one drop of rain, and cause it to come down from heaven. Since, then, the heavens do not of themselves give rain, but at the command of God, how can the idols of the heathens and their vain inventions send rain for us from heaven?" The object of the Prophet is now sufficiently evident, which was to shew, that if God rejected the people, and resolved to punish their sins with the utmost rigour, and in an implacable manner, their salvation was hopeless; for it was not their purpose to flee to idols.

Art not thou, he says, *Jehovah himself*, or alone? *Art not thou Jehovah himself, and our God?*[1] He first mentions the

[1] It is better to regard this line as declaring that God is the giver of rain and showers,—

22. Are there *any* among the vanities of the nations who bring rain?
And do the heavens give showers?
Art thou not he *who givest them*, Jehovah, our God?
So we will look to thee,
For thou makest all these.

To introduce the word "can," borrowed from the *Vulgate*, into the first questions, obscures the passage. "All these" refer, as it appears, to the rain and showers. The perfect tense in Hebrew often includes the past and the present, "For thou hast made and makest all these," &c. So *Gataker* regards the meaning. The *Syriac* has "For thou makest," &c.

name Jehovah, by which is meant the eternal majesty and power of God; and then he joins another sentence,—that he was their God, to remind him of his covenant. Then it is added, *We have looked to thee, for thou hast made all these things.*

Here many, in my judgment, are mistaken, for they apply "these things" to the heavens and the earth, and to all the elements, as though the Prophet declared that God was the creator of the world, and that therefore all things are under his control. But I have no doubt but that he speaks of those punishments which God had already inflicted on the people, and had resolved soon to inflict; for he does not speak here of God's power, which shines forth in the workmanship of the world; but he says, "We have looked to thee, for thou hast made all these things;" that is, from thee alone salvation will come to us, for thou who hast inflicted the wound canst alone heal, according to what is said in another place, "God kills and brings to life, he leads to the grave and restores." (1 Sam. ii. 6.) It is then the same as though the Prophet had said, "We, O Lord, do now flee to thy mercy, for no one but thou alone can help us, as thou art he who has punished our sins. Since then thou hast been our Judge, thou also canst alone deliver us now from our calamities; and no one can resist thee, since the highest power is thine alone. Let all the gods of the heathens unite, yea, all the elements and all creatures, for the purpose of serving us, yet what will all that they can do avail us? As then thou hast made all these things, that is, as these things have not happened to us by chance, but are the effects of thy just vengeance—as thou hast been judge in inflicting these punishments, be now our Physician and Father; as thou hast heavily afflicted us, so now bring comfort and heal those evils which we justly suffer, and indeed through thy judgment." We now understand the real meaning of the Prophet.

Calvin, as far as I can find, stands alone in the sense he attaches to these words. If we take the verb strictly in the past tense, the meaning commonly given is, that God made the heavens, rain, and showers, and that, as he has made them, they are still under his control. But the other meaning is more suitable to the passage,—that God makes the rain and the showers.—*Ed.*

And hence may be learned a useful doctrine,—that there is no reason why punishments, which are signs of God's wrath, should discourage us so as to prevent us from venturing to seek pardon from him; but, on the contrary, a form of prayer is here prescribed for us; for if we are convinced that we have been chastised by God's hand, we are on this very account encouraged to hope for salvation; for it belongs to him who wounds to heal, and to him who kills to restore to life. Now follows—

CHAPTER XV.

1. Then said the Lord unto me, Though Moses and Samuel stood before me, *yet* my mind *could* not *be* toward this people: cast *them* out of my sight, and let them go forth.	1. Et dixit Jehova ad me, Si steterint Moses et Samuel coram facie mea, non est anima (*id est* cor meum) ad populum hunc; emitte à facie mea et exeant.
2. And it shall come to pass, if they say unto thee, Whither shall we go forth? then thou shalt tell them, Thus saith the Lord, Such as *are* for death, to death; and such as *are* for the sword, to the sword; and such as *are* for the famine, to the famine; and such as *are* for the captivity, to the captivity.	2. Et erit, si dixerint tibi, Quò exibimus? (*vel*, egrediemur) tunc dices illis, Sic dicit Jehova, Qui ad mortem, ad mortem, et qui ad gladium, ad gladium, et qui ad famem, ad famem, et qui ad captivitatem, ad captivitatem.

God again repeats what we have before observed,—that as the impieties and sins of the people had arrived at the highest pitch, there was no more room for pardon or for mercy: and though God seems to have rejected altogether the prayer of his servant, we are not yet to think that it was without any benefit. Jeremiah wished indeed to deliver the whole people from destruction; but he did not thus pray inconsiderately and uselessly; for he distinguished between the titular church, as they say, and the chosen seed, for he knew that many were become the degenerated children of Abraham: nor was he unacquainted with what is said in the Psalms, "Who shall dwell in thy tabernacle, and who shall stand on the mount of thy holiness? He who is innocent as to his hands, and is of a pure heart." (Psalm xv. 1, 2.) The Prophet there distinctly shews that hypocrites glory in vain, because they had a free entrance into the

Temple, and sacrificed together with the faithful; for a clean heart and pure hands are required. Jeremiah no doubt fully understood this.

Though then he extended his solicitude to the whole body of the people, he yet knew that there was a chosen seed. So at this day, when we pray, we ought, according to the rule of charity, to include all, for we cannot fix on those whom God has chosen or whom he has rejected; and thus we ought, as far as we can, to promote the salvation of all; and yet we know, as a general truth, that many are reprobate for whom our prayers will avail nothing; we know this, and yet we cannot point out any one as by the finger. So then the prayer of Jeremiah was not useless; but in its very form, as they say, it was not heard, for he wished the whole people to be saved; but as God had resolved to destroy the ungodly, such as were beyond the reach of hope on account of their untamable obstinacy, Jeremiah obtained only in part what he prayed for,—that God would preserve his Church, which then was in a manner hidden.

But it is now said, *If stand before me did Moses and Samuel,*[1] *my soul would not be towards this people.* The meaning is, that though all intercessors came forth in their behalf, they could do nothing, for God had rejected them. Moses and Samuel are here mentioned, but in another place Job and Daniel are named, and for the same reason. (Ezek. xiv. 14.) Moses is mentioned here, because we find that he offered himself, and wished to be, an anathema for his people. "Blot me out of the book of life, or spare this people." (Exod. xxxii. 32.) As then God's wrath had been so often pacified by Moses, he is here mentioned; for when it was all over with the people, he delivered them as it were from eternal death, and this was well and commonly known to the Jews. As to Samuel, we know how celebrated he was,

[1] Noticed here may be an identity of idiom in Hebrew and Welsh: The verb "stand" is in the singular number, though followed by two nominative cases. So it is in Welsh: and were the nominative cases before it, the verb would be in the plural number.

Pe savai Moses a Samuel o'm blaen.

This is the Hebrew, word for word. Both the *Septuagint* and the *Vulgate* retain the singular number of the verb; but they are not grammatically correct.—*Ed.*

and that God had been often pacified by him for the preservation of the whole people; but at length, when he prayed for Saul, God did indeed restrain his immoderate zeal, and forbade him to pray any more, (1 Sam. xvi. 1;) and yet he ceased not to pray. As then there was so great a fervour in Samuel, that he in a manner struggled with God, he is here joined with Moses: "*If,* then, *stand before me did* these two, *my soul,* or my heart, would be alienated from this people, for I shall be no more pacified towards them."

But he speaks of the perverse multitude, which had so often wilfully sought their own destruction; for, as it has appeared elsewhere, the people had never been rejected; and yet we must distinguish between the chaff and the wheat. Judea was, as it were, the threshing-floor of God, on which there was a great heap of chaff, for the multitude had departed from true religion; and there were a few grains found hid in the rubbish. Hence the heart of God was not towards the people, that is, towards the degenerated children of Abraham, who were proud only of their name, while they were covenant breakers; for they had long ago forsaken the true worship of God and all integrity. Therefore the heart of God was not towards them. At the same time he preserved, in a wonderful and in a hidden manner, a remnant.

Now this passage teaches us what James also mentions, that the prayer of the righteous avails much with God; and he brings forward the example of Elijah, who closed heaven by his prayer, so that it rained not for a long time; and who afterwards opened heaven by his prayer, so as to obtain rain from God. (James v. 16-18.) He hence infers that the prayers of the righteous avail much, not only when they pray for themselves, but also when they pray for others; for Elijah had no particular regard for himself, but his object was to gain relief for the whole people. It is indeed certain that the intercession of the saints is highly appreciated by God; and hence it is that we are bidden willingly and freely to make known to one another our necessities, so that we may mutually help and pray for one another. But we must at the same time observe, that they who think themselves to be commended to God by others in their prayers, ought not on that account to become more secure; for it is certain, that as the prayers of the faithful avail the members of Christ, so they do no good to the ungodly and the hypocrites. Nor does God indeed bid us to acquiesce in the confidence, that others pray for us, but bids every one to pray, and also to join their prayers with those of all the members of the Church. Whosoever then desires to profit by the prayers of the saints must also pray himself.

It is true, I allow, that the prayers of the saints sometimes benefit even the ungodly and aliens; for it was not in vain that Christ prayed, "Father, forgive them, for they know not what they do," (Luke xxiii. 34;) nor did Stephen pray in vain when he offered up a similar prayer, (Acts vii. 60;) and I am disposed to agree with what *Augustine* says, that Paul, among others, was the effect of Stephen's prayer. (Serm. i. de Sanctis.) But I am speaking now of what we must do when we find that we are helped by the prayers of the saints, that is, that we are strenuously to perform our part, and strive to shew for our brethren the same solicitude and care as we expect from them. It is then certain beyond a doubt, that each is not only heard when he prays for himself, but that the prayers of the saints avail in behalf of others.

But extremely ridiculous are the Papists, who apply this passage to dead saints: Moses and Samuel, they say, were dead, when God declared what is here said; it is then true that they prayed. The inference is worthy of such teachers, which is as good as the braying of an ass. There is here a supposition made, as though God did say, "If Moses and Samuel were now alive and interceded for them, I would yet remain implacable." But Ezekiel mentions Daniel, who was then living, and he names also Job. We hence see that he makes no distinction between the dead and the living. Therefore the Papists are extremely foolish and stupid when they thus idly prate that the dead pray for the living, on the ground of what is here said of Moses and Samuel. It is not then worth while to refute this ignorant assertion, as it vanishes almost of itself: a brief warning, lest any one should be deluded by such a cavil, is sufficient.[1]

He afterwards bids the Prophet to cast away the people; *cast them away*, or banish them, he says, *from my presence.* He doubtless speaks here in a strong manner, "Let them be gone from me." But yet God shews what he had commanded his Prophet; as though he had said, "Fulfil thou thine office, remember what burden I have laid on thee." Jeremiah had been ordered to denounce exile on the people? he was the herald of divine vengeance. As then he sustained this office, it was his duty to execute the commission which God had given him. We now then apprehend what these words mean, *cast them away.*[2]

But we must again notice here what we have before seen, —that God commends the efficacy of prophetic doctrine, according to what has been said, "I set thee over nations and kingdoms, to plant and to root up, to build and to destroy," (ch. i. 10.) Then God intimates, that so great a power would be in the mouth of his servant, that though the Jews

[1] *Venema,* referring to this notion of the Papists, says, "The words are not that they *stood,* but that *if they stood;* he speaks not of them as dead, but as living, intimating, that if they were alive and interceded for the people, they would not succeed in delivering them." We shall add an observation of *Scott,*—

"This passage fully proves that departed saints do not intercede for us; for it evidently implies that Moses and Samuel did not then stand before the Lord in behalf of Israel or of any in Israel."—*Ed.*

[2] The verb means more properly to send; he was to send them from God's presence by his doctrine, intimating that God disowned and rejected them: and they were to go forth or to go out, that is, from his presence. The allusion is to the sending away a divorced woman,—

Send *them* from my presence, and let them go forth:
2. And it shall be, when they say to thee,
"Where shall we go forth?" that thou shalt say to them,—
Thus saith Jehovah,—"Those for death, to death;
And those for the sword, to the sword;
And those for the famine, to the famine;
And those for captivity, to captivity."

It is observed by *Venema* and *Blayney,* that "death" was that by pestilence. See ch. xiv. 12; xviii. 21. Some were destined for death by pestilence, to this they were to go forth: and so as to the other evils.

The Rabbins say that there are gradations in the evils mentioned here: death by pestilence is less grievous than the sword; the sword than the famine; the famine than captivity; the last being more grievous than all the other evils. See 2 Sam. xxiv. 13, 14; Lam. iv. 9; and Lev. xxvi. 39. The "sword" being the principal weapon, is put here for any violent death inflicted by enemies.—*Ed.*

mocked at his predictions, as if they were vain threatenings to frighten children, they would yet be like thunderbolts; so that Jeremiah would drive away the people, as though he was furnished with a large army and great forces, according to what Paul declares,—that he had power given him to cast down every height that exalted itself against Christ. (2 Cor. x. 5.) As then God claims so great an authority for his prophetic doctrine, when threatening the unbelieving with punishment, let us know that the same extends to all the promises of salvation. Therefore, whenever God offers grace to us by the gospel, and testifies that he will be propitious to us, let us know that heaven is in a manner open to us; and let us not seek any other ground of assurance than his own testimony: and why? because as to the prophets was given the power of binding and loosing, so now the same power is given to the Church, that is, to invite all to be saved who are as yet healable, and to denounce eternal ruin on the reprobate and the obstinate in their wickedness, according to what is said by Christ, "Whatsoever ye shall bind on earth shall be bound in heaven, and whatsoever ye shall loose on earth shall be loosed in heaven." (Matt. xvi. 19; xviii. 18.) For he gave his Apostles the power not only of binding, but also of loosing. And Paul, after having spoken in high terms of the former power, adds, "When your obedience shall be accomplished," (2 Cor. x. 6;) as though he had said, that the gospel was not preached only for this end, to pronounce death on the reprobate, but that it was also a pledge of salvation to all the elect, to them who embraced by true faith the promises offered to them.

He now confirms the previous sentence, *If they shall say, Whither shall we go forth? then shalt thou say to them, Those for death, to death; those for the sword, to the sword; those for the famine, to the famine; those for exile, to exile;* as though he had said, "In vain do they complain of their own miseries." For God, no doubt, had in view the clamorous complaints which prevailed everywhere among the people on account of their very heavy calamities. Thus indeed were hypocrites wont to do; for whenever God spared them, they haughtily insulted the prophets, and boastingly alleged their subsidies and fortresses; but when God's hand pressed hard on them, they became very eloquent in their complaints: "Alas! how far will God go at length? is there to be never an end? and what does all this mean? why does he so severely afflict us? and why does he not at least relieve us in some measure from our miseries?" As then the hypocrites were so querulous in their calamities, God anticipates all these expostulations, and says, "If they say to thee, 'Where shall we flee?' say to them, 'Either to death, or to famine, or to the sword, or to exile;' it is all one with God, and it matters not; for there is no hope of mercy for you any longer, since God has rejected you: know then that it is all over with you, for there is no deliverance for you from God: either the sword, or famine, or some other kind of death will overtake you; ye are in every way past hope."

PRAYER.

Grant, Almighty God, that since thou art graciously pleased to exhort us to repent, and withholdest thine hand, yea, and allowest us the opportunity to repent,—O grant, that we may not obstinately provoke against ourselves thy extreme vengeance, but render ourselves obedient to thee, so that thou mayest not only hear others praying for us, but that our own prayers may also obtain pardon from thee, especially through the intercession of Christ, thine only-begotten Son, who has once for all reconciled thee to us, and whose perpetual intercession is to continue to reconcile us to thee, until we shall appear at length before thee with all our spots and filth wholly washed away, and be made partakers of that glory which has been obtained for us by Christ our Lord. —Amen.

Lecture Fifty-Ninth.

3. And I will appoint over them four kinds, saith the Lord; the sword to slay, and the dogs to tear, and the fowls of the heaven, and the beasts of the earth, to devour and destroy.

3. Et præficiam super eos quatuor familias, dicit Jehova, gladium ad occidendum, et canes ad trahendum, et avem cœlorum et bestiam terræ, ad comedendum et perdendum.

JEREMIAH proceeds with the same subject. He said yesterday that the people were no longer cared for by God, and so that nothing remained for them but in various ways to perish, and that the last punishment would be exile. He now confirms the same thing, and says, that God would prepare against them ravenous birds as well as wild beasts, the sword and dogs;[1] as though he had said, that all animals would be hostile to them, and be the executioners of God's vengeance.

Some render the verb פקד, *pekod*, to visit, but improperly, as I think; for they must give this version, "I will visit four families upon them;" but there is no sense in this, nor can any sense be elicited from it. The meaning most suitable here is to set over,[2] "I will set over them four kinds;" which he calls "four families." And there is to be understood here a contrast: as they thought it hard to obey God, they were now to have over them dogs and wild beasts, and the birds of the air, and the sword. The meaning is, that there would be no end to God's vengeance, and to various punishments, until the Jews were wholly destroyed. He further intimates, that he would have in readiness many to execute his wrath, as he had all creatures under his control. As then he would employ in his service dogs, and birds, and animals, as well as men, it behoved the Jews to feel assured that they in vain had recourse to this or that refuge. We indeed know that men impiously confine the power of God, both with regard to their salvation and the punishment of their sins, for when he passes by any evil they think that

[1] Our version ascribes tearing to dogs, but the verb means to draw or drag about, as rendered by *Calvin*. It is more descriptive of what is done by dogs, and conveys a more horrid idea, and intended doubtless to terrify the Jews. *Blayney* renders it "to drag about," and no doubt correctly. Our version is the *Vulgate:* the *Syriac* is to draw or drag about.—*Ed.*

[2] So *Gataker*, "I will set over them, &c., as in Lev. xxvi. 16; a borrowed speech from officers set over people." The *Syriac* expresses the idea, "I will punish them with four scourges." *Blayney's* version is—

And I will commission against them four species.

But the best rendering is that of *Calvin*, which is also adopted by *Venema*. I give the following version—

And I set over them four kinds, saith Jehovah,—
The sword to kill, and dogs to drag about,
And the bird of heaven and the beast of the earth
To devour, and to pull to pieces.

The "devouring" refers to "the beast of the earth," and the "pulling to pieces" to the bird of heaven, according to the usual style of the Prophets, the order being reversed.—*Ed.*

they have escaped, and promise themselves impunity, as though God indeed were not able every moment to inflict many and various scourges. This then is the reason why the Prophet speaks here of four kinds of judgments. It follows—

4. And I will cause them to be removed into all kingdoms of the earth, because of Manasseh the son of Hezekiah king of Judah, for *that* which he did in Jerusalem.	4. Et ponam eos in commotionem omnibus regnis terræ propter Manasse, filium Ezechiæ, regem Jehudah, (*vel*, regis Jehudah, *parum interest*,) propter ea quæ fecit in Jerusalem.

Jeremiah speaks now of exile. He had hitherto spoken of the sword and famine, and mentioned also other punishments, that their carcases would be dragged about by dogs, and also devoured by wild beasts and ravenous birds ; but he now refers to one kind of punishment only—that God would drive them into exile. And he seems to have taken these words from Moses, for so he speaks in Deut. xxviii., except that ו, *vau*, is placed before ע, *ain*, in the word " commotion," but such a change is common. In other respects there is a perfect agreement.

I will set them, he says, *for a commotion to all the kingdoms of the earth ;* that is, I will cause them to wander in constant fear and trembling. He amplifies the grievousness of exile by the circumstance that they should have no safe rest. They who leave their country for exile do at least find some corner where they take breath ; but God declares that the Jews would be everywhere unsettled and wanderers, so that no place would receive them. And hence God's vengeance became more fully manifest, for these miserable men never found an asylum when scattered through various countries. Though they had habitations in those parts allotted to them by the king of Babylon, they were yet everywhere without any rest. It was not therefore in vain that Moses threatened them with such a punishment, nor was it to no purpose that Jeremiah repeated what had been said by Moses.[1]

[1] *Blayney* rightly observes that the word rendered " to be removed," in our version, has no such meaning. The verb means to move, to agitate, to disquiet, but not to move from one place to another. The noun as found here is rendered " vexation" in Isaiah xxviii. 19, and " trouble" in 2 Chron. xxix. 8. The idea of removing is not given in any of the ver-

He adds the cause, *On account of Manasseh.* But Manasseh was now dead, why then did God transfer the vengeance which he merited to posterity? And this seems inconsistent with another passage found in Ezekiel, "The soul that sinneth it shall die." (Ezek. xviii. 8.) But doubtless God justly punished the wickedness of the people even after the death of that ungodly king, for they ceased not to accumulate evils on evils; as however their impiety appeared especially at that time, he particularly noticed it, that the Jews might understand that they had been long worthy of destruction, and that punishment was not delayed except through the great mercy of God, who had not immediately treated them as they deserved. The Prophet therefore commends the long forbearance of God because their ruin was suspended until that time. And, on the other hand, he shews that they were not so severely treated but that they were worthy of greater and more atrocious punishment; for such had been their obstinacy that they did all they could to draw upon themselves destruction many times.

But another question arises: Manasseh pretended repentance, and God seemed to have forgiven him and the whole people, (2 Kings xxi.; 2 Chron. xxxiii. 12,) why does he now declare that he would take vengeance on sins which had been already buried? But the answer is evident, for the Jews from that time had been in no way better. As

sions, nor in the *Targum*. It is used in two other places by Jeremiah, chap. xxiv. 9; xxix. 18. In both places "vexation, trouble, or disquietude," would be the best rendering. This sentence may be thus translated—

And I will render them a vexation to all the kingdoms of the earth.

Literally it is, "I will give them for a vexation," &c. And so they became, they were a trouble and a disquietude wherever they were; and hence they became, as it is said in chap. xxix. 18, a curse, a hissing, and a reproach among all nations.

Venema gives this rendering—

And I will give them for a shaking to all the kingdoms of the earth.

Which he understands to mean, that they would be given to be shaken, agitated, and disquieted in all the kingdoms of the earth.

Blayney's version is—

And I will give them up to vexation in all kingdoms of the earth.

But this is what the original will hardly bear; the preposition before "kingdoms" is not *in*, but *to*.—*Ed.*

then they had continued to pursue the same sinful courses with Manasseh, it was right that they should at length be rewarded as they deserved ; for, had they become really changed, there would have been a change in God's dealings with them, but inasmuch as their impiety had ever remained the same, and as they gave themselves up to the same vices, a heavier judgment was nigh them, and justly so, because they had abused God's forbearance, who had spared the king as well as themselves on the condition of receiving the pardon offered to them. But since they had hardened themselves, it was right to take such account of their ingratitude and perverseness as to treat them with greater severity.

Farther, Manasseh is called the *son* of Hezekiah, and that for the purpose of enhancing his crime. For as religion had been reformed in the time of Hezekiah, and as that pious king, with great labour and toil, exerted all his powers to restore the true worship of God, it was the duty of Manasseh to follow his example. But he not only built altars to idols, and polluted the whole land with superstitions, but also defiled the very Temple of God. It was thus a horrible, and wholly a diabolical madness in the son, when the right way of worshipping God had been delivered unto him, to be of such a reprobate mind as immediately to overthrow what his father with great labour has so faithfully established. This then was the reason why Jeremiah mentioned to his dishonour the name of his father. And hence we learn that they are worthy of a heavier punishment, who have been religiously brought up from their childhood, and become afterwards degenerated, who, having had pious and godly parents, afterwards abandon themselves to every wickedness. Hence a heavier judgment awaits those who depart from the examples of godly fathers. And this we gather from the very words of the Prophet, who here, by way of reproach, calls Manasseh the *son of Hezekiah*, which yet would have been to his honour, had he been like his father and followed his piety.

And at the same time there is no doubt but that the Prophet indirectly condemns the whole people ; for we know how great opposition pious Hezekiah met with, and how he contended for the faithful worship of God, as though he had been among the Assyrians or the Egyptians. But the perverseness of the people appeared then extreme, when he was put in jeopardy as to the kingdom, because he endeavoured to cleanse the land of Judah from its filth and pollutions; their impiety and ingratitude then shewed, and openly discovered themselves. Afterwards Manasseh overturned as it were in an instant the worship of God, and they all, with great exultation, went immediately after superstition. We hence see that the mouths of the Jews were thus closed, so that they could not object and say, that they obeyed the command of their king; for they willingly followed wicked superstitions. They assented to the king of their own accord, while yet they hardly, and with great unwillingness, were led to obey when God's worship was restored in the time of Hezekiah.

But Manasseh added cruelties to superstitions; for we know that he not only covered the streets of the city with blood, but made it also to flow in streams, as sacred history relates. As, then, the Prophets were so cruelly treated in the time of Manasseh, and as he was not the sole author of this barbarity, but the true servants of God were persecuted to death by the consent of the people, it was hence evident that it was the crime of the whole community. And hence he mentions *Jerusalem,* in order that the Jews might know that the holy city, in which they gloried, had been for a long time the den of robbers, and that the Temple of God had been polluted by wicked superstitions, and even the whole city by unlawful and barbarous slaughters. It now follows—

5. For who shall have pity upon thee, O Jerusalem? or who shall bemoan thee? or who shall go aside to ask how thou doest?

5. Nam quis parcet tibi Jerusalem (*vel,* quis miserebitur tui? *sed* חמל *propriè est ignoscere vel parcere; hìc tamen accipitur pro indulgere vel misereri:* quis *ergo* miserebitur tui Jerusalem?) et quis consolabitur te? et quis locum mutabit ad inquirendum de pace tibi? (*hoc est,* tua: *jungamus* et alterum versum:)

6. Thou hast forsaken me, saith the Lord, thou art gone backward: therefore will I stretch out my hand against thee, and destroy thee; I am weary with repenting.

6. Tu reliquisti me, dicit Jehova; retrorsum abiisti; ideo extendam manum meam super te et perdam te: fatigatus sum pœnitendo.

The Prophet shews here that the severe punishment of which he had spoken could not be deemed unjust, according to what those men thought who were querulous, and ever expostulated with God, and charged him with too much rigour. Lest, then, the Jews should complain, the Prophet says briefly, that all the evils which were nigh at hand were fully due, and so deserved, that they could find no pity, even among men. We know that the worst of men, when the Lord punishes them, have some to condole with them. There is no one so wicked that relatives do not favour him, and that some do not console him. But the Prophet shews that the Jews were not only inexcusable before God, but that they were undeserving of any sympathy from men.

He first says, *Who will pity thee?* and then, *Who will condole with thee?* The verb נוד, *nud,* means properly to give comfort by words, as when relatives, and friends, and neighbours meet together for the purpose of mourning; they hear lamentations, and join in them. But he says that no one would perform this office towards Jerusalem. He adds, in the third place, *And who will turn aside?* or, strictly, change place—*Who will change place to enquire?* or, as some render it, to pray. The verb שאל, *shal,* means properly to ask, and hence sometimes to pray. So, many give this meaning, that there would be no one to pray for the Jews. But if we consider the construction of the sentence, we shall see that the Prophet speaks of that duty of kindness which men cultivate and observe towards one another, by enquiring of their welfare,—"Are all things well with thee?" How dost thou do? Are all things well with thee and thine?" When we thus enquire of the state of any one we shew some concern for him, for love is always solicitous for the welfare of others. The Prophet then says, "Who will turn aside to thee to enquire of thy welfare?" that is, that he may know how thou art, and what is thy state and condition.

We hence see that the Jews are here divested of every complaint, for the whole world would acknowledge them to be unworthy of any commiseration. But the Prophet does not mean that all would act cruelly towards Jerusalem, but rather shews, that such were their crimes that there was no room for courtesy, or for those acts of kindness which men of themselves perform towards one another.[1]

Then follows the reason—*For thou hast forsaken me, saith Jehovah.* Since, then, God had been rejected by the Jews, did not such a defection bring its deserved reward, when they were deprived of every human aid? He afterwards adds, *Backward hast thou gone.* He intimates that there was a continuance in their wicked defection; for they not only forgot God for a time, but departed far from him, so as to become wholly alienated.

It then follows—*And I will stretch out,* &c.; that is, "therefore will I stretch out," &c.; for the copulative is to be taken here as an illative. This may be viewed as in the past or the future tense; for God had in a measure already afflicted the people; but heavier judgments awaited them. I am inclined to regard it as a prediction of what was to come, as it immediately follows, *I am weary with repenting,* that is, "I have so often repented that I cannot possibly be induced now to forgive; for I see that I have been so often deceived, that I cannot bear to be deceived any longer." Some, indeed, give this version,—"I am weary with consoling myself," and נחם, *nuchem,* means both; but the other sense seems to me the most suitable. I doubt not then but that the Prophet means repentance. We indeed know that God changes not his purpose; for men repent because their ex-

[1] There is a general agreement as to the two first clauses of this verse, but not as to the last. The *Syriac* and the *Targum* give the meaning advocated by *Calvin,* with whom *Gataker, Grotius,* and *Blayney* agree. But the *Septuagint* and the *Vulgate* seem to take the other view, that to "pray for peace" is what is meant; and this has been adopted by *Montanus, Castalio,* and *Venema.* But the former is no doubt substantially the right view, though the phrase used, "to salute," or "to enquire of one's welfare," or "how thou doest," is too loose and general. In 1 Sam. xxv. 5 (see also 1 Sam. x. 4) we have the same form of words too loosely rendered, "greet him in my name," in our version. The following verse shews that the rendering ought to be, "wish (or bid) him peace in my name." Literally it is, "Ask for him in my name for peace." So here the literal rendering is,—

Or, who will turn aside to ask for peace for thee?

or, in our language, "to bid thee peace."

The word "turn aside" seems clearly to favour this meaning. In the other case its import does not appear. The intimation is, that no one would deem it worth his while to turn out of his way to express a good wish in behalf of Jerusalem.—*Ed.*

pectation often disappoints them, when things happen otherwise than they had thought; but no such thing can happen to God; and he is said to repent according to our apprehensions. God then repents of his severity whenever he mitigates it towards his people, whenever he withdraws his hand from executing his vengeance, whenever he forgives sins. And this had been often done to the Jews; but they had made a mock of such mercy, and the oftener God spared them the more audaciously did they provoke his wrath. Hence he says, "I am weary with repenting so often;" that is, that he had so often spared them and suspended his judgment.[1]

In short, he deprives the Jews of every excuse, and shews that they acted impiously when they murmured against God, for they allowed no place to his mercy; nay, whenever they found him reconcilable they abused his forbearance with extreme indignity and perverseness. It follows—

7. And I will fan them with a fan in the gates of the land; I will bereave *them* of children, I will destroy my people, *since* they return not from their ways.

7. Et ventilabo ventilabro ipsos in omnibus portis terræ, (*id est,* per omnes portas;) orbavi, perdidi populum meum; à viis suis non recesserunt (*vel,* non reversi sunt, *vel,* non sunt conversi.)

[1] The verse may be thus rendered,—

6. Thou hast broken loose from me, saith Jehovah;
Backward dost thou walk;
But I will stretch my hand over thee and destroy thee;
I have become wearied with repenting.

The verb here used, commonly rendered "forsake," means to loose oneself from restraints: the Jews were bound, as it were, to God by covenant; they broke loose from this bond, they freed themselves from this tie, and went back to idolatry. "Walk," though future, is to be taken here as present. The last line in the *Septuagint* is as follows,—"I will no longer release them;" and in the *Syriac,* "I will no longer spare them." The verb הנחם seems to have been taken as coming from נח, with an ם affixed, and put here in Hiphil—"I am wearied with causing them to rest," or, "with forbearing," as rendered by *Blayney.* But our version, which is that of *Calvin,* seems preferable, and is adopted by *Piscator, Grotius,* and *Venema.* The last indeed proposes the joining of this line with the next verse, which *Blayney* has adopted, and in that case he prefers the reading of the *Septuagint* and *Syriac.* Then the passage would be,—

I am wearied with forbearing them,
or, with suffering them to rest;
7. And I will fan them with a fan in the gates of the land.

He truly says that there is a kind of contrast between the suffering of them to rest quietly, and the fanning of them in the gates of land for the purpose of dispersing them.—*Ed.*

He confirms here the same truth. The verb which I have rendered in the future may be rendered in the past tense, but I still think it to be a prediction of what was to come. But as to what follows, *I have bereaved, I have destroyed*, it must, I have no doubt, be referred to time past.

He then says, *I will fan* or scatter *them*, for the verb זרה, *zare*, means to scatter, but as *with a fan* follows, (the word is derived from the same root,) I wish to retain the repetition. Then it is, *I will fan them with a fan* through *all the gates of the earth.* Many give the meaning, "through the cities," which I do not approve, as it seems a frigid explanation. On the contrary the Prophet means by "the gates of the earth," all countries, for the Jews thought that they should be always safe and quiet in their own cities. By taking a part for the whole, gates do indeed, as it appears elsewhere, signify cities; but as the Jews trusted in their own defences, and thought that they could never be drawn out from these quiet nests, the word gates is in a striking manner transferred to signify any kind of exit; *I will fan* you, says God, but where? *through all gates of the earth*, or through all countries and through all deserts; wherever there is a region open for you there you must pass through. Ye are wont to pass in and out through your gates, and ye have there your quiet homes, but there shall be hereafter to you other cities, other gates, even all countries and all deserts, all ways, and, in short, every sort of passage.[1]

Then follows, *I have bereaved, I have destroyed my people; they have not returned from their own ways.* Here no doubt he condemns the Jews for their sottishness, because they had not repented after having been warned by grievous judgments, which God had executed partly on them and partly on their brethren. For the kingdom of Israel had been cut off: when they saw the ten tribes driven into exile ought they not to have been terrified by such an example? Hence also another Prophet says, "There is no one who

[1] Though *Calvin* has many on his side in his view as to "the gates," yet the most suitable meaning is that presented in our version. God is represented as a fanner, standing in "the gates of the land," that is, in the gates of the cities of the land, and thence fanning or scattering the inhabitants to all parts of the world.—*Ed.*

mourns for the bruising of Joseph." (Amos vi. 6.) God had set before their eyes a sad and dreadful spectacle; they ought then to have acknowledged in the destruction of Israel what they themselves deserved, and to have turned to God. It is then this extreme hardness that God upbraids them with, for though he had bereaved his people, the ten tribes, and destroyed them, and though also the kingdom of Judah had been in a great measure depressed, yet they returned not from their own ways. It hence appeared more fully evident that they deserved the severest judgments, as they were become wholly irreclaimable. He then adds—

8. Their widows are increased to me above the sand of the seas: I have brought upon them, against the mother of the young men, a spoiler at noon-day: I have caused *him* to fall upon it suddenly, and terrors upon the city.

8. Multiplicatæ sunt mihi viduæ ejus supra arenam maris, (præ arena maris:) immisi illis (venire feci illis) super matrem juvenis (*id est,* super turmam, *vel,* multitudinem juvenum) vastatorem in meridie; et projeci (cadere feci, *ad verbum*) super ipsam repentè tumultum et terrores, (*quanquam de his vocibus postea erit aliquid dicendum.*)

He says first, *Multiplied have been his widows;* because the men had been almost all killed in battle. If the Prophet is the speaker, the particle לי, *li,* is redundant, but if the words be referred to God, we know that the people were in such a way under the government of God that he calls the widows his, as he calls the children his who were born Israelites. But in this there is no great importance, only that if we consider God to be speaker the sense will be this, "Behold, it is by no means unknown to me how numerous his widows are: as then I am merciful I have not heedlessly and without reason suffered such slaughters among the people." The Prophet intended to shew that so great was the obstinacy of the Jews that they struggled against all the judgments of God; and it is a proof of dreadful impiety when men rush on heedlessly and pay no attention to any punishments. And this is what the Prophet means when he says that the *widows* were multiplied. And he adds, *More than the sand of the sea.* This was surely a strange thing; so many slaughters were presented to their view that their great perverseness might become more evident, and yet he says that they were not moved.

What follows must be applied to God, *I have made to come to them, on the troop of youths, a waster.*[1] This is an explanation of the former clause, as though he had said, "The reason why there are so many widows is, because God has destroyed all the men." As the Jews might have ascribed this to their enemies, God declares that he was the author of all the slaughters which they had suffered. He then shews that these slaughters were not fortuitous as men suppose who think that fortune prevails mostly in war, for they do not ascribe so much to the wisdom and valour of men as to fortune, being ignorant of the Providence of God. Here then God shews that the whole of the flower of the people had been indeed cut off by the swords of enemies, but that the Chaldeans or the Assyrians had not come of their own accord, or by an impulse of their own, but by a hidden impulse, and that of God, who had resolved to punish that irreclaimable people. This then is the reason why God not only speaks of a waster, but also intimates that the enemies were impelled by his influence, and carried on the war as it were under his banner, authority, and guidance.

He says, *at mid-day,* even when the Jews might have exercised greater watchfulness. But he shews that he was against them, for they were not taken by the craft of their enemies, as had often been the case, nor were they surprised by secret designs, but their enemies attacked them openly and boldly, even at the time when many of their cities were fortified, and the people thought that they had sufficient defences. As the enemies then dared to assail them in the middle of the day, (for such is the meaning of the Hebrew word,) and during the clearest light, it was certainly a fuller proof of God's vengeance; for under such a circumstance the contrivance and counsel of men were not so evident, but

[1] This rendering is the *Targum;* "the mother (and) the youths," is the *Septuagint;* "the mother of a youth," the *Vulgate;* "both mother and youths," the *Syriac;* "the mother and the youths," the *Arabic, Junius* and *Tremellius, Piscator,* and *Gataker* take the "mother" for the chief city, the metropolis, and consider the "youth," or "the chosen one," to be the "waster," signifying Nebuchadnezzar,—"And I will bring to them, against the mother-city, a chosen one, a waster at mid-day." So *Blayney* substantially, only he renders the verb in the past tense.—*Ed.*

the hand of God, which he stretched forth from heaven as it were in an open and visible manner.

He afterwards adds, *And I have cast*, or caused to fall, *upon them suddenly;* some say, the city; others, the enemy; and עיר, *oir*, means a city, and sometimes an enemy; but another explanation seems more probable, that God had sent on them a tumult and terrors, for the word עיר, *oir*, comes from the verb עור, *our*, which signifies to excite. It may therefore be taken for tumult, and this sense I prefer, for they who render the word city, are constrained to adopt a forced and far-fetched explanation, "To fall have I made suddenly the city," that is, cities, "upon them." There is first a change of number, and then, to fall have I made cities, that is, the ruins of cities, upon them, seems an unnatural phrase; but the sense would be most suitable were we to render the word tumult, for what immediately follows is, *and terrors.* Some however render the word בהלות, *belut*, adverbially *suddenly*, and consider that the same thing is said twice. He had said just before, "I have cast upon her suddenly," but now he says, "hastenings." Such is the version, but not suitable, for the two words עיר, *oir*, and בהלות, *belut*, are joined together. I therefore give this simple explanation—that the Jews were suddenly smitten with despair because they thought that their enemies were afar off, and that they had to apprehend no danger. Then it is, *suddenly have I sent upon them a tumult and terrors.*[1] He then adds—

9. She that hath born seven languisheth: she hath given up the ghost; her sun is gone down while *it was* yet day; she hath been ashamed and confounded: and the residue of them will I deliver to the sword before their enemies, saith the Lord.

9. Debilitata est quæ peperit septem, et expiravit anima ejus (*alii vertunt, afflicta fuit, sed* נפח *significat sufflare; videtur autem hîc metaphoricè poni pro expirare:* expiravit *ergo* anima ejus;) ingressus est sol ejus (*hoc est,* occidit sol) in adhuc die (*id est,* cum adhuc esset dies;) confusa est et erubuit: et reliquias ipsorum gladio dabo (ad gladium exponam) coram inimicis ipsorum, dicit Jehova.

[1] "Trembling and haste, (σπουδὴν,)" is the version of the *Septuagint;* "tumult and trembling," of the *Syriac;* "terror and trembling," of the *Arabic;* the *Vulgate* retains only the word "terror." Various have been the explanations of the word עיר, which *Calvin* renders "tumult," consistently with the general tenor of the ancient versions. *Gataker* renders it "watcher;" *Blayney*, "enemy;" and others "city;" but the most suitable to the passage is "tumult," or commotion.—*Ed.*

He proceeds with his narrative; he says, that fruitful women had been weakened, not as we see to be often the case, for by frequent child-bearing we know the strength of women is diminished; but here he speaks of the strength which mothers derive from their children; for a numerous offspring is the support of mothers. She then who has many children seems strong, as she is by so many shields defended. As then mothers were wont to place much dependence on their offspring, he says that they were weakened as to their strength when they were bereaved of all their children, as though they had been barren.

He afterwards adds, that the *soul*, the people, *had expired;* for he speaks not here of women, but of the whole people. For it afterwards follows, *Set hath her sun while it was yet day;* that is, when prosperity seemed certain, God suddenly involved them in adversity, and as it were surrounded them with darkness, when they thought that prosperous fortune was shining on them. He at last says, that they were *confounded and ashamed;* and at the same time he declares, that he would give all who remained to the sword before their enemies; as though he had said, "They have not yet suffered all the punishment allotted to them, for they are not subdued, though I have heavily and severely chastised them; as then they are incurable, the sword shall destroy the remainder; for my vengeance shall not cease to pursue them, until I shall utterly consume them."[1]

[1] The whole passage, including the 7th, 8th and 9th verses, presents difficulties as to the time intended. The verbs, from the middle of the 7th to the last clause in verse the 9th, are all in the past tense, and are so given in the *Septuagint*, *Vulgate*, and the *Targum;* but in the *Syriac* in the future tense. Our version is not uniform. It is better to give the tenses as they are, for the reference seems to be to God's past judgments; and at the end of the 9th verse, God speaks of what he would do,—

7. And I will fan them with a fan in the gates of the land.
I have bereaved, I have destroyed my people;
From their ways have they not turned:
8. Increased to me have their (people) widows
More than the sand of the sea;
I brought on them, on the mother of the youth,
A disaster at mid-day;
I caused to come upon her suddenly
Tumult and terrors:
9. Languish did she who gave birth to seven,

PRAYER.

Grant, Almighty God, that we may not by our hardness so provoke thy judgment against us, as to constrain thee with an armed hand to assail us; but may we through a meek and submissive spirit be so influenced by thy threatenings as to anticipate that vengeance, by which we see that all the reprobate and the perverse have been visited; and may we so endeavour by true repentance to obtain thy favour, that we may receive thy daily blessings and benefits, until we shall at length come to the full and real enjoyment of all those blessings, which have been laid up for us in thy celestial kingdom, through Christ, our Lord.—Amen.

Lecture Sixtieth.

10. Woe is me, my mother, that thou hast born me a man of strife and a man of contention to the whole earth! I have neither lent on usury, nor men have lent to me on usury; *yet* every one of them doth curse me.

10. Hei mihi! mater mea, quod genueris me virum rixæ et virum litis toti terræ: non fœneratus sum et non fœnerati sunt mecum; quisque maledicit mihi.

The Prophet, when he saw that his labour availed nothing, or was not so fruitful as he wished, no doubt felt somewhat like a man, and shewed his own weakness. It must however be observed, that he was so restrained by the secret power of the Holy Spirit, that he did not break forth intemperately, as is the case with many; but he kept the right end so in view, that his sorrows had ever a regard to his object, even to render his labour useful to the people. A clear example of which is seen in these words.

But he addresses his mother, as though he counted his own

Pant for breath did her soul,
Set did her sun during the day time,
Ashamed has she been and confounded:
And the remainder of them to the sword will I give,
In the presence of their enemies, saith Jehova.

As he speaks of bereavement, of widows, and of giving birth to seven, it seems evident, that "the mother of the youth" is a poetical singular, meaning "the mothers of youths," or of young men. Whether mother is to be taken here metaphorically for Jerusalem, is another question; but I think otherwise. The loss of mothers as to their children is what is spoken of. And from having mentioned the case of mothers in their bereavement, the Prophet in the next verse refers to his own mother, and to his own unhappy condition.—*Ed.*

life a curse; what does this mean? "Why," he says, "hast thou begotten me, my mother? Woe to me, that I have been born a man of strife and of contention!" We learn from these words, that the Prophet was not so composed and calm in his mind, but that he felt angry when he saw that he effected less than he wished; and yet it is evident from the context, that all this was expressed for the benefit of the public, even that the Jews might know, that their hardness of heart in despising God's devoted servant, yea, in maliciously opposing him, would not turn out to their benefit. This is the purport of the whole.

He calls himself a *man of strife*, not only because he was constrained to contend with the people, for this he had in common with all prophets. God does not send them to flatter or to please the world; they must therefore contend with the world, for no one is brought to a right state, so as to undertake the yoke of God willingly and submissively, until he is proved guilty. Hence men will never obey God, they will never submit to his word, until they know that they are in a manner condemned; and for this reason have I said, that this evil is common to all prophets,—that they have to contend with the world. But Jeremiah calls himself a *man of strife and contention*, because he was slanderously spoken of throughout Judea, as one who through his moroseness drove the whole people to contentions and strifes. This then is to be referred to the false judgments formed by the people; for there was hardly any one who did not say that he was a turbulent man, and that if he was removed, there would have been tranquillity in the city and throughout the whole land. The same objection is at this day made by the enemies of the truth and godliness; they say, that we needlessly create disturbances, and that if we were quiet, there would be the most delightful peace throughout the whole world, and that dissensions and strifes arise only from us, that we are the fans by which the whole world is kindled into contentions. It was then for this reason that Jeremiah complained that he was born a man of strife and contention; not that he was contentious—not that that he gave any occasion to the people to speak so slanderously of him; for the subject here is not respecting the character of the Prophet, as he knew that his courage was approved by God ; but as he saw that he was urged and charged with these false accusations, he calls himself a *man of strife and a man of contention ;* the last word is from דן, *den,* which means to contend.

But as to the exclamation respecting his *mother,* I have already reminded you that it was an evidence of an intemperate feeling; for had he spoken in a composed state of mind, what had he to do with his mother, so as to make her an associate in the evil he complains of? He indeed seems to ascribe a part of the blame to his mother, because she had given him birth. Now this appears unreasonable. But it may at the same time be easily gathered, that the Prophet was not led away by so great a vehemence, except for the sake of promoting the public good, and that it was for this end that he uttered his complaint ; for it was not his purpose to condemn his mother, though at the first view it appears so ; but though she was innocent, he still shews that he was unjustly loaded with such calumnies, as that he was a man of strife and contention ; as though he had said, "Enquire of my mother, who hath begotten me, whether I was contentious from the womb? has my mother been the cause why ye say that I am a turbulent man and the author of strifes ? Doubtless nothing can be imputed to my mother ; and I am as innocent as she is." We now then see that the Prophet indirectly condemns the wickedness of the people, because they calumniated him, as though he moved tumults and strifes through the whole land ; and this he more fully confirms by the words which follow :—

I have not given on usury, nor have they borrowed of me on usury ;[1] *yet every one curses me.* He shews here that it was not for a private reason that he was hated by the whole people and loaded with calumnies: for whence come hatreds, and strifes, and complaints, and quarrels, and contentions

[1] Not one of the versions, except the *Vulgate,* mentions "usury;" and *Parkhurst* says that the verb does not include the idea. Then the rendering ought to be,

I have not lent, nor have they lent to me.

There had been no money transactions between them, which are commonly the causes of disputes and contentions—*Ed.*

among men, except through unfair dealing in their intercourse with one another? When, therefore, every one is bent on his own private advantage, he ill bears anything to be taken from him. It is indeed a rare thing in the world, that they who carry on business with one another are really friends, and that they wholly approve of each other's conduct; for, as I have already said, covetousness so prevails, that justice and equity disappear among most men. Hence the Prophet says, that he had not *lent on usury.* Under one kind he includes all transactions of life, as though he had said, *Je n'ay point traffiqué,* I have had no contention about money affairs, for I have neither lent nor borrowed money, so that I have had no contention with the people on a private concern, nor have they quarrelled with me as though I had injured them or defrauded them, as though they had suffered any loss on my account: yet they all *curse* me."[1]

We see that the Prophet here testifies that he had not incurred the displeasure of the people through his own fault, or on account of any private concern, but because he had faithfully discharged his duty to God and to his Church. He then brings against the people a most awful accusation, that they carried on war, not with a mortal man, but rather with God himself. We now understand what the Prophet had in view.

But all faithful teachers are here reminded, that if they perform their office strenuously and wisely, they will surely be loaded with many calumnies, and be called tumultuous, or morose, or disturbers of the peace. They ought then to be fortified against such stumblingblocks, so that they may persevere in the course of their calling. They ought at the same time to take heed lest they create enemies through any private concerns. For when the pastors of the Church abstain from every public business, yet when they contend, as

[1] Literally it is,—

The whole of it (the land) is reviling (or cursing) me.

As there is something anomalous in the form of the participle, *Blayney* proposes an emendation, and thinks the right reading to be כלהם קללוני, "All of them curse me." The versions and the *Targum* favour this reading, which is also adopted by the commonly too venturous *Houbigant*, and approved by *Horsley*, one equally venturous and bold. By dropping the ו, as in many copies, the anomaly is removed.—*Ed.*

they ought with the world, all immediately cry out that they are contentious and turbulent; but if the other be added, if they quarrel with this or that man about worldly things, then it cannot be but that the word of God will be evil spoken of through their fault. Hence great care ought to be taken that those who sustain the office of public teaching should not engage in worldly business, and be thus exposed to the necessity of contending about worldly things: they have enough to do, and more than enough, in the warfare in which the Lord has engaged them.

Now when the Prophet says that they all *cursed* him, it was a sad instance of impiety; for he speaks not of heathens but of the seed of Abraham. There was no Church then in the world but at Jerusalem, and yet the Prophet was regarded there as contentious and a man of strife. It ought not then to appear strange to us, that not only professed enemies of Christ load us with reproaches, but that they also curse us who deem themselves to be members of the Church. It now follows—

11. The Lord said, Verily it shall be well with thy remnant; verily I will cause the enemy to entreat thee *well* in the time of evil, and in the time of affliction.

11. Et dixit Jehova, si non reliquiæ tuæ in bonum, si non occurrere fecero tibi in tempore mali, et in tempore afflictionis (*vel,* angustiæ) hostem.

God at the beginning of this verse no doubt intimates that he would be propitious to his servant, and grant him what he asked. We then conclude that the Prophet's prayer was heard; and hence also becomes manifest what I have stated, that the Prophet was not so led away by the force of grief, but that he chiefly regarded the benefit of the people. God then was so propitious to his request, that he said that it would *be well* with his *remnant,* that what remained would be blessed.

Interpreters differ as to the second clause: some apply what is said to the people, *I will make the enemy to meet thee in the time of evil, and in the time of trouble:* and so they take this view, that God at the beginning of the verse answers the Prophet, and intimates that his request was accepted, so that there would be a better and happier end than what then appeared; and they think that God then turns his discourse to the people, "With regard to you, I will make the enemy to meet you in the day of affliction." But this explanation seems forced. I prefer to regard the whole verse as addressed to the Prophet. God promises first that his remnant would be prosperous; and by remnant he means the remaining time or the end of life, as though he had said, "I will at length have pity on thee, so that the things which cause thee the greatest grief shall turn into joy: thine end then shall be more prosperous than thou thinkest." Then the words which follow confirm the previous sentence: for the Prophet might have objected and said, "Then either the people shall be delivered from all trouble, or I shall not escape a part of the calamity." To this God replies and says, "Thou and others must suffer many things, but I will *make the enemy to meet thee*, that is, I will make the enemy to be propitious to thee, and even of his own accord to anticipate thee.

Interpreters differ still farther respecting the verb הפגעתי, *epegoti;* some regard it in a transitive sense, "To meet thee will I make the enemy;" others render the sentence thus, "I will meet the enemy for thee," or, "I will cause the enemy to ask for thee." The verb, פגע, *pego,* means sometimes to meet, either in a good or bad sense; as when one goes as an enemy against another, he is said to meet him; or, when one offers help and shews kindness to another, he is said to meet him. But the word has another meaning, and signifies sometimes to ask, and so some take it here, "I will cause the enemy to ask for thee." But this is far-fetched: God did not send messengers to pacify the Babylonians towards his servant Jeremiah. I prefer to render the words thus, "I will meet the enemy for thee," or, "I will cause the enemy to meet thee;" that is, "I will pacify him by my secret influence, so that he will of himself spare thee and treat thee kindly." And we know that it so happened; for Jeremiah was loosed from his chains and was allowed his liberty, so that he was permitted to go wherever he wished. As then the enemies treated him with so much kindness, it appears evident that what God had before promised was fulfilled.

As to the main thing intended, there is no ambiguity in the words: God promised that the latter end of Jeremiah would be happy, and that though he was to suffer somewhat in the common calamity of the whole people, yet the enemy would treat him kindly, so that his condition would be better and more desirable than that of others.[1]

But why did Jeremiah make this public? why did he give this description? why did he commit it to writing? even that the Jews might understand that they who harassed him, when he had done them no injury, dealt unjustly with him. They had indeed been excited by him, but it was through what his office required, for he could not deny obedience to God. Jeremiah then made public what God only knew before, that he might produce an impression on them, provided any hope of repentance yet remained. And for the same reason also was the promise of God added; for the Jews ought to have been terrified, when they saw that such an end was promised by God to the Prophet; for what must have happened to them, except the curse of God to the utter-

[1] This verse, and the three which follow, have caused considerable variety of opinion. Some, like *Calvin*, *Grotius*, *Henry*, and *Scott*, apply this to the Prophet and the rest to the people; but others, as *Blayney*, consider the whole as addressed to the Prophet, and *Venema* regards the whole as addressed to the people. But what appears the most probable is, that the Prophet is addressed, and in the 11th and 12th verses personally, and then as identified with the people in verses the 13th and 14th. There is no change of person, and this makes it difficult to regard two parties as addressed.

This verse, the 11th, is in the past tense and not in the future, and may be thus rendered,—

Jehovah said,—
Has not thy ministry been for good?
Have I not interposed for thee in the time of evil,
And in the time of distress, with the enemy?

There are various readings for the word I render "ministry," which *Parkhurst* thinks comes from שרת, to serve. Very few readings favour the word which means a "remnant," and of the versions the *Vulgate* alone. The reading mostly countenanced (19 MSS.) is שרותיך, derived from שרה, to loose, or to let go, "Have I not happily let thee go?" In this case לטוב must be rendered adverbially, happily, or fully. *Blayney's* version is,—

Have I not brought thee off advantageously?

But the most natural meaning is what *Parkhurst* proposes, which is approved by *Horsley*, only he renders the sentence in the present tense, "Is not thy ministry for good?" while the only verb in the verse is in the past tense, and so ought this clause to be.—*Ed.*

most? We hence see, that in the complaint of the Prophet, and in the answer given by God, the salvation of the people was regarded; for the complaint contains a most severe reproof, and the answer of God threatens a most dreadful judgment to the rebellious people. It follows—

12. Shall iron break the northern iron and the steel?	12. An conteret ferrum ferrum ab aquilone et æs (*vel*, chalybem?)

This verse also has been taken in different ways by interpreters: some take the word *iron*, when repeated in a different case, "Will iron break iron?" but others think the subject wanting in the clause, and consider people to be understood, "Will the Jews break the iron, even the iron from the north, and not only the iron but the brass also, *or*, the the brass mixed with iron?" There is in reality no difference, but in words only. If we read, "Will the iron break the iron from the north?" the meaning will be, "Though there be great hardness in you, can it yet break that which is in the Assyrians? but ye are not equal to them: make your strength as great as you please, still the Chaldeans will be harder to break you; for if ye are iron, they are brass or steel, and so it will not be possible for you to sustain their violent attacks."

As the meaning of the Prophet is sufficiently evident, I will not insist on words, though the rendering I most approve is this, "Will iron break the iron (the repetition is emphatical) from the north and the brass?"

We here also see that the design of the holy man was, to divest the Jews of that false confidence in which they boasted: for how was it, that they were so refractory, except that they did not dread any misfortune? As then they were secure, predictions had but little weight with them. Hence the Prophet, in order to beat down this ferocity, says, that there would be greater hardness in the Chaldeans, for they would be like iron, yea, and steel also.[1] It follows—

[1] If we consider what is said to the Prophet in chap. i. 18, and in the twentieth verse of this chapter, we shall see the meaning of this verse: he was no doubt the iron and the brass: and the opinion of *Blayney* is probable, that the "enemy" in the previous verse (which is a poetical singular for the plural enemies) is the nominative case to the verb "break."

13. Thy substance and thy treasures will I give to the spoil without price, and *that* for all thy sins, even in all thy borders.	13. Opes tuas et thesauros tuos in direptionem dabo, non in permutatione (*hoc est,* absque pretio,) et propter omne scelus tuum, et propter omnem finem tuum (*vel,* terminum tuum, in omnibus terminis tuis, *ad verbum ; sicuti etiam* in omnibus sceleribus.)

But, there is a difference among interpreters as to the word גבול, *gebul.* I indeed allow that it means a border: but Jeremiah, as I think, when he intended to state things that are different, made use of different forms of speech ; but as the construction is the same, I see not how the word can mean the borders of the land. I hence think that it is to be taken here metaphorically for counsels ; as though he had said, " On account of all thy wicked deeds and on account of all thy ends, that is, of all thy counsels, I will make thy wealth and thy treasures a plunder." For true is that saying of the heathen poet,

There is something where thou goest and to which thou levellest thy bow.[1]

When we undertake any business, we have some end in view. Then the Prophet calls their adulteries, frauds, rapines, violencies and murders, wicked deeds ; but he calls their counsels, borders, such counsels as they craftily took, by which they manifested their depravity and baseness.

Then, in the first place, he declares that God would be a just avenger against their wicked deeds, and against all the ends which the Jews had proposed to themselves ; and at the same time he points out and mentions the kind of punishment they were to have,—that the Lord would give for a plunder all their *wealth and treasures,* and that *without exchanging ;* some read, " without price," and consider the meaning to be,—that the Jews would be so worthless, that no one would buy them : but this is too refined. I doubt not but that the Prophet intimates, that whatever the Jews

God, having before referred to what he had done for the Prophet, now says,—

Can he break the iron,
The iron from the north and the brass ?

God had made him an " iron pillar, and a wall of brass :" and he asks now, was it possible for his enemies to destroy him whom God had thus made. The hardest iron came from the north of Judea. The future tense is to be read here potentially.—*Ed.*

[1] Est aliquid quò tendis et in quod dirigis arcum.—*Per. Sat.* iii. 60.

possessed would become a prey to their enemies, so that it would be taken away from them without any price or bartering; as though he had said, "Your enemies will freely plunder all that you have without any permission from you, and will regard as their own, even by the right of victory, whatever ye think you have so laid up as never to be taken away."[1] He afterwards adds—

14. And I will make *thee* to pass with thine enemies into a land *which* thou knowest not: for a fire is kindled in mine anger, *which* shall burn upon you.	14. Et transire faciam ad hostem in terram quam non cognoscis; quia ignis ascensus est in ira mea (*alii vertunt*, in nare; אפי significat utrunque) super vos ardebit.

He pursues the same subject. He had said, that they would be exposed as a prey to their enemies, so that all their wealth would be plundered with impunity: he now adds, *I will deliver you to the enemy*, that is, I will give you into the hands of your enemies, that they may remove you elsewhere. He afterwards mentions a circumstance, which must have rendered exile much worse; for when any one changes his place and is not led to a distance, the evil is more tolerable; but when any one is carried beyond the sea, or into distant lands, there is a much greater cause for sorrow, as there is no hope of return to one's own country.

[1] This verse and the following are said by *Horsley* to be "very obscure:" and there seems to be no way of understanding them, except we regard the Prophet as classed with the people; and the conclusion of verse fourteenth favours this idea, "On you, עליכם, it shall burn." The Prophet himself did not wholly escape the evils which came on the people. Then this verse and the following I would render thus,—

13. Thy wealth and thy treasures for spoil will I give,
Not for a price, but for all thy sins,
Even in all thy borders;
14. And I will make thine enemies to pass
To a land thou knowest not;
For a fire has been kindled in my wrath,
On you it shall burn.

The "enemy" before is now "enemies." The verb "make to pass," has various readings, owing evidently to the similarity of two letters. The versions, except the *Vulgate*, have "I will make thee to serve thine enemies;" but the received text is the most suitable to the passage. *Blayney's* rendering is,—

I will cause *them* to pass with thine enemies—

By "them" he understands "thy wealth and thy treasures;" but this sort of construction can hardly be admitted; and it seems incongruous.—*Ed.*

Then despair increases the grief. Add to this, that not to hear of one's native land, as though we were in another world, is also a bitter trial.

The Prophet then adds, *Because fire has been kindled in my wrath, and against you it shall burn.* He means that God would be implacable until they were consumed ; for his wrath had been kindled on account of their perverse wickedness.

Now all these things were foretold to them, that they might know that God would execute a just vengeance by making the Chaldeans their conquerors: for they might have thought that this happened by chance, according to what has been said by heathen writers, that the events of war are uncertain, that Mars is indifferent (*Cicero in Epist.*) Thus they ascribe to chance whatever happens through God's providence. That the Jews then might know that they were chastised by God's hand and by his just vengeance, it was necessary that this should have been declared to them: and therefore he speaks now of the Chaldeans and then of God himself, whose agents the Chaldeans were, for they were guided by his hand. He said before, " Will iron break the iron from the north ?" This we have explained of the Chaldeans : but now he turns to God himself, the author of the calamity brought on the Jews: for the Chaldeans could have done nothing, except through his guidance and direction.

Hence he says, *I will cause them to pass over to the enemy, even to a land which they know not.* And the reason which follows ought to have availed to check all their complaints. We indeed know how clamorous the Jews were, for they often accused God of cruelty, as it appears from many passages. The Prophet then, in order to restrain them, says, that the *fire of God's wrath* had been *kindled,* and that it could not be extinguished, but would burn on them, that is, would entirely consume them. At the same time he condemns their obstinacy, for they allowed no place to God's mercy, though often warned. They might indeed have pacified him, had they repented. Hence the Prophet here condemns their sottishness ; for they increased their judgment by a continued progress in their evil ways. He afterwards adds—

15. O Lord, thou knowest: remember me, and visit me, and revenge me of my persecutors; take me not away in thy long-suffering: know that for thy sake I have suffered rebuke.

15. Tu nosti, Jehova; recordare mei, et visita me, et ulciscere me à persecutoribus meis, ne in prorogatione (*vel*, protractione) iræ tuæ tollas me; cognosce sustinuisse me (*id est*, quòd sustinuerim) propter te opprobrium.

The Prophet again turns to God, to shew that he had to do with the deaf. This breaking off in the Prophet's discourse has much more force than if he had pursued regularly his subject. Had he spoken calmly and in uniform order to the people, his address would have been less forcible, than by speaking to them as it were angrily and by severely reproving them, and then immediately by turning from them and addressing God as though bidding adieu to men. Of this we have spoken elsewhere, but it is well to remind you of what we have before noticed. We now perceive the design of the Prophet, in thus abruptly turning from the people to God, and then again from God to the people, even because he indignantly bore the loss of his labour, when the ears of almost all were closed, and when they had become so hardened that they had no fear of God, nor any regard for his teaching. As then the Prophet indignantly bore so great a wickedness, he could not but speak in a hasty manner.

According to this strain, he now says, *Thou knowest, Jehovah; remember me, and visit me, and avenge me of mine enemies.* The Prophet, however, seems here to have been more angry than he ought to have been, for revenge is a passion unbecoming the children of God. How was it, then, that the Prophet was so indignant against the people that he desired revenge? We have said elsewhere that the prophets, though freed from every carnal feeling, might yet have justly prayed for vengeance on the reprobate. We must distinguish between private and public feelings, and also between the passions of the flesh, which keep within no limits, and the zeal of the Spirit. It is certain that the Prophet had no regard to himself when he thus spoke; but he dismissed every regard for himself, and had regard only to the cause of God: for inconsiderate zeal often creeps in, so that we wish all to be condemned of whom we do not approve; and such was the excessive zeal of the disciples, when they said, "Lord, bid fire to descend from heaven to consume them, as was done by Elias." (Luke ix. 54.) But it is necessary not only to be moved by a pious zeal, but also to be guided by a right judgment: and this second requisite was possessed by the Prophet; for he did not let loose the reins to his own zeal, but subjected himself to the guidance of the Holy Spirit. Since, then, these two things were united,—a right zeal, to the exclusion of any private feeling,—and the spirit of wisdom and a right judgment, it was lawful to ask for vengeance on the reprobate, as the Prophet does.

There is further no doubt but that he pitied the people; but he was in a manner freed from the influence of human feelings, and had put off whatever might have disturbed him and led him away from moderation. Though, then, the Prophet was thus emancipated and freed from every kind of perturbation, there is yet no doubt but that he prayed for final judgment on the reprobate; and yet, if there were any healable, he doubtless wished them to be saved, and also prayed anxiously for them.

In short, whenever the prophets were carried away by such a fervour as this, we must understand that they were filled by the Spirit of Christ; and we must know that, when they were thus filled, their whole zeal was directed against the reprobate, while they were at the same time endeavouring to gather together all that could be saved: and the same was the case with David; when he fervently implored destruction on his enemies, he no doubt sustained the person of Christ, as he was filled by his Spirit. (Psalm xxxv. 4-6.) Hence he turned and levelled all his vehemence against the reprobate; but, when there was any hope of salvation, David also, in the spirit of kindness, prayed for the restoration of those who seemed to have already perished. Now, then, when the Prophet says, "Thou knowest, Jehovah; remember me, and visit me, and avenge me of my persecutors," he doubtless does not mean all his persecutors, but those who had been given up and devoted to destruction, and whom he himself knew to be reprobates.[1]

He afterwards shews what he meant by these words—*remember me, and visit me;* for he says, *Take me not away by deferring.* So they render the passage, "Whilst thou bearest with the impiety of this people, and for a time suspendest thy vengeance, let not thy wrath take me away." The word ארך, *arek,* means to defer, to protract, and also to prolong, to extend, and to continue. Hence this meaning is not unsuitable, "Take me not away in the protraction of thy wrath;" that is, "By protracting thy wrath, not only for one day, but for a long time, *take me not away,* involve me not in the same destruction with the reprobate." David also prayed for the same thing, "When thou destroyest the wicked, involve me not with them." (Psalm xxvi. 9.) The sum of the whole is, that the Prophet asks a favour for himself, that God would make a difference between him and the reprobate while he was protracting his wrath; that is, while he was not only taking vengeance on the impiety of the people for a short time, but also while he was adding calamities to calamities, and accumulating evils on evils, and while thus his fire burned for a long time, until the whole land was consumed: and this is the meaning which I prefer, though all the interpreters agree in another.[2]

[1] There are distinctions here made not allowed by the passage. To pray for vengeance on enemies was in accordance with the covenant made with Abraham, "I will bless them that bless thee, and curse him that curseth thee," Gen. xii. 3. See also Gen. xxvii. 29; Numb. xxiv. 9. As they were the enemies of God's servant for delivering his word, they were the enemies of God himself; and they had already been wholly repudiated by God, and given up to judgment.—*Ed.*

[2] The versions favour another view. The *Septuagint* omit the verb, and connect "long-suffering" with the previous clause, "Defend me from my persecutors, not in thy long-suffering;" that is, without delay, as the *Targum* literally expresses it. The *Vulgate* is, "Do not in thy patience take me;" the *Syriac,* "Do not according to thy long-suffering bring me out;" the *Arabic,* "Without delay;" it omits the verb, and connects the words with the former sentence like the *Septuagint.* The words may be thus literally rendered,—

Not in (or, according to) thy long-suffering receive me;

that is, under thy care and protection: he deprecated delay. This is the purport of all the versions, and also of the *Targum.*

Venema divides the clause,—

Let there be no lengthening of thy wrath: receive me;

It must further be noticed that the Prophet, in this prayer, did not so much consult his own advantage as the good of the people,—that they might at length dread the dreadful judgment which was at hand. We have already stated how supine a security prevailed throughout Judea; and they also hoped, that if any calamity happened it would be for a short time, so that, having endured it, they might again live in pleasure and quietness. Hence the Prophet speaks of the *protraction* of God's *wrath*, in order that they might know, as I have already said, that the fire which had been kindled could not be extinguished until they all perished.

PRAYER.

Grant, Almighty God, that as we cease not by our sins daily to provoke thy wrath against us, and are also ungrateful to thee and disobedient to thy heavenly doctrine,—O grant that we may at length know what we have hitherto deserved, and become so displeased with our vices, that being really and from the heart turned to thee, we may above all things seek to be reconciled to thee and received into favour, so that thou mayest rule us by thy Holy Spirit, and confirm us in true obedience and godliness, until we shall at length enjoy that eternal felicity which has been prepared for us in heaven by Christ our Lord.—Amen.

Know that for thee I have borne reproach.

Blayney's version is hardly intelligible,—

Within the length of thine anger comprehend me not.

The meaning of which he says is, " Lengthen not thy resentment as to comprehend me within its limits."

Probably the rendering of *Cocceius* is the best,—

Do not through thy long-suffering take me away;

that is, " Do not bear long with my persecutors, and thus allow them to destroy me."

The verb here used seems simply to take; but it signifies sometimes to take away, and sometimes to take into favour, to take under protection. The most intelligible rendering seems to be as follows:—

15. Thou knowest, Jehova;
Remember me, and visit me,
And take vengeance for me on my persecutors;
Through thy long-suffering *towards them* take me not away;
Know *that* I have for thee borne reproach.

" Take me not away" means " Suffer me not to be taken away." He feared for his life if the vengeance he denounced on the people was not soon executed. See verse 18.—*Ed.*

Lecture Sixty-First.

16. Thy words were found, and I did eat them; and thy word was unto me the joy and rejoicing of mine heart: for I am called by thy name, O Lord God of hosts.

16. Inventi sunt sermones tui, et comedi eos, et fuit sermo tuus mihi in gaudium et lætitiam cordis mei; quia invocatum est nomen tuum super me, Jehova Deus exercituum.

The Prophet had said in the last verse that he was loaded with reproach on God's account; for in his intercourse with his own people he did not incur their hatred for any private affair, but for his faithfulness in the discharge of his duty: hence arose their reproaches and slanders. He now confirms the same thing in other words, and at the same time explains what might have appeared obscure on account of the brief statement which he had made. This verse, then, is explanatory; for the Prophet shews what he meant by saying that he was burdened with reproaches and calumnies on account of God's name.

Found, he says, *by me have been thy words, and I did eat them,* and they turned to me for *joy of heart.* Hence then it was that he was hated by the whole people, because he laboured to obey from the heart and in sincerity the command of God, and to perform the office committed to him. But by saying that *words had been found,* he refers to his calling, as though he had said that he had not sought them as ambitious men are wont to do. We indeed see, with regard to many, that they busy themselves about many things, while they might be at ease and be troublesome to none; but a foolish ambition impels them to seek offices for themselves, and thus they excite against themselves the hatred of many. The Prophet therefore testifies here, that he did not ambitiously seek his office, but that it had been conferred on him from above. We may also take the word in another sense—that the Prophet felt assured that God had sent him; for the word, to find, is often thus taken in Scripture; that is, when anything is perceived and known it is said to be found. But the former view is what I approve, for it is more simple. Then the Prophet says that he was called and made a Prophet, when he expected no such thing; for when he in no way intruded himself, God met him, and in a manner anticipated him: and this we have seen in the first chapter; for he said, for the sake of excusing himself, "Ah! Lord, I cannot speak." (ch. i. 8.) We hence see that the Prophet sought to decline the office rather than to desire it as a vocation of honour. So he now rightly declares that God's *words* had been *found* by him, that is, that they had been gratuitously bestowed on him, according to what the Lord says by Isaiah, "I have been found by them who sought me not, and I have manifested myself to them who asked not for me." (Isaiah lxv. 1; Rom. x. 20.)

This indeed is to be applied to all; but as to the meaning of the term, to find, we see how suitable it is. The Prophet then did not hunt for this honour, nor did he desire any such thing, but the favour of God anticipated him.

He afterwards adds, *I did eat them.* He here testifies that he from the heart, and with a sincere feeling, submitted to God's command. We indeed know that many prattle about heavenly mysteries, and have the words of God on their tongues; but the Prophet says that he had *eaten the words* of God; that is, that he brought forth nothing from the tip of his tongue, as the proverb is, but spoke from the bottom of his heart, while engaged in the work of his calling. Well known and sufficiently common in Scripture is the metaphor of eating. When we are said to eat Christ, (Matt. xxvi. 26,) the reference no doubt is to the union we have with him, because we are one body and one spirit. So also we are said to eat the word of God, not when we only taste and immediately spew it out again, as fastidious men do, but when we receive inwardly and digest what the Lord sets before us. For celestial truth is compared to food, and we know by the experience of faith how fit the comparison is. Since then celestial truth is good to feed spiritually our souls, we are justly said to eat it when we do not reject it, but greedily receive it, and so really chew and digest it that it becomes our nourishment. This then is what is meant by the Prophet; for he did not act a fable on the stage when teaching the people, but performed in real earnest the office committed to him, not like an actor, as the case is with many who boast themselves to be ministers of the word, but he was a faithful and true minister of God.

He then says, that the *word* of God *had been to him the joy and gladness of his heart;* that is, that he delighted in that word, like David, who compares it to honey. (Psalm xix. 11; cxix. 103.) The same manner of speaking is used by Ezekiel, ch. ii. 8; and iii. 1-3; for the Prophet is there bidden to eat the volume presented to him; and then he says that it was to him like honey in sweetness, for he embraced the truth with ardent desire, and made privately such a proficiency in the school of God, that his labours became afterwards publicly useful. We hence see how similar was the case with Jeremiah and Ezekiel; for they not only recited, as is commonly done by those who seek to please the ear, what they had been taught, but they became the disciples of the holy Spirit before they became teachers to the people.[1]

It may however be asked, how could the word of God be so sweet and pleasant to the Prophet, when yet it was so full of bitterness; for we have seen elsewhere that many tears were shed by the holy man, and he had expressed a wish that his eyes would flow, as though they were fountains of water. How then could these things agree—the grief and sorrow which the holy man felt for God's judgments, and the joy and gladness which he now mentions? We have said elsewhere that these two feelings, though apparently repugnant, were connected together in the Prophets; they as men deplored and mourned for the ruin of the people, and yet, through the power of the Spirit, they performed their office, and approved of the just vengeance of God. Thus then the word of God became joy to the Prophet, not that he was not

[1] The received text has "thy words." *Calvin* has followed the *Keri* and the ancient versions, as well as our version; but "words" being mentioned in the previous line, the same thing being meant, it is more proper to use "words" here,—

And thy words were to me for exultation,
And (or, even) for the joy of my heart.

It is no objection that the verb, which precedes in Hebrew the noun "words," is in the singular number; it is the idiom of the language, which is exactly the same in Welsh "Exultation" is the visible effect; "the joy of the heart" is the inward feeling, the hidden cause. It is common in Scripture to mention the effect first, and to go back to the cause.—*Ed.*

touched by a deep feeling for the destruction of the people, but that he rose above all human feelings, so as fully to approve of God's judgments. Hosea says the same thing —" Right are the ways of the Lord; the just will walk in them, but the ungodly will stumble and fall." (Hosea xiv. 9.) The Prophet indeed speaks thus, not of the word itself, but of its execution; but yet the design is the same; for the Prophet Hosea checks the wantonness of the people, because they complained that God was too rigid and severe. Right, he says, are the ways of the Lord; the just will walk in them, that is, they will consent to God, and acknowledge that he acts rightly, even when he punishes for sins; but the ungodly will stumble, according to what the Lord says in another place—" Are my ways perverse and not rather yours?" (Ezek. xviii. 25.) For they said that the Lord's ways were crooked, because they, being soft and delicate, could not endure those severe rebukes, which their own wickedness forced from the holy Prophets. God answers them, and says, that his ways were not crooked, nor thorny, nor tortuous, but that the fault was in the people themselves.

We now then understand the real meaning of this passage. The Prophet knew that nothing was better than to receive whatever proceeded from God; and he testifies that he found sweetness in God's word.

He afterwards adds, *Because on me is called thy name, O Jehovah, God of hosts.* This mode of speaking occurs often in Scripture, but in a different sense. The name of God is indeed called indiscriminately on all, who are deemed his people. As it was formerly given to the whole seed of Abraham, so it is at this day conferred on all who are consecrated to his name by holy baptism, and who boast themselves to be Christians and the sons of the Church; and this belongs even to the Papists. We are called by his name, because he has favoured us with his peculiar grace, for the purity of true and lawful worship exists among us; errors have been removed and his simple truth remains; yet many hypocrites are mixed with the elect of God, so that in a true and well ordered church, the reprobate are called by the name of God; but the elect alone are truly called by his name, as

Paul says, "Let every one who calls on the name of the Lord depart from iniquity," (2 Tim. ii. 19.) There is in this case a mutual connection; for to call on the name of the Lord, and to have his name called on any one, amounts to the same thing. We hence see that the name of God is only truly and really called on those, who not only boast that they are the faithful, but who have been also regenerated by the Holy Spirit.

But the Prophet here refers to his office when he says, that the name of God was called on him; for he had been chosen to his office of teaching; he was not only dignified with the title, but was really approved by God. We now then perceive in what sense he says that God's name was called on him, even because God had laid his hand on him and resolved to employ him in the work of teaching the people. But there are many mercenaries in the Church, and though they do not openly corrupt or adulterate the truth of God, they yet, as Paul says, preach it for gain, (2 Cor. ii. 17.) It must be observed, that God's name was called on Jeremiah, because he was known to God as being true and faithful; and he had not only proved himself to be so to men, but he had been chosen by God to be his faithful messenger.[1]

There is emphasis in the words, *O Jehovah, the God of hosts;* for the Prophet no doubt refers here to the glory of God, that he might with an elevated mind look down, as it were, on so many adversaries, who proudly despised him, as it was difficult to carry on war with the whole people. This then was the reason why he spoke of God's glory in terms so magnificent, by saying, *O Jehovah, the God of hosts.* It follows:—

[1] The connection of this clause is variously understood. It cannot be considered as a reason for the previous clause. *Gataker*, *Grotius*, and others render כי, *that,*—"that thy name was called upon me," regarding it as the cause of his joy, that he was called God's prophet. *Venema* renders it *when*, which seems more suitable. But on viewing the whole passage, we may justly consider this as a reason for the prayer he offers in the previous verse, so that the latter part of that and the beginning of this verse are parenthetic. I would give this version,—

15. Thou knowest, Jehovah;
Remember me and visit me,
And take vengeance for me on my persecutors;

17. I sat not in the assembly of the mockers, nor rejoiced ; I sat alone, because of thy hand : for thou hast filled me with indignation.

17. Non sedi in consilio (*vel* cœtu) derisorum, neque exultavi; propter manum tuam seorsum sedi; quia indignatione replevisti me.

Here the Prophet more fully declares, that he was hated by the whole people because he pleased God. He indeed inveighs against the impiety of those who then bore rule; he does not here so much reprove the common people as the chief men, who exercised authority and administered justice; for when he speaks of the assembly of the ungodly, he no doubt refers to wicked rulers, as the word סוד, *sud*, which means a secret, means also a council. And David (or whosoever was the author of the sixty-ninth Psalm) says, not that he was a sport to the vulgar, but that he was derided by those who sat in the gate, (Psalm lxix. 12;) which means, that he was reproachfully treated by wicked judges, who possessed the chief authority. So also in this place, Jeremiah says, that he did *not sit in the council of mockers.* It is not the same word as in the first Psalm; and סוד, *sud*, is sometimes taken in a good sense, but here in a bad sense; for Jeremiah speaks of the profane despisers of God, who ridiculed everything that was announced in the name of God.[1]

Now it was necessary for the holy man thus to exasperate these impious men, for they were in favour, credit, and authority with the people; and we know that they who were in power do in a manner dazzle the eyes of the vulgar with

Through thy long suffering *towards them* take me not away;
(Know that I have for thee borne reproach;
16. Found have been thy words and I did eat them;
And thy words were to me for exultation,
Even for the joy of my heart;)
Because called on me has been thy name,
Jehovah, *thou* God of hosts.—*Ed.*

[1] *Gataker*, and after him *Blayney*, consider the word, rendered "mockers" by *Calvin* and our version, as meaning "those who make merry;" and the word is so rendered in our version in ch. xxx. 19, and xxxi. 4. The *Septuagint*, the *Vulgate*, and the *Targum*, favour this rendering; the *Syriac* and the *Arabic*, have "mockers." The sense seems to be, that he did not associate with cheerful society. Then the next line is,—

Nor did I exult on account of thy hand.

So all the versions connect the words. The "hand" means, as *Blayney* says, the impulse of the prophetic spirit. See 1 Kings xviii. 46; Ezek. i. 3. He did not inconsiderately rejoice on account of his office, because he was made a prophet.—*Ed.*

their splendour. As they then thus deceived the simple, the Prophet removed the mask, and exclaimed, that he did not sit in their council nor exulted with them. In denying that he was connected with them, he intimates what their conduct and manners were. He therefore shews, that whatever their dignity might be, they were still the impious despisers of God, and were only mockers. The same is the case with us at this day, we are under the necessity directly to expose those masked rulers, who are inflated with their own power and fascinate the people ; for buffoons in tippling-houses and taverns do not so wantonly mock God as those courtiers, who, while consulting respecting the state of the whole earth, and deciding on the affairs of all kingdoms, seem as though they themselves possessed all the power of God ; and we also know that they are profane mockers. Hardly any piety or reverence for God is to be found in the courts of princes ; nay, especially at their councils, the devil reigns, as it were, without control. We are therefore constrained often to speak very strongly against such unprincipled men, who falsely assume the name of God, and by this pretence deceive the common people. By this necessity was Jeremiah constrained to declare, that he had not been in the assembly of such men.

He then adds, *On account of thine hand* (from the presence of thine hand) *I sat apart, because with indignation hast thou filled me.* Here Jeremiah confesses that he had departed from the people ; but he did so, because he could not have otherwise obeyed God. Some consider hand to mean prophecy, and others, a stroke ; and so it is often taken metaphorically ; but I am disposed to take it for command, "On account of thy hand ;" that is, because I attended to what thou hast commanded, nor had I any other object but to obey thee. Hence, *On account of thine hand,* because I regarded thee and wished wholly to submit to thy will, *I sat apart.*

This passage is especially deserving of notice ; for the Prophet was at Jerusalem among the priests, and was one of them, as we found at the beginning of this book. Though then he was a priest, he was constrained to separate himself and to renounce all connection with his colleagues and brethren. As then this was the case with the holy Prophet, why do the Papists try to frighten us by objecting to us our separation, as though it were a most heinous crime? they call us apostates, because we have departed from their assemblies; truly if Jeremiah was an apostate, we need not be ashamed to follow his example, since he was approved by God, though he separated from the whole people, and also from the ungodly priests. Let us at this day openly and boldly confess that we have separated. There is then a separation between us, and one indeed irreconcilable; and accursed were we, if we sought an union with the Papists. We are therefore constrained plainly and openly to repudiate them, and to move heaven and earth rather than to agree with them. We see that there is a rule here prescribed to us by the Holy Spirit through the mouth of Jeremiah. To refute then the calumnies of those who object to us our separation, this very passage is sufficient.

"I sat apart," and true it was so; but no one can say this at this day; for the Lord has gathered to himself many teachers and many disciples. They then who now profess the gospel do not sit apart as Jeremiah. But though all had forsaken him, he yet hesitated not to separate himself from all. But were it necessary for every one of us to become separated and to live apart, were God to scatter each of us through all the regions of the world, so that no one were to strengthen and encourage another, yet we should still stand firm, under the conviction that we sat apart on account of God's hand. Let the Papists then complain as they please, that we are proud, and that we disturb the peace of the whole world, provided we have this answer to give,—That we sit apart on account of God's hand, because we seek to obey God and to follow his call: we can therefore boldly and safely despise and scorn all the reproaches with which they falsely load us.

He afterwards adds, *For thou hast filled me with indignation.*[1] He confirms what he said in the last verse,—that he

[1] "Because all the prophecies thou hast given me are minatory."—*Grotius.*

The meaning may be, "Thou hast filled me with indignant messages."—*Ed.*

had eaten the word of God, that he had not been slightly moved, but had been inflamed with zeal for God: for we cannot really execute the commission given to us unless we be filled with indignation, that is, unless zeal for God burns inwardly, for the prophetic office requires such a fervour. He then adds—

18. Why is my pain perpetual, and my wound incurable, *which* refuseth to be healed? wilt thou be altogether unto me as a liar, *and as* waters *that* fail?	18. Ut quid erit dolor meus fortis, (*vel*, durus,) et plaga mea ægra (*aut*, valida, *aut*, insanabilis, doloris plena; *dicemus postea de voce*,) renuit curari? (*hoc est*, non admittit remedium:) eris mihi sicut mendacium aquarum non fidelium. (*alii vertunt*, eris mihi mendax, aquæ infideles, *hoc est*, tanquam aquæ infideles.)

Before we proceed, we shall shortly refer to the meaning of the passage. Jeremiah has before shewn that he possessed an heroic courage in despising all the splendour of the world, and in regarding as nothing those proud men who boasted that they were the rulers of the Church: but he now confesses his infirmity; and there is no doubt but that he was often agitated by different thoughts and feelings; and this necessarily happens to us, because the flesh always fights against the spirit. For though the Prophet announced nothing human when he declared the truth of God, yet he was not wholly exempt from sorrow and fear and other feelings of the flesh. For we must always distinguish, when we speak of the prophets and the apostles, between the truth, which was pure, free from every imperfection, and their own persons, as they commonly say, or themselves. Nor were they so perfectly renewed but that some remnant of the flesh still continued in them. So then Jeremiah was in himself disturbed with anxiety and fear, and affected with weariness, and wished to shake off the burden which he felt so heavy on his shoulders. He was then subject to these feelings, that is, as to himself; yet his doctrine was free from every defect, for the Holy Spirit guided his mind, his thoughts, and his tongue, so that there was in it nothing human. The Prophet then has hitherto testified that he was called from above, and that he had cordially undertaken the office deputed to him by God, and had faithfully obeyed him: but now he comes to himself, and confesses that he was agitated by many thoughts, which betokened the infirmity of the flesh, and were not free from blame. This then is the meaning.

He says, *Why is my grief strong*, or hard? He intimates that his grief could not be eased by any soothing remedy. He alludes to ulcers, which by their hardness repel all emollients. And for the same purpose he adds, *And my wound weak*, as some render it, for it is from אנש, *anesh*, to be feeble; and hence is אנוש, *anush*, which means man; and it expresses his weakness, as אדם, *adam*, shews his origin, and איש, *aish*, intimates his strength and courage. Others render the words, "and my wound full of pain;" and others, "strong," as he had before called his grief strong. He afterwards thus explains what he meant by the terms he used, *It refuses to be healed.* There is no doubt, as I have already intimated, but that the Prophet here honestly expresses the perturbations of his own mind, and shews that he in a manner vacillated; the wickedness of the people was so great, that he could not so perseveringly execute his office as he ought to have done.[1]

He adds, *Thou wilt be to me as the deception of inconstant waters.* I wonder why some render the words, "Thou wilt be to me deceptive as inconstant waters." The word may indeed be an adjective, but it is doubtless to be rendered as a substantive, "Thou wilt be to me as the deception," and then, "of unfaithful waters," that is, of such as flow not continually: for faithful or constant waters are those which never fail; as the Latins call a fountain inexhaustible whose spring never dries; so the Hebrews call a fountain faithful or constant which never fails either in summer or in drought. On the contrary, they call waters unfaithful which become dry, as when a well, which has no perennial veins, is made dry by great heat; and such also is often the case with large streams.[2]

[1] It is better to retain throughout the figurative language,—

Why has my sore become perpetual,
And my stroke incurable, refusing to be healed?

He mentions "sore" first, the effect; then the "stroke" which caused it. He refers doubtless to the state of his mind: therefore "the sore" and "the stroke" were the sorrow and the grief which he experienced.—*Ed.*

[2] The *Septuagint* and the *Vulgate* strangely refer this to the stroke or

We now see the import of this comparison: but the words are apparently very singular; for the Prophet expostulates with God as though he had been deceived by him, "Thou wilt be to me," he says, "as a vain hope, and as deceptive waters, which fail during great heat, when they are mostly wanted." If we take the words as they appear to mean, they seem to border on blasphemy; for God had not without reason testified before, that he is the Fountain of living water; and he had condemned the Jews for having dug for themselves broken cisterns, and for having forsaken him, the Fountain of living water. Such, no doubt, had He been found by all who trusted in him. What then does Jeremiah mean here by saying, that God was to him as a vain hope, and as waters which continue not to flow? The Prophet, no doubt, referred to others rather than to himself; for his faith had never been shaken nor removed from his heart. He then knew that he could never be deceived; for relying on God's word he greatly magnified his calling, not only before the world, but also with regard to himself: and his glorying, which we have already seen, did not proceed except from the inward feeling of his heart. The Prophet then was ever fully confident, because he relied on God, that he could not be made ashamed; but here, as I have said, he had regard to others. And we have already seen similar passages, and the like expressions will hereafter follow.

There is no doubt but that it was often exultingly alleged that the Prophet was a deceiver: "Let him go on and set before us the words of his God; it has already appeared that his boasting is vain in saying that he has hitherto spoken as a prophet." Since then the ungodly thus harassed the Prophet, he might have justly complained that

the wound in the previous clause, "It has become like the deception of inconstant water:" but the gender of the infinitive added to the verb will not admit of this rendering. It is literally as follows,—

Becoming thou hast become like a deceiver,
Like waters *which* are not constant.

The word אכזב is not a substantive, but an adjective, formed like אכזר, violent. The quotation from *Chardin*, made by *Blayney*, respecting an illusion in the deserts of Arabia, occasioned by the sun's rays on the sand, by which a vast lake appears, is here out of place, as unfaithful or inconstant waters, not unreal, is what is expressed. *Calvin's* view is no doubt correct.—*Ed.*

God was not to him like perennial springs, because they all thought that he was deceived. And we must always bear in mind what I said yesterday,—that the Prophet does not speak here for his own sake, but rather that he might reprove the impiety of the people. It therefore follows—

19. Therefore thus saith the Lord, If thou return, then will I bring thee again, *and* thou shalt stand before me; and if thou take forth the precious from the vile, thou shalt be as my mouth: let them return unto thee; but return not thou unto them.	19. Propterea sic dixit Jehova, Si conversus fueris, ego quoque convertam te; coram facie mea stabis (*hoc est*, ut stes coram me;) et si separaveris (eduxeris *ad verbum*, *hoc est*, si discreveris) pretiosum à vili, tanquam os meum eris: convertantur ipsi ad te, et tu non convertaris ad eos.

From this answer of God we may gather more clearly the design of the Prophet, for his purpose was, in order more fully to prove the people guilty, to set before their eyes as it were his own perverseness. Had he spoken only according to the heroic elevation of his own mind, so as not to appear touched by any human feeling, they might have derided him as hardhearted or a fanatic, for so we find that the proud of this world speak and think of the faithful servants of Christ. They call them melancholy, they consider them as unfeeling, and as they neither dread death, nor are drawn away by the allurements of this life, they think that all this proceeds from brutal savageness. Had then the Prophet only performed the duties of his office, the ungodly might have derided his insensibility, but he wished to set forth his own infirmity, his sorrows, his fears, and his anxieties, that he might thus lead the Jews to view things aright. This answer of God ought then to be connected with the complaint of the Prophet, and we may hence learn the meaning of the whole.

God gives this answer, *If thou wilt be turned, I will turn thee, that thou mayest stand before me.* It is the same as though he had said, that he was reproved by the Lord because he fluctuated amidst the commotions of the people. A similar passage is found in the eighth chapter of Isaiah. The Lord there exhorts his Prophet to separate himself from the people, and not to connect himself with those who might have often easily disturbed him, because they continued not in his word; then he says, " Seal my law for my disciples, sign the testimony," (Isaiah viii. 12, 16,) as though he had said, "Have now nothing to do with so perverse a people." So also now the Lord speaks, *If thou wilt be turned,* that is, if thou wilt not be guided by the false judgments of the people, nor heed what they say of thee, but boldly despise them and persevere in thy separation from them, *I will turn thee,* that is, I will by my spirit so strengthen thee, that they may perceive at length that thou art my faithful servant. Then he adds, *that thou mayest stand before me.* We hence see more plainly what is the meaning of the word "turn" in the second clause, even that the Prophet would render his office approved of God, however clamorous the Jews might be; though they even rose up tumultuously against him, yet he says, thou shalt stand before me. There is implied here a contrast in the word "stand," for though the Prophet should be most violently assailed by the false words of men, yet God would support and sustain him. The rest we defer until to-morrow.

PRAYER.

Grant, Almighty God, that since thou hast at this day plainly made known to us thy will through the gospel of thy Son, so that we may by an unshaken faith embrace what is therein set forth to us,—O grant, that we may learn to be satisfied with thee alone, and to acquiesce in thy truth, and to renounce the whole world, so that we may never be moved by any threats and terrors, nor vacillate when the ungodly seem so proudly disposed to withdraw confidence in thee; but may we render to thee all due honour, so as not only to obey thee but also to perform the offices committed to us, and never to hesitate so to provoke the whole world against us, that howsoever hard our warfare may be we may firmly persevere in the course of thy holy calling, and may thus at length enjoy that triumph, which Christ thy only-begotten Son hath procured for us.—Amen.

Lecture Sixty-Second.

WE began yesterday to explain the passage in which God exhorts the Prophet to be courageous. He indeed uses the word to "turn," but it is the same as though he had said, that it was not wise in him to vacillate, for he ought not to have turned aside by any means from the performance of his office, though the Jews obstinately resisted him. The sum of the whole then is, "If thou turnest thyself I will also restore thee, that thou mayest stand before me."

It then follows, *If thou wilt distinguish the precious from the worthless, thou shalt be as my mouth.* God now expresses what sort of turning he required from his servant, even freely to condemn what was vicious, and boldly to defend what was right, though the whole would oppose him. God then indirectly refers to that fear of Jeremiah by which he was so shaken that he knew not what to do. Hence God reproves his Prophet, and shews that he could not otherwise stand than by distinguishing between the precious and the worthless. Thus all flattery was to be excluded. God then forbids his Prophet to deal gently with the people, or to be influenced by favour so as to spare their vices, and not to defend what was right with that courage which became him.

In these words is briefly comprehended the duty of a true Prophet, even to turn his eyes from men, to heed neither favour nor hatred, but to fix his attention only on the truth, not only to approve of what is right, but also to defend it at the peril of his life, and further, not to spare vices, but freely to reprove them.

What is added, *Thou shalt be as my mouth,* some interpret as though it was said, "Happen to thee shall everything that I have promised," or, "my promise shall not disappoint thee," but this seems to be far-fetched. I therefore take this plain meaning, "I will own thee as a true and faithful servant, if only thou distinguishest what is just from what is unjust, if thou continuest to fight for the truth, and freely reprovest and condemnest vices." The import of the passage is, that those only are deemed by God to be the faithful pastors of the Church, who are not influenced by respect of persons, who do not turn to this or to that side, but rightly judge and according to the law of God; for by the law is the difference to be made between the precious and the worthless, as we are no fit judges but as far as we agree with what God has said. The law then is alone that by which we can distinguish the precious from the worthless.

They who keep to this rule, do justly condemn some and approve of others, because they are only God's heralds, and bring nothing of their own. It hence follows, on the other hand, that those are not God's instruments or ministers, nor are worthy of any honour, who so pervert vices and virtues as to say that light is darkness and that darkness is light. We may, in short, conclude from this passage, that a vocation or a title is not sufficient, except they who are called faithfully discharge their duty to God. It hence follows, that all those who either ambitiously seek the favour of men, or are indulgent to their vices, and by flatteries nourish their corruptions, are impostors: for how much soever they may boast that they are God's servants, yet he himself declares that they are not to be so accounted.

He then adds, *Let them be turned to thee, but be not thou turned to them,* or, thou shalt not be turned to them; but the verbs, being in the future tense, are to be taken as imperatives. He now confirms the previous doctrine,—that he ought not to be submissive to them or to flatter them, but to subdue their perverse minds until they received the yoke of God. The meaning of the words is this,—that the Prophets were sent for this end—not to gratify men, or to soothe them by obsequiousness, but to continue firm and constant in executing their office and to turn refractory men to him, and not to concede anything to them. And doubtless, except this course be pursued, the majesty of God must give place to the humours and fancies of men: for we know how great is the pride of almost the whole world, and also their love of pleasure, so that no one can willingly bear to be reproved. As then the greater part of mankind are so proud and self-indulgent, were the word of God to bend to the humour of this or of that man, what would become of it? there would certainly remain in celestial truth no dignity and no majesty.

We now see why this clause was added: for the precious could not be rightly and justly distinguished from the worthless, except the Prophets continued firm in the course of their calling, and carried on war with the perverseness of men. It is therefore necessary that all faithful teachers in the Church should so conduct themselves, as not to concede to the vices of men nor to cherish their fancies, but to constrain them to undertake the yoke of God. Paul, however, seems to have followed a different course, for he says to the Galatians, "Be ye as I am, for I am as you are." (Gal. iv. 12.) As then he had endeavoured to conform to what they did, and to bear their infirmities, he exhorts them to do the same in return. But it is certain that Paul acted not differently from Jeremiah or other servants of God: and the answer is evident; for Paul in the same Epistle testifies, that if he pleased men, he could not be the servant of Christ, (Gal. i. 10.) He then did not hunt for the favours of men, nor turned aside in the least from the course of his duty to render himself obsequious to men; but he could forgive their infirmities, or bear them, so that he might thereby turn them to himself, or rather restore them to the service of God. For when God thus speaks, *Be not thou turned to them*, he means not Jeremiah personally, but refers to his doctrine. The meaning is, that the truth of God ought not to bend to the will of men; for God changes not, and so his word admits of no change. Whatever then men may expect, this rule must remain fixed and inviolable, that they must submit to God, and that he must be the sovereign, and reduce to submission whatever height or excellency or pride there may be in the world.[1] It then follows—

20. And I will make thee unto this people a fenced brazen wall; and they shall fight against thee, but they shall not prevail against thee: for I *am* with thee to save thee, and to deliver thee, saith the Lord.

20. Et posui te huic populo in murum æneum (æris, *ad verbum*) munitum: ergo pugnabunt contra te, sed non prævalebunt tibi; quia tecum ego sum ad servandum te et ad liberandum te, dicit Jehova.

[1] It is extraordinary what shades of difference appear in the expositions of this verse: but a literal rendering would, I conceive, dissipate them,—

19. Therefore thus said Jehovah,—
If thou returnest and I restore thee,
Before me shalt thou stand;
And if thou bringest forth the precious from the worthless,
As my mouth shalt thou be;
Return shall they to thee,
But thou wilt not return to them.

The return at the beginning of the verse was from the state of mind in

As Jeremiah might have objected and said, that the burden was too heavy for him, if he only attempted to break down the contumacy of the people, for he was alone, and we have seen how great was the ferocity and also the cruelty of his adversaries,—as he might have shunned his commission, it being too much for his strength, hence God comes to his aid and bids him to take courage, for he was fortified by a help from heaven, *I have set thee,* he says, *for a brazen fortified wall to this people.* The word for "fortified" is from בצר, *betsar;* were it בצרה, *betsare,* derived from צור, *tsur,* to besiege, it would much better suit this place. I know not whether the passage has been corrupted: however, I will not depart from the common reading. As then interpreters agree in this, I will change nothing; and indeed the difference is not very material.[1]

We see then what God meant by these words: As the Prophet was almost alone, and God had bidden him to contend with many and powerful enemies, he promises to stand on his side; as though he had said,—"Though thou art defenceless and unarmed, and they are furnished with wealth and great power, thou shalt yet be like a well-fortified city; thou shalt indeed be impregnable, notwithstanding all their assaults and whatever they may attempt against thee."

But God proceeds by degrees; for he first declares that

which he was, to an entire submission to God. The future is here used in the sense of the present. The "precious" was the godly, and the "worthless" the ungodly. The three last lines are promises. See chap. xlii. 2.

Houbigant's explanation of the fourth line is too refined, though approved by *Horsley*. He considers that there is an allusion to Judges xiv. 14. Jeremiah himself was "the worthless" or the mean, being so regarded by the Jews, and "the precious" was the prophetic word. And *Horsley* renders the line thus,—

And if thou wilt bring forth the precious from the mean.

He also approves of *Blayney's* version of the second line, and considers it as expressive of a prompt execution of what is commanded,—

If thou wilt turn as I shall turn thee.

But the first verb is in *Kal,* and the second in *Hiphil,* and therefore cannot be rendered the same.—*Ed.*

[1] All the ancient versions are in favour of the common reading, and there are no MSS. favourable to the proposed emendation. The *Septuagint,* the *Vulgate,* the *Syriac,* and the *Targum,* render it "strong;" and the *Arabic* "fortified." "A strong wall of brass," is the version of *Blayney.* —*Ed.*

his Prophet would be like a brazen and a fortified wall, that is, like an invincible city: for by stating a part for the whole, a wall means a city that is impregnable. It then follows, *They indeed will fight against thee.* This warning was very necessary; for Jeremiah was doubtless willing to serve God in exercising authority over teachable and humble men, and in gently inducing them to render obedience to God; but he is reminded here that he would have many hard contests with a rebellious people, *They will fight,* he says, *against thee.* We see how God does not promise ease to Jeremiah, nor gives him a hope of a better lot in future; but, on the contrary, he exhorts him to fight; and why? because the people would not bear the yoke of God, but kindled into rage against him. But another promise follows, *They shall not prevail against thee,* or overcome thee.

It was indeed necessary for Jeremiah of his own self to disturb the Jews; for nothing would have been more agreeable to them than his silence; and the object of all their attempts was to drive him to despair. But it is not without reason that they are said to fight with him; for it is contrary to nature for men to resist God and to set themselves against him when he invites them to himself; for what can be more natural than for the whole world to hasten to God? It is then something monstrous for men to oppose God, nay, furiously to rise up against him, when he kindly calls them to himself. Hence it is that God here makes the Jews the authors of all this disturbance. For since they loaded the Prophet with the most wicked calumnies, as we have seen, and said, that he was a turbulent man and confounded all things by his morosity, God here shews, on the other hand, that all the commotions and the fightings ought to be attributed to them, because they ought to have obediently received the doctrine set before them.

But though this was said only once to Jeremiah, yet the condition of all God's servants is here set before us as in a mirror; for they cannot perform what God commands them without having to encounter many and grievous assaults; for the world is never so prepared to obey God, but the greater part furiously resists, and, as far as it can, stifles the word of God and checks his ministers.

He states the reason, *For I am with thee to save thee and to deliver thee.*[1] By these words God exhorts his Prophet to prayer; for we know how dangerous is self-security to all the children of God, and especially to teachers. As then they have at all times need of God's aid, they are to be exhorted to have recourse to solitude and prayer. This is the import of the words which God uses, *I am with thee;* as though he had said, "Thou indeed wilt not stand by thyself, or through thine own painstaking, nor wilt thou be a conqueror by carrying on war thyself; but thou must learn to flee to me." It afterwards follows—

21. And I will deliver thee out of the hand of the wicked, and I will redeem thee out of the hand of the terrible.	21. Et liberabo te è manu impiorum (sceleratorum,) et eruam te è manu (*est aliud nomen, sed eodem sensu capitur*) fortium.

This verse contains nothing new, but is a confirmation of the promise which we have seen. God had promised to be with the Prophet; he now shews that there was sufficient strength in his hand to deliver him. How much soever then the Jews might oppose him, God declares here that he alone would be sufficient to break them down. We hence see that there is more expressed in these words than in what he had said before, *I will be with thee to deliver thee;* he now shews the act itself as by the finger. *I will deliver thee.* He had promised his aid; he now says, that his aid would be strong enough to deliver him from the hands of his enemies.

[1] The words here used are remarkably precise and significant. I render the verse thus,—

20. And I will make thee to this people
A wall of brass, fortified:
And they will fight against thee,
But they shall not prevail over thee;
For with thee *will* I *be*,
To save thee and to rescue thee,
Saith Jehovah.

To "save" was to preserve him from the hands of his enemies; but if he fell into their hands, he would rescue him. And this latter idea is more fully expressed in the following verse,—

Yea, I will rescue thee from the hand of the malignant,
And free thee from the grasp of the terrible.—*Ed.*

He says first, *from the hand of the wicked,* that the Jews might know that all their disguises would avail them nothing, for they were condemned by the mouth of God. In the second place, he calls them *strong,* that the Prophet might not be terrified by their power, as was usually the case. For it is very difficult for us not to be disturbed, when we are assailed on every side, and when threats and dangers are in our way. God then here reminds Jeremiah in time, that he would have to fight with the *strong* and valiant, but that all their strength in opposing him would be unavailing, for divine aid would be much stronger. Now follows—

CHAPTER XVI.

1. The word of the Lord came also unto me, saying,

2. Thou shalt not take thee a wife, neither shalt thou have sons or daughters in this place.

3. For thus saith the Lord concerning the sons and concerning the daughters *that are* born in this place, and concerning their mothers that bare them, and concerning their fathers that begat them in this land;

4. They shall die of grievous deaths; they shall not be lamented, neither shall they be buried; *but* they shall be as dung upon the face of the earth: and they shall be consumed by the sword, and by famine; and their carcases shall be meat for the fowls of heaven, and for the beasts of the earth.

1. Et fuit sermo Jehovæ ad me, dicendo,

2. Non accipies tibi uxorem, et non erunt tibi filii et filiæ in hoc loco;

3. Quia sic dicit Jehova super filios et super filias, qui nascentur in loco hoc, et super matres, quæ pepererint illos, et super patres, qui genuerint illos in terra hac;

4. Mortibus ægritudinum (*vel,* agrotationum) morientur, non plangentur, et non sepelientur; in stercus (*id est,* pro stercore) super faciem terræ erunt, et in gladio et fame consumentur (*id est,* per gladium et famem,) et erit cadaver eorum in cibum volucri cœlorum et bestiæ terræ

This is a new discourse, which yet is not unlike many others, except in this particular, that the Prophet was *not to marry a wife nor beget children in the land.* But as to the general subject, he repeats now what he had often said before and confirmed in many places. But the prohibition to marry was full of meaning; it was to shew that the people were wholly given up to destruction. The law of man's creation, we know, was this, "Increase and multiply." (Gen. i. 22; viii. 17; ix. 1, 7.) As then mankind are perpetuated by marriage, here on the contrary God shews that that land was unworthy of this common and even general blessing enjoyed by the whole race of man. It is the same as if he had said, "They indeed as yet live, but a quick destruction awaits them, for I will deprive them of the universal favour which I have hitherto shewed to all mankind."

Marriage is the preservation of the human race: *Take not to thee a wife and beget no children.* We hence see that in the person of Jeremiah God intended to shew the Jews that they deserved to be exterminated from the earth. This is the import of this prophecy.

It may however be asked, whether the Prophet was unmarried? But this has nothing to do with the subject, for he received this command in a vision; and though he might not have been unmarried, he might still have proclaimed this prophecy, that God had forbidden him to marry and to beget children. At the same time, I think it were probable that the Prophet was not married, for as he walked naked, and as he carried on his neck a yoke, so also his celibacy might have been intended to be, as it were, a living representation, in order to produce an effect on the Jews. But, as I have already said, we need not contend about this matter. Every one then is at liberty to judge as he pleases, only I suggest what I deem most probable.

But the reason why God forbad his Prophet to marry, follows, because they were all consigned to destruction. We hence learn that celibacy is not here commended, as some foolish men have imagined from what is here said; but it is the same as though God had said, "There is no reason for any one to set his mind on begetting an offspring, or to think that this would be to his advantage: whosoever is wise will abstain from marriage, as he has death before his eyes, and is as it were near to his grave." The destruction then of the whole people, and the desolation and solitude of the whole land, are the things which God in these words sets forth.

At the same time, they are not threatened with a common kind of death, for he says that they *were to die by the deaths of sicknesses.* He then denounces on them continual languor, which would cause them to pine away with the greatest pain: sudden death would have been more tolerable; and hence David says, while complaining of the prosperity of the ungodly, that there "were no bands in their death." (Psalm lxxiii. 4.) And the same thing is found in the book of Job, that "in a moment of time they descend to the grave," that is, that they flourish and prosper during life, and then die without any pain. (Job xxi. 13.) Hence Julius Cæsar, shortly before he was killed, called this kind a happy death, (*εὐθανασίαν*,) for he thought it a happy thing to expire suddenly. And this is what is implanted in men by nature. Therefore Jeremiah, in order to amplify God's vengeance, says that they would *die by the deaths of sicknesses;*[1] that is, that they would be worn out by daily pains, and pine away until they died.

He adds, *They shall not be lamented nor buried.* We have seen elsewhere, and we shall hereafter see, (Jer. xxii,) that it is a proof of a curse when the dead are not buried, and when no one laments their death: for it is the common duty of humanity for relations and friends who survive, to mourn for the dead and to bury them. But the Prophet seems to mean also something further. I do not indeed exclude this, that God would deprive them of the honour of sepulture and of mourning; but he seems also to intimate, that the destruction of men would be so great that there would be none to perform these offices of humanity. For we lament the dead when leisure is allowed us; but when many are slain in war they are not individually lamented, and then their carcases lie confused, and one grave is not sufficient for such a number. The Prophet there means, that so great would be the slaughter in Judea, that none would be buried, that none would be lamented. The verb which he uses means properly to lament, which is more than to weep: and we have said elsewhere, that in those

[1] More literally, "By the deaths of wastings." The reference is to the famine and also to the sword. *Calvin* has followed the *Vulgate;* "by a pestilential death" is the *Septuagint;* by the death of those who languish by famine" the *Syriac;* and "by a dreadful death" the *Arabic.* The "mortal diseases" of *Blayney* is not proper, for they were not "diseases" but wastings or devastations by the famine and the sword, as stated afterwards.—*Ed.*

countries there were more ceremonies than with us; for all the orientals were much given to various gesticulations; and hence they were not satisfied with tears, but they added lamentation, as though they were in despair.

But the Prophet speaks according to the customs of the age, without approving of this excess of grief. As they were wont not simply to bewail the dead, but also to shew their grief by lamentation, he says, "Their offices shall now cease, for there will not be graves enough for so many thousands: and then if any one wish to mourn, where would he begin?" We also know that men's hearts become hardened, when many thus die through pestilence or war. The import of the whole is, that God's wrath would not be moderate, for he would in a manner empty the land by driving them all away, so that there would be none remaining. God did indeed preserve the elect, though as it were by a miracle; and he afterwards preserved them in exile as in a grave, when they were removed from their own country.

He then adds, That they *would be as dung on the face of the land.* He speaks reproachfully of their carcasses, as though he had said, "They shall be the putridity of the land." As then they had by their filth contaminated the land during life, God declares that after death they would become fœtid like dung. Hence we learn, as I have before said, that it was an evidence of God's curse, when carcases were left unburied; for as God has created us in his own image, so in death he would have some evidence of the dignity and excellency with which he has favoured us beyond brute animals, still to remain. We however know that temporal punishments happen even to the faithful, but they are turned to their good, for the Psalmist complains that the bodies of the godly were cast forth and became food to the birds of heaven. (Psalm lxxix. 2.) Though this is true, yet these two things are by no means inconsistent, that it is a sign of God's wrath when the dead are not buried, and that a temporal punishment does no harm to God's elect; for all evils, as it is well known, turn out to them for good.

It is added, *By the sword and by famine shall they be consumed;* that is, some shall perish by the sword, and some by famine, according to what we have before seen, "Those for the sword, to the sword; those for the famine, to the famine." (ch. xv. 2.) Then he mentions what we have already referred to, *Their carcases shall be for food to the beasts of the earth and to the birds of heaven.*[1] He here intimates, that it would be a manifest sign of his vengeance, when the Jews pined away in their miseries, when the sword consumed some of them, and famine destroyed others, and not only so, but when another curse after death followed them, for the Lord would inflict judgment on their carcases by not allowing them to be buried. How this is to be understood I have already stated; for God's judgments as to the reprobate are evident; but when the godly and the righteous fall under similar punishment, God turns to good what seems in itself to be the sign of a curse. Though famine is a sign of a curse, and also the sword, yet we know that many of God's children perish by famine and by the sword. But in temporal punishments this modification is ever to be remembered,—that God shews himself to be a righteous Judge as to the ungodly and wicked,—and that while he humbles his own people, he is not yet angry with them, but consults their benefit, so that what is in itself adverse to them is turned to their advantage.

PRAYER.

Grant, Almighty God, that as thou anticipatest us by thy word, so that we may not experience thy eternal severity,—O grant, that we may become teachable, and be so displeased with our vices, that we may not provoke more and more thy vengeance, but hasten to seek reconciliation with thee, and that relying on the Mediator whom thou hast given us, we may flee to thy mercy,

[1] I would render the fourth verse thus,—

By deaths of wastings shall they die;
They shall not be lamented, nor buried;
As dung on the face of the ground shall they be:
Yea, by the sword and by the famine shall they be consumed,
And their carcase shall be for meat
To the bird of heaven and to the beast of the earth.

The latter part is a fuller explanation of what was to take place. "As dung," so the *Syriac;* they were scattered like dung. They were to be cast here and there, to be devoured by rapacious birds and beasts.—*Ed.*

until having been cleansed from all our filth, we shall at length be received into thy celestial kingdom, and there appear before thee in that purity from which we are as yet very distant, and shall enjoy that glory which thine only-begotten Son has obtained for us by his own blood.—Amen.

Lecture Sixty-Third.

5. For thus saith the Lord, Enter not into the house of mourning, neither go to lament nor bemoan them: for I have taken away my peace from this people, saith the Lord, *even* loving-kindness and mercies.

5. Quia sic dicit Jehova, Ne ingrediaris domum luctus, et ne eas ad plangendum, et ne movearis propter illos; quia abstuli pacem meam à populo hoc, dicit Jehova, clementiam et miserationes.

As Jeremiah was forbidden at the beginning of the chapter to take a wife, for a dreadful devastation of the whole land was very nigh; so now God confirms what he had previously said, that so great would be the slaughter, that none would be found to perform the common office of lamenting the dead: at the same time he intimates now something more grievous,—that they who perished would be unworthy of any kind office. As he had said before, "Their carcases shall be cast to the beasts of the earth and to the birds of heaven;" so now in this place he intimates, that their deaths would be so ignominious, that they would be deprived of the honour of a grave, and would be buried, as it is said in another place, like asses.

But when God forbids his Prophet to mourn, we are not to understand that he refers to excess of grief, as when God intends to moderate grief, when he takes away from us our parents, or our relatives, or our friends; for the subject here is not the private feeling of Jeremiah. God only declares that the land would be so desolate that hardly one would survive to mourn for the dead.

He says, *Enter not into the house of mourning.* Some render מרזח, *merezach*, a funeral feast; and it is probable, nay, it may be gathered from the context, that such feasts were made when any one was dead.[1] And the same custom

[1] The word is of a general import, to cry aloud or to shout, either for grief or for joy: it is here for grief, and in Amos vi. 7, for joy. The literal rendering here is, "Enter not the house of shouting." The ver-

we see has been observed by other nations, but for a different purpose. When the Romans celebrated a funeral feast, their object was to shake off grief, and in a manner to convert the dead into gods. Hence Cicero condemns Vatinius, because he came clothed in black to the feast of Q. Arius, (*Orat. pro L. Mur.*;) and elsewhere he says, that Tuberonis was laughed at and everywhere repulsed, because he covered the beds with goat's skins, when Q. Maximus made a feast at the death of his uncle Africanus. Then these feasts were among the Romans full of rejoicing; but among the Jews, as it appears, when they lamented the dead, who were their relatives, they invited children and widows, in order that there might be some relief to their sorrow.

However this may be, God intimates by this figurative language, that the Jews, when they perished in great numbers, would be deprived of that common practice, because they were unworthy of having any survivors to bewail them.

Neither go, he says, *to lament*, *nor be moved on their account*;[1] and why? *For I have taken away my peace from this people*, that is, all prosperity; for under the term, peace, the Jews included whatever was desirable. God then says, that he had taken away peace from them, and *his peace*, because he had pronounced that wicked nation accursed. He then adds, that he had taken away his *kindness* and his *mercies*.[2] For the Prophet might have raised an objection

sion of the *Septuagint* is wide of the mark, "Enter not into their bacchanalian assembly, (θίασον.") The *Syriac* omits the word, and the *Vulgate* and *Targum* have "feast."—*Ed.*

[1] The verb means to move, or to nod, either in contempt or in sympathy. The latter is the meaning here: hence to condole is the sense. He was not to go for the purpose of lamenting the dead, or of condoling with the living. To "mourn" is the *Septuagint*, a word of a similar meaning with the preceding; more correct is to "console," as given by the *Vulgate* and the *Targum*.—*Ed.*

[2] These words are omitted by the *Septuagint*, but given by the other versions, and are left out in no copies. The "and" before "kindness" is found in two MSS., and in the *Syriac*, but not in the *Vulgate*: it seems necessary. The passage I thus render,—

For withdrawn have I my peace
From this people, saith Jehovah,
My mercy also and *my* compassions.

There is here a reason given for the preceding prohibitions: the Prophet was to shew no favour, no kindness to the people, and no sympathy with and said, that this was not consistent with the nature of God, who testifies that he is ready to shew mercy; but God meets this objection and intimates, that there was now no place for kindness and mercy, for the impiety of the people had become past all hope. It follows—

6. Both the great and the small shall die in this land: they shall not be buried, neither shall *men* lament for them, nor cut themselves, nor make themselves bald for them:

7. Neither shall *men* tear *themselves* for them in mourning, to comfort them for the dead; neither shall *men* give them the cup of consolation to drink for their father or for their mother.

6. Et morientur magni et parvi in terra hac; non sepelient eos, et non plangent super eos, et non incidet se quisquam, et non fiet calvitium illis;

7. Et non complodent (*vel,* extendent) illis (*quidam legentes* לחם *pro* להם, *vertunt,* non frangent panem; פרס *significat frangere, et interdum dividere, vel ostendere, vel dispergere: non dubium est quin Propheta, sicut alio loco vidimus, intelligat complosionem manuum, vel contorsionem, ubi in vehementi luctu ita brachia huc et illuc projiciuntur, deinde, comploduntur manus: hunc gestum hoc quoque loco exprimit cum dicit,* Et non frangent, *vel,* non complodent manus) ad consolandum (*hoc est,* ad unumquenque consolandum) super mortuo, et non propinabunt illis calicem consolationum super patre suo et super matre sua.

He pursues the same subject: he says that all would die indiscriminately, the common people as well as the chief men, that none would be exempt from destruction; for God would make a great slaughter, both of the lower orders and also of the higher, who excelled in wealth, in honour, and dignity; *Die shall the great and the small.* It often happens in changes that the great are punished; and sometimes the case is that the common people perish, while the nobles are spared: but God declares, that such would be the destruction, that their enemies would make no difference between the common people and the higher ranks, and that if they escaped the hands of their enemies, the pestilence or the famine would prove their ruin.

He adds, *They shall not bury them, nor beat their breast for them;* and then, *they shall not cut themselves, nor make*

them: for God had withdrawn from them his "peace," which means here his favour, and also his mercy or his benignity, as some render the word, and his compassions.—*Ed.*

themselves bald for them.[1] This is not mentioned by the Prophet to commend what the people did; nor did he consider that in this respect they observed the command of the law; for God had forbidden them to imitate the corrupt customs of the heathens. (Lev. xxi. 1.) We have already said, that the orientals were much given to external ceremonies, so that there was no moderation in their lamentations: therefore God intended to correct this excess. But the Prophet here has no respect to the command, that the Jews were to moderate their grief,—what then? He meant to shew, as I have already reminded you, that the slaughters would be so great, that they would cause hardness and insensibility, being so immense as to stun the feelings of men. When any one dies, friends and neighbours meet, and shew respect to his memory; but when pestilence prevails, or when all perish by famine, the greater part become hardened and unmindful of themselves and others, and the offices of humanity are no longer observed. God then shews, that such would be the devastation of the land, that the Jews, as though callous and hardened, would no longer lament for one another. In short, he shews, that together with these dreadful slaughters, such insensibility and hardness would prevail among the Jews, that no husband would think of his wife, and no father of his children; but that all of them would be so astonied by their own evils as to become like the wild beasts.

He says further, *They shall not cut themselves nor pull off their hairs,* as they had used to do. These things are mentioned, as they were commonly done; it cannot be hence concluded, that they were approved by God; for God's de-

[1] The first clause of the verse, as well as the last of the preceding, is omitted in the *Septuagint,* but retained in the *Vulgate, Syriac,* and the *Targum.* The verbs in the next clause ought to be rendered as transitives,—

They shall not bury *them* nor lament for them.

Then the two concluding verbs are to be rendered as impersonals,—

And there shall be no cutting nor making bald for them.

The Welsh is a *literal* version of the Hebrew,—

Ac nid ymdorrir ac nid ymfoelir drostynt.

Nothing can be much more literal. The first verb is in Hithpael, and so the Welsh is; for like Hebrew it has a reciprocal form for its verbs. The last verb is also in Welsh in this form; but it needs not be so, for it might be, *ac ni foelir.—Ed.*

sign was not to pronounce a judgment on their lamentation, on the tearing off of the hair, or on their incisions. It is indeed certain that these practices proceeded from the impetuous feelings of men, and were tokens of impatience; but as I have said, God does not speak here of what was lawful, but of what men were wont to do.

As to that part, where he says, that he had taken away his *kindness* and his *mercies*, he does not mean that he had changed his nature, but his object was to cut off occasion from all who might complain; for men, we know, whenever God's hand presses hard on them, to make them to deplore rightly their miseries, are sufficiently ready to say, that God visits them with too much severity. He therefore shews that they were unworthy of kindness and mercies. At the same time he reminded them that there was no reason for hypocrites to entertain any hope, because Scripture so often commends the kindness of God and his mercy; for since they accumulated sins on sins, God could not do otherwise than come to an extremity with them.

With regard to the seventh verse,[1] we may learn from it what I have already referred to,—that the Jews made funeral feasts, that children and widows might receive some relief to their sorrow; for the Prophet calls it the *cup of consolations*, when friends kindly attended; they had also some ridiculous gesticulations; for no doubt laughter was often excited by mourners among the Jews. But we see that men vied with

[1] *Calvin*, having in his version explained the beginning of this verse, passes it by here. His rendering is, "And they shall not beat their hands together for them, to console *any one* for the dead." He omits one word, rendered, "in mourning" in our version. The *Septuagint*, the *Vulgate*, the *Arabic* and the *Targum* give another meaning. They must have read לחם, "bread," instead of להם, "for them." The difference is so small that we are inclined to think it the true reading, though there be but two MSS. in its favour. The passage itself seems to require this reading,—the verb which precedes it, and the correspondence between the former and latter part of the verse—bread and drink. The verse then would read thus,—

7. And they shall not divide bread to the mourner,
To console him for the dead;
Nor shall they give them to drink the cup of consolations,
Each one for his father and for his mother.

Blayney quotes *Jerome*, who says, "It was usual to carry provisions to mourners, and to make an entertainment, which sort of feasts the Greeks call *περιδειπνα*, and the Latins *parentalia*."—*Ed.*

one another in lamenting for the dead ; for it was deemed a shame not to shew grief at the death of their friends. When tears did not flow, when the nearest relations did not howl for the dead, they thought them inhuman ; hence it was, that there was much dissimulation in their mourning ; and it was foolishly regarded an alleviation to extend the cup of consolation. But as I have said before, the Prophet here did not point out what was right, but borrowed his words from what was commonly practised. It follows—

8. Thou shalt not also go into the house of feasting, to sit with them to eat and to drink.	8. Et domum convivii ne ingrediaris, ut sedeas cum ipsis ad edendum et ad bibendum.

Here the Prophet refers to other feasts, where hilarity prevailed. The meaning then is,—that the people were given up to destruction, so that nothing was better than to depart from them as far as possible. So Jeremiah is prohibited from going at all to them, so that he might not be their associate either in joy or in sorrow ; as though he had said,—'Have no more anything to do with this people ; if they lament their dead, leave them, for they are unworthy of any act of kindness ; and if they make joyful feasts, be far from them, for every intercourse with them is accursed." We now then understand why the Prophet spoke of grief, lamentation and mourning, and then mentioned joy. He afterwards adds,—

9. For thus saith the Lord of hosts, the God of Israel ; Behold, I will cause to cease out of this place in your eyes, and in your days, the voice of mirth, and the voice of gladness, the voice of the bridegroom, and the voice of the bride.	9. Quoniam sic dixit Jehova exercituum, Deus Israel, Ecce ego auferens ab hoc loco, coram oculis vestris, et in diebus vestris, vocem gaudii et vocem lætitiæ, vocem sponsi et vocem sponsæ.

This verse contains a reason for the preceding,—that every connection with that people would be accursed. Yet he states one thing more expressly,—that the time was come in which they were already deprived of all joy ; for the ungodly, even when God most awfully threatens them, strengthen themselves in their security. Hence God intended to give them some presage, that they might before the time know that the saddest calamities were at hand, by which every joy and gladness were to be taken away.

He then says, that the God of *hosts* and the *God of Israel* had spoken. He at the same time deprived them of all hope, though he called himself the God of Israel. Hypocrites were wont either to despise the power of God, or to abuse his goodness. Had not God checked them, they would have deemed as nothing what the prophets threatened ; and how so? Because they depreciated, as far as they could, the power of God. Hence God says, that he is the God of *hosts.* But when they could not in their pride and haughtiness throw down, as it were the power of God, then they betook themselves to another asylum ; they promised to themselves that he would deal indulgently with them ; and thus they deceived themselves. Hence, on the other hand, God calls himself here the *God of Israel,* in order that they might know, that it was of no avail to them, that he had adopted the seed of Abraham ; for they were not the children of Abraham, but aliens, as they had departed from his piety and faith. This served as a preface.

Now when he says, הנני, *enni, Behold me,* he shews that the Jews had no reason to put off the time, and to indulge a vain confidence ; for vengeance was already come. *Behold me,* he says, he thus comes forth and testifies that he is already prepared to execute his judgment. *Behold me,* he says, *taking away from this place, before your eyes, and in your days,* &c. ; their destruction would happen in a short time and before their eyes. I am taking away, he says, *the voice of joy and the voice of gladness,*[1] *the voice of the bridegroom and the voice of the bride.* Here by stating a part for the whole, he intimates that they would become like the dead rather than the living ; for the continuance of the human race is preserved by marriage, as in the offspring mankind are as it were born again, who would otherwise perish daily. Since then there was no more time left for marriages, it was a token of final destruction. This is what the Prophet intimates, when he says, that God would cause the voice of the bridegroom and of the bride to cease, so that there would be no more any congratulations. It follows,—

[1] Rather, "The voice of exultation and the voice of joy;" the most manifest display first—exultation ; and then the most hidden feeling—joy.—*Ed.*

10. And it shall come to pass, when thou shalt shew this people all these words, and they shall say unto thee, Wherefore hath the Lord pronounced all this great evil against us? or what *is* our iniquity? or what *is* our sin that we have committed against the Lord our God.

11. Then shalt thou say unto them, Because your fathers have forsaken me, saith the Lord, and have walked after other gods, and have served them, and have worshipped them, and have forsaken me, and have not kept my law:

12. And ye have done worse than your fathers; (for, behold, ye walk every one after the imagination of his evil heart, that they may not hearken unto me;)

13. Therefore will I cast you out of this land into a land that ye know not, *neither* ye nor your fathers; and there shall ye serve other gods day and night, where I will not shew you favour.

10. Et erit quum annuntiaveris populo huic omnia verba hæc, tunc dicent (*vel,* si diceret) tibi, Cur loquutus est Jehova super nos omne malum hoc magnum? et quæ iniquitas nostra? et quod scelus nostrum, quo sceleratè egimus adversus Jehovam Deum nostrum?

11. Tunc dices illis, Quia dereliquerunt me patres vestri, dicit Jehova, et profecti sunt post deos alienos, et servierunt illis, et adoraverunt illos (*vel,* sese inflexerunt coram illis,) et me reliquerunt et legem meam non servarunt;

12. Et vos deteriores fuistis (deterius egistis) ad faciendum, (*vel,* perpetrandum) quàm patres vestri, et ecce vos profecti estis quisque post pravitatem cordis sui mali, et absque audire me (*hoc est,* ita ut non audieritis me:)

13. Et expellam vos è terra hac ad terram quam non novistis vos et patres vestri, et servietis illic diis alienis die ac nocte; quia non dabo vobis gratiam.

He shews here what we have seen elsewhere,—that the people flattered themselves in their vices, so that they could not be turned by any admonitions, nor be led by any means to repentance. It was a great blindness, nay, even madness, not to examine themselves, when they were smitten by the hand of God; for conscience ought to have been to them like a thousand witnesses, immediately condemning them; but hardly any one was found who examined his own life; and then, though God proved them guilty, hardly one in a hundred willingly and humbly submitted to his judgment; but the greater part murmured and made a clamour, whenever they felt the scourges of God. This evil, as Jeremiah shews, prevailed among the people; and he shewed the same in the fifth chapter.

Hence it is that God says, *When thou shalt declare these words to this people, and they shall say, Wherefore has Jehovah spoken all this great evil against us; what is our iniquity? what is our sin,* that he so rages against us, as though we had acted wickedly against him? God no doubt intended to obviate in time what that perverse people might have said, for he knew that they possessed an untameable disposition. As then he knew that they would be so refractory as to receive no reproof, he confirms his own Prophet, as though he had said, "There is no reason for their perverseness to discourage thee; for they will immediately oppose thee, and treat thee as one doing them a grievous wrong; they will expostulate with thee and deny that they ought to be deemed guilty of so great crimes; if then they will thus petulantly cast aside thy threatenings, there is no reason for thee to be disheartened, for thou shalt have an answer ready for them."

We now see how hypocrites gained nothing, either by their evasions, or by wantonly rising against God and his Prophets. At the same time all teachers are reminded here of their duty, not to vacillate when they have to do with proud and intractable men. As it appeared elsewhere, where God commanded his Prophet to put on a brazen front, that he might boldly encounter all the insults of the people; (chap. i. 18;) the same is the case here, they shall *say to thee,* that is, when thou threatenest them, they will not willingly give way, but they will contend as though thou didst accuse them unjustly, for they will say, "What is our sin? what is our iniquity? what is the wickedness which we have committed against Jehovah our God, that he should declare this great evil against us?" Thus we see that hypocrites vent their rage not only against God's servants, but against God himself, not indeed that they profess openly and plainly to do so. But what is the effect when they cannot bear to be corrected by God's hand, but resist and shew that they do not endure correction with a resigned mind? do they not sufficiently prove that they rebel against God?

But Jeremiah here graphically describes the character of those who struggled with God, for they dared not wholly to deny that they were wicked, but they extenuated as far as they could their sin, like Cain, who ventured not to assert that he was innocent, for he was conscious of having done wrong; and the voice of God, "Where is thy brother?"

strengthened the voice of conscience, but in the meantime he ceased not to utter this complaint, "Greater is my punishment than I can bear." (Gen. iv. 9, 13.) So also Jeremiah introduces the people as speaking, "O, what is our iniquity? and what is the sin which we have committed against Jehovah our God, that he should speak this great evil against us?" They say not that they were wholly without fault, they only object that the atrocity of their sins was not so great as to cause God to be so angry with them, and to visit them with so grievous a punishment. They then exaggerated the punishment, that they might obtain some covering for themselves; and yet they did not say that they were innocent or free from every fault, but they speak of their iniquities and sins as though they had said, "We indeed confess that there is something which God may reprehend, but we do not acknowledge such a mass of sins and iniquities as to cause him thus to thunder against us."

But he then says, *Thou shalt answer them, Because your fathers forsook me; they went after foreign gods, served and worshipped them; and me they forsook and my law they kept not, and ye have done worse.*[1] God in the first place accused their fathers, not that punishment ought to have fallen on their children, except they followed the wickedness of their fathers, but the men of that age fully deserved to be visited with the judgment their fathers merited. Besides well known is that declaration, that God reckons the iniquities of the fathers to their children; (Exodus xx. 5; xxxiv. 7; Deut. v. 9;) and he acts thus justly, for he might justly

[1] The division of these verses, the 11th and the 12th, seems incorrect. Were the latter part of the 11th connected with the 12th, the repetition which now appears would not be perceived. I render the verses thus—

11. Then say to them,
Because your fathers forsook me, saith Jehovah,
And walked after foreign gods,
And served them and bowed down to them:
Yea, me they forsook and my law kept not,
12. And ye have become evil by doing worse than your fathers;
For lo, ye are walking, every man,
After the resolutions of his own evil heart,
So as not to hearken to me.

In the first part their fathers' conduct is set forth; in the second their fathers' conduct and their own. And their "worse" conduct was in not hearkening to the voice of God by his Prophets.—*Ed.*

execute vengeance for sins on the whole human race, according to what Christ says, "On you shall come the blood of all the godly, from righteous Abel to Zachariah the son of Barachiah." (Matt. xxiii. 35; Luke xi. 51.) Thus then the Scripture often declares, that children shall be punished with their fathers, because God will at one time or another require an account of all sins, and thus will make amends for his long forbearance, for as he waits for men and kindly invites them through his patience to repent, so when he sees no hope he inflicts all his scourges. It is hence no wonder that children are more grievously punished after iniquity has prevailed for many ages.

We hence see that these two things are not inconsistent—that God connects the punishment of children with that of their fathers, and that he does not punish the innocent. We indeed see this fulfilled, "The soul that sinneth it shall die; the children shall not bear the iniquity of their fathers, nor the father the iniquity of his child," (Ezek. xviii. 4, 20,) for God never blends children with their fathers except they be their associates in wickedness. But yet there is nothing to prevent God to punish children for the sins of their fathers, especially when they continually rush headlong into worse sins, when the children, as we shall hereafter see, exceed their fathers in all kinds of wickedness.

We further learn from this passage, that they bring forward a vain pretence who allege against us the examples of the Fathers, as we see to be done now by those under the Papacy; for the shield they boldly set up against us is this, that they imitate the examples of the fathers. But God declares here that they were worthy of double punishment who repented not when they saw that their fathers had been ungodly and transgressors of the law.

Let us now notice the sins which God mentions: he says, that they had *forsaken* him. That people could not make any excuse for going astray, like the unhappy heathens, to whom no Prophet had been sent, and no law had been given. Hence the heathens had some excuse more than the Jews. The truth indeed respecting all was, that they were all apostates, for God had bound the human race to himself, and all they who followed superstitions were justly charged with the sin of apostasy; there was yet a greater atrocity of wickedness in the Jewish people, for God had set before them his law, they had been brought up as it were in his school, they knew what true religion was, they were able to distinguish the true God from fictitious gods. We now then see the meaning of the expression, *They have forsaken me:* and it is twice repeated, because it was necessary thus to prove the Jews guilty, that their mouths might be stopped; for we have seen that they were to be thus roused from their insensibility, inasmuch as they would have never yielded nor acknowledged their sins, were they not constrained.

He says further, that *they went after foreign gods, served them, and worshipped them.* Now this statement enhances again their sins, for the Jews preferred their own inventions to the true God, who had by so many signs and testimonies manifested his glory and made known his power among them. As then God had abundantly testified his power, it was by no means an endurable ingratitude in them to follow strange gods, of whom they had only heard. The heathens indeed vainly boasted of their idols, and spread abroad many fables to allure unhappy men to false and corrupt worship, but the Jews knew who the true God was. To believe the fables of the heathens, rather than the law and their own experience, was not this the basest impiety? This then was the reason why God complained that foreign gods were worshipped by them.

Then he adds, *They served and worshipped them.* The verb to serve is often used by the Hebrews to express worship, as we have stated elsewhere; and thus is refuted the folly of the Papists who deny that they are idolaters, because they worship pictures and statues with *dulia,* that is, with service, if we may so render it, and not with *latria,* as though Scripture in condemning idolatry never used this verb. But God condemns here the Jews because they *served* strange gods, because they gave credit to the false and vain fictions of the heathens; and then he adds the outward action, that they prostrated themselves before their idols.

At the end of this verse he shews how he had been forsaken, even because they kept not his *law*. He then confirms what I have already stated, that there was on this account a worse apostasy among the Jews, for they had knowingly and wilfully forsaken the fountain of living water, as we have seen in the second chapter: hence simple ignorance is not what is here reprehended, as though they had sinned through error or want of knowledge, but they had rejected the worship of God as it were designedly. The rest I shall defer till to-morrow.

PRAYER.

Grant, Almighty God, that as we in various ways daily provoke thy wrath against us, and thou ceasest not to exhort us to repent,—O grant, that we may be pliant and obedient and not despise thy kind invitations, while thou settest before us the hope of thy mercy, nor make light of thy threatenings; but that we may so profit by thy word as to endeavour to anticipate thy judgments; and may we also, being allured by the sweetness of thy grace, consecrate ourselves wholly to thee, that thus thy wrath may be turned away from us, and that we may become receivers of that grace which thou offerest to all who truly and from the heart repent, and who desire to have thee propitious to them in Christ Jesus our Lord.—Amen.

Lecture Sixty-Fourth.

I WAS constrained yesterday to leave unfinished the words of the Prophet. He said that the children were *worse* than their fathers, and gave the reason, *Because they followed the wickedness of their evil heart,*[1] *and hearkened not to God.* He seems to have said before the same thing of the fathers: it might then be asked, Why does he say that the children had done worse than their fathers, and pronounce their sins worse? Now we have already seen that sins became worse before God, when the children strengthened themselves in wickedness by following the examples of their fathers. We must also notice, that not only the law had been set before them, but that also Prophets had been often sent to them,

[1] See note in vol. i. p. 187.

who added their reproofs: and this is what Jeremiah seems to have expressed at the end of the verse, by saying that they *hearkened not,* though daily spoken to by the Prophets. It was then their obstinacy that God so severely punished: they had imitated their wicked fathers, and then they not only had despised, but also through their obstinate wickedness had rejected all the warnings which the Prophets gave them.

Then follows a commination, *I will eject you,* he says, or remove you, *from this land to a land which ye know not, nor your fathers,* for they had followed unknown gods, and went after inventions of their own and of others. God now declares that he would be the vindicator of his own glory, by driving them to a land unknown to them and to their fathers. He immediately adds, *There shall ye serve other gods day and night.* We must take notice of this kind of punishment, for nothing could have happened worse to the Jews than to be constrained to adopt false and corrupt forms of worship, as it was a denial of God and of true religion. As this appears at the first view hard, some mitigate it, as though the worship of strange gods would be that servitude into which they were reduced when they became subject to idolators: but this is too remote. I therefore do not doubt but that God abandoned them, because they had violated true and pure worship, and had gone after the many abominations of the heathens; and thus he shews that they were worthy to be thus dealt with, who had in every way contaminated themselves, and as it were plunged themselves into the depth of every thing abominable: and it is certainly probable that they were led by constraint into ungodly ceremonies, when the Chaldeans had the power to treat them, as they usually did, as slaves, without any measure of humanity. It is then hence a probable conjecture that they were drawn to superstitions, and that interminably; so that they were not only forced to worship false gods, but were also constrained to do so by way of sport, as they daily triumphed over them as their conquerors.

And he confirms this clause by what follows, *For I will not,* &c., for the relative **אשר**, *asher,* is here to be taken for a causative particle, *For I will not shew you favour*, or mercy; that is, I will not turn the hearts of your enemies so as to be propitious or kind to you.[1] By these words God shews that he would not only punish them by subjecting them to their enemies, or by suffering them to be driven into exile; but that there would be an additional punishment by rendering their enemies cruel to them; for God can either tame the ferocity of men, or, when he pleases, can rouse them to greater rage and cruelty, when it is his purpose to use them as scourges.

We now then understand the whole design of what the Prophet says, that the Jews who had refused to worship God in their own land would be led away to Chaldea, where they would be constrained, willing or unwilling, to worship strange gods, and that without end or limits. It now follows—

14. Therefore, behold, the days come, saith the Lord, that it shall no more be said, The Lord liveth, that brought up the children of Israel out of the land of Egypt;

15. But, The Lord liveth, that brought up the children of Israel from the land of the north, and from all the lands whither he had driven them: and I will bring them again into their land that I gave unto their fathers.

14. Propterea ecce dies veniunt, dicit Jehova, et non dicetur amplius (*hoc est*, quibus non dicetur amplius,) vivit Jehova, qui eduxit (ascendere fecit, *ad verbum*) filios Israel è terra Egypti;

15. Quin potius, vivit Jehova, qui ascendere fecit filios Israel è terra Aquilonis, et ex omnibus regionibus, ad quas expulerat eos; et reducam ad terram eorum quam dedi patribus vestris.

Jeremiah seems here to promise a return to the Jews; and so the passage is commonly expounded, as though a consolation is interposed, in which the faithful alone are concerned. But I consider the passage as mixed, that the Prophet, in part, speaks in severe terms of the dreadful exile which he foretells, and that he in part blends some consolation; but the latter subject seems to me to be indirectly referred to

[1] The *Targum* and the versions, except the *Syriac*, apply this clause to their enemies, "who will not shew you favour," or mercy; and no doubt this reads better; and the verb in that case would be יתנו; but there is no MS. in its favour. The relative may be regarded in the same way as at the second verse of the first chapter, (To whom the word, &c.,) "To whom I will not shew favour." This kind of idiom evidently exists in Hebrew. However the sense is the same as given in the ancient versions, only according to the Hebrew reading the original cause of the favour is expressly mentioned. The denial of favour proceeded from God's providence, though it was through the instrumentality of their enemies.—*Ed.*

by the Prophet. I therefore think this to be an amplification of what he had said. This is to be kept in mind. He had said, "I will expel you from this land, and will send you to a land unknown to you and to your fathers." Now follows a circumstance which increased the grievousness of exile: they knew how cruel was that servitude from which God had delivered their fathers. Their condition was worse than hundred deaths, when they were driven to their servile works; and also, when all justice was denied them, and when their offspring were from the womb put to death. As then they knew how cruelly their fathers had been treated by the Egyptians, the comparison he states more fully shewed what a dreadful punishment awaited them, for their redemption would be much more incredible.

We now perceive what the Prophet meant, as though he had said, "Ye know from what your fathers came forth, even from a brazen furnace, as it is said elsewhere, and as it were from the depth of death, so that that redemption ought to be remembered to the end of the world; but God will now cast you into an abyss deeper than that of Egypt from which your fathers were delivered; and when from thence he will redeem you, it will be a miracle far more wonderful to your posterity, so that it will almost extinguish, or at least obscure the memory of the first redemption: *It will not then be said any more, Live does Jehovah, who brought the children of Israel from Egypt,* for that Egyptian captivity was far more endurable than what this latter shall be; for ye shall be plunged as it were into the infernal regions; and when God shall rescue you from thence, it will be a work far more wonderful." This I consider to be the real meaning of the Prophet.[1]

Yet his object was at the same time indirectly to give them some hope of their future redemption; but this he did not do avowedly. We ought then to regard what the Prophet had in view, even to strike the Jews, as I have said,

[1] No particular notice is taken of לכן, rendered "therefore," at the beginning of the verse. *Gataker* renders it "notwithstanding;" *Lowth,* "nevertheless," and *Blayney,* "after this." What suits the passage best is "nevertheless." The verse appears to be parenthetic, introduced for the purpose of keeping the people from despair under their sufferings.—*Ed.*

with terror, so that they might know that there was an evil nigh at hand more grievous than what their fathers suffered in Egypt, who yet had been most cruelly oppressed. Then their former liberation would be rendered obscure and not celebrated as before, though it was nevertheless an evidence of the wonderful power of God.

But, it will be rather said, *Live does Jehovah, for he has brought his people from the land of the north;* and for this reason, because there will be less hope remaining for you, when the Chaldeans shall subdue and scatter you like a body torn asunder, and when the name of Israel shall be extinguished, when the worship of God shall be subverted and the Temple destroyed. When therefore all things shall appear to be past remedy, this captivity shall be much more dreadful than that by which your fathers had been oppressed. Therefore, when God restores you, it will be a miracle much more remarkable. And that the Prophet took occasion to give them some hope of God's favour, may be gathered from the end of the verse, when he says, *And I will make them to return to their own land:* but the copulative ought to be rendered as a conditional particle, as though he had said, *When I shall restore them to their own land which I gave to their fathers.* It now follows—

16. Behold, I will send for many fishers, saith the Lord, and they shall fish them; and after will I send for many hunters, and they shall hunt them from every mountain, and from every hill, and out of the holes of the rocks.

16. Ecce ego mitto ad piscatores multos, dicit Jehova, et piscabuntur; et sic (post hæc) mittam ad multos venatores, et venabuntur eos de super omni monte, (*hoc est,* ex omni monte,) et omni colle, et foraminibus (*vel,* cavernis) rupium.

Some explain this of the apostles; but it is wholly foreign to the subject: they think that Jeremiah pursues here what he had begun to speak of; for they doubt not but that he had been speaking in the last verse of a future but a near deliverance, in order to raise the children of God into a cheerful confidence. But I have already rejected this meaning, for their exposition is not well founded. But if it be conceded that the Prophet had prophesied of the liberation of the people, it does not follow that God goes on with the same subject, for he immediately returns to threatenings, as ye will see; and the allegory also is too remote when he speaks of hunters and fishers; and as mention is made of hills and mountains, it appears still more clearly that the Prophet is threatening the Jews, and not promising them any alleviation in their miseries. I therefore connect all these things together in a plain manner; for, having said that the evil which the Jews would shortly have to endure would be more grievous than the Egyptian bondage, he now adds a reason as a confirmation,—

Behold, he says, *I will send to them many fishers,* that they may gather them together on every side. He mentions fishers, as they would draw the children of Israel from every quarter to their nets. He then compares the Chaldeans to fishers, who would so proceed through the whole land as to leave none except some of the most ignoble, whom also they afterwards took away; and to fishers he adds *hunters.* Some understand by fishers armed enemies, who by the sword slew the conquered; and they consider that the hunters were those who were disposed to spare the life of the many, and to drive them into exile; but this appears too refined. Simple is the view which I have stated,—that the Chaldeans were called fishers, because they would empty the whole land of its inhabitants, and that they were called hunters, because the Jews, having been scattered here and there, and become fugitives, would yet be found out in the recesses of hills and rocks.

The two similitudes are exceedingly suitable; for the Prophet shews that the Chaldeans would not have much trouble in taking the Jews, inasmuch as fishers only spread their nets; they do not arm themselves against fishes, nor is there any need; and then all the fish they take they easily take possession of them, for there is no resistance. Thus, then, he shews that the Chaldeans would gain an easy victory, for they would take the Jews as fishes which are drawn into nets. This is one thing. Then, in the second place, he says, that if they betook themselves into recesses of mountains, that if they hid themselves in caverns or holes, their enemies would be like hunters who follow the wild beasts in forests and in other unfrequented places; no brambles, nor thorns, nor any obstructions prevent them from advancing, being led on by a strong impulse; so in like manner no recesses of mountains would be concealed from the Chaldeans, no caverns where the Jews might hide themselves, for they would all be taken. We hence see that he confirms by two similitudes, what he had said in a preceding verse. He afterwards adds—

17. For mine eyes *are* upon all their ways: they are not hid from my face, neither is their iniquity hid from mine eyes.

17. Quia oculi mei super omnes vias ipsorum; non absconditæ sunt à facie mea, et non sunt occultæ iniquitates è regione oculorum meorum, (coram oculis meis; *ad verbum est,* de coram oculis meis.)

The Prophet now shews that the grievous calamity of which he had spoken would be a just reward for the wickedness of the people; for we know that the prophets were endued with the Spirit of God not merely that they might foretell things to come—for that would have been very jejune; but a doctrine was connected with their predictions. Hence the prophets not only foretold what God would do, but at the same time added the causes. There is then now added a doctrine as a seasoning to the prophecy; for the Prophet says that the destruction of the Jews was at hand, because they had long greatly provoked the wrath of God. As there is no end to the evasions of hypocrites, according to what we observed yesterday, God here reminds them of his judgment, as though he had said, "This one thing is sufficient, he knows their iniquities, and he is a fit judge; so they contend in vain, and try in vain, to excuse or to extenuate their fault."

Hence he says that *the eyes* of God *were on all their ways:* and he mentions *all their ways,* because they had not offended only once, or in one way, but they had added sins to sins. *Nor are they hid,* he says: the Prophet presses the matter on their attention; for had he allowed their false pretences, they would have made no end of excuses. He therefore says that their ways *were not hid, nor their iniquities concealed from the eyes* of God. Now follows a confirmation—

18. And first I will recompense their iniquity and their sin double; because they have defiled my land, they have filled

18. Et rependam ab initio duplum iniquitatum eorum et scelerum eorum; quia polluerunt (super polluere ipsos) terram meam in cadaveribus

mine inheritance with the carcases of their detestable and abominable things.

abominationum suarum, et suis inquinamentis repleruut hæreditatem meam.

Jeremiah introduces here nothing new, but proceeds with the subject we observed in the last verse,—that God would not deal with so much severity with the Jews, because extreme rigour was pleasing to him, or because he had forgotten his own nature or the covenant which he had made with Abraham, but because the Jews had become extremely obstinate in their wickedness. As, then, he had said that the *eyes* of God *were on all their ways,* so now he adds that he would *recompense* them as they deserved.

But every word ought to be considered: He says ראשונה, *rashune,* which I render "From the beginning." Some render it more obscurely, "at first,"—I will first recompense them. The word means formerly, and refers to time. The Prophet then, I have no doubt, means what I have already referred to,—that God would punish the fathers and their children, and would thus gather into one mass their old iniquities. We have quoted from the law that God would recompense unto the bosom of children the sins of their fathers; and we have also quoted that declaration of Christ, "Come upon you shall righteous blood from Abel to Zachariah, the son of Barachiah." (Matt. xxiii. 35; Luke xi. 51.) The Prophet now repeats the same thing,—that God, in allotting to the Jews their reward, would collect together as it were all the iniquities which had been as it were long buried, so that he would include the fathers and their children in one bundle, and gather together all their sins, in order that he might consume them as it were in one heap. In this way I explain the term "From the beginning."[1]

[1] The *Septuagint* omit this word, and give this rendering, "And I will recompense their two-fold iniquities," &c., so does the *Vulgate,* only it retains this word, and renders it "first." But the Hebrew will not admit the connection of "two-fold" with "iniquities."

Venema gives the best exposition of this passage, from verse 14 to the end. He considers it a prophecy of the restoration of the people from Babylon. The "fishers" and "the hunters," in verse 16, he regards as the individuals employed by God to gather them from the countries to which they had been dispersed, such as Zerubbabel, Joshuah, Ezra, and Nehemiah. He connects this verse more especially with the latter part

He then adds, *The double of their iniquities and their sins.* The Prophet does not mean that there would be an excess of severity, as though God would not rightly consider what men deserved; but "double" signifies a just and complete measure, according to what is said in Isaiah xl. 2, "The Lord hath recompensed double for all her sins;" that is, sufficiently and more, (*satis supérque,*) as the Latins say. There God assumes the character of a father, and, according to his great kindness, says that the Jews had been more than sufficiently punished. So also in this place, in speaking of punishment, he calls that double, not what would exceed the limits of justice, but because God would shew himself differently to them from what he had done before, when he patiently bore with them; as though he had said, "I will to the utmost punish them; for there will be no remission, no lenity, no mercy." We hence see that what is here designed is only extreme rigour, which yet was just and right; for had God punished a hundred times more severely even those who seemed to have sinned lightly, his justice could not have been questioned as though he had acted cruelly. Since the Jews, then, had in so many ways, and for so long a time, and so grievously sinned, God could not have been thought too severe, when he rendered to them

of verse 17. Having stated that their ways would not be hid from God in their dispersion, the Prophet refers to their previous iniquity as having not been hid from him, and then says in God's name, "And I will first recompense doubly their iniquity," &c., that is before I restore them. These two verses may be thus rendered, the first line being connected with the previous verse,—

17\. For mine eyes *shall be* on all their ways.
Concealed have they not been from me,
Nor hid has been their iniquity from my eyes;
18\. And I will first doubly recompense
Their iniquity and their sin,
Because they have polluted my land
With the vileness of their detestable things,
And with their abominations have filled mine inheritance.

As the previous verse is in the future tense, so the first line in the 17th verse. The "detestable things" were their idols. The version of the *Septuagint* is, "with the dead bodies (θνησιμαίοις) of their abominations;" of the *Vulgate,* "with the carrions (morticînis) of their idols;" and of the *Syriac,* "with the sacrifices of their idols." *Blayney's* rendering is, "by the vileness of their odious practices." The word "carcases" is derived from the *Targum.* Idolatrous practices are evidently the things referred to.—*Ed.*

their reward; and he calls it double because he omitted nothing in order to carry it to the utmost severity. Probably he alludes also to the enemies as being ministers of his vengeance, whose cruelty would be more atrocious than the Jews thought, who imagined some slight remedies for slight sins, as we say, *Il n'y faudra plus retourner*, or, *tout outre.*

He mentions *sins and iniquities,* for Jeremiah had introdued them before as speaking thus, "What is our iniquity? and what is our sin?" Though they could not wholly exculpate themselves, they yet continued to allege some pretences, that they might not appear to be altogether wicked. But here God declares that they were wholly wicked and ungodly; and he adds a confirmation, that they had *polluted the land with the carcases of their abominations.* The Prophet mentions a particular thing, for had he spoken generally, the Jews would have raised a clamour and said, that they were not conscious of being so wicked. That he might then bring the matter home to them, he shews as it were by the finger that their sin was by no means excusable, for they had polluted the land of God with their superstitions; they have polluted, he says, *my land.* He exaggerates their crime by saying, that they polluted the holy land. The earth indeed is God's and its fulness. (Psalm xxiv. 1.) Hence it might be said justly of the whole world, that the land of God is polluted when men act on it an ungodly part. But here God distinguishes Canaan from other countries, because it was dedicated as it were to his name. As God then had set apart that land for himself, that he might be there worshipped, he says, they have *polluted my land.*

And he adds, *With the carcases of their abominations.* It is probable that he calls their sacrifices carcases. For though in appearance their superstitions bore a likeness to the true and lawful worship of God, yet we know that the sacrifices which God had commanded were seasoned by his word as with salt; they were therefore of good odour and fragrance before God. As to the sacrifices offered to idols, they were fœtid carcases, they were mere rottenness, yet the ceremony was altogether alike. But God does not regard the external form, for obedience is better before him than all sacrifices. (1 Sam. xv. 22.) We hence see that there is to be understood a contrast between the carcases and the sweet odour which lawful sacrifices possessed. For as sacrifices, rightly offered according to the rule of the law, pleased God and were said to be of sweet savour, so the victims superstitiously offered having no command of God in their favour, were called filthy carcases.

And he says further, *With their defilements have they filled mine inheritance.* The land of Canaan is called the inheritance of God in the same sense in which the land is before called his land. But in this second clause something more is expressed, as it is the usual manner of Scripture to amplify. It was indeed a grievous thing that the land dedicated to God should be polluted; but when he says, This is *mine inheritance,* that is, the land which I have chosen to dwell in with my people, that it might be to me as it were a kind of an earthly habitation, and that this land was filled with defilements, it was a thing altogether intolerable. We now then see that the Jews were so bridled and checked that they in vain attempted to escape, or thought to gain anything by evasions, for their impiety was intolerable and deserved to be most severely punished by God. I will not proceed further, for it is a new discourse.

PRAYER.

Grant, Almighty God, that as thou hast not given to thy servants a small corner only of the earth to dwell in, but hast designed to extend thy kingdom to the utmost borders of the earth, and to dwell with us, wherever we be, by thine only-begotten Son,—O grant, that we may offer ourselves as sacrifices to thee, and labour also so to regulate our life according to thy word that thy name may be glorified in and by us, till we shall become at length partakers of that celestial and eternal glory, which has been provided for us by Christ our Lord—Amen.

Lecture Sixty-Fifth.

19. O Lord, my strength, and my fortress, and my refuge in the day of affliction, the Gentiles shall come unto thee from the ends of the earth, and shall say, Surely our fathers have inherited lies, vanity, and *things* wherein *there is* no profit.

19. Jehova, robur meum et munitio mea, et refugium in die angustiæ, (*vel*, afflictionis,) ad te Gentes venient è finibus terræ ac dicent, Certè mendacium possederunt patres nostri, vanitas (vanitatem) et nihil in ipsis utile.

WHAT the Prophet has said hitherto might appear contrary to the promises of God, and wholly subversive of the covenant which he had made with Abraham. God had chosen to himself one people from the whole world, now when this people were trodden under foot what could the most perfect of the faithful suppose but that that covenant was rendered void, since God had resolved to destroy the Jews and to obliterate their name? This was then a most grievous trial, and sufficient to shake the strongest minds. The Prophet therefore now returns to the subject, and obviates this temptation; and seeing men in despair he turns to God, and speaks of the calling of the Gentiles, which was sufficient wholly to remove that stumbling-block, which I have mentioned respecting the apostasy and ruin of the chosen people. We now perceive the Prophet's meaning.

When any one reads the whole chapter, he may think that Jeremiah abruptly turns to address God; but what I have stated ought to be borne in mind, for his purpose was to fortify himself and the faithful against the thought I have mentioned, which would have otherwise shaken the faith of them all. And he shews what is best to be done in a troubled and dark state of things, for Satan hunts for nothing more than to involve us in various and intricate disputes, and he is an acute disputant, yea, and a sophist; we are also very ready to receive what he may suggest, and thus it happens that the thoughts which we either attain ourselves or too readily receive when offered by the artifice of Satan, often overwhelm us. There is then no better remedy than to break off such disputes and to turn our eyes and all our thoughts to God. This the Prophet did when he said, *O Jehovah, to thee shall the Gentiles come.*

We now see that Jeremiah sets the conversion of the Gentiles in opposition to the destruction which he had before denounced; for the truth of God and his mercy were so connected with the salvation of the chosen people, that their destruction seemed to obliterate them. Therefore the Prophet sets forth in opposition to this the conversion of the Gentiles, as though he had said, "Though the race of Abraham perishes, yet God's covenant fails not, nor is there any diminution of his grace, for he will convert all the Gentiles to himself." If any one objects and says, that though the Gentiles be converted, yet the covenant of God could not have been valid and perpetual, except the posterity of Abraham were heirs of that grace which God had promised to him. To this there is a ready answer, for when God turned the Gentiles to himself he was mindful of his promise, so as to gather a Church to himself both from the Jews and the Gentiles, as we also know that Christ came to proclaim peace to those afar off and to them who were nigh, according to what Paul teaches. (Eph. ii. 17.) Jeremiah then includes in the calling of the Gentiles what is said elsewhere, "A remnant according to the election of grace." (Rom. xi. 5.) It is an argument from the greater to the less; "God will not retain a few men only, but will gather to himself those who now seem dispersed through the whole world; much more then shall all those of the race of Abraham, who are chosen by God, be saved; and though the great body of the people perish, yet the Lord, who knows his own people, will not suffer them to perish even in the worst state of things."

But as the struggle was difficult, he calls God his *strength*, and *fortress*, and *refuge.* He says עזי ומעזי, *ozi vemozi, ma force et forteresse*, for the two words come from the same root, and we cannot in Latin thus fitly translate them. He then calls God his *strength* and his *fortress*, but both words are derived from a verb which means to be strong. He then adds, *my refuge in the day of affliction.* We here see that God according to circumstances is adorned with names, such as are fit to give us confidence, and as it were to arm us for the purpose of sustaining all the assaults of temptations, for there was not sufficient force and power in that plain declaration, " O Jehovah, the Gentiles shall come to thee," but as the Prophet was reduced to the greatest straits, and, as I have said, his faith must have been greatly tried, he calls God his strength, his fortress, and his refuge in the day of affliction ; as though he had said, " Now is the time when I find how necessary is thy protection, thy strength, thy power ; for though my present miseries, and the approaching ruin dishearten me, yet thou wilt be to me a refuge."

But he says, that *the Gentiles would come from the ends of the earth.*[1] A contrast is to be observed here also ; for the Jews at first worshipped God, as it were in an obscure corner ; but he says, " When that land shall cast out its inhabitants, all nations shall come, not only from neighbouring countries, but also from the extremities of the earth." He adds, that the Gentiles would *say, surely falsehood have our fathers possessed ;* it was *vanity, there was nothing profitable in them.* To possess, here means the same as to inherit ; for we know that one's own inheritance is valuable to him ; and men are as it were fixed in their farms and fields. As then the Gentiles, before they were enlightened, thought their

[1] Though the word rendered here " Gentiles " may be often so translated, yet it does not necessarily mean the heathens. It signifies a people associated together ; and it may mean here the Jewish people in their dispersion, formed into companies or tribes, as *Grotius* thinks ; and a due consideration of the context will lead us to this opinion. They are spoken of in verse 15 as " brought from *all the lands*" whither God had driven them ; and as the idolatry of their fathers is continually mentioned in connection with their own, the confession in this verse seems appropriate to them ; and the last verse, the 21st, clearly refers to the people of Israel. There is nothing in the whole passage (except it be this clause) that has any reference to the conversion of the heathens. I am aware that commentators take the same view of this clause with *Calvin*, yet I fully believe that the " nations " here were the Jews, scattered here and there, as distinct portions of the community, in various parts of the heathen world. The prophet, after having received an assurance of a restoration, makes a thankful acknowledgment to God, and tells us what would be the confession of the returned exiles, which includes the next verse. Then God assures him in the last verse, that such would be the effect of exile as to make them ever afterwards to acknowledge his power and his majesty, which has been remarkably fulfilled ; for the Jews have never been guilty of idolatry since their return from Babylon.—*Ed.*

chief happiness to be in their superstitions, the Prophet says here, by way of concession, that they *possessed falsehood*, as though it was said, "Our fathers thought themselves blessed and happy when they worshipped idols and their own inventions." It was therefore *their heritage*, that is, they thought nothing better or more to be desired than to embrace their idols and their errors; but it was *falsehood*, he says, that is, when they thought that they had a glorious inheritance it was only a foolish imagination; it was, in short, *vanity*, and there was nothing *useful* or profitable *in them*. This confession proves the conversion of the Gentiles by external evidences. When we offend God, not only secretly, but also by bad examples, repentance requires confession. Hence the Prophet shews a change in the Gentiles, for they would of themselves acknowledge that their fathers had been deceived by superstitions; for while they thought that they were acting rightly, they were only under the influence of illusions and fascinations.

But it is not to be doubted but that the Prophet here indirectly condemns the Jews, because they had not departed from the sins of their fathers, though they had been often admonished. *The Gentiles* then *shall come*, and the ignorance of their fathers shall not prevent them from confessing that they and their fathers were guilty before God. Since then the hinderance which from deliberate wickedness held fast the Jews, would not prevail with the Gentiles, it appeared evident how great was the contumacy of the people, who could not be persuaded to forsake the bad examples of their fathers. We now understand what the Prophet means, and for what purpose he introduced this prayer. It follows—

20. Shall a man make gods unto himself, and they *are* no gods?	20. An faciet sibi homo deos? et ipsi non sunt dii.

Some frigidly explain this verse, as though the Prophet said that men are doubly foolish, who form for themselves gods from wood, stone, gold, or silver, because they cannot change their nature; for whatever men may imagine, the stone remains a stone, the wood remains wood. The sense then they elicit from the Prophet's words is this—that they are not gods who are devised by the foolish imaginations of men. But the Prophet reasons differently,—"Can he who is not God make a god?" that is, "can he who is created be the creator?" No one can give, according to the common proverb, what he has not; and there is in man no divine power. We indeed see what our condition is; there is nothing more frail and perishable: as man then is all vanity, and has in him nothing solid, can he create a god for himself? This is the Prophet's argument: it is drawn from what is absurd, in order that men might at length acknowledge, not only their presumption, but their monstrous madness. For when any one is asked as to his condition, he must necessarily confess that he is a creature, and that he is also, as the ancients have said, an ephemeral animal, that his life is like a shadow. Since then men are constrained, by the real state of things, to make such a confession, how comes it that they dare to form gods for themselves? God does not create a god, he creates men; he has created angels, he has created the heavens and the earth, but yet he does not put forth his power to create a new god. Now man, what is he? nothing but vanity; and yet he will create a god though he is no God.[1]

There is no doubt but that the Prophet here, as with new vigour, boldly attacks the Jews. For it seems evident that, when this temptation assailed him—"What can this mean? what will at length happen when God rejects the race of

[1] *Calvin* in this instance follows the *Syriac* version, which is different from all the other ancient versions, and also the *Targum*. *Blayney* gives the same meaning with *Calvin*, which *Horsley* wholly disapproves, and which the Hebrew can hardly admit. The literal rendering is,—

Shall man make for himself gods?
But they are no gods.

As the future may often be rendered potentially, the better version would be this,—

Can man make for himself gods
When they are no gods?

That is, can he make gods of those who are not gods? This is, in my view, a continuation of the confession in the previous verse, which I render as follows,—

"Truly, falsehood have our fathers inherited—vanity,
And they had nothing that profited:
Can man make for himself gods,
When they are no gods?"

"Falsehood" was false religion, the character of which was "vanity," an empty and useless thing: and this is more fully asserted in the next line, which is literally, "And nothing in them," or with them, *i. e.*, the fathers, "that was profitable."—*Ed.*

Abraham whom he had chosen?" he turned to God: but now, having recovered confidence, he inveighs against the ungodly, and says, *can man create gods for himself while yet he is not a god?* The change in the number ought not to be deemed strange; for when there is an indefinite declaration the number is often changed, both in Greek and Latin. If some particular person was intended, the Prophet would not have said, *And they themselves are not gods;* but as he speaks of mankind generally and indefinitely, the sentence reads better when he says, "Shall man make a god? and they," that is men, "are not gods." This remark I have added, because it is probable that those who consider idols to be intended in the last clause have been led astray by the change that is made in the number. It follows,—

21. Therefore, behold, I will this once cause them to know, I will cause them to know mine hand and my might; and they shall know that my name *is* The Lord.	21. Propterea ecce ego cognoscere faciam ipsos hac vice, ostendam ipsis (cognoscere ipsos faciam) manum meam et potentiam meam; et cognoscent quòd nomen meum Jehova.

The Prophet again threatens the Jews, because their impiety was inexcusable, especially when attended with so great an obstinacy. He therefore says that God was already present as a judge: *Behold I,* he says—the demonstrative particle shews the near approach of vengeance—*I will shew at this time:* the words are emphatical, for God indirectly intimates that the Babylonian exile would be an extraordinary event, far exceeding every other which had preceded it. *At this time,* he says—that is, if ye have hitherto been tardy and insensible, or, if the punishments I have already inflicted have not been sufficiently severe—*I will at this time shew to them my hand and my power; and they shall know that my name is Jehovah.*[1]

[1] As the captivity and the restoration of the people are expressly referred to in the previous verses, it seems necessary to connect here the display of God's power with both these events. The restoration was as remarkable an instance of divine interposition as the captivity, if not more so. And the future effect on the people's mind, their preservation from idolatry, is to be ascribed to the power manifested in their restoration as well as in their captivity. "Therefore," at the beginning of the verse, seems to be an inference from what has been said of the captivity and the restoration; and this accounts for the repetition of making known to them his power: God first made known his power in driving them to captivity, and, secondly, in restoring them,—

This way of speaking often occurs in Scripture; but God here, no doubt, reproves the false sentiments with which the Jews were imbued, and by which they were led astray from true religion—for they had devised for themselves many gods; hence he says, *They shall know that my name is Jehovah*, that is, that my name is sacred, and ought not to be given to others. But at the same time he intimates that he would shew to them his power by destroying them, which they had refused to acknowledge in the preservation promised to them. They would indeed have ever found the God of Abraham to be the same, had they not deprived themselves of his favour. As then they had wandered after their own delusions and inventions, God says now, *I will shew to them my hand*, that is, for their ruin; and they shall now know for their own misery what they had refused to acknowledge for their own safety—that I am the only true God.

Here let us first learn that it was wholly a diabolical madness, when men dared to devise for themselves a god; for had they regarded their own beginning and their own end, doubtless they could not have betrayed so much presumption and audacity as to invent a god for themselves. If this only came to the mind of an idolater, "What art thou? whence is thine origin? where goest thou, and what end awaits thee?" all his false imaginations would have instantly fallen to the ground; he would no longer think of forming a god for

Therefore, behold I make known to them, at this time,
And I will make known to them
My hand and my power;
And they shall know that my name is Jehovah.

The *Septuagint* is as follows,—

Therefore, behold I will manifest to them at this time my hand,
And I will make known to them my power;
And they shall know that my name is the Lord.

To remove the word "hand" to the first line has no MS. in its favour; but it shews that they thought that the two verbs had a similar objective case, and the conjunction "and" is supplied before the second verb, as it is also in the *Syriac* and *Arabic*.

It is probable that by the "hand" is meant the infliction of punishment, and is rendered "vengeance" in the *Targum;* and that by "power" or strength is intended what God manifested in the restoration of the people. The combined influence of both was to make them to know that God was really Jehovah, the only supreme, ever the same, true and faithful, without any change. How remarkably has this prophecy been accomplished! The Jews have ever since acknowledged Jehovah as the only true God.—*Ed.*

himself, nor of worshipping anything he might invent. How then does it happen that men proceed to such a madness as to devise gods for themselves, according to their own fancies, except that they know not themselves? It is then no wonder that men are blind in seeking God, when they do not consider nor examine themselves. It hence follows that God cannot be rightly worshipped except men are made humble. And humility is the best preparation for faith, that there may be a submission to the word of God. Idolaters do indeed pretend some kind of humility, but they afterwards involve themselves in such stupidity, that they are unwilling to make any enquiry, so as to make any difference between light and darkness. But true humility leads us to seek God in his word.

But when the Prophet asks this question, "Shall man make a god for himself?" he does not mean, that either the Egyptians or the Assyrians were so ignorant as to think that they could give divinity to wood or stone; but that whatever men dared to invent for themselves as to divine worship, was nothing else but the creation of a god. As soon then as we allow ourselves the liberty to worship God in this or in that way, or to imagine God to be such and such a being, we create gods for ourselves. And as to that point where he says, *They shall know that my name is Jehovah*, we must observe, that what is his own is taken away from God, except we acquiesce in him alone, so as to allow no other divinities to creep in and to be received; for God does not retain his own right or his own glory, except he be regarded as the only true God. Now follows—

CHAPTER XVII.

1. The sin of Judah *is* written with a pen of iron, *and* with the point of a diamond: *it is* graven upon the table of their heart, and upon the horns of your altars.

1. Peccatum (*vel* scelus) Jehudah scriptum est in stylo ferri (ferreo) et in ungue adamantino, exaratum super tabulam cordis eorum et ad cornua altarium vestrorum.

The Prophet teaches us here in other words what we have often already seen,—that the Jews in vain sought refuges, for their sin had so much accumulated that it was very apparent. It indeed often happens, that men fall; but God, who is ever inclined to mercy, forgives them; and they are also often led astray through levity, and thus their sins are not engraven on their hearts. But Jeremiah says, that nothing remained for that nation but to be entirely swept away, because their iniquity was past recovery. Had they been lightly besprinkled with vices, there might have been still a remedy for them; but when their iniquities were engraven on their hearts, on their marrow and bones, what more remained for them? He had said before, "Can the Ethiop change his skin?" chap. xiii. 23: though the Ethiop may change his skin, and also the panther, yet thou art still like thyself. They had so completely imbibed a contempt for God, and also perverseness, that they could not by any means be restored to a right mind. We now then perceive the meaning of the Prophet in this passage.

He says that the *sin of Judah was written with an iron pen, with the point of adamant;* as though he had said, "They are not only slightly imbued with iniquity, for then there might be some healing; but iniquity is engraven on their inmost feelings, as though one had graven it with adamant or with an iron pen." It hence appears, that they were wholly unworthy of pardon, as they were in no way capable of receiving mercy, how much soever God might have been inclined to receive them into favour; for their obstinacy had closed the way of salvation; nor could they apply to themselves the promises, for they require repentance in sinners.

He then adds, *It is graven on the table of their heart;* as though he had said, that they were so addicted to iniquity, that all their inward parts bore the impressions of it. It hence follows that the Jews were so proved to be guilty, that they in vain contrived evasions, for their own conscience condemned them. At the same time, I consider the Prophet as speaking not only of guilt, but also of sin itself, and of their propensity to evil. He means then that the Jews had not only sinned and transgressed God's law in a way not common, but that they were also so given up to wickedness as to delight in the iniquity that was graven on their hearts. He calls by a metaphor the affections or feelings the tables of the heart: for he compares the heart to tables; as writing appears when cut in stone or brass, so when a sinful impression is made on the hearts of men, iniquity itself may be said to be graven on the tables of the heart.

He afterwards adds, *And on the horns of your altars.* He had spoken of the heart, he now proceeds farther,—that there appeared openly an evidence of hidden iniquity. Had he spoken only of their hearts, the Jews might have objected and said, "How canst thou penetrate into our hearts? Art thou God, to examine and try our inward emotions?" But the Prophet adds, that their iniquity was sufficiently known by their altars. He at the same time intimates, that they in vain alleged the name of religion; for under that pretence they especially sinned against God; for they had vitiated his pure worship. And to confirm this very thing he adds—

2. Whilst their children remember their altars and their groves by the green trees upon the high hills.	2. Secundum recordari filios ipsorum (*hoc est,* cum memores erunt filii ipsorum) altarium ipsorum et lucorum ipsorum super arborem frondosam, super colles excelsos.

Interpreters seem not to me to have perceived the design of the Prophet here, at least they have not clearly explained the subject. He proceeds, as I think, with what he said at the end of the last verse,—that the iniquity of Judah was graven on the altars, or on the horns of the altars: how was this? even because they transmitted to posterity whatever they devised as to their ungodly forms of worship. How then was iniquity graven on the horns of the altars? even because it was not a temporary wickedness only, when the Jews cast aside the Law and followed their corrupt superstitions; but, on the contrary, their iniquity flowed down, as it were, by a hereditary right, to their posterity. Justly then does Jeremiah accuse them, that they were not only led away into evil through the whole course of their own lives, but that they also corrupted their children, for they left to them memorials of their own superstitions.

Some give this explanation, "As they remember their

children, so also their altars;" as though the Prophet had said, that idolaters burnt with such ardour, that they held the altars dedicated to their idols as dear to them as their own children. But this view seems too forced. I then have no doubt but that the Prophet here amplifies their wickedness, when he says, that it was graven on the horns of the altars; for their posterity remembered the superstitions, which they had received from their fathers. He mentions also *their groves;*[1] *for on* or near *every shady tree* they built altars; and also *on all high hills.* It follows—

3. O my mountain in the field, I will give thy substance *and* all thy treasures to the spoil, *and* thy high places for sin, throughout all thy borders.	3. Montane, in agro substantiam tuam (*opes tuas,*) omnes thesauros tuos in prædam dabo propter excelsa tua, propter peccatum tuum in omnibus finibus tuis.

The Prophet again repeats, that punishment was nigh the Jews, and that it availed them nothing to seek for themselves recesses and lurking-places, for God would draw them forth from the mountains and expose them as a prey to their enemics.

Some render הררי, *erri,* " O my mountain," &c.; and at the first view this meaning seems appropriate; but as the context requires this to be understood of the Israelites and the Jews, who always resorted to their recesses, when any fear of enemies assailed them, I prefer another rendering. Since then at times of distress they betook themselves to their hiding-places, the Prophet says, that they would in vain attempt to escape, for the mountains would be like the fields: *I will expose,* he says, *as in the field,* or the plain, *your riches and treasures,* that they may become a prey to your enemies. The meaning is, that the Prophet denounces vengeance on the Jews, and at the same time shakes off their foolish confidence, which rendered them secure, so as to despise all the threatenings of God: " Ye think," he says, " that there will be a safe refuge for you on the mountains; but God will draw forth from thence all your possessions, and expose them on the open field, so that they may become an easy prey."

[1] The word rendered " groves," means also idols. See 2 Kings xxiii. 6, where " grove" in our version must mean an idol. What follows here, " near the green tree," shews clearly that " idols," or images, are the things meant; and such is the version given by *Venema* and *Horsley.—Ed.*

He again repeats what he had said, that God would inflict a just punishment on the Jews, because they had sinned very greatly on their high places. By high places he doubtless means all their ungodly and corrupt modes of worship. For God had chosen for himself a Temple on Mount Sion; he designed sacrifices to be offered there: but they, carried away by a foolish zeal, had built for themselves many altars, so that there was no hill where they had not set up some altar or another. By stating then a part for the whole, the Prophet here refers to every thing that was inconsistent with the law of God: and in order to amplify their sin, he says, *In all thy borders;* that is, their impiety was widely and extensively diffused, so that no part of the land was free from their corrupt superstition. Since then the land was throughout contaminated, justly does the Prophet say, "In all thy borders;" he declares that there would be no refuge for them, to preserve them and their treasures from becoming a prey to their enemies. It follows—

4. And thou, even thyself, shalt discontinue from thine heritage that I gave thee; and I will cause thee to serve thine enemies in the land which thou knowest not: for ye have kindled a fire in mine anger, *which* shall burn for ever.	4. Et derelinqueris et in te ab hæreditate tua, quam dedi tibi, et servire te faciam inimicis tuis in terra quam non cognoscis; quia ignem succendistis in excandescentia mea (*vel*, in nare mea, vultu meo) in sæculum usque (*id est*, in perpetuum) ardebit.

Here, as it is a concise mode of speaking, there seems to be some obscurity; but as to the subject handled, the meaning of the Prophet is evident, that they would be *dismissed from their inheritance*, and as it were from their own bowels. Hence he says, *You shall be dismissed from your inheritance;* that is, though ye think yourselves to be beyond the reach of danger, because as yet the city remains safe, and ye continue in it; yet ye shall perish, as they say, living and seeing. *There shall then be a dismissal from the inheritance even as to thee;* that is, "Though the Lord should delay the time and suffer you to remain, yet ye shall be like the dead, for God will destroy you, though he may leave you a pining life." It seems an emphatical expression when the Prophet says that there would be at length a *dismissal* even as to herself: he intimates, that though some of the people would remain alive, they would yet be given up to exile and dispersion. And it was a condition worse than death for the Jews to have their lives continued and to be scattered among their enemies.

And he says, *From the inheritance which I gave to thee;* and he says this that they might not expostulate with him, that their own was taken away from them. "How has the land," he says, "become your inheritance? even because ye have obtained it through my bounty. And now, since ye are so ungrateful, why should I be blamed for taking away what I had given you? or what wrong is done to you? and what can ye object to me? for it has always been my heritage, though for a time I granted it to you. Had ye been thankful to me it would have been yours perpetually; but now when I deprive you of it, this you must ascribe to your own fault."

For the same purpose he adds, *I will make thee to serve thine enemies:* and this was much more grievous than to serve their neighbours by whom they were not hated. But he shews here how dreadful would be their calamity, they being constrained to serve their enemies. He adds, *In a land which thou knowest not.* This is a repetition of what has been said before, and it requires no remark. He in the last place confirms what he had said of their wickedness; *Burn,* he says, *shall fire in my nostril:* but אף, *aph,* may be taken for God's countenance, though it often means anger. As however he says, "Ye have kindled a fire," it seems better to render it here, *In my face.* Further, by the word *I never,* he intimates that God would be implacable to the Jews, for they had so deserved.[1]

[1] The whole of this passage, from the first to the end of the fourth verse, is wanting in the *Septuagint* and *Arabic*, but is found in the other versions and the *Targum*. The many emendations of *Houbigant* and *Horsley* are quite unwarrantable; the first makes his mostly from the *Syriac;* and the second from various readings, and those of no value, except in one or two instances, as "their" instead of "your altars" in the first verse, countenanced by very many MSS.; the other *nine* emendations have, for the most part, nothing of any weight in their favour. The transpositions of *Houbigant* are quite irreconcilable with any thing like errors incidentally committed by scribes. The same objection does not lie against the emendations of *Horsley;* but that *ten* mistakes should occur in the space

PRAYER.

Grant, Almighty God, that as thou kindly invitest us every day to repentance, and shewest thyself ready to be reconciled,—O grant that we may not through our perverseness reject so inestimable a favour, but submit ourselves to thee, and become so displeased with our vices as to be touched with a true and sincere concern for religion, and to labour through the whole course of our life for nothing else but to render ourselves and our duties approved by thee, and thus to glorify thy name, so that we may become at last partakers of that celestial and eternal glory which thine only-begotten Son has attained for us.—Amen.

of four verses is not credible; nor are most of the emendations at all necessary.

The received text is no doubt materially correct, there being no different readings of any weight or suitable, except the one noticed above. The *Vulgate*, the *Syriac*, and *Targum*, differ from one another as much as they do from the Hebrew. They indeed all agree materially as to the beginning of the third verse, in regarding "the mountain" and "the field" as places where the people worshipped idols; and the *Vulgate* and the *Syriac* connect the words with the former verse; and this, I believe, is what ought to be done. Then the passage will read as follows:—

1. The sin of Judah is written by a pen of iron,
By the point of adamant it is graven,
On the tablet of their heart,
And on the horns of their altars:
2. As a memorial to their children
Are their altars and their idols,
Near the green tree, on the high hills,
On the mountains, in the field.—
3. Thy substance, all thy treasures
For a plunder will I give,
Thy high places *also* for sin in all thy borders;
4. And thou shalt be removed, even for thyself,
From thine inheritance which I gave thee;
And I will make thee to serve thine enemies
In a land which thou knowest not;
For a fire have ye kindled in mine anger,
Perpetually shall it burn.

According to the frequent manner of the prophets, the last line in the first verse is connected with the first line, and the third with the second. The sin of Judah was "written" on "the horns of the altars;" it was "graven" on "the tablet of their heart." The services at the altars were visible; the impressions within were seen only by God. They left their altars and their idols to their children. The genitive case in Hebrew may often be rendered by a dative, as here, "A memorial to their children." All emendations as to the beginning of the third verse are unsatisfactory: it will bear the rendering above; "for thyself," that is, for thine own fault.—*Ed.*

Lecture Sixty-Sixth.

5. Thus saith the Lord, Cursed *be* the man that trusteth in man, and maketh flesh his arm, and whose heart departeth from the Lord:

6. For he shall be like the heath in the desert, and shall not see when good cometh; but shall inhabit the parched places in the wilderness, *in* a salt land and not inhabited.

5. Sic dicit Jehova, Maledictus vir qui confidit in homine, et ponit carnem brachium suum, et à Jehova aversum est cor ejus:

6. Et erit quasi myrica (*sic vertunt communiter*) in deserto, et non videbit cum veniet bonum (*id est*, fœcunditas,) et habitabit in siccitatibus in deserto, in terra salsuginis, et quæ non habitatur.

The Prophet, I doubt not, prefixed this sentence to many of his discourses, for it was necessary often to repeat it, as the Jews were so refractory in their minds. We have already seen how sharply he inveighed against their false confidence: but it was necessary to lay down this truth. He then wrote once for all what he had often said. And this deserves to be especially observed, for we shall not sufficiently understand how needful this truth was, unless we consider the circumstances: the Prophet had often found that the promises as well as the threatenings of God were disregarded, that his doctrine was despised, and that he had to do with a proud people, who, relying on their own defences, not only esteemed as nothing what was brought before them under the authority of God, but also, as it were, avowedly rejected it. This then was the reason why the Prophet not only once, but often exhorted the people to repent, by setting before them this truth, that *accursed* are they who trust in men.

Flesh here is to be taken for man, as we may easily gather from the context. It was a common thing with the Hebrews to state the same thing twice: In the first clause *man* is mentioned, and in the second *flesh:* and *arm* means power or help. The meaning is, that all are accursed who trust in man. But the word *flesh* is no doubt added in the second line by way of contempt, according to what is done in Isaiah xxxi. 3, where the Prophet says, "The Egyptian is man and not God, flesh and not spirit." He calls the Egyptians flesh by way of contempt, as though he had said that there was nothing strong or firm in them, and that the aid which the

Jews expected from them would be evanescent. So it is in this place, though the Prophet, according to the common usage, repeats in the second clause what he had said in the first, he yet expresses something more, that men are extremely sottish when they place their salvation in a thing of nought; for, as we have said, there is nothing solid or enduring in flesh. As men therefore quickly vanish away, what can be more foolish than to seek safety from them?

But it must be observed that the Prophet had spoken thus, because the Jews, in looking now to the Assyrians and then to the Egyptians, thought to gain sufficient defence against God himself, though they might not have expressly or avowedly despised God: but we shall hereafter see that God cannot be otherwise deemed than of no account, when safety is sought from mortal man. As then this false confidence was an hinderance to the Jews to rely on the favour of God, and to lead them to repentance, the Prophet said *Accursed is the man who trusts in man.*

It seems to be a sentence abruptly introduced; but as we have observed, the doctrine of the Prophet could not have been confirmed, had he not shaken off from his people the presumption through which they were blinded, for they thought the Egyptians would be to them like a thousand gods. We shall thus understand the design of the Prophet, if we bear in mind what was the condition of the Jews, and what were the difficulties the Prophet had to contend with, while he was daily threatening them and labouring to restore them to God. But no progress was made, and why? because all God's promises were coldly received, for they thought themselves ever safe and secure, while the Egyptians were kind to them and promised them help: his threatenings also were coldly received, because they hesitated not to set up as their shield, and as the strongest fortress, the aid which they expected from the Egyptians. Hence the Prophet was constrained to cry out, not only once, or ten times, but a hundred times, *accursed is he who trusts in man and makes flesh his arm.*[1]

[1] Like the Hebrew, there is no need of the verb is, or be, after "cursed,"

This is however a general truth. We also, at this day, advance general truths, which we apply to individual cases. The spirit then declares here generally, that all are *accursed* who *trust* in men. We indeed know that men are in various ways deceived while they trust in men: they begin with themselves, and seek in this and in that thing a ground of security; for every one is inflated with vain and false confidence, either in his own prudence or dexterity or power. There is then no one who does not trust in himself before he trusts in others: I speak even of the most wretched. It is indeed what men ought to be ashamed of; but there is no one so contemptible but that he swells with some secret pride, so that he esteems something in himself, and even ascribes to himself some high dignity. Then they who seem prudent in their own eyes take aids to themselves from every quarter, and in these they acquiesce. But when men look behind and before, they gather help to themselves from all parts of the world: however their goings around are useless, and not only so, but they turn out to their own destruction, for God not only derides in this place the folly of them who trust in flesh, but declares that they are accursed. This curse of God ought to strike us with terror; for we hence learn that God is highly displeased with all those who seek their own salvation in the world and in creatures.

It is added, *And from Jehovah turned away is his heart.* Hypocrites draw this to their own advantage; for there is no one who will not object and say, that he does not so trust in man as to take away or diminish anything from the glory of God. Were all asked, from the least to the greatest, every one would boldly say that he leaves God's honour entire, and never wishes to take anything from it: this would be the common saying. But yet, when confidence is reposed in the flesh, God is deprived of his own honour. These two things are no less contrary, the one to the other, than light is to darkness. Hence the Prophet intended here

in Welsh: the sentence is more emphatical without it. In that language, too, the future tense of "trust" is understood as the present,—

Melldigedig y gwr yr hwn a hydero mewn dyn.

It is a denunciation, not an imprecation; therefore "be," introduced into the English version, is not proper.—*Ed.*

to shew that these two things cannot be connected together—to put confidence in the flesh and in God at the same time. When water is blended with fire, both perish; so, when one seeks in part to trust in God and in part to trust in men, it is the same as though he wished to mix heaven and earth together, and to throw all things into confusion. It is, then, to confound the order of nature, when men imagine that they have two objects of trust, and ascribe half of their salvation to God, and the other half to themselves or to other men. This is the meaning of the Prophet.

Let us then know that all those who place the least portion of their hope in men do in part depart from God, and therefore turn aside from him. In short, the Holy Spirit declares, briefly indeed, but very solemnly, that all are apostates and deserters from God who turn to men and fix their hope in them. But if this declaration be true as to the present life, when we treat of eternal life, it is doubtless a twofold madness if we ascribe it, even in the smallest degree, either to our own righteousness or to any other virtues. He who looks for aid from men is pronounced accursed by God, even when he expects from them what belongs to this frail life, which soon vanishes; but when we hope for eternal life and the inheritance of heaven from ourselves or from other creatures, how much more detestable it is? Let us then observe this inference, so that the truth taught here by the Prophet may keep us dependent on God only.

But here a question may be raised,—Are we not to hope for help from those men whom God may employ to assist us, and who are not only the instruments of his favour and aid, but who are also as it were his hands? for whenever men assist us, it is the same as though God stretched forth his hands from heaven. Why, then, should we not look for aid from men whom God has appointed as ministers of his favour to us? But there is great emphasis in the word *trust;* for it is indeed lawful to look to men for what is given to them; but we ought to trust in God alone, and to hope for all things from him, as well as to pray for them: and this will hereafter appear more clearly. But we must now only briefly observe, that when we seek from men what is given them by

God, we detract nothing from his power, who chooses his ministers as he pleases. But this is a rare thing; for when anything is done to us by men, we forget God, and our thoughts are drawn downwards to men, so that God loses a part of his honour; and when anything, even the least, is taken away from him, he condemns us, as we deserve. We ought especially to observe what he declares here, that *turned away* from him is the *heart* of man whenever he places his hope in the flesh.

He adds a similitude for the purpose of confirming his doctrine, *He shall be like a tamarisk*, or a juniper, as some render it. The word ערער, *oror*, means a copse. But the Jews themselves are not agreed; some think it to be the juniper, and others the tamarisk; but we may hold it as certain that it was a useless shrub, not fruit-bearing: for those Jews are mistaken, in my judgment, who consider it to be the juniper, for some fruit grows on branches of that. It was a shrub or a tree, as I think, unknown to us now.[1]

[1] It is rendered "a wild tamarisk—*ἀγριομυρίκη*," by the *Septuagint*; "a tamarisk," by the *Vulgate* and the *Targum*; and "a log," or "a trunk," by the *Syriac*. *Gataker* considers that no particular tree is meant, but that it means a "solitary" or a "barren" tree, agreeably, in his view, with what is contrasted with it in the 8th verse. *Blayney* renders it, "a blasted tree," of which *Horsley* approves. The word is a reduplicate of a verb, which means to be bare; and the wild tamarisk may suitably be thus designated, as it bears a very few leaves. The idea of being "blasted" is foreign to the word.

But *Venema* contends that the reference is not to any tree, but to a person dwelling in solitude; and he renders the passage thus,—

And he shall be like the naked in solitude,
Nor shall he see when good cometh;
And *is like him* who inhabits parched spots in the desert,
A land of salt and not inhabited.

The words "see" and "inhabit," appear doubtless more suitable when the passage is thus rendered; yet what is said of the "tree" in verse 8 is equally metaphorical. What seems most agreeable to the whole context is such a rendering as follows:—

And he shall be like a bare *tree* in the desert,
Which perceives not when good cometh;
For it inhabits parched spots in the wilderness,
The land of salt and not inhabited.

It is sometimes the case that it is proper in our language to render the copulative ו by "which;" not that it properly means that, but the meaning cannot be otherwise seen. The connection here is with the "bare" tree; it is bare, and perceives or knows not when good comes, for it inhabits parched places. This seems to be the meaning.—*Ed.*

Then he says that they were like shrubs which *grow in the desert, which see not fruitfulness,* but *dwell in droughts, in a land of brine.* The Hebrews call barren land the land of brine or of salt: and he enlarges on the subject by saying, *Which is not inhabited:* for where nothing grows there are no inhabitants. The object of the Prophet, then, was merely to shew, that their hopes who look to men would be vain; for God would frustrate them, so that they could never succeed.

But we must notice also the other part of the simile; for the Prophet does not compare the unbelieving to dry branches, but to shrubs, which have roots, and bear the appearance of having some life. Such are the unbelieving, while success, as they say, smiles on them; they think themselves happy, and so they become hardened in their own false counsels, and reject every instruction, and, as though they were freed from the authority of God, they rejected all his prophets. Hence the Prophet, conceding something to them, says, that they were like shrubs, which indeed have roots and leaves, but no fruit, and which also dry up when heat comes. As then the heat of the sun consumes whatever moisture, beauty, and life, may appear in shrubs, so also God would scorch and dry up the hopes of the unbelieving, though they may think that they have roots to preserve them and their life. A similar declaration is found in Psalm cxxix. 6, where it is said that the unbelieving are like the grass which grows on the housetops; for such grass appears conspicuous in a high place, while the wheat grows in the low fields, and is even trodden under foot; but that grass, the more elevated it is, the sooner it dries up and perishes without bringing forth any fruit; so also are the unbelieving, who for a time glory and exult over God's children, and look down on them from their high place, because they are simple and lowly; but as from the corn comes food to us, and that very corn is blessed, so also the elect bring forth fruit in their low and despised condition, while the unfaithful, who occupy elevated stations, vanish away without producing any fruit. It is the same thing that the Prophet means here. These two parts of the comparison ought therefore to be particularly noticed. It follows—

7. Blessed *is* the man that trusteth in the Lord, and whose hope the Lord is:

8. For he shall be as a tree planted by the waters, and *that* spreadeth out her roots by the river, and shall not see when heat cometh, but her leaf shall be green; and shall not be careful in the year of drought, neither shall cease from yielding fruit.

7. Benedictus vir qui confidit in Jehova, et cujus est Jehova fiducia (*ad verbum,* et erit Jehova fiducia ejus :)

8. Et erit tanquam arbor plantata prope aquas, et prope rivum emittet (*hoc est,* quæ emittit) radices suas, et non videbit cum veniet æstus, et erit folium ejus viride, et anno prohibitionis non timebit, et non desinet à faciendo fructu (*hoc est,* à proferendo fructu.)

Observed ought to be the order which the Prophet keeps; for he could not have profitably spoken of this second part had he not first taken away that false confidence to which the Jews had long cleaved; for when any one casts seed on an uncultivated soil, what fruit can there be to his labour? As then it is necessary to make use of the plough before the seed is sown, so also, when we seek to teach profitably, it is necessary to pull up the vices which have their roots in the hearts of men; and this especially must be the case when we treat of faith in God alone, and of sincere calling on his name. And the Prophet had a particular reason for what he did, because the Jews had long hardened themselves in false confidences, so that they disregarded God in two respects,—they despised his threatenings, and also made no account of his gracious promises. The Prophet then could have effected nothing had he not pursued this method,—that is, to correct the evil by which they had been long tainted; for noxious weeds must be first taken away before there can be any room for the corn to grow.

But had he spoken only negatively, that is, had he only condemned their false confidence, it would not have been sufficient. The Jews indeed might have said, that they had been deceived in placing their hopes in the Egyptians; but this might have happened through some bad men: and by looking for aid elsewhere, when disappointed, they would indeed have condemned their own counsels, but would yet have remained in suspense and anxious, without seeking

God. Hence we see how suitably the Prophet began by condemning the Jews for placing confidence in men, and then how wisely he added this second part; for, as I have said, it was not enough to speak as it were negatively, without inviting them to return to God. But this is often the case in the present day; for we see that many laugh at those superstitions which have hitherto prevailed under the Papacy; but yet no religion appears in them. It is enough for them to ridicule these mummeries; but it would have been better for them to be retained in the fear of God, even by some superstition, than thus to expose evil, and yet to have no reverence for God. It is the same absurdity as to pull down a bad house and to leave man under the open air; for what end can such a thing be done? for he who is compelled to leave his house had something to cover him for a time. Hence it is not sufficient to destroy what is bad, except a good building succeeds.

This is the method and order which the Prophet observed: After having said, that all they are accursed who confide in men, he now adds, *Blessed is the man who trusts in Jehovah;* as though he had said, that men are wholly inexcusable in relying on themselves or on others, when God willingly offers himself to them. What then is it that prevents men from having their safety secured? Their own sin in rejecting the grace of God, which is freely offered to them; but they prefer to deceive themselves, and to ascribe to themselves and to others what justly belongs to God alone.

We see then that the ingratitude of the whole world is here condemned by the Prophet when he says, that all who *trust in Jehovah* are *blessed:* for had God concealed himself there would have been some covering for ignorance; and also a defence of this kind might have been made,—"What else could we do? We sought the aid which was within our reach: had God called us to himself or allowed us to come to him, we would have been very willing; but as he has forsaken us, it was indeed the last refuge of despair to consider what was to be done, and to seek from every quarter aids for ourselves." Hence the Prophet here shews that all such defences were frivolous, for God had freely invited them to himself; for to no purpose would he have said, that they are blessed who trust in Jehovah, had not God set himself forth as their confidence.

But we must notice what farther confirms this sentence, which is in itself very clear, *And whose confidence Jehovah is.* No additional light seems to be given to the preceding truth; and then what ambiguity does it contain which requires an explanation? *Blessed is the man who trusts in Jehovah;* even children can understand this: the words, then, of the Prophet are either superfluous, or there is some reason why he repeats what is so clear. Doubtless the unbelief, which every one of us finds in himself, is the best teacher; for even they who seem to have real confidence in God, yet falter when some trial assails them. Since then it is a common thing with us to look around to various quarters when any danger is near, we may hence easily know that we do not hope in God. What then seems to us so easy, we find in reality to be very difficult: and hence the Prophet, after having said, that they are blessed who trust in God, has mentioned this in the second place, *And whose hope is God;* as though he had said, "The world knows not what it is to trust in God: though every one boldly testifies this, and even boastingly declares that he trusts in God, yet not one in a thousand finds that he understands this, or has ever known what it is from the heart to hope in God." We now see that this repetition is not superfluous or unmeaning.

He then adds a comparison, answerable to that in the former clause, *He shall be like a tree planted by the waters, which sends its roots upon,* or nigh *the river, which shall not see when heat comes.* Here the Prophet points out the difference between the true servants of God, who trust in him, and those who are inflated with their own false imaginations, so that they seek safety either from themselves or from others: he had said of the unbelieving, that they are like tamarisks, which flourish for a time, but never bring forth any fruit, and are also soon dried up by the heat; but he says now as to the faithful, that they are like trees planted by the waters, and send their roots to the river. The tamarisks have the appearance of life, but there is no moisture in a dry soil; so their roots quickly dry up; but the servants of God, they are planted, as it were, in a moist soil, irrigated continually by streams of water. Hence the Prophet adds, that this tree *shall not see the heat when it comes.*

He indirectly intimates that God's children are not exempt from adversities; for they feel the heat of the sun, like trees, who are exposed to it; but moisture is supplied, and the juice diffuses itself through all the branches: hence the Prophet says, that the leaf was *green,* even by means of the moisture which the earth supplied, being itself watered. The Prophet then intimates, that though God's children feel great heats, as well as the unbelieving, for this is common to both, they shall yet be kept safe; for though the sun dries up by its great heat, there is yet a remedy; for the root has moisture, derived from the irrigation of water.

We now then see how suitable is every part of the comparison. He says farther, that it shall *not be careful.* The verb דאג, *dag,* means to fear and to be careful; it means also sometimes to grieve, and so some render it here, "It will not grieve:" but the other meaning seems better to me,—that the tree planted nigh streams of waters is *not afraid of heat;* and then he adds, *nor shall it cease from producing fruit.*[1]

Nearly the same similitude is found in Psalm i. 3, only that the fear of God and meditation on his law are mentioned, and not hope: "Blessed is the man, &c., who medi-

[1] The verbs here are all futures, but ought to be rendered in our language, as they are in *Syriac,* in the present tense,—

And he shall be like a tree *which is* planted by waters,
And nigh the stream sends forth its roots,
Which perceives not when heat comes;
And its leaf is flourishing,
And in the year of drought it suffers not,
And never ceases from bringing forth fruit.

The verb דאג, when applied to the mind, means agitation, commotion, trouble, disturbance: but here, as applied to a tree, it must mean a withering effect, a disturbance as to the process of growing. Joined with a negative, it may therefore be rendered, "it suffers not," or, it withers not, according to the *Targum,* which applies it to the leaf, but not correctly. "It will not fear" is the rendering of the *Septuagint;* of the *Vulgate,* "it will not be careful," as in our version; and of *Blayney,* "it is without concern." None of these give the secondary meaning of the verb, which it evidently has here.—*Ed.*

tates on the law of God;" but Jeremiah speaks here expressly of the hope which ought to be put in God alone. Yet the two Prophets well agree together as to this truth,—that all their hopes are accursed, by which men inebriate themselves, while they seek salvation in themselves or in the world, and make more account of their own counsels, virtues, power, or the aids they expect from others, than of God himself and of his promises: for he who really meditates on the law of God day and night, well knows thereby, where to put his trust for salvation, both temporal and eternal. It follows—

9. The heart *is* deceitful above all *things*, and desperately wicked: who can know it?

10. I the Lord search the heart, *I* try the reins, even to give every man according to his ways, *and* according to the fruit of his doings.

9. Insidiosum cor præ omnibus (super omnia) et perversum (*vertunt quidam; alii*, durum; *alii*, ægrotum; *possumus vertere*, vitiosum, *vel*, morbidum;) quis cognoscet illud?

10. Ego Jehova exquirens (*vel*, explorans) cor, examinans renes, ad dandum (*id est*, ut dem, ut reddam) cuique secundum vias ejus, secundum fructum operum ejus.

What is taught here depends on what is gone before; and therefore they ought to be read together. Many lay hold on these words and mutilate them without understanding the design of the Prophet. This is very absurd: for we ought first to see what the prophets had in view, and by what necessity or cause they were led to speak, what was their condition, and then the general doctrine that may be gathered from their words. If we wish to read the prophets with benefit, we must first consider the reason why a thing is spoken, and then elicit a general doctrine. Thus we shall be able rightly to apply this passage to a common use, if we first understand why the Prophet said, that the *heart of man was insidious*. He wished, no doubt, to be more earnest with the Jews; for he saw that they had so much wantonness and obstinacy, that a simple and plain doctrine would not have penetrated into their hearts. The declaration, that they are accursed who trust in men, and that no blessedness can be expected except we rely on God, ought to have been sufficient to move them; but when he saw that there was no sufficient power in such a declaration, he added, " I see how it is, the *heart is wicked and vicious;* so ye think that you have so much craftiness, that ye can with impunity deride God and his ministers: *I*, says Jehovah, *I will inquire and search;* for it belongs to me to examine the hearts of men."

We hence see that there is an implied reproof, when he says, that the *heart is insidious* and *wicked;*[1] as though he had said, "Ye think yourselves in this instance wise; is not God also wise?" Isaiah says ironically the same, "Woe to them who go down to Egypt and make secret covenants, and who trust in horses, as though they could deceive me: ye are wise, I also have a portion of wisdom." (Isaiah xxxi. 1.) Notice especially the expression, "Ye are wise, &c.;" that is, "Ye are not alone wise; leave to me some portions of wisdom, so that I may be wise like yourselves." So also in this place, "Ye are deceitful and insidious, and think that I can be deceived:" for astute men are ever pleased with their own counsels, and seek to deceive God with mere trumperies. "Ye are," he says, "very cunning; but I, Jehovah, will search both your hearts and your reins." I cannot finish the whole to-day.

[1] The early versions and the *Targum* are neither consistent nor satisfactory as to the beginning of this verse: "Deep is the heart above all things, and it is man," *Septuagint;* "Depraved is the heart of all, and inscrutable," *Vulgate;* "Hard in heart is man above all things," *Syriac;* "The heart, deeper than anything, is human," *Arabic;* "Deceitful is the heart above all things, and it is strong," *Targum.* Correct, no doubt, is the first clause in the *Targum,* but not the last.

Critics agree as to the first word, "deceitful," but not as to the word rendered in our version "desperately wicked." It occurs in all *nine* times, and four times in other parts of Jeremiah, ch. xv. 18; xvii. 16; xxx. 12, 15; and it is rendered "incurable," except in ch. xvii. 16. It means to be so bad as to be past endurance or past remedy. *Blayney* renders it here, "past all hope;" and *Horsley*, "incurable," which is perhaps the best word,—

Deceitful the heart above every thing,
And incurable it is, who can know it?

The meaning is, that it is incurably deceitful; hence the question, "Who can know it?"—*Ed.*

PRAYER.

Grant, Almighty God, that as we are wholly nothing and less than nothing, we may know our nothingness, and having cast away all confidence in the world as well as in ourselves, we may learn to flee to thee as suppliants, and so put our trust in thee for our present life and for eternal salvation, that thou alone mayest be glorified: and may we be devoted to thee through the whole course of our life, and so persevere in humility and in calling on thy name, that thou mayest not only for once bring us help, but that we may know that thou art always present with those who truly and from the heart call upon thee, until we shall at length be filled with the fulness of all those blessings, which are laid up for us in heaven by Christ our Lord.—Amen.

Lecture Sixty-Seventh.

WE began yesterday to explain that passage where the Prophet says, that the *heart is insidious,* or fallacious and wicked, so that no one can penetrate into those deceits which are concealed within it. We referred to the Prophet's object in saying this,—that the Jews might know that their cunning was in vain, while they hid their thoughts as it were under the earth, that is, while they thought that by their false pretences they could deceive God as well as men.

He says then what he takes as granted, "I know that you have a fallacious heart." This indeed they did not allow; for they made a specious pretext and boasted of their wisdom, and not of deceit and guile. But the Prophet speaks plainly and expresses the fact as it was, "There is in you," he says, "a fallacious and a wicked heart: hence is the confidence, which inebriates you; for ye think that your deceits cannot be discovered." Then in astonishment he asks, *Who can search it?* but the answer immediately follows, *I—I Jehovah;* that is, "It belongs to one to search the heart and the reins, and so nothing can escape me."[1] The

[1] The beginning of this verse is an answer to the previous question, "Who can know it?" The best rendering would be this,—

I Jehovah,—who search the heart and try the reins,
And *that* in order to give to every man
According to his ways, according to the fruit of his doings.—*Ed.*

meaning then is, that when men try to deceive God, they gain nothing, for God knows how to take the wise in their own craftiness, and to discover all their guiles and deceits. Then he adds for what end is this done, *That I may render to every one according to his ways, according to the fruit of his works.*

By these words he means that they, after having for a long time made many evasions, would yet be brought to judgment, willing or unwilling; for they could not possibly deprive God of his right, that he should not be the judge of the world, and thus render to each the reward of his own works: for the Prophet does not speak of merits or of virtues, but only shews that how much soever the ungodly might hide themselves, they could not yet escape the tribunal of God, but that they must at last render an account to him.

We may further gather from this passage a general truth, —that the recesses of the heart are so hidden, that no judgment can be formed of man by any human being. We indeed know that there are appearances of virtue in many; but it belongs to God alone to search the hearts of men and to try the reins. Rashly then do many form an estimate of man's character according to their own apprehensions or the measure of their own knowledge; for the heart of man is ever false and deceitful. If any one objects and says, that Jeremiah speaks of the Jews then living, there is an answer given by Paul, " Whatsoever things are written in the Law pertain to all." (Rom. xv. 4.) Described then is here the character of all mankind, until God regenerates his elect. As then there is no purity except from the Spirit of God, as long as men continue in their own nature, their hearts are full of deceits and frauds. So the fairest splendour is nothing but hypocrisy, which is abominable in the sight of God. Let us proceed—

11. *As* the partridge sitteth *on eggs,* and hatcheth *them* not; *so* he that getteth riches, and not by right, shall leave them in the midst of his days, and at his end shall be a fool.

11. Perdix quæ congregat et non parit, qui facit (*hoc est,* acquirit, *vel,* comparat) divitias, idque non in judicio (*id est,* non rectè) in medio dierum suorum relinquet illas, et in exitu suo erit nihili.

The Prophet no doubt intended only to shew that those who enriched themselves by unlawful means, or heaped together great wealth, would yet be subject to the curse of God, so that whatever they may have got through much toil and labour would vanish away from them ; for God would empty them of all they possessed. There is therefore no ambiguity in the meaning of the Prophet, or in the subject itself. But as to the words, interpreters do not agree : the greater part, however, incline to this view,—That as the partridge gathers the eggs of others, which she does not hatch, so also he who accumulates wealth, shall at length have nothing, for God will deprive him. But the passage seems to me to be plainly this;—*Whosoever makes*, or procures or acquires, *riches, and that not by right*, that is, not rightly nor honestly, but by wicked and artful means, *shall leave them in the midst of his days, and at last shall be of no account*, or shall be a mockery : for נבל, *nabal*, means a thing of nought ; some render it fool, and rightly, for so it often means.

But there is a similitude employed, *As the partridge gathers eggs and produces not*. To produce may be here explained in two ways ; it may be applied to the pullets or to the eggs. Some consider the word, קרא, *kora*, to be masculine : then it is, The partridge, that is, the male, *gathers*, or lays on *eggs which he has not produced*, or did not lay. But to produce may also mean to hatch.[1]

[1] It is evident from 1 Sam. xxvi. 20, that the partridge is meant ; and it appears from a quotation which *Parkhurst* makes from *Buffon*, under the word קרא, that the *red* partridge is referred to here ; for the male of the red kind in eastern countries sits on eggs as well as the female. This explains what appears intricate in this passage ; for the word is masculine, and the verbs are in the same gender. What is here stated respecting the partridge is what often happens, the nest being often disturbed ; and then the eggs become useless. It is a case of this kind that is here referred to,—

A partridge sitting and not hatching,
Is he who gets wealth, and not by right ;
In the midst of his day shall he leave it,
And at his end shall be a fool.

The reason why the partridge sits and hatches not, is intimated in the second clause, when it is said that the getter of wealth leaves it in the midst of his day : various things often compel the partridge to leave its eggs, such as dogs, cattle, &c. : and then nothing is brought forth. So the rich man is constrained to quit his wealth before he derives any benefit from it. This seems to be the comparison.—*Ed.*

It may be now asked, how can this similitude be applied to the subject in hand? The Rabbins, according to their practice, have devised fables; for they imagine that the partridge steals all the eggs of other birds which she can find, and gathers them into one heap; and then that the pullets, when hatched, fly away, as by a certain hidden instinct, they understand that it is not their mother. But neither Aristotle nor Pliny say any such thing of partridges. They indeed say that the bird is full of cunning, and mention several instances; but they refer to no such thing as that the partridge collects thus stealthily its eggs. These things then are fables, which it would be very absurd to believe. But it is said of partridges with one consent, by Aristotle and Pliny, as well as by others, that it is a very lustful bird. So great is their lust, that the males seek after the eggs, and lest the females should lay on them, they break them with their beaks or scatter them with their feet. There is also, as they say, great lust in the females, but a greater concern for their brood: they therefore hide their eggs, except when lust at times compels them to return to the males; and then they lay their eggs in their presence; and the male, when it finds an egg, breaks it with his feet. Hence great is the difficulty to protect the brood; for before the female hatches the eggs, they are often forced out by the male. I doubt not therefore but that the real meaning of the Prophet is this,—that while partridges so burn with love to their brood, they are at the same time led away by their own lust, and that while they conceal their eggs, the male cunningly steals them, so that their labour proves useless. Now the Prophet says, "that all those who accumulate riches in an unjust manner are like partridges; for they are compelled to leave riches unlawfully got in the midst of their days." The pur-

There are many MSS. and the marginal reading, in favour of "days" for "day:" but the latter is more poetical: man's day is his life. "A fool,"—so the versions, and more suitable here than any other word: he will then appear to all to have acted foolishly and not wisely; and he will find himself to have so acted, though he thought himself before to be very wise.

Some consider the word to be a proper name, Nabal, whose history we have in 1 Sam. xxv. 10-39; and they render the line thus,—

And at his end shall be a Nabal.—*Ed.*

port of the whole is, that whosoever seeks to become rich by means of injustice and wrong, will be exposed to the curse of God, so that at last he will not enjoy his ill-gotten wealth.

If any one will object and say, that many who are avaricious, perfidious and rapacious, do enjoy their riches: I answer, that there is no true enjoyment, when there is no use made of them and no security for them. If we duly consider how the avaricious possess what they have plundered, we shall find that they always gape for more plunder and are like the partridges; for they lay eggs as it were, and yet no fruit appears. Before any fruit is brought forth, or at least before it comes to them, they become destitute in the midst of their days. And though God permits them to hold hidden riches, yet they derive, as it is well known, no benefit from them: nay, their cupidity, as it is insatiable, is a dropsy; for they are always thirsty; and the very mass of wealth so inflames their avarice, that the richest of them has less than he who is contented with a moderate and even with a small fortune. It is then certain, that those who, even to death, possess ill-gotten wealth, do not yet really enjoy it; for they always lay on their eggs, and yet, as I have said, they derive no benefit. And then the more remarkable judgment of God may be noticed; for in a moment the richest are reduced to the extremest poverty; and though they think to make their children happy by leaving them a large patrimony, they yet leave them nothing but what proves to be snares to them all their life, and turns to their ruin. However this may be, experience sufficiently proves the truth of the old proverb, "What is ill-got is ill-spent." And this is what the Prophet means, when he compares to partridges those who accumulate riches, *not by right*, as he says.

An exception is to be here noticed; for a just man may become rich, as God made Abraham rich; but he became not rich by frauds and plunder and cruelty: the blessing of God made him rich. But they who by wrong and injustice accumulate wealth must necessarily at length be destroyed by God.

He says first, *In the midst of his days shall he leave them;* that is, even while he has money shut up in his chest, while he has his granaries and his cellars full, even then his wealth shall vanish away. We see that where there is the greatest abundance, the master himself is hungry and famishing; he cannot eat so as to satisfy his hunger, while he could feed hundreds. Thus then his wealth disappears and vanishes in his hands. He afterwards adds, *at his end he will be nothing,* or he will be a mockery, or he will be a fool. The world indeed esteems those alone wise, who are provident, who are attentive to their own gain, and who plunder on every side, and tenaciously hold what has once come to their hands; but the Lord here condemns them all for their folly and vanity. I think, at the same time, that the slaves of money are here called men of nought and contemptible. It follows:—

12. A glorious high throne from the beginning *is* the place of our sanctuary.

12. Solium gloriæ excelsum (vel, celsitudo; מרום *enim tam adjectivè capitur quam substantivè*) ab initio locus sanctuarii nostri.

No doubt the Prophet refers to the singular favour which God granted the Jews, when he chose for himself an habitation among them. It was an incomparable honour when God was pleased to dwell in the midst of that people. Hence the Prophet exclaims, that the *throne of glory and of loftiness was the place of his sanctuary,* which God had chosen in that land. But we must understand the design of the Prophet; for the Holy Spirit sometimes commemorates the blessings of God, to raise the minds of men to confidence, or to rouse them to make sacrifices of praise. Here is then a twofold object, when the Scripture sets before us the blessings of God; it is first, that we may be fully persuaded, that he will be always a father to us, for he who begins is wont to bring his work to an end, according to what is said in Psalm cxxxviii. 8, "The work of thine hands thou wilt not forsake." And then, the Scripture sometimes encourages us to render thanks to God, when it shews how bountifully he has dealt with us. But here is a reproof when the Prophet says, that the *glorious throne* of God was among the Jews, as though God appeared there openly and in a visible form; for Judea, so to speak, was as it were a terrestrial heaven; for God had consecrated to himself mount Sion, that he might dwell there.

We now then understand why the Prophet here extols the dignity to which God had raised the Jews, when he had commanded a temple for himself to be built on mount Sion. Some will have a particle of comparison to be understood, "As a throne of glory;" that is, as heaven itself in height, so is the place of our sanctuary; but we may take the words simply as they are. We must at the same time repudiate the Rabbinical comment,—that God before the creation of the world had built the temple, as he had appointed the Messiah and other things. But these are foolish trifles. Yet this passage has afforded the Jews an occasion for fabling; for it is said *from the beginning,* מראשון, *merashun.* If the throne of God, that is, the sanctuary, [they say] was from the beginning, it then follows that it was created before heaven and earth. But this is disproved by this single consideration,—that he speaks not here of time but of the order of things, and that that order is not according to the essence of things, but according to the providence of God. *From the beginning* then *was the throne of God glorious* in Judea, even because God in his eternal counsel had determined to choose the race of Abraham, and then to raise up in that nation the throne of David, and from thence to extend salvation to the whole world.[1] Predestination therefore is the antiquity of the throne of which the Prophet now speaks. Hence the most suitable view is this,—that God had honoured the Jews with a singular privilege, because he had purposed to dwell among them, not otherwise

[1] If we connect "from the beginning" with the following words, and not with "high," which seems to give a better meaning, we shall get rid of the Rabbinical figment; and it seems also right to join with this verse the first words in the next, as it has been done by the *Septuagint,*—

A throne of glory on high,
Is from the beginning the place of our sanctuary,—
The hope of Israel.

Or we may render the first line thus,—

The glorious throne of the most high.

For so we find מרום rendered in Psalm lvi. 2.—*Ed.*

than in heaven, so that their condition became more excellent than all human glory. It now follows,—

13. O Lord, the hope of Israel, all that forsake thee shall be ashamed, *and* they that depart from me shall be written in the earth, because they have forsaken the Lord, the fountain of living waters.

13. Spes (*vel,* expectatio) Israel Jehova, quicunque abs te discedunt (*vel,* qui te derelinquunt, עזבוך; *hoc verbo nuper fuerat usus de perdicibus loquens*) pudefient; qui deficiunt à me in terra scribentur; quia dereliquerunt (*idem est verbum*) fontem aquarum viventium Jehovam.

It appears more clear from this verse why the Prophet had commended before the excellency of his own nation, even that by the comparison their impiety might appear less excusable; for the more bountiful God had dealt with them, the more atrocious was their sin of ingratitude. As then the Jews had been raised high, so that their elevation appeared eminent through the whole world, the more detestable became their contumacy against God, and also their ingratitude in rejecting and despising a favour so remarkable, when they forsook him and followed idols, vain hopes, and their own false counsels. It is the same as though the Prophet had said,—"What does it avail you, that God dwells among you, and that the Temple is as it were his earthly habitation, where he converses familiarly with you? what benefit is this to you? for no one accepts of this favour; nay, we wilfully, and as it were designedly, cast away from us this kindness which is freely offered to us."

We hence see that all this ought to be read together,—that the throne of God was in Judea, but that the people in the meantime malignantly and wickedly rejected the favour offered them.

But the Prophet turns to God, that he might rouse the Jews, for such was their perverseness that he in vain taught them. And he says, *Jehovah, the expectation of Israel! whosoever forsake thee shall be made ashamed;* as though he had said,—"The ungodly multitude which accepts not the dignity by which our race excels all other nations, receives no benefit. God indeed dwells in the midst of us, but hardly one in a hundred cleaves to him; nay, almost all treacherously forsake him; but notwithstanding all their glory, they shall be made ashamed who thus reject the kindness of God." The Prophet, in short, reminds the Jews how vainly and presumptuously they gloried, because God had adopted their race; for a reciprocity was required, so that they were to respond to God and receive his benefits. But when they perversely rejected his favour, what could have remained for them?

Hence he says, *Ashamed shall all they be made who forsake thee.* By the word forsake, he intimates that the Jews had been favoured by God; for this could not have been said in the same sense, and in an equal degree of the heathens, as the heathens had never been gathered by God into one body; but the Jews alone had enjoyed this favour. When therefore he had manifested himself to them, and testified that he would be their Father, he was forsaken by them. This defection, of which the Jews alone were guilty, is noticed, because God had sought them for himself; he had also come to them, and made with them a covenant. As then they were thus brought nigh to God, this defection was the more execrable. This is what the Prophet means.

He now adds, *And they who depart shall be written in the earth.* Literally it is, "Who depart from me;" but the י, *iod*, at the end, as many think, is a servile letter. And some think that the word is a verb, and that the י, *iod*, at the beginning denotes the future tense, and they regard the י, *iod*, at the end to be for ו, *vau*, יסורו, *isuru*, "Who depart." Others suppose it to be a noun, and read יסורי, *isuri*, for וסורים, *vasurim.*[1] As to the meaning, it is evident that the Prophet designed here to shake off from the Jews the vain glory with which they were inflated, when they boasted that they were the people of God, the holy race of Abraham, the royal priesthood; all these things he ridicules as vain, as

[1] The reading of the *Keri* and of many MSS. is no doubt to be adopted, and the final ם, as is sometimes the case, is dropped. It would then be, according to the *Septuagint*, וסורים. Our version is the *Vulgate*. I would connect "earth" or land with this word,—

And apostates in the land shall they be recorded.

This would be their designation; they were to be handed down to posterity as apostates in the very land which God gave them. The reason why the ם is dropped is the connection of the word with "land," though preceded by ב.—*Ed.*

though he had said,—" Away with all these boastings, which are all false ; ye are apostates, therefore your name shall be written in the earth." No doubt the earth here is set in opposition to heaven ; and Scripture sometimes says, that the name of the wicked shall be a reproach on earth. But as they often acquire a celebrated and honourable name on earth, the Prophet makes a concession and says, " Be it so ; let the world regard you as the holy race of Abraham, the blessed seed and the chosen people ; let, in short, every one of you claim for himself whatever he pleases, but your name shall be on earth, and shall be blotted out from heaven ; there will be no inheritance above for you, no portion in the kingdom of God." He in short intimates, that the Jews would have no place before God and his angels, for they were unworthy that God should regard them as his children, since they had wickedly denied him. He then grants them a name on earth ; but it is the same as though he had said, that they wickedly lied in boasting that they were a chosen people, since they themselves, as far as they could, obliterated the election of God.

He afterwards adds, *Because they have forsaken Jehovah, the fountain of living waters.* The Prophet confirms what he had said, lest the Jews should think that they were too severely rebuked, when he said that their name was blotted out from heaven : Ye *have forsaken,* he says, *the fountain of living waters.* " What does this mean ? God (according to what is said in the second chapter) manifested himself to you ; is there not in him a full and sufficient happiness for you ? What more can be sought for by a mortal man than to enjoy his God, in whom there is the fulness of all blessings ? God has offered himself to you, and his bounty has ever been extended to you, as though he were a fountain from which you might draw enough to satisfy you ; but ye have forsaken this fountain. You must therefore perish through thirst, and justly so, for your ingratitude has been so great as to despise these remarkable and invaluable favours of God." It now follows—

14. Heal me, O Lord, and I shall be healed; save me, and I shall be saved: for thou *art* my praise.	**14. Sana me Jehova, et sanabor; serva me, et salvus ero; quia laus mea tu es.**

Here the Prophet, as though terrified, hides himself under the wings of God, for he saw that apostasy and every kind of wickedness prevailed everywhere throughout the land; he saw that the principal men of his nation were wicked despisers of God, and that they vainly boasted of their own descent, while yet destitute of all care for justice and uprightness. When therefore he saw that the land was thus infected, in order that fainting might not overcome him, he presents himself to God, as though he had said, "What shall become of me, Lord? for I am here surrounded with wickedness; wherever I turn I find nothing but what allures and leads me away from true religion and the sincere worship of thy name. What then will be the case if thou forsakest me? I shall be immediately seized, and it will be all over with me, for there is no safety in the whole land, and no healing: it is as though pestilence prevailed, so that no one can go forth lest he should meet with some contagion." Thus the Prophet in this passage, on seeing the whole land so polluted with crimes that there was not a corner free from them, flees to God for help, and says, "O Lord, I cannot be safe except thou keep me; I cannot be pure except my purity comes from thee." We now understand the design of the Prophet, and how this verse is connected with the preceding verses.

He says first, *Heal me, and I shall be healed;* as though he had said that he was now diseased, having contracted a taint from corrupt practices. He therefore seeks healing from God alone, and through his gracious help. And for the same reason he adds that then only he should be *safe* when saved by God.

We are taught by these words, that whenever stumbling-blocks come in our way, we ought to call on God with increasing ardour and earnestness. For every one of us must well know his own infirmity; even when we have not to fight, our own weakness does not suffer us to stand uncorrupted; how then will it be with us, when Satan assails our faith with his most cunning devices? While therefore we now see all things in the world in a corrupted state, so that we are allured by a thousand things from the true worship of God, let us learn by the example of the Prophet to hide ourselves under the wings of God, and to pray that he may heal us, for we shall not only be apparently vicious, but many corruptions will immediately devour us, except God himself bring us help. Hence the worse the world is, and the greater the licentiousness of sin, the more necessity there is for praying God to keep us by his wonderful power, as it were in the very regions of hell.

A general truth may be also gathered from this passage, that it is not in man to stand or to keep himself safe, so as to be preserved, but that this is the peculiar kindness of God; for if man had any power to preserve himself, so as to continue pure and unpolluted in the midst of corruptions, no doubt Jeremiah would have been endued with such a gift; but he confesses that there is no hope of healing and of salvation, except through the special favour of God. For what else is healing but purity of life? as though he had said, "O Lord, it is not in me to preserve that integrity which thou requirest:" and hence he says, *Heal me, and I shall be healed.* And then, when he speaks of salvation, he no doubt intended to testify, that it is not enough for the Lord to help us once or for a short time, except he continues to help us to the end. Therefore the beginning, as well as the whole progress of salvation, is here ascribed by him to God. It hence follows that all that the sophists vainly talk about free-will is reduced to nothing. They indeed confess that it is not in man's power to save himself; but they afterwards pull down and subvert what they seem to confess, for they say that the grace of the Spirit concurs with free-will, and that man saves himself while God is co-operating with him. But all this is mere trifling; for the Prophet here not only implores help, and prays God to succour his infirmity, but he confesses that it is God's work alone to heal and to save him.

And this he further confirms by saying, *Thou art my praise;*[1] for he thus declares that he effected nothing, but

[1] Both the object and the ground of praise: Thou art he whom I praise or glorify; or, Thou art he who givest me an occasion to praise. "Thou art my boasting (καύχημα,") is the *Septuagint*. —*Ed.*

that all the praise for his salvation was due alone to God; for how can God be said to be our praise, except when we glory in him alone? according to what is said in the ninth chapter. If men claim even the least thing for themselves, they cannot call God their praise. The Prophet then acknowledges here that he contributed nothing towards the preservation of his purity, but that this was wholly the work of God. And then he confirms his own hope, as he doubted not but he would be heard by God, for he asks of him whatever was necessary for his salvation.

We have then this general rule, that if we desire to obtain from him the beginning and the end of our salvation, his praise must be given to him, so that we may glory in him alone. If then we own ourselves destitute of all power, and flee to God under the consciousness of such a want, we shall doubtless obtain whatever is needful for us; but if we are inflated with the conceit of our own power, or of our own righteousness, the door is closed against us. We now then see the benefit of this confirmation; it assures the faithful that they shall find in God whatever they may want, for they do not obscure the glory of God by transferring to themselves what peculiarly belongs to him, but confess that in him dwells what they cannot find in themselves. The rest I defer till to-morrow.

PRAYER.

Grant, Almighty God, that we may learn, whether in want or in abundance, so to submit ourselves to thee, that it may be our only and perfect felicity to depend on thee and to rest in that salvation, the experience of which thou hast already given us, until we shall reach that eternal rest, where we shall enjoy it in all its fulness, when made partakers of that glory, which has been procured for us by the blood of thine only-begotten Son.—Amen.

Lecture Sixty-Eighth.

15. Behold, they say unto me, Where *is* the word of the Lord? let it come now.	15. Ecce ipsi dicunt mihi, Ubi est sermo Jehovæ? veniat nunc.

HERE Jeremiah complains of the obstinate contempt of

the people; he found them not only uncourteous but even petulant towards God, so that they hesitated not to discredit all prophecies, to despise the promises, and boldly to reject all threatenings. The Prophet had often threatened them; and when God delayed the time, they made a wrong use of his forbearance, as it is commonly the case with the reprobate. Nor did they deem it enough even to add sins to sins, but they openly and petulantly provoked God, "*Where is the word?* many years have now elapsed since thou hast continually spoken of war, of famine, and of pestilence; but we still remain quiet, and God spares us; where then is the *word of Jehovah*, which thou hast announced?"

We now then see how great was the wilfulness of this people, for the teaching of Jeremiah became not only useless but was treated with ridicule. They had however heard much before from the mouth of Isaiah, "Alas! when the Lord calls you to ashes and sackcloth, ye say, "Let us eat and drink, to-morrow we shall die." "As I live, saith the Lord, not forgiven to you shall be this iniquity." (Isaiah xxii. 12-14.) God then had sworn by his own glory that their sin would be inexpiable, because they continued obstinately in their vices, and were in no degree terrified by the threatenings of the prophets. We however see that they ever became worse and worse. Isaiah was dead when they thus spoke in contempt and mockery, *Where is the word of Jehovah? let it now come*, as though they designedly provoked God, like one who despises his enemy, and says, "Oh! thou art indeed to be dreaded, if thou art to be believed; let us now see thy power, shew to us what thou canst do." Thus contemptibly did they utter their scoffs, when God by his servants made known to them the approaching ruin which they deserved. We see, in short, that the Prophet shews here that they had come to a hopeless state.[1] It follows—

16. As for me, I have not hastened from *being* a pastor to follow thee: neither have I desired the woeful day; thou knowest: that which came out of my lips was *right* before thee.

16. Ego autem non festinavi, ut essem pastor post te, et diem doloris non concupivi, tu nosti: quod egressum est è labiis meis, coram facie tua fuit.

[1] The *Targum* thus paraphrases the verse,—
Behold they say to me, "Where is what thou hast prophesied in the name of the Lord? let it be now confirmed."

The Prophet here implores God as his defender, having found his own nation so refractory, that they could in no way be brought to a right mind. There is yet no doubt but he intended to double their fear in thus testifying that he brought nothing of his own, but faithfully executed the command of God, that he did not presumptuously undertake the office of a teacher, but obeyed the call of God, as though he had said, that they (as we shall find in another place) did not resist a mortal man, but God himself. He therefore refers the matter to God, as though he had said, "Contend with God; for what have I to do with you, or you with me? For I do not plead my own cause, nor came I forth through any desire of my own; but as God has committed to me this office, it was necessary for me to obey. As then I am only the instrument of God, what will you at last gain after having quarrelled ever so much? No doubt God will shew that he is an adversary to you, and can ye conquer him?" We now understand the object of the Prophet.

But we have said elsewhere that the Prophet fled to God when he found no equity or rectitude in the world; yea, when all were deaf and so blinded that there was no hope of obtaining notice. When therefore men are thus perverted in their minds, we must necessarily have recourse to God. So the Prophet does now, as he had done before, leaving men he addresses his words to God; and this kind of apostrophe has more force than if he had charged them with perverseness.

But I, he says, *I have not hastened.* Here interpreters differ; for אוץ, *auts,* means sometimes to hasten, and sometimes to be slow, two contrary things. It signifies also to be careful and to abominate or to dislike; and so some render it here, "I have not disliked, so as not to become a pastor;" for מן, *men,* in Hebrew is often taken as a negative. Others give this version, "I have not been careful," or anxious, "I have not cared to become a pastor." But a meaning more suitable to the context may be given to the words, that the Prophet *hastened not,* for it follows, *and I have not coveted.* These two expressions, לא אצתי, *la atsati,*

Their language was similar to that of those mentioned in 2 Peter iii. 4. --*Ed.*

and לא התאויתי, *la ethaviti*, correspond the one with the other, "I have not hastened," and, "I have not coveted;" and both is a denial of his temerity. Many indeed thrust themselves, as we shall see in the twenty-third chapter, without being called by God; they run of themselves, and are led astray by foolish imaginations.

The Prophet says first, that he had *not hastened to be a pastor after God*, literally; for many are ruled by ambition, which leads them to undertake more than what is right for them, and they do not regard what may please God. Hence the Prophet says in the first place, that he had *not hastened*, and then that he had *not coveted*, which is not different in meaning, but is a confirmation of the same thing. But let us first bear in mind that he thus proves the impiety of the people, for they fought against God himself the author of his call. How so? had he hastened, that is, had he through foolish zeal obtruded himself, the Jews might have justly contended with him, and might have done so with impunity; but as he had waited for the call of God, they had no ground to contend with him, and by opposing the servant of God, they discovered their own impiety.[1]

Jeremiah prescribes here a law for all prophets and teachers, and that is, that they are not to aspire to this office as many do, who, as we have already said, are guided by ambition. He then alone is to be deemed a lawful minister

[1] It is singular how variously the early versions and the *Targum* have rendered the first half of this verse. Various, too, have been the opinions of critics. The first verb means to *hasten*, in a transitive, and in an intransitive sense, to *urge*, and to be *urgent*, *forward*, or *hasty*. It is used here evidently intransitively. Then the literal rendering seems to be this,—

> But I have not been more forward than a pastor after thee, *or* following thee.

The meaning seems to be, that he did not exceed his commission; and this is confirmed by the latter part of the verse. The preposition מ has often the meaning of "more than," or above.

The word "woeful" is the same with what is rendered "desperately wicked" in verse 9. Its meaning is, to be bad beyond recovery; and when applied to day, it may be properly rendered "irretrievable." I thus render the two lines,—

> But I—I have not been forwarder than a pastor following thee,
> And the irretrievable day have I not desired.

This day was the day of exile which he had foretold. Then the words, "thou knowest," stand connected with what follows.—*Ed.*

and prophet of God and a teacher in his church who is not led by the impulse of his own flesh, nor by inconsiderate zeal, but to whom God extends his hand, and who being called obeys. The beginning then is obedience, if we wish to become lawful teachers. This is one thing.

In the second place he shews, that those who are called to the office of teaching are not endued with a sovereign power, so that they can announce whatever pleases them, but that they are pastors for God. God indeed would have his prophets to take the lead, so as to point out the way to the rest of the people, and he thus honours them with no common dignity. He would have them to be heads or leaders, or ensign-bearers, but still he himself retains his own peculiar honour; hence no one ever so presides over God's Church as to be the chief pastor, for God takes away nothing from himself by transferring the office of teaching to his ministers, but on the contrary he remains complete in his own authority. In short, he does not resign, as they say, his own right, but substitutes those who teach in his own place, and in such a way as still to retain what peculiarly belongs to him. Hence these words ought to be carefully noticed, *I have not hastened to become a pastor after thee*, that is, that he might follow God. Whosoever then takes so much liberty as not to follow God, but is carried away by his own spirit, is to be repudiated, and deserves not to be reckoned among lawful pastors.

But this passage seems to militate against what is declared by Paul when he says, that he who desires the episcopate seeks an excellent work. (1 Tim. iii. 1.) Paul does not there condemn, it is said, the desire, he only reminds us how difficult and arduous is the office of a bishop. To this we may readily answer, that Paul there does not speak of that foolish ardour by which many are inflamed, while they do not consider their own abilities, or rather their own weakness; but he says, that if any offers himself to God for the office of teaching, he is to think and duly to consider that it is no common work. He ought then rather to restrain himself, while bearing in mind how difficult it is to fulfil all the duties of a good bishop. But Jeremiah here refers to what we have seen in the first chapter, for he even dreaded the prophetic office, and confessed that he was not able to speak. As then he alleged his own stammering, he was very far from having any corrupt desire. There is then nothing inconsistent in the words, that Jeremiah did not desire the office of a pastor, and that whosoever desires the episcopate desires an excellent work.

He now adds a confirmation, *The day of grief*, he says, *have I not desired.* Some think the verb to be passive, but I have rendered it with others as an active verb, yet some read, "And the day of affliction, or of sorrow, has not been wished for by me." But there is, in reality, no difference. He confirms what he had said, for he saw clearly, when God chose him a Prophet, that he would be drawn into hard contests; "Why, he says, should I covet the prophetic office? It would have been an insane ambition." He found out from the very beginning the consequence of undertaking the office, that he had to contend with the whole people, yea, with every one of them, "I knew how great would be their stubbornness, and how great also would be their cruelty; how then could I have wished of mine own accord to run into danger, and to throw myself into so many troubles and so many sorrows?" Jeremiah then shews from what he had apprehended as to the issue, that he had not been led by any hasty desire.

If one objects and says, that many are notwithstanding led away by a foolish ambition to undergo dangers and troubles which they cannot but foresee. To this I answer, that the Prophet assumes the fact as it was, that not only known to him from the beginning was whatever he afterwards experienced, for he had well considered what the people were, but that he had been also constrained by God's command to renounce his own will. Many hasten because they consider not the difficulties of the office. Hardly one in a hundred at this day duly considers how difficult and arduous it is rightly to discharge the pastoral office. Hence many are led to undertake it as an easy duty, and of no great importance. Afterwards experience too late teaches them, that they have foolishly desired what was unknown to them. Some think that they possess great skill and activity, and also promise themselves great things on account of their own capacities, learning, and judgment; but they afterwards very soon find how scanty is a furniture, as they say, of this kind, for aptness for the work fails them at the very outset, and not in the middle of their course. Some also, while seeing that they are to have many and grievous contests, dread nothing and put on an iron front, as though they were born to fight. Others there are who, in desiring the office of teachers, are mercenaries. We indeed know that all God's servants are miserable as to this world, and according to the perceptions of men, for they must carry on war against the prevailing dispositions of all, and thus displease men that they may please God; but mercenaries, who have no religion and adulterate God's word, desire the office, and why? because they see that they can deal in a pleasing manner with men, for they will carefully avoid everything that may offend. But this was not the case with the Prophet; hence he assumes, as I have said, this fact, that he sincerely engaged in his office of teaching, and was not induced by any other motive than that of promoting the wellbeing of the people.

He says that *he hastened not;* how so? "I should have been," he says, "altogether insane had I been led by an inconsiderate zeal, for I know that I should have to contend, and to contend not with one man only, but with the whole people, yea, with every one of them." Hence he calls the warfare which awaits all true pastors, *the day of sorrow,* for if they please men they cannot be the servants of God. And of this fact he makes God a witness, *Thou knowest.* Men of wind profess boldly enough that they have nothing in view but to serve God, that they do not rashly enter on their course; but the Prophet here sets himself in God's presence, and is not anxious to secure the approbation of men, being content with that of God alone.[1]

[1] The *Targum* connects "thou knowest" with what follows; and such is the version of *Blayney,* and more suitable it is to the passage,—

Thou knowest what has gone forth from my lips,
Before thy face has it been.—*Ed.*

And then he adds, *Before thy face has been whatever has proceeded from my lips.* By these words he intimates, that he had not vainly spoken whatever came to his mind, but what he had received from God himself, and that before God was everything which had proceeded from his mouth. We hence learn, that it is not enough for one to have been once called, except he faithfully delivers what he has received from God himself. It now follows—

17. Be not a terror unto me: thou *art* my hope in the day of evil.	17. Ne sis mihi in terrorem; protectio mea tu in die mali.
18. Let them be confounded that persecute me, but let not me be confounded; let them be dismayed, but let not me be dismayed: bring upon them the day of evil, and destroy them with double destruction.	18. Pudefiant qui persequuntur me, et non pudefiam ego; terreantur illi, et non terrear ego; inducas super eos diem mali, et duplici contritione contere eos.

Now the Prophet, having appealed to God as a witness to his integrity, prays him to shew himself as his patron and defender. Thus he again implores God's aid, *Be not thou,* he says, *a terror to me,* that is, "Suffer me not while pleading thy cause to be terrified." By the word, terror, he means such a dread as stupifies all the feelings. It would have indeed been wholly unreasonable for the Prophets to fail in constancy and firmness, for it belonged to God to rule them by his Spirit, and to support them by his grace, from the time he committed to them their office. Since then no one is of himself fit to discharge the duties of a faithful teacher, God must necessarily succour and aid those whom he calls and sends to the work. This is now what the Prophet speaks of when he says, *Be not to me a terror*, that is, "Be not to me a cause of dread by depriving me of constancy and firmness, so as to render me an object of ridicule to all;" and why? because *thou art my protection,* or my hope, for the word means both.

Thou art then *my protection* (of this meaning I mostly approve) *in the day of evil,* that is, "I have chosen thee as my protector, as though thou wert a shield to me; as then I have promised myself the favour of having thee as my help, see that I be not left destitute, since I have to fight for thee and under thy banner." Hence he adds, *Ashamed let them be who persecute me, and let not me be ashamed; terrified let them be, and let not me be terrified.*

The Prophet, as we have seen, had a hard contest, not only with one man or with a few, but with the whole people, and then it is probable that there were many sects, for when he cried against the avaricious, there was a commotion instantly made by all those who lived on plunder; when he spoke against the indulgence of lust, there was a second conspiracy against him; when he condemned drunkenness and intemperance, there was a new combination formed to oppose him. We hence see how all the ungodly in all parts and for various reasons assailed the Prophet, he was therefore constrained to pray, as he now does, *Ashamed let them be who persecute me,* even because they now testified that they were evidently the enemies of God, for he had no private concern with them, but faithfully obeyed the command of God. As then he knew them to be God's avowed enemies, he hesitated not to ask God himself to oppose them.[1]

We must yet notice what we have said in other places, that the Prophet was not only influenced by a holy and pious zeal, but was also governed by the wisdom of the Spirit. This I again repeat, for there are many foolish imitators, who always appeal to the vehemence which the Prophets shewed, while they themselves are carried away by a violent rather than by a vehement impulse. But we must first see whether the Holy Spirit guides us, lest we

[1] I would render the 18th verse thus,—

18. Ashamed let my persecutors be,
That I may not be ashamed;
Dismayed let them be,
That I may not be dismayed;
Bring on them the day of evil,
And doubly with breaking break them.

There was a contest between the Prophet and his enemies; the shame and dismay of his enemies would deliver him from shame and dismay. The copulative ו may often be rendered *that, ut.* The two last lines refer to the two preceding couplets in an inverted order. "The day of evil" was to dismay his enemies, and "the breaking" was to make them ashamed. The breaking was that of the spirit or of the heart; it means sorrow, trouble, such as brings men to a state of helplessness; it does not mean destruction. The line may be thus rendered,—

And doubly with depression depress them.

The word doubly, means what is extreme.—*Ed.*

should utter imprecations against the very elect; and then we must beware of being influenced by the feelings of our flesh, and intemperate zeal is ever to be feared, for it is a rare gift so to burn with zeal as to join with it the moderation that is required. As then there is always something turbulent in our zeal, we must remember that the Prophets never uttered a word but as the Spirit guided their tongues, and then that they had no regard to themselves, and, thirdly, that they were so calm and composed in their ardour that they were not guilty of excess.

The Prophet no doubt fully knew that all those were reprobate on whom he imprecated God's vengeance, but as it does not belong to us to distinguish between the elect and the reprobate, let us learn to suspend and check our zeal, so that it may not be too fervid, for we may often mistake, if we follow generally what the Prophet says here, *Bring on them the day of evil, and with a double breach break them.* Were we thus to speak indiscriminately of all, our zeal would often hit the very children of God. We must therefore bear in mind, that before the Prophet uttered this imprecation he was taught by the Spirit of God that he had to do with reprobate and irreclaimable men. Now a new discourse follows—

19. Thus said the Lord unto me, Go and stand in the gate of the children of the people, whereby the kings of Judah come in, and by the which they go out, and in all the gates of Jerusalem;

19. Sic dixit mihi Jehova, Vade et sta in porta filiorum populi; per quam ingrediuntur reges Jehudah, et per quam egrediuntur, (*ad verbum*, è qua egrediuntur in ipsa; *sed* בו *est supervacuum*,) et omnibus portis Jerusalem:

20. And say unto them, Hear ye the word of the Lord, ye kings of Judah, and all Judah, and all the inhabitants of Jerusalem, that enter in by these gates:

20. Et dic illis, Audite sermonem Jehovæ, reges Jehudah, et totus Jehudah, et omnes incolæ Jerusalem, qui ingredimini per has portas:

21. Thus saith the Lord, Take heed to yourselves, and bear no burden on the sabbath-day, nor bring *it* in by the gates of Jerusalem.

21. Sic dicit Jehova, Custodite vos, (*vel*, cavete vobis,) in animabus vestris, ne inferatis onus die sabbathi, (ne tollatis,) et inferatis per portas Jerusalem.

This discourse is no doubt to be separated from the preceding one, and whosoever divided the chapters was deficient in judgment as to many other places as well as here. Now the meaning is, that so great and so gross was the contempt of the law, that they neglected even the observance of the Sabbath; and yet we know that hypocrites are in this respect very careful, nay, Isaiah upbraided the men of his day that they made so much of their sanctity to consist in the outward observance of days. (Isaiah i. 13.) But, as I have already said, the Jews were so audacious in the time of Jeremiah that they openly violated the Sabbath, men were become so lost, as we commonly say, as not to pretend any religion. The licentiousness of the people was so great that they had no shame; nay, they all openly shewed that they had wholly cast away the yoke of God and of his law. When this was the case at Jerusalem, what can we think was done in obscure villages where so much religion did not exist? for if there was any right teaching, if there was any appearance of religion, it must have been at Jerusalem.

We now then see that the Prophet was sent by God to charge the people with this gross and base contempt of the law; as though he had said, "Go to now, and pretend that you retain at least some religion: yet even in this small matter, the observance of the Sabbath, ye are deficient, for *ye bring burdens,* that is, ye carry on business on the Sabbath as on other days. As then there is not among you even an external sanctity as to the Sabbath, why do you go on with your evasions? for your impiety is sufficiently proved." We now see what the Prophet means, and what the import of this discourse is which we are now to explain.

He says first, that he was sent, *go,* to bring this message. He had been indeed chosen before a prophet; but he speaks here of a special thing which he was commissioned to do: and he says that he was sent *to the chief gate of the city, through which the kings entered in and went out and the whole people;*[1] and then that he was sent *to all the gates.* By

[1] There is a peculiarity in the phraseology of the original as to the relative "which," after "the gate of the city;" literally it is, "which they enter through it the kings of Judah, and which they go out through it." In Welsh there is exactly the same form of expression,—*Yr hwn yr â trwyddo frenhinoedd Iwda,* &c. Had this been the Welsh version, it would have been literally the Hebrew, and more consonant than the present version with the idiom of the language.—*Ed.*

these words he means, that it was not God's will that the profanation of the Sabbath should be partially made known, but be everywhere proclaimed, in order that he might shame not only the king but also the whole people. The prophets usually spoke first in the Temple, and then they went to the gates, where there was a larger concourse of people. But Jeremiah had here something unusual; for God intended most clearly to condemn the Jews for their base and inexcusable contempt of the Sabbath.

He then adds, *Thou shalt say to them, Hear the word of Jehovah, ye kings of Judah, and let all the people hear, and let all the citizens of Jerusalem* hear, *who enter in at these gates.* The Prophet was commanded to begin with the king himself, who ought to have repressed so great a licentiousness. It was therefore an intolerable indifference in the king silently to bear this contempt of religion, especially in a matter so easy and so evident; for he could not have pretended that he was unacquainted with it: it was indeed the same as though the Jews intended to triumph against God, and to shew that his law was deemed of no value. Hence the profanation of the Sabbath was a proof of their shamelessness, as they thereby shewed that they cared nothing either for God or for his law. We shall hereafter see how great that wickedness was; but I shall defer the subject, as I cannot now discuss it at large, and a more convenient opportunity will offer itself.

He bids them to *attend,* or to beware *in their souls.* Some render the words, "As your souls are precious to you." But I take souls, not for their lives, but for the affections of their hearts; as though he had said, "Take heed carefully of yourselves, that this may be laid up in your inmost heart." The word נפש, *nuphesh,* means often the heart, the seat of the affections. It is said in Deut. iv. 15, "Take heed to yourselves, לנפשותיכם, *lanupheshuticam,* to your souls:" here it is, בנפשותיכם, *benupheshuticam,* "in your souls;" but there, "to" or "for your souls," as also in Joshua xxiii. 11. But the same thing is meant, and that is, that they were to take great heed, to take every care, to exert every effort, and, in short, every faculty of their souls. *Take heed* then *carefully*,[1] he says, take heed with every thought and faculty of your soul, *that ye carry no burden on the Sabbath-day, and that ye bring it not through the gates of Jerusalem.* It was a thing not difficult to be observed; and further, it was a most shameless transgression of the law; for, as I have said, by this slight matter they shewed that they despised the law of God, while yet the observance of the Sabbath was a thing of great importance: it was important in itself, but to observe it was easy. Hence appeared the twofold impiety of the people,—because they despised God's singular favour, of which the seventh day was an evidence; and, because they were unwilling to take rest on that day, and in so easy a matter, they hesitated not, as it were, to insult God, as it has been before said.

Hence we ought to notice also what he says in these words, *Carry no burden, and bring it not through* THE GATES *of Jerusalem:* and this was emphatically added; for it was not lawful even in the fields or in desert places to do anything on the Sabbath; but it was extremely shameful to carry a burden through the gates of Jerusalem; it was as though they wished publicly to reproach and despise God. Jerusalem was a public place; and it was as though one was not content privately to do dishonour to his neighbour or his brother, but must shew his ill-nature openly and in the light of day. Thus the Jews were not only reproachful towards God, but also dared to shew their impiety in his own renowned city, and, in short, in his very sanctuary. The rest we must defer.

PRAYER.

Grant, Almighty God, that as thou hast not only in former times sent thy prophets, but makest the testimony of thy will to be declared to us daily,—O grant, that we may learn to render ourselves teachable and submissive to thee, and so willingly bear thy yoke, that thy holy word may gain among us that reverence which it deserves: and may we so submit ourselves to thee, while

[1] "Guard ye your souls" is the version of the *Septuagint*, *Vulgate*, and the *Turgum;* but that of the *Syriac* is, "Take heed to yourselves;" which is no doubt the meaning, as the word soul, נפש, is often used for one's self.—*Ed.*

thou speakest to us by men, that we may at length enjoy a view of thy glory, in which will consist our perfect felicity; and that we may not only contemplate thy glory face to face, but also hear thee thyself speaking, and so speaking, that we shall delight in that sweetness, which is laid up for us in hope, through Christ, our Lord.—Amen.

Lecture Sixty-Ninth.

22. Neither carry forth a burden out of your houses on the Sabbath-day, neither do ye any work; but hallow ye the Sabbath-day, as I commanded your fathers.

22. Et ne efferatis onus è domibus vestris die Sabbathi, et omne opus ne faciatis (nullum opus faciatis,) et sanctificetis diem Sabbathi, quemadmodum præcepi patribus vestris.

We stated in our last lecture why the Prophet so severely reproved the Jews for neglecting an external rite. It seems indeed a thing in itself of small moment to rest on one day; and God by Isaiah clearly declares, (Isaiah i. 13,) that he cares not for that external worship, for hypocrites think they have done all their duty when they rest on the seventh day; but God denies that he approved of such a service, it being like a childish play. We know what Paul says, that the exercises of the body do not profit much. (1 Tim. iv. 8.) This was not written when Jeremiah spoke, but it must have been written in the hearts of the godly. It might then, at the first view, appear a strange thing, that the Prophet insisted so much on a thing of no great moment: but the reason I have briefly explained, and that was,—because the gross impiety of the people was thereby plainly detected, for they despised God in a matter that could easily be done. Men often excuse themselves on the ground of difficulty,—"I could wish to do it, but it is too onerous for me." They could not have alleged this as to the sanctification of the Sabbath; for what can be easier than to rest for one day? Now, when they carried their burdens and did their work on the Sabbath as on other common days, it was, as it were, designedly to shake off the yoke, and to shew openly that they wholly disregarded the authority of the law.

Another reason must also be noticed, which I have not yet stated: God did not regard the external rite only, but rather the end, of which he speaks in Ex. xxxi. 13, and in Ezek. xx. 12. In both places he reminds us of the reason why he commanded the Jews to keep holy the seventh day, and that was, that it might be to them a symbol of sanctification. "I have given my Sabbaths," he says, "to you, that ye might know that I am your God who sanctifies you." If then we consider the end designed by the Sabbath-day, we cannot say that it was an unimportant rite: for what could have been of more importance to that ancient people than to acknowledge that they had been separated by God from other nations, to be a holy and a peculiar people to him, nay, to be his inheritance?

And it appears from other places that this command was typical. We learn especially from Paul that the Sabbath-day was enjoined in order that the people might look to Christ; for well known is the passage in Col. ii. 16, where he says that the Sabbath as well as other rites were types of Christ to come, and that he was the substance of them. And the Apostle also, in the Epistle to the Hebrews, iv. 9, shews that we are to understand spiritually what God had formerly commanded respecting the seventh day, that is, that men should rest from their works, as God rested from his works after he had finished the creation of the world: and Isaiah, in the fifty-eighth chapter, teaches us with sufficient clearness what the design of the Sabbath is, even that the people should cease from their own pleasure; for it was to be a day of rest, in which they were truly to worship God, and to leave off pursuing any of the lusts of their own flesh. And God did not simply forbid them to do some things; but he says, "Thou shalt rest from all thy work." (Ex. xx. 10; Deut. v. 14.) To come to the Temple, to offer sacrifices, and to circumcise infants, were indeed works; but we cannot say that it was a human work to circumcise infants, for they obeyed God's command in thus presenting to him their offspring; and it was the same when they came to sing God's praises and to offer sacrifices.

We now then perceive that the design as to the ancient people was, that they might know that they were to rest from all the works of the flesh; and God, that he might more easily bend them to obedience, set before them his own example; for there is nothing more to be desired than a mutual agreement between us and God. For this reason God says, "I rested the seventh day from all my works: therefore, rest ye also now from your works." (Ex. xx. 11.) God had no doubt chosen the seventh day, that men might devote themselves wholly to the consideration of his works. However this may be, we see that the principal thing on the seventh day was the worship of God. And even heathen writers, whenever they speak of the Sabbath, mention it as the difference between the Jews and the rest of the world. It was, in short, a general profession of God's worship, when they rested on the seventh day. When they now regarded it as nothing, by carrying their burdens and violating their sacred rest, it was doubtless nothing less than wantonly to cast away the yoke of God, as though they openly boasted that they despised whatever he had commanded. There was then in the violation of the Sabbath a public defection from the law. As then the Jews had become apostates, Jeremiah with severity justly condemns them; and hence he says that their extreme impiety was sufficiently proved, because they thus disregarded the seventh day.

He says further, *Carry not a burden from your houses.* Under one thing he includes every worldly business, by which they violated the Sabbath, though he afterwards adds also what is general, *And do no work, but sanctify the Sabbath, as I commanded your fathers.* To sanctify the Sabbath-day is to make it different from the other days; for sanctification is the same as separation: they ought not then to have done their own concerns on that day as on other days; for it was a day consecrated to God. He then adds, that it was a day which he commanded their *fathers* to keep holy. He doubtless claims here authority for the law on the ground of time; as though he had said, that he did not introduce the law on that day or on the day before, but that from the time he gathered the people for himself, the precept concerning the observance of the Sabbath had been given, as it was evident; for God at the beginning thus spoke by Moses, "Remember the seventh day," &c.

(Ex. xx. 8.) As then the whole law of God and the whole of religion fell to the ground through the violation of the Sabbath, the Prophet rightly reminded them here that this day was commanded to be observed by their *fathers.* We may add further, that they were not ignorant of the memorable punishment by which God had sanctioned the observance of the Sabbath, when by his command he who gathered wood on that day was stoned to death. It now follows—

23. But they obeyed not, neither inclined their ear, but made their neck stiff, that they might not hear, nor receive instruction.

23. Et non audierunt, et non inclinarunt aurem suam, et obduraverunt cervicem suam non audiendo et non recipiendo disciplinam.

Here the Prophet exaggerates their crime,—that the Jews had not now begun for the first time to violate this precept of the Law; for he reminds them that the Sabbath had been before violated by their fathers. We have said elsewhere that men are less excusable when the children follow the bad examples of their fathers. This is indeed what the world does not commonly think; for we see at this day, that most men boast of the examples of their fathers, when they wish to reject both the Law and the Prophets and the gospel: they think themselves to be defended by a strong shield, when they can object to us and say that the fathers had done otherwise. But we have seen from many passages how frivolous is such a defence; and Jeremiah here confirms the same thing, by saying that the crime of the people was the more atrocious, because their fathers had many ages before begun to despise this command of God.

But they heard not,[1] he says, *nor inclined their ear, but hardened their neck.* By these words he shews most clearly that their fathers had not sinned through inadvertence or ignorance, but because they had hardened themselves in the

[1] Our version, "they obeyed not," is the *Targum.* The *Septuagint* and the *Vulgate* have the same rendering with that of *Calvin.* The verb is שמע, which is to hear, to hearken, to listen. The charge of not hearing God's word, was often brought by the prophets against the Jews. They would not hear or attend to what was said to them, not that they did not obey it. This is the case still with all who are perverted by superstition and tradition; they will not hear the word of God, and its authority is wholly disregarded. Anything about tradition and the Church will be attended to; but God's word is neglected; they will not hear it.—*Ed.*

contempt of God. It often happens that men, rightly taught, go astray through ignorance, as their want of knowledge may prevent them to understand what they hear: but when men incline not their ear, but harden their neck, their obstinacy becomes manifest, for they knowingly and wilfully reject God. Such perverseness then does Jeremiah here set forth by the various expressions he employs, as we have seen done in other places.

As to the hardening of the *neck*, it is a metaphor, as stated elsewhere, taken from untameable oxen. God compares his law to a yoke, and for the best reason; for as the oxen are tamed that they may labour and are trained to obey when the yoke is laid on them; so also God proves our obedience, when he rules us by his law, for we otherwise wander after our lusts. As therefore God corrects and checks in us by his law, all the unruly passions of the flesh, he is said to lay his yoke on us. Now, if we are intractable and do not submit to the authority of God, we are said to harden our neck. Jeremiah speaks afterwards without a metaphor, and says, *That they heard not, nor received instruction*, or correction.[1] The word מוסר, *musar*, means teaching or correction. The import of the whole is, that the Jews were not only unteachable when the will of God was plainly made known to them, but that they were also refractory and perverse in their spirit: for when to teaching were added exhortations the more to stimulate them, and when to these were added threatenings, yet God could not by any means subdue their wantonness. It now follows—

24. And it shall come to pass, if ye diligently hearken unto me, saith the Lord, to bring in no burden through the gates of this city on the sabbath-day, but hallow the sabbath-day, to do no work therein;

25. Then shall there enter into the gates of this city kings and princes sitting upon the throne of

24. Et erit, si audiendo audieritis me, dicit Jehova, ne efferatis onus per portas urbis hujus die Sabbathi, et ad sanctificandum diem (*hoc est, si sanctificatis diem,*) non agendo in eo quicquam operis;

25. Tunc (*copula enim hic accipitur pro adverbio temporis*) ingredientur per portas urbis hujus Reges

[1] The verse may be thus rendered,—

And they hearkened not, nor inclined their ear;
But hardened their neck,
So as not to hear, and not to receive correction.

They were reproved and warned, but they refused to be corrected.—*Ed.*

David, riding in chariots and on horses, they, and their princes, the men of Judah, and the inhabitants of Jerusalem; and this city shall remain for ever.

et principes, sedentes super solium Davidis, vecti curru et equis, ipsi et proceres eorum, vir Jehudah, et incolæ Jerusalem, et habitabitur urbs hæc in perpetuum.

Jeremiah introduced, as I have said, a condemnation as to the fathers, that he might make the Jews of his age ashamed of themselves, lest they should imitate the example of those whom they saw to have been disobedient to God. He yet shews, that God would be reconciled to them, provided they from the heart repented; as though he had said, —"Your fathers indeed provoked, for many years, and even for ages, the vengeance of God; but as he is ever inclined to mercy, he is ready to forgive you, if only you cease to follow your fathers and return to him." In short, he promises them pardon for the time past, if they turned to God.

If by hearing ye will hear, he says, *so as to carry no burden through the gates of this city on the sabbath-day*, and to sanctify (this is connected with "hear") *the sabbath-day, so that ye do no work on it; then shall enter through the gates of this city kings and princes*, &c. He first promises them a perpetuity as to the kingdom; and it was the chief happiness of the people to have a king from the posterity of David; for thus they saw as it were with their eyes the favour of God present with them, inasmuch as David and his posterity were visible pledges of God's favour. And we must remember also, that that kingdom was a type of a better kingdom, which had not yet been plainly discovered. Hence in the posterity of David the Jews beheld Christ, until he was manifested. For this reason I said, that they were miserable without a king, and that the perpetuity of the kingdom was a main part of their happiness. This is the reason why Jeremiah now sets before them, as a singular benefit, the continuance of David's kingdom among them, provided they observed the sabbath-day: and thus God did not only strictly demand what he had a right to do, but also allured them by the sweetness of his promise, according to his usual manner. He may indeed in one word command what he pleases; but when he invites us by promises, he has a regard to our infirmity.

But it may be here asked, Was the rest on the seventh day of such a moment, that God should on that account promise to them the perpetuity of the kingdom? The answer has been already given, that is, that the end, which was spiritual, was connected with the outward rite; for God commanded the people to keep holy this day, that they might have a manifest symbol, as it has been said, of their own sanctification. When therefore the Prophet thus speaks, *If ye carry no burden through the gates of this city*, that is, If ye observe the sabbath-day, the perpetuity of the kingdom shall be secured to you,—when he thus speaks, he had doubtless, as I have said, a regard to a true observance of the day, which consists not in the naked rite, but included something greater and more excellent, even that they might learn by self-denial to render themselves up to God to be ruled by him; for God will not work in us, unless we first renounce our own reason and the thoughts and feelings of our flesh. In the observance of the Sabbath, therefore, is briefly included the whole of religion: hence he says, *Enter in shall kings and princes, sitting on the throne of David.*

Noticed also ought to be the state of things at that time: It was a time when the country was nearly in ruins and the kingdom greatly weakened, so that the kings and the whole people were daily exposed to danger. When therefore there were hardly any means to defend the city and to support the kingdom, Jeremiah promised it, as a special favour from God, that the kings and the princes would be rendered secure. From the family of David, as it is well known, were descended the royal counsellors; and hence he says of the counsellors as well as of the king, that they would sit on the throne of David: and he further says, They shall *ride in a chariot and on horses, they the kings and their princes;* and he adds, *the men of Judah*, &c. He extends the promise to the whole body of the people; after having spoken of the chief men, he then adds, that the whole community would be partakers of this blessing and favour of God; for the kingdom was formed, that the whole people might know that they were under God's care and protection. It was not then without reason that Jeremiah states here that this blessing would be conferred in common on the whole people.

And inhabited, he says, *shall be the city perpetually.* For the same reason he also adds this; for Jerusalem was then in great danger; nay, there were new terrors daily, and there was a horrible desolation in every part, for the whole country had been visited with many calamities. Jeremiah therefore promised now what in a manner seemed incredible, that is, that the city would be made safe, if they truly and faithfully worshipped God, and testified that by observing the Sabbath. The meaning is, that it would be their own fault, if they found not the aid of God sufficient for them, that even if they were besieged by enemies, yet God would be a sure protector of their safety, provided they became his true and faithful servants. He afterwards adds—

26. And they shall come from the cities of Judah, and from the places about Jerusalem, and from the land of Benjamin, and from the plain, and from the mountains, and from the south, bringing burnt-offerings, and sacrifices, and meat-offerings, and incense, and bringing sacrifices of praise, unto the house of the Lord.

26. Et venient ex urbibus Jehudah, et ex circuitibus (*hoc est,* ex toto circuitu) Jerusalem, et ex terra Benjamin, et ex planitie, et ex monte (*hoc est,* ex montibus, *vel,* regionibus montanis,) et à meridie, afferentes holocaustum, sacrificium, et oblationem (מנחה) et thus, et afferentes confessionem (*vel,* laudem,) in domum Jehovæ.

Here he mentions the second part of the blessing; for the whole people would be preserved safe in the possession of their kingdom and priesthood, as in both the favour of God appeared; for both the king and the priest were types of Christ. For as by the priesthood they knew that God was propitious to them, they being reconciled to him by sacrifices, and as by the kingdom they knew that God was the protector and guardian of their safety, so these two things constituted a real and complete happiness. Hence the Prophet, having mentioned one of these things, now proceeds to the other,—

They shall come from the cities of Judah and from the whole circuit of Jerusalem, and from the land of Benjamin, and from other places, to offer sacrifices in the Temple. Sacrifices of themselves could not indeed save the people; but Jeremiah assumed this principle,—that reconciliation was not in vain promised to the people by the sacrifices; for sins were really atoned, and God as it were came forth to gather a people for himself. It was the same as though God said, that he would by all means be gracious to them, if only they observed the Sabbath, that is, if they with a pure heart devoted themselves to his service. The country, as I have said, was in a great measure laid waste; but the Prophet, after having spoken of the city, now adds, that all Judea would become inhabited, for from thence they would ascend to the Temple to offer sacrifices. After having mentioned the whole circuit, he names the *land of Benjamin*, the half tribe of whom, as it is well known, had continued in the faith, and had not separated from the family of David; indeed a part of the city was in the tribe of Benjamin.

He afterwards adds, *the plain and the mountains*, as though he had said, God's worshippers would come from all the neighbouring region to celebrate the feasts and to offer sacrifices as usual.

At last he mentions *burnt-offering, sacrifice, and oblation*, מנחה, *meneche;* the three principal offerings. But Jeremiah wished to shew briefly that God would cause religion to flourish and prevail among them as before. But after having spoken of the external worship, he then refers to the end, *They shall bring*, he says, *confession*, or praise, תודה, *tude*, into the Temple.[1] Here by one word Jeremiah includes the chief thing in sacrifices, as we may learn from Psalm l. 14, 23; where it is said, "sacrifice praise unto God." God there rejects the sacrifices which were offered by the Jews without a

[1] It is more consistent with the rest of the passage to regard this word as meaning "sacrifice of praise," or thanksgiving, or confession. There were sacrifices of this kind especially prescribed; see Lev. vii. 12-15, and the word is often taken in this sense, without the word "sacrifice" being connected with it. Offerings according to the Law are the things which are here mentioned: and the same verb "bring," precedes תודה, as in the previous instances, when "burnt-offering, sacrifice," &c., are named.

The *Septuagint*, as in many other instances, give only a verbal translation, "praise;" "oblation," is the *Vulgate;* "thanksgiving," the *Syriac;* and "sacrifice of confession," the *Targum*.

All the words are singular in Hebrew—burnt-offering—sacrifice—oblation, (or meat-offering)—incense—thanksgiving. It would be well to retain the singular in a version.—*Ed.*

right motive: he then shews what he required, commanding them to sacrifice praise. So now Jeremiah teaches us that the design of all sacrifices was to celebrate the name of God, that is, that the Jews might profess that they owed all things to him, that they received their life and their safety freely from him: in short, they were thereby to testify their gratitude before God. So at this day this truth remains the same, though the types have been abolished: we do not offer calves or oxen or rams, but the sacrifice of praise, by confessing and proclaiming his benefits and blessings, according to what the Apostle says in Hebrews xiii. 15. But what ought to prevail among us apart from types, was formerly accompanied with types; and yet this truth was observed by the Jews in common with us,—that while they offered their sacrifices under the Law, they were to testify their gratitude by visible symbols. Let us proceed—

27. But if ye will not hearken unto me to hallow the sabbath-day, and not to bear a burden, even entering in at the gates of Jerusalem on the sabbath-day; then will I kindle a fire in the gates thereof, and it shall devour the palaces of Jerusalem, and it shall not be quenched.

27. Quòd si non audietis me ad sanctificandum diem sabbathi, et non tollendo onus, et ingrediendo per portas Jerusalem die sabbathi; tunc accendam ignem in portis ejus, et vorabit palatia Jerusalem, et non extinguetur.

Now, on the other hand, the Prophet terrifies them, if they hearkened not to the promises of God. God first kindly allures us; but when he sees us to be refractory, he deals with us according to the hardness of our hearts. He therefore now adds threatenings to promises. He had said, that the Jews would be happy, if they worshipped and served God faithfully; for their priesthood and their kingdom would be continued to them.

But he now adds, *If ye will not obey, so as to sanctify the sabbath-day, and not to carry a burden on it, and not to enter through the gates of Jerusalem,* that is, for the purpose of doing business (for it was lawful for them, as it is well known, to go out of the city, but by entering he means the transaction of business)—*If* then *ye will not hearken to me* in this respect, *then,* he says, *I will kindle a fire in the gates* of this city. We see the design of the Prophet,—that he would have the Jews to entertain a sure hope of their safety, provided they repented, and provided the pure and uncorrupted worship of God prevailed among them ; but that, on the other hand, he wished to fill them with terror, if they went on in their obstinacy.

No doubt this commination greatly offended them ; for we know how self-confident they were, and how foolishly they boasted that the city, in which God had his habitation, could not be demolished ; and yet the Prophet declares here that the destruction of the holy city was nigh at hand, if they violated the sabbath-day as they had been accustomed to do. But that this punishment might not seem to be too severe, he shews that the people were inexcusable, if they rejected these plain warnings : he says, *If ye will not hearken to me ;* for they might have otherwise objected and said, that they had been deceived, as they did not think that there was so great a sin in violating the Sabbath. Jeremiah now excludes all such evasions, for he says in effect, " Behold I am present with you by God's authority ; if ye will violate the Sabbath as hitherto, what excuse can you make ? Have you not been proved guilty of open impiety ? for God has spoken ; and how is it that ye reject his teaching ?" We thus see that this, *If ye will not hearken to me so as to sanctify the Sabbath,* was said to anticipate an objection.

He then adds, *Devour shall the fire the gates of the city, and shall not be extinguished,* that is, shall not be extinguished until it shall consume the whole city and its gates. We indeed know that assemblies were then held at the gates, and that they were therefore places of great importance. As to the *fire* it is to be taken metaphorically for destruction ; and yet we know that even fire was kindled by the Chaldeans ; for they deemed it not enough to demolish the city, but proceeded still farther : hence the Temple was burnt, and the houses were consumed by fire. We ought however to explain the words of the Prophet as meaning simply this—that God's vengeance would be like fire, destroying and consuming all things, so that not even the gates would remain. Something usually remains when cities are demolished to the foundations ; but God threatens the Jews with something more grievous—that the city would not be in a common way destroyed, but be so wholly consumed that nothing would remain. We shall proceed to-morrow.

PRAYER.

Grant, Almighty God, that as thou dost not now prescribe to us one day on which we are to testify that we are sanctified by thee, but commandest us to observe a sacred rest through our whole life, so as to renounce ourselves and the world,—O grant, that we may really contemplate this rest, and so crucify the old man, that being effectually united to thine only-begotten Son, we may become also partakers of that resurrection in which he has led the way, and be gathered into that celestial kingdom which he has procured for us by his death and resurrection, after having so fought in this world, under thy banner, that thou mayest ever reign in us and rule and govern us by thy Spirit, so that nothing throughout life may be our own doing, but that we suffer ourselves to be governed by thee, until thou at length become to us all in all.—Amen.

CHAPTER XVIII.

Lecture Seventieth.

1. The word which came to Jeremiah from the Lord, saying,

2. Arise, and go down to the potter's house; and there I will cause thee to hear my words.

3. Then I went down to the potter's house; and, behold, he wrought a work on the wheels.

4. And the vessel that he made of clay was marred in the hand of the potter: so he made it again another vessel, as seemed good to the potter to make *it*.

5. Then the word of the Lord came to me, saying,

6. O house of Israel, cannot I do with you as this potter? saith the Lord. Behold, as the clay *is* in the

1. Sermo qui fuit ad Jeremiam à Jehova, dicendo,

2. Surge, et descende in domum figuli, et faciam audire[1] te verba mea.

3. Et descendi in domum figuli, et ecce ipse faciens opus super lapide (super typo; *alii vertunt*, super rotam:)

4. Et corruptum fuit vas, quod ipse faciebat ex luto (lutum, *ad verbum*) in manu figuli; et reversus est, et fecit vas aliud sicut rectum fuit in oculis figuli ut faceret:

5. Et fuit sermo Jehovæ ad me, dicendo,

6. Annon sicut figulus hic potero vobis facere, domus Israel? dicit Jehova: ecce sicut lutum in manu

[1] Both the *Septuagint* and the *Vulgate* improperly render the verb "thou shalt hear;" but the *Targum* retains the causative sense, "I will cause thee to hear."—*Ed.*

potter's hand, so *are* ye in mine hand, O house of Israel.

figuli, ita vos in manu mea, domus Israel.

The sum of what is here taught is, that as the Jews gloried in God's singular favour, which yet had been conferred on them for a different purpose, even that they might be his sacred heritage, it was necessary to take from them a confidence of this kind; for they at the same time heedlessly despised God and the whole of his law. We indeed know that in God's covenant there was a mutual stipulation—that the race of Abraham were faithfully to serve God, as God was prepared to perform whatever he had promised; for it was the perpetual law of the covenant, "Walk before me and be perfect," which was once for all imposed on Abraham, and extended to all his posterity. (Gen. xvii. 1.) As then the Jews thought that God was by an inviolable compact bound to them, while they yet proudly rejected all his prophets, and polluted, and even as far as they could, abolished, his true worship, it was necessary to deprive them of that foolish boasting by which they deluded themselves. Hence the Prophet was commanded to go down to the potter's house, that he might relate to the people what he saw there, even that the potter, according to his own will and pleasure, made and re-made vessels.

It seems indeed at the first view a homely mode of speaking; but if we examine ourselves we shall all find, that pride, which is innate in us, cannot be corrected except the Lord draws us as it were by force to see clearly what it is, and except he shews us plainly what we are. The Prophet might have attended to God speaking to him at his own house, but he was commanded to go down to the house of the potter—not indeed for his own sake, for he was willing to be taught—but that he might teach the people, by adding this sign as a confirmation to his doctrine.

He then relates what had been enjoined him, that he descended into the potter's house; and then he relates what he saw there—that when the potter formed a vessel *it was marred*, and that he then made another vessel from the same clay, and, as it seems, one of a different form; for there is a peculiar emphasis in these words, *as it seemed right in his eyes.* The application is afterwards added—*cannot I, as the potter, change you, O house of Israel? Doubtless, ye are in my hand as the clay in the hand of the potter;* that is, I have no less power over you than the potter over his work and his earthen vessels.[1]

We now see what this doctrine contains—that men are very foolish when they are proud of their present prosperous condition, and think that they are as it were fixed in a state of safety; for in a single moment God can cast down those whom he has raised up, and also raise up on high those whom he has before brought down to the ground. This is even well known by heathens, for moderation is commended by them, which they describe thus—"That no one ought to be inflated in prosperity, nor succumb in adversity." But no one is really influenced by this thought, except he who acknowledges that we are ruled by the hand of God: for they who dream that fortune rules in the world set up their own wisdom, their own wealth, and their own strongholds. It must then necessarily be, that they always delude themselves with some vain hope or another. Until then men are brought to know that they are so subject to God's power that their condition can in a single moment be changed, according to his will, they will never be humble as they ought to be. This doctrine therefore was entitled to special notice, especially when we consider how foolishly the Jews had abused the privilege with which God had favoured Abraham and all his posterity; it was therefore an admonition altogether necessary. Besides, if we come to ourselves, we shall find that it requires a great effort to learn to humble ourselves, as Peter reminds us, under the mighty hand of God. (1 Peter v. 6.)

[1] The proper rendering of the former part of this verse, according to *Gataker* and *Venema*, is as follows,—

"And marred was the vessel which he made, as the clay *was* in the hand of the potter."

Though there be readings, and many, which have ב instead of כ before "clay," yet the received text is the most suitable. The word "clay" is omitted in the *Septuagint.* The meaning is, that the vessel was marred, while it was yet as a soft clay in the hand of the potter, after he had formed it on the stones. As to "potter," the noun here is used instead of the pronoun, "in his hand," which is often the case in Hebrew. The pronoun "his" is what is given by the *Septuagint* and the *Vulgate.—Ed.*

With regard to the words we must observe that האבנים, *eabenim*, is a word in the dual number. The Prophet no doubt meant the moulds, *des moules;* for they who render it "wheel" seem not to understand the subject.[1] The Prophet evidently refers to the moulds, made either of stone, or of wood, or of white clay; and this the number sufficiently proves. He then saw the potter with his moulds, *avec ses moules*, so that when he had formed one vessel it was marred; then he took the same clay and formed another vessel, and that according to his own will. I have already stated why it was necessary for the Prophet to go down to the potter's house: he did so that he might afterwards lead the Jews to see their own case in a more vivid manner; for we know what a powerful effect a representation of this kind produces, when a scene like this is set before our eyes. Naked doctrine would have been frigid to slothful and careless men; but when a symbol was added, it had much greater effect. This then was the reason why God ordered the Prophet to see what the potter was doing.

Now, in the application, we must notice how things correspond: As the clay is at the will and under the power of the potter, so men are at the will of God: God then is compared to the potter. There is indeed no comparison between things which are equal, but the Prophet argues from the less to the greater. Then God, with respect to men, is said to be the potter, for we are the clay before him. We must also notice the variety in what was formed: from the same clay one vessel is made, then another different from the first. These three things that are compared ought to be specially observed. It is then said, *cannot I, as the potter, do with you, O house of Israel?* God includes here two of these compari-

[1] "On the stones," is the *Septuagint;* "on the wheel," the *Vulgate* and the *Targum;* "on the anvil," the *Syriac.*

"There can be no doubt," says *Blayney*, "that the machine is intended on which the potters formed their earthen vessels; and the appellation οἱ λίθοι, "the stones," will appear very proper if we consider this machine as consisting of a pair of circular stones, placed upon one another like millstones, of which the lower was immovable, but the upper one turned upon the foot of a spindle or axis, and had motion communicated to it by the feet of the potter sitting at his work, as may be learned from Eccles. xxxviii. 29. Upon the top of this upper stone, which was flat, the clay was placed, which the potter, having given the stone the due velocity, formed into shape with his hands."

sons: he compares himself to the potter, and he compares the people to clay. We know that God has much greater power over men than a mortal man over the clay; for however he may form it into vessels he is yet not the creator of the clay. Then much greater authority has God over men than the potter over the clay. But the comparison, as I have said, is of the greater with the less, as though he had said, "The potter can form the clay at his will; am I inferior to him? or, is not my power at least equal to the power of the artificer, who is a mortal and of an abject condition?" Then he adds, *with you*, or to you, *O house of Israel?* as though he had said, "Trust ye in your own excellency as you please, yet ye are not better than the clay, when ye consider what I am and what I can do to you."

We have now seen two of the comparisons; the third follows—that God can turn us here and there, and change us at his will. Then how foolishly do men trust in their present good fortune; for in a single moment their condition can be altered, as there is nothing certain on the earth.

But we must bear in mind what I have already stated—that vain was the confidence by which the Jews deluded themselves; for they thought that God was bound to them, and so they promised themselves a state of perpetuity, and, as though they could with impunity despise the whole law, they ever boasted that the covenant, by which God had adopted the seed of Abraham, was hereditary. Now the Prophet shews that the covenant was in such a way hereditary, that yet the Jews ought to have regarded it as it were an adventitious benefit, as though he had said, "What God gave you he can take away at any time; there is then nothing certain to you, except so far as God will be propitious to you." In short, he reminds them that the whole of their safety depended on God's gratuitous favour, as though he had said, "Ye have nothing as your own, but what God has conferred on you is at his will and pleasure; he can to-day take away even what he had yesterday given you. What meaneth then this foolish boasting, when ye say that ye are exempted from the common lot of men?"

The Jews might indeed have rightly disregarded all the

dangers of the world, for God had gathered them under his own protection; they would indeed have been safe under his guardianship, had they observed mutual faithfulness, so as to be really his people as he had promised to be their God; but as they esteemed as nothing his whole law, and made void the covenant in which they foolishly gloried, the Prophet, as we see, did not without reason shake off that confidence by which they deceived themselves.

We may hence gather a useful doctrine: With regard to the whole race of man there is nothing certain or permanent in this life; for God can change our condition at any time, so as to cast down the rich and the eminent from their elevation, and also to raise up the most despised of men, according to what is said in Psalm cxiii. 7. And we know this to be true, not only as to individuals, but also as to nations and kingdoms. Many kings have so increased their power as to think themselves beyond the reach of harm; and yet we have seen that God laid them prostrate as by a sudden whirlwind: so also it has happened to powerful nations. With regard then to the condition of mankind, God shews here as in a mirror, or by a vivid spectacle, that sudden changes are often in the world, which ought to awaken us from our torpor, so that no one of us may dare to promise himself another day, or even another hour, or another moment. This is one thing; but this doctrine has a peculiar application to us; for as God has by a peculiar favour separated us from the rest of the world, so he would have us to depend wholly on his mere good will. Faith indeed ought to be tranquil, nay, it ought to disregard whatever may bring on us any terror or anxiety; but faith, where has it its seat? In heaven. Then courage is required in all the children of God, so that they may with a quiet mind disregard all the changes of the world. But we must see that the tranquillity of faith be well founded, that is, in humility. For as we cast our anchor in heaven, so also, with regard to ourselves, we ought always to lie low and be humble. Whosoever then flies in vain confidence boasts in vain of faith, and falsely pretends that he trusts in God. Let it then ever come to our minds, and constantly recur to us, that our condition is not through ourselves safe and secure, but through the gratuitous goodness of God. We now see the application of this doctrine. The Prophet proceeds,—

7. *At what* instant I shall speak concerning a nation, and concerning a kingdom, to pluck up, and to pull down, and to destroy *it;*

8. If that nation, against whom I have pronounced, turn from their evil, I will repent of the evil that I thought to do unto them.

9. And *at what* instant I shall speak concerning a nation, and concerning a kingdom, to build, and to plant *it;*

10. If it do evil in my sight, that it obey not my voice, then I will repent of the good wherewith I said I would benefit them.

7. Subitò loquar contra gentem et contra regnum, ad evellendum et eradicandum (*alii vertunt,* ad frangendum, *vel,* conterendum) et ad perdendum.

8. Et conversa fuit gens illa à malo suo (*hoc est,* à malitia sua,) de qua (*vel,* pro qua) locutus sum adversus illam; et (*potius,* tunc; *copula* valet hic adverbium temporis) pœnitebit me super malo, quod cogitaveram ut facerem ei.

9. Et repentè loquar super gentem et super regnum, ad ædificandum et ad plantandum;

10. Quod si fecerit malum coram oculis meis, ut non audiat vocem meam, tunc pœnitebit me super bono, quod locutus fueram ut benefacerem ei.

This is a fuller application of the Prophet's doctrine; for he had said generally before, that the people were in God's hand as the clay is in the hand of the potter; but he adds here what is more popular or comprehensive,—that all men are in the hand of God, so that he now favours one nation with his blessing, and then deprives them of it, and that he raises up those whom he had previously brought low.

I have said that this part of the doctrine is more popular or comprehensive, for he refers to repentance. When Paul adduced this similitude,—that we are in the power of God as the clay is in the hand of the potter, he spoke not in so popular a manner: for he did not speak of repentance, but ascended higher and said, that before the world was created, it was in God's power to determine what he pleased respecting every individual, and that we are now formed according to his will, so that he chooses one and rejects the other. Paul then did not refer to faithfulness nor to repentance, but spoke of the hidden purpose of God, by which he has predestinated some to salvation and some to destruction. (Rom. ix. 21.) Isaiah also seems to have had the same thing in view ; for he says only, " Woe to them who rise up against their Maker." (Isaiah xlv. 9.) Cannot I determine, saith God, with regard to men, as the potter, who forms the clay as he pleases ? We must then maintain this principle,—that men are thus formed according to God's will, so that all must become mute ; for uselessly do the reprobate make a clamour, object and say, " Why hast thou formed us thus ?" Has not the potter, says Paul, power, &c. ? This is what must be said of God's hidden predestination.

But Jeremiah here accommodates his doctrine to the people, that he might shew, that God had by a gratuitous covenant chosen and adopted the seed of Abraham in such a way, that he could still repudiate the unworthy, even all those who despised so great a favour.

We now see the various applications of this doctrine ; God determined, before the creation of the world, what he pleased respecting each individual ; but his counsel is hid, and to us incomprehensible. There is here a more familiar application made,—that God at one time takes away his blessings, and that at another he raises men as it were from death, that he might set them on high, according as he pities those who truly and from the heart turn to him, or is offended with the ingratitude of such as reject his offered favours.

Hence he says, *Suddenly will I speak against a nation and against a kingdom, to pull down, to root up,* or to extirpate, *and to destroy.* By saying *suddenly,* he reminds the Jews of their origin ; for what was their condition when the Lord stretched out his hand to them, and brought them from that wretched bondage in which they lived ? as though he had said, " Consider from whence God raised you, and then acknowledge that he raised you in a wonderful manner and beyond human expectation ; for in the same day ye were of all the most miserable, and of all the most happy ; one night not only brought you from death into life, but carried you from the deepest abyss above all earthly happiness, as though ye rode on the clouds." God then *suddenly* spoke.[1]

[1] " At length," or finally—πέρας, is the *Septuagint ;* " suddenly," the *Vulgate ;* but the *Targum* renders the word here, " At one time," and in ver. 9, " At another time ;" and this seems to be the meaning of רגע, when

But he refers also to punishment; God speaks of a nation and of a kingdom, to do it good; and he speaks again, in order to pull down, to destroy a nation and a kingdom. How then comes it, that they who seem for a time to flourish and to be most happy, suddenly perish? Because God punishes men for their ingratitude. And how comes it, that they, who were trodden under foot by all, suddenly rise? Because the Lord pities them.

But the Prophet speaks first of punishment; *Suddenly*, he says, *will I speak of a nation and of a kingdom, to pull down, to extirpate and to destroy;* that is, even they who seem far from all danger shall find that they are exposed to my judgment. But *if a nation*, he says, *turns from its wickedness, against whom I have spoken, then I will repent of the evil,* &c. The Prophet no doubt intended to shut up the mouths of the Jews, who, as we have before seen, continually contended with God; for he could not convince them that the punishments were just which God inflicted on them for their sins. As then they were thus perverse in their wickedness, and hypocrisy also had hardened them the more, the Prophet says here in God's name, "When I speak against a nation and threaten final ruin, if it repents, I shall be immediately reconciled to it; there is therefore no ground for the Jews to expostulate with me, as though I dealt with them too severely; for they shall find me reconcilable if

repeated, as it is here. Let it be so rendered, and let the future verb which comes after it be viewed as present, which is often the case in Hebrew, and the whole passage may be literally rendered, without giving an unusual meaning to the copulative, ו,—

7. At one time I speak of a nation and of a kingdom,
In order to pluck up and to pull down and to destroy;
8. And that nation returns from its evil,
Against which I had spoken,
And I repent of the evil
Which I had thought of doing to it:
9. And at another time I speak of a nation and of a kingdom,
In order to build and to plant;
And it doeth evil in mine eyes,
So as not to hear my voice;
And I repent of the good
Which I had spoken of doing to it,
or of making good to it.

The whole is a striking narrative of God's dealings with nations and kingdoms.—*Ed.*

they repent from the heart." It follows then, that their obstinacy was the cause why God proceeded in his judgments, for the repentance of God means no other thing than what Scripture says elsewhere, that he is merciful, slow to wrath, and ready to forgive. (Num. xiv. 18; Psalm ciii. 8.) He then here testifies, that nothing hindered the Jews from being in a better state but their own perverseness.

On the other hand, he affirms, that the lost are restored, when the Lord *speaks suddenly of a nation and of a kingdom, to build and to plant;* as though it was said,—"I will not only forgive, but I am ready to bestow blessings on those whom I had previously rejected as mine enemies." Then God amplifies his goodness when he says, that he will not only forgive the sins of men, so as freely to pardon them, but that he is ready to bestow on them all kinds of blessings, if they seek to be reconciled to him.

Now follows the opposite clause, *But if it will do evil before mine eyes, so as not to hear my voice;* that is, when a nation has been planted through my kindness, (for this is required by the context,) *then I will repent,* &c. By this denunciation is meant, that God would tread in the dust those whom he had favoured with singular benefits, on account of the abuse made of them; as though he had said, "When I promise bountifully and freely to a nation or a kingdom everything that can be wished, except my favour and goodness be rightly received, then I repent of the good done to it." The meaning is, that the way of pardon is always open, when a sinner turns to God, and that it is in vain for men to boast of God's promises, except they in fear and obedience submit themselves to him.

Both these things were necessary; that is, that the Jews should know that God would be entreated if they repented, and that his promises could not be extended to those who were guilty of such gross abuse as a total disregard of his law and his prophets. Then the Prophet mentions here the ordinary course,—that as soon as men repented, they might safely and fully expect good things from God, for he is inclined to mercy; and then, that no nation, however it may excel in gifts, ought to indulge a foolish confidence and to use its present glory as means to despise its giver, for God can take away what he has given. The real import of the whole then is, that we cannot expect to enjoy the benefits which God bestows on us, except we persevere in faithfulness and in the fear of him. It is indeed certain that God's blessings do not depend on worthiness in men; but still he will not have his bounty to be despised, as was the case with the Jews, and at this day it is a common thing in the world. It now follows,—

11. Now therefore go to, speak to the men of Judah, and to the inhabitants of Jerusalem, saying, Thus saith the Lord, Behold, I frame evil against you, and devise a device against you: return ye now every one from his evil way, and make your ways and your doings good.

12. And they said, There is no hope: but we will walk after our own devices, and we will every one do the imagination of his evil heart.

11. Et nunc (agedum) dic ad virum Jehudah (*hoc est,* ad unumquemque,) et incolas Jerusalem, dicendo (alloquere omnes Judæos et incolas Jerusalem,) sic dicit Jehova, Ecce ego fingo super vos malum, et cogito super vos cogitationem; revertimini igitur quisque à via sua mala, et rectas facite vias vestras et studia vestra.

12. Et dixerunt, Actum est; quia post cogitationes nostras ambulabimus, et quisque pravitatem cordis sui mali faciemus.

The Prophet is now bidden to turn his discourse to the Jews, that he might apply the doctrine of repentance, to which he had referred; for a doctrine generally stated, as it is well known, is less efficient. He then contends here, as it were, in full force with his own nation: *Say* then *to the Jews and the inhabitants of Jerusalem,* who indeed ought to have shewn the way to others, but were themselves the worst of all, *return ye,* he says, *every one from his evil way.* Here God shews, that what he had before stated generally, applied peculiarly to the Jews,—that he is reconcilable when a sinner returns to him, and that they who disregard and despise his goodness cannot possibly escape unpunished.

Return ye, he says, *every one from his evil way, and make right your ways;* why so? *For behold I frame for you an evil, and I think for you a thought;* that is, "Vengeance is now prepared and is suspended over your heads, except ye turn in due time; but if ye truly and from the heart repent, I am ready to receive you." We see how God includes the two things before referred to: He had previously said, "If I speak against a nation, and it turns from its sins, I immediately repent; but when I promise to be a father to a nation or a kingdom, I do not allow myself and my bounty to be despised, which men do when they reject what I offer." But he now says, *Behold, I think*,[1] &c.; this refers to the former clause, the threatenings; and then when he adds, *Return ye*, he promises pardon; for as it has been said elsewhere and often, there can be no exhortation to repentance without a hope of favour, as God cannot be feared, except there be propitiation with him, according to what is said in Psalm cxxx. 4.

God then shews in this verse, that he was ready to receive the Jews if they repented; but that if they continued perverse as they were wont to be, he would not suffer them to go unpunished, for he thought of evil for them. But this thought included the effect, the execution, as he was the potter, in whose hand and power they were.

Then the Prophet adds what shews how hopeless was the impiety of the people, for all his labour was in vain. It was indeed a monstrous stupidity, when they could not be terrified by God's threatenings nor allured by his kind promises. But the Prophet meant also to shew, that God tried all means to restore the people from ruin to life and salvation, but that all means were tried in vain, owing to the irreclaimable character of the people. I cannot finish the subject to-day; I must therefore defer it till to-morrow.

PRAYER.

Grant, Almighty God, that since we stand or fall at thy will, we may be conscious of our weakness and frailty, and constantly remember that not only our life is a shadow, but that we are wholly nothing, and thus learn to trust in thee alone, and to depend on thee alone and on thy good pleasure; and as it is thine to begin and to complete whatever belongs to our salvation, may

[1] More is meant by this word than expressed, which is often the case in all languages. "I contrive with respect to you a contrivance," is perhaps the most literal rendering. "Device" is taken commonly in a bad sense.—*Ed.*

we in real fear and trembling submit ourselves to thee, and proceed in the course of our calling, ever calling on thee, and casting all our cares into thy bosom, until being at length freed from all dangers, we shall be gathered into that eternal and blessed rest which has been obtained for us by the blood of thine only-begotten Son.—Amen.

Lecture Seventy-First.

The Prophet, having related that he had denounced on the Jews the vengeance of God, adds now, how proudly they despised his threatenings. And their sin was on this account enhanced, because a hope of pardon remained for them, provided they returned to God. But the Prophet says, that they expressly refused to do so. *They said*, נואש, *nuash*, which we render, "It is all over," though interpreters in general render it, "It is past hope." We have spoken of this word in chapter second, and the Prophet now repeats the same thing,—that the Jews were obstinately given to superstitions, and also to perverted counsels, thinking that they could well provide for their own safety and drive away all dangers by connecting themselves, at one time with the Assyrians, and at another with the Egyptians. But as the verb יאש, *iash*, may be taken as signifying, to be weary, as we learn from the twelfth chapter of Ecclesiastes; it may perhaps be not unsuitably rendered here, "We are become weary;" that is, we are unwilling to consume so much labour in vain; for the ungodly took this as a reason for their obstinacy, that they had laboured long and much in something or another; and pride hardened them, and they said, "Have we not hitherto laboured in vain?" Now this meaning, "We have become wearied," does not appear unsuitable, by which they implied, "Thou oughtest to have called us back at the beginning; but now we have nearly finished the whole journey and are not far distant from the goal; it cannot then be that we shall return to the starting place, for it would be absurd for us to spend so much labour in vain and to no purpose." Nor is this meaning disapproved of by those who regard the word as a noun, "It is weariness," that is, "It is now too late to reprove us, for we have now followed this way for many years."[1]

With regard to the main subject, there is but little difference. But the meaning would be clearer were we thus to paraphrase it, "Labour more than enough has been already spent; thou comest then not in due time."

Isaiah in chap. lvii. verse 10, seems to have reproved the Jews for what was praiseworthy, if this declaration of Jeremiah be right; for he spoke thus, "For ye have wearied yourselves in your ways, and no one has said נואש, *nuash;* and Jeremiah reproves them here for having said נואש, *nuash.* These two places then seem inconsistent. But when Isaiah spoke thus, he reproved the insensibility of the Jews, for even experience, which is said to be the teacher of fools, had not made them weary; for when they had so often found by their own calamities that they had been at one time deceived by the Assyrians, and at another by the Egyptians, it was an instance of palpable madness not to learn at length by long experience, and to confess, "We have surely laboured in vain." We thus see in what sense Isaiah blamed them for not saying, "It is weariness;" that is, because they did not consider that their labour had been in vain. But our Prophet here has another thing in view,—that the Jews were unwilling to lose their toil, but went on in their course obstinately, for they had hardened themselves so as to persist in their corrupt habit of sinning.

It follows, *For after our thoughts we shall go, and every one will do the wickedness of his evil heart.*[2] Doubtless they did not thus speak openly, for they did not avowedly boast that they were ungodly and despisers of God: but the Prophet did not regard what they said, but what their conduct proved, for the Jews were wont to set up their own devices and the fallacies of Satan against the word of God. No

[1] The variety of the versions is remarkable as to the word נואש; "We shall be men, *or* act manly," is the *Septuagint;* "We have despaired," the *Vulgate;* "We shall perish," the *Syriac.* See note in vol. i. p. 122. It is a participle, and may be rendered "Hopeless." *Blayney's* version is, "It is a thing not to be hoped."—*Ed.*

[2] More literally,—

For after our own contrivances shall we go;
And we shall do, each, the resolutions of his evil heart.—*Ed.*

wonder then that the Prophet charges them with these impious and sacrilegious words, that they resolved to follow their own thoughts, and the wickedness of their own hearts, rather than to submit to God and to obey his word.

We hence see that hypocrites gain nothing by obtruding their vain mummeries, for God cannot be dealt with sophistically or cunningly. Condemnation then awaits all the ungodly, however they may by disguises cover their wickedness; for whatever is contrary to sound doctrine, is a sinful device, a fallacy of Satan, and, in a word, the impiety of a corrupt heart. Whosoever indeed turns aside from the plain teaching of the prophets, and from the teaching of the law, follow their own thoughts, or the figments of their own hearts. It hence follows that they try evasions in vain, for when they reject pure doctrine they set up their own inventions. In the same sense we are to take the words "his own evil heart," לבו הרע, *labu ero;* they never confessed that their heart was evil or wicked, and yet the Prophet charged them with having uttered the words here stated, for he considered, as I have said, what their conduct proved, and not the evasions by which hypocrites usually attempt to deceive God. It now follows—

13. Therefore thus saith the Lord, Ask ye now among the heathen, who hath heard such things? the virgin of Israel hath done a very horrible thing.

13. Propterea sic dicit Jehova, Interrogate agedum inter gentes, quis audierit secundum hoc (quis unquam audierit aliquid simile?) fœditatem (*vel,* portentum) patravit valdè virgo Israel.

God shews here that the Jews were become wholly irreclaimable, for they arrived at the highest pitch of impiety, when they were so daring as to reject the salvation offered to them; for what had the Prophet in view but to extricate them from ruin? God himself by his Prophet wished to secure their safety. How great then was their ingratitude to reject God's paternal care, and not to give ear to the Prophet who was to be a minister of salvation to them? Now as they were extremely deaf and stupid, God turns to the Gentiles.

Enquire, or ask, he says, *among the Gentiles, Has any one heard such a thing?* as though he had said, "I will no more contend with those brute animals, for there is no reason in them; but the Gentiles, destitute of the light of knowledge, can be made witnesses of so gross an impiety." And he says the same thing in chap. ii. 10, "Go, pass through the isles and survey the whole world, has any nation forsaken its own gods, and yet they are no gods?" As though he had said, "Religion so much prevails among wretched idolaters, that they continue stedfast in their superstitions; as they consider it a dreadful thing to change their god, they therefore shun it as a monstrous thing. Hence it is, that they are devoted to their superstitions, for the god whom they have once received, they think it the highest impiety to forsake, while yet they are no gods; but my people have forsaken me, who am the fountain of living water." Jeremiah repeats now the same thing in other words, that such an example could not be found among heathens.

He then adds, *A base thing has the virgin of Israel done.* Some indeed render שערות, *shorret,* "a monstrous thing," and it may be thus taken metaphorically, for the verb שער, *shor,* means to count, to think; and this meaning may be adopted here; but as in many places it signifies baseness, I will not depart from that common meaning.[1] He says then, that it was an extremely base thing for the people to forsake him. He does not call the people *the virgin of* Israel by way of honour, but to augment their reproach. For God, as we have before seen, had espoused the people to himself; and so it was their duty to observe conjugal fidelity, as a virgin espoused by a husband, who ought not to regard any other, for she is not to look for any other after she has pledged her faith. But the people of Israel, who ought to have been as it were the bride of God, sinned most basely, yea, most disgracefully and infamously, when they prostituted

[1] It is rendered in the *Septuagint* and *Vulgate* as a noun in the plural number, and more suitably in this place,—

13. Therefore thus saith Jehovah,
Enquire I pray among the nations,
Who hath heard such things as these—
The horrible things *which* she hath fully done,
The virgin of Israel.

The particle מאד, *much, very much,* &c., must from its position be construed with the verb, and not with "horrible." It may be rendered, "which she hath done excessively."—*Ed.*

themselves to wicked counsels as well as to superstitions. He now adds comparisons, by which he more fully exposes their wickedness,—

14. Will *a man* leave the snow of Lebanon *which cometh* from the rock of the field? *or* shall the cold flowing waters that come from another place be forsaken?

15. Because my people hath forgotten me, they have burnt incense to vanity, and they have caused them to stumble in their ways *from* the ancient paths, to walk in paths, *in* a way not cast up.

14. An relinquet è rupe agri nivem Libani? an relinquentur aquæ alienæ et frigidæ fluentes?

15. Quia oblitus est mei populus meus, frustra suffitum faciunt (*vel,* adolent,) dum corruere eos fecerunt (*copula enim explicitivè accipitur, vel causaliter*) in viis suis (*vel,* ipsorum,) semitis sæculi, ut ambularent per semitas, viam non calcatam (*quamquam* כשל *significat etiam impingere, vel, offendere, ideo verti posset,* et eos impingere fecerunt in viis suis.)

As I have just said, God here enhances the sin of the people by a twofold comparison; for when one can draw water in his own field, and find there a spring, what folly will it be for him to run to a distance to seek water? And then, when water does not spring up near, but flows from a distance in a pure and cold stream, who will not be satisfied with such water? and if he seeks to find the spring, will not all laugh at such madness? Now God was like a living fountain, and at Jerusalem was the spring where the Jews might drink to their full; and God's blessings flowed also to them as it were through various channels, so that nothing was wanting to them. We then see that here is condemned a twofold madness in the people, that they despised God's kindness which was near at hand, as though one close to Mount Libanus refused its cold waters, or as though one would not draw water from a river without going to the spring-head. Since then God offered himself to them in every way, and presented his bounty to them, it was a madness extremely base and inexcusable to reject flowing waters and the fountain itself.

We now perceive the meaning of this passage. It is doubtless natural for all to be satisfied with present blessings, especially when nothing better can anywhere else be found. When one has a fountain in his own field, why should he go elsewhere to drink? This would be monstrous. Dost thou want water? God supplies thee with it; take it from thine own fountain. If one objects and says, "That fountain I dislike; I wish to know whether better waters can be found at a distance." This we see is a proof of brutal stupidity; for if the water which flows be cold and pure, and he dislikes it, because he wishes to go to the spring, he shews his own folly, whoever he may be. If, for instance, any one at this day would not drink the waters of the Rhone, which flows by here, and would not taste of the springs, but would run to the fountain and spring-head of the Rhone, would he not deserve to perish through thirst? God then shews that the Jews were so void of all sense and reason, that they ought to have been deemed detestable by all; and therefore in the application, when he says, *My people have forgotten me*, both clauses ought to be repeated. This indeed by itself would have been obscure, or at least not sufficiently explicit; but God here in substance repeats what he had said before, that he is the fountain of living water which was offered to the Jews; and also that his bounty flowed through various channels like living and cold waters. As then the people forgat God they were doubly ungrateful, for they refused to drink of the fountain itself, and disdained the cold and flowing waters, which were not hot to occasion a nausea; they were also pure and liquid, having no impure mixture in them.[1]

[1] The general drift of this verse is no doubt given here, though the version seems not to be correct. The early versions and the *Targum* are all different, and hardly present any meaning at all. The versions of *Blayney* and *Horsley* are not much better. *Venema* appears to have given the most satisfactory version, which is as follows,—

Will *any one* forsake for a rock
A field *irrigated by* the snow of Libanus?
Shall for strange waters
Be abandoned cold streams?

To make the two clauses alike, the preposition מ is put before "waters," which is found before "rock." "Strange waters" were those conducted to a place by artificial means. But to give מ the meaning which it often has, *rather than*, the verse may be thus rendered,—

Shall it be forsaken, rather than the rock,
The field *watered by* the snow of Libanus?
Shall they be abandoned rather than strange waters,
The cooling streams (or rills)?

He again calls them *his people*, but for the sake of reproaching them ; for the less excusable was their perverseness, when God in an especial manner offered himself to them, and they refused his offered bounty. Had this been done by heathens it would have been no small sin, though God had not favoured them with any remarkable privilege, but when the Jews had been chosen in preference to all others, it was as it were a monstrous thing that they *forgot God*, even him whom they had known. He was unknown to heathens, but he had made himself known to the Jews ; hence this forgetfulness, with which the Prophet charged them, could not have proceeded from ignorance, but from determined perverseness.

He afterwards adds, *In vain*[1] *they burn incense to me, since to stumble*, &c., (the copulative is to be rendered as a causal particle.) When he says, *in vain they burn incense*, it is to anticipate an objection. For we know that the Jews trusted in their ceremonial rites, so when they were reproved by the Prophets they had ever ready this answer, " We are the worshippers of God, for we constantly go up to the Temple, and he has promised that the incense which we offer shall be to him a sweet odour." He at the same time includes under this word all the sacrifices, for it is said generally of them all, " A sweet odour shall ascend before the Lord." Then by mentioning one thing he denotes all that external worship in which the Jews were sufficiently assiduous. But as the whole was nothing but hypocrisy, when the integrity of the heart was absent, the Prophet here dissipates this vain objection, and says, " In vain do they set forth their ceremonial rites, that they attend very regularly to their sacri-

The change proposed in the last verb is unnecessary, as both verbs are nearly of the same meaning. The second line literally rendered is, " The field of the snow of Libanus ;" so called as being irrigated by the melted snow from that mountain. To prefer a rocky dry ground for such a field, symbolized the conduct of the Jews, as well as to prefer waters brought by pipes from a distance to refreshing streams.—*Ed.*

[1] So the *Septuagint*, the *Vulgate*, and the *Targum*, but the *Syriac* and *Arabic* are like our version, " to vanity," the idol being often so called: and this is the most suitable rendering here, as it shews the object of their worship when they forsook Jehovah. The word may be rendered " to a lie," or, what is meant, " to a false god." See Rom. i. 25.—*Ed.*

fices, and that they do not neglect anything in the external worship of God: it is all in vain," he says.

This truth is often referred to by the Prophets, and ought to be well known by the godly; yet we see how difficult it is to bring the world to believe it. Hypocrisy ever prevails, and men think that they perform all that is required of them when some kind of religion appears among them. But God, as we have before seen, has regard to the heart itself or integrity; yet this is what the world cannot comprehend. Therefore the Prophets do not without reason so often inculcate the truth, that inward piety, connected with integrity of heart, alone pleases God.

He afterwards mentions the cause—that they *made them to stumble in their ways.* He means here no doubt the false teachers, who allured the people from the true and simple worship of God, and corrupted wholesome doctrine by their many fictions. And it is a common thing in Hebrew to leave a word, as we have said elsewhere, to be understood: they then *made them to stumble,* or to fall. The meaning is, that the sacrifices of the people could not be approved by God, because the whole of religion was corrupted. And the crime the Prophet names was, that the people were drawn aside from the right way, that is, from the law, which is alone the rule of piety and uprightness.

But we hence learn how frivolous is the excuse of those who say, that they follow what they have learnt from the fathers, and what has been delivered to them from the ancients, and received by universal consent; for God here declares, that the destruction of the people would follow, because they suffered themselves to be deceived by false prophets.

As to the words *in their ways,* or in their own ways, interpreters differ; and many apply the pronoun הם, *em,* to the false Prophets; but I prefer the other view, that they made them to stumble in their right ways, for by errors they led them away from the right course. When therefore he says, *in their ways,* the words are to be taken in a good sense; for God had pointed out the right way to the people. He then calls the doctrine of the law the ways to which the people had been accustomed. Then follows the expression, *the paths of ages,* which is to be taken in the same sense. But we must notice the contrast between those *paths,* and *the way not trodden.*[1]

This brevity may be deemed obscure; I will therefore give a more explicit explanation. The Prophet calls those the ways of the people in which they had been fully taught; and this took away every colour of defence; for the people could not object and say that they had been deceived, as though they had not known what was right; for they had not only been taught, but had also been led as it were by the hand, so that the way of the law ought to have been well known by them. Then he adds, *the paths of ages;* for as the law had not been introduced a short time before, but for many ages, this antiquity ought to have strengthened their faith in God's law. We now see how these two things bear on what is said, that the Jews, being deceived by false teachers, *fell* or stumbled in those *ways* to which they had been accustomed; and then *in the paths of ages,* that is, in the doctrine long before received, and whose authority had been for many ages established. On the other hand, he says that the Jews had been drawn to paths and to a *way not trodden,* that is, had been led from the right way into error. And he farther aggravates their sin by saying, that they preferred to go astray rather than to keep the way which had been trodden by their fathers.

But it may be here asked, whether this change in itself ought to be condemned, since we despise antiquity, or rather regard what is right? To this the easy reply is, that the

[1] I propose the following rendering of the verse,—

For forsaken me have my people;
To vanity they burn incense,
And make them stumble in their ways,
The paths of ages;
So that they walk in the tracks
Of a way not prepared;
literally, not cast up or raised.

That "they" were the false priests is evident, because to burn incense was the office of the priests. To stumble in God's ways is to transgress his law; and these "ways" were "the paths of ages," or, of antiquity, or, "ancient paths," as they had for ages been made known to the people.—*Ed.*

Prophet speaks here in the name of God: therefore this principle ought to be maintained, that there is no right way but what God himself has pointed out. Had any one else come and boasted antiquity, the Prophet would have laughed to scorn such boasting, and why? for what antiquity can be in men who vanish away? and when we count many ages, there is nothing constant and sure among men. It ought then to be noticed, that God was the author of that way which the Prophet complains had been forsaken by the people. Now the things which follow harmonize together, that the people had strayed from the way which they had long kept; for the Jews, as it has been said, had not followed any men, but God himself, who had been pleased to stretch forth his hand to them and to shew them the sure way of salvation; and we must also observe what sort of people were the fathers, even such as had followed God, and when they had such examples, they ought to have been more and more stimulated to imitate them.

It was therefore an inexcusable wickedness to forsake a way found good by long experience, *the way of ages*, which had been approved for a long time, and to depart into paths not trodden, for by no example of the saints who were alone the true fathers, had they been led to devise for themselves new and fictitious modes of worship, and also to depart from the plain doctrine of the law. Had any one answered, that these ways had been long trodden, because they had both the Assyrians and the Egyptians as associates in their superstitions, such an exception could not be admitted, for the Prophet, as I have said, does not speak indiscriminately of any kind of examples, but of the examples of the fathers, who had been ruled and led by the Lord. It follows—

16. To make their land desolate, *and* a perpetual hissing: every one that passeth thereby shall be astonished, and wag his head.

16. Ad ponendum terram eorum in vastitatem, (*hoc est*, ut ponam terram eorum in vastitatem,) in sibila perpetua; quisquis transibit per eam obstupescet et movebit caput.

The Prophet again denounces the punishment which they deserved, that *desolation* awaited the land. It would be, he says, their reward to have the land reduced to a solitude, and also to *perpetual hissings.* The word עולם, *oulam,* which the Prophet had just used, is here also used, but in a different sense, for when he said, *the paths of ages,* he referred to past time, but now to a future time. As then the Jews had alienated themselves from the ways of ages, that is, from the eternal verity of God, so now he says, that their land would be for the hissings of ages, for the dreadful calamity now at hand would not be for a few years but to the end of the world.

And in the second clause he expresses more clearly what he meant by eternal hissings, that *every one passing through it would be astonished* and *move* or shake *his head,*[1] as one does either in amazement, or in contempt, or in abhorrence; this kind of speaking often occurs in the Prophets. The land of Canaan, after having been given to the Jews, became as it were an extraordinary country, in which all kinds of opulence appeared, for God poured upon it the invaluable treasures of his bounty, so that the very sight of it filled all with admiration; on the other hand, it became the scene of horror and an object of hissing when God cursed it. A confirmation then follows—

17. I will scatter them as with an east wind before the enemy; I will shew them the back, and not the face, in the day of their calamity.

17. In vento orientali, (*vel,* per ventum orientalem; *quidam legunt* כ *loco* ב, *et dicunt,* tanquam ventus orientalis; *sed quod ad mentem Prophetæ spectat nulla est ambiguitas,* per ventum *ergo* orientalem,) dispergam eos coram facie inimici; cervicem, non faciem ostendam ipsis (videre ipsos faciam) in die calamitatis ipsorum, (*vel,* interitus, *ut alii vertunt.*)

Though no word of comparison is expressed, if we read ב, *beth,* and not כ, *caph,* yet the Prophet employs a comparison, for God did not drive away the Jews by an eastern wind, but as the force of that wind is violent in Judea, the eastern wind often means a storm or a whirlwind, as though he had said, "As by a whirlwind or a storm will I cast them out."[2] *I will disperse* or dissipate *them,* he says, *before the face of the enemy.* He means that enemies would come to

[1] More literally, "And shall nod with his head."—*Ed.*

[2] Many copies read ב, though all the versions retain the כ; "As a burning wind will I scatter them," is the version of the *Septuagint* and the *Vulgate;* "As a hot wind," &c., is the *Syriac.—Ed.*

exterminate the Jews from the land; and he adds another thing, that these enemies would be full of terror, for God would give them the force of a whirlwind or a storm to disperse and scatter the Jews, for being terrified by God they would not dare to withstand.

Then follows a commination, that God would *turn to them the neck*, or the back, *and not the face in the day of calamity.* It sometimes happens that we are severely chastised by God, he thus often tries his faithful people when he subjects them to the will of the ungodly; but yet all remedy is not taken away from them, as they find consolation in God's mercy, for as he casts down so he raises up, as he puts to death so he gives life, according to what is said in 1 Sam. ii. 6. But God here denounces a punishment without any prospect of pardon or alleviation, *I will scatter them*, he says, as by an east wind before their enemies. Then he adds, "In vain shall they flee to me and seek my mercy, though otherwise it is offered to all, yet then they shall implore it in vain, for it is decreed not to pardon them. I will shew to them my back, (or neck, for עֹרֶף, *oreph*, is the hinder part of the head, but here it means the back,) they shall then find that I am turned away from them, so that they shall not be set before my eyes." For it is an invaluable consolation when God is pleased to look on our miseries, but he deprives the Jews of this hope, for he would turn to them his back in *the day of slaughter*. I cannot proceed farther now.

PRAYER.

Grant, Almighty God, that we may in due time anticipate thy wrath, and never so kindle it by our perverseness as to preclude every remedy; and then also when thou for a time chastisest us, do not wholly cast us away, but let this resort ever remain to us, to seek thee in the day of calamity and to find thee accessible, so that being reunited to thee we may find that thou rememberest mercy even in wrath, until we shall enjoy a full and real participation of thy favour and paternal love in thy celestial kingdom, which has been procured for us by the blood of thine only-begotten Son.—Amen.

Lecture Seventy-Second.

18. Then said they, Come, and let us devise devices against Jeremiah; for the law shall not perish from the priest, nor counsel from the wise, nor the word from the prophet: come, and let us smite him with the tongue, and let us not give heed to any of his words.

18. Et dixerunt, Venite, et cogitemus contra Jeremiam cogitationes, quia non peribit Lex à sacerdote, et consilium à sapiente, et sermo à Propheta: venite, et percutiamus eum lingua, neque attendamus ad cunctos sermones ejus.

HERE Jeremiah relates how great was the fury which seized the minds of those on whom he had denounced the vengeance of God. It was no doubt a dreadful thing to hear, that when they should be in a state of despair, no aid from God could be expected: for this is the import of what we have observed,—"In the day of their calamity I will shew them my back and not my face;" that is, "They shall see my back and not my face." As then there was no hope of pardon remaining for them, was it not a monstrous stupidity not to be moved and humbled, when they saw that God was thus angry with them? But the Prophet shews, that his denunciation was heedlessly despised by them; nay, that there was such obstinacy in their wickedness, that they then more stoutly prepared themselves for battle. For he says that they avowedly conspired against him, after he had warned them of God's dreadful judgment.

And he introduces them as encouraging one another, *Come, and let us think thoughts against Jeremiah.* We may observe what it was that they set up against God's judgment, even their own counsels and purposes: this was in a word to transfer authority from God to themselves. They thus deprived God of his right, and sought to occupy his throne, as though they were the judges and could subject to their own will whatever the Prophet had declared. It is indeed probable, that they did not avowedly or designedly carry on war with God; for hypocrites raise up for themselves mists and clouds, by which they wilfully bring darkness on themselves. In the meantime a diabolical fury possesses them, so that they make no account of God; for were they really to consider the truth brought to them, they might easily understand it. Whence then is this violent fury and madness, that when they seek to contend with man, they really fight with God? Even because their impiety and pride, as I have said, so blinds them, that they hesitate not to rob God of his honour, and thus they put themselves in his place.

The same thing is to be seen now under the whole Papacy: for when they conspire among themselves to oppose plain truths, they do not ask at the mouth of God, nor regard anything taught in the Scriptures, but are satisfied with trumpeting forth their rotten decrees, or rather dreams, in which there is nothing, however futile, which they do not regard as an oracle: and when they bring forth their bulls, they think themselves sufficiently fortified, as though God were deprived of his own right. But this will appear more fully from the context.

They said, *For perish shall not the law from the priest.*[1] This reason, which they added, shews whence that security arose, through which they hesitated not to reject the words of the Prophet: there were priests and prophets who occupied a place in the Church, and who boasted of their titles, though they were nothing but mere masks, having no care to possess what their calling required. Thus the vizarded priests were satisfied with an honourable vocation, and cared nothing for the account that was to be rendered to God: and thus in all ages hypocrites have abused the gifts of God. This is seen most clearly under the Papacy. For doubtless when all things are well examined, we find that the Pope and all his party mainly rely on these weapons; for when

[1] It would be better to render this, "The law cannot perish," &c.; for the future with a negative may often be thus rendered: כי, translated, "For," often means *certainly, truly, surely, doubtless,* and might be so translated here,—

Surely, not perish can the law from the priests,
Or counsel from the wise,
Or the word from the Prophet.

These things they thought were impossibilities. How like are errors and the delusions of men in every age! "The word" was what the prophets taught and preached: hence "the word" in the New Testament often means the preaching of the gospel.—*Ed.*

they are a hundred times conquered by proofs from Scripture, they still strenuously defend themselves with this one shield,—That the Church cannot err, that the Church is represented by the Pope, the bishops, and the whole clergy, and also that those whom they call prelates are successors of the Apostles: and so they boastingly thunder out a continual succession from Peter. They at length conclude, that the Church of Rome is the mother of all the faithful, and also that the Holy Spirit dwells there; for whosoever succeeds in the place of Peter and occupies his chair, is endued with the same spirit and the same authority. We hence see, that the Papists at this day contend with us with no other weapons than those with which all the ungodly reprobates assailed Jeremiah.

They said first, that it would be enough if they had their own thoughts, that is, if they resolved among themselves what was necessary to be done; for under the word thoughts, they included decrees as well as deliberations; as though they had said,—"We possess an ordinary jurisdiction; for God has set us over his Church: whatever then proceeds from us, ought to be deemed inviolable. The reason is, because the law cannot perish from the priest, and counsel cannot perish from the wise, nor the word from the Prophets." These three things were very speciously brought against Jeremiah; nor could it have been denied, but that there were legitimate priests as to their vocation, that there was also a church, and that the elders, who were connected with the priests, justly boasted of their dignity; and lastly, that the people ever had their prophets. We hence see that they could have alleged very specious pretences against God's Prophet, by which they might have easily deceived the simple. If a comparison be made, doubtless the whole Papal system cannot justly have any such pretensions; but they are far inferior to those of the Jews. For when they say that they represent the Church, *that* is disputed; and they are at length constrained to come to this point—to define what the Church is: and when it is settled what the Church is, we are then to inquire whether the bishops or prelates are legitimate. Now their calling is not founded on the word of God; for they are all schismatics; and this appears from their own canons, as there is among them, at this day, no canonical election. It then follows that their calling, of which they are so foolishly and arrogantly proud, comes to nothing. But let us allow them to be lawful ministers, and their calling to be approved according to God's word, it does not yet hence follow that they are true ministers of God, that is, because they hold an ordinary station and jurisdiction in the Church. For we find that in all ages the Church of God has been subject to the evil of having wolves occupying the place of pastors, of having impious and perfidious men daring to oppose God in his own name.

As it thus happened formerly, neither the Pope nor all his masked bishops can shew any difference in the present day, why we ought not to dread wolves: how so? "There were formerly," says the Apostle, "false prophets, so also there will be false teachers among you." (2 Peter ii. 1.) He shews that at this time no less than formerly we ought to beware of false bishops, of false prophets, and of false teachers, however high their titles may be. When therefore the Papists vainly boast that the Church cannot err, they are justly objects of ridicule; for we see who those are whom they follow: as formerly the manifest enemies of God contended with Jeremiah, even so now they openly oppose God by this vain pretence only—they are priests, they are prophets, they are elders or presbyters, that is, they hold an ordinary jurisdiction. But this passage is sufficient to confute their folly; for they bring words instead of proof, and rely only on this argument—"The Church cannot err:" and what the Prophet relates further, "The law cannot perish from the priest," means the same thing. But we find elsewhere what God threatened, even that a dreadful judgment was at hand, when the wise would become blind, when the priests and prophets would become foolish and fatuitous. (Hosea ix. 7; Isaiah xxix. 14.) But we may hence learn on what condition and for what purpose God everywhere honours the ministers and pastors of the Church with high eulogies: it is not certainly that they may be proud through a false pretence, but that they may faithfully execute their office.

However this may be, we see that it is a false confidence, when pastors allege that the law and the word or the truth, cannot depart from them, because they are, and are called priests.

They added, *Come and let us smite him with the tongue.* They again magnify their own authority, as the Papists do at this day, who, standing as it were on high, look down on us with contempt, and say, "We must not dispute with heretics, for things formerly settled, and which the Church has once decreed, must not be called in question." For it seems very strange to them, and even unbecoming, when we ask a hearing and wish the controversies, by which the world is now disturbed, to be decided and removed, by the law, and the prophets, and the gospel. "What! are then the Church's decrees to be reduced to nothing? The Scripture is a nose of wax; it has nothing sure or certain; it can be twisted to favour any party, and hypocrites always pervert the word of God; and therefore it follows that there is nothing certain or clear in the Scripture." This is to smite with the tongue, as we see to have been done to Jeremiah,—"Why should we dispute with that man, who so daringly threatens us, as though he was superior to others? but he is only one of the people; what need then of long disputation; for we have authority, and it will be enough by one word to determine, that whatever he brings is to be rejected. There is then no reason why we should weary ourselves by a long contest; for our tongue, as they say, decisively settles what is right."

We see how the ungodly dared to set forward their own decrees, by which they tried to overwhelm the prophetic word and to take away the authority of Jeremiah. Whenever then men thus elevate themselves, so as to seek to smite God's servants with the tongue, and to suppress his word when spoken by them, we understand how to regard them, and what weight belongs to all their decrees or determinations.[1]

[1] This phrase, "Let us smite him with the tongue," is thus literally rendered by the *Septuagint*, the *Vulgate*, and the *Arabic;* but by the *Syriac*, "Let us smite his tongue," and paraphrased by the *Targum*, "Let us testify against him false testimonies." "With *our* tongue," is *Piscator's;* that is, by accusations to the king; "For *his* tongue," is *Junius's;* that is, for his denunciations; "On the tongue," is *Blayney's;* that is, on the

But the end of this verse shews more clearly how wantonly they despised every truth; for it is a proof of hopeless contumacy when no attention is paid to the prophetic word: *Let us not attend,* they said; that is, "Let us not care for what he says, and let us boldly despise whatever he may speak." The Prophet, as I have said, meant by this expression to shew, that they were so blinded by a diabolical impulse, that they hesitated not to reject whatever proceeded from God, to close their ears and designedly to neglect it, as is usual with the wholly wicked. No less contempt is now to be seen under the Papacy; for were they calmly to hear us, were they to consider with tranquil minds and meek hearts what we allege, doubtless the matter would soon be settled between us. But their only resolution is, not to hear; for they are content with this fallacious prejudice,—that as they represent the Church, it is in their power to condemn whatever we say, and that when they have condemned us, there is no need of any disputation.

But we are hence reminded, that when men are guilty of many vices, there is yet some hope of salvation remaining, provided they are not unteachable, and do not with resolute confidence reject what is proposed to them from the law, and the prophets, and the gospel. For as there are many diseases, and those grievous and dangerous, which yet may be healed, so also we ought to conclude that men are healable, as long as they bear to be taught, to be admonished and reproved; but when with closed ears they pass by every truth, when they despise all counsels, when they esteem as nothing God's threatenings and reproofs, then their salvation is hopeless. It follows—

19. Give heed to me, O Lord, and hearken to the voice of them that contend with me.	19. Attende, Jehova, ad me, et audi vocem litigatorum meorum (*hoc est,* rixantium mecum.)

As the Prophet saw that his labour as to men was use-

offending part, an allusion to a mode of punishment that was practised; or, as *Gataker* suggests, in order to stop his mouth.

The most probable meaning is, that they meant to accuse him before the authorities; therefore "with the tongue," as countenanced by the best versions, is the best rendering.

"Let us accuse him, let us speak so ill of him, that no man may attend to him, but that all may flee from him," *Cocceius.—Ed.*

less, he turned to God, as we find he had done often before. This way of speaking, no doubt, had more force than if he had continued to address the people. He might indeed have said, "Miserable men! where are you rushing headlong? what means this madness? what at last do ye think will be the end, since ye are resisting God, being obstinate against his Spirit? for ye cannot extinguish the light by your perverseness or by your effrontery." The Prophet might have thus reproved them; but it betokens more vehemence, when he leaves men and addresses God himself. This apostrophe then ought to be carefully noticed, for we hence gather that the madness of the Jews was reprobated, inasmuch as the Prophet did not deign to contend with them. But he notwithstanding said, "As they do not attend, *attend thou, Jehovah, to me.*" He saw that he was despised by God's enemies, and by this prayer he intimates, that his doctrine was in force before God, and retained its own importance and could not fail. Hence he says, *Jehovah, regard me, and hear the voice of those who contend with me.*

Here Jeremiah asks two things,—that God would undertake his cause, and that he would take vengeance on the wantonness of his enemies. And this passage deserves especial notice, for it is a support which can never fail us, when we know that our service is approved by God, and that as he prescribes to us what to say, so what proceeds from him shall ever possess its own weight, and that it cannot be effected by the ingratitude of the world, that any portion of the authority of celestial truth should be destroyed or diminished. Whenever then the ungodly deride us, and elude or neglect the truth, let us follow the example of the Prophet, let us ask God to look on us; but this cannot be done, except we strive with a sincere heart to execute what he has committed to us. Then a pure conscience will open a door for us, so that we may be able confidently to call on God as our guardian and defender, whenever our labour is despised by men.

He asks, in the second place, that God would *hear the voice of those who contended* with him.[1] We hence conclude,

[1] "The voice of my justification," is the *Septuagint;* "the voice of my

that the wicked gain nothing by their pride, for they provoke God more and more, when they thus oppose his pure doctrine and contend against his prophets and faithful teachers. Since then we see that the ungodly effect nothing, except that they kindle God's wrath the more, we ought to go on more courageously in the discharge of our office; for even when for a time they suppress by their great clamours the truth of God, he will yet check them, and so check them, that the doctrine, which is now subverted by unjust calumnies, may shine forth more fully. He afterwards adds—

20. Shall evil be recompensed for good? for they have digged a pit for my soul. Remember that I stood before thee to speak good for them, *and* to turn away thy wrath from them.

20. An reddetur pro bono malum? quia foderunt foveam animæ meæ; recordare quòd steterim coram facie tua ad loquendum pro ipsis in bonum, ad avertendam iracundiam tuam ab ipsis.

The Prophet in this verse exaggerates the sin of his enemies, for they not only were ferocious against God, but also forgot everything humane, and wickedly assailed the Prophet himself. Impiety is indeed more detestable than inhumanity, inasmuch as God is far above all mortals; but inhumanity has in it more baseness; for it is, so to speak, more gross and more evident. The ungodly often hide their perfidy; but when they come to act towards men, then it appears immediately what they are. Hence the Prophet, having made known the impiety of his enemies, now adds, that they, when tried by the judgment of men, were found to be wholly intolerable, for they rendered a shameful reward to an innocent man who was sedulous in securing their salvation. We now understand the meaning of the Prophet.

Though it often happens that evil is rendered for good, and ingratitude is a common vice, yet nature itself detests ingratitude; hence it has been said that there is no law against the ungrateful, because ingratitude seems a monstrous thing. As then nature dictates that merit deserves a reward, and this ought to be a fixed principle in the hearts

adversaries," the *Vulgate;* "the voice of my oppression," the *Syriac;* "the voice of my strife," the *Arabic.* But the best is our version and that of *Calvin.* The *Septuagint,* the *Vulgate,* and the *Syriac* are wholly wrong; for the verb ריב never means any one of the ideas which they convey.—*Ed.*

of all, the Prophet reasons according to the common sense and judgment of all mankind.

Shall evil, he says, *be rendered for good? for they have digged a pit for my soul?*[1] and yet I prayed for them, and endeavoured to turn away the wrath of God. Since I have set myself humbly to pray for their salvation, how great is their savageness and inhumanity in persecuting me? But as he saw that it was vain to speak to the deaf, he again appeals to God as a witness to his integrity; *Remember,* he says, *that I stood before thy face to speak for them;* as though he had said, "Even if malignity prevent men to own what I am, and how I have conducted myself towards them, God will be to me a sufficient witness, and I shall be satisfied with his judgment." It then follows—

21. Therefore deliver up their children to the famine, and pour out their *blood* by the force of the sword; and let their wives be bereaved of their children, and *be* widows; and let their men be put to death; *let* their young men *be* slain by the sword in battle.

21. Propterea pone filios eorum ad famem (*hoc est,* projice, *vel,* prostitue ad famem,) et diffunde (*vel,* diffluere fac) eos ad manus gladii, et sint mulieres eorum orbæ et viduæ, et viri eorum sint percussi ad mortem (lethaliter,) juvenes eorum sint percussi gladio in prælio.

The Prophet seems here to have been driven through indignation to utter imprecations which are not consistent with a right feeling; for even if Christ had not said with his own mouth, that we are to pray for those who curse us, the very law of God, ever known to the holy fathers, was sufficient. Jeremiah then ought not to have uttered these curses, and to have imprecated final destruction on his enemies, though they fully deserved it. But it must be observed, that he was moved not otherwise than by the Holy Spirit, to become thus indignant against his enemies; for he could not have been excused on the ground that indignation often transgresses the bounds of patience, for the children of God ought

[1] It is better to render these lines like the *Septuagint* and *Vulgate,*—

Is not evil rendered for good?
For they have dug a pit for my soul.

Or thus,—

Should evil be rendered for good?—
For they have dug a pit for me.

So should "soul" be rendered here and in many other places. There is here an allusion to the practice of digging pits to take wild beasts.—*Ed.*

to bear all injuries to the utmost; but, as I have said, the Prophet here has announced nothing rashly, nor did he allow himself to wish anything as of himself, but obediently proclaimed what the Holy Spirit dictated, as his faithful instrument.

We have said elsewhere, that the first thing to be noticed is, that when we pray for any evil on the wicked, we ought not to act on private grounds; for he who has a regard to himself, will ever be led away by too strong an impulse; and even when our prayers are calmly and rightly formed, we are yet ever wrong, when we consult our private advantages or redress our own injuries. This is one thing. And secondly, we ought to have that wisdom which distinguishes between the elect and the reprobate. But as God bids us to suspend our judgment, inasmuch as we cannot surely know what will take place to-morrow, we ought not to imitate indiscriminately the Prophet in praying God to destroy and scatter ungodly men of whom we despair; for, as it has been stated, we are not certain what has been decreed in heaven. In short, whosoever is disposed, after the example of Jeremiah, to pray for a curse on his enemies, must be ruled by the same spirit, according to what Christ said to his disciples; for as God destroyed the wicked at the request of Elijah, the Apostles wished Christ to do the same by fire from heaven; but he said, "Ye know not by what spirit ye are ruled." (Luke ix. 55.) They were unlike Elijah, and yet wished like apes to imitate what he did.

But, as I have said, let first all regard to our own benefit or loss be dismissed, when we would shew ourselves indignant against the wicked; and secondly, let us have the spirit of wisdom and discretion; and lastly, let all the turbulent feelings of the flesh be checked, for as soon as anything human be mixed with our prayers, some confusion will ever be found. There was nothing turbulent in this imprecation of Jeremiah, for the Spirit of God ruled his heart and his tongue, and then he forgot himself; and lastly, he knew that they were reprobate and already doomed to final ruin. He therefore hesitated not, through the prophetic spirit, to imprecate on them what we here read. And there is no doubt but that he was ever solicitous for the remnant, for he knew that there were some faithful; and though they were unknown, he yet prayed God for them. But he fulminates here against the reprobate who were already given up to ruin. This is the reason why he hesitated not to pray that they might be delivered up to *famine* and given to the *sword,*[1] so that their *women* might be *bereaved* and become *widows,* and their *men* put to *death,*[2] and their *youth* smitten by the *sword.* It now follows—

22. Let a cry be heard from their houses, when thou shalt bring a troop suddenly upon them; for they have digged a pit to take me, and hid snares for my feet.

22. Audiatur clamor ex ædibus eorum cum induxeris super eos exercitum repentè; quia foderunt foveam ad capiendum me, laqueos occultarunt pedibus meis.

He proceeds with his imprecation: he then wishes that a *cry* should he heard from the *houses,* as though he had said, "Let there be no refuge for them when their calamity shall happen." For his own house is to every one his place of safety in a disordered state of things. The Prophet then wished them to be slain by their enemies even when concealed in their houses; for it appears from the preceding verse that he meant slaughter. For why should a cry be, except on account of enemies breaking in and raging against them, while they, being not able to defend their life, were driven to lamentations and howlings? *Let a cry* then *be heard from their houses, when thou bringest an army upon*

[1] The rendering of this line is various: our version, "pour out," &c., cannot be sustained; nor "drain them," &c., by *Blayney.* The idea generally given by the versions and the *Targum* to the verb, is that of giving up, delivering, committing. The *Syriac* seems to give the original correctly, "deliver them into the hands of the sword;" only the verb נגרה, signifies to draw or drive rather than to deliver. Perhaps the literal rendering would be, "drive them on the hands of the sword," as though the sword was a person with hands stretched out to receive what might come in its way: but "hands" in this instance mean power; so that the best version would be,

And deliver them into the power of the sword.

[2] Literally, "the slain of death," as in the next line, "the smitten of the sword." The two lines are literally thus,—

And let their men be the slain of death;
Their youths the smitten of the sword in battle.

"Death" here, notwithstanding what Horsley has said, evidently means pestilence. See chap. xv. 2. The "men" were those past the time of service, and "youths" or young men were those fit for war.—*Ed.*

them suddenly; and he adds, *For they have digged a pit to take me.*

The Prophet indeed seems here to be the defender of his own cause: but there is no doubt, but that apart from anything personal, he hated the impiety of those of whom he speaks, because they insidiously assailed him, when yet he was doing the work of God. For the Prophet neither sowed nor reaped for himself, but only laboured to obey God. When therefore they artfully assailed and circumvented him, what was it but openly to carry on war with God? Let us then remember, that the Prophet does not here complain of troubles which he underwent, or of injuries, but that he only pleads a public cause; for these ungodly men treated him perfidiously, while he was doing nothing else but spending his labour for God, and indeed for their salvation. At last he adds—

23. Yet, Lord, thou knowest all their counsel against me to slay *me:* forgive not their iniquity, neither blot out their sin from thy sight, but let them be overthrown before thee; deal *thus* with them in the time of thine anger.

23. Et tu Jehovah nosti omnia consilia eorum super me in mortem; ne propitius sis (*vel,* placabilis) super iniquitate eorum, et peccatum eorum (*vel,* scelus eorum) à facie tua ne deleas (*quidam existimant* תמחי *esse in kal, et* י poni loco ה,) et sint impingentes coram facie tua, in die excandescentiæ tuæ fac cum ipsis.

I shall not be able to explain this verse to-day.

PRAYER.

Grant, Almighty God, that since thou exhortest us daily, and even constantly to repent, by the doctrine of thy Gospel, and shewest thyself to us reconcilable,—O grant, that we may not disregard so incomparable a benefit, but with resigned minds devote ourselves wholly to thee, and that we may not so far provoke thy wrath as to be altogether rejected by thee, and to find at last that there is no mercy for us; but may we anticipate extreme judgment, while the time of thy good-will continues, and thus embrace the benefit of reconciliation which thou offerest to us, so that being thankful to thee and accepted in thine only-begotten Son, we may proceed in the course of our vocation, until we shall at length enjoy that eternal inheritance which thine only-begotten Son has obtained for us by his own blood.—Amen.

Lecture Seventy-Third.

THE words of the last verse of the eighteenth chapter we gave yesterday. Let us now see what the Prophet means by them, and what fruit we ought to gather from them. He says, that God was a witness of the wickedness of his enemies—that all their counsels had in view his destruction. There is, moreover, to be understood a contrast,—that the Prophet, as we have before seen, cared faithfully for their salvation. It was then a most base ingratitude in them to plot the death of the holy Prophet, who was not only innocent, but highly deserved their thanks for labouring for their salvation. We hence conclude that they deserved no mercy. *Thou knowest,* he says, *their counsel, that what they consult among themselves tends to bring death on me: be not thou then propitious to their iniquity, and blot not out their sin.*

We said in our last lecture that this vehemence, as it was dictated by the Holy Spirit, is not to be condemned, nor ought it to be made an example of, for it was peculiar to the Prophet to know that they were reprobates: and we also shewed why no common law is to be made from particular examples; for Jeremiah was endued with the spirit of wisdom and judgment, and zeal also for God's glory so ruled in his heart, that the feelings of the flesh were wholly subdued, or at least brought under subjection; and farther, he pleaded not a private cause. We said in the last place, that it was oracular; for God designed to make it known, that they who thus obstinately resisted true doctrine were reprobate and irreclaimable. As all these things fall not to our lot, we ought not indiscriminately to imitate Jeremiah in this prayer: for that would then apply to us which Christ said to his disciples, "Ye know not what spirit governs you." (Luke ix. 55.)

And doubtless it ought to fill us with dread when we hear, *Be not propitious* to them, *nor blot out their sin.* God testifies in many places that he is gracious and inclined to mercy, and that when he is angry it is only for a moment. (Num. xiv. 18; Psalm ciii. 8; xxx. 5.) There seems then a great difference between the words of the Prophet and these testimonies, by which God makes known his own nature. But we have said already that the destruction of the people, against whom the Prophet thus prayed, had been made evident to him: and we must also bear in mind what we have stated, that he did not include the people without exception; for he knew that there was a seed remaining among them. He then confined his imprecation to the reprobate and irreclaimable, as he knew that they were already doomed to ruin, even by the eternal purpose of God: and as they had over and over again destroyed themselves, he boldly declares that God would never be propitious to them.

To the same purpose is what follows, *Let them ever stumble before thy face.* He mentions *face* here for manifest judgment; for the wicked exult as long as he spares them. The Prophet then would have God to sit on his throne, that he might appear as a Judge, and thus check the wantonness of those who despised his judgment, being constrained to know that they could not escape. There is also a contrast to be understood here between the presence and the absence of God. For hypocrites think that God is absent as long as he is indulgent to them and does not take vengeance: hence they grow wanton, as though they had a permission to deceive him: but when God constrains them to acknowledge what they are unwilling to do, they are said to stand in his presence; for they are pressed too near to render it possible for them to evade, and willing or unwilling they are held fast, as the Lord proves that he is their Judge. We hence see the meaning of the expression when the Prophet says, *Let them stumble before thy face.*

He in the last place adds, *In the time of thy wrath deal* thus *with them.* The manner of his presence is set forth. There is, however, no doubt but that the Prophet here checks both himself and all the godly, that they may not be hasty, for we are often too precipitant in our wishes; for we would that God would fulminate every moment from heaven. This hastiness ought to be moderated; and the Prophet here prescribes to us the rule of moderation, by saying, *In the time of thy wrath;* as though he had said, " Even though thou deferrest and seemest now to connive at these great crimes, yet the time will eventually come in which thou wilt take vengeance on the reprobate."

Whenever then the Scripture speaks of the time of God's wrath, let us know that under this form of speaking there is an exhortation to patience, so that excessive ardour may not lead us beyond the limits of moderation, but that we may wait with resigned minds until the due time of judgment comes. This is one thing; but at the same time the Prophet expresses also something more: for he would have the reprobate of whom he speaks, to be so involved in endless judgment as never to be able to extricate themselves. It is said in Psalm cvi. 4, "Remember me, O Lord, with the favour of thy people," that is, "O Lord, this only I ask, to be joined to thy people; for even when thy Church is afflicted and deemed miserable, it will still be enough for me to be of the number of those whom thou honourest with thy paternal favour." The favour then of God's people is that paternal regard which he entertains for his Church. So, on the other hand, *the time* of *wrath* is that judgment by which God devotes the reprobate to eternal perdition, so that there is no hope of salvation remaining for them. *Deal* thou *with them*, but when? even in *the time of thy wrath;* that is, deal with them as thou art wont to deal with thine irreclaimable enemies, to whom thou wilt never be reconcilable.[1] This is the meaning. Now another discourse follows.

CHAPTER XIX.

1. Thus saith the Lord, Go and get a potter's earthen bottle, and *take* of the ancients of the people, and of the ancients of the priests;

1. Sic dicit Jehova, Vade et acquire (*alii vertunt,* posside; *et* קנה *significat utrunque, sed hic non convenit verbum possidendi;* acquire tibi) lagenam figuli testaceam, et quidem cum senioribus populi, et cum senioribus sacerdotum:

[1] The last line in the *Syriac* is,—

In the time of thine indignation act against them.

"Take vengeance on them," is the paraphrase of the *Targum*. *Horsley* would have it, "deal with them," leaving out "*thus*" in our version. It is no doubt an expression which includes more than what is stated. It may be rendered "do for them," that is, wholly destroy them.—*Ed.*

2. And go forth unto the valley of the son of Hinnom, which *is* by the entry of the east gate, and proclaim there the words that I shall tell thee:

3. And say, Hear ye the word of the Lord, O kings of Judah, and inhabitants of Jerusalem; Thus saith the Lord of hosts, the God of Israel, Behold, I will bring evil upon this place, the which whosoever heareth, his ears shall tingle.

2. Et egredere ad vallem filii Hinnom, quæ est in introitu portæ orientalis, (*alii vertunt,* fictilis,) et clama illic (*hoc est,* alta voce pronuntia) sermones quos loquutus fuero ad te;

3. Et dices, Audite sermonem Jehovæ, reges Jehudah et incolæ Jerusalem, Sic dicit Jehova exercituum, Deus Israel, Ecce adduco malum super locum hunc, de quo quisque audierit, tinnient aures ejus.

We see that the Prophet was sent by God to shew the people that there was no firmness in that state of which hypocrites boasted; for God, who had favoured the people of Israel with singular benefits, did no less retain them in his own possession than the potter. The Prophet had before shewn to the Jews that the potter formed his vessels as he pleased, and also, that when he had taken the clay and the vessel did not please him, he formed another. This prophecy has a similar import, and yet it is different, as we shall presently see. The Prophet is here bidden to buy an earthen vessel of the potter, and at the meeting of the people to break it, that all might understand that they were like earthen vessels, and that being thus admonished of their fragility, they might no longer be proud, as though they possessed a firm and perpetual state of happiness.

The main object of the two visions is, however, the same: for the Jews thought that they were not subject to the common lot of men, because they had been chosen as a peculiar people; nor would they have gloried in vain with regard to that inestimable privilege, had there been a mutual agreement between God and them; but as they were covenant-breakers, their glorying was vain and foolish, in thinking that God was bound to them. For what right had they to claim this privilege? God indeed had adopted the whole race of Abraham, but there was a condition introduced, "Walk before me and be perfect." (Gen. xvii. 2.) When they all had become apostates, the covenant, as to them, was abolished. Then God could not have been called, as it were, to an account, as though he had violated his covenant with them, for he owed them nothing. They had become aliens; for through their wickedness and perfidy they had departed from him. God then designed to shew how vain and how false was their confidence, when they said, "We are a holy race, we are God's heritage;" because they had wholly departed from the covenant which God had made with their fathers.

But in the form adopted, as I have said, there is some difference. The Prophet had before introduced the potter to shew that there was no less power in God than in a mortal man, because we are before him as the clay, so that he can form and destroy his vessels as he pleases: but here the Prophet shews, that though the Jews had been formed for a time, and so formed as to have been like an excellent and a beautiful vessel, yet it was not a perpetual condition. And it is probable that when they had heard that God could, like the potter, form and re-form them, they had devised an evasion, according to what men usually do who deal sophistically with God,—"O, be it so, the potter can from the same clay form both a precious and a worthless vessel; but we are the precious vessel, and God has given us that form; for when he made a covenant with Abraham, he adorned him with this singular distinction: he afterwards brought our fathers out of Egypt, and then there was a better form added; and since at length he raised a kingdom among us with this promise, that the throne of David would be perpetual, it cannot possibly be otherwise than that we are to continue in our state." Hence the Prophet expresses here more than in the former prophecy, that not only God had the power of a potter in forming his vessels, but that when the vessel is already formed and possesses great splendour, it can again be broken: he stated this lest the Jews should object by saying, that the state in which they were under David and his posterity would be perpetual. He says, "This is nothing: for the earthen vessel, though splendid and elegant in its form, can yet be broken in the third or fourth year no less than at the time when it is formed, and can be broken for ever," according to what is afterwards implied by the similitude.

We shall proceed now to the words: he says, *Go and get*

for thee an earthen vessel. The Rabbins think the name given to the vessel to be factitious, as the grammarians say, that is, made from its sound; for it appears to have been a flagon or a bottle; and as the bottle has a narrow mouth, it makes this sound, *bakbuk,* when we drink from it; and hence they think the name is derived. There is, however, no ambiguity as to the thing itself, that the word means a bottle, not only made of earth, but also either of glass or of wood. By adding the word חרש, *cheresh,* he specifies what it was; but בקבק, *bekbek,* is a general word. He then adds what is literally, *From the elders,* and interpreters think that the words "bring with thee" are to be understood; and as to the sense I agree with them, for we shall hereafter see, that in the presence of those who went with him he broke the vessel: it then follows that the elders here spoken of were taken by Jeremiah as his companions; but as מ, *mem,* sometimes means "with," as in the fifty-seventh chapter of Isaiah, (verse 8,) "and made thee a covenant with them, מהם," I take it to be of the same meaning here; and this is doubtless suitable here, for he was to go *with the elders of the people and with the elders of the priests.*[1]

And he adds, *Enter into the valley of the son of Hinnom, which is at the entrance of the east gate,* rendered by some "of the earthen gate," for which I see no reason; but I leave this to be examined by those who are more versed in the language. It is indeed thought that ש, *shin,* is changed here into ס, *samech;* but if we take the word as it is, it means "solar," for חרס, *cheras,* from which חרסית, *cherasit,* is derived, signifies the sun; and it seems to have been called the solar gate by way of excellency, because it looked toward the rising sun.[2] I do not yet oppose the idea of those

[1] The literal rendering of this verse I conceive to be the following,—

"Thus saith Jehovah, go and get a bottle from the maker of earthenware, and *some* of the elders of the people and of the elders of the priests."

The מ, *of,* or *from,* before elders, implies a part; and it is the idiom of the language not to put in "some,"—"get (or take) from the elders," &c. He was first to get the bottle, and then some of the elders. The *Vulgate* very strangely represents the Prophet as taking the bottle from the elders, omitting the ו, and as taking it from both elders!—*Ed.*

[2] It appears that the valley of Hinnom was not to the east, but to the

who think that the Prophet alludes to חרש, *cheresh*, of which he had spoken, and that he calls it the east gate, though it was as it were an earthen gate; for the two letters ש, *shin*, and ס, *samech*, as it is well known, are closely allied. *Cry there*, he says, *the words which I shall speak to thee.*

I come now to the subject: God bids his Prophet to get from the potter an earthen vessel, and to do so in the presence of the elders; for it was necessary to have witnesses in a matter so important; and as the public safety of the people was concerned, it was God's purpose, lest the prophecy should be despised, that there should be present the gravest witnesses, suitable, and, as they say, authorized, or approved; and he calls them the *elders* of the *people* and of the *priests;* and no doubt they were chosen from a great number, even from among the priests who were chief. There were also Levites of the sons of Aaron; but there were then chief priests a large number; but, as they say, it was a turbulent rabble. They were chosen from those first orders who ruled the Church, and Jeremiah calls them the *elders* of the priests. There were also others chosen from the people who presided over the Church. And we know that there were two public functionaries, or, as they say, a twofold government: the priests were the rulers of the Church with regard to the law, so that their government was spiritual; there were also the elders of the people who managed civil affairs; but there were some things in which they ruled in common. We now then see what the Prophet meant by saying that he was bidden to call witnesses to see what is afterwards stated, and that they were taken partly from the priests and partly from the people.

south of Jerusalem. See Joshua xv. 8. The *Keri* and several copies read החרסית, and it is given untranslated by the *Septuagint*, the *Syriac*, and the *Arabic*. It is rendered " earthen" by the *Vulgate*, as though the ס, as *Calvin* mentions, is substituted for ש. In this case it might be rendered " the potsherd"—" at the entrance of the gate, The potsherd." It was the gate, before which did lie all the broken vessels, and the dirt and filth from the Temple. For this reason it may be that the *Targum* renders it here, " the gate of the dunghill."

Parkhurst, however, takes the word as it is in the text, and gives this version, " the gate of the burnings," so called because of the practice of burning children in the valley opposite the gate. See chap. vii. 31. All these names would properly designate the south gate.—*Ed.*

He says, *Enter into the valley of the son of Hinnom.* This valley was in the suburbs, and was called תפת, *Tophet,* as we shall hereafter see. It is thought that this name is derived from drums, because they did beat drums when infants were killed, lest their cry should excite any feeling of humanity. But we shall again say something on the etymology of this word. In this valley they were accustomed to sacrifice and offer their children by casting them into the fire. Many indeed performed this in a different way, by purifying their children and carrying them round the fire, so that they felt only the flame and escaped unhurt. But there were those who wished to shew their zeal above others, whose ambition drove them farther, and they killed their children and then burnt them. But of this matter I have spoken elsewhere, and I shall now only briefly notice it. This opinion is not what is commonly received; but it seems to me that it may be gathered from many parts of Scripture, that many killed their children, and that some only purified them. However this may have been, God justly abominated the sacrifice; for his will was that sacrifices should be offered only in one place. When any one offered a calf or a lamb in any other place than at Jerusalem, it was a spurious sacrifice; and the Jews ought to have followed what God had prescribed, and not to have done anything presumptuously, for obedience is ever better than any sacrifices.

But here there was a double crime; they left the Temple and sought to obtrude on God sacrifices against his expressed will; and then there was another crime still more atrocious, for they devoted their children to Baalim or to Baal, and not to the only true God. (I pass by now their slaughter and burning.) This then was the reason why the Prophet was commanded to go to this place. How detestable that service was to God appears clear from this, that the prophets give the name of hell to the valley of Hinnom, גיא הנם, *gia-enom.* And we know that at the time of Christ it was the common name for hell; and whenever Christ speaks of Gehenna, he uses the word according to its common acceptation at that time. The word has indeed been corrupted by the Greeks, for it is properly גיא הנם, *gia-enom.* But what does the word mean in the gospel? Hell itself; and whence was its origin? We indeed know how great and how incurable was the madness of those who gave themselves up to their own superstitions; for though the prophets strongly condemned the place, yet the people proceeded in their usual idolatry; it was therefore necessary to give the place a disgraceful name in order to render it more abominable.

It is now added, that the place was *by the entrance of the east gate.* As it was especially a celebrated gate, and as the sun, rising there, reminded them to behold the light which God had kindled for them in his law, it was a monstrous stupidity proudly to tread, as it were, under foot the law of God in so renowned a place, and to profane his worship, as though they openly wished to shew that they esteemed as nothing what God had commanded. If any still think that there is an allusion to the word חרש, *cheresh,* before used, I offer no opposition; that is, though this gate was indeed oriental, it was yet as it were an earthen gate.

He says, *Cry there,* or, proclaim with a clear voice, *the words which I shall speak to thee.* The Prophet no doubt said this expressly, in order to add more weight to his prophecy. He indeed did nothing but by God's command; but as his authority was not acknowledged by the Jews, he here testifies for their sakes that he would say nothing but what God himself would command. This preface then confirmed the authority of his prophecy, so that the Jews might not reject what he might say, as though it came from Jeremiah himself.

But a general doctrine may be hence gathered,—that ministers are to bring forward nothing but what they have learnt from God himself. For though Jeremiah was a great man and endued with excellent gifts, yet he was not to bring one word or a syllable as from himself: how great then must be the presumption of those who seek to be superior to him by bringing their inventions, and at the same time demand to be deemed oracles? This passage confirms the doctrine of Peter, who says, "He who speaks, let him speak the words of God." (1 Peter iv. 11.)

He now adds, *Hear ye the word of Jehovah.* This is a

confirmation of the former sentence. We hence see why it was said, *Cry*, or, with a clear voice proclaim, what I shall say to thee; it was, that they might know that he spake not according to his own ideas as a man, but that he was a celestial herald to proclaim what God commanded. *Hear*, he says, *ye kings of Judah and inhabitants of Jerusalem*. We see how the Prophet did not spare even kings, according to what God had before commanded him, that he should act boldly and shew no respect of persons, (chap. i. 8.) He then faithfully performed his office, as he did not flatter kings, and was not terrified by their dignity and power. But he addressed them first, and then the people, because they who had most grievously sinned, were made rightly to bear the first reproof. We hence see what that passage means, "Reprove mountains and chide hills," (Micah vi. 1;) and also this passage, "I have set thee over nations and kingdoms," (chap. i. 10:) for heavenly truth ought to bring under subjection, as Paul says, everything high in the world, so that all the pride of man may be subdued. (2 Cor. x. 5.) Kings indeed do very ill bear to be thus boldly treated; for they wish to be exempt from every law and to be free from every yoke. But if they now acknowledge not their subjection to God's word, they must at last come before his tribunal; and then they shall find how perversely they have abused their power. As to teachers, they ought, small and great, to teach after the example of Jeremiah; they ought to reprove and to rebuke, when necessary, without shewing any respect of persons.

Thus saith Jehovah of hosts, and the God of Israel, Behold, I am bringing an evil on this place, of which whosoever shall hear, tingle shall his ears. The prophetic word had more power when the Jews were brought to the very place where the event was exhibited. He might have said the same thing in the Temple or in the gate or in the palace of the king: but his prophecy would not have been so effectual. We indeed know how much tardiness there is in men in general; but so great was then the obstinacy of the Jews, that however forcibly the truth might have been set forth, yet it was received with so much indifference, that it was neglected. God then intended to shew to them, as it were, the event itself. He says, *Jehovah of hosts and the God of Israel;* and he used these words, that they might know, as we have stated elsewhere, that they had to do with God, whose power is dreaded even by angels. And in order to shake off their foolish boasting, that they were the children of Abraham,—" God," he says, " has sufficient power to chastise you, and the same is the God of Israel, whose name ye falsely and absurdly pretend to profess." These subjects I only in a brief manner handle, because I have explained them more fully elsewhere.

He says that such a calamity was nigh that place as would make the *ears to tingle:* when there is a violent noise, our ears are stunned, and there is at the same time a certain tingling or ringing. When a man is killed, or when ten or twelve men are slain, there is a dreadful cry; but in a great tumult occasioned by men perishing, such is the noise that it stuns in a manner the ears, like that which proceeds from cataracts; for the violent noise of the Nile, they say, causes some degree of deafness. So also the Prophet says here, *I am bringing,* says God, *a calamity on this place,* which shall not only terrify those who will hear of it, but also render them quite astonished, so that their *ears shall tingle,* as is the case when there is a violent and dreadful noise. The cause follows—

4. Because they have forsaken me, and have estranged this place, and have burnt incense in it unto other gods, whom neither they nor their fathers have known, nor the kings of Judah, and have filled this place with the blood of innocents;

5. They have built also the high places of Baal, to burn their sons with fire *for* burnt-offerings unto Baal, which I commanded not, nor spake *it,* neither came *it* into my mind.

4. Propterea quòd reliquerunt me et alienarunt locum hunc, et suffitum fecerunt in eo diis extraneis, quos non noverunt ipsi neque patres ipsorum, neque reges Jehudah; et impleverunt locum hunc sanguine innocentium;

5. Et extruxerunt excelsa (ædificarunt excelsa) ipsi Baal, ad comburendum filios suos igne in holocaustum ipsi Baal; quod non mandavi et non loquutus sum, et non ascendit super cor meum (*vel,* in cor meum.)

The reason is given why God would so severely deal with that place. We indeed know that hypocrites are ever ready with their answer; as soon as God threatens them, they bark and bring forward their evasions. The Prophet then shews that the judgment announced would be just, lest the Jews should pretend that it was extreme.

God first complains that he had been forsaken by them, because they had changed the worship which had been prescribed in his Law. And this is what ought to be carefully considered; for no one would have willingly confessed what Jeremiah charged upon them all; they would have said,—"We have not forsaken God, for we are the children of Abraham; but what we wish to do is to add to his worship; and why should it be deemed a reproach to us, if we are not content with our own simple form of worship, and add various other forms? and we worship God not only in the Temple, but also in this place; and further, we do not spare our own children." But God shews by one expression that these were frivolous evasions; for he is not acknowledged except what he orders and commands is obediently received. Let us know, that God is forsaken as soon as men turn aside from his pure word, and that all are apostates who turn here and there, and do not follow what God approves.

Then he says that they had *alienated the place.* God had consecrated to himself the whole of Judea: he would not indeed have sacrifices offered to him in every place; but when the Jews worshipped him, as they were taught by Moses and the prophets, the whole land was as it were an altar and a temple to him. Then God complains that his authority in that part of the suburbs was taken away; as though he had said,—"The whole of Judea is my right and my jurisdiction, and Jerusalem is the royal palace in which I dwell; but ye, deluded beings, do by force take away my right and transfer it to another, as though one gave to a robber a place nigh a royal residence." Thus God justly complains that they had *alienated* that *place.*[1]

But we must remember the reason, which immediately

[1] Perhaps the idea would be better expressed, if we were to say, "They had alienized the place," or heathenized it, made it a heathen place. To alienate is to transfer a right or property from one to another. This was indeed true, for they separated as it were the place from God and transferred it to heathen deities. But the idea here seems to be, that they made the place heathenish: "and have heathenized this place." "Alienated" is the *Septuagint;* "made it alien," the *Vulgate;* "polluted," the *Syriac;* and "defiled," the *Targum.—Ed.*

follows, because they had *burned incense* to Baal. They pretended, no doubt, the name of God; but yet it was a most preposterous superstition, when they worshipped inferior gods, as the Papists do at this day. The word Baal is sometimes used in the singular number by the prophets, and sometimes in the plural: but what is Baal? a patron. They were not content with one patron, but every one desired a patron for himself: hence under the words Baal and Baalim, the prophets characterized all fictitious modes of worship: when they worshipped God's name, they blended the worship of patrons, who had not been made known to them; hence he adds, *They have made incense in it to foreign gods.* He afterwards says, that these foreign gods were such as neither they nor their fathers nor their kings knew. By saying that they were gods unknown to their fathers as well as to themselves and to their kings, he no doubt calls their attention to the doctrine of the law, and to the many certain proofs by which they had found that he was the only true God.

The Jews might have raised such an objection as the Papists do at this day,—that their modes of worship were not devised in their time, but that they had derived them from their ancestors. But God regarded as nothing those kings and the fathers, who had long before degenerated from true and genuine religion. It must be here observed, that true knowledge is connected with verity: for they who had first contrived new forms of worship, doubtless followed their own foolish imaginations; as when any one in the present day asks the Papists, why they weary themselves so much with their superstitions, good intention is ever their shield,—"O, we think that this is pleasing to God." Therefore rightly does God here repudiate their inventions as wholly vain, for they possess nothing solid or permanent. At the same time, he by implication condemns the Jews for rejecting his law, whose authority had been established among them, so that they ought not to have entertained any doubt: for it would have been the greatest ingratitude to say, "We know not who introduced the Law!" God had indeed sanctioned the law by so many miracles, that it could not have been disputed; and they had also found by many evidences and proofs that he was the only true God. He had then been known by their fathers as well as by their kings, even by David and by all his godly successors. Hence their crime was exaggerated, by seeking for themselves foreign gods.

Now we also see how foolishly the Papists lay hold on this passage and similar passages, in order to commend their abominations by the pretext of antiquity: for vain are their disguises when they say, " O, we have been thus taught by our ancestors, and we have the authority of kings." But the Prophet here does not speak of fathers indiscriminately; but by fathers he means those who had embraced the true and pure worship of God, as they had been taught by the law; and those kings were alone worthy of imitation, who had faithfully worshipped God according to the doctrine of the law: and thus he excludes all those fathers and kings who had degenerated from the law of Moses.

He at last adds, that that place was *filled with the blood of innocents;* for there they killed their children. And by this circumstance Jeremiah again amplifies the wickedness of the people; for they had not only despised God and his law, but also cruelly destroyed their innocent infants; and thus he proved them guilty not only of impiety and profaneness in vitiating the worship of God, but also of brutal and barbarous savageness in not sparing innocent blood.

PRAYER.

Grant, Almighty God, that since thou hast been pleased to shew to us the way in which we cannot err, provided we obey thee,—O grant, that we may render ourselves really teachable and ready to obey, and never undertake anything but what we know is approved by thee, nor turn aside on the right hand or on the left; but continue in that form of worship which thou hast prescribed to us in thy word, so that we may be able to bear witness, not only before the world, but before thee and the holy angels, that we obediently follow thee; and may we never blend anything of our own, but with submissive minds worship thee alone, and strive to render ourselves wholly subject to thee, until having at length rendered to thee due service through the whole course of our life, we shall reach that blessed rest which thy Son has procured for us by his own blood.—Amen.

Lecture Seventy-Fourth.

6. Therefore, behold, the days come, saith the Lord, that this place shall no more be called Tophet, nor The valley of the son of Hinnom, but The valley of slaughter.

6. Propterea ecce dies veniunt, dicit Jehova, et non (*hoc est*, quibus non) vocabitur locus hic amplius Thopheth et vallis filii Hinnon, sed vallis interfectionis.

WE saw in the last Lecture that the Prophet was sent by God's bidding to the house of the potter, that he might there take an earthen bottle, carry it to Tophet, and there explain the judgment of God, which was nigh at hand on account of his worship being violated. And he shewed why the Jews deserved reproof, even because they made incense to Baal, built groves and high places for themselves, and committed their sons and daughters to the fire: they were not only profane towards God, but also cruel towards innocent souls. Now, lest they pretended an excuse, he also added, that such a thing never came to God's mind; and this is worthy of notice, because God by this one expression fulminates against all those inventions with which men delight themselves. As then there is no command, it follows that whatever is thus attempted is frivolous and useless.

He now denounces punishment, *The days are coming*, or shall come, *in which this place shall no more be called Tophet, nor The valley of the son of Hinnom, but The valley of slaughter.* This seemed incredible to the Jews; for they had chosen that place for themselves to perform their superstitions: they thought therefore that a great part of their safety depended on their false worship.

As to the word Tophet, some think that it is to be taken simply for hell, or for eternal death; but this cannot by any means be admitted. More probable is their opinion who derive it from תף, *teph,* which means a drum; for they think that they did beat drums when infants were killed, that their cries might not be heard. But as this is only a conjecture, I know not whether another reason may be given. Some derive the word from יפה, *iphe,* which signifies to be decorous or beautiful; and this etymology has something apparently in its favour. And perhaps it ought to be so taken in Job xvii. 6, where the holy man complains that he was become a proverb, and that he had been תפת, *Tophet,* in the presence of all. There are indeed some who explain the word there as signifying something monstrous, and thus take it in a bad sense. But it seems rather to have been put in contrast with the former clause,—he had been a pleasant spectacle, but he was now become detestable. But they who take the word there as meaning hell, do so entirely without any reason, for that Job perished, seeing and knowing his perdition, as they say, is a forced view. I doubt not then but that he said, that he had been תפת, *Tophet;* that is, an object of joy and of praise, but that he was then a sad and mournful spectacle. And it is certain that this name, תפת, *Tophet,* was given to the valley of Hinnom, because of the hilarity and joy which thence arose to the people; for they thought that God was propitious to them, when they so sedulously offered there their sacrifices, and yet they provoked his wrath. Then Tophet is to be taken in a good sense, when we regard the origin of the word. It is indeed true that in Isaiah xxx. 33, Tophet is to be taken for Gehenna; but it may be that the prophets had now begun so to execrate the place as to call hell indiscriminately Gehinnon and Tophet; for the word Gehenna, as we have stated elsewhere, had its origin from the same place; it is indeed corrupted, but its origin is not doubtful. Now, the reason why the prophets and other faithful men called the place hell, was plainly this,—because the devil reigned in that place, when God's worship became vitiated, and the whole of true religion was subverted; and especially, because superstition became so deeply fixed in the hearts of the people, that it could not be rooted up except by an extraordinary force and power.

However this may have been, we may conclude from this passage, as well as from other passages, that this name was given on account of the joy experienced there, even because they thought themselves altogether happy, as God was pacified towards them. But what does Jeremiah say? This place shall be no more *called Tophet, nor The valley of the son of*

Hinnom, but The valley of slaughter. This seemed, as I have said, incredible to the Jews. But it however behoved the Prophet boldly to declare what was to be. It afterwards follows,—

7. And I will make void the counsel of Judah and Jerusalem in this place; and I will cause them to fall by the sword before their enemies, and by the hands of them that seek their lives; and their carcases will I give to be meat for the fowls of the heaven, and for the beasts of the earth.	7. Et exinaniam consilium Jehudah et Jerusalem in loco hoc, et prosternam eos in gladio coram inimicis ipsorum, et in manu quærentium animam eorum, et ponam (dabo) cadaver eorum in cibum volucri cœli (*hoc est,* avibus cœli, *est enallage*) et bestiæ (*hoc est,* bestiis) terræ.

This amplification farther exasperated the minds of the people,—that they in vain trusted that this place would be to them a fortress. For, as we have already stated, they had persuaded themselves that it was abundantly sufficient to reconcile them with God, when they spared not their own children, and so zealously performed their acts of worship. And hypocrites are commonly inflated with this presumption, for they prefer what pleases them to what pleases God; they regard not what the law bids, what God approves, but they adore their own inventions. Since then almost all the superstitious are filled with such a presumption, God here rightly declares, that he would *make void their counsels.*[1]

It is indeed certain that there is neither wisdom nor counsel in deluded men, while they thus devise new and frivolous modes of worship, for these are sheer mummeries. But we ought to observe what Paul says in Col. ii. 23, that all the fictions which men devise for themselves have in them some appearance of wisdom; for we know that wherever our imagination may carry us, we think ourselves wise, and that whatever God prescribes becomes insipid to us. Then the Prophet concedes "counsel," though improperly, to frivolous and vain inventions, but not without reason, for experience teaches us sufficiently, that men ever take great delight in their superstitions, for they wish to subject God as it were to their own will. He then says, by way of concession, that the

[1] "The plain meaning is, I will frustrate all your plots and projects, whereby you think to escape and to secure yourselves, and make them as vain and empty as this earthen bottle is."—*Gataker.*

counsels of the whole people, especially of the city Jerusalem, would be made *void*, which was above others the teacher of errors, while yet the doctrine of the law ought especially to have prevailed there. And it may be also that there is an allusion to that word בקבק, *bekbek*, which we have before seen, and which the Prophet will repeat again, for it means to make void or empty, though some think it to be a factitious word, because the sound, bekbek, is produced while the bottle is emptied. However this may be, the allusion is still sufficiently striking.

He afterwards adds, *And I will lay them prostrate by the sword before their enemies, and by the hand of those who seek their life.* In this second part, the Prophet intimates that the hatred entertained by their enemies towards the Jews would not be common. Wars are carried on sometimes in such a way, that the conquerors are satisfied with the spoils; but the Prophet intimates, that the cruelty of their enemies would be such, that they would seek the life of the whole people, and delight in slaughter; as though he had said, that they would be deadly enemies and altogether implacable. He will again repeat these words, and in the same sense.

He then adds, *I will give your carcase to be meat to the birds of heaven, and to the beasts of the field.*[1] We have said elsewhere that it is deemed a punishment inflicted by heaven when the carcases of the dead remain unburied; for it is the last office of humanity to bury the dead. And this is a distinction which God would have to be between men and brute animals, for animals have not the honour of a burial. It has also been ever granted as a singular privilege to men to be buried, in order to set forth the hope of resurrection. When, therefore, a burial is denied, it is a proof of extreme dishonour. It has indeed often happened that the saints have been without a burial; but temporal punishment is ever turned to salvation to God's children. As to the reprobate it must be deemed a judgment from God, when he casts away their carcases, as then there is no difference between them and animals. But I have treated this subject

[1] The words are in the singular number—"The bird of heaven and the beast of the field."—*Ed.*

more fully elsewhere, and I shall not proceed with it now. It follows—

8. And I will make this city desolate, and an hissing; every one that passeth thereby shall be astonished and hiss, because of all the plagues thereof.	8. Et ponam urbem hanc in stuporem et sibilum; quisquis transibit per eam stupebit et sibilabit super omnem plagam ejus.

Jeremiah proceeds with his denunciation, and it was necessary for him to add this amplification, that he might penetrate into their hard and perverse hearts; for had he employed only a single sentence, or a common mode of speaking, in describing their calamity and the ruin of the city, they would not have been at all moved. Hence he enlarges on the subject, and advances with greater vehemence, and always speaks in the person of God, that his denunciation might have greater weight.

I will set, &c. Here is to be noticed a second reason; for it was not enough that a calamity should be denounced on the Jews, without adding this, that it was inflicted by God's hand, and that thus the punishment of their wickedness was just. Then he says, I will *set this city for an astonishment;* for so in this place the word שמה *sheme* ought to be rendered, inasmuch as the reason afterwards follows, *astonished shall be whosoever shall pass through it.*[1] He adds also, *for a hissing*, which is rather a mark of detestation than of scorn; yet the desolation of the whole land, and also the ruin of the holy city in which God had chosen an habitation for himself, might have filled all with terror, and ought justly to have done so. *Whosoever*, he says, *shall pass through shall be astonished, and shall hiss on account of all her stroke;*[2] for it was not to be a common calamity, but

[1] *Blayney* gives the same meaning,—

"And I will make this city an object of astonishment and of hissing." The *Vulgate* and the *Syriac* are the same; but the *Septuagint* and the *Targum* have "desolation" instead of "astonishment." The word שמה signifies both, as in Hebrew the same word often expresses the cause and the effect: desolation is the cause, astonishment is the effect. The primary meaning is what is given mostly by the *Septuagint*, and very seldom the secondary. The literal rendering of the sentence is,—

"And I will set this city for an astonishment and for a hissing."—*Ed.*

[2] *Plagam;* the original word is considered to be in the plural number, and means strokes, stripes, scourges, but not plagues in the usual sense of the word—pestilences: it may be rendered smitings, or more properly, in-

one in which might be seen God's dreadful judgment. It follows—

9. And I will cause them to eat the flesh of their sons, and the flesh of their daughters, and they shall eat every one the flesh of his friend, in the siege and straitness wherewith their enemies, and they that seek their lives, shall straiten them.

9. Et pascam eos carne filiorum suorum et carne filiarum suarum, et vir carnem proximi sui comedent (*hoc est,* singuli comedent carnem proximi sui) in afflictione et angustia, qua angent (*vel,* constringent) eos hostes ipsorum, et qui quærent animam ipsorum.

Here the Prophet goes farther—that so atrocious would be the calamity, that even fathers and mothers would not abstain from their children, but would devour their flesh. This was indeed monstrous. It has sometimes happened that husbands, in a state of extreme despondency, have killed their wives and children, (anxious to exempt them from the lust of enemies,) or have kindled a fire in the midst of the forum, to cast their children and wives on the pile, and afterwards to die themselves; but it was more barbarous and brutal for a father to eat the flesh of his son. The Prophet then describes an unusual vengeance of God, which could not be classed among the calamities which usually happen to mankind.

We know that this was also done in the last siege of that city; for Josephus shews at large that mothers in a brutal manner slew their children, and that they so lay in wait for one another that they snatched at anything to eat. This was also an evidence of God's dreadful vengeance.

But it was no wonder that God visited in such an awful manner the sins of those who had in such various ways, and for so long a time, provoked him: for if we compare the Jews with other nations, we shall find that their impiety, and ingratitude, and perverseness, exceeded the crimes of all nations. Then justly did God inflict such a punishment, which even at this day cannot be referred to without horror. The whole indeed is to be ascribed to his judgment; for it was he who fed[1] the fathers with the flesh of their children;

flictions. It occurs three times in Deut. xxviii. 59, and is rendered plagues, but it ought to be smitings or inflictions; and so here, "on account of all her inflictions."—*Ed.*

[1] The expression, according to the Hebrew, is, "I will cause them to eat." What a punishment! Those who sacrificed their children to their

for as they had sacrificed their sons and their daughters to demons, as before stated, so it was necessary that the vengeance of God should be openly pointed out as by the finger. This was done when God imprinted marks on the bodies of children, which even the blind could not but perceive.

He adds, *In the tribulation*[1] *and straitness with which their enemies shall straiten them.* We have said that those who had been long besieged, and were not able to resist, have been often reduced to the necessity to freeing their wives, or their children, or themselves, from dishonour; but to protract life in the manner here mentioned was altogether brutal. It follows—

10. Then shalt thou break the bottle in the sight of the men that go with thee.	10. Et conteras lagenam in oculis virorum qui proficiscentur (*vel,* qui profecti fuerint) tecum.

Jeremiah summoned witnesses, that the confirmation of the prophecy might be more fully attested to the people. With regard to the history of this transáction we may add, that he was first sent to the house of the potter, from whence he procured the bottle; he then went to Tophet, and there spoke against their impious and corrupt superstitions; and at last, to seal the prophecy, he broke the bottle in the presence of the witnesses whom he had brought with him. And we have said that it was necessary thus to deal with a people, not only ignorant and stupid, but, which is worse, perverse and obstinate. There was not only importance in the sign, that they might thence learn the doom of the city and of the whole land, but it was also a solemn sealing of the prophecy; and on this account he was commanded to break the vessel, even that he might shew, by a visible act, the near approach of God's vengeance, of which the Jews had no apprehension. It follows—

11. And shalt say unto them, Thus saith the Lord	11. Et dices ad eos, Sic dicit Jehova exercituum, Ita confringam populum hunc

idols were judicially brought to such straits as to be driven to eat their own children! God often punishes men in a way that corresponds with their sin. Through superstitious madness the Jews willingly offered their children in sacrifice to demons; and through the extreme cravings of hunger they were constrained to eat their own children!—*Ed.*

[1] The word is מצור, which means a siege, as well as tribulation or distress; and the former is the most suitable word here; and so it is rendered by the *Targum* and the early versions, except the *Syriac.*—*Ed.*

of hosts, Even so will I break this people, and this city, as *one* breaketh a potter's vessel, that cannot be made whole again: and they shall bury *them* in Tophet, till *there be* no place to bury.

et urbem hanc, sicut quis confringit vas figuli, (*hoc est*, vas testaceum; *vel*, vas fragile, figulinum,) quod non poterit reparari amplius: et in Thopheth sepelientur; quia non erit locus ad sepeliendum (*ad verbum*, à non loco ad sepeliendum.)

The Prophet again confirms what he had shewn by the external symbol, and he does this by a new command from God. We know that signs are wholly useless when the word of God does not shine forth, as we see that superstitious men always practise many ceremonies, but they are only histrionic acts. But God never commanded his prophets to shew any sign without adding doctrine to it. This is what we see was done on this occasion; for Jeremiah spoke against impious superstitions, and as a celestial herald denounced punishment; he then sealed the prophecy by breaking the bottle, and a repetition of the doctrine follows again, *Thus shalt thou say to them.* This is not said of the Prophet's companions, the pronoun is without an antecedent, but the whole people are the persons referred to.

Thus saith Jehovah, I will so break this people and this city. He mentions the city, in which they thought they had an impregnable fortress, because the temple of God was there. But as they had profaned the temple and polluted the city with their crimes, Jeremiah reminded them that no confidence or hope was to be placed in the city. Then he says, *As one breaks a vessel which cannot be repaired,* &c. Here again he shews that they were wholly to perish, so as no more to rise again. We indeed know that sometimes those who are most grievously afflicted retain some remnants of strength, and are at length restored to their former vigour; but the Prophet shews that the approaching calamity would be wholly irremediable. It is no objection to say, that God afterwards restored the people, and that the city and the temple were rebuilt, for all this was nothing to the ungodly men of that age, as their memory wholly perished. A curse and God's vengeance remained on the heads of those who thus continued obstinate in their wickedness; and hence those who returned from exile are said in Psalm cii. 19, to have been a people created again, as though they rose up as new men, "A people, who shall be created, shall praise the Lord."

He then says, *Buried shall they be in Tophet, for there will be no place elsewhere.*[1] They had chosen that place at a time when they thought that they had some evidence of God's favour, and a cause for joy; but he declares that that place would be filled with dead bodies, for they would flee in great numbers into the city, which afterwards would become so full of dead bodies that no room for burial could be found except in Tophet. It follows—

12. Thus will I do unto this place, saith the Lord, and to the inhabitants thereof, and *even* make this city as Tophet.	12. Sic faciam loco huic, dicit Jehova, et incolis ejus; et ad ponendum (et ponam) urbem hanc sicut Thopheth.

As he had said before that the valley would be the place of slaughter, that thence it might take its name, so now he declares the same as to the city; "As then Tophet shall be the valley of slaughter, so shall Jerusalem be."[2] They were no doubt kindled into rage (as we shall see in the next chapter) on hearing this prophecy; but yet God purposed, however irreclaimable and refractory they were, to let them know what was approaching, and though they did not believe the words of the Prophet, God touched and even deeply wounded their consciences, so that before the event came they were miserable. For the same purpose he adds—

13. And the houses of Jerusalem, and the houses of the kings of Judah, shall be defiled as the place of Tophet, because of all the houses upon whose roofs they have burnt incense unto all the host of heaven, and have poured out drink-offerings unto other gods.	13. Et erunt domus Hierusalem et domus regum Jehudah, sicut locus Thopheth immundæ; ad omnes domos in quibus suffitum fecerunt super tecta eorum universæ militiæ cœlorum, et libarunt libamen diis alienis.

He describes, as I have said, more at large what he had briefly expressed, for he had spoken of the city; but as the

[1] This is evidently the meaning, and not that given in our version. See note in vol. i. p. 415.—*Ed.*

[2] The ellipsis in the last clause is what often occurs in Hebrew; it may be supplied in our language by *that*,—

"Thus will I do to this place, saith Jehovah, and to its inhabitants, and *that* to make this city like Tophet."

The full sentence is, "and thus will I do to make," &c.—*Ed.*

belief of that was difficult, he now enumerates particulars, as though he had said, that Jerusalem was a wide city and splendidly built, for there were there many large and elegant houses, and the royal palaces, yet he says, that all these things would not prevent God to demolish the whole city. And this deserves particular notice, for we know that Satan dazzles our eyes whenever he suggests anything that gives a hope of defence, but what God threatens we think is vain, and as it were fabulous, or at least produces no effect on us. Since then so gross an hypocrisy prevailed in the hearts of the people, the Prophet rightly tried to shake off from them whatever might deceive them.

Hence he says, *The houses of Jerusalem*, &c.—these were many and splendid—*and the houses of the kings of Judah*, their palaces either within or without the city *shall be as the place of Tophet;* that is, no house shall be exempt from slaughter, and no palace shall protect its inhabitants. They shall be *unclean*, he says, that is, on account of dead bodies, for men slain would be found everywhere; and this is, as it is well known, often mentioned in Scripture as a pollution or defilement. *With regard to all the houses;* some read, "On account of all the houses," and ל, *lamed*, is often a causal preposition. But it seems rather to be taken here as explanatory; and hence I render the words, *With regard to all the houses*, so that the Prophet speaks of all the houses *in which they made incense.*[1] As then there was no house free from sacrilege, he says that God's vengeance would penetrate into all houses without any exception.

He says also, *On the roofs*, with the view of condemning them for their effrontery; for they raised their baseness as a standard, that it might be seen at a distance. They indeed thought that God was delighted with such a service; but how came they to entertain such a foolish persuasion,

[1] "On account of all the houses," is the *Septuagint* and the *Targum;* "all the houses," is the *Vulgate* and the *Syriac*, being put in apposition with "the houses of Jerusalem," &c.

The words which follow are literally,—"which they have burned incense on their roofs," which we properly render in our language, "on whose roofs they have burned incense;" but the *Welsh* is literally the Hebrew, *Y rhai yr arogldarthasant ar eu pennau,*—"which they incensed on their roofs;" but "incensed" in this sense is not used.—*Ed.*

except through their neglect and contempt of the law, and also through a mad presumption in giving more credit to their own fictions than to certain truth. The Prophet then justly condemns them, for they had cast off all shame, and went up to the roofs of their houses, that their doings might be more open. Then he mentions the *whole host of heaven;* and says further, that they had *poured a libation to foreign gods.* We see that many kinds of superstitions prevailed among the people; for he spoke of Baal in the singular number, he mentioned also Baalim, patrons, and he now adds, the whole host of heaven; that is, the sun, the moon, and all the stars.

We hence see that the Jews kept no limits as to their sacrileges, which is usually the case with all the ungodly; for as soon as men begin to turn aside from the pure and genuine worship of God, they sink into the lowest depths. It is then this wantonness that the Prophet now refers to, when he intimates that their various forms of worship were so increased, that they had devised as many gods as there are stars in heaven; which is similar to what is said elsewhere, "According to the number of thy cities, O Judah, are thy gods," (chap. ii. 28; xi. 13.)

14. Then came Jeremiah from Tophet, whether the Lord had sent him to prophesy; and he stood in the court of the Lord's house, and said to all the people,

15. Thus saith the Lord of hosts, the God of Israel, Behold, I will bring upon this city, and upon all her towns, all the evil that I have pronounced against it, because they have hardened their necks, that they might not hear my words.

14. Et venit (reversus est) Jeremias é Thopheth, quo miserat eum Jehova ad prophetandum; et stetit in atrio domus Jehovæ, et dixit ad totum populum,

15. Sic dicit Jehova exercituum, Deus Israel, Ecce ego adduco super urbem hanc et super omnes urbes ejus omne malum quod loquutus sum super eam, quia obduraverunt cervicem suam, ut non audirent sermones meos.

Jeremiah had been led to the very place, when he foretold the punishment, which was nigh at hand, on account of the superstitions of Tophet or of the valley of Hinnom. That his doctrine might be more efficacious, God intended that he should preach before the very altar and in the very valley, then well known for ungodly and false modes of worship. He says now that he went to the Temple and delivered there the same message. We hence learn how great must have been the stupidity and indifference of the people, for the repetition of the prophecy was not unnecessary. For as God knew that the Jews were extremely tardy and slow, he caused them to be warned twice by his servant, and in two different places.

Jeremiah, it is said, *returned from Tophet, where God had sent him to prophesy;* which last words were added, that we may not suppose that he without reason preached in the valley of Hinnom. God then commanded Jeremiah to denounce there, as it were in the very place, on the Jews their own destruction. *And he stood*, it is added, *in the court of Jehovah's house.* As it was not lawful for the people to enter into the Temple, they usually assembled in the court, which was a part of the Temple. Then Jeremiah *stood* there; for he had to speak, not to a few, or in a corner, but to the whole people, and to make them witnesses of his prophecy. But we read here nothing new; for, as it has been stated, he was bidden to declare twice the same thing—the approaching calamity; and he was so bidden, because the Jews were so hardened, that they could not easily be moved. That he connects other cities with Jerusalem is not to be wondered at; he thereby intimates, that the whole land was guilty before God, and that therefore desolation was near at hand, as to all the towns and cities; as though he had said, "God will not spare Jerusalem, though it has been hitherto his sanctuary; but as lesser cities are not innocent, they shall also feel the hand of God together with Jerusalem."

The reason is subjoined, *Because they have hardened* their neck. He again confirms what we have before observed,—that they had fallen, not through ignorance, but through perverseness; for they had learned with sufficient clearness from the law what was right, and they had also been often warned by the prophets. Hence then their wickedness appeared and their untameable spirit, for they had heard the sound doctrine of the law, and had many to warn them.

Now this passage teaches us that there is no pardon left for us, when we, as it were, avowedly reject the yoke of God. And this ought to be carefully noticed, for we see how difficult it is to subdue men, even when they confess that the word of God is what they hear. Since then there is in all mankind an innate perverseness, that hardly one in a hundred allows himself to be ruled by God's word, it behoves us seriously to consider what is here said,—that they are unworthy of mercy who harden their neck. Hence it is said in Psalm xcv. 8, "Harden not your hearts like your fathers." And a clearer definition follows, *That they might not hear my words.* Though there be hardness in all mortals, yet when the doctrine of salvation is made known and not received, then a greater impiety and pride shew themselves; for in that case, men hear God speaking, and yet rob him of his authority. It then follows, that the more clearly God makes known his truth, the less ground of excuse there is; for then especially comes to light the impiety of men, and their disdain seems incapable of being subdued.

PRAYER.

Grant, Almighty God, that since thou hast been pleased to prescribe a rule for us, by which we may truly and purely worship thee,—O grant, that we may follow this plain rule, and never indulge our own imaginations, nor trifle with thee through our own fancies or through the foolish wisdom of our flesh, but continue in thy law, and in the doctrine which thine only-begotten Son, our Lord, has delivered to us, so that we may advance more and more in the knowledge of that glory, the foretaste of which thou givest us now, until we shall at length fully and perfectly enjoy it, when we shall be gathered into that celestial kingdom, which thy Son has procured for us by his own blood.—Amen.

A TRANSLATION

OF

CALVIN'S VERSION OF JEREMIAH.

CHAPTERS I.—XIX.

CHAPTER I.

1 The words of Jeremiah, the son of Hilkiah, *one* of the priests who
2 were in Anathoth, in the land of Benjamin: even the word of
Jehovah came to him in the days of Josiah, the son of Amon,
3 the king of Judah, in the tenth year of his reign; and it came
in the days of Jehoiakim, the son of Josiah, the king of Judah,
to the end of the eleventh year of Zedekiah, the son of Josiah,
the king of Judah, to the transmigration of Jerusalem in the
fifth month.

4 And the word of Jehovah came to me, saying,—

5 Before I formed thee in the womb, I knew thee;
Before thou camest forth from the womb, I sanctified thee;
A prophet to the nations have I made thee.

6 And I said,—
Ah! Lord Jehovah,
Behold, I know not how to speak, for I am a child.

7 And Jehovah said to me,—
Say not, I am a child;
For wheresoever I send thee, thou shalt go;
And whatsoever I command thee, thou shalt say:
8 Fear not their face, for I am with thee,
To deliver thee, saith Jehovah.

9 And Jehovah extended his hand and touched my mouth;
and Jehovah said to me,—
Behold, I have put my words in thy mouth;
10 See, I have set thee to-day
Over nations and over kingdoms,
To pull down and to destroy,
To root up and to demolish,
To build and to plant. (i. 47)

11 Then the word of Jehovah came to me, saying, What seest

thou, Jeremiah? And I said, The rod of a watcher *is what* I
12 see. Then Jehovah said to me, Thou hast rightly seen, for I
watch over my word to do it.
13 And the word of Jehovah came to me again, saying, What
seest thou? And I said, A pot boiling *is what* I see; its face
14 is towards the north. And Jehovah said to me,—

From the north shall break forth an evil
On all the inhabitants of the land:
15 For behold, I am calling all the families
Of the kingdoms of the north, saith Jehovah;
And they shall come, *and* set shall each his throne,
At the entrance of the gates of Jerusalem,
And on all its walls around,
And on all the cities of Judah:
16 And I will execute my judgments on them
For all their wickedness;
Because they have forsaken me,
And have burnt incense to strange gods,
And bowed down to the works of their own hands. (i. 58)

17 Thou then, gird thy loins and arise,
And speak to them whatsoever I command thee;
Fear not their face,
Lest I dismay thee before them.
18 And I, behold I have made thee this day
A fortified city, an iron pillar,
And a brazen wall, as to the whole land,
Against the kings of Judah,
Against his princes, against his priests,
Against the people of the land:
19 And they shall fight with thee,
But shall not prevail over thee,
For with thee am I, saith Jehovah, to deliver thee.

CHAPTER II.

1 And the word of Jehovah came to me, saying,—
2 Go and cry in the ears of Jerusalem,
Saying, Thus saith Jehovah,—
I remember thee for *my* kindness to thine youth
And *my* love at thy espousal,
When thou didst follow me in the desert,
In a land not sown. (i. 70)
3 Holiness *was* Israel to Jehovah,
The first-fruits of his increase:
Whosoever devour him shall be punished,
Evil shall ccme upon them, saith Jehovah.

4 Hear the word of Jehovah, ye house of Jacob,
And all the families of the house of Israel:
5 Thus saith Jehovah,—
What iniquity did your fathers find in me?
For they alienated themselves from me,
And walked after vanity, and became vain; (i. 75)
6 And they said not, "Where is Jehovah,
Who brought us out of the land of Egypt,
And led us through the wilderness,
In a land waste and rugged,
In a land horrible and deadly,
In a land through which none passed,
And in which no man dwelt?" (i. 79)
7 And I brought you into a fertile land,
To eat its fruit and its abundance;
But ye entered and polluted my land,
And my heritage have ye made an abomination:
8 The priests said not, "Where is Jehovah?"
And they who handled the law, knew not me;
And the pastors dealt treacherously with me,
And the prophets prophesied by Baal,
And after things which did not profit, they walked.

9 Therefore still will I contend with you, saith Jehovah;
And with your children's children will I contend.
10 For pass over to the isles of Chittim, and see;
And to Kedar send, and consider diligently;
And see whether such a thing as this has been done—
11 Has a nation changed its gods,
Though they are no gods?
Yet my people have changed their glory
Unto that which does not profit.
12 Be astonished, ye heavens, at this, and terrified,
Be ye wholly desolated, saith Jehovah: (i. 92)
13 Surely, two evils have my people done,—
Me have they forsaken, the fountain of living waters,
And dug have they for themselves cisterns,
Broken cisterns, which hold no waters!

14 Is Israel a servant? Is he one born in the house?
Why is he become a prey?
15 Over him roar the lions,
They have raised their voice;
They have made his land waste;
His cities are burnt up,
Without an inhabitant.
16 Even the children of Noph and Thaphanes
Do break thy crown.

17 Hast thou not done this for thyself,
By forsaking Jehovah thy God,
While he was leading thee in the way?
18 And now what hast thou to do in the way to Egypt,
That thou mightest drink the waters of the Nile?
And what hast thou to do in the way to Assyria,
That thou mightest drink of the water of the river?
19 Chastise thee shall thine own wickedness,
And thy apostasies, they shall punish thee;
And thou shalt understand and know,
That it is an evil and a bitter thing for thee
To have forsaken Jehovah thy God,
And that my fear has not been in thee,
Saith the Lord, Jehovah of hosts.

20 For of old have I broken thy yoke,
Have I burst thy bands;
But thou hast said, "I will not serve;"
For on every high hill and under every shady tree
Hast thou rambled like a harlot. (i. 107)
21 I indeed planted thee a choice vine,
Altogether a good seed;
How then art thou turned to me
A degenerated foreign vine!
22 Even though thou washest thyself with nitre,
And multipliest to thee the herb of the fuller;
Yet imprinted is thine iniquity
Before my face, saith the Lord Jehovah.
23 How canst thou say, "I am not polluted,
After Baalim have I not gone?"
See thy ways in the valley,
Know what thou hast done,—
Thou swift dromedary, traversing her ways,—
24 A wild she-ass, used to the desert,
In her own lust snuffing up the wind she meets with:
Who can thence bring her back?
Whosoever seeks her, needs not weary himself;
In her month will he find her. (i. 118)
25 Keep thy foot from being unshod,
And thy throat from thirst:
Yet thou hast said, "It is all over;
No, for I have loved strangers,
And after them will I go."
26 As there is shame to a thief when caught,
So ashamed shall be the house of Israel,
Their kings and their princes,
Their priests and their prophets,—
27 Who say to the wood, "My father art thou;"

And to the stone, "Thou hast begotten me:"
For they have turned to me the back, not the face;
But in the time of their calamity they say,
"Arise and save us."
28 But where are thy gods,
Which thou hast made for thyself?
Let them arise, if they can save thee
In the time of thy calamity;
For according to the number of thy cities
Have been thy gods, O Judah!
29 Why do ye contend with me?
Ye have all dealt perfidiously with me, saith Jehovah.
30 In vain have I chastised your children;
Correction they received not;
Devoured has the sword your prophets,
As a destroying lion.

31 O generation! see ye the word of Jehovah;
Have I been a desert to Israel, or a land of darkness?
Wherefore have my people said,—
"We have ruled, we will come no more to thee." (i. 135)
32 Can a maid forget her ornaments,
A spouse her attire?
But my people have forgotten me,
Days without number.
33 Why trimmest thou thy ways to seek love?
Thou hast even thus taught wickedness by thy ways.
34 Even in thy skirts is found
The blood of the souls of the poor innocents;
Not in digging under have they been found,
But on account of all these things: (i. 143)
35 Yet thou hast said, "Surely I am clean;
Only let his fury depart from me."
Behold I will contend with thee in judgment,
Because thou hast said, "I have not sinned."
36 Why ramblest thou so much to change thy ways?
Even of Egypt shalt thou be ashamed,
As thou hast been ashamed of Assyria.
37 Even now for this thou shalt go forth,
And thine hands on thine head;
For abhorred hath Jehovah thy confidences,
And in them thou shalt not prosper. (i. 151)

CHAPTER III.

1 It is said, when a man puts away his wife,
And she goes from him to another man,

Shall he return to her again?
Would not the land be thus greatly polluted?
But thou hast played the harlot with many friends;
Yet return to me, saith Jehovah.
2 Raise thine eyes to the high places,
And see where thou hast played the harlot:
By the ways thou didst sit for them,
As the Arabian in the desert;
And polluted hast thou the land
With thy whoredoms and thy wickedness.
3 Restrained therefore have been the showers,
And the late rain has not been;
Yet the front of a strumpet has been thine,
Thou hast refused to be ashamed.
4 Wilt thou not hereafter cry to me,—
"My Father, the guide of my youth art thou?
5 Will he keep *wrath* for ever?
Will he reserve it perpetually?"
Behold, thou hast spoken,
And hast done evils with all thy might. (i. 162)

6 And Jehovah said to me in the days of Josiah the king,—
Hast thou seen what the apostate Israel has done?
She went on every high mountain
And under every shady tree,
And played there the harlot:
7 And I said, after she had done all these things,
"Return to me;" but she returned not;
And see this did her perfidious sister Judah.
8 And I saw, that when for all these things,
Because rebellious Israel had played the harlot,
I had dismissed her and given her a bill of divorce,
Yet fear did not her perfidious sister Judah,
But went and played also the harlot. (i. 166)
9 And it happened through the levity of her whoredom,
That she polluted the land,
And played the harlot with stone and with wood.
10 And yet after all this, returned to me
Has not her perfidious sister Judah,
With her whole heart, but feignedly, saith Jehovah.

11 And Jehovah said to me,—
Justified herself has apostate Israel
Rather than perfidious Judah:
12 Go and publish these words towards the north,
And say, Return, rebellious Israel, saith Jehovah;
I will not let fall my wrath upon you,
For I am merciful, saith Jehovah;

I will not keep it for ever :
13 But know thine iniquity,
That against Jehovah thy God thou hast acted wickedly,
And prostituted thy ways to strangers
Under every shady tree ; (i. 176)
And to my voice thou didst not hearken, saith Jehovah.
14 Return, ye rebellious children, saith Jehovah ;
For I am your husband ;
And I will take you, one from a city,
And two from a family, and bring you to Sion ;
15 And will give you pastors according to my heart,
And they shall feed you with knowledge and understanding.

16 And it shall be, when ye shall multiply and increase
In the land, in those days, saith Jehovah,
That they will no more say,—
" The ark of the covenant of Jehovah ;"
And it shall not come to mind,
And they shall not remember nor visit it ;
Even *this* shall not be done any more. (i. 185)
17 At that time they shall call Jerusalem,
The throne of Jehovah ;
And assemble to it shall all nations,
For the name of Jehovah, even to Jerusalem ;
And walk shall they no more
After the evil hardness of their own hearts. (i. 186)
18 In those days shall come
The house of Judah with the house of Israel ;
Together shall they come from the land of the north,
To the land which I have given
For an inheritance to your fathers.

19 But I said, How shall I put thee among the children,
And give thee the desirable land,
The heritage coveted by hosts of nations ?
And I said, " My Father," shalt thou call me,
And from me thou wilt not depart. (i. 189)
20 Surely as a woman deals perfidiously with her partner,
So hast thou dealt perfidiously with me,
O house of Israel, saith Jehovah.
21 A voice on high places was heard,
The weeping of the prayers of the children of Israel ;
Because they had perverted their way,
And forgotten Jehovah their God. (i. 192)
22 " Return, ye rebellious children,
I will heal your transgressions."

" Behold we come to thee,

For thou art Jehovah our God:
23 Surely deceit *is* from the hills,
From the multitude of mountains;
Surely, in Jehovah our God
Is the salvation of Israel. (i. 194)
24 Even shame hath devoured the labour
Of our fathers, from our youth,
Even their sheep and their cattle,
Their sons and their daughters.
25 We have lain down in our shame,
And our reproach hath covered us,
Because with Jehovah our God
We have dealt wickedly, we and our fathers,
From our childhood even to this day, (i. 196)
And have not attended to the voice of Jehovah our God."

CHAPTER IV.

1 If thou wilt return, Israel, saith Jehovah,
Return to me;
Even if thou wilt take away
Thine abominations from my sight,
And wilt not wander: (i. 199)
2 And thou shalt swear, "Live does Jehovah,
In truth, in judgment, and in righteousness;"
Then bless themselves in him shall nations,
And in him shall they glory. (i. 202)

3 For thus saith Jehovah
To the men of Judah and to Jerusalem,—
Plough again the first ploughing,
And sow not among thorns:
4 Be ye circumcised to Jehovah,
And take away the foreskin of your heart,
Ye men of Judah and inhabitants of Jerusalem;
Lest my fury go forth like fire,
And burn that none may quench it;
On account of the evil of your doings.

5 Proclaim ye in Judah,
And publish in Jerusalem, and say,
"Sound the trumpet in the land;"
Call, assemble, yea, say,—
"Be assembled, and let us enter into fortified cities;"
6 Raise the standard in Sion;
Flee, stay not, for an evil do I bring
From the north, even a great ruin. (i. 208)

7 Ascended has the lion from his thicket,
And the waster of nations is gone forth;
He is come forth from his place,
To make thy land a waste;
Thy cities shall be destroyed,
So as to be without an inhabitant.
8 For this gird yourselves with sackcloth,
Lament and howl; for turned away from us
Is not the fury of Jehovah's wrath.
9 And it shall be in that day, saith Jehovah,
That perish shall the heart of the king,
And the heart of the princes;
And amazed shall be the priests,
And the prophets shall be astonished. (i. 212)

10 Then I said, Ah! Lord Jehovah!
Surely, deceiving thou hast deceived
This people and Jerusalem, by saying,
"Peace shall be to you;"
Yet reached has the sword to the soul. (i. 214)
11 At that time it shall be said
To this people and to Jerusalem,—
A dry wind from the heights of the desert
Shall be towards the way of the daughter of my people,
Not to fan nor to cleanse;
12 A wind stronger than this shall come for me;
Now also will I pronounce judgments on them. (i. 217)
13 Behold as clouds shall he ascend,
And as a whirlwind his chariots;
Swifter than eagles his horses:
Wo to us! for we are lost.

14 Cleanse from evil the heart, Jerusalem;
That thou mayest be saved:
How long will remain within thee
The thoughts of vanity! (i. 221)
15 For a voice proclaims from Dan
And publishes ruin from Mount Ephraim.
16 Rehearse it to the nations;
Behold, publish against Jerusalem,—
Besiegers come from a remote land,
And raise over the cities of Judah their voice;
17 As keepers of the field they shall be over her around;
Because she hath provoked me, saith Jehovah.
18 Thy way and thy doings have done this for thee;
This is thy wickedness, though it be bitter,
Though it reaches to thy heart. (i. 227)

19 My bowels! my bowels! I am in pain;
The walls of my heart!
My heart is in a tumult within me;
I will not be silent, for the sound of the trumpet
Has my soul heard,
And the clamour of war has it heard. (i. 229)
20 Calamity on calamity is cried;
For destroyed is the whole land;
Suddenly destroyed are my tents,
In an instant my curtains.
21 How long shall I see the standard—
Shall I hear the sound of the trumpet?

22 Because foolish are my people,
Me have they not known;
Sottish children are they,
And they are not intelligent;
Acute are they for evil,
But how to do good they know not.

23 I beheld the land, and lo, it was waste and without form;
And the heavens, and they had no light:
24 I beheld the mountains, and lo, they trembled;
And all the hills were shaking:
25 I beheld, and lo, there was no man,
And every bird of the heavens was fled:
26 I beheld, and lo, Carmel was a desert;
And all its cities were destroyed,
At the presence of Jehovah,
At the presence of the burning of his wrath.
27 For thus saith Jehovah,
Laid waste shall be the whole land;
But an end will I not make.
28 For this mourn shall the land,
And black shall become the heavens above;
For I have spoken, I have purposed,
And will not repent nor be turned from this.
29 At the voice of the horseman and of the bowmen,
Flee shall the whole city;
They shall penetrate into thick clouds,
They shall ascend into rocks;
Every city shall be forsaken,
And no man shall dwell in them. (i. 245)
30 And thou, wretched one, what wilt thou do?
Though thou puttest on crimson,
Though thou deckest thyself with ornaments of gold,
Though thou adornest with paint thine eyes,
In vain wilt thou decorate thyself;

Hate thee will thy lovers,
Thy life will they seek.
31 Surely, the voice of one in travail have I heard,
The distress as of one giving birth to a first-begotten,
The voice of the daughter of Sion;
Who mourns, who spreads her hands,—
"Wo to me now! for fainted has my soul
On account of murderers." (i. 251)

CHAPTER V.

1 Go round through the streets of Jerusalem,
And see, I pray, and know,
Inquire also in its cross-ways,
Whether ye shall find a man,
Whether there be any, who doeth judgment,
Who seeketh the truth,
And I will spare it. (i. 252)

2 Though they say, "Live does Jehovah;"
Yet in this they swear falsely.
3 Jehovah! are not thine eyes on the truth?
Thou hast smitten them,
But they have not grieved;
Thou hast consumed them,
But they have not received correction:
They have made their faces harder than a rock,
They have refused to return.
4 But I said, Surely the poor are these;
They have acted foolishly,
Because they knew not the way of Jehovah,
The judgment of their God:
5 I will go to the great and speak to them,
For they know the way of Jehovah,
The judgment of their God:
But these have altogether broken the yoke,
They have burst the bonds.
6 Therefore smite them shall the lion from the forest,
The wolf of the desert shall spoil them,
The leopard shall watch over their cities;
Whosoever goeth out shall be torn:
For manifold are their transgressions,
Increased are their defections.

7 How for this shall I spare thee?
Thy children have forsaken me,
And have sworn by one that is not a god;

When I fully satisfied them, they committed adultery,
And at the house of the harlot they assembled:
8 Fed horses! rising early in the morning,
Every one at his neighbour's wife neigheth.
9 Should I not for these things visit? saith Jehovah,
And on such a nation as this
Shall not my soul be avenged?
10 Ascend her walls and demolish,
But an end make not;
Take away her foundations,
For they are not Jehovah's:
11 For by transgressing they have transgressed against me,
The house of Israel and the house of Judah, saith Jehovah.
12 They have denied Jehovah and said,
"He is not, and come on us shall no evil;
Yea, the sword and the famine we shall not see:
13 And the prophets shall be wind,
For the word is not in them:
Thus shall it be done to them."

14 Therefore, thus saith Jehovah, the God of hosts,—
Because you have uttered this word,
Behold, I will make my words in thy mouth fire,
And this people wood,
And it shall devour them:
15 Behold I will bring on you a nation from far,
O house of Israel, saith Jehovah,
A strong nation, an ancient nation,
A nation whose language thou knowest not,
And understandest not what it says: (i. 286)
16 Their quiver *is* like an open sepulchre,
All of them *are* valiant;
17 And they will devour thy harvest and thy bread;
They will devour thy sons and thy daughters,
They will devour thy flocks and thy herds,
They will devour thy vine and thy fig-tree;
To want shall they reduce thy fortified cities,
To which thou trustest, by the sword:
18 But even in those days, saith Jehovah,
I will not make with you an end.

19 And it shall be, when ye say,
"Why hath Jehovah our God done to us
All these things?" that thou wilt say to them,—
As ye have forsaken me,
And served foreign gods in your land,
So shall ye serve foreigners in a land not your own.

20 Declare this in the house of Jacob,
And publish it in Judah, saying,—
21 Hear this, I pray,
Ye foolish people and void of heart,
Who have eyes and see not,
Who have ears and hear not:
22 Will ye not fear me? saith Jehovah;
Will ye not at my presence tremble?
Who have set the sand a bound to the sea,
By a perpetual decree that it cannot pass it;
Though its waves rage, yet they cannot prevail;
Though they roar, yet they cannot pass over it.
23 But this people hath a perverse and rebellious heart;
They have turned aside and departed:
24 And they have not said in their heart,—
Let us now fear Jehovah our God,
Who giveth rain, both the early
And the latter shower in its season,
Who keeps to us the appointed weeks of harvest.

25 Your iniquities have prevented these things,
And your sins have restrained good from you.
26 For found among my people are the wicked;
They look, as though they would set snares;
A trap they set, in which they catch men. (i. 303)
27 As a cage is full of birds
So their houses are full of fraud:
Therefore they are increased and become rich;
28 They are become fat, they shine;
They even surpass the deeds of the wicked:
The cause they judge not,
The cause of the fatherless, yet they prosper;
And the judgment of the poor they judge not. (i. 306)
29 Shall I not for this visit, saith Jehovah?
On such a nation as this
Shall not my soul be avenged?

30 A monstrosity and baseness is in the land!
31 The prophets prophesy falsely,
And the priests rule by their means; (i. 309)
And my people wish it to be so:
But what will ye do at the end of it?

CHAPTER VI.

1 Be assembled, ye children of Benjamin,
From the midst of Jerusalem,

And in Tekoa sound the trumpet;
In Beth-haccerem also set up a sign;
For evil is seen from the north,
And great distress.
2 To a quiet and delicate *woman*
Have I likened the daughter of Sion:
3 To her shall come shepherds and their flocks;
They shall pitch their tents near her around,
Feed shall each in his own place.

4 Prepare ye war against her:
" Arise ye, and let us ascend at mid-day;
Alas for us! for declined has the day,
For extended are the evening shadows:
5 Arise, and let us ascend in the night,
And let us demolish her palaces." (i. 319)
6 For thus saith Jehovah of hosts,—
Cut ye down wood,
And form against Jerusalem a mound;
It is a city of visitation,
Entire oppression is in the midst of her:
7 As a fountain casts out its waters,
So she casts out her wickedness;
Violence and plunder is heard of in her;
Before me continually is grief and smiting.
8 Be thou instructed, O Jerusalem,
Lest my soul be torn from thee,
Lest I make thee a desert,
A land not inhabited.

9 Thus saith Jehovah of hosts,—
By gleaning they shall glean, as a vine,
The remnant of Israel:
Turn back thine hand,
As a grape-gatherer into the baskets. (i. 326)
10 To whom shall I speak and protest,
That they may hear?
Behold, uncircumcised is their ear,
And they cannot hear;
Behold, the word of Jehovah *is* to them a reproach;
They delight not in it.
11 Of Jehovah's indignation therefore am I full,
I am wearied with refraining
To pour it on the children in the streets,
And on the assembly of young men also;
For the husband with his wife shall be taken,
The aged with the full of days:
12 And turned shall be their houses to aliens,

Their fields and their wives in like manner;
For I will stretch out my hand
On the inhabitants of the land, saith Jehovah:
13 For from the least to the greatest of them,
Every one is given to covetousness;
And from the prophet to the priest,
Every one acts deceitfully;
14 And healed have they the wound
Of the daughter of my people slightly
By saying, "Peace, peace," when there was no peace. (i.336)
15 Were they ashamed, that they had done abomination?
Even of shame they were not ashamed,
And how to blush they knew not:
Fall therefore shall they among the fallen;
At the time of their visitation
They shall perish, saith Jehovah. (i. 339)

16 Thus said Jehovah,—
Stand in the ways and see,
Inquire also concerning the old paths,
Which is the right way, and walk ye in it,
That ye may find rest to your soul:
And they said, "We will not walk *in it*."
17 I also set over them watchmen,
That they might attend to the sound of the trumpet;
But they said, "We will not attend."
18 Hear therefore, ye nations,
And know, thou assembly, what shall be to them:
19 Hear, thou land; behold I bring an evil
On this people, the fruit of their thoughts;
Because to my words they have not hearkened,
And my law have they despised.
20 To what purpose is this to me?
Incense cometh from Sheba,
And the sweet cane from a far country;
Your burnt-offerings are not acceptable,
And your sacrifices are not pleasant to me.
21 Therefore thus saith Jehovah,—
Behold, I lay before this people stumblingblocks;
And stumble shall fathers and sons alike;
Neighbour and friend, they shall perish.

22 Thus saith Jehovah,—
Behold, a people shall come from the north country,
And a great nation shall be roused
From the sides of the earth:
23 On the bow and spear shall they lay hold;
They are cruel and will not spare;

Their voice, like the sea, will roar,
And on horses shall they mount;
Arrayed shall they be as men for war,
Against thee, O daughter of Sion.
24 We have heard its fame;
Relaxed are our hands,
Anguish has laid hold on us,
The pain as of one in travail.
25 Go not forth into the field,
Nor walk by the way;
For the sword of the enemy
Is a terror on every side.
26 Daughter of my people! gird on sackcloth,
And roll thyself in the dust;
Make thee mourning, as for an only son,
Most bitter lamentation;
For suddenly shall come on thee the spoiler.

27 A tower have I made thee to my people,—
A fortress; that thou mightest know
And try their ways:
28 All are entire apostates,
Walking in detraction;
Brass and iron *are they*;
All of them are corrupters. (i. 358)
29 Burnt are the bellows by the fire,
Entire is the lead,
In vain has melted the melter;
For the wicked have not been refined:
30 Reprobate silver shall they call them,
Because rejected them has Jehovah. (i. 360)

CHAPTER VII.

1 The word which came to Jeremiah from Jehovah, saying,—
2 Stand in the gate of the house of Jehovah,
And proclaim there this word, and say,—
Hear the word of Jehovah, all ye Judah,
Who enter through these gates to worship Jehovah:
3 Thus saith Jehovah of hosts, the God of Israel,—
Make good your ways and your doings,
And I will dwell with you in this place:
4 Trust not in words of falsehood, by saying,
"The temple of Jehovah, the temple of Jehovah,
The temple of Jehovah, are *these buildings*." (i. 364)
5 Surely, if by making good ye make good
Your ways and your doings,

If by doing ye do judgment
Between man and his neighbour,
6 If the stranger, the orphan and the widow,
Ye oppress not, and innocent blood
Ye shed not in this place,
And after strange gods
Ye walk not to your hurt,—
7 Then will I cause you to dwell in this place,
In the land which I gave to your fathers,
For ever and ever.

8 Behold, ye trust in words of falsehood,
Which are without profit.
9 Will ye steal, kill, and commit adultery,
Swear falsely, burn incense to Baal,
And walk after alien gods,
Whom ye do not know;
10 And come and stand before me in this house,
Which is called by my name, and say,
"We have been made free
To do all these abominations?" (i. 373)
11 Is this house, called by my name,
Become a den of robbers in your eyes?
Even I, behold I see, saith Jehovah.
12 But go now to my place in Shilo,
Where I made to dwell my name at first,
And see what I did there,
For the wickedness of my people Israel:
13 And now, because ye have done
All these works, saith Jehovah,
And I spoke to you, rising early,
And when I spoke, ye heard not,
When I called you, ye answered not;
14 I will therefore do to this place,
Which is called by my name,
In which ye trust—
Even to the place which I gave to you
And to your fathers, as I did to Shilo;
15 And I will cast you out from my presence,
As I have cast out all your brethren,
The whole seed of Ephraim.
16 And thou, pray not for this people,
And raise not for them a cry and a prayer,
And intercede not with me;
For I will not hear thee. (i. 384)

17 Seest thou not what they do in the cities of Judah
And in the streets of Jerusalem?

18 Children gather wood,
And fathers kindle a fire,
And women knead a dough,
To make cakes for the queen of heaven;
And they pour libations to alien gods,
That they may provoke me to wrath! (i. 387)
19 Do they provoke me to wrath, saith Jehovah?
Is it not to the shame of their own faces?
20 Therefore thus saith the Lord Jehovah,—
Behold my wrath, even my fury,
It shall be poured on this place,
Upon men and upon beast,
Upon the tree of the field and the fruit of the land;
And it shall burn, and none shall quench *it*.

21 Thus saith Jehovah of hosts, the God of Israel,—
Your burnt-offerings add to your sacrifices,
And eat ye the flesh:
22 For I spoke not to your fathers,
Nor commanded them in the day,
In which I brought them out of the land of Egypt,
Concerning burnt-offerings and sacrifices;
23 But this is what I commanded them, saying,—
"Hear my voice,
And I will be to you a God,
And you shall be to me a people;
And walk ye in all the ways
Which I have commanded you,
That it may be well with you:"
24 Yet they heard not, nor inclined their ear;
But walked in perverse counsels,
In the wickedness of their own evil heart,
And went backward and not forward.
25 From the day in which your fathers came out
From the land of Egypt, to this day,
Have I sent to you all my servants, the prophets,
Every day rising early and sending *them*:
26 Yet they heard not nor inclined their ear,
But hardened their neck;
They have acted more perversely than their fathers.
27 Thou also shalt say to them all these words,
But they will not hear thee;
And thou shalt call to them,
But they will not answer thee:
28 Therefore say to them,—This is a nation,
Which have not hearkened to the voice
Of Jehovah, their God,
And have not received correction:

Perished has the truth,
And cut off has it been from their mouth.

29 Shave off thy hair and cast it away,
Raise on the heights a lamentation;
For rejected thee has Jehovah;
And forsaken hath he the generation of his wrath:
30 For the children of Judah have done evil
Before mine eyes, saith Jehovah;
They have set their abominations in the house,
On which my name is called, to pollute it;
31 And they have built the high places of Tophet,
Which is in the valley of the son of Hinnom,
To burn their sons and their daughters in the fire;
Which I have not commanded,
Nor has it ever come into my heart.
32 Therefore, behold the days come, saith Jehovah,
That it shall no more be called Tophet,
And The valley of the son of Hinnom,
But, The valley of slaughter;
And they shall bury in Tophet,
For *elsewhere* there will be no place:
33 And the carcases of this people shall be for meat
To the birds of heaven and to the beasts of the earth;
And there will be none to frighten them:
34 And to cease will I make, from the cities of Judah
And from the streets of Jerusalem,
The voice of joy and the voice of gladness,
The voice of the bridegroom and the voice of the bride;
For to a waste shall the land be reduced.

CHAPTER VIII.

1 In that day, saith Jehovah, they shall bring forth
The bones of the kings of Judah,
And the bones of his princes,
And the bones of the priests,
And the bones of the prophets,
And the bones of the citizens of Jerusalem,
Out of their graves;
2 And they shall spread them before the sun,
And the moon, and all the host of heaven,
Which they have loved and served,
And after which they have walked,
And which they have sought,
And before which they have bowed themselves;
They shall not be gathered nor buried;

For dung on the face of the land shall they be:
3 And chosen shall be death,
Rather than life, by all the residue,
Who shall remain of this wicked nation,
Who shall remain in all the places
Where I shall drive them, saith Jehovah of hosts.

4 Thou shalt also say to them, Thus saith Jehovah,—
Shall not they who have fallen rise again?
If any one turns aside shall he not return?
5 Why rebel does this people at Jerusalem
With a perpetual rebellion?
They have held fast deceit,
They have refused to return.
6 I hearkened and heard; they will not speak aright;
There is no one who repents of his wickedness,
And says, "What have I done?"
Every one turns to his own course,
Like a horse who rushes into battle. (i. 425)
7 Even the stork in the heavens knows its times;
The turtle also, and the swallow and the crane,
Observe the time of their journey;
But my people know not the judgment of Jehovah.
8 How say ye, "We are wise
And the law of Jehovah is with us:"
Surely, behold in vain
Hath the writer prepared his pen,
In vain are the scribes!
9 Ashamed are the wise, terrified and taken;
Behold the word of Jehovah have they rejected;
And wisdom, what is it to them! (i. 432)
10 I will therefore give their wives to aliens,
And their fields to inheritors;
For from the least even to the greatest,
Every one is given to covetousness;
From the prophet even to the priest,
All have acted deceitfully;
11 And healed have they the wound
Of the daughter of my people slightly,
By saying, "Peace, peace," when there was no peace.
12 Had they shame, that they had done abomination?
Even of shame they were not ashamed,
And how to blush they knew not:
Fall therefore shall they with the fallen;
At the time of their visitation
They shall perish, saith Jehovah.

13 Destroying, I will destroy them, saith Jehovah;

No grapes *shall be* on the vine,
And no figs on the fig-tree;
The leaf also shall fall,
And what I gave them shall pass from them.
14 Why do we sit still? Assemble ye,
And let us enter into fortified cities,
And let us rest there:
Surely, Jehovah our God hath made us silent,
And given us waters of gall to drink:
Because we have sinned against Jehovah. (i. 442)
15 We looked for peace, but there was nogood;
For time of healing, but behold terror.
16 From Dan is heard the snorting of his horses;
At the sound of the neighing of his strong ones,
Tremble does the whole land;
For they will come and devour
The land and its abundance,
The city and its inhabitants.
17 For behold, I will send among you
Serpents and basilisks,
Which will not be charmed;
And they shall bite you, saith Jehovah.

18 I would strengthen myself against grief:
But within me my heart is weak.
19 Behold the voice of the crying
Of the daughter of my people from a far country!
"Is not Jehovah in Sion?
Is not her king within her?"—
Why have they provoked me to wrath
With their images, with foreign vanities?
20 Past has the harvest, ended is the summer,
And we have not been saved! (i. 452)
21 For the hurt of the daughter of my people
I am hurt, I am become black;
Astonishment has laid hold on me.
22 Is there no balm in Gilead?
Is there no physician there?
For why is not restored
The healing of the daughter of my people! (i. 456)

CHAPTER IX.

1 Who will make my head waters
And mine eye a fountain of tears!
Then would I bewail, day and night,
The slain of the daughter of my people.

2 Who will set me in the desert,
In the lodging of travellers!
Then would I leave my people
And depart from them:
For all of them are adulterers,
An assembly of perfidious men.
3 And they shoot lies with their tongue as with a bow;
But not for truth are they strong in the land;
For from evil to evil they proceed; (i. 462)
And me they know not, saith Jehovah.
4 And every one of his friend take ye heed,
And in a brother trust ye not;
For every brother by supplanting will supplant,
And every friend walks fraudulently:
5 And a man deceives his neighbour,
And the truth he speaks not;
They have taught their tongues to speak falsehood;
With doing evil they weary themselves.

6 Thou dwellest in the midst of deceit;
Through deceit they refuse
To know me, saith Jehovah. (i. 469)
7 Therefore thus saith Jehovah of hosts,—
Behold, I will try them, and will prove them;
For how should I deal
With the daughter of my people?
8 A sharpened arrow is their tongue,
Falsehood it speaks;
His mouth speaks peace to his neighbour,
But within he sets up intrigues.
9 For this shall I not visit, saith Jehovah,
On such a nation as this
Shall not my soul be avenged?

10 For the mountains will I raise up weeping and wailing,
For the pastures of the wilderness, lamentation;
Because they are laid waste,
So that there is not a man passing through,
And they hear not the voice of cattle;
From the bird of heaven to the beast,
Have they fled, have they departed. (i. 475)
11 I will also make Jerusalem heaps,
A place for dragons;
And the cities of Judah will I make a waste,
So that there shall be no inhabitant.

12 Who is a wise man to understand this?
And to whom has Jehovah's mouth spoken,

That he may declare why the land is to perish—
Is to be laid waste like the desert,
So that no man should pass through? (i. 480)
13 Then Jehovah said,—
Because they have forsaken my law,
Which I have set before them,
And hearkened not to my voice,
Nor walked according to it;
14 But walked after the imaginations
Of their own hearts, and after Baalim,
As their fathers taught them;
15 Therefore, thus saith Jehovah of hosts,
The God of Israel,—Behold,
I will feed this people with bitterness,
And will give them the water of gall to drink;
16 I will also scatter them among the nations,
Whom they have not known nor their fathers,
And I will send after them the sword,
Until I shall have consumed them.

17 Thus saith Jehovah of hosts,—
Attend ye and call for the mourning women,
That they may come,
And send for those who are skilful,
That they may come.
18 And let them hasten and make a wailing for us,
That our eyes may let fall tears,
And our eyelids drop down waters. (i. 489)
19 For a voice of wailing is heard from Sion,
" How we are wasted! How greatly shamed!
Because we have left the land,
They have cast down our dwellings."
20 Therefore hear, ye women, the word of Jehovah,
And let your ears receive the word of his mouth,
And teach your daughters wailing,
And each one her friend lamentation:
21 For come up is death to our windows,
It has entered into our palaces,
To cut off the infant from the street,
The young men in the broad places. (i. 493)
22 Speak, thus saith Jehovah,
Fall shall the carcases of men
As dung on the face of the field,
And as the handful after the reaper,
And none gathering *it*.

23 Thus saith Jehovah,—
Let not the wise glory in his wisdom,

And let not the brave glory in his courage,
Let not the rich glory in his riches;
24 But in this let him glory who glorieth,
In understanding, and in knowing me,
That I am Jehovah, who doeth mercy,
Judgment and righteousness in the land;
For in these things I delight, saith Jehovah. (i. 502)

25 Behold the days are coming, saith Jehovah,
That I will visit every one circumcised,
Who is in uncircumcision,—
26 Egypt and Judah and Edom,
The sons of Ammon and Moab,
And all those who are in extreme recesses,
Who dwell in the wilderness;
For all these nations are uncircumcised,
And the whole house of Israel,
They are uncircumcised in heart.

CHAPTER X.

1 Hear ye the word which Jehovah speaks to you, O house of Israel:
2 Thus saith Jehovah,—
The way of the Gentiles learn not,
And of the signs of heaven be not afraid,
For fear them do the Gentiles:
3 Because the rites of the heathens are vanity,
For a tree from the forest does *one* cut—
The work of the craftsman's hands by the ax;
4 With silver and gold they beautify it,
With nails and hammer they make it fast,
That it should not move;
5 As a palm, erect, but they speak not;
And being raised, they are raised, for they cannot walk:
Fear them not, for they cannot do evil,
And to do good is not in their power. (ii. 14)

6 From no time has been found *any*
Like thee, Jehovah; great *art* thou,
And great is thy name in power.
7 Who should not fear thee, king of nations?
For to thee this belongs;
For among all the wise of the nations,
And in all their kingdoms,
From no time has there been *one* like thee. (ii. 28)

8 Even in this one thing they are foolish and fatuitous—
The teaching of vanities the wood is:
9 Silver, extended, is from Tarshish brought,
And gold from Ophas,—
The work of the artificer and of the melter's hands;
Hyacinth and purple *are* their garments,
The work of the wise, all of them.
10 But Jehovah is God, the truth,
God, the life and the king of ages:
Through his fury tremble will the earth,
And the nations will not bear his wrath.

11 Thus shall ye say to them,—
The gods who made not the heaven and the earth,
Let them perish from the earth and from under heaven:
12 He who made the earth by his power,
Who set in order the world by his wisdom,
And by his understanding extended the heavens,—
13 At his voice *there is* abundance of waters in the heavens,
And he makes vapours to ascend from the extremity of the earth;
Lightnings he makes for rain,
And brings the wind from his treasures. (ii. 31)
14 Foolish is every man through *his* knowledge,
Ashamed is every maker of the graven image,
For a falsehood is the molten image,
And there is no breath in them.
15 Vanity they are, the work of illusions;
At the time of their visitation they shall perish.
16 But not like them *is* the portion of Jacob,
For the Creator of all things is he,
And Israel *is* the rod of his inheritance;
Jehovah of hosts is his name.

17 Gather from the land thy treasures
Thou who dwellest in a fortress:
18 For thus saith Jehovah,—
Behold I will cast out *as* with a sling
The inhabitants of the land at this time,
And I will straiten them,
That they may find *what they deserve.*
19 Wo is me on account of my bruising!
Full of pain is the smiting given to me! and I said,—
Surely it is my stroke, and I will bear it:
20 My tent is pulled down,
And all my cords are broken;
My sons are gone from me, and there are none—
No one to extend any more my tent,

And to set up my curtains!
21 For infatuated are the pastors,
And Jehovah have they not sought;
Therefore have they not prospered,
And all that was in their pastures has been destroyed.
22 A sound of rumour! lo, it comes,
And a great tumult, from the land of the north,
To make the cities of Judah a waste,
The habitation of dragons!

23 I know Jehovah,
That his way is not in the power of man,
That it is not in man who walketh to guide his steps.
24 Chastise me, Jehovah, but only in moderation;
Not in thy wrath, lest thou shouldest consume me:
25 Pour thy wrath on the nations, who know thee not,
And on the families who have not called on thy name;
For they have devoured Jacob,
Yea, they have devoured and consumed him,
And his tents have they laid waste.

CHAPTER XI.

1 The word which came to Jeremiah from Jehovah, saying,—
2 Hear ye the words of this covenant; and say ye to the men
3 of Judah and to the inhabitants of Jerusalem: and thou shalt
say to them, Thus saith Jehovah, the God of Israel,—Cursed
4 is the man who hears not the words of this covenant, which
I commanded your fathers in the day in which I brought them
out of the land of Egypt, from the iron furnace, saying,—Hear
ye my voice, and do according to all those things which I have
commanded you; and ye shall be to me a people and I will
5 be to you a God; that I may confirm the oath which I sware
to your fathers, to give them a land flowing with milk and
honey, according to what it is at this day. And I answered
and said, Amen, Jehovah.
6 And Jehovah said to me, Proclaim these words in the cities of
Judah and in the streets of Jerusalem, saying,—
Hear the words of this covenant and do them;
7 For protesting I protested to your fathers,
In the day in which I brought them
Out of the land of Egypt, to this day,
Rising up early and protesting, and saying,—
8 "Hear ye my voice:"
Yet they heard not, nor inclined their ear,
But walked, every one of them,
After the wickedness of his own evil heart:

I have therefore brought on them
All the words of this covenant,
Which I commanded them to do,
But they did them not. (ii. 84)

9 And Jehovah said to me,—
Found out is a conspiracy,
Among the men of Judah and the citizens of Jerusalem:
10 Returned are they to the iniquities of their forefathers,
Who refused to hear my words,
But walked after foreign gods to serve them:
Broken have the house of Israel and the house of Judah
My covenant, which I made with their fathers.
11 Therefore thus saith Jehovah,—
Behold, I will bring upon you an evil,
From which ye shall not be able to escape;
And they shall cry to me, but I will not hear them:
12 And go shall the cities of Judah and the citizens of Jerusalem,
And cry to the gods to whom they have offered incense;
But by saving they will not save them
In the time of *their* affliction:
13 For according to the number of thy cities
Have been thy gods, O Judah;
And according to the number of streets of Jerusalem,
Have ye set up altars for reproach—
Altars to offer incense to Baal. (ii. 94)
14 And thou, pray not for this people,
And raise not for them a cry and a prayer;
For I will not hear them at the time
When they shall cry to me for their distress.

15 What has my beloved to do in mine house,
While she commits abomination with many?
And the flesh of the sanctuary is taken from thee;
For when thou didst evil, thou didst then glory. (ii. 102)
16 A green olive, fair in fruit *and* form,
Hath Jehovah called thy name;
At the noise of great tumult hath he kindled a *fire* on it,
And broken down are its branches: (ii. 105)
17 For Jehovah of hosts who planted thee
Hath spoken against thee an evil,
For the wickedness of the house of Israel
And of the house of Judah,
Which they have done for themselves,
To provoke me by offering incense to Baal.

18 Jehovah hath made me to know, and I knew it;

Thou didst then discover to me their works.
19 But I was like a lamb *or* an ox
Led to be slain; and I knew not
That they meditated thoughts against me:
"Let us spoil with wood his bread,
And cut him off from the land of the living;
And let his name be remembered no more." (ii. 113)
20 Now, Jehovah of hosts, who judgest righteously,
Who searchest the reins and the heart,
Let me see thy vengeance on them,
For to thee have I revealed my cause.

21 Therefore thus saith Jehovah
To the men of Anathoth, who seek thy life and say,
"Prophesy thou not in the name of Jehovah,
That thou mayest not die by our hand;"
22 Therefore thus saith Jehovah of hosts,—
Behold, I will visit them;
Their young men shall die by the sword,
Their sons and their daughters shall die by famine,
23 And there shall be no remnant of them;
For I will bring evil on the men of Anathoth,
In the year of their visitation.

CHAPTER XII.

1 Just *art* thou, Jehovah, though I contend with thee;
Yet of judgments will I speak to thee:
How long shall the way of the ungodly prosper?
Secure are all they who by transgressing transgress. (ii. 121)
2 Thou hast planted them, they have even taken root;
They have grown, they have even produced fruit:
Nigh art thou in their mouth,
But far from their reins.
3 But thou, Jehovah, knowest me,
Thou seest me and hast tried my heart towards thee;
Draw them forth as sheep for the slaughter,
And prepare them for the day of destruction.
4 How long shall mourn the land,
And the grass of every field wither,
For the wickedness of those who dwell in it?
Consumed are the beasts and the birds,
Because they have said, "He shall not see our end." (ii. 129)

5 If with footmen thou hast run,
And they have wearied thee,
How canst thou contend with horsemen?
In the land of peace thou hast trusted,

How then canst thou do in the rising of Jordan?
6 Truly, even thy brethren and the house of thy father,
Even these act perfidiously towards thee;
Yea, they cry after thee with a loud voice:
Trust them not, even when they speak good things to thee.

7 I have forsaken my house,
I have left my heritage;
I have given up the darling of my soul
Into the hand of her enemies!
8 My heritage has become to me like a lion in the forest;
It has sent forth its voice against me;
Therefore have I hated it.
9 Is my heritage to me a speckled bird?
Is there not a bird around over it?
Come, gather yourselves all ye beasts of the field;
Come to devour it. (ii. 140)
10 Many shepherds have destroyed my vineyard,
They have trodden under foot my portion,
They have made my choice portion a desolate wilderness;
11 They have made it a desolation,
It mourns to me, being desolate;
Desolate is become the whole land;
Though no one hath laid it to heart.
12 On all high places in the wilderness have come destroyers;
For the sword of Jehovah hath devoured,
From one end to the other end of the land;
There is no peace to any flesh.
13 They have sown wheat,
And thorns have they reaped;
An heritage have they got, but have not succeeded:
Ashamed have they been of your produce,
Through the burning of the wrath of Jehovah. (ii. 149)

14 Thus saith Jehovah,—
As to all my evil neighbours,
Who touch my heritage,
Which I have inherited, *even* my people Israel,
Behold, I will pluck them up from their land,
And the house of Judah
Will I pluck up from the midst of them.
15 And it shall be, after I draw them out,
That I shall return and shew mercy to them,
And will restore them, every one to his heritage,
And every one to his own land.
16 And it shall be, that if by learning they will learn
The ways of my people,
To swear by my name, "Live does Jehovah,"
As they taught my people to swear by Baal,

They shall then be built up
In the midst of my people:
17 But if they will not hear,
I will then pluck up that nation,
Plucking *it* up and destroying *it*, saith Jehovah.

CHAPTER XIII.

1 Thus saith Jehovah to me,—
Go and get thee a linen belt, and put it on thy loins, and
2 in water set it not. So I got for me a belt, as Jehovah had
3 commanded, and put it on my loins. Then came the word of
4 Jehovah to me again, saying,—Take the belt which thou hast
got, which is on thy loins, and rise, go to Euphrates and hide
5 *it* there in the hole of a rock. Then I went and hid it by
6 Euphrates, as Jehovah had ordered me. And it was, that at
the end of many days, Jehovah said to me, Rise and go to
Euphrates, and take thence the belt which I commanded thee
7 to hide there. So I went to Euphrates, and digged, and took
the belt from the place where I had hid it; and behold the belt
8 was marred, *and* it was good for nothing. Then came the
word of Jehovah to me, saying,—

9 Thus saith Jehovah,—
In this way will I mar the excellency of Judah
And the great excellency of Jerusalem:
10 This wicked people, who refuse to hear my words,
Who walk in the wickedness of their own heart,
And walk after foreign gods,
That they may serve them and worship them,—
Shall be even as this belt,
Which is good for nothing.
11 For as the belt cleaves to the loins of man,
So had I joined to me the whole house of Israel
And the whole house of Judah, saith Jehovah,
That they might be to me a people and a name,
Yea, a praise and a glory;
But they hearkened not.

12 Thou shalt also say this word to them, Thus saith Jehovah,
the God of Israel,—Every bottle shall be filled with wine. When
they shall say to thee, Knowing do we not know, that every
13 bottle shall be filled with wine? then shalt thou say to them,—
Thus saith Jehovah,—
Behold, I will fill with drunkenness
All the inhabitants of this land,
And all the kings who sit for David on his throne,
The priests also and the prophets,
And all the inhabitants of Jerusalem;
14 And I will dash them, every one against his brother,

The fathers also and the sons together, saith Jehovah :
I will not spare, nor will I be propitious,
Nor shew pity until I destroy them.

15 Hear ye and attend, be not lifted up,
For Jehovah hath spoken :
16 Give to Jehovah your God the glory,
Before he makes it to grow dark,
And before your feet stumble at the dark mountains,
And *before* he turns the light ye hope for
Into the shadow of death,
And makes it thick darkness. (ii. 179)
17 But if ye will not hear this,
In secret will my soul mourn for pride,
And weeping my eye will weep
And run down with tears ;
For led captive is the flock of Jehovah.

18 Say to the king and to the queen,
Be ye humbled, lie ye down,
For come down from your heads
Shall the crown of your glory.
19 The cities of the south are closed up,
And there is no one to open *them* ;
For carried away has been all Judah,
He has been carried away completely. (ii. 185)

20 Raise ye your eyes,
And behold them who come from the north :
Where is the flock, which has been given to thee,
The sheep of thy glory ?
21 What wilt thou say when he visits thee ?
But thou hast taught them to be leaders over thy head ;
Shall not sorrows lay hold on thee,
As on a woman in travail ?

22 But if thou wilt say in thine heart,
" Why have these evils happened to me ?"
For the multitude of thine iniquity
Are thy skirts discovered,
And naked are made thy heels.
23 Can the Ethiop change his skin,
And the panther his spots ?
Even so can ye do good,
Who have been taught evil. (ii. 192)
24 I will therefore scatter them like the stubble,
That passeth away by the wind of the desert.
25 This thy lot *is* the portion of thy measures
From me, saith Jehovah,
For thou hast forgotten me,
And thou hast trusted in falsehood ;

26 And I also will uncover thy skirts on thy face,
That seen may be thy shame.
27 Thy adulteries and thy neighings,
The thought of thy whoredom,
On the mountains, in the field, have I seen,
Even thine abominations;
Wo to thee, Jerusalem!
Wilt thou not at length be made clean?
How long yet!

CHAPTER XIV.

1 The word which came to Jeremiah respecting the drought:
2 Mourned has Judah,
And his gates have been weakened;
They are become black on the ground,
And the cry of Jerusalem has gone up: (ii. 205)
3 And their chiefs sent the common people to the waters;
They came to the cisterns, they found no water;
They returned with empty vessels;
They were confounded and ashamed,
And they covered their head:
4 For the chapt ground, as there was no rain in the land,
Ashamed were the husbandmen,
And they covered their head:
5 Moreover the hind brought forth young in the field,
And forsook it, for there was no grass:
6 And the wild asses stood on the cliffs,
They drew in wind like serpents;
Fail did their eyes, for there was no grass (ii. 209)

7 Though our iniquities testify against us, O Jehovah,
Deal *with us* for thine own name's sake;
For multiplied have our defections,
Against thee have we done wickedly.
8 Hope of Israel! Saviour art thou
In the time of trouble;
Why shouldest thou be as a stranger in the land?
As a traveller, turning aside to pass the night?
9 Why shouldest thou be as a man terrified?
As a strong man, who yet cannot save?
Thou art in the midst of us, O Jehovah,
And on us is thy name called,
Forsake us not. (ii. 214)

10 Thus saith Jehovah of this people:
As they have loved to wander,
And have not restrained their feet,
Therefore Jehovah has not been pleased with them;
He will now remember their iniquities,

And visit their sins.
11 Jehovah said also to me:
Pray not for this people for *their* good:
12 When they fast I will not hear their cry;
And when they offer a sacrifice and an oblation,
I will not be pleased with them;
For with the sword and with famine,
And with pestilence, will I consume them.

13 And I said, Ah! Lord Jehovah,
Behold, the prophets say to them,—
"Ye shall not see the sword,
And famine shall not be to you,
Nay, sure peace will I give you in this place."
14 Then said Jehovah to me,—
Falsehood do the prophets prophesy in my name;
I have not sent them nor commanded them,
Nor have I spoken to them;
A false vision and divination,
Yea, vanity and the deceit of their own heart,
Do they of themselves prophesy to you. (ii. 226)

15 Therefore, thus saith Jehovah, of the prophets who prophesy in
my name, and I have not sent them, and who say, The sword
and the famine shall not be in this land,—By the sword and
16 famine shall these prophets be consumed; and the people, to
whom they have prophesied, shall be cast out in the streets of
Jerusalem through the famine and the sword, and there will be
none to bury them,—they, their wives, and their sons, and their
daughters; and I will pour upon them their own wickedness.
17 Therefore shalt thou say to them this word,—
Run down shall mine eyes with tears
Day and night, and they shall not rest,
For with a great breach is broken down
The virgin, the daughter of my people;
The stroke *is* very grievous:
18 If I go out to the field, behold the slain with the sword!
And if I enter the city, behold the sorrowful with famine!
For both the prophet, and the priest,
Go round through the land, and know not *what to do.*

19 Repudiating hast thou repudiated Judah?
Has thy soul abominated Sion?
Why hast thou *so* smitten us, that we have no healing?
We have looked for peace, and there is no good,
And for time of healing, and behold terror!
20 We know, O Jehovah, our wickedness,
And the iniquity of our fathers;
For we have done wickedly against thee.
21 Reject not, for thy name's sake,

Overthrow not the throne of thy glory;
Remember, render not void,
Thy covenant with us. (ii. 240)
22 Are there any among the vanities of the Gentiles,
Who can cause it to rain?
And can they give rain from heaven?
Art not thou thyself, Jehovah, our God?
And we have looked to thee,
For thou hast done all these things.

CHAPTER XV.[1]

1 Then Jehovah said to me:
Though Moses and Samuel stood before me,
My soul would not be towards this people;
Send *them* from my presence, and let them depart.
2 And it shall be, if they say to thee,
" Whither shall we go forth?"
Then shalt thou say to them,—
Thus saith Jehovah,—
They who are for death, to death,
And they who are for the sword, to the sword,
And they who are for the famine, to the famine,
And they who are for captivity, to captivity:
3 And I will set over them four kinds, saith Jehovah,—
The sword to kill, and the dogs to drag,
And the bird of heaven, and the beast of the earth,
To devour and to destroy:
4 And I will set them a vexation,
To all the kingdoms of the earth,
For Manasse, the son of Hezekiah, king of Judah,
On account of what he did in Jerusalem.

5 For who will pity thee, O Jerusalem?
And who will condole with thee?
And who will turn aside
To inquire of thy welfare?
6 Thou hast forsaken me, saith Jehovah;
Backward hast thou gone;
I will therefore stretch my hand against thee,
And I will destroy thee;
I am wearied with repenting:
7 And I will fan them with a fan
Through all the gates of the earth;
I have bereaved, I destroyed my people;
From their own ways they have not returned:
8 Multiplied have their widows to me

[1] The beginning of this chapter is evidently connected with the end of the last, and ought not to have been separated.—*Ed.*

Above the sand of the sea;
I brought to them, on the troop of youths,
A waster at mid-day;
And I cast on them suddenly
A tumult and terrors.
9 Weakened did she become who had born seven,
Expire did her soul,
Go down did her sun while it *was yet* day,
Confounded has she been and ashamed:
And the remainder of them to the sword will I give,
Before their enemies, saith Jehovah. (ii. 266)

10 Wo to me, my mother!
That thou hast born me a man of strife,
And a man of contention to the whole land:
I have not lent on usury,
And they have not on usury lent to me;
Yet every one curses me.
11 And Jehovah said,—
Surely thy latter end shall be well;
Surely I will cause to meet thee the enemy,
In the time of evil and in the time of distress. (ii. 273)
12 Shall iron break
The iron from the north and the steel!
13 Thy wealth and thy treasures
To plunder will I give,
Not in exchange, but for all thy wickedness,
And for all thy counsels:
14 And I will make *thee* to pass to the enemy
Into a land which thou knowest not;
For a fire is kindled in my wrath,
On you it shall burn.

15 Thou knowest, O Jehovah,
Remember me and visit me,
And avenge me on my persecutors,
Lest thou shouldest take me away
By protracting thy wrath:
Know that for thee have I borne reproach. (ii. 280)
16 Found were thy words, and I did eat them;
And thy word was my joy and the gladness of my heart;
For called on me was thy name,
O Jehovah, the God of hosts.
17 I sat not in the assembly of mockers,
Nor exulted on account of thy hand;
I sat apart, for with indignation
Hast thou filled me.
18 Why is my pain strong, and my stroke incurable,
And refuses to be healed?

Wilt thou be to me
As the deception of unfaithful waters?

19 Therefore, thus saith Jehovah,—
If thou wilt be turned, then I will turn thee,
That thou mayest stand before me;
And if thou separatest the precious from the worthless,
As my mouth shalt thou be:
Let them turn to thee, but turn not thou to them.
20 I have even made thee to this people
A wall of brass, fortified;
They shall therefore fight against thee,
But over thee they shall not prevail;
For with thee am I to save thee,
And to deliver thee, saith Jehovah:
21 Yea, I will save thee from the hand of the wicked,
And deliver thee from the hand of the strong. (ii. 300)

CHAPTER XVI.

1 Then came the word of Jehovah to me, saying,—
2 Take not to thee a wife,
And have no sons and daughters in this place:
3 For thus saith Jehovah,—
As to the sons and daughters, born in this place,
And as to the mothers who shall bear them,
And as to the fathers, who shall beget them in this land—
4 With deaths of sicknesses shall they die,
They shall not be lamented nor buried;
As dung on the face of the earth shall they be;
With the sword also and the famine shall they be consumed,
And their carcases shall be for meat
To the birds of heaven, and to the beasts of the earth. (ii. 305)
5 For thus saith Jehovah,—
Enter not the house of mourning
Nor go to lament, nor be moved for them;
For I have taken away my peace
From this people, saith Jehovah,
My kindness *also* and mercies:
6 And die shall they, great and small, in this land;
They shall not be buried,
Nor shall any lament for them nor cut themselves,
Nor shall baldness be made for them;
7 And they shall not for them smite the hand,
To console them for the dead;
Nor shall they drink to them the cup of consolations,
For their father or for their mother. (ii. 310)
8 The house of feasting also enter not,
To sit with them to eat and to drink;
9 For thus saith Jehovah of hosts, the God of Israel,—

Behold, I will take away from this place,
Before your eyes and in your days,
The voice of joy and the voice of gladness,
The voice of the bridegroom and the voice of the bride.

10 And it shall be, when thou declarest to this people
All these words, that they will say to thee,—
"Why has Jehovah spoken against us
All this great evil?
And what is our iniquity? and what is our sin?
Which we have wickedly done against Jehovah, our God."
11 Then thou shalt say to them,—
Because your fathers forsook me, saith Jehovah:
For they went after foreign gods,
And served them and bowed down to them,
And me they forsook, and my law they did not keep;
12 And worse are ye become than your fathers;
For, behold, ye have walked, every one of you,
After the wickedness of his own evil heart,
So as not to hearken to me.
13 I will therefore cast you out of this land,
Into a land which ye have not known, nor your fathers,
And there shall ye serve foreign gods, day and night;
For I will shew you no favour.

14 Therefore, behold, the days will come, saith Jehovah,
When it shall be no more said, Live does Jehovah,
Who brought up the children of Israel from the land of Egypt:
15 But, Live does Jehovah, who has brought up
The children of Israel, from the land of the north,
And from all the lands to which he had driven them;
For I will restore them to the land
Which I gave to their fathers.
16 Behold, I will send for many fishers, saith Jehovah;
And they shall fish them;
And afterwards I will send for many hunters,
And they shall hunt them from every mountain,
And from every hill and holes of rocks:
17 For mine eyes are on all their ways;
They are not hid from my face,
Nor are their iniquities hid from mine eyes:
18 And I will render double, from the beginning,
For their iniquities and their sins;
For they have polluted my land
With the carcases of their abominations;
And with their defilements
Have they filled mine inheritance. (ii. 325)

19 O Jehovah, my strength and my fortress,
And my refuge in the day of distress,

To thee shall come the Gentiles
From the extremities of the earth, and shall say,—
"Surely falsehood did our fathers inherit;
Vanity and nothing profitable had they."
20 Can men make gods for themselves,
When they themselves are no gods? (ii. 333)
21 Therefore, behold, I will make them to know at this time,
I will make them to know
My hand and my power;
And they shall know that my name is Jehovah.

CHAPTER XVII.

1 The sin of Judah is written
With a pen of iron, with the point of adamant,
It is graven on the tablet of their hearts,
And on the horns of your altars:
2 For their children remember
Their altars and their groves,
Under the shady tree, on high hills.
3 Dweller on mountains! in the field will I give for spoil
Thy wealth *and* all thy treasures,
Because of thy high places,
Because of thy sin in all thy borders:
4 And dismissed shalt thou be, even thyself,
From thine inheritance which I gave thee;
And I will make thee to serve thine enemies
In a land which thou knowest not;
For ye have kindled a fire in my wrath,
Perpetually shall it burn. (ii. 342)

5 Thus saith Jehovah,—
Cursed *is* the man who trusts in man,
And makes flesh his arm,
And whose heart turns away from Jehovah:
6 And he shall be like a tamarisk in the desert,
And shall not see when good comes,
And shall dwell in dryness in the desert,
In the land of salt and not inhabited.
7 Blessed *is* the man who trusts in Jehovah,
And whose hope Jehovah is:
8 And he shall be like a tree,
That is planted near waters,
And nigh the stream sends its roots,
And shall not see when heat comes;
And green shall be its leaf,
And in the year of drought it shall not fear,
Nor cease from bringing forth fruit. (ii. 347)

9 Insidious is the heart above all things,
And vicious,—who can know it?
10 I Jehovah, who search the heart
And try the reins, to give to every one,
According to his ways,
According to the fruit of his doings. (ii. 354)
11 A partridge, which gathers and produces not,
Is he who gains riches, and not by right;
In the midst of his days he leaves them,
And at his end he is nothing.

12 A high throne of glory, from the beginning,
Is the place of our sanctuary.
13 The hope of Israel *art thou*, Jehovah;
All who thee forsake shall be ashamed:
They who turn aside shall on the earth be written;
For they have forsaken
The fountain of living waters, even Jehovah.
14 Heal me, O Jehovah,
And I shall be healed;
Save me, and I shall be saved,
For my praise art thou.

15 Behold they say to me,—
"Where is the word of Jehovah? let it now come."
16 But I hastened not to be a pastor following thee,
And the day of grief I desired not, thou knowest:
What went forth from my lips,
Before thy face has it been.
17 Be not to me a terror;
My protector *art* thou in the day of evil.
18 Ashamed let them be who persecute me,
And let not me be ashamed;
Terrified let them be,
And let not me be terrified:
Bring upon them the day of evil,
And with a double breach break them.

19 Thus said Jehovah to me,—
Go and stand in the gate of the children of the people, through
which the kings of Judah enter, and through which they go
20 out, and in all the gates of Jerusalem; and say to them,—
Hear the words of Jehovah, ye kings of Judah, and all Judah,
and all the inhabitants of Jerusalem, who enter in through these
21 gates, Thus saith Jehovah,—
Take heed to yourselves,
And bring not a burden on the Sabbath-day,
Yea, bring it not through the gates of Jerusalem;
22 Nor bring a burden from your houses
On the Sabbath-day, nor do any work,

But sanctify the Sabbath-day,
As I commanded your fathers;
23 Though they heard not nor inclined their ear,
But hardened their neck,
So as not to hear nor receive correction:
24 And it shall be, if by hearing
Ye will hear me, saith Jehovah,
So as not to bring a burden
Through the gates of the city on the Sabbath-day,
And if ye sanctify the Sabbath-day
By doing on it no work;
25 Then shall enter through the gates of this city
Kings and princes, sitting on David's throne,
Riding in chariots and on horses,
They and their princes, the men of Judah
And the inhabitants of Jerusalem,
And inhabited shall be this city perpetually:
26 And come shall they from the cities of Judah,
And from the circuits of Jerusalem,
And from the land of Benjamin,
And from the plain, and the mountain, and the south,
Bringing burnt-offering and sacrifice,
And oblation and incense,
And bringing praise, to the house of Jehovah. (ii. 388)
27 But if ye will not hearken to me,
So as to sanctify the Sabbath-day,
And not to bring a burden, nor enter
Through the gates of Jerusalem on the Sabbath-day;
Then will I kindle a fire in its gates,
And it shall devour the palaces of Jerusalem,
And it shall not be extinguished.

CHAPTER XVIII.

1 The word which came to Jeremiah from Jehovah, saying,—
2 Rise and go down to the potter's house, and I will cause thee
3 to hear my words. And I went down to the potter's house,
4 and, behold, he was making a work on the stone: and the
vessel was marred, which he made of the clay in the hand of
the potter; and he again made another vessel, as it seemed
5 good in the eyes of the potter to make. And the word of
Jehovah came to me, saying,—
6 Cannot I as this potter do to you,
O house of Israel? saith Jehovah.
Behold, as the clay is in the hand of the potter,
So are ye in my hand, O house of Israel.
7 Suddenly will I speak of a nation and a kingdom,
To pull down and to eradicate and to destroy:
8 If that nation turn from its evil,

For which I spoke against it;
Then will I repent of the evil
Which I had thought of doing to it.
9 Suddenly also will I speak of a nation and a kingdom,
To build up and to plant:
10 But if it do evil before mine eyes,
So as not to hearken to my voice;
Then will I repent of the good
Which I had said that I would do to it. (ii. 398)

11 And now, I pray, say to the men of Judah and to the inhabitants of Jerusalem, saying,—
Thus saith Jehovah,—
Behold, I frame for you an evil,
And I think for you a thought;
Return ye then, every one from his evil way,
And make right your ways and your doings.
12 And they said,—
It is all over;
For after our own thoughts will we walk,
And we will do, every one,
The wickedness of his own evil heart.
13 Therefore thus saith Jehovah,—
Ask, I pray, among the heathens,
Who hath heard such a thing?
A monstrous thing hath the virgin of Israel done.
14 Will *any one* leave the snow of Libanus from the rock of the field?
Will waters brought from another place,
And cold streams, be relinquished? (ii. 408)
15 For forgotten me have my people;
In vain do they offer incense,
Since they have made them to stumble
In their ways—the paths of ages,
That they might walk in paths—
In a way not trodden;
16 To make their land a desolation,
A perpetual hissing:
Whosoever shall pass through it
Shall be astonished and shake his head.
17 By the east wind will I scatter them
Before the face of the enemy;
The back and not the face will I shew them
In the day of their calamity.

18 And they said,—
Come, and let us think thoughts against Jeremiah;
For perish shall not the law from the priest,
Nor counsel from the wise,
Nor the word from the prophet:

And let us smite him with the tongue,
And not attend to any of his words.
19 Hearken, O Jehovah, to me,
And hear the voice of those who contend with me.
20 Shall evil be rendered for good?
For they have digged a pit for my soul:
Remember that I stood before thee
To speak good for them—
To turn away from them thy wrath.
21 Therefore give their children up to famine,
And deliver them into the hands of the sword,
And let their wives be bereaved and be widows,
And their men be smitten to death,
And their youths be smitten with the sword in battle:
22 Let a cry be heard from their houses,
When thou bringest on them an army suddenly;
For they have dug a pit to take me,
And snares have they hid for my feet.
23 And thou, Jehovah, who knowest their counsels
To be against me for death,
Be not propitious to their iniquity,
And their sin from thy sight blot not out,
But let them stumble before thee;
In the time of thy wrath deal thus with them.

CHAPTER XIX.

1 Thus saith Jehovah,—
Go and get a potter's vessel, even with the elders of the
2 people and with the elders of the priests; and enter into the
valley of Hinnom, which is at the entrance of the oriental
gate, and proclaim there the words which I shall speak to
3 thee: and thou shalt say, Hear the word of Jehovah, ye kings
of Judah and the inhabitants of Jerusalem,—
Thus saith Jehovah of hosts, the God of Israel,—
Behold I bring an evil on this place,
The which whosoever hears, tingle shall his ears:
4 Because they have forsaken me,
And have alienated this place,
And have made incense in it to foreign gods,
Whom they have not themselves known,
Nor their fathers, nor the kings of Judah,
And have filled this place
With the blood of innocents:
5 And they have built high places to Baal,
To burn their sons with fire,
For a burnt-offering to Baal;
Which I have not commanded nor spoken of,
And *which* came not into my mind.

6 Therefore behold the days shall come, saith Jehovah,
When this place shall no more be called Tophet,
Nor The valley of the son of Hinnom,
But, The valley of slaughter:
7 And void will I make the counsel of Judah
And of Jerusalem in this place,
And lay them prostrate by the sword before their enemies,
And by the hand of those who seek their life;
And I will give their carcases for meat
To the birds of heaven and to the beasts of the earth;
8 And I will set this city
For an astonishment and for hissing;
Whosoever shall pass through it shall be astonished,
And shall hiss on account of all her stroke:
9 And I will feed them with the flesh of their sons,
And with the flesh of their daughters;
And they shall eat, every one the flesh of his friend,
In the tribulation and straitness,
By which their enemies shall straiten them,
And those who seek their life.

10 Then shalt thou break the bottle in the presence of the men
11 who shall go with thee; and thou shalt say to them,—
Thus saith Jehovah of hosts,—
So will I break this people and this city,
As one breaks an earthen vessel,
Which can no more be repaired:
And in Tophet shall they be buried,
For there will be no *other* place to bury *them*:
12 Thus will I do to this place,
Saith Jehovah, and to its inhabitants,
I will even make this city like Tophet;
13 For the houses of Jerusalem,
And the houses of the kings of Judah,
Shall be, like the place of Tophet, unclean,
Even all the houses, on whose roofs
They have made incense to all the host of heaven,
And poured a libation to foreign gods.

14 Then came Jeremiah from Tophet, where Jehovah had sent
him to prophesy, and stood in the court of the house of Je-
hovah, and said to the whole people,—
15 Thus saith Jehovah of hosts, the God of Israel,—
Behold, I will bring upon this city
And upon all her towns, all the evil
Which I have pronounced against her;
Because they have hardened their neck,
That they might not hear my words.

END OF VOLUME SECOND.

Geneva